W9-CEX-860

COMPETITIVE COLLEGES

THOMSON

PETERSON'S

Australia • Canada • Mexico • Singapore • Spain • United Kingdom • United States

THO

PET

About The Thomson Corporation and Peterson's

With revenues approaching US$6 billion, The Thomson Corporation (www.thomson.com) is a leading global provider of integrated information solutions for business, education, and professional customers. Its Learning businesses and brands (www.thomsonlearning.com) serve the needs of individuals, learning institutions, and corporations with products and services for both traditional and distributed learning.

Peterson's, part of The Thomson Corporation, is one of the nation's most respected providers of lifelong learning online resources, software, reference guides, and books. The Education Supersite[SM] at www.petersons.com—the Internet's most heavily traveled education resource—has searchable databases and interactive tools for contacting U.S.-accredited institutions and programs. In addition, Peterson's serves more than 105 million education consumers annually.

For more information, contact Peterson's, 2000 Lenox Drive, Lawrenceville, NJ 08648; 800-338-3282; or find us on the World Wide Web at www.petersons.com/about.

ISSN 0887-0152
ISBN 0-7689-1045-5 (sponsor version)
     0-7689-0820-5 (trade version)

Printed in Canada

10 9 8 7 6 5 4 3 2 1   04 03 02

CONTENTS

WHY SHOULD YOU CONSIDER A COMPETITIVE COLLEGE?

Excellent colleges typically take great care in admitting students. For them, selecting the entering class is, as Bill Fitzsimmons, Dean of Admissions and Financial Aid at Harvard University, describes it: a process of "sculpting" the best possible class from the pool of qualified applicants. The goal of an admission committee is to bring together a community of students who can learn from one another, each one bringing their own particular talents, skills, and experiences that will contribute to the development of all the others.

Students who have excelled in high school want to go on excelling. They need an educational environment that will push them, test them, help them go beyond their past accomplishments. They require a college that "fits," one that will help them develop into what they can uniquely become.

At the start, you'll likely find that everyone's list of "best" colleges is very much alike. Except for adding the most popular regional schools or schools serving an unusual interest or a family's traditional alma mater, your initial list and your classmates' basic lists probably will include the Ivy League schools and one or more of up to a dozen other similarly prestigious colleges and universities. The one quality shared by these schools is prestige. It certainly can be argued

that it helps to graduate from a prestigious college. But prestige is a limited and very expensive factor upon which to base one's college choice. You and we know that there are truly excellent college choices beyond the eight Ivy League schools and a newsstand magazine's designated top schools. One of these "other" college choices could very well be the best fit for your particular requirements and goals.

We make only one assumption in *Competitive Colleges: Top Colleges for Top Students*. This is that the most influential factor in determining your experience on campus is the other students you will find there. In selecting colleges for inclusion in this book, we measure the competitiveness of the admission environment at colleges. This is measured over a meaningful period of time by entering-class statistics, such as GPA, class rank, and test scores. The 400 colleges selected for inclusion in this book routinely attract and admit an above-average share of the nation's high-achieving students.

Selecting a college is a great adventure, and Peterson's wants to guide you in this quest. For additional information on the colleges listed in this book, be sure to check out Peterson's Web sites: *www.petersons.com* and *www.bestcollegepicks.com*.

UNDERSTANDING THE COLLEGE ADMISSION PROCESS

BY **TED SPENCER,** Director of Undergraduate Admissions at the University of Michigan

The process you are about to begin, that of choosing a college, can be very challenging, sometimes frustrating, but most often rewarding. As Director of Admissions at a large, selective university, I would like to provide some basic information about the admission process that should help you get into the college of your choice. Although each competitive college or university has its own distinctive qualities and goals, the process of applying to them is strikingly similar. The following will give you the basic information you need to know to help you plan and apply to college.

GATHERING INFORMATION

How do you get the information you need to choose a college? Although colleges publish volumes of information about themselves that they are willing to mail or give out in person, another way to find out about them is through a guide such as *Competitive Colleges: Top Colleges for Top Students.*

The major difference between the college-published materials and this book is that the colleges present only the most appealing picture of themselves and are perhaps, then, somewhat less objective. As a student seeking information about college, you should review both the information provided in books like this one and the information sent by the colleges. Your goal should be to use all of the available literature to assist you in developing your list of the top five or ten colleges in which you are interested.

Chances are that if you are a top student and you have taken the PSAT, SAT I, SAT II, ACT, PACT, or AP (Advanced Placement) tests, you will receive a great deal of material directly from many colleges and universities. Colleges purchase lists of names of students taking these exams and then screen the list for students they think will be most successful at their institutions. Some colleges will also automatically mail course catalogs, posters, departmental brochures, and pamphlets, as well as videocassettes. If you do not

receive this information but would like a sample, write or call that particular college.

My advice is to take a look at the materials you receive and then use them to help you decide (if you don't already know) about the type of college you would like to attend. Allow the materials to help you narrow your list of top schools by comparing key facts and characteristics.

OTHER HELPFUL SOURCES

Published information about colleges, printed by the colleges, is certainly an important way to narrow your choices. But there are at least five other means of learning more about colleges and universities:

- *High School Counselors.* Most high school counselors have established positive relationships with the college representatives in your state as well as with out-of-state universities where large numbers of their students apply. As you attempt to gain more information while narrowing your choice of colleges, the high school counselor can give you a fairly accurate assessment of colleges to which you will have the best chance of gaining admission.

- *Parents.* Because most prospective students and their parents are at that stage in life in which they view issues in different ways, students tend to be reluctant to ask parents' opinions about college choices. However, you may find that parents are very helpful because they often are actively gathering information about the colleges that they feel are best suited for you. And not only do they gather information—you can be sure that they have thoroughly read the piles of literature that colleges have mailed to you. Ask your parents questions about what they have read and also about the colleges from which they graduated. As alumni of schools on your list, parents can be a very valuable resource.

• *College Day/Night/Fairs Visitation.* One of the best ways to help narrow your college choices is to meet with a person representing a college while they are visiting your area or high school. In fact, most admission staff members spend a good portion of the late spring and fall visiting high schools and attending college fairs. In some cases, college fairs feature students, faculty members, and alumni. Before attending one of these sessions, you should prepare a list of questions you would like to ask the representatives. Most students want to know about five major areas: academic preparation, the admission process, financial aid, social life, and job preparation. Most college representatives can be extremely helpful in addressing these questions as well as the many others that you may have. It is then up to you to decide if their answers fit your criteria of the college you are seeking.

• *Alumni.* For many schools, alumni are a very important part of the admission process. In some cases, alumni conduct interviews and even serve as surrogate admission officers, particularly when admission office staff cannot travel. As recent graduates, alumni can talk about their own experience and can give balance to the materials you have received from the college or university.

• *Campus Visits.* Finally, try to schedule a campus visit as part of your information-gathering process. By the time you begin thinking about a campus visit, you should have narrowed down your college shopping list. Hopefully your short list of colleges will have met your personal and educational goals. Before deciding which schools to visit, you should sort the materials into piles of "definitely not interested," "definitely interested," or "could be interested." Next, in an effort to make sure that the reality lives up to the printed viewbook, you should schedule a visit and see firsthand what the college is really like. Most colleges and universities provide daily campus tours to both prospective and admitted students. The tours for prospective students are generally set up to help you answer questions about the following: class size and student-to-teacher ratio; size of the library, residence halls, and computer centers; registration and faculty advising; and

retention, graduation rates, and career placement planning. Since the tours may not cover everything you came prepared to ask about, be sure to ask questions of as many staff, students, and faculty members as possible before leaving the campus.

THE ADMISSION PROCESS

ADMISSION CRITERIA

After you go through the process of selecting a college or narrowing your choices to a few schools, the admission process now focuses on you—your academic record and skills—and judgment will be passed on these pieces of information for admission to a particular school. The first things you should find out about each college on your priority list are the admission criteria—what it takes to get in:

1. Does the college or university require standardized tests—the ACT or SAT I? Do they prefer one or the other, or will they accept either?
2. Do they require SAT II Subject Tests and, if so, which ones?
3. Are Advanced Placement scores accepted and, if so, what are the minimums needed?
4. In terms of grades and class rank, what is the profile of a typical entering student?

It is also important to find out which type of admission notification system the college uses—rolling or deferred admission. On a rolling system, you find out your status within several weeks of applying; with the deferred system, notification is generally made in the spring. For the most part, public universities and colleges use rolling admission and private colleges generally use delayed notification.

THE APPLICATION

The application is the primary vehicle used to introduce yourself to the admission office. As with any introduction, you should try to make a good first impression. The first thing you should do in presenting your application is to find out what the college or university wants from you. This means you should read the application carefully to learn the following:

1. Must the application be typed, or can you print it?

2. Is there an application fee and, if so, how much is it?

3. Is there a deadline and, if so, when is it?

4. What standardized tests are required?

5. Is an essay required?

6. Is an interview required?

7. Should you send letters of recommendation?

8. How long will it take to find out the admission decision?

9. What other things can you do to improve your chances of admission?

My advice is to submit your application early. It does not guarantee admission, but it is much better than submitting it late or near the deadline. Also, don't assume that colleges using rolling admission will always have openings close to their deadlines. Regardless of when you submit it, make sure that the application is legible and that all the information that is requested is provided.

TRANSCRIPTS

While all of the components of the application are extremely important in the admission process, perhaps the single most important item is your transcript because it tells: (1) what courses you took; (2) which courses were college-preparatory and challenging; (3) class rank; and (4) grades and test scores.

- *Required Course Work.* Generally speaking, most colleges look at the high school transcript to see if the applicant followed a college-preparatory track while in high school. So, if you have taken four years of English, math, natural science, social sciences, and foreign language, you are on the right track. Many selective colleges require four years of English; three years each of math, natural science, and social science; and two years of a foreign language. It is also true that some selective colleges believe students who are interested in majoring in math and science need more than the minimum requirements in those areas.

- *Challenging Courses.* As college admission staff members continue to evaluate your transcript, they also look to see how demanding your course load has been during high school. If the high school offered Advanced Placement or Honors courses, the expectation of most selective colleges

is that students will have taken seven or more honors classes or four or more AP courses during their four years in high school. However, if you do elect to take challenging courses, it is also important that you make good grades in those courses. Quite often, students ask, "If I take honors and AP courses and get a 'C,' does that count more than getting a 'B' or higher in a strictly college-prep course?" It's a difficult question to answer, because too many C's and B's can outweigh mostly A's. On the other hand, students who take the more challenging courses will be better prepared to take the more rigorous courses in college. Consequently, many colleges will give extra consideration when making their selections to the students who take the more demanding courses.

- *Transcript Trends.* Because the courses you take in high school are such a critical part of the college decision-making process, your performance in those courses indicates to colleges whether you are following an upward or downward trend. Beginning with the ninth grade, admission staff look at your transcript to see if you have started to develop good academic habits. In general, when colleges review your performance in the ninth grade, they are looking to see if you are in the college-preparatory track.

By sophomore year, students should begin choosing more demanding courses and become more involved in extracurricular activities. This will show that you are beginning to learn how to balance your academic and extracurricular commitments. Many admission officers consider the sophomore year to be the most critical and telling year for a student's future success.

The junior year is perhaps the second-most-important year in high school. The grades you earn and the courses you take will help to reinforce the trend you began in your sophomore year. At the end of your junior year, many colleges will know enough about the type of student you are to make their admission decision.

The upward and positive trend must continue, however, during your senior year. Many selective schools do not use senior grades in making their admission decisions. However, almost all review the final transcript, so your last year needs to show a strong performance to the end. The research shows that students who finish their senior year with strong grades will start their freshman year in college with strong grades.

THE APPLICATION REVIEW PROCESS

WHAT'S NEXT?

At this point, you have done all you can do. So you might as well sit back and relax, if that's possible, and wait for the letters to come in the mail. Hopefully, if you've evaluated all the college materials you were sent earlier and you prepared your application carefully and sent it to several colleges, you will be admitted to either your first, second, or third choice. It may help your peace of mind, however, to know what happens to your application after the materials have been submitted.

Once your application is received by the admission office, it is reviewed, in most cases by noncounseling staff, to determine if you have completed the application properly. If items are missing, you will receive a letter of notification identifying additional information that must be provided. Be sure to send any additional or missing information the college requests back to them as soon as possible. Once your application is complete, it is then ready for the decision process.

READER REVIEW

The process by which the decision is finalized varies from school to school. Most of the private colleges and universities use a system in which each application is read by 2 or more admission staff members. In some cases, faculty members are also readers. If all of the readers agree on the decision, a letter is sent. Under this system, if the readers do not agree, the application will be reviewed by a committee or may be forwarded to an associate dean, dean, or director of admission for the final decision. One advantage to this process is that each applicant is reviewed by several people, thereby eliminating bias.

COMMITTEE REVIEW

At some universities, a committee reviews every application. Under that system, a committee member is assigned a number of applications to present. It is that member's responsibility to prepare background information on each applicant and then present the file to the committee for discussion and a vote. In this process, every applicant is voted on.

COUNSELOR REVIEW

The review process that many selective public institutions use is one in which the counselor responsible for a particular school or geographical territory makes the final decision. In this case, the counselor who makes the admission decision is also the one who identified and recruited the student, thereby lending a more personal tone to the process.

COMPUTER-GENERATED REVIEW

Many large state universities that process nearly 20,000 applications a year have developed computer-generated guidelines to admit their applicants. If applicants meet the required GPA and test scores, they are immediately notified of the decision.

Once the decisions are made using one of these methods, colleges use a variety of ways to notify students. The common methods used are early action or early decision, rolling admission, and deferred admission.

A WORD OF ADVICE

When you start the admission process, do so with the idea of exploring as many college opportunities as you can. From the very beginning, avoid focusing on just one college or, for that matter, one type of college. Look at private, public, large, small, highly selective, selective—in short, a variety of colleges and universities. Take advantage of every available resource, including students, parents, counselors, and college materials, in order to help identify the colleges that will be a great fit for you.

Finally, the most important thing you can do is to build a checklist of what you want out of the college experience and then match your list with one of the many wonderful colleges and universities just waiting for you to enroll.

Applying to Professional Colleges for Art and Music

by **Theresa Bedoya,** Vice President for Admission and Financial Aid, Maryland Institute, College of Art

The term "competitive" will have a different meaning if you are applying to a professional college specializing in art or music. The goal of selective art and music colleges is to admit students of extraordinary talent. Since you are using this resource as part of your college search, you most likely have distinguished yourself academically. But to gain admission to the music and art colleges listed in this book, you will also need to be competitive in your achievements in the arts.

ADMISSION CRITERIA

In order to choose the most talented students from those who apply, most professional art and music colleges require evidence of talent, skill, ability, experience, and desire as demonstrated in an audition or by a portfolio of artwork. Each art and music college has expectations and academic requirements particular to the program of study you choose.

Admission will be based upon the review of traditional criteria such as your grade point average, level of course work, test scores, essays, and interviews. However, for most professional colleges, the evaluation of your portfolio or your audition will supersede the review of all other criteria for admission. (Many visual arts colleges even prescreen potential applicants through review of the portfolio prior to application in order to determine eligibility for admission. This process, which occurs early in the senior year, allows students the opportunity to gain valuable guidance early in the admission process. It also creates a more "acceptable" pool of applicants and is the reason that acceptance rates at many visual arts colleges appear to be higher than other selective

institutions.) In some cases, the evaluation of your talent and academic achievement will be given equal weight.

In contrast, most comprehensive colleges and universities offering majors in art and music will rely on academic criteria to make an admission decision. The portfolio or audition, if required, will play a secondary role. You should take these factors into account when deciding whether to apply to art and music schools or to colleges and universities that offer art and music programs.

PREPARING FOR YOUR PORTFOLIO REVIEW OR AUDITION

If you are interested in the visual arts, you should gain as much studio experience as possible in order to develop a strong portfolio. Take full advantage of your high school art program and enroll in extra Saturday or summer classes or seek private tutoring. Exhibit your artwork when the opportunity is provided. Become better informed as an artist by studying art history and the works of contemporary artists.

If you plan to study music, remember that experience and confidence need to be clearly evident in your audition. Therefore, become involved as much as possible in your own high school music activities as well as local, district, and state youth orchestras, choirs, and performance ensembles. The more you perform and study, the more confident you will be on stage.

Contact the schools to which you are applying early in the process to learn how and when they will receive your portfolio or conduct your audition.

PAYING FOR COLLEGE

BY DON BETTERTON, Director of Financial Aid at Princeton University

Regardless of which college a student chooses, higher education requires a major investment of time, energy, and money. By taking advantage of a variety of available resources, most students can bring the education that is right for them within reach.

A NOTE OF ENCOURAGEMENT

While there is no denying that the cost of an education at some competitive colleges can be high, it is important to recognize that, although the rate of increase in costs during the last ten years has outpaced gains in family income, there are more options available to pay for college than ever before.

Many families find it is economically wise to spread costs out over a number of years by borrowing money for college. A significant amount of government money, both federal and state, is available to students. Moreover, colleges themselves have expanded their own student aid efforts considerably. In spite of rapidly increasing costs, most competitive colleges are still able to provide financial aid to all admitted students with demonstrated need.

In addition, many colleges have developed ways to assist families who are not eligible for need-based assistance. These include an increasing number of merit scholarships as well as various forms of parental loans. There also are a number of organizations that give merit awards based on a student's academic record, talent, or special characteristics. Thus, regardless of your family's income, if you are academically qualified and knowledgeable about the many different sources of aid, you should be able to attend the college of your choice.

ESTIMATING COSTS

If you have not yet settled on specific colleges and you would like to begin early financial planning, estimate a budget. By calculating a 5 percent increase on 2001–02 charges, we can estimate 2002–03 expenses at a typical competitive college as follows: tuition and fees, about $21,830; room and board, about $7500; and an allowance for books and miscellaneous

expenses, about $2260. Thus a rough budget (excluding travel expenses) for the year is $31,590.

IDENTIFYING RESOURCES

There are essentially four sources of funds you can use to pay for college:

1. Money from your parents
2. Need-based scholarships or grants from a college or outside organization
3. Your own contribution from savings, loans, and jobs
4. Assistance unrelated to demonstrated financial need.

All of these are considered by the financial aid office, and the aid "package" given to a student after the parental contribution has been determined usually consists of a combination of scholarships, loans, and campus work.

THE PARENTAL CONTRIBUTION

The financial aid policies of most colleges are based on the assumption that parents should contribute as much as they reasonably can to the educational expenses of their children. The amount of this contribution varies greatly, but almost every family is expected to pay something.

Because there is no limit on aid eligibility based solely on income, the best rule of thumb is *apply for financial aid if there is any reasonable doubt about your ability to meet college costs.* Since it is generally true that applying for financial aid does not affect a student's chances of being admitted, any candidate for admission should apply for aid if his or her family feels they will be unable to pay the entire cost of attendance. (In spite of considerable publicity on the subject, there are still only a handful of competitive colleges that practice need-sensitive admissions.)

Application for aid is made by completing the Free Application for Federal Student Aid (FAFSA). In addition, many competitive colleges will require you to also file a separate application called PROFILE, since they need more detailed information to award their own funds. The financial aid section of a college's admission information booklet will tell you which financial aid application is required, when it should be filed, and whether a separate aid form of the college's own design is also necessary.

Colleges use the same government formula (the Federal Methodology) to determine eligibility for federal and state student aid. This process of coming up with an expected contribution from you (the student) and your parents is called "need analysis." The information on the FAFSA—parental and student income and assets, the number of family members, and the number attending college as well as other variables—is analyzed to derive the Expected Family Contribution (EFC).

You can estimate how much your parents might be asked to contribute for college by consulting the Approximate Expected Family Contribution Chart. Keep in mind that the actual parental contribution is determined on campus by a financial aid officer, using the government formula as a guideline.

Competitive colleges that also require the PROFILE will have at their disposal information they will analyze in addition to what is reported on the FAFSA. The net result of this further examination (for example, adding the value of the family home to the equation) will usually increase the expected parental contribution compared to the Federal Methodology.

Parental Borrowing

Some families who are judged to have sufficient resources to be able to finance their children's college costs find that lack of cash at any moment prevents them from paying college bills without difficulty. Other families prefer to use less current income by extending their payments over more than four years. In both instances, these families rely on borrowing to assist with college payments. Each year parental loans become a more important form of college financing.

The PLUS program, part of the Federal Family Education Loan Program, is designed to help both aid and non-aid families. It allows parents to pay their share of educational costs by borrowing at a reasonable interest rate, with the backing of the federal government. The up to 9 percent loans are available through both the Direct Loan and FFEL programs. Many competitive colleges, state governments, and

commercial lenders also have their own parental loan programs patterned along the lines of PLUS. For more information about parental loans, contact a college financial aid office or your state higher education department.

NEED-BASED SCHOLARSHIP OR GRANT ASSISTANCE

Need-based aid is primarily available from federal and state governments and from colleges themselves. It is not necessary for a student to apply directly for a particular scholarship at a college; the financial aid office will match an eligible applicant with the appropriate fund.

The Federal Pell Grant is by far the largest single form of federal student assistance; an estimated 4 million students receive awards annually. Families with incomes of up to $25,000 (higher when other family assets are relatively low) may be eligible for grants up to $3125.

For state scholarships, students should check with the department of higher education about eligibility requirements. Aid applicants are expected to apply directly to outside organizations for any scholarships for which they may be eligible.

It is particularly important to apply for a Federal Pell Grant and a state scholarship. Application for both Pell and state scholarships is made by checking the appropriate box on the FAFSA. (Aid recipients are required to notify the college financial aid office about outside awards, as colleges take into consideration grants from all sources before assigning scholarships from their own funds.)

THE STUDENT'S OWN CONTRIBUTION

All undergraduates, not only those who apply for financial aid, can assume responsibility for meeting a portion of their college expenses by borrowing, working during the academic year and the summer, and contributing a portion of their savings. Colleges require aid recipients to provide a "self-help" contribution before awarding scholarship money because they believe students should pay a reasonable share of their own educational costs.

Student Loans

Many students will be able to borrow to help pay for college. Colleges administer three loans (all backed by the federal government): the Direct Stafford Loan,

FFEL Stafford Loan, and the Federal Perkins Loan. Students must demonstrate financial need to be eligible for either the Direct Stafford or the Perkins Loan.

Note: Rather than providing FFEL Stafford Loans, many colleges have made arrangements to participate in the Direct Stafford Loan Program. As far as the student is concerned, the loan terms are essentially the same.

Summer Employment

All students, whether or not they are receiving financial aid, should plan to work during the summer months. Students can be expected to save from $800 to $1850 before their freshman year and $1500 to $2550 each summer while enrolled in college. It is worthwhile for a student to begin working while in high school to increase the chance of finding summer employment during college vacations.

Term-Time Employment

Colleges have student employment offices that find jobs for students during the school year. Aid recipients on work-study receive priority in placement, but once they have been assisted, non-aid students are helped as well. Some jobs relate closely to academic interests; others should be viewed as a source of income rather than intellectual stimulation. A standard 8- to 12-hour-per-week job does not normally interfere with academic work or extracurricular activities and results in approximately $1550 to $2250 in earnings during the year.

Student Savings

Student assets accumulated prior to starting college are available to help pay college bills. The need analysis system expects 35 percent of each year's student savings to go toward college expenses. This source can often be quite substantial, particularly when families have accumulated large sums in the student's name (or in a trust fund with the student as the beneficiary). If you have a choice whether to keep college savings in the parents' name or the student's name, you should realize that the contribution rate on parental assets is 12 percent, compared to 35 percent for the student's savings.

AID NOT REQUIRING NEED AS AN ELIGIBILITY CRITERION

There are scholarships available to students whether or not they are eligible for need-based financial aid. Awards based on merit are given by certain state scholarship programs, and National Merit Scholarship winners usually receive a $2500 stipend regardless of family financial circumstances. Scholarships and prizes are also awarded by community organizations and other local groups. In addition, some parents receive tuition payments for their children as employment benefits. Most colleges offer merit scholarships to a limited group of highly qualified applicants. The selection of recipients for such awards depends on unusual talent in a specific area or on overall academic excellence.

The Reserve Officers' Training Corps sponsors an extensive scholarship program that pays for tuition and books and provides an expense allowance of $1500 per school year. The Army, Air Force, and Navy/Marine Corps have ROTC units at many colleges. High school guidance offices have brochures describing ROTC application procedures.

A Simple Method for Estimating Family Contribution

The chart that follows will enable parents to make an approximation of the yearly amount the national financial aid need analysis system will expect them to pay for college.

To use the chart, you need to work with your income, assets, and size of your family. Read the instructions below and enter the proper amounts in the spaces provided.

1. Parents' total income before taxes

   A. Adjusted gross income (equivalent to tax return entry; use actual or estimated) _____ A

   B. Nontaxable income (Social Security benefits, child support, welfare, etc.) _____ B

   Total Income: A + B _____ ①

2. Parents' total assets

   C. Total of cash, savings, and checking accounts _____ C

   D. Total value of investments (stocks, bonds, real estate other than home, etc.) _____ D

   Total Assets: C + D _____ ②

3. Family size (include student, parents, other dependent children, and other dependents) _____ ③

Now find the figures on the chart that correspond to your entries in ①, ②, and ③ to determine your approximate expected parental contribution, interpolating as necessary.

4. Estimated parental contribution from chart _____ ④

If there will be more than one family member in college half-time or more, divide the figure above by the number in college.

5. Estimated parental contribution for each person in college _____ ⑤

6. Student's savings _____ × .35 = _____ ⑥

7. Finally, add the estimated parental contribution in ⑤ and the estimated student contribution in ⑥ to arrive at the total estimated family contribution _____ ⑦

This number can be compared to college costs to determine an approximate level of need.

Approximate Expected Family Contribution Chart

Assets	Family Size	Income Before Taxes: $20,000	30,000	40,000	50,000	60,000	70,000	80,000	90,000	100,000
$20,000	3	$220	2,100	3,200	5,400	8,700	11,800	14,800	17,600	20,400
	4	0	1,400	2,000	4,000	7,400	10,500	13,400	15,900	19,300
	5	0	300	1,300	3,000	6,200	9,300	12,200	15,100	18,100
	6	0	0	600	2,100	5,000	7,800	10,800	13,700	16,600
$30,000	3	$220	2,100	3,200	5,400	8,700	11,800	14,800	17,600	20,400
	4	0	1,400	2,000	4,000	7,400	10,500	13,400	15,900	19,300
	5	0	300	1,300	3,000	6,200	9,300	12,200	15,100	18,100
	6	0	0	600	2,100	5,000	7,800	10,800	13,700	16,600
$40,000	3	$220	2,200	3,300	5,600	8,900	11,900	14,900	14,700	21,700
	4	0	1,500	2,100	4,100	7,500	10,700	13,600	16,000	20,400
	5	0	400	1,400	3,100	6,300	9,400	12,300	15,200	18,100
	6	0	0	600	2,200	5,100	8,000	11,000	13,900	16,700
$50,000	3	$600	2,500	3,800	6,200	9,500	12,500	15,500	18,300	21,200
	4	0	1,800	2,400	4,600	8,200	11,300	14,200	16,700	20,000
	5	0	600	1,600	3,500	6,900	10,000	12,900	15,700	18,700
	6	0	0	900	2,500	5,700	8,600	11,600	14,500	17,300
$60,000	3	$800	2,900	4,200	6,700	10,100	13,100	16,000	18,900	21,800
	4	140	2,000	2,700	5,100	8,700	11,900	14,800	17,600	20,600
	5	0	900	1,900	3,900	7,500	10,600	13,500	16,300	19,300
	6	0	0	1,200	2,900	6,300	9,200	12,200	15,100	17,900

	Assets	$20,000	30,000	40,000	50,000	Income Before Taxes 60,000	70,000	80,000	90,000	100,000
	$80,000									
FAMILY SIZE	3	$1,400	3,500	5,100	7,800	11,000	14,200	17,100	20,000	22,900
	4	600	2,600	3,400	6,100	9,800	12,900	15,700	18,300	21,600
	5	0	1,400	2,500	4,800	8,600	11,700	14,600	17,400	20,400
	6	0	300	1,700	3,600	7,300	10,200	13,200	16,000	19,100
	$100,000									
FAMILY SIZE	3	$1,800	4,400	6,100	8,900	12,300	15,300	18,200	21,100	24,000
	4	1,200	3,300	4,200	7,200	10,900	14,000	16,800	15,400	22,700
	5	100	1,900	3,200	5,800	9,700	12,800	15,600	18,500	21,500
	6	0	900	2,300	4,400	8,400	11,400	14,400	17,200	20,100
	$120,000									
FAMILY SIZE	3	$2,500	5,300	7,300	10,100	13,400	16,300	19,300	22,300	25,100
	4	1,700	4,100	5,100	8,400	12,100	15,200	18,000	20,600	23,900
	5	600	2,500	4,000	6,900	10,800	13,900	16,600	19,600	22,600
	6	250	1,400	2,900	5,400	9,600	12,500	15,500	18,300	21,200
	$140,000									
FAMILY SIZE	3	$3,200	6,500	8,400	11,200	14,500	17,400	20,400	23,300	26,200
	4	2,300	5,100	6,200	9,500	13,200	16,200	19,100	21,700	25,000
	5	1,200	3,200	4,900	8,100	11,900	15,100	17,900	20,800	23,800
	6	800	1,900	3,700	6,500	10,700	13,600	16,500	19,400	22,400

WHAT'S INSIDE AND ONLINE

Before the Competitive Art and Music Colleges and the Competitive Colleges and Universities sections, you will find brief explanations, in profile format, of the information found in each college's full-page description.

 Colleges with this icon are sponsors of this book. These colleges have arranged for copies of *Competitive Colleges: Top Colleges for Top Students* to reach outstanding students.

In an effort to provide you with more convenient ways to apply, many colleges accept common applications, which make it easier for you to apply to several colleges at once. This reduces the amount of time you have to spend repeatedly entering information as well as the risk of errors. Once you have completed your applications, you can then print them and mail them.

COLLEGEQUEST.COM

One of the most comprehensive Web resources for college-bound students can be found at CollegeQuest.com. CollegeQuest provides information and tools that will help you prepare, search, apply, and pay for college. If you are preparing for the SAT or ACT, you will find test dates, valuable test-taking tips, and full-length practice tests. You can search Peterson's complete college database to find the colleges that best fit your needs and then view in-depth profiles or do a side-by-side comparison of selected colleges. The site will keep you on track with a personal organizer and college calendar that provides general reminders, test dates, and key dates for every college that you add to your personal list. The financial aid section provides a complete overview of how financial aid works, a free scholarship search of over 800,000 awards, and a family contribution estimator that will help your family calculate how much you will be expected to contribute toward the cost of college. All of these tools are supplemented with informative articles, as well as an Advice Center and Expert Forum, where admissions and financial aid experts are available to answer your questions.

BESTCOLLEGEPICKS.COM

Peterson's college search tool, BestCollegePicks, encourages you to focus on what *you* believe is most important in a college experience. You'll have the unique opportunity to select a college that best matches your own goals, values, and interests.

This groundbreaking tool is based on research conducted by Dr. Robert Zemsky at the University of Pennsylvania's Institute for Higher Education Research. It measures colleges according to the type of graduates they produce, rather than criteria such as average SAT scores and student-faculty ratios. Data are provided by college graduates who reveal what they actually did after graduation—in terms of work, additional schooling, and more. Choose the college that's right for you by logging on to BestCollegePicks.com.

PETERSONS.COM

Petersons.com offers valuable information about educational opportunities at all levels. A searchable database leads users to applicable institutional sites where they will find an overview of the institution. Features include online applications and "instant inquiry" e-mail. Visit the most comprehensive education resource on the Web at www.petersons.com.

SPONSOR LIST

These Sponsors arranged for copies of *Competitive Colleges: Top Colleges for Top Students* to reach outstanding students—students eager to learn more about top schools. This icon appears in each Sponsor's profile:

Agnes Scott College
Albion College
Albright College
Alfred University
Allegheny College
Alma College
American University
Amherst College
Asbury College
Augustana College (IL)
Babson College
Baldwin-Wallace College
Barnard College
Baylor University
Belmont University
Beloit College
Bennington College
Berry College
Bethel College (MN)
Birmingham-Southern College
Boston College
Boston University
Brandeis University
Brown University
Bryn Mawr College
Bucknell University
Buena Vista University
Butler University
Calvin College
Canisius College
Carnegie Mellon University
Carroll College (MT)
The Catholic University of America
Central College (IA)
Chapman University
Christian Brothers University
Claremont McKenna College
Clarkson University
Clemson University
College of New Jersey
College of Saint Benedict

College of the Atlantic
College of the Holy Cross
The College of Wooster
Colorado State University
Cooper Union for the Advancement of Science and Art
Cornell University
Dartmouth College
David Lipscomb University
Davidson College
Denison University
DePauw University
Drake University
Earlham College
Eckerd College
Elizabethtown College
Embry-Riddle Aeronautical University
Emerson College
Emory University
Eugene Lang College, New School University
Florida Institute of Technology
Florida State University
Fordham University
Georgetown College (KY)
Georgia State University
Gettysburg College
Gordon College
Goucher College
Grove City College
Hamilton College
Hampshire College
Harding University
Harvard University
Haverford College
Heidelberg College
Hendrix College
Hillsdale College
Hiram College
Hobart and William Smith Colleges

Illinois College
Illinois Institute of Technology
Illinois Wesleyan University
Iowa State University of Science and Technology
Ithaca College
John Carroll University
Johns Hopkins University
Juniata College
Kettering University
Lafayette College
Lake Forest College
Lawrence Technological University
Lawrence University
Lebanon Valley College
Lehigh University
Le Moyne College
List College, Jewish Theological Seminary of America
Loyola College in Maryland
Loyola University Chicago
Lycoming College
Lyon College
Mannes College of Music, New School University
Marietta College
Marquette University
Maryland Institute College of Art
Maryville College
Mercer University
Messiah College
Miami University (OH)
Michigan Technological University
Middlebury College
Millsaps College
Mills College
Morehouse College
Mount Holyoke College
Mount St. Mary's College
Mount Union College
Muhlenberg College

Nazareth College of Rochester
New College of Florida
New Jersey Institute of Technology
New York School of Interior Design
North Carolina School of the Arts
North Central College
Oberlin College
Oglethorpe University
Ohio Northern University
Ohio Wesleyan University
Pitzer College
Polytechnic University,
    Brooklyn Campus
Pomona College
Presbyterian College
Princeton University
Providence College
Quincy University
Quinnipiac University
Randolph-Macon Woman's College
Reed College
Regis University
Rensselaer Polytechnic Institute
Rice University
Ripon College
Rochester Institute of Technology
Rockhurst University
Saint Francis University
St. John's College (MD)
St. John's College (NM)
Saint John's University (MN)
Saint Joseph's University
St. Lawrence University
Saint Louis University
Saint Mary's College of California
St. Mary's College of Maryland
St. Norbert College
Samford University

Sarah Lawrence College
Seattle University
Siena College
Simon's Rock College of Bard
Simpson College
Skidmore College
Smith College
Southern Methodist University
Southwestern University
Southwest Missouri State University
State University of New York
    at Binghamton
State University of New York
    at Buffalo
Stevens Institute of Technology
Susquehanna University
Swarthmore College
Sweet Briar College
Syracuse University
Texas Christian University
Texas Tech University
Transylvania University
Trinity College (CT)
Trinity University
Tulane University
Union College (NY)
Union University
United States Air Force Academy
United States Merchant Marine
    Academy
United States Military Academy
The University of Alabama in
    Huntsville
The University of Arizona
University of Colorado at Boulder
University of Dayton
University of Georgia
University of Illinois at Chicago

University of Illinois at
    Urbana-Champaign
The University of Iowa
University of Maryland,
    College Park
University of Michigan
University of Minnesota,
    Twin Cities Campus
University of Redlands
University of Rhode Island
University of Rochester
University of St. Thomas
University of San Diego
University of Scranton
University of South Carolina
University of Southern California
University of the Sciences in
    Philadelphia
Valparaiso University
Villanova University
Virginia Military Institute
Virginia Polytechnic Institute and
    State University
Wabash College
Wartburg College
Washington College
Washington University in St. Louis
Wellesley College
Wells College
Wesleyan College
Wesleyan University
Western Maryland College
Westminster College
Westmont College
Whittier College
Whitworth College
Williams College

COMPETITIVE ART AND MUSIC COLLEGES

Art or Music College Name

SETTING ■ PUBLIC/PRIVATE ■ INSTITUTIONAL CONTROL ■ COED?
CITY, STATE

Web site: www.website.com
Contact: Contact name and address
Telephone: Telephone number **Fax:** Fax number
E-mail: E-mail address

Academics
- Degrees awarded
- Challenging opportunities and special programs
- Most frequently chosen fields
- Faculty, including student-faculty ratio
- Cooperative programs

Facilities and Resources
- Performance facilities/studio space
- Exhibition halls and galleries
- Library facilities
- Special media collections

Applying
- Required documentation and standardized tests
- Portfolio/audition information
- GPA minimum
- Interviews
- Deadlines

Sponsoring schools are able to submit a brief message in order to highlight special programs or opportunities that are available or to more fully explain their particular commitment to higher education. That message appears in this box.

Getting in Last Year
- Number who applied
- Percent accepted
- Number enrolled (percent)
- Percent h.s. achievers
- Average GPA
- SAT I/ACT performance
- Number of National Merit Scholars
- Number of class presidents
- Number of valedictorians

The Student Body
- How many students on campus and number who are undergrads
- Where they come from
- Percent from in-state
- Who they are:
  —Women and men
  —Ethnic makeup
  —International students

Graduation and After
- Percent graduating in 4, 5, or 6 years
- Percent pursuing further study, with most popular fields, if provided
- Percent with job offers within 6 months
- How many organizations recruit on campus
- Major academic awards won by students

Financial Matters
- Tuition and fees
- Room and board
- Percent of need met
- Average financial aid received per undergraduate

ART CENTER COLLEGE OF DESIGN

Suburban setting ■ Private ■ Independent ■ Coed
Pasadena, California

Web site: www.artcenter.edu
Contact: Ms. Kit Baron, Vice President of Student Services, 1700 Lida Street,
Pasadena, CA 91103-1999
Telephone: 626-396-2373 **Fax:** 626-795-0578
E-mail: admissions@artcenter.edu

Getting in Last Year
1,129 applied
65% were accepted
43 enrolled (6%)
3.10 average high school GPA

The Student Body
1,465 total
1,377 undergraduates
43 home states and territories
81% from California
37 home countries, other than U.S.
39.7% women, 60.3% men
1.5% African American
0.7% American Indian
31.6% Asian American
9.7% Hispanic American
17.4% international students

Graduation and After
60% graduated in 4 years
13% graduated in 5 years
7% graduated in 6 years
94% had job offers within 6 months
200 organizations recruited on campus

Financial Matters
$21,110 tuition and fees (2001–02)
50% average percent of need met
$13,573 average financial aid amount received
per undergraduate (2000–01 estimated)

Academics

Art Center awards bachelor's and master's **degrees**. Challenging opportunities include advanced placement credit, accelerated degree programs, and independent study. Special programs include internships and summer session for credit.

The most frequently chosen **baccalaureate** field is visual/performing arts. A complete listing of majors at Art Center appears in the Majors Index beginning on page 430.

The **faculty** at Art Center has 66 full-time members. The student-faculty ratio is 12:1.

Art Center offers exchange programs with Occidental College and California Institute of Technology. Exchange programs include cross-registration in classes and use of libraries and other facilities.

Facilities and Resources

Art Center's facilities are housed in a contemporary steel and glass structure that affords views of the Los Angeles valleys. Computer graphics equipment includes 60 Silicon Graphics workstations, 115 Macintosh computers, and a range of peripheral hardware and digital and audio equipment. Two galleries house both student work and traveling shows. State-of-the-art photography and industrial design facilities combine traditional equipment with state-of-the-art technology.

225 **computers** are available on campus that provide access to the Internet. The **library** has 73,595 books and 385 subscriptions. Other features are a rare book room, a CD-ROM workstation, and 180 laser discs of rare features, animation, and advertising.

Applying

Art Center requires an essay, a high school transcript, and portfolio, and in some cases SAT I or ACT. It recommends an interview and a minimum high school GPA of 3.0. Application deadline: rolling admissions; 3/1 priority date for financial aid. Deferred admission is possible.

Portfolios are the single most important component of the application. Academic credentials and experience are also weighed heavily. Students apply directly to one major, so the college requires portfolios to focus on that area.

CLEVELAND INSTITUTE OF MUSIC

URBAN SETTING ■ PRIVATE ■ INDEPENDENT ■ COED
CLEVELAND, OHIO

Web site: www.cim.edu
Contact: Mr. William Fay, Director of Admission, 11021 East Boulevard,
    Cleveland, OH 44106-1776
Telephone: 216-795-3107 **Fax:** 216-791-1530
E-mail: cimadmission@po.cwru.edu

Academics

Cleveland Institute of Music awards bachelor's, master's, and doctoral **degrees**. Challenging opportunities include advanced placement credit, accelerated degree programs, and a senior project. Special programs include internships, summer session for credit, off-campus study, and Army and Air Force ROTC. A complete listing of majors at Cleveland Institute of Music appears in the Majors Index beginning on page 430.

The **faculty** at Cleveland Institute of Music has 31 full-time members. The student-faculty ratio is 7:1.

In 1969, The Cleveland Institute of Music (CIM) and Case Western Reserve University established a Joint Music Program at both the undergraduate and graduate levels. Each institution continues activities peculiar to it: CIM concentrates on the education and training of professionals skilled in the arts of performance, composition, and related musical disciplines, while Case Western Reserve University pursues and develops studies in the fields of music history, musicology, and music education.

Facilities and Resources

Facilities include classrooms, teaching studios, practice rooms, the CIM library, an orchestra library, a specially designed eurhythmics studio, an opera workshop and studio, and a music store. In addition, there are two concert and recital halls, electronic music studios, an annex, and dormitory.

Student rooms are linked to a campus network. 25 **computers** are available on campus that provide access to the Internet. The **library** has 47,500 books and 110 subscriptions. Audiovisual facilities include a sound-recording collection of 18,000 CDs, records, audio- and videotapes, reel-to-reel tapes, laser discs, and CD-ROMs.

Applying

Cleveland Institute of Music requires an essay, SAT I or ACT, a high school transcript, 2 recommendations, and audition. It recommends an interview. Application deadline: 12/1; 2/15 for financial aid. Early and deferred admission are possible.

Acceptance for study is determined by musical talent and achievement. Audition appointments are scheduled by the Admission Office only upon receipt of application.

Getting in Last Year
355 applied
29% were accepted
55% from top tenth of their h.s. class

The Student Body
382 total
224 undergraduates
37 home states and territories
17% from Ohio
13 home countries, other than U.S.
0.9% African American
12.1% Asian American
2.7% Hispanic American
12.9% international students

Graduation and After
90% pursued further study (90% arts and
    sciences)

Financial Matters
$20,312 tuition and fees (2001–02)
$6200 room and board
80% average percent of need met
$13,885 average financial aid amount received
    per undergraduate (2000–01)

CORCORAN COLLEGE OF ART AND DESIGN

URBAN SETTING ■ PRIVATE ■ INDEPENDENT ■ COED
WASHINGTON, DISTRICT OF COLUMBIA

Getting in Last Year
198 applied
62% were accepted
46 enrolled (37%)
4% from top tenth of their h.s. class
3.10 average high school GPA
35% had SAT verbal scores over 600
18% had SAT math scores over 600
34% had ACT scores over 24
2% had SAT verbal scores over 700
2% had SAT math scores over 700

The Student Body
372 undergraduates
19 home states and territories
12% from District of Columbia
21 home countries, other than U.S.
67.5% women, 32.5% men
6.6% African American
12.2% Asian American
7.5% Hispanic American

Graduation and After
37% graduated in 4 years
7% graduated in 5 years

Financial Matters
$17,000 tuition and fees (2001–02)
$6800 room and board
27% average percent of need met
$7588 average financial aid amount received
   per undergraduate

Web site: www.corcoran.edu
Contact: Ms. Anne E. Bowman, Director of Admissions, 500 17th Street, NW, Washington, DC 20006-4804
Telephone: 202-639-1814 or toll-free 888-CORCORAN (out-of-state) **Fax:** 202-639-1830
E-mail: admofc@corcoran.org

Academics

Corcoran awards associate and bachelor's **degrees**. Challenging opportunities include advanced placement credit, independent study, and a senior project. Special programs include internships, summer session for credit, and off-campus study.

The most frequently chosen **baccalaureate** field is visual/performing arts. A complete listing of majors at Corcoran appears in the Majors Index beginning on page 430.

The **faculty** at Corcoran has 26 full-time members, 73% with terminal degrees. The student-faculty ratio is 8:1.

Corcoran participates in the Alliance of Independent Colleges of Art and Design (AICAD) Student Mobility Program. Through the Visual Arts Community Outreach Program (VACOP), students teach art fundamentals in the Washington, DC, metropolitan area. Corcoran is nationally accredited by the National Association of Schools of Art and Design (NASAD).

Facilities and Resources

Corcoran remains one of the few examples of the "museum-art school," maintaining its original relationship with the Corcoran Gallery of Art. Studios are accessible 7 days a week; fine arts majors have semiprivate studios; photography majors have unlimited access to department facilities; graphic design majors have studios in Georgetown and 3 computer labs. Seniors exhibit annually in the Museum's Hemicycle gallery.

45 **computers** are available on campus that provide access to the Internet. The **library** has 20,518 books and 148 subscriptions. Other media resources include computers for word processing and Internet access, televisions, VCRs, and slide projectors.

Applying

Corcoran requires SAT I or ACT, a high school transcript, portfolio, and a minimum high school GPA of 2.5, and in some cases an essay, an interview, and 2 recommendations. It recommends an essay, an interview, 2 recommendations, and a minimum high school GPA of 3.0. Application deadline: rolling admissions; 3/15 priority date for financial aid. Early and deferred admission are possible.

The portfolio is very important relative to all other admission criteria. Writing samples are welcome.

THE CURTIS INSTITUTE OF MUSIC

URBAN SETTING ■ PRIVATE ■ INDEPENDENT ■ COED
PHILADELPHIA, PENNSYLVANIA

Contact: Mr. Christopher Hodges, Admissions Officer, 1726 Locust Street,
Philadelphia, PA 19103-6107
Telephone: 215-893-5262 **Fax:** 215-893-7900

Academics

Curtis awards bachelor's and master's **degrees**. Challenging opportunities include
advanced placement credit and accelerated degree programs. Off-campus study is a
special program. A complete listing of majors at Curtis appears in the Majors Index
beginning on page 430.

The **faculty** at Curtis has 80 members.

Students who have completed Curtis' liberal arts requirements may enroll at no cost
at the University of Pennsylvania for additional courses not available at Curtis under a
reciprocal agreement between the two schools.

Facilities and Resources

Curtis Hall, a 250-seat auditorium with splendid acoustics and facilities for recording, is
used for student recitals, alumni and faculty concerts, organ lessons and practice, master
classes, school assemblies, orchestra rehearsals, and recording sessions. Curtis Opera
Studio, a black-box theater that seats 125, has recording capabilities and is used primarily
by the vocal studies department for opera performances, dance and movement classes,
rehearsals, and master classes.

The **library** has 70,000 books. The library contains more than 65,000 volumes of
music, scores, and books and more than 14,000 recordings, including scholarly editions
of the works of 60 composers as well as authoritative editions of the standard repertoire.

Applying

Curtis requires an essay, SAT I, a high school transcript, recommendations, and audition.
Application deadline: 1/15. Early admission is possible.

Because the school's enrollment has always been limited to the exceptional candidate,
the audition process is extremely competitive.

Getting in Last Year
671 applied
7% were accepted

The Student Body
168 total
148 undergraduates
24 home states and territories
22 home countries, other than U.S.

Financial Matters
$695 tuition and fees (2001–02)

FASHION INSTITUTE OF TECHNOLOGY

URBAN SETTING ■ PUBLIC ■ STATE AND LOCALLY SUPPORTED ■ COED
NEW YORK, NEW YORK

Getting in Last Year
4,469 applied
36% were accepted
1,021 enrolled (64%)
7% from top tenth of their h.s. class
3.30 average high school GPA

The Student Body
10,786 total
10,680 undergraduates
52 home states and territories
74% from New York
80 home countries, other than U.S.
82% women, 18% men
7.4% African American
0.2% American Indian
10.6% Asian American
10.1% Hispanic American
14.9% international students

Graduation and After
86% had job offers within 6 months
95 organizations recruited on campus

Financial Matters
$3366 resident tuition and fees (2001–02)
$7894 nonresident tuition and fees (2001–02)
$7535 room and board
80% average percent of need met
$5997 average financial aid amount received
per undergraduate

Web site: www.fitnyc.suny.edu
Contact: Mr. Jim Pidgeon, Director of Admissions, Seventh Avenue at 27th Street, New York, NY 10001-5992
Telephone: 212-217-7675 or toll-free 800-GOTOFIT (out-of-state) **Fax:** 212-217-7481
E-mail: fitinfo@sfitva.cc.fitsuny.edu

Academics

FIT awards associate, bachelor's, and master's **degrees**. Challenging opportunities include advanced placement credit, an honors program, and a senior project. Special programs include cooperative education, internships, summer session for credit, and study-abroad.

The most frequently chosen **baccalaureate** fields are business/marketing, visual/performing arts, and engineering/engineering technologies. A complete listing of majors at FIT appears in the Majors Index beginning on page 430.

The **faculty** at FIT has 211 full-time members. The student-faculty ratio is 13:1.

In 1986, FIT established an affiliation with the Politecnico Internazionale della Moda in Florence, Italy. FIT-sponsored study-abroad programs are available in Australia, Canada, England, France, Italy, and Spain. Through FIT's membership in the College Consortium for International Studies, additional semester-abroad opportunities are also available.

Facilities and Resources

The Fred P. Pomerantz Art and Design Center houses photography studios and darkrooms, painting and printmaking rooms, a sculpture studio, a graphics laboratory, a model-making workshop, and a toy design workshop. Student presentations are staged in the Kate Murphy Amphitheatre. Other facilities include the Marvin Feldman Center, the 800-seat Morris W. and Fannie B. Haft Auditorium, the Quick Response Center, the Design/Research Lighting Laboratory, and the Peter G. Scotese Computer-Aided Design and Communications Center.

Student rooms are linked to a campus network. 450 **computers** are available on campus that provide access to the Internet. The **library** has 154,015 books. The library carries an international assortment of sketchbooks, periodicals, slides, films, and extensive clippings files. Its special collections contain rare books, original fashion sketches, photographs, and archives. The Shirly Goodman Resource Center houses the Gladys Marcus Library and the Museum at FIT.

Applying

FIT requires an essay, a high school transcript, and portfolio for art and design programs. It recommends SAT I or ACT. Application deadline: 1/1; 3/1 priority date for financial aid. Deferred admission is possible.

The Juilliard School

Urban setting ■ Private ■ Independent ■ Coed
New York, New York

Web site: www.juilliard.edu
Contact: Ms. Mary K. Gray, Associate Dean for Admissions, 60 Lincoln Center Plaza, New York, NY 10023-6588
Telephone: 212-799-5000 ext. 527 **Fax:** 212-724-0263
E-mail: webmaster@juilliard.edu

Academics

Juilliard awards bachelor's, master's, and doctoral **degrees**. Challenging opportunities include accelerated degree programs, student-designed majors, double majors, and a senior project. Off-campus study is a special program. A complete listing of majors at Juilliard appears in the Majors Index beginning on page 430.

The **faculty** at Juilliard has 119 full-time members. The student-faculty ratio is 4:1.

The Juilliard School, Columbia University, and Barnard College have a cooperative program offering students combined music conservatory and liberal arts education. A joint-degree program offers academically and musically gifted students the opportunity to earn both a Bachelor of Arts and a Master of Music degree in five years.

Another cross-registration program opens individual courses for academic credit at Juilliard to qualified students in the three undergraduate liberal arts schools. Juilliard also maintains a nonformalized and limited exchange with the Royal Academy of Music in London.

Facilities and Resources

Juilliard's modern Lincoln Center home includes 15 two-story rehearsal studios, 84 practice rooms, and 35 teaching studios housing more than 250 Steinway pianos, a large permanent instrument collection, and 28 classrooms. Juilliard features 4 auditoriums: the Juilliard Theater seats 933 people and has a movable ceiling; Paul Recital Hall seats 278; Morse Recital Hall, suitable for various types of performances, seats 200; and the Drama Theater seats 206 and is equipped with a complete theatrical lighting system.

In-house scenery and costume shops produce materials for all of Juilliard's fully staged opera, dance, and drama presentations.

34 **computers** are available on campus that provide access to the Internet. The **library** has 80,793 books and 220 subscriptions. Other media resources include 47,000 performance and study scores, 14,000 musical recordings, and a listening lab. Students have access to the world-wide OCLC database, the latest notation software (Finale), state-of-the-art sequencing software, and Yamaha DX7 synthesizers. Juilliard's archives feature the Ruth Dana Collection of First and Early Editions of Franz Liszt's Piano Music; the Rare Libretto Collection; Leonard Rose's Collection of Cello Music; and several works by Belgian violinist-composer Eugene Ysaye.

Applying

Juilliard requires an essay, a high school transcript, and audition. Application deadline: 12/1; 3/1 priority date for financial aid. Early admission is possible.

The members of the Juilliard faculty believe personal auditions are the means by which they may best judge talent and potential and consider the audition the most important factor in determining admission status.

Getting in Last Year
1,624 applied
9% were accepted
119 enrolled (83%)

The Student Body
813 total
506 undergraduates
38 home states and territories
22% from New York
24 home countries, other than U.S.
51.2% women, 48.8% men
10.3% African American
13.8% Asian American
5.3% Hispanic American
22.9% international students

Graduation and After
70% graduated in 4 years
3% graduated in 5 years
2% graduated in 6 years

Financial Matters
$19,000 tuition and fees (2001–02)
$7500 room and board
76% average percent of need met
$16,372 average financial aid amount received per undergraduate (2000–01 estimated)

Manhattan School of Music

Urban setting ■ Private ■ Independent ■ Coed
New York, New York

Getting in Last Year
699 applied
40% were accepted
87 enrolled (31%)

The Student Body
831 total
395 undergraduates
35 home states and territories
38% from New York
30 home countries, other than U.S.
51.6% women, 48.4% men
4.4% African American
0.8% American Indian
9.8% Asian American
5.9% Hispanic American
29.3% international students

Graduation and After
37% graduated in 4 years
4% graduated in 5 years
3% graduated in 6 years
60% pursued further study (60% arts and sciences)
25 organizations recruited on campus

Financial Matters
$21,500 tuition and fees (2001–02)
$7200 room only
47% average percent of need met
$12,599 average financial aid amount received per undergraduate

Web site: www.msmnyc.edu
Contact: Mrs. Amy Anderson, Director of Admission, 120 Claremont Avenue, New York, NY 10027
Telephone: 212-749-2802 ext. 4449 **Fax:** 212-749-3025
E-mail: admission@msmnyc.edu

Academics
MSM awards bachelor's, master's, and doctoral **degrees** and post-bachelor's and post-master's certificates. Challenging opportunities include advanced placement credit and a senior project. Off-campus study is a special program.

The most frequently chosen **baccalaureate** field is visual/performing arts. A complete listing of majors at MSM appears in the Majors Index beginning on page 430.

The **faculty** at MSM has 40 full-time members, 38% with terminal degrees. The student-faculty ratio is 8:1.

MSM has a cross-registration program with Barnard College.

Facilities and Resources
Facilities of note at MSM include the 1,000-seat Borden Auditorium, the 250-seat Hubbard Recital Hall (with organ), the 60-seat Pforzheimer Recital Hall, the 35-seat Myers Recital Hall and Recording Studio, and two electronic music studios.

10 **computers** are available on campus that provide access to the Internet. The **library** has 71,400 books and 93 subscriptions.

Applying
MSM requires an essay, a high school transcript, 1 recommendation, audition, and a minimum high school GPA of 2.0. It recommends SAT I or ACT, an interview, and a minimum high school GPA of 3.0. Application deadline: 12/1; 3/15 priority date for financial aid.

Auditions are by far the most important part of the application process. Transcripts and TOEFL scores (for international students) are also very important; essays are somewhat important.

MANNES COLLEGE OF MUSIC, NEW SCHOOL UNIVERSITY

URBAN SETTING ■ PRIVATE ■ INDEPENDENT ■ COED
NEW YORK, NEW YORK

Web site: www.mannes.edu
Contact: Ms. Allison Scola, Director of Enrollment, 150 West 85th Street, New York, NY 10024-4402
Telephone: 212-580-0210 ext. 246 or toll-free 800-292-3040 (out-of-state)
Fax: 212-580-1738
E-mail: mannasadmissions@newschool.edu

Academics

Mannes awards bachelor's and master's **degrees** and post-master's certificates. Challenging opportunities include advanced placement credit, accelerated degree programs, double majors, and a senior project. Summer session for credit is a special program.

The most frequently chosen **baccalaureate** field is visual/performing arts. A complete listing of majors at Mannes appears in the Majors Index beginning on page 430.

The **faculty** at Mannes has 4 full-time members. The student-faculty ratio is 2:1.

Mannes students may take liberal arts courses in other New School Divisions: at Eugene Lang College or through the Adult Division. Mannes students will also interact with students at Parsons School of Design or the School of Dramatic Arts.

Facilities and Resources

Mannes is located in a Federal-style building on Manhattan's Upper West Side. The building houses classrooms, practice rooms, offices, a student lounge, and a spacious library with study carrels and a listening room. Two concert halls are available; the larger seats 300, the smaller—suitable for student recitals—seats 50. Additional performance opportunities are available through the use of facilities at the New School's downtown campus.

475 **computers** are available on campus for student use. The 3 **libraries** have 368,390 books and 1,155 subscriptions.

Applying

Mannes requires a high school transcript, 1 recommendation, audition, and a minimum high school GPA of 2.5. Application deadline: 12/15; 3/1 priority date for financial aid. Deferred admission is possible.

Students are required to pass entrance examinations in their major field of study. (Accompanists will be provided for students auditioning in voice and orchestral instruments.) Placement tests in theory, ear training, and dictation are also required.

Mannes College of Music, a division of New School University, holds a proud place at the forefront of American music education. Throughout its 75 years of existence, it has led the way with programs considered among the best in the world for broad musical training and the encouragement of artistic growth. Its distinguished faculty includes some of New York City's most prominent musicians as well as internationally known ensembles. In an age of mass education, Mannes maintains small classes and an intimate atmosphere that permits a close and sustained contact among students, faculty members, and the administration.

Getting in Last Year
268 applied
37% were accepted
43 enrolled (44%)

The Student Body
278 total
127 undergraduates
17 home states and territories
47% from New York
33 home countries, other than U.S.
64.6% women, 35.4% men
4.1% African American
6.6% Asian American
4.1% Hispanic American
42.1% international students

Graduation and After
45% pursued further study (45% arts and sciences)

Financial Matters
$20,246 tuition and fees (2001–02)
$9612 room and board
57% average percent of need met
$10,815 average financial aid amount received per undergraduate

MARYLAND INSTITUTE, COLLEGE OF ART

URBAN SETTING ■ PRIVATE ■ INDEPENDENT ■ COED
BALTIMORE, MARYLAND

Web site: www.mica.edu
Contact: Mr. Hans Ever, Director of Undergraduate Admission, 1300 Mount
    Royal Avenue, Baltimore, MD 21217-4191
Telephone: 410-225-2222 **Fax:** 410-225-2337
E-mail: admissions@mica.edu

Getting in Last Year
1,693 applied
46% were accepted
321 enrolled (41%)
21% from top tenth of their h.s. class
3.58 average high school GPA
41% had SAT verbal scores over 600
31% had SAT math scores over 600
8% had SAT verbal scores over 700
3% had SAT math scores over 700
4 valedictorians

The Student Body
1,333 total
1,195 undergraduates
46 home states and territories
26% from Maryland
50 home countries, other than U.S.
61.2% women, 38.8% men
3.6% African American
0.5% American Indian
6.4% Asian American
3.7% Hispanic American
4.9% international students

Graduation and After
51% graduated in 4 years
10% graduated in 5 years
2% graduated in 6 years
23% pursued further study (16% arts and sciences, 7% education)
30% had job offers within 6 months
40 organizations recruited on campus

Financial Matters
$21,080 tuition and fees (2001–02)
$6640 room and board

Academics
MICA awards bachelor's and master's **degrees** and post-bachelor's certificates. Challenging opportunities include advanced placement credit, accelerated degree programs, student-designed majors, double majors, independent study, and a senior project. Special programs include internships, summer session for credit, off-campus study, study-abroad, and Army ROTC.

The most frequently chosen **baccalaureate** fields are visual/performing arts and education. A complete listing of majors at MICA appears in the Majors Index beginning on page 430.

The **faculty** at MICA has 113 full-time members, 74% with terminal degrees. The student-faculty ratio is 10:1.

MICA is a member of the Association of Independent Colleges of Art and Design (AICAD). Through this association qualified Institute students can participate in a semester-long program in Manhattan or can spend up to one year at any of more than 30 member schools across the country and in Canada. MICA also offers study abroad opportunities in England, France, Japan, Italy, the Netherlands, Scotland, Greece, Canada, Israel, and Mexico. MICA participates in an academic exchange program with the nearby Johns Hopkins University, Goucher College, Loyola College, Notre Dame College, the University of Baltimore, and the Peabody Conservatory of Music.

Facilities and Resources
Students have 24-hour access to individual and shared studio space. More than 250,000 square feet of institutional facilities in 6 buildings are dedicated to studio and classroom space, including 9 galleries that total over 5,600 square feet. MICA has a 250-seat auditorium and a state-of-the-art media lecture room with a color projection system, sound and video playback, and multimedia computer projection. Computer classrooms, a 3-D imaging lab, a computerized writing lab, and a digital video facility provide access to more than 235 computers for students in every major.

Student rooms are linked to a campus network. 240 **computers** are available on campus that provide access to email and the Internet. The 2 **libraries** have 50,000 books and 305 subscriptions. The Media Resources Collection houses more than 100,000 slides.

Applying
MICA requires an essay, a high school transcript, and art portfolio, and in some cases SAT I or ACT. It recommends an interview and 3 recommendations. Application deadline: 1/15; 3/1 priority date for financial aid. Early and deferred admission are possible.

The portfolio of artwork should demonstrate talent, ability, and experience and is considered very important. Level of course work, GPA, test scores, and essays are also weighed heavily.

Massachusetts College of Art

Urban setting ■ Public ■ State-supported ■ Coed
Boston, Massachusetts

Web site: www.massart.edu

Contact: Ms. Kay Ransdell, Dean of Admissions, 621 Huntington Avenue, Boston, MA 02115-5882

Telephone: 617-232-1555 ext. 235 **Fax:** 617-879-7250

E-mail: admissions@massart.edu

Academics

MassArt awards bachelor's and master's **degrees** and post-bachelor's certificates. Challenging opportunities include student-designed majors, double majors, independent study, and a senior project. Special programs include internships, summer session for credit, off-campus study, and study-abroad.

The most frequently chosen **baccalaureate** fields are visual/performing arts and education. A complete listing of majors at MassArt appears in the Majors Index beginning on page 430.

The **faculty** at MassArt has 67 full-time members, 75% with terminal degrees. The student-faculty ratio is 13:1.

MassArt is a member of the Professional Arts Consortium (ProArts), an association of neighboring Boston colleges (Berklee College of Music, Boston Architectural Center, the Boston Conservatory, Emerson College, and the School of the Museum of Fine Arts) that prepare their students to be professionals in the visual and performing arts and architecture. MassArt participates in the College Academic Program Sharing (CAPS) and the Public College Exchange Program, through which students can cross-register at the majority of Massachusetts state colleges and universities.

MassArt participates in the mobility program of the Association of Independent Colleges of Art and Design (AICAD), coordinates exchange programs with 3 schools in England (The Chelsea School of Art and Design, London; The West Surrey College of Art and Design; The Central Saint Martin's School of Art and Design, London) and has exploratory exchange programs with 2 schools in the Netherlands (the Rietveld Academy, Amsterdam; the Royal Academy of Visual Arts, The Hague), and one with the Universitat de Barcelona in Spain and with the Fachhochschule in Wiesbaden, Germany.

Facilities and Resources

The main Huntington/Bakalar Galleries comprise 9,000 square feet. An additional 30,000 square feet of exhibition space are student programmed. Student studio space totals 250,000 square feet. Performance spaces include the 500-seat main auditorium, an 18,000-square-foot flexible space, an analog/digital sound studio, and a variety of smaller studio spaces for video and interrelated media projects.

250 **computers** are available on campus for student use. The **library** has 231,586 books and 757 subscriptions. Other media resources include 700 films, 1,500 videotapes, 100,000 slides, sound recordings, posters, a rare book collection, the Gunn Associate pictorial reference file (90,000 images collected from periodicals between 1939 and 1965), and the College's archives, consisting of manuscripts, artwork, and rare publications.

Applying

MassArt requires an essay, SAT I or ACT, a high school transcript, portfolio, and a minimum high school GPA of 2.9. It recommends recommendations. Application deadline: 3/1; 3/15 priority date for financial aid. Early and deferred admission are possible.

The portfolio should consist of a minimum of 15 recent art works presented in slide format. The portfolio is very important, although transcripts and test scores, as well as motivation and drive shown in a required Statement of Purpose, are also important.

Getting in Last Year

1,133 applied
46% were accepted
236 enrolled (45%)
17% from top tenth of their h.s. class
3.23 average high school GPA
35% had SAT verbal scores over 600
23% had SAT math scores over 600
8% had SAT verbal scores over 700
2% had SAT math scores over 700

The Student Body

2,245 total
2,133 undergraduates
26 home states and territories
78% from Massachusetts
58 home countries, other than U.S.
65.2% women, 34.8% men
3.5% African American
0.1% American Indian
3.4% Asian American
3.6% Hispanic American
5.1% international students

Graduation and After

5% pursued further study
8 organizations recruited on campus

Financial Matters

$4068 resident tuition and fees (2001–02)
$13,198 nonresident tuition and fees (2001–02)
$7742 room and board

New England Conservatory of Music

Urban setting ■ Private ■ Independent ■ Coed
Boston, Massachusetts

Getting in Last Year
731 applied
56% were accepted
97 enrolled (24%)
3.05 average high school GPA

The Student Body
772 total
381 undergraduates
44 home states and territories
25% from Massachusetts
36 home countries, other than U.S.
47% women, 53% men
3.7% African American
0.6% American Indian
8.7% Asian American
2.8% Hispanic American
18.5% international students

Graduation and After
20 organizations recruited on campus

Financial Matters
$21,800 tuition and fees (2001–02)
$9400 room and board
71% average percent of need met
$16,467 average financial aid amount received
  per undergraduate

Web site: www.newenglandconservatory.edu
Contact: Dean of Enrollment Services, 290 Huntington Avenue, Boston, MA
  02115-5000
Telephone: 617-585-1101 **Fax:** 617-585-1115
E-mail: admissions@newenglandconservatory.edu

Academics

NEC awards bachelor's, master's, and doctoral **degrees** and post-bachelor's certificates. Challenging opportunities include advanced placement credit, double majors, independent study, and a senior project. Special programs include internships, summer session for credit, and off-campus study.

The most frequently chosen **baccalaureate** field is visual/performing arts. A complete listing of majors at NEC appears in the Majors Index beginning on page 430.

The **faculty** at NEC has 76 full-time members. The student-faculty ratio is 7:1.

NEC participates in a double-degree program with Tufts University. Students in the double-degree program earn a Bachelor of Music degree from NEC and a Bachelor of Arts or Bachelor of Science degree from Tufts University. Cross-registration is also available at Northeastern University and Simmons College.

Facilities and Resources

NEC has more than 150 practice rooms ranging in size from 180 to more than 500 square feet. Most rooms are equipped with Steinway grand pianos, while some hold upright pianos. There are locked practice rooms for percussion, harpsichord, and organ.

48 **computers** are available on campus that provide access to the Internet. The 2 **libraries** have 75,674 books and 255 subscriptions. Other media resources include 110,000 volumes of music, books, sound and video recordings, and microforms. Special collections include early scores and manuscripts.

Applying

NEC requires an essay, SAT I or ACT, a high school transcript, 2 recommendations, audition, and a minimum high school GPA of 2.75. Application deadline: 12/3; 2/2 priority date for financial aid. Deferred admission is possible.

Audition and/or portfolio review are judged as most important admission criteria.

New York School of Interior Design

Urban setting ■ Private ■ Independent ■ Coed
New York, New York

Web site: www.nysid.edu
Contact: Mr. Douglas Robbins, Admissions Associate, 170 East 70th Street, New York, NY 10021-5110
Telephone: 212-472-1500 ext. 204 or toll-free 800-336-9743 **Fax:** 212-472-1867
E-mail: admissions@nysid.edu

Academics
NYSID awards associate, bachelor's, and master's **degrees**. Challenging opportunities include advanced placement credit, independent study, and a senior project. Special programs include internships and summer session for credit.

The most frequently chosen **baccalaureate** field is visual/performing arts. A complete listing of majors at NYSID appears in the Majors Index beginning on page 430.

The student-faculty ratio is 8:1.

Facilities and Resources
Facilities include an extensive design library, materials library of manufacturers' catalogs and samples, a new lighting design laboratory, a computer-aided design (CAD) lab, and gallery spaces that host a variety of exhibitions each year, including the annual student exhibition. NYSID also has a large open studio space.

50 **computers** are available on campus that provide access to the Internet. The **library** has 10,000 books and 88 subscriptions. Other media resources include architecture, art, and interior design videos, collections of rare folios, material samples, and product information.

Applying
NYSID requires an essay, SAT I or ACT, a high school transcript, 2 recommendations, portfolio, and a minimum high school GPA of 2.5, and in some cases an interview. It recommends an interview. Application deadline: rolling admissions; 5/1 priority date for financial aid. Deferred admission is possible.

The quality of an applicant's portfolio is given equal consideration in relation to other admission requirements. Applicants who exhibit exceptional talent or ability are considered for scholarships.

Manhattan, with its world-famous museums, showrooms, and architectural landmarks, is home to the New York School of Interior Design (NYSID). NYSID is a single-major college dedicated solely to the study of interior design. Facilities include a lighting lab, a computer-aided design (CAD) lab, and an extensive reference library. Many NYSID graduates have gone on to find work in the best design and architectural firms in New York City and around the world. The Bachelor of Fine Arts degree is a FIDER-accredited program.

Getting in Last Year
103 applied
53% were accepted
166 enrolled (302%)
3.00 average high school GPA
3% had SAT verbal scores over 600
2% had SAT math scores over 600

The Student Body
640 total
631 undergraduates
15 home states and territories
83% from New York
30 home countries, other than U.S.
86.7% women, 13.3% men

Graduation and After
5% graduated in 5 years
15% graduated in 6 years

Financial Matters
$16,940 tuition and fees (2001–02)
50% average percent of need met
$3500 average financial aid amount received per undergraduate

North Carolina School of the Arts

Urban setting ■ Public ■ State-supported ■ Coed
Winston-Salem, North Carolina

Web site: www.ncarts.edu
Contact: Ms. Sheeler Lawson, Director of Admissions, 1533 South Main Street, PO Box 12189, Winston-Salem, NC 27127-2188
Telephone: 336-770-3290 **Fax:** 336-770-3370
E-mail: admissions@ncarts.edu

The School's mission encompasses not only the performing arts but the moving image and visual arts as well. The relationship between students and their teachers, that of apprentice to master, is the heart of the School. The members of a resident faculty of 100 artists have had successful careers on Broadway, in Hollywood, and as members of great orchestras and dance companies and theaters of the world. School of the Arts alumni have distinguished themselves in such famous places as the Metropolitan Opera, the Houston Ballet, the Great Lakes Theater Festival, the Merce Cunningham Dance Company, Broadway, and Hollywood.

Getting in Last Year
698 applied
45% were accepted
187 enrolled (59%)
15% from top tenth of their h.s. class
3.48 average high school GPA
38% had SAT verbal scores over 600
27% had SAT math scores over 600
51% had ACT scores over 24
8% had SAT verbal scores over 700
3% had SAT math scores over 700
7% had ACT scores over 30

The Student Body
789 total
708 undergraduates
40 home states and territories
48% from North Carolina
21 home countries, other than U.S.
43.2% women, 56.8% men
10% African American
0.4% American Indian
2.1% Asian American
1.7% Hispanic American
1.8% international students

Graduation and After
40% graduated in 4 years
5% graduated in 5 years

Financial Matters
$2877 resident tuition and fees (2001–02)
$12,282 nonresident tuition and fees (2001–02)
$4920 room and board
79% average percent of need met
$7851 average financial aid amount received per undergraduate (2000–01)

Academics
NCSA awards bachelor's and master's **degrees**. A senior project is a challenging opportunity.

The most frequently chosen **baccalaureate** field is visual/performing arts. A complete listing of majors at NCSA appears in the Majors Index beginning on page 430.

The **faculty** at NCSA has 126 full-time members, 69% with terminal degrees. The student-faculty ratio is 8:1.

Facilities and Resources
Facilities include 71 music practice rooms; 27 teaching studios; 3 large rehearsal halls; a 600-seat concert auditorium housing a Kenan Organ and Hamburg and Steinway grand pianos; a 56-seat recital hall; electronic and film music composition studios equipped with state-of-the-art MIDI instruments; and a historic 1,380-seat theater with state-of-the-art stage, electronic, and sound equipment, rehearsal and warm-up rooms, dressing rooms, sound and light projection booths, and orchestra pit.

20 **computers** are available on campus for student use. The 2 **libraries** have 85,672 books and 48,546 subscriptions. Other media resources include 40,000 music scores, 36,000 records, CDs, and tapes.

Applying
NCSA requires SAT I or ACT, a high school transcript, 2 recommendations, and audition, and in some cases an essay and an interview. Application deadline: rolling admissions; 3/1 priority date for financial aid.

In addition to the transcripts, test scores, and references, admission to NCSA is based on talent and potential as assessed in an audition before the arts faculty.

PARSONS SCHOOL OF DESIGN, NEW SCHOOL UNIVERSITY

URBAN SETTING ■ PRIVATE ■ INDEPENDENT ■ COED
NEW YORK, NEW YORK

Web site: www.parsons.edu

Contact: Ms. Nadine M. Bourgeois, Director of Admissions and Associate Dean of Enrollment Management, 66 Fifth Avenue, New York, NY 10011-8878

Telephone: 212-229-8910 or toll-free 800-252-0852

E-mail: parsadm@newschool.edu

Academics

Parsons awards associate, bachelor's, and master's **degrees**. Challenging opportunities include advanced placement credit, accelerated degree programs, an honors program, independent study, and a senior project. Special programs include internships, summer session for credit, off-campus study, and study-abroad.

The most frequently chosen **baccalaureate** fields are visual/performing arts and architecture. A complete listing of majors at Parsons appears in the Majors Index beginning on page 430.

The **faculty** at Parsons has 56 full-time members. The student-faculty ratio is 11:1.

Students enrich their education by taking part in mobility or exchange programs arranged between Parsons and other art and design colleges. Parsons offers study-abroad opportunities in Israel, the Netherlands, Great Britain, and Sweden. Parsons participates in exchange programs with the 31 schools of the Alliance of Independent Colleges of Art and Design (AICAD). Parsons is also affiliated with a number of two-year schools whose graduates may transfer to Parsons to complete their degrees.

Facilities and Resources

The students at Parsons work within 3 designated buildings that house studios equipped for specific fields of work.

705 **computers** are available on campus that provide access to e-mail and the Internet. The 3 **libraries** have 368,390 books and 1,155 subscriptions. Other media resources include visual, printed, and online services and links to the libraries of New York University and Cooper Union for the Advancement of Science and Art. Parsons is also connected to the Smithsonian Collection in Washington, DC.

Applying

Parsons requires SAT I or ACT, a high school transcript, portfolio, home examination, and a minimum high school GPA of 2.0, and in some cases an essay and an interview. It recommends a minimum high school GPA of 3.0. Application deadline: rolling admissions; 3/1 priority date for financial aid.

The portfolio requirement plays a key role in the decision-making process of the admissions committee.

Getting in Last Year

1,690 applied
44% were accepted
361 enrolled (49%)
25% had SAT verbal scores over 600
28% had SAT math scores over 600
6% had SAT verbal scores over 700
6% had SAT math scores over 700

The Student Body

2,733 total
2,311 undergraduates
42 home states and territories
53% from New York
57 home countries, other than U.S.
74.6% women, 25.4% men
3.8% African American
0.2% American Indian
20% Asian American
6.7% Hispanic American
29% international students

Graduation and After

5% pursued further study (5% arts and sciences)
100 organizations recruited on campus

Financial Matters

$23,126 tuition and fees (2001–02)
$9612 room and board
66% average percent of need met
$13,129 average financial aid amount received per undergraduate

RHODE ISLAND SCHOOL OF DESIGN

URBAN SETTING ■ PRIVATE ■ INDEPENDENT ■ COED
PROVIDENCE, RHODE ISLAND

Getting in Last Year
2,004 applied
41% were accepted
418 enrolled (51%)
30% from top tenth of their h.s. class
3.30 average high school GPA
51% had SAT verbal scores over 600
53% had SAT math scores over 600
15% had SAT verbal scores over 700
10% had SAT math scores over 700

The Student Body
2,119 total
1,845 undergraduates
51 home states and territories
6% from Rhode Island
53 home countries, other than U.S.
2.7% African American
0.2% American Indian
11.3% Asian American
4.6% Hispanic American
11.9% international students

Graduation and After
5% pursued further study (5% arts and sciences)
96% had job offers within 6 months
50 organizations recruited on campus

Financial Matters
$23,397 tuition and fees (2001–02)
$6830 room and board
70% average percent of need met
$14,900 average financial aid amount received per undergraduate

Web site: www.risd.edu
Contact: Mr. Edward Newhall, Director of Admissions, 2 College Street, Providence, RI 02905-2791
Telephone: 401-454-6300 or toll-free 800-364-RISD **Fax:** 401-454-6309
E-mail: admissions@risd.edu

Academics

RISD awards bachelor's, master's, and first-professional **degrees**. Challenging opportunities include advanced placement credit and a senior project. Special programs include internships, off-campus study, and study-abroad.

The most frequently chosen **baccalaureate** fields are visual/performing arts and architecture. A complete listing of majors at RISD appears in the Majors Index beginning on page 430.

The **faculty** at RISD has 139 full-time members, 73% with terminal degrees. The student-faculty ratio is 11:1.

RISD offers cross-registration with neighboring Brown University and participates in the mobility program of the Association of Independent Colleges of Art and Design (AICAD). Students may also consider a unique international study opportunity through the International Exchange Program. RISD currently has exchange agreements with 26 schools in 15 other countries.

Facilities and Resources

RISD's 13-acre urban campus has 40 buildings encompassing one million square feet of space. Each of 17 studio disciplines has its own facility offering studios, classrooms, and specialized facilities such as shops and computer labs. There are 11 galleries on campus available for the exhibition of student work. The 45 galleries in RISD's Museum of Art display selections from the permanent collection of 100,000 works of art, and the Nature Lab contains more than 70,000 items of natural history.

Student rooms are linked to a campus network. 300 **computers** are available on campus that provide access to the Internet. The **library** has 95,161 books and 423 subscriptions. Other media resources include an image collection of 550,000 slides, photos, and clippings.

Applying

RISD requires an essay, SAT I or ACT, a high school transcript, and portfolio, drawing assignments. It recommends 3 recommendations. Application deadline: 2/15; 2/15 priority date for financial aid. Early and deferred admission are possible.

The portfolio should contain 8 to 20 slides of a student's best work. The portfolio is very important in relation to the other criteria, although the application is a combination of all the required elements. For architecture students, the portfolio is less crucial.

SAN FRANCISCO CONSERVATORY OF MUSIC

URBAN SETTING ■ PRIVATE ■ INDEPENDENT ■ COED
SAN FRANCISCO, CALIFORNIA

Web site: www.sfcm.edu
Contact: Susan Dean, Director of Admissions, 1201 Ortega Street, San
  Francisco, CA 94122-4411
Telephone: 415-759-3431 **Fax:** 415-759-3499
E-mail: admit@sfcm.edu

Academics

SFCM awards bachelor's and master's **degrees** and post-master's certificates. Challenging opportunities include advanced placement credit and independent study.

The most frequently chosen **baccalaureate** field is visual/performing arts. A complete listing of majors at SFCM appears in the Majors Index beginning on page 430.

The **faculty** at SFCM has 24 full-time members, 54% with terminal degrees. The student-faculty ratio is 6:1.

Facilities and Resources

Performance spaces include the 333-seat Hellman Hall and 50-seat Agnes Albert Performance Hall. Hellman Hall is considered one of the finest concert halls of its size in northern California. It also includes one of the few professional recording studios in a Bay Area concert hall. Both halls are available for formal and informal student concerts. Practice rooms are available to enrolled students at no charge. Almost all practice rooms have windows and most overlook the Conservatory courtyard.

7 **computers** are available on campus that provide access to the Internet. The **library** has 36,821 books and 80 subscriptions. The Conservatory Library collection includes video recordings pertinent to music study. These recordings are primarily opera performances, music history lectures, and a collection of Conservatory master classes and concerts.

Applying

SFCM requires SAT I or ACT, a high school transcript, 2 recommendations, and audition. It recommends SAT I. Application deadline: 2/1; 3/1 priority date for financial aid. Early admission is possible.

The audition is the most important criterion used to determine eligibility for admission to the program.

Getting in Last Year
116 applied
63% were accepted
21 enrolled (29%)
3.34 average high school GPA
46% had SAT verbal scores over 600
27% had SAT math scores over 600
9% had SAT verbal scores over 700
7% had SAT math scores over 700

The Student Body
275 total
146 undergraduates
28 home states and territories
51% from California
16 home countries, other than U.S.
56.2% women, 43.8% men
3.4% African American
1.4% American Indian
12.3% Asian American
6.8% Hispanic American
19.9% international students

Graduation and After
61% graduated in 4 years
4% graduated in 5 years
50% pursued further study (45% arts and sciences, 5% education)
2 organizations recruited on campus

Financial Matters
$20,780 tuition and fees (2001–02)
71% average percent of need met
$14,235 average financial aid amount received per undergraduate (1999–2000)

WESTMINSTER CHOIR COLLEGE OF RIDER UNIVERSITY

SMALL-TOWN SETTING ■ PRIVATE ■ INDEPENDENT ■ COED
PRINCETON, NEW JERSEY

Web site: westminster.rider.edu
Contact: Elizabeth S. Rush, Assistant Director of Admissions, 101 Walnut Lane, Princeton, NJ 08540-3899
Telephone: 609-921-7144 ext. 221 or toll-free 800-96-CHOIR **Fax:** 609-921-2538
E-mail: wccadmission@rider.edu

Getting in Last Year
193 applied
67% were accepted
80 enrolled (62%)
3.40 average high school GPA
33% had SAT verbal scores over 600
35% had SAT math scores over 600
6% had SAT verbal scores over 700
8% had SAT math scores over 700
1 class president

The Student Body
446 total
340 undergraduates
40 home states and territories
36% from New Jersey
59.7% women, 40.3% men

Financial Matters
$18,230 tuition and fees (2001–02)
$7670 room and board
79% average percent of need met
$12,804 average financial aid amount received per undergraduate (2000–01 estimated)

Academics

Westminster awards bachelor's and master's **degrees**. Challenging opportunities include advanced placement credit, an honors program, double majors, independent study, and a senior project. Special programs include internships, summer session for credit, and off-campus study.

The most frequently chosen **baccalaureate** field is visual/performing arts. A complete listing of majors at Westminster appears in the Majors Index beginning on page 430.

The **faculty** at Westminster has 35 full-time members. The student-faculty ratio is 7:1.

Westminster has a cooperative program with Princeton University permitting limited undergraduate and graduate student cross-registration. For graduate students there is a similar affiliation with Princeton Theological Seminary. An arrangement also exists by which graduates holding the Master of Music degree with a major in sacred music may apply for advanced standing in the doctoral program at Drew University. A cooperative program between Westminster and the New School for Music Study exists for students in the Master of Piano Performance and Pedagogy program.

Facilities and Resources

Westminster performance facilities include the Fine Arts Theater (550 seats), Bristol Hall (350 seats), Williamson Hall (100 seats), Scheide Hall (100 seats), and the Playhouse/Opera Theatre (300 seats).

60 **computers** are available on campus for student use. The **library** has 55,000 books and 160 subscriptions. Special collections include the Erik Routley Hymnology Collection and the archives of the Organ Historical Society. The Westminster Performance Collection contains 420,000 copies of 6,000 titles for study and performances and a single-copy reference of 45,000 individual octavos, the largest collection of its kind.

Applying

Westminster requires an essay, SAT I or ACT, a high school transcript, 2 recommendations, and audition, music examination. It recommends an interview and a minimum high school GPA of 2.5. Application deadline: rolling admissions; 3/1 priority date for financial aid. Deferred admission is possible.

Auditions play a very important role in the decision-making process. Westminster accepts applicants based on indicators of musical talent and academic achievement.

COMPETITIVE COLLEGES AND UNIVERSITIES

COLLEGE OR UNIVERSITY NAME

SETTING ■ PUBLIC/PRIVATE ■ INSTITUTIONAL CONTROL ■ COED?
CITY, STATE

Web site: www.website.com
Contact: Contact name and mailing address
Telephone: Telephone number **Fax:** Fax number
E-mail: E-mail address

> **S**ponsoring schools are able to submit a brief message in order to highlight special programs or opportunities that are available or to more fully explain their particular commitment to higher education. That message appears in this box.

Academics
- Degrees awarded
- Most frequently chosen fields
- Faculty, including student-faculty ratio

The Student Body
- How many students on campus and number who are undergrads
- Percent of women and men
- Where students come from
- Percent of students from in-state
- Who they are (international students and ethnic makeup)
- How many students come back for the sophomore year

Facilities and Resources
- Computer resources
- Network, e-mail, and online services
- Library facilities

Campus Life
- Organizations, activities, and student participation
- Fraternities and sororities
- Sports ("m" for men, "w" for women; neither "m" nor "w" means both)

Campus Safety
- Late-night transport/escort service
- Emergency telephone alarm devices
- 24-hour patrols
- Electronically operated residence hall entrances

Applying
- Required documentation and standardized tests
- GPA minimum
- Interviews
- Deadlines

Getting in Last Year
- Number who applied
- Percent accepted
- Number enrolled (percent)
- Percent h.s. achievers
- Average GPA
- SAT I/ACT performance
- Number of National Merit Scholars
- Number of class presidents
- Number of valedictorians

Graduation and After
- Percent graduating in 4, 5, or 6 years
- Percent pursuing further study, with most popular fields, if provided
- Percent with job offers within 6 months
- How many organizations recruit on campus
- Major academic awards won by students

Financial Matters
- Tuition and fees
- Room and board
- Percent of need met
- Average financial aid received per undergraduate

AGNES SCOTT COLLEGE

URBAN SETTING ■ PRIVATE ■ INDEPENDENT RELIGIOUS ■ WOMEN ONLY
DECATUR, GEORGIA

Web site: www.agnesscott.edu

Contact: Ms. Stephanie Balmer, Associate Vice President for Enrollment and
Director of Admission, 141 East College Avenue, Atlanta/Decatur, GA
30030-3797

Telephone: 404-471-6285 or toll-free 800-868-8602 **Fax:** 404-471-6414

E-mail: admission@agnesscott.edu

Agnes Scott College is committed to a 21st-century curriculum that emphasizes academic excellence through the liberal arts and sciences and is enhanced by experience-based learning, including internships, collaborative research, independent study, and study abroad. Programs such as the First-Year Seminars, Atlanta Semester, Global Awareness and Global Connections, and Language Across the Curriculum enrich the Agnes Scott experience. In the last 10 years, Agnes Scott has had 5 Fulbright scholars, 4 Goldwater scholars, and an NCAA semifinalist; it ranks 7th nationally in the percentage of graduates who earn PhD's in education and 15th in the area of humanities. Atlanta, the South's most dynamic and international city, provides opportunities for fun as well as for internships, community service, and cultural events. Agnes Scott is an excellent value in terms of academic quality, personalized attention, and a residential community with a student-governed honor system.

Getting in Last Year
709 applied
74% were accepted
223 enrolled (42%)
42% from top tenth of their h.s. class
3.66 average high school GPA
57% had SAT verbal scores over 600
41% had SAT math scores over 600
72% had ACT scores over 24
18% had SAT verbal scores over 700
6% had SAT math scores over 700
22% had ACT scores over 30

Graduation and After
64% graduated in 4 years
1% graduated in 5 years
**25% pursued further study (10% arts and
sciences, 6% law, 2% education)**
45% had job offers within 6 months
73 organizations recruited on campus

Financial Matters
$17,670 tuition and fees (2001–02)
$7280 room and board
99% average percent of need met
**$17,749 average financial aid amount received
per undergraduate (1999–2000)**

Academics

Agnes Scott awards bachelor's and master's **degrees** and post-bachelor's certificates. Challenging opportunities include advanced placement credit, accelerated degree programs, student-designed majors, double majors, independent study, and a senior project. Special programs include internships, summer session for credit, off-campus study, study-abroad, and Navy and Air Force ROTC.

The most frequently chosen **baccalaureate** fields are social sciences and history, psychology, and English. A complete listing of majors at Agnes Scott appears in the Majors Index beginning on page 430.

The **faculty** at Agnes Scott has 81 full-time members, 96% with terminal degrees. The student-faculty ratio is 10:1.

Students of Agnes Scott

The student body totals 885, of whom 869 are undergraduates. Students come from 39 states and territories and 24 other countries. 55% are from Georgia. 3.9% are international students. 22.3% are African American, 0.2% American Indian, 5% Asian American, and 4% Hispanic American. 75% returned for their sophomore year.

Facilities and Resources

Student rooms are linked to a campus network. 263 **computers** are available on campus that provide access to the Internet. The **library** has 209,747 books and 905 subscriptions.

Campus Life

There are 60 active organizations on campus, including a drama/theater group, newspaper, choral group, and marching band. No national or local **sororities**.

Agnes Scott is a member of the NCAA (Division III). **Intercollegiate sports** include basketball, cross-country running, soccer, softball, swimming, tennis, volleyball.

Campus Safety

Student safety services include shuttle bus service, security systems in apartments, public safety facility, surveillance equipment, late-night transport/escort service, 24-hour emergency telephone alarm devices, and 24-hour patrols by trained security personnel.

Applying

Agnes Scott requires an essay, SAT I or ACT, a high school transcript, and 2 recommendations, and in some cases SAT II Subject Tests. It recommends an interview and a minimum high school GPA of 3.0. Application deadline: 3/1; 3/1 priority date for financial aid. Early and deferred admission are possible.

ALBERTSON COLLEGE OF IDAHO

SMALL-TOWN SETTING ■ PRIVATE ■ INDEPENDENT ■ COED
CALDWELL, IDAHO

Web site: www.albertson.edu
Contact: Brandie Allemand, Associate Dean of Admission, 2112 Cleveland
  Boulevard, Caldwell, ID 83605-4494
Telephone: 208-459-5305 or toll-free 800-224-3246 **Fax:** 208-459-5757
E-mail: admission@albertson.edu

Academics

Albertson awards bachelor's **degrees**. Challenging opportunities include advanced placement credit, student-designed majors, an honors program, double majors, independent
study, and a senior project. Special programs include internships, off-campus study, and
study-abroad.

The most frequently chosen **baccalaureate** fields are social sciences and history,
biological/life sciences, and business/marketing. A complete listing of majors at
Albertson appears in the Majors Index beginning on page 430.

The **faculty** at Albertson has 69 full-time members, 96% with terminal degrees. The
student-faculty ratio is 11:1.

Students of Albertson

The student body is made up of 778 undergraduates. 54% are women and 46% are men.
Students come from 18 states and territories and 11 other countries. 71% are from
Idaho. 2.4% are international students. 0.5% are African American, 0.8% American
Indian, 3.6% Asian American, and 4.2% Hispanic American. 73% returned for their
sophomore year.

Facilities and Resources

Student rooms are linked to a campus network. 200 **computers** are available on campus
that provide access to online course syllabi, course assignments, course discussion and
the Internet. The 2 **libraries** have 181,146 books and 822 subscriptions.

Campus Life

There are 55 active organizations on campus, including a drama/theater group,
newspaper, and choral group. 19% of eligible men and 19% of eligible women are
members of national **fraternities**, national **sororities**, local fraternities, and local sororities.

Albertson is a member of the NAIA. **Intercollegiate sports** (some offering scholarships) include baseball (m), basketball, golf, skiing (cross-country), skiing (downhill), soccer, softball (w), tennis (w), volleyball (w).

Campus Safety

Student safety services include late-night transport/escort service, 24-hour emergency
telephone alarm devices, 24-hour patrols by trained security personnel, student patrols,
and electronically operated dormitory entrances.

Applying

Albertson requires an essay, SAT I or ACT, a high school transcript, and 1 recommendation. It recommends an interview. Application deadline: 6/1; 2/15 priority date for
financial aid. Early and deferred admission are possible.

Getting in Last Year

631 applied
98% were accepted
227 enrolled (37%)
31% from top tenth of their h.s. class
3.5 average high school GPA
33% had SAT verbal scores over 600
39% had SAT math scores over 600
60% had ACT scores over 24
6% had SAT verbal scores over 700
4% had SAT math scores over 700
7% had ACT scores over 30
11 National Merit Scholars

Graduation and After

22% pursued further study
69% had job offers within 6 months
20 organizations recruited on campus

Financial Matters

$19,330 tuition and fees (2001–02)
$4400 room and board
71% average percent of need met
$10,920 average financial aid amount received
  per undergraduate (2000–01 estimated)

ALBION COLLEGE

SMALL-TOWN SETTING ■ PRIVATE ■ INDEPENDENT RELIGIOUS ■ COED
ALBION, MICHIGAN

Web site: www.albion.edu
Contact: Doug Kellar, Associate Vice President for Enrollment, 611 East
 Porter Street, Albion, MI 49224
Telephone: 517-629-0600 or toll-free 800-858-6770
E-mail: admissions@albion.edu

Albion College is located in south-central Michigan and ranks fourth in the nation for students involved in summer research. Outstanding internships are offered on every continent (except Antarctica). Albion is among the top 85 private liberal arts colleges for the number of alumni who are corporate executives, including CEOs of *Newsweek,* Dow Corning, NYNEX, and Saab USA. All students with a GPA of 3.2 or better are accepted into law school, including Harvard, Michigan, Columbia, Northwestern, Notre Dame, Vanderbilt, and Wisconsin. Albion is ranked seventh in Yahoo's *Most Wired Colleges in the USA.*

Academics

Albion awards bachelor's **degrees**. Challenging opportunities include advanced place-ment credit, student-designed majors, an honors program, double majors, independent study, and a senior project. Special programs include internships, summer session for credit, off-campus study, and study-abroad.

The most frequently chosen **baccalaureate** fields are business/marketing, social sci-ences and history, and biological/life sciences. A complete listing of majors at Albion ap-pears in the Majors Index beginning on page 430.

The **faculty** at Albion has 121 full-time members, 93% with terminal degrees. The student-faculty ratio is 12:1.

Students of Albion

The student body is made up of 1,548 undergraduates. 55.6% are women and 44.4% are men. Students come from 28 states and territories and 19 other countries. 89% are from Michigan. 1.5% are international students. 1.9% are African American, 0.3% American Indian, 1.9% Asian American, and 0.8% Hispanic American. 86% returned for their sophomore year.

Facilities and Resources

Student rooms are linked to a campus network. 257 **computers** are available on campus that provide access to the Internet. The **library** has 348,542 books and 1,528 subscrip-tions.

Campus Life

There are 122 active organizations on campus, including a drama/theater group, newspaper, radio station, choral group, and marching band. 40% of eligible men and 40% of eligible women are members of national **fraternities** and national **sororities**.

Albion is a member of the NCAA (Division III). **Intercollegiate sports** include baseball (m), basketball, cross-country running, football (m), golf, soccer, softball (w), swimming, tennis, track and field, volleyball (w).

Campus Safety

Student safety services include late-night transport/escort service, 24-hour emergency telephone alarm devices, 24-hour patrols by trained security personnel, student patrols, and electronically operated dormitory entrances.

Applying

Albion requires an essay, a high school transcript, and 1 recommendation, and in some cases an interview. It recommends a minimum high school GPA of 3.0. Application deadline: 5/1; 2/15 priority date for financial aid. Early and deferred admission are pos-sible.

Getting in Last Year
1,297 applied
87% were accepted
451 enrolled (40%)
31% from top tenth of their h.s. class
3.50 average high school GPA
40% had SAT verbal scores over 600
41% had SAT math scores over 600
62% had ACT scores over 24
6% had SAT verbal scores over 700
9% had SAT math scores over 700
12% had ACT scores over 30
2 National Merit Scholars
17 class presidents
16 valedictorians

Graduation and After
70% graduated in 4 years
1% graduated in 5 years
40% pursued further study (54% arts and
  sciences, 18% medicine, 13% education)
69% had job offers within 6 months
36 organizations recruited on campus

Financial Matters
$19,620 tuition and fees (2001–02)
$5604 room and board
96% average percent of need met
$16,620 average financial aid amount received
  per undergraduate

ALBRIGHT COLLEGE

SUBURBAN SETTING ■ PRIVATE ■ INDEPENDENT RELIGIOUS ■ COED
READING, PENNSYLVANIA

Web site: www.albright.edu
Contact: Mr. Gregory E. Eichhorn, Vice President for Enrollment
Management, P.O. Box 15234, 13th and Bern Streets, Reading, PA
19612-5234
Telephone: 610-921-7260 or toll-free 800-252-1856 **Fax:** 610-921-7294
E-mail: admission@alb.edu

Academics
Albright awards bachelor's **degrees**. Challenging opportunities include advanced placement credit, accelerated degree programs, student-designed majors, an honors program, double majors, independent study, and a senior project. Special programs include internships, summer session for credit, off-campus study, and study-abroad.

The most frequently chosen **baccalaureate** fields are business/marketing, psychology, and social sciences and history. A complete listing of majors at Albright appears in the Majors Index beginning on page 430.

The **faculty** at Albright has 88 full-time members, 85% with terminal degrees. The student-faculty ratio is 14:1.

Students of Albright
The student body is made up of 1,809 undergraduates. 57.3% are women and 42.7% are men. Students come from 25 states and territories and 20 other countries. 73% are from Pennsylvania. 4.1% are international students. 7.4% are African American, 0.5% American Indian, 2.2% Asian American, and 3.3% Hispanic American. 74% returned for their sophomore year.

Facilities and Resources
Student rooms are linked to a campus network. 271 **computers** are available on campus that provide access to the Internet. The 2 **libraries** have 208,457 books and 2,280 subscriptions.

Campus Life
There are 70 active organizations on campus, including a drama/theater group, newspaper, radio station, and choral group. 29% of eligible men and 32% of eligible women are members of national **fraternities** and national **sororities**.

Albright is a member of the NCAA (Division III). **Intercollegiate sports** include badminton (w), baseball (m), basketball, cross-country running, field hockey (w), football (m), golf (m), soccer, softball (w), swimming, tennis, track and field, volleyball (w), wrestling (m).

Campus Safety
Student safety services include late-night transport/escort service, 24-hour emergency telephone alarm devices, 24-hour patrols by trained security personnel, student patrols, and electronically operated dormitory entrances.

Applying
Albright requires an essay, SAT I or ACT, a high school transcript, 1 recommendation, and secondary school report (guidance department). It recommends an interview. Application deadline: rolling admissions; 3/1 priority date for financial aid. Early and deferred admission are possible.

I t used to be acceptable to enter college undecided about a major; in fact, it was expected. But things have changed, and today there is more pressure on students to choose a major as soon as they walk on campus. Pressure doesn't lead to wise decisions, so Albright has developed a program, the Alpha Program, specially designed for the undecided student. Through a structured package of academic guidance, peer support, special events, and career counseling, the Alpha Program helps students to choose not only the right major, but also the right career and the right future.

Getting in Last Year
2,502 applied
73% were accepted
402 enrolled (22%)
19% from top tenth of their h.s. class
3.2 average high school GPA
16% had SAT verbal scores over 600
15% had SAT math scores over 600
29% had ACT scores over 24
2% had SAT verbal scores over 700
1% had SAT math scores over 700
3% had ACT scores over 30
4 class presidents
4 valedictorians

Graduation and After
57% graduated in 4 years
5% graduated in 5 years
1% graduated in 6 years
32% pursued further study (12% arts and sciences, 9% law, 5% business)
68% had job offers within 6 months
50 organizations recruited on campus

Financial Matters
$21,300 tuition and fees (2001–02)
$6342 room and board
82% average percent of need met
$16,749 average financial aid amount received per undergraduate

---

ALFRED UNIVERSITY
RURAL SETTING ■ PRIVATE ■ INDEPENDENT ■ COED
ALFRED, NEW YORK

Web site: www.alfred.edu
Contact: Mr. Scott Hooker, Director of Admissions, Alumni Hall, Alfred, NY 14802-1205
Telephone: 607-871-2115 or toll-free 800-541-9229 **Fax:** 607-871-2198
E-mail: admwww@alfred.edu

With more than 60 majors and programs of study, high-technology opportunities, and top-notch facilities, Alfred University provides its students an outstanding academic experience in an up-close-and-personal learning environment. Through research, co-op and internship opportunities, active learning, and study abroad, students gain extensive knowledge that makes them more marketable for graduate or professional school placement or securing employment within the workforce. All students are encouraged to value diversity, tolerance, and interdisciplinary work.

Getting in Last Year
2,048 applied
75% were accepted
495 enrolled (32%)
19% from top tenth of their h.s. class
32% had SAT verbal scores over 600
34% had SAT math scores over 600
5% had SAT verbal scores over 700
4% had SAT math scores over 700
9 National Merit Scholars
7 valedictorians

Graduation and After
48% graduated in 4 years
16% graduated in 5 years
1% graduated in 6 years
24% pursued further study
113 organizations recruited on campus

Financial Matters
$19,196 tuition and fees (2001–02)
$8016 room and board
92% average percent of need met
$18,239 average financial aid amount received per undergraduate

Academics
Alfred awards bachelor's, master's, and doctoral **degrees** and post-master's certificates. Challenging opportunities include advanced placement credit, accelerated degree programs, student-designed majors, an honors program, double majors, independent study, and a senior project. Special programs include cooperative education, internships, summer session for credit, off-campus study, study-abroad, and Army ROTC.

The most frequently chosen **baccalaureate** fields are visual/performing arts, engineering/engineering technologies, and business/marketing. A complete listing of majors at Alfred appears in the Majors Index beginning on page 430.

The **faculty** at Alfred has 173 full-time members, 93% with terminal degrees. The student-faculty ratio is 12:1.

Students of Alfred
The student body totals 2,443, of whom 2,115 are undergraduates. 53% are women and 47% are men. Students come from 38 states and territories and 12 other countries. 69% are from New York. 1.6% are international students. 3.8% are African American, 0.5% American Indian, 2% Asian American, and 3.6% Hispanic American. 77% returned for their sophomore year.

Facilities and Resources
Student rooms are linked to a campus network. 390 **computers** are available on campus that provide access to the Internet. The 2 **libraries** have 317,832 books and 1,507 subscriptions.

Campus Life
There are 90 active organizations on campus, including a drama/theater group, newspaper, radio station, television station, and choral group. 20% of eligible men and 11% of eligible women are members of national **fraternities**, national **sororities**, local fraternities, and local sororities.

Alfred is a member of the NCAA (Division III). **Intercollegiate sports** include basketball, cross-country running, equestrian sports, football (m), golf, lacrosse, skiing (downhill), soccer, softball (w), swimming, tennis, track and field, volleyball (w).

Campus Safety
Student safety services include late-night transport/escort service, 24-hour emergency telephone alarm devices, and student patrols.

Applying
Alfred requires an essay, SAT I or ACT, a high school transcript, and 1 recommendation, and in some cases an interview and portfolio. It recommends SAT II: Writing Test and an interview. Application deadline: 2/1. Early and deferred admission are possible.

ALLEGHENY COLLEGE
SMALL-TOWN SETTING ■ PRIVATE ■ INDEPENDENT RELIGIOUS ■ COED
MEADVILLE, PENNSYLVANIA

Web site: www.allegheny.edu
Contact: Ms. Megan K. Murphy, Dean of Admissions and Enrollment
Management, 520 North Main Street, Box 5, Meadville, PA 16335
Telephone: 814-332-4351 or toll-free 800-521-5293 **Fax:** 814-337-0431
E-mail: admiss@allegheny.edu

Academics
Allegheny awards bachelor's **degrees**. Challenging opportunities include advanced placement credit, accelerated degree programs, student-designed majors, double majors, independent study, and a senior project. Special programs include internships, off-campus study, study-abroad, and Army ROTC.

The most frequently chosen **baccalaureate** fields are social sciences and history, biological/life sciences, and psychology. A complete listing of majors at Allegheny appears in the Majors Index beginning on page 430.

The **faculty** at Allegheny has 135 full-time members, 93% with terminal degrees. The student-faculty ratio is 13:1.

Students of Allegheny
The student body is made up of 1,879 undergraduates. 52.6% are women and 47.4% are men. Students come from 35 states and territories and 14 other countries. 67% are from Pennsylvania. 1.2% are international students. 2.3% are African American, 0.3% American Indian, 1.6% Asian American, and 1.3% Hispanic American. 88% returned for their sophomore year.

Facilities and Resources
Student rooms are linked to a campus network. 245 **computers** are available on campus that provide access to the Internet. The **library** has 266,096 books and 3,100 subscriptions.

Campus Life
There are 78 active organizations on campus, including a drama/theater group, newspaper, radio station, television station, and choral group. 17% of eligible men and 30% of eligible women are members of national **fraternities** and national **sororities**.

Allegheny is a member of the NCAA (Division III). **Intercollegiate sports** include baseball (m), basketball, cross-country running, football (m), golf (m), lacrosse (w), soccer, softball (w), swimming, tennis, track and field, volleyball (w).

Campus Safety
Student safety services include local police patrol, late-night transport/escort service, 24-hour emergency telephone alarm devices, 24-hour patrols by trained security personnel, and student patrols.

Applying
Allegheny requires an essay, SAT I or ACT, a high school transcript, and 2 recommendations. It recommends SAT II Subject Tests, SAT II: Writing Test, and an interview. Application deadline: 2/15; 2/15 for financial aid. Early and deferred admission are possible.

Allegheny's historic campus, in a natural setting of great beauty, is home to an active community of students who thrive on challenge and make the most of opportunity. The College is known for providing an exceptional education in the sciences as well as the humanities and social sciences, with a high value placed on experiential learning and civic education. Small classes and a low student-faculty ratio allow students to work with professors and other students in a dynamic learning environment. Faculty members often bring students in on their own research projects, creating opportunities usually reserved for graduate students at other schools.

Getting in Last Year
2,530 applied
79% were accepted
489 enrolled (25%)
37% from top tenth of their h.s. class
3.69 average high school GPA
51% had SAT verbal scores over 600
50% had SAT math scores over 600
66% had ACT scores over 24
11% had SAT verbal scores over 700
7% had SAT math scores over 700
13% had ACT scores over 30
15 National Merit Scholars
20 valedictorians

Graduation and After
62% graduated in 4 years
7% graduated in 5 years
1% graduated in 6 years
32% pursued further study (7% law, 5% arts and sciences, 4% education)
77% had job offers within 6 months
63 organizations recruited on campus

Financial Matters
$22,490 tuition and fees (2001–02)
$5290 room and board
95% average percent of need met
$18,348 average financial aid amount received per undergraduate

ALMA COLLEGE

SMALL-TOWN SETTING ■ PRIVATE ■ INDEPENDENT RELIGIOUS ■ COED
ALMA, MICHIGAN

Web site: www.alma.edu
Contact: Mr. Paul Pollatz, Director of Admissions, Admissions Office, Alma, MI 48801-1599
Telephone: 989-463-7139 or toll-free 800-321-ALMA **Fax:** 989-463-7057
E-mail: admissions@alma.edu

Alma's undergraduates thrive on challenging academic programs in a supportive, small-college atmosphere. The College is committed to a liberal arts curriculum with opportunities for one-on-one research and publication with faculty members whose first priority is teaching. Students enjoy small classes in modern facilities, including the new Alan J. Stone Center for Recreation. Alma College offers excellent preparation for professional careers in business, law, medicine, the arts, and a wide range of other fields.

Getting in Last Year
1,237 applied
82% were accepted
308 enrolled (30%)
37% from top tenth of their h.s. class
3.50 average high school GPA
59% had ACT scores over 24
9% had ACT scores over 30
11 valedictorians

Graduation and After
56% graduated in 4 years
14% graduated in 5 years
2% graduated in 6 years
40% pursued further study (12% arts and sciences, 3% engineering, 3% law)
61% had job offers within 6 months
30 organizations recruited on campus

Financial Matters
$16,602 tuition and fees (2001–02)
$5984 room and board
91% average percent of need met
$15,010 average financial aid amount received per undergraduate

Academics
Alma awards bachelor's **degrees**. Challenging opportunities include advanced placement credit, accelerated degree programs, student-designed majors, double majors, independent study, and a senior project. Special programs include internships, summer session for credit, off-campus study, study-abroad, and Army ROTC.

The most frequently chosen **baccalaureate** fields are business/marketing, education, and social sciences and history. A complete listing of majors at Alma appears in the Majors Index beginning on page 430.

The **faculty** at Alma has 82 full-time members, 89% with terminal degrees. The student-faculty ratio is 13:1.

Students of Alma
The student body is made up of 1,366 undergraduates. 58.9% are women and 41.1% are men. Students come from 21 states and territories and 19 other countries. 97% are from Michigan. 1.1% are international students. 1.3% are African American, 0.7% American Indian, 1.2% Asian American, and 1.5% Hispanic American. 85% returned for their sophomore year.

Facilities and Resources
Student rooms are linked to a campus network. 621 **computers** are available on campus that provide access to the Internet. The **library** has 176,278 books and 1,178 subscriptions.

Campus Life
There are 123 active organizations on campus, including a drama/theater group, newspaper, radio station, choral group, and marching band. 33% of eligible men and 22% of eligible women are members of national **fraternities**, national **sororities**, local fraternities, and local sororities.

Alma is a member of the NCAA (Division III). **Intercollegiate sports** include baseball (m), basketball, cross-country running, football (m), golf, soccer, softball (w), swimming, tennis, track and field, volleyball (w).

Campus Safety
Student safety services include 24-hour emergency telephone alarm devices and 24-hour patrols by trained security personnel.

Applying
Alma requires SAT I or ACT, a high school transcript, 2 recommendations, and a minimum high school GPA of 3.0. It recommends an essay and an interview. Application deadline: rolling admissions; 2/21 priority date for financial aid. Early and deferred admission are possible.

American University

SUBURBAN SETTING ■ PRIVATE ■ INDEPENDENT RELIGIOUS ■ COED
WASHINGTON, DISTRICT OF COLUMBIA

Web site: www.american.edu
Contact: Dr. Sharon Alston, Director of Admissions, 4400 Massachusetts
Avenue, NW, Washington, DC 20016-8001
Telephone: 202-885-6000 **Fax:** 202-885-1025
E-mail: afa@american.edu

American University attracts academically distinctive and intensely engaged students who want to understand how the world works. American's diverse campus community; location in Washington, D.C.; study-abroad options; and emphasis on the practical application of knowledge prepare students to be major contributors in their fields.

Academics

AU awards associate, bachelor's, master's, doctoral, and first-professional **degrees** and post-bachelor's certificates. Challenging opportunities include advanced placement credit, accelerated degree programs, student-designed majors, an honors program, double majors, independent study, and a senior project. Special programs include cooperative education, internships, summer session for credit, off-campus study, study-abroad, and Army and Air Force ROTC.

The most frequently chosen **baccalaureate** fields are social sciences and history, business/marketing, and communications/communication technologies. A complete listing of majors at AU appears in the Majors Index beginning on page 430.

The **faculty** at AU has 489 full-time members. The student-faculty ratio is 14:1.

Students of AU

The student body totals 10,693, of whom 5,851 are undergraduates. 61.7% are women and 38.3% are men. Students come from 53 states and territories and 122 other countries. 7% are from District of Columbia. 11.2% are international students. 5.7% are African American, 0.2% American Indian, 4.2% Asian American, and 4.5% Hispanic American. 85% returned for their sophomore year.

Facilities and Resources

Student rooms are linked to a campus network. 600 **computers** are available on campus that provide access to online course support and the Internet. The 2 **libraries** have 725,000 books and 3,600 subscriptions.

Campus Life

There are 151 active organizations on campus, including a drama/theater group, newspaper, radio station, television station, and choral group. 14% of eligible men and 16% of eligible women are members of national **fraternities** and national **sororities**.

AU is a member of the NCAA (Division I). **Intercollegiate sports** (some offering scholarships) include basketball, cross-country running, field hockey (w), golf (m), lacrosse (w), soccer, swimming, tennis, track and field, volleyball (w), wrestling (m).

Campus Safety

Student safety services include late-night transport/escort service, 24-hour emergency telephone alarm devices, 24-hour patrols by trained security personnel, and electronically operated dormitory entrances.

Applying

AU requires an essay, SAT I or ACT, a high school transcript, 2 recommendations, and a minimum high school GPA of 2.0. It recommends SAT II Subject Tests, an interview, and a minimum high school GPA of 3.0. Application deadline: 2/1; 3/1 for financial aid. Early and deferred admission are possible.

Getting in Last Year
10,359 applied
68% were accepted
1,422 enrolled (20%)
25% from top tenth of their h.s. class
3.23 average high school GPA
58% had SAT verbal scores over 600
51% had SAT math scores over 600
78% had ACT scores over 24
13% had SAT verbal scores over 700
8% had SAT math scores over 700
18% had ACT scores over 30

Graduation and After
63% graduated in 4 years
5% graduated in 5 years
3% graduated in 6 years
85% had job offers within 6 months
200 organizations recruited on campus

Financial Matters
$22,481 tuition and fees (2001–02)
$9063 room and board
71% average percent of need met
$21,913 average financial aid amount received per undergraduate

AMHERST COLLEGE

SMALL-TOWN SETTING ■ PRIVATE ■ INDEPENDENT ■ COED
AMHERST, MASSACHUSETTS

Web site: www.amherst.edu
Contact: Mr. Thomas Parker, Dean of Admission and Financial Aid, PO Box 5000, Amherst, MA 01002
Telephone: 413-542-2328 **Fax:** 413-542-2040
E-mail: admission@amherst.edu

Amherst seeks talented students who have demonstrated their passion for learning along with a willingness to be involved in the world around them. With its dynamic, dedicated faculty, Amherst is a lively intellectual and cultural community in which students are active members; small classes and a wide variety of extracurricular offerings provide many opportunities for exploration. An open curriculum, with majors ranging from neuroscience to law, jurisprudence, and social thought, allows students substantial freedom to pursue their goals.

Getting in Last Year
5,175 applied
19% were accepted
430 enrolled (44%)
83% from top tenth of their h.s. class
92% had SAT verbal scores over 600
91% had SAT math scores over 600
91% had ACT scores over 24
61% had SAT verbal scores over 700
57% had SAT math scores over 700
58% had ACT scores over 30
80 National Merit Scholars
37 valedictorians

Graduation and After
84% graduated in 4 years
8% graduated in 5 years
2% graduated in 6 years
30% pursued further study
63% had job offers within 6 months
74 organizations recruited on campus

Financial Matters
$27,258 tuition and fees (2001–02)
$7100 room and board
100% average percent of need met
$24,229 average financial aid amount received per undergraduate

Academics

Amherst College awards bachelor's **degrees**. Challenging opportunities include student-designed majors, an honors program, double majors, independent study, and a senior project. Special programs include off-campus study and study-abroad.

The most frequently chosen **baccalaureate** fields are social sciences and history, English, and biological/life sciences. A complete listing of majors at Amherst College appears in the Majors Index beginning on page 430.

The **faculty** at Amherst College has 179 full-time members, 93% with terminal degrees. The student-faculty ratio is 9:1.

Students of Amherst College

The student body is made up of 1,631 undergraduates. 48.8% are women and 51.2% are men. Students come from 56 states and territories and 29 other countries. 16% are from Massachusetts. 4.2% are international students. 8.8% are African American, 11.2% Asian American, and 7.6% Hispanic American. 97% returned for their sophomore year.

Facilities and Resources

Student rooms are linked to a campus network. 161 **computers** are available on campus that provide access to the Internet. The 6 **libraries** have 916,830 books and 5,878 subscriptions.

Campus Life

There are 100 active organizations on campus, including a drama/theater group, newspaper, radio station, and choral group. No national or local **fraternities** or **sororities**.

Amherst College is a member of the NCAA (Division III). **Intercollegiate sports** include baseball (m), basketball, cross-country running, field hockey (w), football (m), golf, ice hockey, lacrosse, soccer, softball (w), squash, swimming, tennis, track and field, volleyball (w).

Campus Safety

Student safety services include late-night transport/escort service, 24-hour emergency telephone alarm devices, 24-hour patrols by trained security personnel, student patrols, and electronically operated dormitory entrances.

Applying

Amherst College requires an essay, SAT I or ACT, 3 SAT II Subject Tests, a high school transcript, and 3 recommendations. Application deadline: 12/31; 2/1 priority date for financial aid. Deferred admission is possible.

Arkansas Tech University

SMALL-TOWN SETTING ■ PUBLIC ■ STATE-SUPPORTED ■ COED
RUSSELLVILLE, ARKANSAS

Web site: www.atu.edu

Contact: Ms. Shauna Donnell, Director of Enrollment Management, L.L. "DOC" Bryan Student Services Building, Suite 141, Russellville, AR 72801-2222

Telephone: 501-968-0404 or toll-free 800-582-6953 (in-state) **Fax:** 501-964-0522

E-mail: tech.enroll@mail.atu.edu

Academics

Arkansas Tech awards associate, bachelor's, and master's **degrees**. Challenging opportunities include advanced placement credit, accelerated degree programs, an honors program, double majors, independent study, and a senior project. Special programs include internships, summer session for credit, off-campus study, study-abroad, and Army ROTC.

The most frequently chosen **baccalaureate** fields are education, business/marketing, and computer/information sciences. A complete listing of majors at Arkansas Tech appears in the Majors Index beginning on page 430.

The **faculty** at Arkansas Tech has 210 full-time members, 66% with terminal degrees. The student-faculty ratio is 20:1.

Students of Arkansas Tech

The student body totals 5,576, of whom 5,205 are undergraduates. 51.8% are women and 48.2% are men. Students come from 30 states and territories and 35 other countries. 94% are from Arkansas. 1.5% are international students. 4.2% are African American, 1.3% American Indian, 1% Asian American, and 1.4% Hispanic American. 64% returned for their sophomore year.

Facilities and Resources

Student rooms are linked to a campus network. 258 **computers** are available on campus that provide access to the Internet. The **library** has 229,450 books and 1,245 subscriptions.

Campus Life

There are 90 active organizations on campus, including a drama/theater group, newspaper, radio station, television station, choral group, and marching band. 5% of eligible men and 3% of eligible women are members of national **fraternities**, national **sororities**, local fraternities, and local sororities.

Arkansas Tech is a member of the NCAA (Division II). **Intercollegiate sports** (some offering scholarships) include baseball (m), basketball, cross-country running (w), football (m), golf (m), tennis (w), volleyball (w).

Campus Safety

Student safety services include late-night transport/escort service, 24-hour patrols by trained security personnel, and electronically operated dormitory entrances.

Applying

Arkansas Tech requires SAT II: Writing Test, SAT I or ACT, a high school transcript, and a minimum high school GPA of 2.0, and in some cases ACT COMPASS, an interview, and 2 recommendations. Early and deferred admission are possible.

Getting in Last Year
2,685 applied
52% were accepted
1,239 enrolled (88%)
3.22 average high school GPA
34% had ACT scores over 24
3% had ACT scores over 30

Graduation and After
18% graduated in 4 years
17% graduated in 5 years
2% graduated in 6 years
56% had job offers within 6 months
92 organizations recruited on campus

Financial Matters
$2976 resident tuition and fees (2001–02)
$6132 nonresident tuition and fees (2001–02)
$3280 room and board
54% average percent of need met
$4389 average financial aid amount received per undergraduate

ASBURY COLLEGE

SMALL-TOWN SETTING ■ PRIVATE ■ INDEPENDENT RELIGIOUS ■ COED
WILMORE, KENTUCKY

Web site: www.asbury.edu
Contact: Mr. Stan F. Wiggam, Dean of Admissions, 1 Macklem Drive,
Wilmore, KY 40390
Telephone: 859-858-3511 ext. 2142 or toll-free 800-888-1818 **Fax:**
859-858-3921
E-mail: admissions@asbury.edu

With a commitment to academic excellence and spiritual vitality, Asbury College's 1,350 students study, worship, live, and serve on a brick-and-columned campus 20 minutes from Lexington, Kentucky. A 4-year, multidenominational, Christian, liberal arts institution, Asbury's character-building emphasis has earned it national recognition and *U.S. News & World Report* ranks the College second overall among Southern comprehensive colleges. Students from more than 40 states and 10 nations foster a diverse community. Experienced, credentialed scholars teach classes, and there is a student-faculty ratio of 14:1. Asbury College offers more than 45 majors, including media communication, teacher education, business, psychology, and biochemistry.

Getting in Last Year
848 applied
84% were accepted
331 enrolled (46%)
32% from top tenth of their h.s. class
3.54 average high school GPA
47% had SAT verbal scores over 600
35% had SAT math scores over 600
58% had ACT scores over 24
11% had SAT verbal scores over 700
6% had SAT math scores over 700
13% had ACT scores over 30
3 National Merit Scholars
26 valedictorians

Graduation and After
36% graduated in 4 years
13% graduated in 5 years
1% graduated in 6 years
83 organizations recruited on campus

Financial Matters
$14,764 tuition and fees (2001–02)
$3794 room and board
83% average percent of need met
$10,010 average financial aid amount received per undergraduate (1999–2000)

Academics
Asbury College awards bachelor's and master's **degrees**. Challenging opportunities include advanced placement credit, double majors, independent study, and a senior project. Special programs include internships, summer session for credit, study-abroad, and Army and Air Force ROTC.

The most frequently chosen **baccalaureate** fields are English, education, and philosophy. A complete listing of majors at Asbury College appears in the Majors Index beginning on page 430.

The **faculty** at Asbury College has 91 full-time members, 74% with terminal degrees. The student-faculty ratio is 12:1.

Students of Asbury College
The student body totals 1,352, of whom 1,328 are undergraduates. 59% are women and 41% are men. Students come from 42 states and territories and 14 other countries. 27% are from Kentucky. 1.1% are international students. 1.1% are African American, 0.3% American Indian, 0.6% Asian American, and 1.1% Hispanic American. 81% returned for their sophomore year.

Facilities and Resources
Student rooms are linked to a campus network. 290 **computers** are available on campus for student use. The **library** has 150,449 books and 5,203 subscriptions.

Campus Life
There are 35 active organizations on campus, including a drama/theater group, newspaper, radio station, television station, and choral group. No national or local **fraternities** or **sororities**.

Asbury College is a member of the NAIA and NCCAA. **Intercollegiate sports** include baseball (m), basketball, cross-country running, soccer, softball (w), swimming, tennis, volleyball (w).

Campus Safety
Student safety services include late night security personnel, late-night transport/escort service, 24-hour emergency telephone alarm devices, and electronically operated dormitory entrances.

Applying
Asbury College requires an essay, SAT I or ACT, a high school transcript, 3 recommendations, and a minimum high school GPA of 2.5, and in some cases an interview. Application deadline: rolling admissions; 3/1 priority date for financial aid. Early and deferred admission are possible.

Augustana College

Suburban setting ■ Private ■ Independent Religious ■ Coed
Rock Island, Illinois

Web site: www.augustana.edu
Contact: Mr. Martin Sauer, Director of Admissions, 639 38th Street, Rock Island, IL 61201-2296
Telephone: 309-794-7341 or toll-free 800-798-8100 **Fax:** 309-794-7422
E-mail: admissions@augustana.edu

Academics

Augie awards bachelor's **degrees**. Challenging opportunities include advanced placement credit, accelerated degree programs, an honors program, double majors, independent study, and a senior project. Special programs include internships, summer session for credit, and study-abroad.

The most frequently chosen **baccalaureate** fields are biological/life sciences, business/marketing, and health professions and related sciences. A complete listing of majors at Augie appears in the Majors Index beginning on page 430.

The **faculty** at Augie has 142 full-time members, 91% with terminal degrees. The student-faculty ratio is 12:1.

Students of Augie

The student body is made up of 2,232 undergraduates. 57.2% are women and 42.8% are men. Students come from 28 states and territories and 19 other countries. 88% are from Illinois. 0.6% are international students. 2.4% are African American, 0.1% American Indian, 1.6% Asian American, and 2.7% Hispanic American. 87% returned for their sophomore year.

Facilities and Resources

Student rooms are linked to a campus network. 600 **computers** are available on campus that provide access to the Internet. The 4 **libraries** have 227,357 books and 1,870 subscriptions.

Campus Life

There are 109 active organizations on campus, including a drama/theater group, newspaper, radio station, and choral group. 36% of eligible men and 40% of eligible women are members of local **fraternities** and local **sororities**.

Augie is a member of the NCAA (Division III). **Intercollegiate sports** include baseball (m), basketball, cross-country running, football (m), golf, soccer, softball (w), swimming, tennis, track and field, volleyball (w), wrestling (m).

Campus Safety

Student safety services include late-night transport/escort service, 24-hour emergency telephone alarm devices, 24-hour patrols by trained security personnel, and electronically operated dormitory entrances.

Applying

Augie requires SAT I or ACT and a high school transcript, and in some cases an essay, an interview, and 2 recommendations. Application deadline: rolling admissions; 4/1 priority date for financial aid. Deferred admission is possible.

> Augustana College seeks to develop in students the characteristics of liberally educated persons: clarity of thought and expression, curiosity, fair-mindedness, appreciation for the arts and cultural diversity, intellectual honesty, and a considered set of personal values and commitments. Students combine exploration of the arts, sciences, and humanities with in-depth study in their major field(s), guided by an excellent, committed faculty; they grow personally and socially through participation in wide extracurricular and cocurricular opportunities on one of the most beautiful campuses in the country. Special features include innovative interdisciplinary first-year course sequences, foreign study, and internships—both domestic and international.

Getting in Last Year
2,622 applied
77% were accepted
552 enrolled (27%)
31% from top tenth of their h.s. class
3.50 average high school GPA
67% had ACT scores over 24
17% had ACT scores over 30

Graduation and After
30% pursued further study (21% arts and sciences, 4% medicine, 3% law)
67% had job offers within 6 months
189 organizations recruited on campus

Financial Matters
$18,720 tuition and fees (2001–02)
$5397 room and board
88% average percent of need met
$14,664 average financial aid amount received per undergraduate

Augustana College

Urban setting ■ Private ■ Independent Religious ■ Coed
Sioux Falls, South Dakota

Getting in Last Year
1,389 applied
85% were accepted
426 enrolled (36%)
28% from top tenth of their h.s. class
3.55 average high school GPA
39% had SAT verbal scores over 600
48% had SAT math scores over 600
56% had ACT scores over 24
7% had SAT verbal scores over 700
6% had SAT math scores over 700
9% had ACT scores over 30
1 National Merit Scholar
35 valedictorians

Graduation and After
49% graduated in 4 years
13% graduated in 5 years
1% graduated in 6 years
21% pursued further study (10% arts and sciences, 4% medicine, 2% law)
94% had job offers within 6 months
50 organizations recruited on campus

Financial Matters
$19,938 comprehensive fee (2001–02)
91% average percent of need met
$13,343 average financial aid amount received per undergraduate

Web site: www.augie.edu
Contact: Robert Preloger, Vice President for Enrollment, 2001 South Summit Avenue, Sioux Falls, SD 57197
Telephone: 605-274-5516 ext. 5504 or toll-free 800-727-2844 ext. 5516 (in-state), 800-727-2844 (out-of-state) **Fax:** 605-274-5518
E-mail: info@inst.augie.edu

Academics
Augustana awards bachelor's and master's **degrees**. Challenging opportunities include advanced placement credit, accelerated degree programs, student-designed majors, an honors program, double majors, independent study, and a senior project. Special programs include cooperative education, internships, summer session for credit, off-campus study, and study-abroad.

The most frequently chosen **baccalaureate** fields are business/marketing, education, and health professions and related sciences. A complete listing of majors at Augustana appears in the Majors Index beginning on page 430.

The **faculty** at Augustana has 113 full-time members, 88% with terminal degrees. The student-faculty ratio is 12:1.

Students of Augustana
The student body totals 1,807, of whom 1,774 are undergraduates. 65.2% are women and 34.8% are men. Students come from 28 states and territories and 9 other countries. 48% are from South Dakota. 1.8% are international students. 0.7% are African American, 0.3% American Indian, 0.5% Asian American, and 0.3% Hispanic American. 76% returned for their sophomore year.

Facilities and Resources
Student rooms are linked to a campus network. 360 **computers** are available on campus that provide access to the Internet. The 2 **libraries** have 234,515 books and 1,085 subscriptions.

Campus Life
There are 55 active organizations on campus, including a drama/theater group, newspaper, radio station, and choral group. No national or local **fraternities** or **sororities**.

Augustana is a member of the NCAA (Division II). **Intercollegiate sports** (some offering scholarships) include baseball (m), basketball, cross-country running, football (m), golf, soccer (w), softball (w), tennis, track and field, volleyball (w), wrestling (m).

Campus Safety
Student safety services include late-night transport/escort service, 24-hour emergency telephone alarm devices, 24-hour patrols by trained security personnel, and electronically operated dormitory entrances.

Applying
Augustana requires SAT I or ACT, a high school transcript, 1 recommendation, minimum ACT score of 20, and a minimum high school GPA of 2.5, and in some cases an essay. It recommends an interview. Application deadline: 8/1; 3/1 priority date for financial aid. Early and deferred admission are possible.

Austin College

Suburban setting ■ Private ■ Independent Religious ■ Coed
Sherman, Texas

Web site: www.austinc.edu
Contact: Ms. Nan Massingill, Vice President for Institutional Enrollment, 900 North Grand Avenue, Suite 6N, Sherman, TX 75090-4400
Telephone: 903-813-3000 or toll-free 800-442-5363 **Fax:** 903-813-3198
E-mail: admission@austinc.edu

Academics

AC awards bachelor's and master's **degrees**. Challenging opportunities include advanced placement credit, accelerated degree programs, student-designed majors, an honors program, double majors, independent study, and a senior project. Special programs include internships, summer session for credit, off-campus study, and study-abroad.

The most frequently chosen **baccalaureate** fields are business/marketing, social sciences and history, and biological/life sciences. A complete listing of majors at AC appears in the Majors Index beginning on page 430.

The **faculty** at AC has 85 full-time members, 98% with terminal degrees. The student-faculty ratio is 13:1.

Students of AC

The student body totals 1,261, of whom 1,227 are undergraduates. 55.8% are women and 44.2% are men. Students come from 30 states and territories and 28 other countries. 89% are from Texas. 2.4% are international students. 4.6% are African American, 0.8% American Indian, 8.5% Asian American, and 6.9% Hispanic American. 83% returned for their sophomore year.

Facilities and Resources

Student rooms are linked to a campus network. 165 **computers** are available on campus that provide access to the Internet. The **library** has 201,354 books and 1,364 subscriptions.

Campus Life

There are 50 active organizations on campus, including a drama/theater group, newspaper, and choral group. 21% of eligible men and 19% of eligible women are members of local **fraternities** and local **sororities**.

AC is a member of the NCAA (Division III). **Intercollegiate sports** include baseball (m), basketball, cross-country running, football (m), golf (m), soccer, swimming, tennis, track and field, volleyball (w).

Campus Safety

Student safety services include late-night transport/escort service, 24-hour emergency telephone alarm devices, 24-hour patrols by trained security personnel, and electronically operated dormitory entrances.

Applying

AC requires an essay, SAT I or ACT, a high school transcript, and 2 recommendations, and in some cases an interview. It recommends an interview and a minimum high school GPA of 3.0. Application deadline: 8/15; 4/1 priority date for financial aid. Early and deferred admission are possible.

Getting in Last Year
1,004 applied
80% were accepted
313 enrolled (39%)
40% from top tenth of their h.s. class
53% had SAT verbal scores over 600
53% had SAT math scores over 600
73% had ACT scores over 24
9% had SAT verbal scores over 700
11% had SAT math scores over 700
17% had ACT scores over 30
5 National Merit Scholars
18 valedictorians

Graduation and After
34% pursued further study (10% education, 6% arts and sciences, 6% medicine)
45% had job offers within 6 months
18 organizations recruited on campus

Financial Matters
$15,963 tuition and fees (2001–02)
$6187 room and board
97% average percent of need met
$16,447 average financial aid amount received per undergraduate

AZUSA PACIFIC UNIVERSITY

SMALL-TOWN SETTING ■ PRIVATE ■ INDEPENDENT RELIGIOUS ■ COED
AZUSA, CALIFORNIA

Web site: www.apu.edu
Contact: Mrs. Deana Porterfield, Dean of Enrollment, 901 East Alosta
    Avenue, PO Box 7000, Azusa, CA 91720-7000
Telephone: 626-812-3016 or toll-free 800-TALK-APU
E-mail: admissions@apu.edu

Getting in Last Year
2,257 applied
70% were accepted
763 enrolled (48%)
26% from top tenth of their h.s. class
3.59 average high school GPA
52% had SAT verbal scores over 600
29% had SAT math scores over 600
45% had ACT scores over 24
7% had SAT verbal scores over 700
4% had SAT math scores over 700
7% had ACT scores over 30

Graduation and After
47% graduated in 4 years
10% graduated in 5 years
5% graduated in 6 years
150 organizations recruited on campus

Financial Matters
$17,495 tuition and fees (2001–02)
$6230 room and board
74% average percent of need met
$6859 average financial aid amount received
    per undergraduate (1998–99)

Academics
APU awards bachelor's, master's, doctoral, and first-professional **degrees**. Challenging opportunities include advanced placement credit, accelerated degree programs, freshman honors college, an honors program, double majors, and a senior project. Special programs include cooperative education, internships, summer session for credit, off-campus study, study-abroad, and Army ROTC.

The most frequently chosen **baccalaureate** fields are business/marketing, liberal arts/general studies, and education. A complete listing of majors at APU appears in the Majors Index beginning on page 430.

The **faculty** at APU has 217 full-time members, 73% with terminal degrees. The student-faculty ratio is 16:1.

Students of APU
The student body totals 6,835, of whom 3,654 are undergraduates. 63.7% are women and 36.3% are men. Students come from 43 states and territories and 50 other countries. 82% are from California. 2.5% are international students. 3.1% are African American, 0.5% American Indian, 5% Asian American, and 12.4% Hispanic American. 79% returned for their sophomore year.

Facilities and Resources
300 **computers** are available on campus that provide access to the Internet. The 3 **libraries** have 147,377 books and 1,411 subscriptions.

Campus Life
Active organizations on campus include a drama/theater group, newspaper, choral group, and marching band. APU has Multi-Ethnic Student Alliance (MESA).

APU is a member of the NAIA. **Intercollegiate sports** (some offering scholarships) include baseball (m), basketball, cross-country running, football (m), golf (m), soccer, softball (w), tennis (m), track and field, volleyball.

Campus Safety
Student safety services include late-night transport/escort service, 24-hour emergency telephone alarm devices, 24-hour patrols by trained security personnel, student patrols, and electronically operated dormitory entrances.

Applying
APU requires an essay, SAT I or ACT, a high school transcript, 2 recommendations, and a minimum high school GPA of 2.5, and in some cases an interview. Application deadline: 7/1; 8/1 for financial aid, with a 3/2 priority date. Early and deferred admission are possible.

Babson College

Suburban setting ■ Private ■ Independent ■ Coed
Babson Park, Massachusetts

Web site: www.babson.edu
Contact: Mrs. Monica Inzer, Dean of Undergraduate Admission and Student Financial Services, Office of Undergraduate Admission, Mustard Hall, Babson Park, MA 02457-0310
Telephone: 800-488-3696 or toll-free 800-488-3696 **Fax:** 781-239-4006
E-mail: ugradadmission@babson.edu

Academics

Babson awards bachelor's and master's **degrees**. Challenging opportunities include advanced placement credit, student-designed majors, freshman honors college, an honors program, independent study, and a senior project. Special programs include internships, summer session for credit, off-campus study, study-abroad, and Army, Navy and Air Force ROTC. A complete listing of majors at Babson appears in the Majors Index beginning on page 430.

The **faculty** at Babson has 163 full-time members. The student-faculty ratio is 9:1.

Students of Babson

The student body totals 3,328, of whom 1,719 are undergraduates. 37.2% are women and 62.8% are men. Students come from 42 states and territories and 64 other countries. 47% are from Massachusetts. 19.1% are international students. 2.7% are African American, 0.3% American Indian, 8.2% Asian American, and 3.8% Hispanic American. 89% returned for their sophomore year.

Facilities and Resources

Student rooms are linked to a campus network. 350 **computers** are available on campus that provide access to the Internet. The 2 **libraries** have 129,401 books and 1,224 subscriptions.

Campus Life

There are 47 active organizations on campus, including a drama/theater group, newspaper, radio station, and choral group. 8% of eligible men and 13% of eligible women are members of national **fraternities** and national **sororities**.

Babson is a member of the NCAA (Division III). **Intercollegiate sports** include baseball (m), basketball, cross-country running, field hockey (w), golf, ice hockey (m), lacrosse, skiing (downhill), soccer, softball (w), swimming, tennis, track and field, volleyball (w).

Campus Safety

Student safety services include late-night transport/escort service, 24-hour emergency telephone alarm devices, 24-hour patrols by trained security personnel, and electronically operated dormitory entrances.

Applying

Babson requires an essay, SAT I or ACT, a high school transcript, and 2 recommendations. It recommends SAT II: Writing Test and SAT II Subject Test in math. Application deadline: 2/1; 2/15 for financial aid. Deferred admission is possible.

Babson College is among the most innovative, integrated, entrepreneurial business schools in the world. Babson students are part of a community that believes in the power of ideas, revels in innovation, and makes an impact on the world. They are immersed in an environment that fosters leadership, teamwork, creativity, and communication. Babson students bring a diverse range of experience to the classroom. As a result, Babson students leave with 3 things: a top-notch business degree, a network of contacts all over the world, and wonderful, lifelong friends.

Getting in Last Year
3,127 applied
35% were accepted
398 enrolled (37%)
49% from top tenth of their h.s. class
2.83 average high school GPA
53% had SAT verbal scores over 600
80% had SAT math scores over 600
5% had SAT verbal scores over 700
17% had SAT math scores over 700
3 valedictorians

Graduation and After
77% graduated in 4 years
4% graduated in 5 years
1% graduated in 6 years
2% pursued further study (2% law)
96% had job offers within 6 months
301 organizations recruited on campus

Financial Matters
$24,544 tuition and fees (2001–02)
$8746 room and board
99% average percent of need met
$18,147 average financial aid amount received per undergraduate (2000–01 estimated)

BALDWIN-WALLACE COLLEGE

SUBURBAN SETTING ■ PRIVATE ■ INDEPENDENT RELIGIOUS ■ COED
BEREA, OHIO

Web site: www.bw.edu
Contact: Mrs. Julie Baker, Director of Undergraduate Admission, 275 Eastland Road, Berea, OH 44017-2088
Telephone: 440-826-2222 or toll-free 877-BWAPPLY (in-state) **Fax:** 440-826-3830
E-mail: admit@bw.edu

Founded in 1845, Baldwin-Wallace was among the first colleges to admit students without regard to race or gender. That spirit of inclusiveness and innovation continues today. The academic program, rooted in the liberal arts yet balanced by abundant opportunities for career exploration and application, is designed to prepare students to make a living . . . and a life worth living. It's a program committed to quality and distinguished by a personalized approach to learning that celebrates each student. "Quality education with a personal touch" is more than a slogan at B-W. It's a statement of purpose. It *is* Baldwin-Wallace.

Getting in Last Year
2,090 applied
85% were accepted
701 enrolled (39%)
30% from top tenth of their h.s. class
3.50 average high school GPA
39% had SAT verbal scores over 600
43% had SAT math scores over 600
50% had ACT scores over 24
6% had SAT verbal scores over 700
8% had SAT math scores over 700
6% had ACT scores over 30
1 National Merit Scholar
26 valedictorians

Graduation and After
48% graduated in 4 years
16% graduated in 5 years
2% graduated in 6 years
24% pursued further study
80% had job offers within 6 months
120 organizations recruited on campus

Financial Matters
$16,330 tuition and fees (2001–02)
$5680 room and board
97% average percent of need met
$13,822 average financial aid amount received per undergraduate

Academics
B-W awards bachelor's and master's **degrees**. Challenging opportunities include advanced placement credit, accelerated degree programs, student-designed majors, an honors program, double majors, independent study, and a senior project. Special programs include internships, summer session for credit, off-campus study, study-abroad, and Army and Air Force ROTC.

The most frequently chosen **baccalaureate** fields are business/marketing, education, and social sciences and history. A complete listing of majors at B-W appears in the Majors Index beginning on page 430.

The **faculty** at B-W has 162 full-time members, 79% with terminal degrees. The student-faculty ratio is 15:1.

Students of B-W
The student body totals 4,884, of whom 3,993 are undergraduates. 61.7% are women and 38.3% are men. Students come from 29 states and territories and 23 other countries. 91% are from Ohio. 1.2% are international students. 3.8% are African American, 0.2% American Indian, 1% Asian American, and 1.4% Hispanic American. 84% returned for their sophomore year.

Facilities and Resources
Student rooms are linked to a campus network. 386 **computers** are available on campus that provide access to the Internet. The 3 **libraries** have 200,000 books and 12,960 subscriptions.

Campus Life
There are 140 active organizations on campus, including a drama/theater group, newspaper, radio station, and choral group. 22% of eligible men and 23% of eligible women are members of national **fraternities** and national **sororities**.

B-W is a member of the NCAA (Division III). **Intercollegiate sports** include baseball (m), basketball, cross-country running, football (m), golf, soccer, softball (w), swimming, tennis, track and field, volleyball (w), wrestling (m).

Campus Safety
Student safety services include late-night transport/escort service, 24-hour emergency telephone alarm devices, 24-hour patrols by trained security personnel, student patrols, and electronically operated dormitory entrances.

Applying
B-W requires an essay, SAT I or ACT, a high school transcript, 1 recommendation, and a minimum high school GPA of 2.6. It recommends an interview and a minimum high school GPA of 3.2. Application deadline: rolling admissions; 9/1 for financial aid, with a 5/1 priority date. Deferred admission is possible.

BARD COLLEGE

RURAL SETTING ■ PRIVATE ■ INDEPENDENT ■ COED
ANNANDALE-ON-HUDSON, NEW YORK

Web site: www.bard.edu
Contact: Ms. Mary Inga Backlund, Director of Admissions, Ravine Road, PO
 Box 5000, Annandale-on-Hudson, NY 12504
Telephone: 845-758-7472 **Fax:** 845-758-5208
E-mail: admission@bard.edu

Academics

Bard awards bachelor's, master's, and doctoral **degrees**. Challenging opportunities include advanced placement credit, accelerated degree programs, student-designed majors, double majors, independent study, and a senior project. Special programs include internships, off-campus study, and study-abroad. A complete listing of majors at Bard appears in the Majors Index beginning on page 430.

The **faculty** at Bard has 113 full-time members. The student-faculty ratio is 9:1.

Students of Bard

The student body totals 1,515, of whom 1,343 are undergraduates. 55.9% are women and 44.1% are men. Students come from 50 states and territories and 48 other countries. 26% are from New York. 5.6% are international students. 2.7% are African American, 0.4% American Indian, 2.8% Asian American, and 4.8% Hispanic American. 86% returned for their sophomore year.

Facilities and Resources

Student rooms are linked to a campus network. 150 **computers** are available on campus that provide access to the Internet. The 4 **libraries** have 275,000 books and 1,400 subscriptions.

Campus Life

There are 70 active organizations on campus, including a drama/theater group, newspaper, radio station, and choral group. No national or local **fraternities** or **sororities**.

Bard is a member of the NCAA (Division III) and NAIA. **Intercollegiate sports** include basketball, cross-country running, fencing, rugby, soccer, squash, tennis, volleyball.

Campus Safety

Student safety services include late-night transport/escort service, 24-hour emergency telephone alarm devices, 24-hour patrols by trained security personnel, student patrols, and electronically operated dormitory entrances.

Applying

Bard requires an essay, a high school transcript, and 3 recommendations, and in some cases an interview. It recommends SAT II Subject Tests, SAT I or ACT, an interview, and a minimum high school GPA of 3.0. Application deadline: 1/15; 3/15 for financial aid, with a 2/15 priority date. Early and deferred admission are possible.

Getting in Last Year

2,970 applied
44% were accepted
358 enrolled (27%)
61% from top tenth of their h.s. class
3.60 average high school GPA
82% had SAT verbal scores over 600
71% had SAT math scores over 600
94% had ACT scores over 24
32% had SAT verbal scores over 700
22% had SAT math scores over 700
17% had ACT scores over 30
63 National Merit Scholars
31 class presidents
16 valedictorians

Graduation and After

55% pursued further study (43% arts and
 sciences, 5% law, 3% business)
60% had job offers within 6 months
198 organizations recruited on campus

Financial Matters

$26,170 tuition and fees (2001–02)
$7742 room and board
87% average percent of need met
$20,092 average financial aid amount received
 per undergraduate

Barnard College

Urban setting ■ Private ■ Independent ■ Women Only
New York, New York

Web site: www.barnard.edu
Contact: Ms. Jennifer Gill Fondiller, Dean of Admissions, 3009 Broadway,
New York, NY 10027
Telephone: 212-854-2014 **Fax:** 212-854-6220
E-mail: admissions@barnard.edu

Barnard is a small, selective liberal arts college for women, located in New York City. Its superb faculty, more than half of whom are women, is made up of leading scholars as well as accessible and dedicated teachers. Barnard's unique affiliation with Columbia University, which is just across the street, gives students a vast selection of additional course offerings and extracurricular activities, NCAA Division I Ivy League athletic competition, and a fully coeducational social life. Its location means that students have access to thousands of internships and excellent cultural, intellectual, and social resources.

Academics

Barnard awards bachelor's **degrees**. Challenging opportunities include advanced placement credit, accelerated degree programs, student-designed majors, an honors program, double majors, independent study, and a senior project. Special programs include internships, off-campus study, and study-abroad.

The most frequently chosen **baccalaureate** fields are social sciences and history, English, and psychology. A complete listing of majors at Barnard appears in the Majors Index beginning on page 430.

The **faculty** at Barnard has 183 full-time members, 94% with terminal degrees. The student-faculty ratio is 10:1.

Students of Barnard

The student body is made up of 2,261 undergraduates. Students come from 51 states and territories and 27 other countries. 39% are from New York. 2.8% are international students. 5.2% are African American, 0.5% American Indian, 20.7% Asian American, and 6.1% Hispanic American. 93% returned for their sophomore year.

Facilities and Resources

Student rooms are linked to a campus network. 150 **computers** are available on campus that provide access to the Internet. The **library** has 198,020 books and 900 subscriptions.

Campus Life

There are 100 active organizations on campus, including a drama/theater group, newspaper, radio station, television station, choral group, and marching band. No national or local **sororities**.

Barnard is a member of the NCAA (Division I). **Intercollegiate sports** include archery, basketball, crew, cross-country running, fencing, field hockey, lacrosse, soccer, softball, swimming, tennis, track and field, volleyball.

Campus Safety

Student safety services include 4 permanent security posts, late-night transport/escort service, 24-hour emergency telephone alarm devices, and 24-hour patrols by trained security personnel.

Applying

Barnard requires an essay, SAT II: Writing Test, SAT I and SAT II or ACT, a high school transcript, and 3 recommendations. It recommends an interview. Application deadline: 1/1; 2/1 for financial aid. Early and deferred admission are possible.

Getting in Last Year
4,074 applied
33% were accepted
541 enrolled (40%)
78% from top tenth of their h.s. class
3.83 average high school GPA
89% had SAT verbal scores over 600
86% had SAT math scores over 600
91% had ACT scores over 24
37% had SAT verbal scores over 700
29% had SAT math scores over 700
33% had ACT scores over 30
4 National Merit Scholars

Graduation and After
72% graduated in 4 years
9% graduated in 5 years
3% graduated in 6 years
22% pursued further study (6% arts and sciences, 5% medicine, 4% law)
67% had job offers within 6 months
106 organizations recruited on campus

Financial Matters
$24,036 tuition and fees (2001–02)
$9658 room and board
100% average percent of need met
$22,676 average financial aid amount received per undergraduate

BATES COLLEGE

SUBURBAN SETTING ■ PRIVATE ■ INDEPENDENT ■ COED
LEWISTON, MAINE

Web site: www.bates.edu
Contact: Mr. Wylie L. Mitchell, Dean of Admissions, 23 Campus Avenue,
Lewiston, ME 04240-6028
Telephone: 207-786-6000 **Fax:** 207-786-6025
E-mail: admissions@bates.edu

Academics

Bates awards bachelor's **degrees**. Challenging opportunities include advanced placement
credit, accelerated degree programs, student-designed majors, an honors program,
double majors, independent study, and a senior project. Special programs include internships, off-campus study, and study-abroad.

The most frequently chosen **baccalaureate** fields are social sciences and history,
English, and physical sciences. A complete listing of majors at Bates appears in the
Majors Index beginning on page 430.

The **faculty** at Bates has 163 full-time members. The student-faculty ratio is 10:1.

Students of Bates

The student body is made up of 1,767 undergraduates. Students come from 50 states and
territories and 68 other countries. 11% are from Maine. 5.1% are international students.
1.9% are African American, 0.2% American Indian, 3.2% Asian American, and 1.6%
Hispanic American. 93% returned for their sophomore year.

Facilities and Resources

Student rooms are linked to a campus network. 1,150 **computers** are available on
campus that provide access to the Internet. The **library** has 524,830 books and 2,012
subscriptions.

Campus Life

There are 80 active organizations on campus, including a drama/theater group,
newspaper, radio station, television station, and choral group. No national or local
fraternities or **sororities**.

Bates is a member of the NCAA (Division III). **Intercollegiate sports** include
baseball (m), basketball, crew, cross-country running, field hockey (w), football (m), golf,
lacrosse, skiing (cross-country), skiing (downhill), soccer, softball (w), squash, swimming,
tennis, track and field, volleyball (w).

Campus Safety

Student safety services include late-night transport/escort service, 24-hour emergency
telephone alarm devices, 24-hour patrols by trained security personnel, student patrols,
and electronically operated dormitory entrances.

Applying

Bates requires an essay, a high school transcript, and 3 recommendations. It recommends
an interview. Application deadline: 1/15; 1/15 for financial aid. Early and deferred admission are possible.

Getting in Last Year

4,264 applied
33% were accepted
582 enrolled (42%)
57% from top tenth of their h.s. class
91% had SAT verbal scores over 600
94% had SAT math scores over 600
30% had SAT verbal scores over 700
31% had SAT math scores over 700

Graduation and After

17% pursued further study
75 organizations recruited on campus

Financial Matters

$34,100 comprehensive fee (2001–02)
100% average percent of need met
$22,434 average financial aid amount received
per undergraduate

BAYLOR UNIVERSITY

URBAN SETTING ■ PRIVATE ■ INDEPENDENT RELIGIOUS ■ COED
WACO, TEXAS

Web site: www.baylor.edu
Contact: Mr. James Steen, Director of Admission Services, PO Box 97056, Waco, TX 76798-7056
Telephone: 254-710-3435 or toll-free 800-BAYLOR U **Fax:** 254-710-3436
E-mail: admissions_office@baylor.edu

A s a selective Baptist university, Baylor is committed to educating the whole student—mind, body, and spirit. Each student enjoys the individual attention of a dedicated faculty, the options afforded by a comprehensive range of challenging academic programs, and a supportive environment that fosters intellectual, social, and spiritual growth. Baylor's strong core curriculum, based on the liberal arts, crosses all majors and emphasizes analytical skills and ethical practices. With competitive financial assistance packages, Baylor strives to help families from all financial backgrounds achieve their dreams of the best education possible. Students should visit Baylor and discover why it is frequently cited as a best value.

Getting in Last Year
7,986 applied
79% were accepted
2,801 enrolled (44%)
39% from top tenth of their h.s. class
39% had SAT verbal scores over 600
48% had SAT math scores over 600
61% had ACT scores over 24
8% had SAT verbal scores over 700
10% had SAT math scores over 700
8% had ACT scores over 30
55 National Merit Scholars

Graduation and After
265 organizations recruited on campus

Financial Matters
$12,804 tuition and fees (2001–02)
$5494 room and board
66% average percent of need met
$9975 average financial aid amount received per undergraduate

Academics

Baylor awards bachelor's, master's, doctoral, and first-professional **degrees** and post-master's certificates. Challenging opportunities include advanced placement credit, accelerated degree programs, student-designed majors, an honors program, double majors, and a senior project. Special programs include internships, summer session for credit, study-abroad, and Air Force ROTC.

The most frequently chosen **baccalaureate** fields are business/marketing, education, and health professions and related sciences. A complete listing of majors at Baylor appears in the Majors Index beginning on page 430.

The **faculty** at Baylor has 697 full-time members, 78% with terminal degrees. The student-faculty ratio is 18:1.

Students of Baylor

The student body totals 14,221, of whom 12,190 are undergraduates. 57.8% are women and 42.2% are men. Students come from 50 states and territories and 70 other countries. 83% are from Texas. 1.7% are international students. 5.6% are African American, 0.5% American Indian, 5.1% Asian American, and 7.5% Hispanic American. 85% returned for their sophomore year.

Facilities and Resources

Student rooms are linked to a campus network. 1,300 **computers** are available on campus that provide access to the Internet. The 9 **libraries** have 1,084,438 books and 9,106 subscriptions.

Campus Life

There are 275 active organizations on campus, including a drama/theater group, newspaper, radio station, television station, choral group, and marching band. 15% of eligible men and 17% of eligible women are members of national **fraternities**, national **sororities**, local fraternities, and local sororities.

Baylor is a member of the NCAA (Division I). **Intercollegiate sports** (some offering scholarships) include baseball (m), basketball, cross-country running, football (m), golf, soccer (w), softball (w), tennis, track and field, volleyball (w).

Campus Safety

Student safety services include bicycle patrols, late-night transport/escort service, 24-hour emergency telephone alarm devices, 24-hour patrols by trained security personnel, and electronically operated dormitory entrances.

Applying

Baylor requires an essay, SAT I or ACT, and a high school transcript. It recommends an interview. Application deadline: rolling admissions; 3/1 priority date for financial aid. Early and deferred admission are possible.

BELMONT UNIVERSITY
URBAN SETTING ■ PRIVATE ■ INDEPENDENT RELIGIOUS ■ COED
NASHVILLE, TENNESSEE

Web site: www.belmont.edu
Contact: Dr. Kathryn Baugher, Dean of Enrollment Services, 1900 Belmont Boulevard, Nashville, TN 37212-3757
Telephone: 615-460-6785 or toll-free 800-56E-NROL **Fax:** 615-460-5434
E-mail: buadmission@mail.belmont.edu

Academics
Belmont awards bachelor's, master's, and doctoral **degrees** and post-bachelor's certificates. Challenging opportunities include advanced placement credit, accelerated degree programs, student-designed majors, an honors program, double majors, independent study, and a senior project. Special programs include cooperative education, internships, summer session for credit, study-abroad, and Army ROTC.

The most frequently chosen **baccalaureate** fields are visual/performing arts, business/marketing, and liberal arts/general studies. A complete listing of majors at Belmont appears in the Majors Index beginning on page 430.

The **faculty** at Belmont has 206 full-time members, 64% with terminal degrees. The student-faculty ratio is 11:1.

Students of Belmont
The student body totals 3,129, of whom 2,617 are undergraduates. 60.3% are women and 39.7% are men. Students come from 51 states and territories and 11 other countries. 41% are from Tennessee. 0.4% are international students. 3.4% are African American, 0.2% American Indian, 1.5% Asian American, and 1.3% Hispanic American. 73% returned for their sophomore year.

Facilities and Resources
Student rooms are linked to a campus network. 250 **computers** are available on campus that provide access to the Internet. The **library** has 178,660 books and 1,476 subscriptions.

Campus Life
There are 54 active organizations on campus, including a drama/theater group, newspaper, radio station, television station, choral group, and marching band. 6% of eligible men and 8% of eligible women are members of national **fraternities**, national **sororities**, local fraternities, and local sororities.

Belmont is a member of the NCAA (Division I). **Intercollegiate sports** (some offering scholarships) include baseball (m), basketball, cross-country running, golf, soccer, softball (w), tennis, track and field, volleyball (w).

Campus Safety
Student safety services include bicycle patrol, late-night transport/escort service, 24-hour emergency telephone alarm devices, 24-hour patrols by trained security personnel, and electronically operated dormitory entrances.

Applying
Belmont requires an essay, SAT I or ACT, a high school transcript, recommendations, resume of activities, and a minimum high school GPA of 3.0, and in some cases an interview. Application deadline: 5/1. Early and deferred admission are possible.

Belmont University brings together the best of liberal arts and professional education in a Christian community of learning and service. Located in Nashville on the former Belle Monte estate, Belmont offers a campus rich in heritage with the conveniences and advantages of one of the fastest-growing cities in the nation. Belmont students benefit from an education marked by personal attention from professors; special academic opportunities, such as the Belmont Undergraduate Research Symposium, studies abroad, and the honors program; and outstanding internship opportunities in many areas, including business, health care, education, communication arts, and the music industry.

Getting in Last Year
1,265 applied
74% were accepted
510 enrolled (54%)
30% from top tenth of their h.s. class
3.24 average high school GPA
39% had SAT verbal scores over 600
33% had SAT math scores over 600
56% had ACT scores over 24
7% had SAT verbal scores over 700
5% had SAT math scores over 700
7% had ACT scores over 30
21 valedictorians

Graduation and After
33% graduated in 4 years
17% graduated in 5 years
1% graduated in 6 years
22% pursued further study
79% had job offers within 6 months
180 organizations recruited on campus

Financial Matters
$13,400 tuition and fees (2001–02)
$5666 room and board
46% average percent of need met
$7123 average financial aid amount received per undergraduate

BELOIT COLLEGE

SMALL-TOWN SETTING ■ PRIVATE ■ INDEPENDENT ■ COED
BELOIT, WISCONSIN

Web site: www.beloit.edu
Contact: Mr. James S. Zielinski, Director of Admissions, 700 College Street, Beloit, WI 53511-5596
Telephone: 608-363-2500 or toll-free 800-356-0751 **Fax:** 608-363-2075
E-mail: admiss@beloit.edu

At Beloit College, students invent themselves. From 49 states, 58 countries, the District of Columbia, and the U.S. Virgin Islands, Beloit students come from many different places and go in many different directions. There is no standardized, stereotypical way to graduate from Beloit. The raw materials Beloit provides begin with an extraordinary faculty and a curriculum that emphasizes an international outlook, interdisciplinary studies, and experiential learning opportunities that include numerous study-abroad, independent research, and internship possibilities. Through investigation and scholarship, students explore Beloit's many resources and are guided by faculty mentors in the directions that best fit them and enable them to achieve their fullest intellectual, professional, and personal development.

Academics

Beloit awards bachelor's **degrees**. Challenging opportunities include advanced placement credit, student-designed majors, double majors, independent study, and a senior project. Special programs include internships, summer session for credit, off-campus study, and study-abroad.

The most frequently chosen **baccalaureate** fields are social sciences and history, visual/performing arts, and biological/life sciences. A complete listing of majors at Beloit appears in the Majors Index beginning on page 430.

The **faculty** at Beloit has 93 full-time members, 99% with terminal degrees. The student-faculty ratio is 11:1.

Students of Beloit

The student body is made up of 1,273 undergraduates. 59.3% are women and 40.7% are men. Students come from 49 states and territories and 58 other countries. 20% are from Wisconsin. 9.7% are international students. 3.7% are African American, 0.5% American Indian, 4.1% Asian American, and 3.5% Hispanic American. 89% returned for their sophomore year.

Facilities and Resources

Student rooms are linked to a campus network. 152 **computers** are available on campus that provide access to the Internet. The **library** has 243,779 books and 980 subscriptions.

Campus Life

There are 100 active organizations on campus, including a drama/theater group, newspaper, radio station, television station, and choral group. 15% of eligible men and 5% of eligible women are members of national **fraternities** and local **sororities**.

Beloit is a member of the NCAA (Division III). **Intercollegiate sports** include baseball (m), basketball, cross-country running, football (m), golf, soccer, softball (w), swimming, tennis, track and field, volleyball (w).

Campus Safety

Student safety services include late-night transport/escort service, 24-hour emergency telephone alarm devices, 24-hour patrols by trained security personnel, and electronically operated dormitory entrances.

Applying

Beloit requires an essay, SAT I or ACT, a high school transcript, and 1 recommendation, and in some cases an interview. It recommends an interview. Application deadline: 2/1; 3/1 priority date for financial aid. Early and deferred admission are possible.

Getting in Last Year
1,529 applied
66% were accepted
309 enrolled (31%)
31% from top tenth of their h.s. class
3.54 average high school GPA
67% had SAT verbal scores over 600
50% had SAT math scores over 600
75% had ACT scores over 24
20% had SAT verbal scores over 700
8% had SAT math scores over 700
25% had ACT scores over 30
8 National Merit Scholars
10 valedictorians

Graduation and After
31% pursued further study
70% had job offers within 6 months

Financial Matters
$22,404 tuition and fees (2001–02)
$5078 room and board
100% average percent of need met
$17,560 average financial aid amount received per undergraduate

BENNINGTON COLLEGE

SMALL-TOWN SETTING ■ PRIVATE ■ INDEPENDENT ■ COED
BENNINGTON, VERMONT

Web site: www.bennington.edu
Contact: Mr. Deane Bogardus, Director of Admissions, One College Drive, Bennington, VT 05201
Telephone: 802-440-4312 or toll-free 800-833-6845 **Fax:** 802-440-4320
E-mail: admissions@bennington.edu

Academics
Bennington awards bachelor's and master's **degrees** and post-bachelor's certificates. Challenging opportunities include student-designed majors, independent study, and a senior project. Special programs include internships, off-campus study, and study-abroad.

The most frequently chosen **baccalaureate** fields are visual/performing arts, interdisciplinary studies, and social sciences and history. A complete listing of majors at Bennington appears in the Majors Index beginning on page 430.

The **faculty** at Bennington has 61 full-time members, 67% with terminal degrees. The student-faculty ratio is 9:1.

Students of Bennington
The student body totals 673, of whom 537 are undergraduates. 67.8% are women and 32.2% are men. Students come from 48 states and territories and 23 other countries. 4% are from Vermont. 11% are international students. 1.1% are African American, 0.2% American Indian, 1.7% Asian American, and 2.4% Hispanic American. 79% returned for their sophomore year.

Facilities and Resources
Student rooms are linked to a campus network. 60 **computers** are available on campus that provide access to the Internet. The 3 **libraries** have 121,000 books and 500 subscriptions.

Campus Life
There are 20 active organizations on campus, including a drama/theater group, newspaper, radio station, and choral group. No national or local **fraternities** or **sororities**.

This institution has no intercollegiate sports.

Campus Safety
Student safety services include late-night transport/escort service, 24-hour emergency telephone alarm devices, and 24-hour patrols by trained security personnel.

Applying
Bennington requires an essay, SAT I or ACT, a high school transcript, an interview, and 2 recommendations. Application deadline: 1/1; 3/1 priority date for financial aid. Early and deferred admission are possible.

A Bennington education imparts more than a body of knowledge or an excellent liberal arts education. It imparts an approach to life—the belief that the way to get things done is to do them. The College was founded almost 7 decades ago on the premise that people learn best by pursuing that which most interests them and by working closely with teachers who are themselves actively engaged in their fields. Self-directedness is central; the power of the Bennington experience has everything to do with the role students have in shaping their education, and the result is lifelong confidence, adaptability, and independence of mind.

Getting in Last Year
719 applied
65% were accepted
182 enrolled (39%)
48% from top tenth of their h.s. class
3.54 average high school GPA
64% had SAT verbal scores over 600
41% had SAT math scores over 600
19% had SAT verbal scores over 700
8% had SAT math scores over 700

Graduation and After
69% graduated in 4 years

Financial Matters
$25,000 tuition and fees (2001–02)
$6350 room and board
75% average percent of need met
$19,417 average financial aid amount received per undergraduate

BEREA COLLEGE
SMALL-TOWN SETTING ■ PRIVATE ■ INDEPENDENT ■ COED
BEREA, KENTUCKY

Getting in Last Year
1,871 applied
32% were accepted
425 enrolled (70%)
26% from top tenth of their h.s. class
3.35 average high school GPA
32% had SAT verbal scores over 600
27% had SAT math scores over 600
49% had ACT scores over 24
5% had SAT verbal scores over 700
3% had SAT math scores over 700
5% had ACT scores over 30

Graduation and After
125 organizations recruited on campus

Financial Matters
$205 tuition and fees (2001–02)
$4099 room and board
87% average percent of need met
$20,849 average financial aid amount received per undergraduate

Web site: www.berea.edu
Contact: Mr. Joseph Bagnoli, Director of Admissions, CPO 2220, Berea, KY 40404
Telephone: 859-985-3500 or toll-free 800-326-5948 **Fax:** 859-985-3512
E-mail: admissions@berea.edu

Academics
Berea awards bachelor's **degrees**. Challenging opportunities include advanced placement credit, student-designed majors, an honors program, double majors, independent study, and a senior project. Special programs include internships, summer session for credit, off-campus study, and study-abroad.

The most frequently chosen **baccalaureate** fields are business/marketing, home economics/vocational home economics, and engineering/engineering technologies. A complete listing of majors at Berea appears in the Majors Index beginning on page 430.

The **faculty** at Berea has 131 full-time members, 88% with terminal degrees. The student-faculty ratio is 11:1.

Students of Berea
The student body is made up of 1,674 undergraduates. 56.5% are women and 43.5% are men. Students come from 45 states and territories and 64 other countries. 43% are from Kentucky. 14.6% are African American, 0.7% American Indian, 1.3% Asian American, and 0.6% Hispanic American. 83% returned for their sophomore year.

Facilities and Resources
Student rooms are linked to a campus network. 260 **computers** are available on campus that provide access to the Internet. The 3 **libraries** have 242,893 books and 2,029 subscriptions.

Campus Life
There are 70 active organizations on campus, including a drama/theater group, newspaper, and choral group. No national or local **fraternities** or **sororities**.

Berea is a member of the NAIA. **Intercollegiate sports** include baseball (m), basketball, cross-country running, golf (m), soccer, softball (w), swimming, tennis, track and field, volleyball (w).

Campus Safety
Student safety services include crime prevention programs, late-night transport/escort service, 24-hour emergency telephone alarm devices, 24-hour patrols by trained security personnel, and electronically operated dormitory entrances.

Applying
Berea requires an essay, SAT I or ACT, a high school transcript, an interview, and financial aid application. It recommends 2 recommendations. Application deadline: 4/1 priority date for financial aid.

BERRY COLLEGE

SMALL-TOWN SETTING ■ PRIVATE ■ INDEPENDENT RELIGIOUS ■ COED
MOUNT BERRY, GEORGIA

Web site: www.berry.edu
Contact: Mr. George Gaddie, Dean of Admissions, PO Box 490159, 2277
Martha Berry Highway, Mount Berry, GA 30149-0159
Telephone: 706-236-2215 or toll-free 800-237-7942 **Fax:** 706-290-2178
E-mail: admissions@berry.edu

Academics
Berry awards bachelor's and master's **degrees**. Challenging opportunities include
advanced placement credit, accelerated degree programs, student-designed majors, an
honors program, double majors, independent study, and a senior project. Special
programs include cooperative education, internships, summer session for credit, and
study-abroad.

The most frequently chosen **baccalaureate** fields are business/marketing, education,
and social sciences and history. A complete listing of majors at Berry appears in the
Majors Index beginning on page 430.

The **faculty** at Berry has 150 full-time members, 82% with terminal degrees. The
student-faculty ratio is 12:1.

Students of Berry
The student body totals 2,038, of whom 1,846 are undergraduates. 63.1% are women
and 36.9% are men. Students come from 34 states and territories and 27 other countries.
84% are from Georgia. 1.5% are international students. 2% are African American, 0.1%
American Indian, 0.8% Asian American, and 1.4% Hispanic American. 75% returned for
their sophomore year.

Facilities and Resources
Student rooms are linked to a campus network. 100 **computers** are available on campus
that provide access to the Internet. The 2 **libraries** have 264,714 books and 1,364
subscriptions.

Campus Life
There are 71 active organizations on campus, including a drama/theater group,
newspaper, television station, and choral group. No national or local **fraternities** or
sororities.

Berry is a member of the NAIA. **Intercollegiate sports** (some offering scholarships)
include baseball (m), basketball, cross-country running, golf, soccer, tennis, track and
field.

Campus Safety
Student safety services include late-night transport/escort service, 24-hour emergency
telephone alarm devices, and 24-hour patrols by trained security personnel.

Applying
Berry requires SAT I or ACT and a high school transcript. Application deadline: 7/28;
4/1 priority date for financial aid. Early and deferred admission are possible.

Berry College is an
independent, coeducational
college with fully accredited
arts, sciences, and professional
programs as well as specialized
graduate programs in education and
business administration. The College
serves humanity by inspiring and
educating students regardless of
their economic status and
emphasizes a comprehensive
educational program committed to
high academic standards, Christian
values, and practical work
experiences. The campus is an
unusually beautiful environment with
approximately 28,000 acres of land.
Fields, forests, lakes, and mountains
provide scenic beauty in a protected
natural setting. The College is
located in Rome, Georgia, 65 miles
northwest of Atlanta and 65 miles
south of Chattanooga.

Getting in Last Year
1,948 applied
82% were accepted
539 enrolled (34%)
36% from top tenth of their h.s. class
3.61 average high school GPA
43% had SAT verbal scores over 600
35% had SAT math scores over 600
52% had ACT scores over 24
10% had SAT verbal scores over 700
5% had SAT math scores over 700
14% had ACT scores over 30
2 National Merit Scholars
13 valedictorians

Graduation and After
35% graduated in 4 years
8% graduated in 5 years
1% graduated in 6 years
31% pursued further study
99% had job offers within 6 months
103 organizations recruited on campus

Financial Matters
$13,450 tuition and fees (2001–02)
$5730 room and board
90% average percent of need met
$12,500 average financial aid amount received
per undergraduate

BETHEL COLLEGE

SUBURBAN SETTING ■ PRIVATE ■ INDEPENDENT RELIGIOUS ■ COED
ST. PAUL, MINNESOTA

Web site: www.bethel.edu
Contact: Mr. Jay Fedje, Director of Admissions, 3900 Bethel Drive, St. Paul, MN 55112
Telephone: 651-638-6242 or toll-free 800-255-8706 ext. 6242 **Fax:** 651-635-1490
E-mail: bcoll-admit@bethel.edu

Getting in Last Year
1,580 applied
67% were accepted
638 enrolled (60%)
27% from top tenth of their h.s. class
50% had SAT verbal scores over 600
45% had SAT math scores over 600
57% had ACT scores over 24
10% had SAT verbal scores over 700
10% had SAT math scores over 700
10% had ACT scores over 30
6 National Merit Scholars

Graduation and After
51% graduated in 4 years
6% graduated in 5 years
1% graduated in 6 years
75% had job offers within 6 months
100 organizations recruited on campus

Financial Matters
$16,815 tuition and fees (2001–02)
$5960 room and board
86% average percent of need met
$13,986 average financial aid amount received per undergraduate

Academics
Bethel awards associate, bachelor's, and master's **degrees**. Challenging opportunities include advanced placement credit, accelerated degree programs, student-designed majors, freshman honors college, an honors program, double majors, independent study, and a senior project. Special programs include internships, summer session for credit, off-campus study, study-abroad, and Army, Navy and Air Force ROTC.

The most frequently chosen **baccalaureate** fields are education, business/marketing, and health professions and related sciences. A complete listing of majors at Bethel appears in the Majors Index beginning on page 430.

The **faculty** at Bethel has 146 full-time members. The student-faculty ratio is 16:1.

Students of Bethel
The student body totals 2,991, of whom 2,700 are undergraduates. 61% are women and 39% are men. Students come from 38 states and territories. 72% are from Minnesota. 0.3% are international students. 0.8% are African American, 0.3% American Indian, 2% Asian American, and 0.9% Hispanic American. 86% returned for their sophomore year.

Facilities and Resources
Student rooms are linked to a campus network. 367 **computers** are available on campus that provide access to the Internet. The 2 **libraries** have 156,000 books and 4,045 subscriptions.

Campus Life
Active organizations on campus include a drama/theater group, newspaper, radio station, television station, and choral group. No national or local **fraternities** or **sororities**.

Bethel is a member of the NCAA (Division III). **Intercollegiate sports** include baseball (m), basketball, cross-country running, football (m), golf (m), ice hockey, soccer, softball (w), tennis, track and field, volleyball (w).

Campus Safety
Student safety services include late-night transport/escort service, 24-hour emergency telephone alarm devices, 24-hour patrols by trained security personnel, student patrols, and electronically operated dormitory entrances.

Applying
Bethel requires an essay, SAT I, ACT, or PSAT, a high school transcript, and 2 recommendations, and in some cases an interview. It recommends an interview. Application deadline: 3/1; 4/15 priority date for financial aid. Deferred admission is possible.

Biola University

Suburban setting ■ Private ■ Independent Religious ■ Coed
La Mirada, California

Web site: www.biola.edu
Contact: Mr. Greg Vaughan, Director of Enrollment Management, 13800
Biola Avenue, La Mirada, CA 90639
Telephone: 562-903-4752 or toll-free 800-652-4652 **Fax:** 562-903-4709
E-mail: admissions@biola.edu

Academics

Biola awards bachelor's, master's, and doctoral **degrees**. Challenging opportunities
include advanced placement credit, accelerated degree programs, freshman honors college, an honors program, double majors, independent study, and a senior project. Special
programs include cooperative education, internships, summer session for credit, off-
campus study, study-abroad, and Army and Air Force ROTC.

The most frequently chosen **baccalaureate** fields are business/marketing,
philosophy, and communications/communication technologies. A complete listing of
majors at Biola appears in the Majors Index beginning on page 430.

The **faculty** at Biola has 154 full-time members. The student-faculty ratio is 18:1.

Students of Biola

The student body totals 4,317, of whom 2,949 are undergraduates. 60.9% are women
and 39.1% are men. Students come from 43 states and territories and 40 other countries.
79% are from California. 4.3% are international students. 3.6% are African American,
0.4% American Indian, 8.1% Asian American, and 8.2% Hispanic American. 83%
returned for their sophomore year.

Facilities and Resources

Student rooms are linked to a campus network. 115 **computers** are available on campus
that provide access to the Internet. The **library** has 259,285 books and 1,188 subscriptions.

Campus Life

There are 33 active organizations on campus, including a drama/theater group,
newspaper, radio station, television station, and choral group. No national or local
fraternities or **sororities**.

Biola is a member of the NAIA. **Intercollegiate sports** (some offering scholarships)
include baseball (m), basketball, cross-country running, soccer, softball (w), swimming,
tennis (w), track and field, volleyball (w).

Campus Safety

Student safety services include access gates to roads through the middle of campus, late-
night transport/escort service, 24-hour emergency telephone alarm devices, 24-hour
patrols by trained security personnel, student patrols, and electronically operated dormitory entrances.

Applying

Biola requires an essay, SAT I or ACT, a high school transcript, an interview, and 2
recommendations. It recommends a minimum high school GPA of 3.0. Application
deadline: 6/1; 3/2 priority date for financial aid. Early and deferred admission are possible.

Getting in Last Year
2,351 applied
55% were accepted
650 enrolled (50%)
45% from top tenth of their h.s. class
3.56 average high school GPA
39% had SAT verbal scores over 600
36% had SAT math scores over 600
56% had ACT scores over 24
8% had SAT verbal scores over 700
5% had SAT math scores over 700
10% had ACT scores over 30

Graduation and After
39% graduated in 4 years
10% graduated in 5 years
2% graduated in 6 years
50% had job offers within 6 months
130 organizations recruited on campus

Financial Matters
$17,410 tuition and fees (2001–02)
$5445 room and board
78% average percent of need met
$13,651 average financial aid amount received
per undergraduate (2000–01 estimated)

BIRMINGHAM-SOUTHERN COLLEGE

URBAN SETTING ■ PRIVATE ■ INDEPENDENT RELIGIOUS ■ COED
BIRMINGHAM, ALABAMA

Web site: www.bsc.edu
Contact: Ms. DeeDee Barnes Bruns, Vice President for Admission and
Financial Aid, Box 549008, Birmingham, AL 35254
Telephone: 205-226-4696 or toll-free 800-523-5793 **Fax:** 205-226-3074
E-mail: admissions@bsc.edu

The College continues to be recognized as one of the nation's leading liberal arts colleges by *National Review, U.S. News & World Report,* and *Money* magazine. Special features of the curriculum are the Interim Term and the Honors Program, as well as undergraduate research, the Hess Center for Leadership and Service, and international study programs. The Interim Term (January) provides an opportunity for independent study, foreign and domestic trips, and internships with government and private organizations. The College has been recognized for its outstanding track record of graduate admission to medical, law, and graduate schools and job placement.

Getting in Last Year
1,047 applied
92% were accepted
388 enrolled (40%)
43% from top tenth of their h.s. class
3.35 average high school GPA
53% had SAT verbal scores over 600
44% had SAT math scores over 600
81% had ACT scores over 24
12% had SAT verbal scores over 700
6% had SAT math scores over 700
21% had ACT scores over 30
13 National Merit Scholars
28 valedictorians

Graduation and After
39% pursued further study (13% arts and sciences, 8% business, 7% medicine)
34 organizations recruited on campus

Financial Matters
$17,185 tuition and fees (2001–02)
$5980 room and board
82% average percent of need met
$14,189 average financial aid amount received per undergraduate

Academics

Birmingham-Southern awards bachelor's and master's **degrees** and post-bachelor's certificates. Challenging opportunities include advanced placement credit, accelerated degree programs, student-designed majors, an honors program, double majors, independent study, and a senior project. Special programs include internships, summer session for credit, off-campus study, study-abroad, and Army and Air Force ROTC.

The most frequently chosen **baccalaureate** fields are business/marketing, visual/performing arts, and biological/life sciences. A complete listing of majors at Birmingham-Southern appears in the Majors Index beginning on page 430.

The **faculty** at Birmingham-Southern has 98 full-time members, 92% with terminal degrees. The student-faculty ratio is 12:1.

Students of Birmingham-Southern

The student body totals 1,424, of whom 1,347 are undergraduates. 59.8% are women and 40.2% are men. Students come from 28 states and territories. 77% are from Alabama. 0.1% are international students. 6.7% are African American, 0.5% American Indian, 2.6% Asian American, and 0.5% Hispanic American. 84% returned for their sophomore year.

Facilities and Resources

Student rooms are linked to a campus network. 156 **computers** are available on campus for student use. The **library** has 170,103 books and 1,155 subscriptions.

Campus Life

There are 70 active organizations on campus, including a drama/theater group, newspaper, radio station, and choral group. 47% of eligible men and 58% of eligible women are members of national **fraternities** and national **sororities**.

Birmingham-Southern is a member of the NCAA (Division I). **Intercollegiate sports** (some offering scholarships) include baseball (m), basketball, cross-country running, golf, riflery (w), soccer, softball (w), tennis, volleyball (w).

Campus Safety

Student safety services include vehicle safety inspection, late-night transport/escort service, 24-hour emergency telephone alarm devices, 24-hour patrols by trained security personnel, and electronically operated dormitory entrances.

Applying

Birmingham-Southern requires an essay, SAT I or ACT, a high school transcript, 1 recommendation, and a minimum high school GPA of 2.0, and in some cases an interview. It recommends an interview. Application deadline: rolling admissions; 3/1 priority date for financial aid. Early and deferred admission are possible.

BOSTON COLLEGE

SUBURBAN SETTING ■ PRIVATE ■ INDEPENDENT RELIGIOUS ■ COED
CHESTNUT HILL, MASSACHUSETTS

Web site: www.bc.edu

Contact: Mr. John L. Mahoney Jr., Director of Undergraduate Admission,
140 Commonwealth Avenue, Devlin Hall 208, 140 Commonwealth Avenue,
Chestnut Hill, MA 02167-3809

Telephone: 617-552-3100 or toll-free 800-360-2522 **Fax:** 617-552-0798

E-mail: ugadmis@bc.edu

Academics

BC awards bachelor's, master's, doctoral, and first-professional **degrees** and post-master's certificates (also offers continuing education program with significant enrollment not reflected in profile). Challenging opportunities include advanced placement credit, accelerated degree programs, student-designed majors, freshman honors college, an honors program, double majors, and independent study. Special programs include internships, summer session for credit, off-campus study, study-abroad, and Army, Navy and Air Force ROTC.

The most frequently chosen **baccalaureate** fields are business/marketing, social sciences and history, and communications/communication technologies. A complete listing of majors at BC appears in the Majors Index beginning on page 430.

The **faculty** at BC has 645 full-time members, 98% with terminal degrees. The student-faculty ratio is 13:1.

Students of BC

The student body totals 13,510, of whom 9,000 are undergraduates. 52.7% are women and 47.3% are men. Students come from 53 states and territories and 63 other countries. 28% are from Massachusetts. 1.3% are international students. 4.3% are African American, 0.3% American Indian, 8.5% Asian American, and 5.3% Hispanic American. 95% returned for their sophomore year.

Facilities and Resources

Student rooms are linked to a campus network. 200 **computers** are available on campus for student use. The 7 **libraries** have 1,976,743 books and 21,121 subscriptions.

Campus Life

There are 140 active organizations on campus, including a drama/theater group, newspaper, radio station, television station, choral group, and marching band. No national or local **fraternities** or **sororities**.

BC is a member of the NCAA (Division I). **Intercollegiate sports** (some offering scholarships) include baseball (m), basketball, cross-country running, fencing, field hockey (w), football (m), golf, ice hockey, lacrosse, sailing, skiing (downhill), soccer, softball (w), swimming, tennis, track and field, volleyball (w), water polo (m), wrestling (m).

Campus Safety

Student safety services include late-night transport/escort service, 24-hour emergency telephone alarm devices, 24-hour patrols by trained security personnel, and electronically operated dormitory entrances.

Applying

BC requires an essay, SAT II: Writing Test, SAT I and SAT II or ACT, a high school transcript, and 2 recommendations. Application deadline: 1/2; 2/1 priority date for financial aid. Early and deferred admission are possible.

Boston College is a school with international stature strengthened by the more than 450-year tradition of Jesuit education, which emphasizes rigorous academic development grounded in the arts and sciences and a commitment to the development of the whole person. Through opportunities to participate in honors programs, research with faculty members, independent study, study abroad, and service learning, students are challenged to fulfill their potential as scholars. With artistic, cultural, service, social, religious, and athletic opportunities that abound on campus and throughout the city of Boston, students are challenged to fulfill their potential as caring, thoughtful individuals and future leaders in society.

Getting in Last Year
19,059 applied
34% were accepted
2,103 enrolled (33%)
69% from top tenth of their h.s. class
78% had SAT verbal scores over 600
85% had SAT math scores over 600
22% had SAT verbal scores over 700
30% had SAT math scores over 700
7 National Merit Scholars

Graduation and After
16% pursued further study (5% law, 4% arts and sciences, 4% business)

Financial Matters
$24,470 tuition and fees (2001–02)
$8860 room and board
100% average percent of need met
$18,830 average financial aid amount received per undergraduate (2000–01)

BOSTON UNIVERSITY
URBAN SETTING ■ PRIVATE ■ INDEPENDENT ■ COED
BOSTON, MASSACHUSETTS

Web site: www.bu.edu
Contact: Ms. Kelly A. Walter, Director of Undergraduate Admissions, 121 Bay State Road, Boston, MA 02215
Telephone: 617-353-2300 **Fax:** 617-353-9695
E-mail: admissions@bu.edu

Boston University (BU) has 11 undergraduate schools and colleges with more than 130 programs of study in areas as diverse as biochemistry, theatre arts, physical therapy, elementary education, and broadcast journalism. Students can customize their own major, either through the Boston University Collaborative Degree Program or the University Professors. BU has an international student body, with students from every state and more than 100 countries. In addition, opportunities to excel exist in all areas of study through research, internships, directed study, and honors programs.

Getting in Last Year
27,562 applied
48% were accepted
3,601 enrolled (27%)
58% from top tenth of their h.s. class
3.5 average high school GPA
75% had SAT verbal scores over 600
83% had SAT math scores over 600
91% had ACT scores over 24
20% had SAT verbal scores over 700
22% had SAT math scores over 700
29% had ACT scores over 30
38 National Merit Scholars
101 valedictorians

Graduation and After
55% graduated in 4 years
13% graduated in 5 years
2% graduated in 6 years
25% pursued further study
500 organizations recruited on campus

Financial Matters
$26,228 tuition and fees (2001–02)
$8750 room and board
93% average percent of need met
$23,838 average financial aid amount received per undergraduate

Academics
Boston University awards bachelor's, master's, doctoral, and first-professional **degrees** and post-master's certificates. Challenging opportunities include advanced placement credit, accelerated degree programs, student-designed majors, an honors program, double majors, independent study, and a senior project. Special programs include cooperative education, internships, summer session for credit, off-campus study, study-abroad, and Army, Navy and Air Force ROTC.

The most frequently chosen **baccalaureate** fields are communications/communication technologies, social sciences and history, and business/marketing. A complete listing of majors at Boston University appears in the Majors Index beginning on page 430.

The **faculty** at Boston University has 2,350 full-time members, 43% with terminal degrees. The student-faculty ratio is 12:1.

Students of Boston University
The student body totals 27,756, of whom 17,602 are undergraduates. 59.7% are women and 40.3% are men. Students come from 52 states and territories and 102 other countries. 24% are from Massachusetts. 7.3% are international students. 2.6% are African American, 0.3% American Indian, 12.1% Asian American, and 5% Hispanic American. 85% returned for their sophomore year.

Facilities and Resources
Student rooms are linked to a campus network. 750 **computers** are available on campus that provide access to research and educational networks and the Internet. The 19 **libraries** have 2,266,999 books and 30,689 subscriptions.

Campus Life
There are 380 active organizations on campus, including a drama/theater group, newspaper, radio station, choral group, and marching band. 5% of eligible men and 7% of eligible women are members of national **fraternities** and national **sororities**.

Boston University is a member of the NCAA (Division I). **Intercollegiate sports** (some offering scholarships) include basketball, crew, cross-country running, field hockey (w), golf, ice hockey (m), lacrosse (w), soccer, softball (w), swimming, tennis, track and field, wrestling (m).

Campus Safety
Student safety services include security personnel at residence hall entrances, self-defense education, well-lit sidewalks, late-night transport/escort service, 24-hour emergency telephone alarm devices, 24-hour patrols by trained security personnel, and electronically operated dormitory entrances.

Applying
Boston University requires an essay, SAT I or ACT, a high school transcript, and 2 recommendations, and in some cases SAT II Subject Tests, SAT II: Writing Test, an interview, and audition, portfolio. It recommends a minimum high school GPA of 3.0. Application deadline: 1/1; 2/15 priority date for financial aid. Early and deferred admission are possible.

BOWDOIN COLLEGE

SMALL-TOWN SETTING ■ PRIVATE ■ INDEPENDENT ■ COED
BRUNSWICK, MAINE

Web site: www.bowdoin.edu
Contact: Ms. Rose Woodd, Receptionist, 5000 College Station, Brunswick, ME 04011-8441
Telephone: 207-725-3958 **Fax:** 207-725-3101
E-mail: admissions@bowdoin.edu

Academics

Bowdoin awards bachelor's **degrees**. Challenging opportunities include advanced placement credit, accelerated degree programs, student-designed majors, double majors, and independent study. Special programs include off-campus study and study-abroad.

The most frequently chosen **baccalaureate** fields are social sciences and history, business/marketing, and foreign language/literature. A complete listing of majors at Bowdoin appears in the Majors Index beginning on page 430.

The **faculty** at Bowdoin has 151 full-time members, 95% with terminal degrees. The student-faculty ratio is 10:1.

Students of Bowdoin

The student body is made up of 1,635 undergraduates. 49.4% are women and 50.6% are men. Students come from 52 states and territories and 29 other countries. 14% are from Maine. 3.4% are international students. 3.1% are African American, 0.6% American Indian, 7% Asian American, and 3.1% Hispanic American. 94% returned for their sophomore year.

Facilities and Resources

Student rooms are linked to a campus network. 462 **computers** are available on campus that provide access to the Internet. The 7 **libraries** have 914,339 books and 2,742 subscriptions.

Campus Life

There are 87 active organizations on campus, including a drama/theater group, newspaper, radio station, television station, and choral group. No national or local **fraternities** or **sororities**.

Bowdoin is a member of the NCAA (Division III). **Intercollegiate sports** include baseball (m), basketball, cross-country running, field hockey (w), football (m), golf, ice hockey, lacrosse, sailing, skiing (cross-country), skiing (downhill), soccer, softball (w), squash, swimming, tennis, track and field, volleyball (w).

Campus Safety

Student safety services include self-defense education, whistle program, late-night transport/escort service, 24-hour emergency telephone alarm devices, 24-hour patrols by trained security personnel, student patrols, and electronically operated dormitory entrances.

Applying

Bowdoin requires an essay, a high school transcript, and 3 recommendations. It recommends an interview. Application deadline: 1/1; 2/15 for financial aid. Early and deferred admission are possible.

Getting in Last Year
4,536 applied
24% were accepted
452 enrolled (42%)
79% from top tenth of their h.s. class
90% had SAT verbal scores over 600
91% had SAT math scores over 600
47% had SAT verbal scores over 700
38% had SAT math scores over 700
20 National Merit Scholars
40 valedictorians

Graduation and After
15% pursued further study (5% arts and sciences, 3% law, 3% medicine)
85% had job offers within 6 months
50 organizations recruited on campus

Financial Matters
$27,280 tuition and fees (2001–02)
$7000 room and board
100% average percent of need met
$22,919 average financial aid amount received per undergraduate

BRADLEY UNIVERSITY

URBAN SETTING ■ PRIVATE ■ INDEPENDENT ■ COED
PEORIA, ILLINOIS

Web site: www.bradley.edu

Contact: Ms. Nickie Roberson, Director of Admissions, 1501 West Bradley Avenue, 100 Swords Hall, Peoria, IL 61625-0002

Telephone: 309-677-1000 or toll-free 800-447-6460

E-mail: admissions@bradley.edu

Getting in Last Year
4,736 applied
76% were accepted
1,110 enrolled (31%)
32% from top tenth of their h.s. class
50% had SAT verbal scores over 600
54% had SAT math scores over 600
72% had ACT scores over 24
10% had SAT verbal scores over 700
12% had SAT math scores over 700
14% had ACT scores over 30
17 National Merit Scholars
57 valedictorians

Graduation and After
49% graduated in 4 years
18% graduated in 5 years
1% graduated in 6 years
96% pursued further study
97% had job offers within 6 months
374 organizations recruited on campus

Financial Matters
$15,340 tuition and fees (2001–02)
$5630 room and board
82% average percent of need met
$12,131 average financial aid amount received per undergraduate

Academics

Bradley awards bachelor's and master's **degrees**. Challenging opportunities include advanced placement credit, accelerated degree programs, student-designed majors, an honors program, double majors, independent study, and a senior project. Special programs include cooperative education, internships, summer session for credit, off-campus study, study-abroad, and Army ROTC.

The most frequently chosen **baccalaureate** fields are business/marketing, engineering/engineering technologies, and communications/communication technologies. A complete listing of majors at Bradley appears in the Majors Index beginning on page 430.

The **faculty** at Bradley has 328 full-time members, 82% with terminal degrees. The student-faculty ratio is 14:1.

Students of Bradley

The student body totals 5,996, of whom 5,167 are undergraduates. 54.3% are women and 45.7% are men. Students come from 44 states and territories and 48 other countries. 86% are from Illinois. 1.7% are international students. 4.8% are African American, 0.3% American Indian, 2% Asian American, and 1.4% Hispanic American. 86% returned for their sophomore year.

Facilities and Resources

Student rooms are linked to a campus network. 2,000 **computers** are available on campus that provide access to the Internet. The **library** has 524,945 books and 1,965 subscriptions.

Campus Life

There are 220 active organizations on campus, including a drama/theater group, newspaper, radio station, television station, and choral group. 36% of eligible men and 33% of eligible women are members of national **fraternities** and national **sororities**.

Bradley is a member of the NCAA (Division I). **Intercollegiate sports** (some offering scholarships) include baseball (m), basketball, cross-country running, golf, soccer (m), softball (w), tennis, track and field (w), volleyball (w).

Campus Safety

Student safety services include bicycle patrol, late-night transport/escort service, 24-hour emergency telephone alarm devices, 24-hour patrols by trained security personnel, and electronically operated dormitory entrances.

Applying

Bradley requires SAT I or ACT and a high school transcript. It recommends an essay, an interview, recommendations, and a minimum high school GPA of 3.0. Application deadline: rolling admissions; 3/1 priority date for financial aid. Early and deferred admission are possible.

BRANDEIS UNIVERSITY

SUBURBAN SETTING ■ PRIVATE ■ INDEPENDENT ■ COED
WALTHAM, MASSACHUSETTS

Web site: www.brandeis.edu
Contact: Mr. Michael Kalafatas, Director of Admissions, 415 South Street,
   Waltham, MA 02254-9110
Telephone: 781-736-3500 or toll-free 800-622-0622 (out-of-state) **Fax:**
   781-736-3536
E-mail: sendinfo@brandeis.edu

Academics
Brandeis awards bachelor's, master's, and doctoral **degrees** and post-bachelor's
certificates. Challenging opportunities include advanced placement credit, student-
designed majors, double majors, independent study, and a senior project. Special
programs include internships, summer session for credit, off-campus study, study-abroad,
and Army and Air Force ROTC.

The most frequently chosen **baccalaureate** fields are social sciences and history,
biological/life sciences, and psychology. A complete listing of majors at Brandeis appears
in the Majors Index beginning on page 430.

The **faculty** at Brandeis has 326 full-time members, 94% with terminal degrees. The
student-faculty ratio is 8:1.

Students of Brandeis
The student body totals 4,882, of whom 3,081 are undergraduates. 56.4% are women
and 43.6% are men. Students come from 52 states and territories and 54 other countries.
25% are from Massachusetts. 6.1% are international students. 2.4% are African
American, 0.2% American Indian, 9.8% Asian American, and 2.4% Hispanic American.
93% returned for their sophomore year.

Facilities and Resources
Student rooms are linked to a campus network. 104 **computers** are available on campus
that provide access to educational software and the Internet. The 3 **libraries** have
1,060,323 books and 16,119 subscriptions.

Campus Life
There are 184 active organizations on campus, including a drama/theater group,
newspaper, radio station, television station, and choral group. No national or local
fraternities or **sororities**.

Brandeis is a member of the NCAA (Division III). **Intercollegiate sports** include
baseball (m), basketball, cross-country running, fencing, golf (m), sailing, soccer (w),
softball (w), swimming, tennis, track and field, volleyball (w).

Campus Safety
Student safety services include late-night transport/escort service, 24-hour emergency
telephone alarm devices, 24-hour patrols by trained security personnel, and electronically operated dormitory entrances.

Applying
Brandeis requires an essay, SAT I and SAT II or ACT, a high school transcript, and 2
recommendations. It recommends an interview and a minimum high school GPA of 3.0.
Application deadline: 1/31. Deferred admission is possible.

Getting in Last Year
6,653 applied
41% were accepted
736 enrolled (27%)
65% from top tenth of their h.s. class
3.50 average high school GPA
87% had SAT verbal scores over 600
85% had SAT math scores over 600
32% had SAT verbal scores over 700
37% had SAT math scores over 700
21 National Merit Scholars

Graduation and After
79% graduated in 4 years
4% graduated in 5 years
1% graduated in 6 years
23% pursued further study (11% arts and
   sciences, 6% law, 3% medicine)
110 organizations recruited on campus

Financial Matters
$27,076 tuition and fees (2001–02)
$7405 room and board
84% average percent of need met
$21,076 average financial aid amount received
   per undergraduate

Brigham Young University

Suburban setting ■ Private ■ Independent Religious ■ Coed
Provo, Utah

Web site: www.byu.edu
Contact: Mr. Erlend D. Peterson, Dean of Admissions and Records, Provo, UT 84602-1001
Telephone: 801-378-2539 **Fax:** 801-378-4264
E-mail: admissions@byu.edu

Getting in Last Year
10,293 applied
65% were accepted
5,186 enrolled (77%)
54% from top tenth of their h.s. class
3.76 average high school GPA
88% had ACT scores over 24
25% had ACT scores over 30
133 National Merit Scholars

Graduation and After
23% pursued further study
79% had job offers within 6 months
600 organizations recruited on campus

Financial Matters
$3060 tuition and fees (2001–02)
$4780 room and board
37% average percent of need met
$3602 average financial aid amount received per undergraduate (2000–01)

Academics
BYU awards bachelor's, master's, doctoral, and first-professional **degrees**. Challenging opportunities include advanced placement credit, accelerated degree programs, freshman honors college, an honors program, double majors, independent study, and a senior project. Special programs include cooperative education, internships, summer session for credit, off-campus study, study-abroad, and Army and Air Force ROTC.

The most frequently chosen **baccalaureate** fields are education, business/marketing, and social sciences and history. A complete listing of majors at BYU appears in the Majors Index beginning on page 430.

The **faculty** at BYU has 1,562 full-time members, 66% with terminal degrees. The student-faculty ratio is 20:1.

Students of BYU
The student body totals 32,771, of whom 29,815 are undergraduates. 50.6% are women and 49.4% are men. Students come from 53 states and territories and 107 other countries. 30% are from Utah. 3.3% are international students. 0.3% are African American, 0.6% American Indian, 2.6% Asian American, and 2.5% Hispanic American. 91% returned for their sophomore year.

Facilities and Resources
Student rooms are linked to a campus network. 1,800 **computers** are available on campus that provide access to the Internet. The 3 **libraries** have 2,552,288 books and 16,201 subscriptions.

Campus Life
There are 140 active organizations on campus, including a drama/theater group, newspaper, radio station, television station, choral group, and marching band. No national or local **fraternities** or **sororities**.

BYU is a member of the NCAA (Division I). **Intercollegiate sports** (some offering scholarships) include baseball (m), basketball, cross-country running, football (m), golf, gymnastics (w), soccer (w), swimming, tennis, track and field, volleyball.

Campus Safety
Student safety services include late-night transport/escort service, 24-hour emergency telephone alarm devices, 24-hour patrols by trained security personnel, and electronically operated dormitory entrances.

Applying
BYU requires an essay, ACT, a high school transcript, an interview, and 1 recommendation. Application deadline: 2/15. Early and deferred admission are possible.

BROWN UNIVERSITY

URBAN SETTING ■ PRIVATE ■ INDEPENDENT ■ COED
PROVIDENCE, RHODE ISLAND

Web site: www.brown.edu
Contact: Mr. Michael Goldberger, Director of Admission, Box 1876,
Providence, RI 02912
Telephone: 401-863-2378 **Fax:** 401-863-9300
E-mail: admission_undergraduate@brown.edu

Academics
Brown awards bachelor's, master's, doctoral, and first-professional **degrees**. Challenging opportunities include advanced placement credit, accelerated degree programs, student-designed majors, an honors program, double majors, independent study, and a senior project. Special programs include internships, summer session for credit, off-campus study, study-abroad, and Army ROTC.

The most frequently chosen **baccalaureate** fields are social sciences and history, liberal arts/general studies, and biological/life sciences. A complete listing of majors at Brown appears in the Majors Index beginning on page 430.

The **faculty** at Brown has 745 full-time members, 98% with terminal degrees. The student-faculty ratio is 8:1.

Students of Brown
The student body totals 7,774, of whom 5,999 are undergraduates. 54.3% are women and 45.7% are men. Students come from 52 states and territories and 72 other countries. 4% are from Rhode Island. 6.2% are international students. 6.1% are African American, 0.5% American Indian, 14.4% Asian American, and 6.6% Hispanic American. 97% returned for their sophomore year.

Facilities and Resources
Student rooms are linked to a campus network. 400 **computers** are available on campus that provide access to the Internet. The 7 **libraries** have 3,000,000 books and 17,000 subscriptions.

Campus Life
There are 240 active organizations on campus, including a drama/theater group, newspaper, radio station, television station, choral group, and marching band. 10% of eligible men and 3% of eligible women are members of national **fraternities**, national **sororities**, and coed fraternity.

Brown is a member of the NCAA (Division I). **Intercollegiate sports** include baseball (m), basketball, crew, cross-country running, equestrian sports (w), fencing, field hockey (w), football (m), golf, gymnastics (w), ice hockey, lacrosse, skiing (downhill) (w), soccer, softball (w), squash, swimming, tennis, track and field, volleyball (w), water polo, wrestling (m).

Campus Safety
Student safety services include late-night transport/escort service, 24-hour emergency telephone alarm devices, 24-hour patrols by trained security personnel, and electronically operated dormitory entrances.

Applying
Brown requires an essay, SAT I and SAT II or ACT, a high school transcript, and 2 recommendations. It recommends SAT II: Writing Test. Application deadline: 1/1; 2/1 for financial aid. Early and deferred admission are possible.

Brown is a university/college with a renowned faculty that teaches students in both the undergraduate college and the graduate school. The unique, nonrestrictive curriculum allows students freedom in selecting their courses, and they may choose their concentration from 83 areas, complete a double major, or pursue an independent concentration. The 140-acre campus is set in a residential neighborhood (National Historic District) and features state-of-the-art computing facilities and an athletics complex. A real sense of community exists on campus, as every student has an academic adviser, and there are several peer counselors in the residence halls.

Getting in Last Year
16,606 applied
16% were accepted
1,401 enrolled (51%)
87% from top tenth of their h.s. class
86% had SAT verbal scores over 600
91% had SAT math scores over 600
94% had ACT scores over 24
51% had SAT verbal scores over 700
55% had SAT math scores over 700
61% had ACT scores over 30
174 valedictorians

Graduation and After
79% graduated in 4 years
13% graduated in 5 years
2% graduated in 6 years
35% pursued further study (10% arts and sciences, 10% law, 9% medicine)
60% had job offers within 6 months
400 organizations recruited on campus

Financial Matters
$27,172 tuition and fees (2001–02)
$7578 room and board
100% average percent of need met
$22,093 average financial aid amount received per undergraduate

BRYN MAWR COLLEGE

SUBURBAN SETTING ■ PRIVATE ■ INDEPENDENT ■ WOMEN ONLY
BRYN MAWR, PENNSYLVANIA

Web site: www.brynmawr.edu
Contact: Ms. Elizabeth Mosier, Acting Director of Admissions, 101 North Merion Avenue, Bryn Mawr, PA 19010
Telephone: 610-526-5152 or toll-free 800-BMC-1885 (out-of-state)
E-mail: admissions@brynmawr.edu

Bryn Mawr is a residential liberal arts college for women that values critical, creative, and independent habits of thought and expression. Located in suburban Philadelphia, Bryn Mawr offers the benefits of proximity to the city with its rich cultural and social resources. An extraordinarily close relationship with neighboring Haverford College allows students to take classes—and even major—on either campus. At the heart of Bryn Mawr is a serious and important education that transforms students' relationship to the world and prepares them to do whatever they choose with dedication and success.

Getting in Last Year
1,522 applied
60% were accepted
338 enrolled (37%)
62% from top tenth of their h.s. class
81% had SAT verbal scores over 600
71% had SAT math scores over 600
31% had SAT verbal scores over 700
14% had SAT math scores over 700
10 valedictorians

Graduation and After
76% graduated in 4 years
3% graduated in 5 years
1% graduated in 6 years
20% pursued further study
52% had job offers within 6 months
60 organizations recruited on campus

Financial Matters
$24,990 tuition and fees (2001–02)
$8590 room and board
96% average percent of need met
$22,848 average financial aid amount received per undergraduate

Academics

Bryn Mawr awards bachelor's, master's, and doctoral **degrees**. Challenging opportunities include advanced placement credit, accelerated degree programs, student-designed majors, an honors program, double majors, independent study, and a senior project. Special programs include summer session for credit, off-campus study, study-abroad, and Air Force ROTC.

The most frequently chosen **baccalaureate** fields are social sciences and history, foreign language/literature, and English. A complete listing of majors at Bryn Mawr appears in the Majors Index beginning on page 430.

The **faculty** at Bryn Mawr has 146 full-time members, 96% with terminal degrees. The student-faculty ratio is 9:1.

Students of Bryn Mawr

The student body totals 1,756, of whom 1,333 are undergraduates. Students come from 48 states and territories and 44 other countries. 20% are from Pennsylvania. 7.7% are international students. 3.8% are African American, 15% Asian American, and 3% Hispanic American. 89% returned for their sophomore year.

Facilities and Resources

Student rooms are linked to a campus network. 200 **computers** are available on campus that provide access to the Internet. The 3 **libraries** have 932,423 books and 4,045 subscriptions.

Campus Life

There are 100 active organizations on campus, including a drama/theater group, newspaper, and choral group. No national or local **sororities**.

Bryn Mawr is a member of the NCAA (Division III). **Intercollegiate sports** include badminton, basketball, crew, cross-country running, field hockey, lacrosse, soccer, swimming, tennis, track and field, volleyball.

Campus Safety

Student safety services include shuttle bus service, awareness programs, bicycle registration, security Website, late-night transport/escort service, 24-hour emergency telephone alarm devices, 24-hour patrols by trained security personnel, and electronically operated dormitory entrances.

Applying

Bryn Mawr requires an essay, SAT I and SAT II or ACT, a high school transcript, and 3 recommendations. It recommends an interview. Application deadline: 1/15; 1/15 for financial aid. Early and deferred admission are possible.

BUCKNELL UNIVERSITY

SMALL-TOWN SETTING ■ PRIVATE ■ INDEPENDENT ■ COED
LEWISBURG, PENNSYLVANIA

Web site: www.bucknell.edu
Contact: Mr. Mark D. Davies, Dean of Admissions, Lewisburg, PA 17837
Telephone: 570-577-1101 **Fax:** 570-577-3538
E-mail: admissions@bucknell.edu

Academics

Bucknell awards bachelor's and master's **degrees**. Challenging opportunities include advanced placement credit, student-designed majors, an honors program, double majors, independent study, and a senior project. Special programs include internships, summer session for credit, off-campus study, study-abroad, and Army ROTC.

The most frequently chosen **baccalaureate** fields are social sciences and history, engineering/engineering technologies, and business/marketing. A complete listing of majors at Bucknell appears in the Majors Index beginning on page 430.

The **faculty** at Bucknell has 289 full-time members, 91% with terminal degrees. The student-faculty ratio is 12:1.

Students of Bucknell

The student body totals 3,587, of whom 3,430 are undergraduates. 48.7% are women and 51.3% are men. Students come from 48 states and territories and 33 other countries. 33% are from Pennsylvania. 1.6% are international students. 2.9% are African American, 0.4% American Indian, 5.4% Asian American, and 2.6% Hispanic American. 94% returned for their sophomore year.

Facilities and Resources

Student rooms are linked to a campus network. 350 **computers** are available on campus that provide access to the Internet. The **library** has 432,730 books and 2,789 subscriptions.

Campus Life

There are 120 active organizations on campus, including a drama/theater group, newspaper, radio station, and choral group. 51% of eligible men and 58% of eligible women are members of national **fraternities** and national **sororities**.

Bucknell is a member of the NCAA (Division I). **Intercollegiate sports** include baseball (m), basketball, crew, cross-country running, field hockey (w), football (m), golf, lacrosse, soccer, softball (w), swimming, tennis, track and field, volleyball (w), water polo, wrestling (m).

Campus Safety

Student safety services include well-lit pathways, self-defense education, safety/security orientation, late-night transport/escort service, 24-hour emergency telephone alarm devices, 24-hour patrols by trained security personnel, and student patrols.

Applying

Bucknell requires an essay, SAT I or ACT, a high school transcript, and 2 recommendations. It recommends an interview. Application deadline: 1/1; 1/1 for financial aid. Deferred admission is possible.

With 3,350 undergraduates and 200 graduate students, Bucknell is the largest of the top 40 "national liberal arts colleges" and one of just 5 among the group that is a university. Its combination of an intimate college experience and the extensive choices offered by a distinguished university gives students opportunities they won't find elsewhere. With the help of committed professors who provide sound advice, students find many ways to add breadth, depth, and imagination to their program of study.

Getting in Last Year
8,033 applied
39% were accepted
913 enrolled (29%)
60% from top tenth of their h.s. class
72% had SAT verbal scores over 600
85% had SAT math scores over 600
89% had ACT scores over 24
15% had SAT verbal scores over 700
25% had SAT math scores over 700
32% had ACT scores over 30

Graduation and After
83% graduated in 4 years
3% graduated in 5 years
1% graduated in 6 years
20% pursued further study (7% arts and sciences, 3% engineering, 3% law)
97% had job offers within 6 months
211 organizations recruited on campus

Financial Matters
$25,335 tuition and fees (2001–02)
$5761 room and board
99% average percent of need met
$19,500 average financial aid amount received per undergraduate (2000–01 estimated)

BUENA VISTA UNIVERSITY

SMALL-TOWN SETTING ■ PRIVATE ■ INDEPENDENT RELIGIOUS ■ COED
STORM LAKE, IOWA

Web site: www.bvu.edu
Contact: Ms. Louise Cummings-Simmons, Director of Admissions, 610 West
Fourth Street, Storm Lake, IA 50588
Telephone: 712-749-2351 or toll-free 800-383-9600
E-mail: admissions@bvu.edu

Located in America's heartland, Buena Vista University prepares students for successful careers by offering a balance between traditional liberal arts courses and innovative experiential learning opportunities that require the practical application of knowledge. Long a leader in information technology, BVU is currently at the forefront nationally in providing "anytime, anywhere" online access by creating a campuswide wireless network and providing its students with notebook computers.

Getting in Last Year
1,172 applied
85% were accepted
380 enrolled (38%)
22% from top tenth of their h.s. class
3.36 average high school GPA
37% had ACT scores over 24
4% had ACT scores over 30
22 valedictorians

Graduation and After
41% graduated in 4 years
6% graduated in 5 years
4% graduated in 6 years
15% pursued further study (2% arts and sciences, 2% business, 1% medicine)
97% had job offers within 6 months
50 organizations recruited on campus

Financial Matters
$17,846 tuition and fees (2001–02)
$4982 room and board
93% average percent of need met
$17,618 average financial aid amount received per undergraduate

Academics
BVU awards bachelor's and master's **degrees**. Challenging opportunities include advanced placement credit, student-designed majors, freshman honors college, an honors program, double majors, independent study, and a senior project. Special programs include internships, summer session for credit, off-campus study, and study-abroad.

The most frequently chosen **baccalaureate** fields are education, social sciences and history, and communications/communication technologies. A complete listing of majors at BVU appears in the Majors Index beginning on page 430.

The **faculty** at BVU has 82 full-time members, 61% with terminal degrees. The student-faculty ratio is 15:1.

Students of BVU
The student body totals 1,392, of whom 1,292 are undergraduates. 51% are women and 49% are men. Students come from 18 states and territories and 6 other countries. 85% are from Iowa. 1.8% are international students. 1.1% are African American, 0.3% American Indian, 1.8% Asian American, and 1.2% Hispanic American. 72% returned for their sophomore year.

Facilities and Resources
Student rooms are linked to a campus network. 400 **computers** are available on campus that provide access to the Internet. The **library** has 153,084 books and 698 subscriptions.

Campus Life
There are 50 active organizations on campus, including a drama/theater group, newspaper, radio station, television station, choral group, and marching band. No national or local **fraternities** or **sororities**.

BVU is a member of the NCAA (Division III). **Intercollegiate sports** include baseball (m), basketball, cross-country running, football (m), golf, soccer, softball (w), swimming, tennis, track and field, volleyball (w), wrestling (m).

Campus Safety
Student safety services include night security patrols, late-night transport/escort service, 24-hour emergency telephone alarm devices, and electronically operated dormitory entrances.

Applying
BVU requires SAT I or ACT, a high school transcript, and recommendations, and in some cases an essay and an interview. It recommends a minimum high school GPA of 3.0. Application deadline: 6/1; 6/1 priority date for financial aid. Early and deferred admission are possible.

BUTLER UNIVERSITY

URBAN SETTING ■ PRIVATE ■ INDEPENDENT ■ COED
INDIANAPOLIS, INDIANA

Web site: www.butler.edu

Contact: Mr. William Preble, Dean of Admissions, 4600 Sunset Avenue, Indianapolis, IN 46208-3485

Telephone: 317-940-8100 ext. 8124 or toll-free 888-940-8100 **Fax:** 317-940-8150

E-mail: admission@butler.edu

Academics

Butler awards associate, bachelor's, master's, and first-professional **degrees** and post-bachelor's certificates. Challenging opportunities include advanced placement credit, accelerated degree programs, an honors program, double majors, independent study, and a senior project. Special programs include cooperative education, internships, summer session for credit, off-campus study, study-abroad, and Army and Air Force ROTC.

The most frequently chosen **baccalaureate** fields are business/marketing, education, and health professions and related sciences. A complete listing of majors at Butler appears in the Majors Index beginning on page 430.

The **faculty** at Butler has 257 full-time members, 82% with terminal degrees. The student-faculty ratio is 13:1.

Students of Butler

The student body totals 4,264, of whom 3,424 are undergraduates. 63% are women and 37% are men. Students come from 43 states and territories and 40 other countries. 60% are from Indiana. 1.7% are international students. 3.6% are African American, 0.1% American Indian, 2% Asian American, and 1.2% Hispanic American. 81% returned for their sophomore year.

Facilities and Resources

Student rooms are linked to a campus network. 250 **computers** are available on campus that provide access to e-mail and the Internet. The 2 **libraries** have 345,415 books and 2,202 subscriptions.

Campus Life

There are 100 active organizations on campus, including a drama/theater group, newspaper, radio station, television station, choral group, and marching band. 25% of eligible men and 25% of eligible women are members of national **fraternities** and national **sororities**.

Butler is a member of the NCAA (Division I). **Intercollegiate sports** (some offering scholarships) include baseball (m), basketball, cross-country running, football (m), golf, lacrosse (m), soccer, softball (w), swimming, tennis, track and field, volleyball (w).

Campus Safety

Student safety services include late-night transport/escort service, 24-hour emergency telephone alarm devices, 24-hour patrols by trained security personnel, and electronically operated dormitory entrances.

Applying

Butler requires an essay, SAT I or ACT, and a high school transcript, and in some cases an interview and audition. It recommends SAT II Subject Tests. Application deadline: 8/15; 3/1 priority date for financial aid. Deferred admission is possible.

At Butler University, students are actively engaged in the learning experience from the minute they step on campus. With small class sizes, students receive direct access to faculty members, personalized attention, and hands-on learning opportunities. Participation in research is an opportunity that is rarely offered to undergraduates; at Butler, students not only have the chance to participate in research with faculty members, they also originate research projects and develop them into professional presentations and publications. Butler students receive research grants through the Butler Summer Institute and present their projects at the Undergraduate Research Conference, hosted by Butler every April.

Getting in Last Year
3,168 applied
85% were accepted
933 enrolled (35%)
44% from top tenth of their h.s. class
3.60 average high school GPA
40% had SAT verbal scores over 600
49% had SAT math scores over 600
77% had ACT scores over 24
5% had SAT verbal scores over 700
8% had SAT math scores over 700
16% had ACT scores over 30
12 National Merit Scholars
67 valedictorians

Graduation and After
48% graduated in 4 years
14% graduated in 5 years
7% graduated in 6 years
19% pursued further study (7% arts and sciences, 4% medicine, 2% law)
68% had job offers within 6 months
125 organizations recruited on campus

Financial Matters
$19,130 tuition and fees (2001–02)
$6450 room and board
$14,900 average financial aid amount received per undergraduate

CALIFORNIA INSTITUTE OF TECHNOLOGY

SUBURBAN SETTING ■ PRIVATE ■ INDEPENDENT ■ COED
PASADENA, CALIFORNIA

Web site: www.caltech.edu
Contact: Ms. Charlene Liebau, Director of Admissions, 1200 East California
Boulevard, Pasadena, CA 91125-0001
Telephone: 626-395-6341 or toll-free 800-568-8324 **Fax:** 626-683-3026
E-mail: ugadmissions@caltech.edu

Getting in Last Year
3,365 applied
15% were accepted
214 enrolled (42%)
98% from top tenth of their h.s. class
99% had SAT verbal scores over 600
100% had SAT math scores over 600
80% had SAT verbal scores over 700
98% had SAT math scores over 700
53 National Merit Scholars
85 valedictorians

Graduation and After
71% graduated in 4 years
12% graduated in 5 years
3% graduated in 6 years
Graduates pursuing further study: 26% arts
and sciences, 20% engineering, 3% medicine
40% had job offers within 6 months
211 organizations recruited on campus

Financial Matters
$21,120 tuition and fees (2001–02)
$6543 room and board
100% average percent of need met
$20,202 average financial aid amount received
per undergraduate (2000–01 estimated)

Academics
Caltech awards bachelor's, master's, and doctoral **degrees**. Challenging opportunities
include student-designed majors, double majors, and independent study. Special
programs include internships, off-campus study, study-abroad, and Army and Air Force
ROTC.

The most frequently chosen **baccalaureate** fields are engineering/engineering
technologies, physical sciences, and biological/life sciences. A complete listing of majors
at Caltech appears in the Majors Index beginning on page 430.

The **faculty** at Caltech has 294 full-time members, 98% with terminal degrees. The
student-faculty ratio is 3:1.

Students of Caltech
The student body totals 2,058, of whom 942 are undergraduates. Students come from 47
states and territories and 33 other countries. 42% are from California. 9.8% are international students. 1.9% are African American, 0.3% American Indian, 24.5% Asian
American, and 6.9% Hispanic American. 97% returned for their sophomore year.

Facilities and Resources
Student rooms are linked to a campus network. 600 **computers** are available on campus
that provide access to the Internet. The 11 **libraries** have 2,878,000 books and 3,200
subscriptions.

Campus Life
There are 85 active organizations on campus, including a drama/theater group,
newspaper, and choral group. No national or local **fraternities** or **sororities**.

Caltech is a member of the NCAA (Division III). **Intercollegiate sports** include
baseball (m), basketball, cross-country running, fencing, golf, soccer (m), swimming, tennis, track and field, volleyball (w), water polo (m).

Campus Safety
Student safety services include late-night transport/escort service, 24-hour emergency
telephone alarm devices, and 24-hour patrols by trained security personnel.

Applying
Caltech requires an essay, SAT I, SAT II: Writing Test, SAT II Subject Test in math and
either physics, chemistry, or biology, a high school transcript, and 3 recommendations.
Application deadline: 1/1; 1/15 priority date for financial aid. Early and deferred admission are possible.

CALIFORNIA POLYTECHNIC STATE UNIVERSITY, SAN LUIS OBISPO

SMALL-TOWN SETTING ■ PUBLIC ■ STATE-SUPPORTED ■ COED
SAN LUIS OBISPO, CALIFORNIA

Web site: www.calpoly.edu
Contact: Mr. James Maraviglia, Director of Admissions and Evaluations, San Luis Obispo, CA 93407
Telephone: 805-756-2311 **Fax:** 805-756-5400
E-mail: admprosp@calpoly.edu

Academics

Cal Poly State University awards bachelor's and master's **degrees**. Challenging opportunities include advanced placement credit, an honors program, double majors, independent study, and a senior project. Special programs include cooperative education, internships, summer session for credit, off-campus study, study-abroad, and Army ROTC.

The most frequently chosen **baccalaureate** fields are engineering/engineering technologies, business/marketing, and agriculture. A complete listing of majors at Cal Poly State University appears in the Majors Index beginning on page 430.

The **faculty** at Cal Poly State University has 654 full-time members, 73% with terminal degrees. The student-faculty ratio is 20:1.

Students of Cal Poly State University

The student body totals 18,079, of whom 17,066 are undergraduates. 44.7% are women and 55.3% are men. Students come from 48 states and territories and 41 other countries. 96% are from California. 0.7% are international students. 0.9% are African American, 0.9% American Indian, 11% Asian American, and 10.5% Hispanic American. 89% returned for their sophomore year.

Facilities and Resources

Student rooms are linked to a campus network. 1,880 **computers** are available on campus for student use. The **library** has 1,151,800 books and 2,617 subscriptions.

Campus Life

There are 360 active organizations on campus, including a drama/theater group, newspaper, radio station, choral group, and marching band. 8% of eligible men and 9% of eligible women are members of national **fraternities**, national **sororities**, local fraternities, and local sororities.

Cal Poly State University is a member of the NCAA (Division I). **Intercollegiate sports** (some offering scholarships) include baseball (m), basketball, cross-country running, equestrian sports, football (m), golf (m), gymnastics (w), soccer, softball (w), swimming, tennis, track and field, volleyball (w), wrestling (m).

Campus Safety

Student safety services include late-night transport/escort service, 24-hour emergency telephone alarm devices, 24-hour patrols by trained security personnel, student patrols, and electronically operated dormitory entrances.

Applying

Cal Poly State University requires SAT I or ACT and a high school transcript. Application deadline: 11/30; 3/2 priority date for financial aid. Early admission is possible.

Getting in Last Year
18,755 applied
47% were accepted
3,003 enrolled (34%)
30% from top tenth of their h.s. class
3.63 average high school GPA
34% had SAT verbal scores over 600
56% had SAT math scores over 600
62% had ACT scores over 24
4% had SAT verbal scores over 700
11% had SAT math scores over 700
8% had ACT scores over 30

Graduation and After
15% pursued further study
90% had job offers within 6 months
630 organizations recruited on campus

Financial Matters
$2153 resident tuition and fees (2001–02)
$8057 nonresident tuition and fees (2001–02)
$6594 room and board
80% average percent of need met
$6765 average financial aid amount received per undergraduate

CALVIN COLLEGE

SUBURBAN SETTING ■ PRIVATE ■ INDEPENDENT RELIGIOUS ■ COED
GRAND RAPIDS, MICHIGAN

Web site: www.calvin.edu
Contact: Mr. Dale D. Kuiper, Director of Admissions, 3201 Burton Street, SE, Grand Rapids, MI 49546-4388
Telephone: 616-957-6106 or toll-free 800-688-0122 **Fax:** 616-957-6777
E-mail: admissions@calvin.edu

Calvin brings together some remarkable minds—4,300 students and 290 professors who chose this institution because it values both intellect and faith. Through intellectual curiosity, spirited interaction, and conscientious work, Calvin people tackle some big questions—always questioning, always analyzing—exploring what it means to work for renewal in God's world.

Getting in Last Year
1,920 applied
98% were accepted
1,031 enrolled (55%)
28% from top tenth of their h.s. class
3.5 average high school GPA
43% had SAT verbal scores over 600
52% had SAT math scores over 600
71% had ACT scores over 24
13% had SAT verbal scores over 700
15% had SAT math scores over 700
16% had ACT scores over 30
25 National Merit Scholars
41 valedictorians

Graduation and After
20% pursued further study (5% arts and sciences, 2% education, 2% medicine)
73% had job offers within 6 months
295 organizations recruited on campus

Financial Matters
$14,870 tuition and fees (2001–02)
$5180 room and board
88% average percent of need met
$11,390 average financial aid amount received per undergraduate

Academics
Calvin awards bachelor's and master's **degrees** and post-bachelor's certificates. Challenging opportunities include advanced placement credit, accelerated degree programs, student-designed majors, an honors program, double majors, independent study, and a senior project. Special programs include cooperative education, internships, summer session for credit, off-campus study, study-abroad, and Army ROTC.

The most frequently chosen **baccalaureate** fields are business/marketing, social sciences and history, and education. A complete listing of majors at Calvin appears in the Majors Index beginning on page 430.

The **faculty** at Calvin has 284 full-time members, 85% with terminal degrees. The student-faculty ratio is 15:1.

Students of Calvin
The student body totals 4,258, of whom 4,221 are undergraduates. 56% are women and 44% are men. Students come from 48 states and territories and 33 other countries. 61% are from Michigan. 7.8% are international students. 0.9% are African American, 0.4% American Indian, 2.3% Asian American, and 1.2% Hispanic American. 86% returned for their sophomore year.

Facilities and Resources
Student rooms are linked to a campus network. 659 **computers** are available on campus that provide access to the Internet. The **library** has 700,000 books and 2,660 subscriptions.

Campus Life
There are 52 active organizations on campus, including a drama/theater group, newspaper, radio station, and choral group. No national or local **fraternities** or **sororities**.

Calvin is a member of the NCAA (Division III). **Intercollegiate sports** include baseball (m), basketball, cross-country running, golf, soccer, softball (w), swimming, tennis, track and field, volleyball (w).

Campus Safety
Student safety services include crime prevention programs, crime alert bulletins, late-night transport/escort service, 24-hour emergency telephone alarm devices, 24-hour patrols by trained security personnel, student patrols, and electronically operated dormitory entrances.

Applying
Calvin requires an essay, SAT I or ACT, a high school transcript, 1 recommendation, and a minimum high school GPA of 2.5. It recommends ACT. Application deadline: 8/15; 2/15 priority date for financial aid. Deferred admission is possible.

CANISIUS COLLEGE

URBAN SETTING ■ PRIVATE ■ INDEPENDENT RELIGIOUS ■ COED
BUFFALO, NEW YORK

Web site: www.canisius.edu
Contact: Miss Penelope H. Lips, Director of Admissions, 2001 Main Street, Buffalo, NY 14208-1098
Telephone: 716-888-2200 or toll-free 800-843-1517 **Fax:** 716-888-3230
E-mail: inquiry@canisius.edu

Academics

Canisius awards associate, bachelor's, and master's **degrees**. Challenging opportunities include advanced placement credit, student-designed majors, an honors program, independent study, and a senior project. Special programs include internships, summer session for credit, off-campus study, study-abroad, and Army ROTC.

The most frequently chosen **baccalaureate** fields are education, social sciences and history, and business/marketing. A complete listing of majors at Canisius appears in the Majors Index beginning on page 430.

The **faculty** at Canisius has 209 full-time members, 92% with terminal degrees. The student-faculty ratio is 16:1.

Students of Canisius

The student body totals 4,870, of whom 3,378 are undergraduates. 52.8% are women and 47.2% are men. Students come from 33 states and territories and 26 other countries. 93% are from New York. 81% returned for their sophomore year.

Facilities and Resources

Student rooms are linked to a campus network. 208 **computers** are available on campus that provide access to the Internet. The 2 **libraries** have 318,789 books and 9,637 subscriptions.

Campus Life

There are 95 active organizations on campus, including a drama/theater group, newspaper, radio station, and choral group. 3% of eligible men and 3% of eligible women are members of national **fraternities** and national **sororities**.

Canisius is a member of the NCAA (Division I). **Intercollegiate sports** (some offering scholarships) include baseball (m), basketball, cross-country running, football (m), golf (m), ice hockey (m), lacrosse, riflery, soccer, softball (w), swimming (w), tennis, track and field, volleyball (w).

Campus Safety

Student safety services include crime prevention programs, closed-circuit television monitors, late-night transport/escort service, 24-hour emergency telephone alarm devices, 24-hour patrols by trained security personnel, and electronically operated dormitory entrances.

Applying

Canisius requires SAT I or ACT and a high school transcript, and in some cases an interview. It recommends an essay, an interview, and recommendations. Application deadline: rolling admissions; 2/15 priority date for financial aid. Early and deferred admission are possible.

C anisius College is one of 28 Jesuit colleges in the nation and the premier private college in western New York. Canisius offers more than 50 academic majors and several teaching programs, which expose students to learning, travel and research events, and the expertise of world-renowned figures. Canisius College prepares leaders— intelligent, caring, faithful individuals—who are able to pursue and promote excellence in their professions, communities, and service to humanity.

Getting in Last Year
3,276 applied
81% were accepted
719 enrolled (27%)
19% from top tenth of their h.s. class
3.38 average high school GPA
23% had SAT verbal scores over 600
28% had SAT math scores over 600
46% had ACT scores over 24
2% had SAT verbal scores over 700
3% had SAT math scores over 700
10% had ACT scores over 30
12 valedictorians

Graduation and After
34% graduated in 4 years
16% graduated in 5 years
1% graduated in 6 years
25% pursued further study (11% arts and sciences, 6% medicine, 4% law)
68.6% had job offers within 6 months
30 organizations recruited on campus

Financial Matters
$17,536 tuition and fees (2001–02)
$7160 room and board
82% average percent of need met
$14,905 average financial aid amount received per undergraduate

CARLETON COLLEGE

SMALL-TOWN SETTING ■ PRIVATE ■ INDEPENDENT ■ COED
NORTHFIELD, MINNESOTA

Web site: www.carleton.edu
Contact: Mr. Paul Thiboutot, Dean of Admissions, 100 South College Street, Northfield, MN 55057
Telephone: 507-646-4190 or toll-free 800-995-2275 **Fax:** 507-646-4526
E-mail: admissions@acs.carleton.edu

Getting in Last Year
4,065 applied
37% were accepted
516 enrolled (34%)
68% from top tenth of their h.s. class
90% had SAT verbal scores over 600
88% had SAT math scores over 600
94% had ACT scores over 24
49% had SAT verbal scores over 700
42% had SAT math scores over 700
51% had ACT scores over 30
88 National Merit Scholars
59 valedictorians

Graduation and After
16% pursued further study (8% arts and sciences, 2% education, 2% law)
65% had job offers within 6 months
70 organizations recruited on campus

Financial Matters
$30,780 comprehensive fee (2001–02)
100% average percent of need met
$18,334 average financial aid amount received per undergraduate (2000–01)

Academics

Carleton awards bachelor's **degrees**. Challenging opportunities include advanced placement credit, accelerated degree programs, student-designed majors, double majors, independent study, and a senior project. Special programs include internships, off-campus study, and study-abroad.

The most frequently chosen **baccalaureate** fields are social sciences and history, physical sciences, and biological/life sciences. A complete listing of majors at Carleton appears in the Majors Index beginning on page 430.

The **faculty** at Carleton has 184 full-time members, 95% with terminal degrees. The student-faculty ratio is 10:1.

Students of Carleton

The student body is made up of 1,948 undergraduates. 52.4% are women and 47.6% are men. Students come from 50 states and territories and 26 other countries. 23% are from Minnesota. 2.3% are international students. 3.9% are African American, 0.4% American Indian, 8.6% Asian American, and 3.6% Hispanic American. 96% returned for their sophomore year.

Facilities and Resources

Student rooms are linked to a campus network. 275 **computers** are available on campus that provide access to the Internet. The 2 **libraries** have 629,099 books and 1,555 subscriptions.

Campus Life

There are 134 active organizations on campus, including a drama/theater group, newspaper, radio station, and choral group. No national or local **fraternities** or **sororities**.

Carleton is a member of the NCAA (Division III). **Intercollegiate sports** include baseball (m), basketball, cross-country running, football (m), golf, skiing (cross-country), skiing (downhill), soccer, softball (w), swimming, tennis, track and field, volleyball (w), wrestling (m).

Campus Safety

Student safety services include late-night transport/escort service, 24-hour emergency telephone alarm devices, 24-hour patrols by trained security personnel, student patrols, and electronically operated dormitory entrances.

Applying

Carleton requires an essay, SAT I or ACT, a high school transcript, and 2 recommendations. It recommends SAT II Subject Tests, SAT II: Writing Test, and an interview. Application deadline: 1/15; 2/15 priority date for financial aid. Early and deferred admission are possible.

CARNEGIE MELLON UNIVERSITY

URBAN SETTING ■ PRIVATE ■ INDEPENDENT ■ COED
PITTSBURGH, PENNSYLVANIA

Web site: www.cmu.edu
Contact: Mr. Michael Steidel, Director of Admissions, 5000 Forbes Avenue, Warner Hall, Room 101, Pittsburgh, PA 15213
Telephone: 412-268-2082 **Fax:** 412-268-7838
E-mail: undergraduate-admissions@andrew.cmu.edu

Academics

CMU awards bachelor's, master's, and doctoral **degrees** and post-master's certificates. Challenging opportunities include advanced placement credit, accelerated degree programs, student-designed majors, freshman honors college, an honors program, double majors, independent study, and a senior project. Special programs include cooperative education, internships, summer session for credit, off-campus study, study-abroad, and Army, Navy and Air Force ROTC.

The most frequently chosen **baccalaureate** fields are engineering/engineering technologies, social sciences and history, and computer/information sciences. A complete listing of majors at CMU appears in the Majors Index beginning on page 430.

The **faculty** at CMU has 778 full-time members, 98% with terminal degrees. The student-faculty ratio is 10:1.

Students of CMU

The student body totals 8,588, of whom 5,310 are undergraduates. 37.8% are women and 62.2% are men. Students come from 52 states and territories and 61 other countries. 24% are from Pennsylvania. 10.9% are international students. 3.8% are African American, 0.4% American Indian, 21.8% Asian American, and 4.6% Hispanic American. 93% returned for their sophomore year.

Facilities and Resources

Student rooms are linked to a campus network. 450 **computers** are available on campus that provide access to the Internet. The 3 **libraries** have 961,507 books and 5,714 subscriptions.

Campus Life

There are 100 active organizations on campus, including a drama/theater group, newspaper, radio station, choral group, and marching band. 15% of eligible men and 11% of eligible women are members of national **fraternities**, national **sororities**, and local sororities.

CMU is a member of the NCAA (Division III). **Intercollegiate sports** include basketball, cross-country running, football (m), golf (m), riflery (m), soccer, swimming, tennis, track and field, volleyball.

Campus Safety

Student safety services include late-night transport/escort service, 24-hour emergency telephone alarm devices, 24-hour patrols by trained security personnel, and electronically operated dormitory entrances.

Applying

CMU requires an essay, SAT II Subject Tests, SAT I or ACT, a high school transcript, and 1 recommendation, and in some cases SAT II: Writing Test and portfolio, audition. It recommends an interview. Application deadline: 1/1; 2/15 priority date for financial aid. Early and deferred admission are possible.

First envisioned by steel magnate and philanthropist Andrew Carnegie, Carnegie Mellon University has steadily built upon its foundations of excellence and innovation to become one of America's leading universities. Carnegie Mellon's unique approach to education—giving students opportunities to become experts in their chosen fields while studying a broad range of course work across disciplines—helps students become leaders and problem solvers today and tomorrow. The University offers more than 90 majors and minors across 6 undergraduate colleges. Whether students are interested in creating the technology of tomorrow or getting their break on Broadway, a Carnegie Mellon education can take them there.

Getting in Last Year
16,696 applied
31% were accepted
1,318 enrolled (25%)
72% from top tenth of their h.s. class
3.61 average high school GPA
77% had SAT verbal scores over 600
96% had SAT math scores over 600
97% had ACT scores over 24
27% had SAT verbal scores over 700
67% had SAT math scores over 700
50% had ACT scores over 30

Graduation and After
61% graduated in 4 years
13% graduated in 5 years
3% graduated in 6 years
20% pursued further study (9% arts and sciences, 7% engineering, 2% medicine)
60% had job offers within 6 months
945 organizations recruited on campus

Financial Matters
$25,872 tuition and fees (2001–02)
$7264 room and board
77% average percent of need met
$15,821 average financial aid amount received per undergraduate (2000–01 estimated)

CARROLL COLLEGE

SMALL-TOWN SETTING ■ PRIVATE ■ INDEPENDENT RELIGIOUS ■ COED
HELENA, MONTANA

Web site: www.carroll.edu
Contact: Ms. Candace A. Cain, Director of Admission, 1601 North Benton
  Avenue, Helena, MT 59625-0002
Telephone: 406-447-4384 or toll-free 800-992-3648 **Fax:** 406-447-4533
E-mail: enroll@carroll.edu

A t Carroll College, students expect more. Carroll College maintains an excellent reputation for academics, preprofessional programs, and placement in graduate schools. Carroll's courses are demanding, but the College's low student-faculty ratio means students receive the personal attention—in the classroom and beyond—to succeed academically, spiritually, and personally. Helena, located midway between Yellowstone and Glacier National Parks, is surrounded by outdoor recreational areas and offers a safe, rural environment.

Academics

Carroll awards associate and bachelor's **degrees**. Challenging opportunities include advanced placement credit, accelerated degree programs, student-designed majors, freshman honors college, an honors program, double majors, independent study, and a senior project. Special programs include cooperative education, internships, summer session for credit, study-abroad, and Army ROTC.

The most frequently chosen **baccalaureate** fields are business/marketing, biological/life sciences, and education. A complete listing of majors at Carroll appears in the Majors Index beginning on page 430.

The **faculty** at Carroll has 79 full-time members, 67% with terminal degrees. The student-faculty ratio is 14:1.

Students of Carroll

The student body is made up of 1,347 undergraduates. 60.9% are women and 39.1% are men. Students come from 26 states and territories and 10 other countries. 68% are from Montana. 2% are international students. 0.2% are African American, 1% American Indian, 0.5% Asian American, and 2% Hispanic American. 81% returned for their sophomore year.

Facilities and Resources

Student rooms are linked to a campus network. 91 **computers** are available on campus that provide access to the Internet. The 2 **libraries** have 89,003 books and 2,721 subscriptions.

Campus Life

There are 35 active organizations on campus, including a drama/theater group, newspaper, radio station, and choral group. No national or local **fraternities** or **sororities**.

Carroll is a member of the NAIA. **Intercollegiate sports** (some offering scholarships) include basketball, football (m), golf (w), soccer (w), swimming, volleyball (w).

Campus Safety

Student safety services include late-night transport/escort service.

Applying

Carroll requires an essay, SAT I or ACT, a high school transcript, 1 recommendation, and a minimum high school GPA of 2.0, and in some cases SAT II Subject Tests, SAT II: Writing Test, and an interview. It recommends an interview and a minimum high school GPA of 3.0. Application deadline: 6/1. Deferred admission is possible.

Getting in Last Year
842 applied
89% were accepted
344 enrolled (46%)
28% from top tenth of their h.s. class
3.46 average high school GPA
29% had SAT verbal scores over 600
26% had SAT math scores over 600
55% had ACT scores over 24
5% had SAT verbal scores over 700
4% had SAT math scores over 700
9% had ACT scores over 30
12 class presidents
26 valedictorians

Graduation and After
27% graduated in 4 years
6% graduated in 5 years
1% graduated in 6 years
22% pursued further study (7% arts and sciences, 3% business, 3% engineering)
57% had job offers within 6 months
108 organizations recruited on campus

Financial Matters
$12,816 tuition and fees (2001–02)
$5168 room and board
81% average percent of need met
$11,435 average financial aid amount received per undergraduate

CASE WESTERN RESERVE UNIVERSITY

URBAN SETTING ■ PRIVATE ■ INDEPENDENT ■ COED
CLEVELAND, OHIO

Web site: www.cwru.edu
Contact: Mr. William T. Conley, Dean of Undergraduate Admission, 10900 Euclid Avenue, Cleveland, OH 44106
Telephone: 216-368-4450
E-mail: admission@po.cwru.edu

Academics

CWRU awards bachelor's, master's, doctoral, and first-professional **degrees** and post-bachelor's certificates. Challenging opportunities include advanced placement credit, accelerated degree programs, student-designed majors, an honors program, double majors, independent study, and a senior project. Special programs include cooperative education, internships, summer session for credit, off-campus study, study-abroad, and Army and Air Force ROTC.

The most frequently chosen **baccalaureate** fields are engineering/engineering technologies, biological/life sciences, and business/marketing. A complete listing of majors at CWRU appears in the Majors Index beginning on page 430.

The **faculty** at CWRU has 562 full-time members, 95% with terminal degrees. The student-faculty ratio is 8:1.

Students of CWRU

The student body totals 9,216, of whom 3,381 are undergraduates. 39.4% are women and 60.6% are men. Students come from 51 states and territories and 29 other countries. 62% are from Ohio. 3.4% are international students. 4.5% are African American, 0.2% American Indian, 13.7% Asian American, and 2% Hispanic American. 90% returned for their sophomore year.

Facilities and Resources

Student rooms are linked to a campus network. 100 **computers** are available on campus that provide access to software library, CD-ROM databases and the Internet. The 7 **libraries** have 14,520 subscriptions.

Campus Life

There are 100 active organizations on campus, including a drama/theater group, newspaper, radio station, choral group, and marching band. 36% of eligible men and 17% of eligible women are members of national **fraternities**, national **sororities**, and local sororities.

CWRU is a member of the NCAA (Division III). **Intercollegiate sports** include baseball (m), basketball, cross-country running, fencing, football (m), golf (m), soccer, softball (w), swimming, tennis, track and field, volleyball (w), wrestling (m).

Campus Safety

Student safety services include crime prevention programs, late-night transport/escort service, 24-hour emergency telephone alarm devices, 24-hour patrols by trained security personnel, student patrols, and electronically operated dormitory entrances.

Applying

CWRU requires an essay, SAT I or ACT, a high school transcript, and 1 recommendation. It recommends SAT II Subject Tests and an interview. Application deadline: 2/1; 2/1 priority date for financial aid. Early and deferred admission are possible.

Getting in Last Year

4,663 applied
74% were accepted
738 enrolled (22%)
69% from top tenth of their h.s. class
78% had SAT verbal scores over 600
88% had SAT math scores over 600
93% had ACT scores over 24
32% had SAT verbal scores over 700
47% had SAT math scores over 700
51% had ACT scores over 30
56 National Merit Scholars

Graduation and After

49% graduated in 4 years
23% graduated in 5 years
3% graduated in 6 years
39% pursued further study (10% arts and sciences, 10% medicine, 8% engineering)
96% had job offers within 6 months
191 organizations recruited on campus

Financial Matters

$21,168 tuition and fees (2001–02)
$6250 room and board
99% average percent of need met
$20,418 average financial aid amount received per undergraduate

THE CATHOLIC UNIVERSITY OF AMERICA

URBAN SETTING ■ PRIVATE ■ INDEPENDENT RELIGIOUS ■ COED
WASHINGTON, DISTRICT OF COLUMBIA

Web site: www.cua.edu
Contact: Ms. Michelle D. Petro-Siraj, Executive Director of Undergraduate
Admission, 102 McMahon Hall, Washington, DC 20064
Telephone: 202-319-5305 or toll-free 202-319-5305 (in-state), 800-673-2772
(out-of-state) **Fax:** 202-319-6533
E-mail: cua-admissions@cua.edu

The Catholic University of America, situated on 144 residential, tree-lined acres in Washington, D.C., offers the beauty of a traditional collegiate campus and the excitement of the nation's capital. Catholic University, founded by the U.S. Catholic bishops, is the national university of the Catholic church. Catholic University is a valuable resource for employers looking to fill top internships. Undergraduates work in congressional offices, executive agencies, professional associations, research institutes, lobbying groups, and media organizations. Overseas programs include internships with the British and Irish parliaments. At Catholic University, undergraduate students can apply to six schools: arts and sciences, which includes politics, business, communications, premed, and prelaw; architecture and planning; engineering; music; nursing; and philosophy.

Getting in Last Year
2,191 applied
85% were accepted
614 enrolled (33%)
18% from top tenth of their h.s. class
3.34 average high school GPA
43% had SAT verbal scores over 600
36% had SAT math scores over 600
53% had ACT scores over 24
9% had SAT verbal scores over 700
5% had SAT math scores over 700
8% had ACT scores over 30

Graduation and After
61% graduated in 4 years
9% graduated in 5 years
1% graduated in 6 years
88% had job offers within 6 months
160 organizations recruited on campus

Financial Matters
$20,950 tuition and fees (2001–02)
$8382 room and board
78% average percent of need met
$14,234 average financial aid amount received
per undergraduate (2000–01 estimated)

Academics

CUA awards bachelor's, master's, doctoral, and first-professional **degrees** and post-master's certificates. Challenging opportunities include advanced placement credit, accelerated degree programs, student-designed majors, freshman honors college, an honors program, double majors, independent study, and a senior project. Special programs include internships, summer session for credit, off-campus study, study-abroad, and Army, Navy and Air Force ROTC.

The most frequently chosen **baccalaureate** fields are social sciences and history, architecture, and visual/performing arts. A complete listing of majors at CUA appears in the Majors Index beginning on page 430.

The **faculty** at CUA has 360 full-time members, 92% with terminal degrees. The student-faculty ratio is 10:1.

Students of CUA

The student body totals 5,510, of whom 2,587 are undergraduates. 54.3% are women and 45.7% are men. Students come from 51 states and territories and 33 other countries. 6% are from District of Columbia. 2.7% are international students. 6.8% are African American, 0.2% American Indian, 3.3% Asian American, and 4.2% Hispanic American. 82% returned for their sophomore year.

Facilities and Resources

Student rooms are linked to a campus network. 450 **computers** are available on campus that provide access to the Internet. The 8 **libraries** have 1,429,026 books and 11,200 subscriptions.

Campus Life

There are 55 active organizations on campus, including a drama/theater group, newspaper, radio station, and choral group. 1% of eligible men and 1% of eligible women are members of national **fraternities**, national **sororities**, and local sororities.

CUA is a member of the NCAA (Division III). **Intercollegiate sports** include baseball (m), basketball, cross-country running, field hockey (w), football (m), lacrosse, soccer, softball (w), swimming, tennis, track and field, volleyball (w).

Campus Safety

Student safety services include controlled access of academic buildings, late-night transport/escort service, 24-hour emergency telephone alarm devices, 24-hour patrols by trained security personnel, and electronically operated dormitory entrances.

Applying

CUA requires an essay, SAT I or ACT, a high school transcript, and 1 recommendation. It recommends SAT II Subject Tests, SAT II: Writing Test, and a minimum high school GPA of 2.8. Application deadline: 2/15; 2/1 for financial aid, with a 1/15 priority date. Early and deferred admission are possible.

Cedarville University

Rural setting ■ Private ■ Independent Religious ■ Coed
Cedarville, Ohio

Web site: www.cedarville.edu
Contact: Mr. Roscoe Smith, Director of Admissions, 251 North Main Street, Cedarville, OH 45314-0601
Telephone: 937-766-7700 or toll-free 800-CEDARVILLE **Fax:** 937-766-7575
E-mail: admiss@cedarville.edu

Academics

Cedarville awards associate, bachelor's, and master's **degrees**. Challenging opportunities include advanced placement credit, accelerated degree programs, an honors program, double majors, independent study, and a senior project. Special programs include internships, summer session for credit, off-campus study, study-abroad, and Army and Air Force ROTC.

The most frequently chosen **baccalaureate** fields are education, business/marketing, and communications/communication technologies. A complete listing of majors at Cedarville appears in the Majors Index beginning on page 430.

The **faculty** at Cedarville has 184 full-time members, 61% with terminal degrees. The student-faculty ratio is 16:1.

Students of Cedarville

The student body totals 2,951, of whom 2,943 are undergraduates. 54% are women and 46% are men. Students come from 43 states and territories and 10 other countries. 33% are from Ohio. 0.3% are international students. 0.6% are African American, 0.2% American Indian, 1.1% Asian American, and 0.7% Hispanic American. 86% returned for their sophomore year.

Facilities and Resources

Student rooms are linked to a campus network. 1,850 **computers** are available on campus that provide access to software packages. The **library** has 139,026 books and 4,112 subscriptions.

Campus Life

There are 49 active organizations on campus, including a drama/theater group, newspaper, radio station, and choral group. No national or local **fraternities** or **sororities**.

Cedarville is a member of the NAIA and NCCAA. **Intercollegiate sports** (some offering scholarships) include baseball (m), basketball, cross-country running, golf (m), soccer, softball (w), tennis, track and field, volleyball (w).

Campus Safety

Student safety services include late-night transport/escort service, 24-hour emergency telephone alarm devices, 24-hour patrols by trained security personnel, student patrols, and electronically operated dormitory entrances.

Applying

Cedarville requires an essay, SAT I or ACT, a high school transcript, 2 recommendations, and a minimum high school GPA of 3.0, and in some cases an interview. Application deadline: rolling admissions; 3/1 priority date for financial aid. Early and deferred admission are possible.

Getting in Last Year

2,103 applied
73% were accepted
833 enrolled (54%)
31% from top tenth of their h.s. class
3.60 average high school GPA
48% had SAT verbal scores over 600
45% had SAT math scores over 600
73% had ACT scores over 24
14% had SAT verbal scores over 700
9% had SAT math scores over 700
15% had ACT scores over 30
19 National Merit Scholars
58 valedictorians

Graduation and After

54% graduated in 4 years
13% graduated in 5 years
2% graduated in 6 years
Graduates pursuing further study: 4% theology, 2% medicine, 2% arts and sciences
99% had job offers within 6 months
328 organizations recruited on campus

Financial Matters

$12,624 tuition and fees (2001–02)
$4929 room and board
41% average percent of need met
$9761 average financial aid amount received per undergraduate (2000–01)

CENTENARY COLLEGE OF LOUISIANA

SUBURBAN SETTING ■ PRIVATE ■ INDEPENDENT RELIGIOUS ■ COED
SHREVEPORT, LOUISIANA

Web site: www.centenary.edu
Contact: Dr. Eugene Gregory, Vice President of College Relations, 2911
    Centenary Blvd, PO Box 41188, Shreveport, LA 71134-1188
Telephone: 318-869-5131 or toll-free 800-234-4448 **Fax:** 318-869-5005
E-mail: jtmartin@centenary.edu

Getting in Last Year
737 applied
86% were accepted
261 enrolled (41%)
30% from top tenth of their h.s. class
45% had SAT verbal scores over 600
45% had SAT math scores over 600
68% had ACT scores over 24
9% had SAT verbal scores over 700
10% had SAT math scores over 700
16% had ACT scores over 30

Graduation and After
27% graduated in 4 years
17% graduated in 5 years
2% graduated in 6 years
40 organizations recruited on campus

Financial Matters
$15,800 tuition and fees (2001–02)
$4800 room and board
76% average percent of need met
$11,397 average financial aid amount received
    per undergraduate

Academics

Centenary awards bachelor's and master's **degrees**. Challenging opportunities include advanced placement credit, student-designed majors, an honors program, double majors, independent study, and a senior project. Special programs include internships, summer session for credit, off-campus study, and study-abroad.

The most frequently chosen **baccalaureate** fields are business/marketing, visual/performing arts, and biological/life sciences. A complete listing of majors at Centenary appears in the Majors Index beginning on page 430.

The **faculty** at Centenary has 74 full-time members, 89% with terminal degrees. The student-faculty ratio is 12:1.

Students of Centenary

The student body totals 1,049, of whom 910 are undergraduates. 61.5% are women and 38.5% are men. Students come from 38 states and territories and 18 other countries. 3.4% are international students. 5.7% are African American, 1.1% American Indian, 1.1% Asian American, and 2.5% Hispanic American. 74% returned for their sophomore year.

Facilities and Resources

Student rooms are linked to a campus network. The 2 **libraries** have 186,564 books and 59,899 subscriptions.

Campus Life

There are 34 active organizations on campus, including a drama/theater group, newspaper, radio station, and choral group. 25% of eligible men and 20% of eligible women are members of national **fraternities** and national **sororities**.

Centenary is a member of the NCAA (Division I). **Intercollegiate sports** (some offering scholarships) include baseball (m), basketball, cross-country running, golf, gymnastics (w), riflery, soccer, softball (w), tennis, volleyball (w).

Campus Safety

Student safety services include late-night transport/escort service, 24-hour emergency telephone alarm devices, 24-hour patrols by trained security personnel, and electronically operated dormitory entrances.

Applying

Centenary requires an essay, SAT I or ACT, a high school transcript, 1 recommendation, and a minimum high school GPA of 2.0, and in some cases SAT II Subject Tests. It recommends an interview and class rank. Application deadline: 2/15; 2/15 priority date for financial aid. Early and deferred admission are possible.

CENTRAL COLLEGE

SMALL-TOWN SETTING ■ PRIVATE ■ INDEPENDENT RELIGIOUS ■ COED
PELLA, IOWA

Web site: www.central.edu
Contact: John Olsen, Vice President for Admission and Student Enrollment
Services, 812 University Street, Pella, IA 50219-1999
Telephone: 641-628-7600 or toll-free 800-458-5503 **Fax:** 641-628-5316
E-mail: admissions@central.edu

Academics

Central awards bachelor's **degrees**. Challenging opportunities include advanced placement credit, student-designed majors, freshman honors college, an honors program, and a senior project. Special programs include internships, summer session for credit, off-campus study, and study-abroad.

The most frequently chosen **baccalaureate** fields are business/marketing, education, and parks and recreation. A complete listing of majors at Central appears in the Majors Index beginning on page 430.

The **faculty** at Central has 89 full-time members, 80% with terminal degrees. The student-faculty ratio is 13:1.

Students of Central

The student body is made up of 1,425 undergraduates. 57.6% are women and 42.4% are men. Students come from 34 states and territories. 84% are from Iowa. 0.7% are international students. 0.4% are African American, 0.1% American Indian, 0.9% Asian American, and 1.4% Hispanic American. 80% returned for their sophomore year.

Facilities and Resources

Student rooms are linked to a campus network. 168 **computers** are available on campus for student use. The 4 **libraries** have 198,000 books and 924 subscriptions.

Campus Life

There are 72 active organizations on campus, including a drama/theater group, newspaper, radio station, and choral group. 15% of eligible men and 7% of eligible women are members of local **fraternities** and local **sororities**.

Central is a member of the NCAA (Division III). **Intercollegiate sports** include baseball (m), basketball, cross-country running, football (m), golf, soccer, softball (w), tennis, track and field, volleyball (w), wrestling (m).

Campus Safety

Student safety services include late-night transport/escort service, 24-hour emergency telephone alarm devices, student patrols, and electronically operated dormitory entrances.

Applying

Central requires SAT I or ACT and a high school transcript, and in some cases an essay, an interview, and 3 recommendations. It recommends an interview and a minimum high school GPA of 2.0. Application deadline: rolling admissions; 3/1 priority date for financial aid. Early and deferred admission are possible.

> *"Challenging yet supportive"* describes Central College in Pella, Iowa. Students establish one-to-one relationships with their professors, while the curriculum engages students and prepares them for a career or graduate school. More than 99% of Central's May 2001 graduates either accepted professional employment or enrolled in a graduate school of their choice within 6 months of graduation. Central is recognized by *U.S. News & World Report* as the 8th-ranked comprehensive college in the Midwest and also as a "great school at a great price." Nearly 50% of Central's graduates study overseas in one of the College's 8 international programs.

Getting in Last Year
1,438 applied
87% were accepted
412 enrolled (33%)
26% from top tenth of their h.s. class
3.47 average high school GPA
49% had ACT scores over 24
5% had ACT scores over 30
38 valedictorians

Graduation and After
58% graduated in 4 years
5% graduated in 5 years
18% pursued further study (10% arts and sciences, 5% medicine, 2% business)
94% had job offers within 6 months
68 organizations recruited on campus

Financial Matters
$15,714 tuition and fees (2001–02)
$5492 room and board
75% average percent of need met
$12,363 average financial aid amount received per undergraduate (2000–01 estimated)

CENTRE COLLEGE

SMALL-TOWN SETTING ■ PRIVATE ■ INDEPENDENT RELIGIOUS ■ COED
DANVILLE, KENTUCKY

Web site: www.centre.edu

Contact: Mr. J. Carey Thompson, Dean of Admission and Financial Aid, 600
West Walnut Street, Danville, KY 40422-1394

Telephone: 859-238-5350 or toll-free 800-423-6236 **Fax:** 859-238-5373

E-mail: admission@centre.edu

Getting in Last Year
1,265 applied
82% were accepted
299 enrolled (29%)
56% from top tenth of their h.s. class
3.73 average high school GPA
68% had SAT verbal scores over 600
66% had SAT math scores over 600
89% had ACT scores over 24
25% had SAT verbal scores over 700
19% had SAT math scores over 700
24% had ACT scores over 30
37 valedictorians

Graduation and After
71% graduated in 4 years
2% graduated in 5 years
40% pursued further study (34% arts and
  sciences, 21% law, 13% medicine)
70% had job offers within 6 months
25 organizations recruited on campus

Financial Matters
$24,000 comprehensive fee (2001–02)
100% average percent of need met
$18,519 average financial aid amount received
  per undergraduate

Academics

Centre awards bachelor's **degrees**. Challenging opportunities include advanced placement credit, student-designed majors, double majors, independent study, and a senior
project. Special programs include internships, off-campus study, study-abroad, and Army
and Air Force ROTC.

The most frequently chosen **baccalaureate** fields are social sciences and history,
biological/life sciences, and English. A complete listing of majors at Centre appears in
the Majors Index beginning on page 430.

The **faculty** at Centre has 90 full-time members, 98% with terminal degrees. The
student-faculty ratio is 11:1.

Students of Centre

The student body is made up of 1,070 undergraduates. 55% are women and 45% are
men. Students come from 37 states and territories and 7 other countries. 72% are from
Kentucky. 1.4% are international students. 3.2% are African American, 0.3% American
Indian, 1.9% Asian American, and 0.5% Hispanic American. 89% returned for their
sophomore year.

Facilities and Resources

Student rooms are linked to a campus network. 150 **computers** are available on campus
that provide access to the Internet. The 2 **libraries** have 152,721 books and 2,076
subscriptions.

Campus Life

There are 76 active organizations on campus, including a drama/theater group,
newspaper, and choral group. 60% of eligible men and 65% of eligible women are
members of national **fraternities** and national **sororities**.

Centre is a member of the NCAA (Division III). **Intercollegiate sports** include
baseball (m), basketball, cross-country running, field hockey (w), football (m), golf, soccer, softball (w), swimming, tennis, track and field, volleyball (w).

Campus Safety

Student safety services include late-night transport/escort service, 24-hour emergency
telephone alarm devices, 24-hour patrols by trained security personnel, and electronically operated dormitory entrances.

Applying

Centre requires an essay, SAT I or ACT, a high school transcript, and 1 recommendation. It recommends an interview. Application deadline: 2/1; 3/1 for financial aid.
Early and deferred admission are possible.

CHAPMAN UNIVERSITY

SUBURBAN SETTING ■ PRIVATE ■ INDEPENDENT RELIGIOUS ■ COED
ORANGE, CALIFORNIA

Web site: www.chapman.edu
Contact: Mr. Michael O. Drummy, Associate Dean for Enrollment Services
and Chief Admission Officer, One University Drive, Orange, CA 92866
Telephone: 714-997-6711 or toll-free 888-CUAPPLY **Fax:** 714-997-6713
E-mail: admit@chapman.edu

Academics

Chapman awards bachelor's, master's, and first-professional **degrees**. Challenging
opportunities include advanced placement credit, accelerated degree programs, an
honors program, double majors, independent study, and a senior project. Special
programs include cooperative education, internships, summer session for credit, study-
abroad, and Army and Air Force ROTC.

The most frequently chosen **baccalaureate** fields are visual/performing arts, busi-
ness/marketing, and social sciences and history. A complete listing of majors at Chapman
appears in the Majors Index beginning on page 430.

The **faculty** at Chapman has 217 full-time members, 79% with terminal degrees.
The student-faculty ratio is 13:1.

Students of Chapman

The student body totals 4,192, of whom 3,127 are undergraduates. 55.7% are women
and 44.3% are men. Students come from 40 states and territories and 35 other countries.
67% are from California. 86% returned for their sophomore year.

Facilities and Resources

278 **computers** are available on campus that provide access to the Internet. The 2
libraries have 203,915 books and 2,121 subscriptions.

Campus Life

There are 65 active organizations on campus, including a drama/theater group,
newspaper, radio station, and choral group. 10% of eligible men and 15% of eligible
women are members of national **fraternities** and national **sororities**.

Chapman is a member of the NCAA (Division III). **Intercollegiate sports** include
baseball (m), basketball, crew, cross-country running, football (m), golf, soccer, softball
(w), swimming (w), tennis, track and field (w), volleyball (w), water polo.

Campus Safety

Student safety services include full safety education program, late-night transport/escort
service, 24-hour emergency telephone alarm devices, and 24-hour patrols by trained
security personnel.

Applying

Chapman requires an essay, SAT I or ACT, a high school transcript, 1 recommendation,
and a minimum high school GPA of 2.75. It recommends SAT II Subject Tests, an
interview, and a minimum high school GPA of 3.5. Application deadline: 1/31; 3/2 priority date for financial aid. Early and deferred admission are possible.

D etermining the cost of a
Chapman education at the
beginning of the
application process is now possible
through Chapman's Early Aid
Estimator program. In the early fall,
all high school seniors and
prospective transfer students in
Chapman's inquiry database are
furnished with an estimator form
that can be completed and returned
to Chapman for analysis at no
charge. Using in-house needs
analysis software and merit
eligibility formulas, Chapman
responds with an estimate of the
student's aid and scholarship
eligibility. Under the previous
system, students were unable to
receive this information until
admission had been determined and
aid notification had been sent,
usually in late spring.

Getting in Last Year
2,195 applied
77% were accepted
744 enrolled (44%)
41% from top tenth of their h.s. class
3.55 average high school GPA
39% had SAT verbal scores over 600
43% had SAT math scores over 600
50% had ACT scores over 24
6% had SAT verbal scores over 700
5% had SAT math scores over 700
5% had ACT scores over 30
12 National Merit Scholars
16 class presidents
9 valedictorians

Graduation and After
70 organizations recruited on campus

Financial Matters
$22,256 tuition and fees (2001–02)
$7712 room and board
100% average percent of need met
$17,767 average financial aid amount received
per undergraduate (2000–01)

Christendom College

RURAL SETTING ■ PRIVATE ■ INDEPENDENT RELIGIOUS ■ COED
FRONT ROYAL, VIRGINIA

Getting in Last Year
197 applied
81% were accepted
102 enrolled (64%)
25% from top tenth of their h.s. class
3.50 average high school GPA
54% had SAT verbal scores over 600
46% had SAT math scores over 600
66% had ACT scores over 24
26% had SAT verbal scores over 700
8% had SAT math scores over 700
14% had ACT scores over 30
2 National Merit Scholars
3 class presidents
2 valedictorians

Graduation and After
63% graduated in 4 years
2% graduated in 5 years
20% pursued further study (8% arts and sciences, 6% theology, 4% law)
80% had job offers within 6 months
5 organizations recruited on campus

Financial Matters
$11,980 tuition and fees (2001–02)
$4700 room and board
90% average percent of need met
$9125 average financial aid amount received per undergraduate

Web site: www.christendom.edu
Contact: Mr. Paul Heisler, Director of Admissions, 134 Christendom Drive, Front Royal, VA 22630-5103
Telephone: 540-636-2900 ext. 290 or toll-free 800-877-5456 ext. 290 **Fax:** 540-636-1655
E-mail: admissions@christendom.edu

Academics
Christendom awards associate, bachelor's, and master's **degrees**. Challenging opportunities include advanced placement credit, accelerated degree programs, double majors, and a senior project. Special programs include cooperative education, internships, summer session for credit, and study-abroad.

The most frequently chosen **baccalaureate** fields are social sciences and history, philosophy, and English. A complete listing of majors at Christendom appears in the Majors Index beginning on page 430.

The **faculty** at Christendom has 20 full-time members, 75% with terminal degrees. The student-faculty ratio is 12:1.

Students of Christendom
The student body totals 407, of whom 331 are undergraduates. 57.4% are women and 42.6% are men. Students come from 48 states and territories and 4 other countries. 21% are from Virginia. 2.7% are international students. 0.6% are African American, 0.3% American Indian, 1.5% Asian American, and 2.7% Hispanic American. 83% returned for their sophomore year.

Facilities and Resources
17 **computers** are available on campus that provide access to the Internet. The **library** has 70,850 books and 395 subscriptions.

Campus Life
There are 15 active organizations on campus, including a drama/theater group, newspaper, and choral group. No national or local **fraternities** or **sororities**.

This institution has no intercollegiate sports.

Campus Safety
Student safety services include night patrols by trained security personnel, late-night transport/escort service, and 24-hour emergency telephone alarm devices.

Applying
Christendom requires an essay, SAT I or ACT, a high school transcript, and 2 recommendations. It recommends an interview and a minimum high school GPA of 3.0. Application deadline: rolling admissions; 4/1 priority date for financial aid. Early admission is possible.

CHRISTIAN BROTHERS UNIVERSITY

URBAN SETTING ■ PRIVATE ■ INDEPENDENT RELIGIOUS ■ COED
MEMPHIS, TENNESSEE

Web site: www.cbu.edu
Contact: Ms. Courtney Fee, Dean of Admission, 650 East Parkway South,
Memphis, TN 38104
Telephone: 901-321-3205 or toll-free 800-288-7576 **Fax:** 901-321-3202
E-mail: admissions@cbu.edu

Academics

CBU awards bachelor's and master's **degrees**. Challenging opportunities include advanced placement credit, accelerated degree programs, an honors program, double majors, and a senior project. Special programs include internships, summer session for credit, off-campus study, study-abroad, and Army, Navy and Air Force ROTC.

The most frequently chosen **baccalaureate** fields are business/marketing, psychology, and engineering/engineering technologies. A complete listing of majors at CBU appears in the Majors Index beginning on page 430.

The **faculty** at CBU has 111 full-time members, 83% with terminal degrees. The student-faculty ratio is 14:1.

Students of CBU

The student body totals 2,123, of whom 1,659 are undergraduates. 55.3% are women and 44.7% are men. Students come from 30 states and territories and 28 other countries. 83% are from Tennessee. 4.8% are international students. 28% are African American, 0.3% American Indian, 3.7% Asian American, and 1.6% Hispanic American. 73% returned for their sophomore year.

Facilities and Resources

Student rooms are linked to a campus network. 300 **computers** are available on campus that provide access to on-line class listings, e-mail, course assignments and the Internet. The **library** has 100,000 books and 537 subscriptions.

Campus Life

There are 23 active organizations on campus, including a drama/theater group, newspaper, and choral group. 24% of eligible men and 20% of eligible women are members of national **fraternities**, national **sororities**, and local sororities.

CBU is a member of the NCAA (Division II). **Intercollegiate sports** (some offering scholarships) include baseball (m), basketball, cross-country running, golf (m), soccer, softball (w), tennis, volleyball (w).

Campus Safety

Student safety services include late-night transport/escort service, 24-hour emergency telephone alarm devices, 24-hour patrols by trained security personnel, student patrols, and electronically operated dormitory entrances.

Applying

CBU requires an essay, SAT I or ACT, a high school transcript, and a minimum high school GPA of 2.5, and in some cases recommendations. It recommends an interview. Application deadline: 8/23; 2/15 priority date for financial aid. Early and deferred admission are possible.

> **C**hristian Brothers University (CBU) is located in the center of the friendly Southern city of Memphis, Tennessee. Situated on a beautiful 70-acre campus, Christian Brothers University encourages a true sense of excellence and achievement that embodies the history and the tradition of the Christian Brothers. CBU offers a low student-faculty ratio and is known for the high academic caliber of its students and the caring commitment of its faculty. At Christian Brothers University, education is and always will be student centered. Outstanding acceptance rates for medical and law school, along with a high graduate placement rate, are proof that CBU's graduates are prepared for the future.

Getting in Last Year

888 applied
82% were accepted
289 enrolled (40%)
28% from top tenth of their h.s. class
3.38 average high school GPA
27% had SAT verbal scores over 600
42% had SAT math scores over 600
46% had ACT scores over 24
8% had SAT verbal scores over 700
13% had SAT math scores over 700
10% had ACT scores over 30

Graduation and After

30% pursued further study
85.7% had job offers within 6 months
211 organizations recruited on campus

Financial Matters

$15,300 tuition and fees (2001–02)
$4520 room and board
74% average percent of need met
$11,887 average financial aid amount received per undergraduate

CLAREMONT MCKENNA COLLEGE

SMALL-TOWN SETTING ■ PRIVATE ■ INDEPENDENT ■ COED
CLAREMONT, CALIFORNIA

Web site: www.claremontmckenna.edu
Contact: Mr. Richard C. Vos, Vice President/Dean of Admission and
    Financial Aid, 890 Columbia Avenue, Claremont, CA 91711
Telephone: 909-621-8088
E-mail: admission@mckenna.edu

Claremont McKenna College (CMC) offers a traditional liberal arts education with a twist: within the context of a liberal arts curriculum, CMC focuses on economics, government, and international relations as it prepares students for leadership in business, government, and other professions. CMC's enrollment of approximately 1,000 students ensures a personalized educational experience. However, with 4 other colleges—Harvey Mudd, Pitzer, Pomona, and Scripps—and 2 graduate schools right next door, CMC students also have access to the academic, intellectual, social, and athletic resources typical of a medium-sized university.

Getting in Last Year
2,898 applied
29% were accepted
262 enrolled (32%)
81% from top tenth of their h.s. class
92% had SAT verbal scores over 600
93% had SAT math scores over 600
45% had SAT verbal scores over 700
51% had SAT math scores over 700
17 National Merit Scholars
18 class presidents
20 valedictorians

Graduation and After
82% graduated in 4 years
4% graduated in 5 years
26% pursued further study (42% law, 11% arts and sciences, 8% business)
64% had job offers within 6 months
200 organizations recruited on campus

Financial Matters
$24,540 tuition and fees (2001–02)
$8160 room and board
100% average percent of need met
$21,769 average financial aid amount received per undergraduate

Academics
CMC awards bachelor's **degrees**. Challenging opportunities include advanced placement credit, accelerated degree programs, student-designed majors, an honors program, double majors, independent study, and a senior project. Special programs include internships, off-campus study, study-abroad, and Army, Navy and Air Force ROTC. A complete listing of majors at CMC appears in the Majors Index beginning on page 430.
    The **faculty** at CMC has 139 full-time members. The student-faculty ratio is 7:1.

Students of CMC
The student body is made up of 1,044 undergraduates. 46.6% are women and 53.4% are men. Students come from 47 states and territories and 22 other countries. 59% are from California. 3.1% are international students. 3.9% are African American, 0.4% American Indian, 15.3% Asian American, and 9.3% Hispanic American. 94% returned for their sophomore year.

Facilities and Resources
Student rooms are linked to a campus network. 120 **computers** are available on campus for student use. The 4 **libraries** have 2,028,793 books and 6,028 subscriptions.

Campus Life
There are 280 active organizations on campus, including a drama/theater group, newspaper, radio station, and choral group. No national or local **fraternities** or **sororities**.
    CMC is a member of the NCAA (Division III). **Intercollegiate sports** include baseball (m), basketball, cross-country running, football (m), golf (m), soccer, softball (w), swimming, tennis, track and field, volleyball (w), water polo.

Campus Safety
Student safety services include late-night transport/escort service, 24-hour emergency telephone alarm devices, 24-hour patrols by trained security personnel, student patrols, and electronically operated dormitory entrances.

Applying
CMC requires an essay, SAT I or ACT, a high school transcript, 2 recommendations, and a minimum high school GPA of 3.0. It recommends SAT II Subject Tests and an interview. Application deadline: 1/1; 2/1 for financial aid. Early and deferred admission are possible.

CLARKSON UNIVERSITY

SMALL-TOWN SETTING ■ PRIVATE ■ INDEPENDENT ■ COED
POTSDAM, NEW YORK

Web site: www.clarkson.edu
Contact: Mr. Brian T. Grant, Director of Enrollment Operations, Holcroft
House, Potsdam, NY 13699
Telephone: 315-268-6479 or toll-free 800-527-6577 **Fax:** 315-268-7647
E-mail: admission@clarkson.edu

Academics

Clarkson awards bachelor's, master's, and doctoral **degrees**. Challenging opportunities include advanced placement credit, accelerated degree programs, student-designed majors, an honors program, double majors, independent study, and a senior project. Special programs include cooperative education, internships, summer session for credit, off-campus study, study-abroad, and Army and Air Force ROTC.

The most frequently chosen **baccalaureate** fields are engineering/engineering technologies, interdisciplinary studies, and business/marketing. A complete listing of majors at Clarkson appears in the Majors Index beginning on page 430.

The **faculty** at Clarkson has 165 full-time members, 90% with terminal degrees. The student-faculty ratio is 17:1.

Students of Clarkson

The student body totals 2,949, of whom 2,610 are undergraduates. 25.5% are women and 74.5% are men. Students come from 41 states and territories and 35 other countries. 76% are from New York. 3.5% are international students. 2.4% are African American, 0.8% American Indian, 2.9% Asian American, and 1.3% Hispanic American. 87% returned for their sophomore year.

Facilities and Resources

Student rooms are linked to a campus network. 250 **computers** are available on campus that provide access to the Internet. The **library** has 235,876 books and 845 subscriptions.

Campus Life

There are 54 active organizations on campus, including a drama/theater group, newspaper, radio station, and television station. 14% of eligible men and 14% of eligible women are members of national **fraternities**, national **sororities**, and local fraternities.

Clarkson is a member of the NCAA (Division III). **Intercollegiate sports** (some offering scholarships) include baseball (m), basketball, cross-country running, golf (m), ice hockey (m), lacrosse, skiing (cross-country), skiing (downhill), soccer, swimming, tennis, volleyball (w).

Campus Safety

Student safety services include late-night transport/escort service, 24-hour emergency telephone alarm devices, 24-hour patrols by trained security personnel, and electronically operated dormitory entrances.

Applying

Clarkson requires SAT I or ACT, a high school transcript, and 1 recommendation. It recommends SAT II Subject Tests and an interview. Application deadline: 3/15; 3/1 priority date for financial aid. Early and deferred admission are possible.

C larkson is a blend of vivid contrasts—high-powered academics in a cooperative and friendly community, technically oriented students who enjoy people, and a technology-rich learning environment that serves as a gateway to outstanding outdoor recreational opportunities in the Adirondack region and to numerous social and cultural activities at 4 area colleges. Clarkson's students are described as hard-working, outgoing, energized team players; the academic programs as relevant, flexible, and nationally respected; and the teachers as approachable, concerned, accomplished, and inspiring. Clarkson alumni, students, and faculty members share an exceptionally strong bond and the lifetime benefits that come from a global network of personal and professional ties.

Getting in Last Year
2,584 applied
81% were accepted
724 enrolled (35%)
36% from top tenth of their h.s. class
3.47 average high school GPA
38% had SAT verbal scores over 600
61% had SAT math scores over 600
7% had SAT verbal scores over 700
13% had SAT math scores over 700
2 National Merit Scholars
23 valedictorians

Graduation and After
52% graduated in 4 years
16% graduated in 5 years
1% graduated in 6 years
17% pursued further study (3% business, 3% engineering, 2% arts and sciences)
99% had job offers within 6 months
163 organizations recruited on campus

Financial Matters
$21,800 tuition and fees (2001–02)
$8084 room and board
88% average percent of need met
$10,904 average financial aid amount received per undergraduate

CLEMSON UNIVERSITY

SMALL-TOWN SETTING ■ PUBLIC ■ STATE-SUPPORTED ■ COED
CLEMSON, SOUTH CAROLINA

Web site: www.clemson.edu
Contact: Ms. Audrey Bodell, Assistant Director of Undergraduate Admissions, 105 Sikes Hall, PO Box 345124, Clemson, SC 29634
Telephone: 864-656-5460 **Fax:** 864-656-2464
E-mail: cuadmissions@clemson.edu

C lemson's honors program, known as Calhoun College, is designed for academically talented students who wish to cultivate a lifelong love of learning and to prepare for lives as leaders and change-agents. The honors experience includes a core of interdisciplinary courses and opportunities for independent research. Under the administration of Calhoun College, the Dixon Fellows Program helps prepare students to compete for prestigious postgraduate scholarships, such as Rhodes, Marshall, Truman, and Fulbright. Housing for 300 Calhoun scholars is available in Holmes Hall, located in the heart of Clemson's beautiful campus.

Academics

Clemson awards bachelor's, master's, and doctoral **degrees**. Challenging opportunities include advanced placement credit, accelerated degree programs, an honors program, double majors, and a senior project. Special programs include cooperative education, internships, summer session for credit, study-abroad, and Army and Air Force ROTC.

The most frequently chosen **baccalaureate** fields are business/marketing, engineering/engineering technologies, and education. A complete listing of majors at Clemson appears in the Majors Index beginning on page 430.

The **faculty** at Clemson has 964 full-time members, 87% with terminal degrees. The student-faculty ratio is 16:1.

Students of Clemson

The student body totals 17,101, of whom 13,975 are undergraduates. 45.3% are women and 54.7% are men. Students come from 52 states and territories and 62 other countries. 70% are from South Carolina. 0.6% are international students. 7.9% are African American, 0.2% American Indian, 1.6% Asian American, and 0.9% Hispanic American. 88% returned for their sophomore year.

Facilities and Resources

Student rooms are linked to a campus network. 1,000 **computers** are available on campus for student use. The 2 **libraries** have 1,648,741 books and 5,978 subscriptions.

Campus Life

There are 250 active organizations on campus, including a drama/theater group, newspaper, radio station, television station, choral group, and marching band. 15% of eligible men and 22% of eligible women are members of national **fraternities** and national **sororities**.

Clemson is a member of the NCAA (Division I). **Intercollegiate sports** (some offering scholarships) include baseball (m), basketball, crew (w), cross-country running, football (m), golf (m), soccer, swimming, tennis, track and field, volleyball (w).

Campus Safety

Student safety services include late-night transport/escort service, 24-hour emergency telephone alarm devices, 24-hour patrols by trained security personnel, and electronically operated dormitory entrances.

Applying

Clemson requires SAT I or ACT and a high school transcript. It recommends an essay, an interview, and recommendations. Application deadline: 5/1; 4/1 priority date for financial aid. Early and deferred admission are possible.

Getting in Last Year
11,432 applied
51% were accepted
2,543 enrolled (43%)
45% from top tenth of their h.s. class
3.64 average high school GPA
37% had SAT verbal scores over 600
51% had SAT math scores over 600
59% had ACT scores over 24
6% had SAT verbal scores over 700
10% had SAT math scores over 700
15% had ACT scores over 30
20 National Merit Scholars
100 valedictorians

Graduation and After
35% graduated in 4 years
27% graduated in 5 years
6% graduated in 6 years
85% had job offers within 6 months
392 organizations recruited on campus

Financial Matters
$5090 resident tuition and fees (2001–02)
$11,284 nonresident tuition and fees (2001–02)
$4532 room and board
72% average percent of need met
$7244 average financial aid amount received per undergraduate

COE COLLEGE

URBAN SETTING ■ PRIVATE ■ INDEPENDENT RELIGIOUS ■ COED
CEDAR RAPIDS, IOWA

Web site: www.coe.edu
Contact: Mr. Dennis Trotter, Vice President of Admission and Financial Aid, 1220 1st Avenue, NE, Cedar Rapids, IA 52402-5070
Telephone: 319-399-8500 or toll-free 877-225-5263 **Fax:** 319-399-8816
E-mail: admission@coe.edu

Academics

Coe awards bachelor's and master's **degrees**. Challenging opportunities include advanced placement credit, accelerated degree programs, student-designed majors, an honors program, double majors, independent study, and a senior project. Special programs include internships, summer session for credit, off-campus study, study-abroad, and Army and Air Force ROTC.

The most frequently chosen **baccalaureate** fields are business/marketing, social sciences and history, and psychology. A complete listing of majors at Coe appears in the Majors Index beginning on page 430.

The **faculty** at Coe has 72 full-time members, 92% with terminal degrees. The student-faculty ratio is 12:1.

Students of Coe

The student body totals 1,311, of whom 1,280 are undergraduates. 55.8% are women and 44.2% are men. Students come from 40 states and territories and 20 other countries. 62% are from Iowa. 4.6% are international students. 2% are African American, 0.1% American Indian, 0.9% Asian American, and 1% Hispanic American. 79% returned for their sophomore year.

Facilities and Resources

Student rooms are linked to a campus network. 189 **computers** are available on campus that provide access to the Internet. The 2 **libraries** have 206,290 books and 818 subscriptions.

Campus Life

There are 65 active organizations on campus, including a drama/theater group, newspaper, radio station, and choral group. 27% of eligible men and 20% of eligible women are members of national **fraternities** and national **sororities**.

Coe is a member of the NCAA (Division III). **Intercollegiate sports** include baseball (m), basketball, cross-country running, football (m), golf, soccer, softball (w), swimming, tennis, track and field, volleyball (w), wrestling (m).

Campus Safety

Student safety services include late-night transport/escort service, 24-hour emergency telephone alarm devices, 24-hour patrols by trained security personnel, and electronically operated dormitory entrances.

Applying

Coe requires an essay, SAT I or ACT, a high school transcript, and 1 recommendation. It recommends an interview and a minimum high school GPA of 3.0. Application deadline: 3/1; 3/1 priority date for financial aid. Early and deferred admission are possible.

Getting in Last Year

1,219 applied
77% were accepted
302 enrolled (32%)
28% from top tenth of their h.s. class
3.59 average high school GPA
35% had SAT verbal scores over 600
41% had SAT math scores over 600
59% had ACT scores over 24
6% had SAT verbal scores over 700
4% had SAT math scores over 700
7% had ACT scores over 30
14 valedictorians

Graduation and After

53% graduated in 4 years
6% graduated in 5 years
1% graduated in 6 years
24% pursued further study (14% arts and sciences, 3% business, 2% education)
98% had job offers within 6 months
90 organizations recruited on campus

Financial Matters

$19,340 tuition and fees (2001–02)
$5410 room and board
96% average percent of need met
$18,813 average financial aid amount received per undergraduate

COLBY COLLEGE

SMALL-TOWN SETTING ■ PRIVATE ■ INDEPENDENT ■ COED
WATERVILLE, MAINE

Web site: www.colby.edu

Contact: , Dean of Admissions and Financial Aid, Office of Admissions and Financial Aid, 4800 Mayflower Hill, Waterville, ME 04901-8848

Telephone: 207-872-3168 or toll-free 800-723-3032 **Fax:** 207-872-3474

E-mail: admissions@colby.edu

Getting in Last Year
3,909 applied
34% were accepted
488 enrolled (37%)
64% from top tenth of their h.s. class
84% had SAT verbal scores over 600
90% had SAT math scores over 600
93% had ACT scores over 24
31% had SAT verbal scores over 700
35% had SAT math scores over 700
28% had ACT scores over 30
18 valedictorians

Graduation and After
85% graduated in 4 years
3% graduated in 5 years
Graduates pursuing further study: 12% arts and sciences, 4% law, 2% medicine
75% had job offers within 6 months
66 organizations recruited on campus

Financial Matters
$34,290 comprehensive fee (2001–02)
100% average percent of need met
$20,792 average financial aid amount received per undergraduate

Academics
Colby awards bachelor's **degrees**. Challenging opportunities include advanced placement credit, student-designed majors, an honors program, double majors, independent study, and a senior project. Special programs include internships, off-campus study, study-abroad, and Army ROTC.

The most frequently chosen **baccalaureate** fields are social sciences and history, biological/life sciences, and area/ethnic studies. A complete listing of majors at Colby appears in the Majors Index beginning on page 430.

The **faculty** at Colby has 157 full-time members, 96% with terminal degrees. The student-faculty ratio is 11:1.

Students of Colby
The student body is made up of 1,809 undergraduates. 52.1% are women and 47.9% are men. Students come from 47 states and territories and 50 other countries. 11% are from Maine. 4.9% are international students. 2.2% are African American, 0.3% American Indian, 3.9% Asian American, and 2.1% Hispanic American. 94% returned for their sophomore year.

Facilities and Resources
Student rooms are linked to a campus network. 300 **computers** are available on campus that provide access to the Internet. The 3 **libraries** have 620,705 books and 1,835 subscriptions.

Campus Life
There are 90 active organizations on campus, including a drama/theater group, newspaper, radio station, and choral group. No national or local **fraternities** or **sororities**.

Colby is a member of the NCAA (Division III). **Intercollegiate sports** include baseball (m), basketball, crew, cross-country running, field hockey (w), football (m), golf, ice hockey, lacrosse, skiing (cross-country), skiing (downhill), soccer, softball (w), squash, swimming, tennis, track and field, volleyball (w).

Campus Safety
Student safety services include campus lighting, student emergency response team, self-defense education, property id program, party monitors, late-night transport/escort service, 24-hour emergency telephone alarm devices, 24-hour patrols by trained security personnel, and electronically operated dormitory entrances.

Applying
Colby requires an essay, SAT I or ACT, a high school transcript, and 2 recommendations. It recommends an interview. Application deadline: 1/1; 2/1 for financial aid. Early and deferred admission are possible.

Colgate University

Rural setting ■ Private ■ Independent ■ Coed
Hamilton, New York

Web site: www.colgate.edu
Contact: Mr. Gary L. Ross, Dean of Admission, 13 Oak Drive, Hamilton, NY 13346-1383
Telephone: 315-228-7401 **Fax:** 315-228-7544
E-mail: admission@mail.colgate.edu

Academics

Colgate awards bachelor's and master's **degrees**. Challenging opportunities include advanced placement credit, student-designed majors, an honors program, double majors, independent study, and a senior project. Special programs include off-campus study, study-abroad, and Army ROTC. A complete listing of majors at Colgate appears in the Majors Index beginning on page 430.

The **faculty** at Colgate has 236 full-time members, 97% with terminal degrees. The student-faculty ratio is 11:1.

Students of Colgate

The student body totals 2,785, of whom 2,781 are undergraduates. 50.8% are women and 49.2% are men. Students come from 48 states and territories and 27 other countries. 31% are from New York. 97% returned for their sophomore year.

Facilities and Resources

Student rooms are linked to a campus network. 577 **computers** are available on campus that provide access to software applications and the Internet. The 2 **libraries** have 634,874 books and 2,314 subscriptions.

Campus Life

There are 100 active organizations on campus, including a drama/theater group, newspaper, radio station, television station, choral group, and marching band. 34% of eligible men and 33% of eligible women are members of national **fraternities**, national **sororities**, and local fraternities.

Colgate is a member of the NCAA (Division I). **Intercollegiate sports** include basketball, crew, cross-country running, field hockey (w), football (m), golf (m), ice hockey, lacrosse, soccer, softball (w), swimming, tennis, track and field, volleyball (w).

Campus Safety

Student safety services include late-night transport/escort service, 24-hour emergency telephone alarm devices, 24-hour patrols by trained security personnel, student patrols, and electronically operated dormitory entrances.

Applying

Colgate requires an essay, SAT I and SAT II or ACT, a high school transcript, and 3 recommendations. Application deadline: 1/15; 2/1 for financial aid. Deferred admission is possible.

Getting in Last Year

6,059 applied
37% were accepted
740 enrolled (33%)
61% from top tenth of their h.s. class
3.61 average high school GPA
81% had SAT verbal scores over 600
87% had SAT math scores over 600
93% had ACT scores over 24
28% had SAT verbal scores over 700
32% had SAT math scores over 700
58% had ACT scores over 30
25 valedictorians

Graduation and After

85% graduated in 4 years
4% graduated in 5 years
1% graduated in 6 years
16% pursued further study (5% law, 3% arts and sciences, 3% medicine)
82% had job offers within 6 months
87 organizations recruited on campus

Financial Matters

$27,025 tuition and fees (2001–02)
$6455 room and board
100% average percent of need met
$22,950 average financial aid amount received per undergraduate

THE COLLEGE OF NEW JERSEY

SUBURBAN SETTING ■ PUBLIC ■ STATE-SUPPORTED ■ COED
EWING, NEW JERSEY

Web site: www.tcnj.edu
Contact: Ms. Lisa Angeloni, Dean of Admissions, PO Box 7718, Ewing, NJ 08628
Telephone: 609-771-2131 or toll-free 800-624-0967 **Fax:** 609-637-5174
E-mail: admiss@tcnj.edu

The College of New Jersey (TCNJ) is one of today's best buys in American higher education. Students choose TCNJ for its location between Philadelphia and New York City, its impressive academic strength, and its comfortable size—all at a remarkably affordable cost. College programs stress leadership skills, public service, and serious scholarship. The College community is both friendly and diverse, both challenging and fun. Opportunities abound for study abroad, internships, undergraduate research, and artistic expression. Students who demonstrate curiosity, initiative, and enthusiasm find TCNJ eager to help them grow.

Getting in Last Year
5,988 applied
51% were accepted
1,262 enrolled (41%)
61% from top tenth of their h.s. class
64% had SAT verbal scores over 600
79% had SAT math scores over 600
13% had SAT verbal scores over 700
20% had SAT math scores over 700
15 National Merit Scholars
14 valedictorians

Graduation and After
59% graduated in 4 years
20% graduated in 5 years
1% graduated in 6 years
26% pursued further study (8% education, 7% arts and sciences, 6% business)
65% had job offers within 6 months
265 organizations recruited on campus

Financial Matters
$6661 resident tuition and fees (2001–02)
$10,409 nonresident tuition and fees (2001–02)
$6764 room and board
$2562 average financial aid amount received per undergraduate (1999–2000)

Academics
TCNJ awards bachelor's and master's **degrees**. Challenging opportunities include advanced placement credit, an honors program, double majors, independent study, and a senior project. Special programs include internships, summer session for credit, off-campus study, study-abroad, and Army and Air Force ROTC.

The most frequently chosen **baccalaureate** fields are business/marketing, education, and social sciences and history. A complete listing of majors at TCNJ appears in the Majors Index beginning on page 430.

The **faculty** at TCNJ has 334 full-time members, 88% with terminal degrees. The student-faculty ratio is 12:1.

Students of TCNJ
The student body totals 6,847, of whom 5,973 are undergraduates. 59% are women and 41% are men. Students come from 22 states and territories and 12 other countries. 95% are from New Jersey. 0.2% are international students. 5.7% are African American, 0.1% American Indian, 4.8% Asian American, and 5.1% Hispanic American. 96% returned for their sophomore year.

Facilities and Resources
Student rooms are linked to a campus network. 800 **computers** are available on campus that provide access to the Internet. The **library** has 520,000 books and 4,700 subscriptions.

Campus Life
There are 150 active organizations on campus, including a drama/theater group, newspaper, radio station, and choral group. 20% of eligible men and 20% of eligible women are members of national **fraternities**, national **sororities**, local fraternities, and local sororities.

TCNJ is a member of the NCAA (Division III). **Intercollegiate sports** include baseball (m), basketball, cross-country running, field hockey (w), football (m), golf (m), lacrosse (w), soccer, softball (w), swimming, tennis, track and field, wrestling (m).

Campus Safety
Student safety services include late-night transport/escort service, 24-hour emergency telephone alarm devices, 24-hour patrols by trained security personnel, student patrols, and electronically operated dormitory entrances.

Applying
TCNJ requires an essay, SAT I or ACT, a high school transcript, and a minimum high school GPA of 2.0, and in some cases an interview and art portfolio or music audition. Application deadline: 2/15; 6/1 for financial aid, with a 3/1 priority date. Early and deferred admission are possible.

COLLEGE OF SAINT BENEDICT
COORDINATE WITH SAINT JOHN'S UNIVERSITY (MN)
SMALL-TOWN SETTING ■ PRIVATE ■ INDEPENDENT RELIGIOUS ■ WOMEN ONLY
SAINT JOSEPH, MINNESOTA

Web site: www.csbsju.edu
Contact: Ms. Mary Milbert, Dean of Admissions, 37 South College Avenue, St. Joseph, MN 56374
Telephone: 320-363-5308 or toll-free 800-544-1489 **Fax:** 320-363-5010
E-mail: admissions@csbsju.edu

Academics
St. Ben's awards bachelor's **degrees**. Challenging opportunities include advanced placement credit, accelerated degree programs, student-designed majors, an honors program, double majors, independent study, and a senior project. Special programs include internships, off-campus study, study-abroad, and Army ROTC.

The most frequently chosen **baccalaureate** fields are business/marketing, English, and health professions and related sciences. A complete listing of majors at St. Ben's appears in the Majors Index beginning on page 430.

The **faculty** at St. Ben's has 137 full-time members, 77% with terminal degrees. The student-faculty ratio is 14:1.

Students of St. Ben's
The student body is made up of 2,100 undergraduates. Students come from 31 states and territories and 24 other countries. 86% are from Minnesota. 3.7% are international students. 0.5% are African American, 0.2% American Indian, 1.8% Asian American, and 1.1% Hispanic American. 88% returned for their sophomore year.

Facilities and Resources
Student rooms are linked to a campus network. 350 **computers** are available on campus that provide access to the Internet. The 3 **libraries** have 853,351 books and 8,916 subscriptions.

Campus Life
There are 80 active organizations on campus, including a drama/theater group, newspaper, radio station, and choral group. No national or local **sororities**.

St. Ben's is a member of the NCAA (Division III). **Intercollegiate sports** include basketball, cross-country running, golf, gymnastics, skiing (cross-country), soccer, softball, swimming, tennis, track and field, volleyball.

Campus Safety
Student safety services include well-lit pathways, late-night transport/escort service, 24-hour emergency telephone alarm devices, 24-hour patrols by trained security personnel, student patrols, and electronically operated dormitory entrances.

Applying
St. Ben's requires an essay, SAT I or ACT, and a high school transcript, and in some cases recommendations. It recommends an interview and a minimum high school GPA of 3.0. Application deadline: rolling admissions; 3/15 priority date for financial aid. Early and deferred admission are possible.

Through a partnership of 2 national liberal arts colleges, the College of Saint Benedict (for women) and Saint John's University (for men) come together to offer one exceptional education. Enriched by a Catholic and Benedictine tradition, the colleges promote an integrated learning experience that combines a challenging academic program with extensive opportunities for international study, leadership, service, spiritual growth, and cultural and athletic involvement. The colleges' residential campuses, set amid the woods and lakes of central Minnesota, are excellent places for active students to become fully immersed in their college education.

Getting in Last Year
1,431 applied
82% were accepted
556 enrolled (47%)
43% from top tenth of their h.s. class
3.7 average high school GPA
56% had SAT verbal scores over 600
53% had SAT math scores over 600
66% had ACT scores over 24
15% had SAT verbal scores over 700
7% had SAT math scores over 700
14% had ACT scores over 30
4 National Merit Scholars

Graduation and After
68% graduated in 4 years
7% graduated in 5 years
11% pursued further study (5% arts and sciences, 2% education, 2% law)
82% had job offers within 6 months
135 organizations recruited on campus

Financial Matters
$18,315 tuition and fees (2001–02)
$5606 room and board
78% average percent of need met
$15,507 average financial aid amount received per undergraduate

THE COLLEGE OF ST. SCHOLASTICA

SUBURBAN SETTING ■ PRIVATE ■ INDEPENDENT RELIGIOUS ■ COED
DULUTH, MINNESOTA

Web site: www.css.edu
Contact: Mr. Brian Dalton, Vice President for Enrollment Management, 1200
  Kenwood Avenue, Duluth, MN 55811-4199
Telephone: 218-723-6053 or toll-free 800-249-6412 **Fax:** 218-723-6290
E-mail: admissions@css.edu

Getting in Last Year
960 applied
31% were accepted
298 enrolled (99%)
28% from top tenth of their h.s. class
3.55 average high school GPA
29% had SAT verbal scores over 600
36% had SAT math scores over 600
48% had ACT scores over 24
7% had SAT verbal scores over 700
7% had SAT math scores over 700
5% had ACT scores over 30
12 valedictorians

Graduation and After
49% graduated in 4 years
6% graduated in 5 years
4% graduated in 6 years
31% pursued further study
61.8% had job offers within 6 months
3 organizations recruited on campus

Financial Matters
$17,180 tuition and fees (2001–02)
$5198 room and board
84% average percent of need met
$15,050 average financial aid amount received
  per undergraduate

Academics
St. Scholastica awards bachelor's and master's **degrees**. Challenging opportunities
include advanced placement credit, accelerated degree programs, student-designed
majors, an honors program, double majors, independent study, and a senior project.
Special programs include internships, summer session for credit, off-campus study,
study-abroad, and Army and Air Force ROTC.

The most frequently chosen **baccalaureate** fields are health professions and related
sciences, business/marketing, and biological/life sciences. A complete listing of majors at
St. Scholastica appears in the Majors Index beginning on page 430.

The **faculty** at St. Scholastica has 113 full-time members, 43% with terminal
degrees. The student-faculty ratio is 12:1.

Students of St. Scholastica
The student body totals 2,231, of whom 1,700 are undergraduates. 70.3% are women
and 29.7% are men. Students come from 22 states and territories. 89% are from Minnesota. 0.5% are international students. 1.1% are African American, 1.1% American
Indian, 0.9% Asian American, and 0.6% Hispanic American. 76% returned for their
sophomore year.

Facilities and Resources
Student rooms are linked to a campus network. 160 **computers** are available on campus
that provide access to the Internet. The 2 **libraries** have 122,492 books and 828
subscriptions.

Campus Life
There are 45 active organizations on campus, including a drama/theater group,
newspaper, and choral group. No national or local **fraternities** or **sororities**.

St. Scholastica is a member of the NCAA (Division III) and NAIA. **Intercollegiate
sports** include baseball (m), basketball, cross-country running, ice hockey (m), soccer,
softball (w), tennis, volleyball (w).

Campus Safety
Student safety services include student door monitor at night, late-night transport/escort
service, 24-hour emergency telephone alarm devices, 24-hour patrols by trained security
personnel, and electronically operated dormitory entrances.

Applying
St. Scholastica requires SAT I or ACT and a high school transcript, and in some cases an
interview and a minimum high school GPA of 2.0. It recommends an essay, PSAT, an
interview, and recommendations. Application deadline: rolling admissions; 3/15 priority
date for financial aid. Early and deferred admission are possible.

COLLEGE OF THE ATLANTIC

SMALL-TOWN SETTING ■ PRIVATE ■ INDEPENDENT ■ COED
BAR HARBOR, MAINE

Web site: www.coa.edu
Contact: Ms. Sarah G. Baker, Director of Admission, 105 Eden Street, Bar Harbor, ME 04609-1198
Telephone: 207-288-5015 ext. 233 or toll-free 800-528-0025 **Fax:** 207-288-4126
E-mail: inquiry@ecology.coa.edu

Academics

COA awards bachelor's and master's **degrees**. Challenging opportunities include advanced placement credit, accelerated degree programs, student-designed majors, independent study, and a senior project. Special programs include cooperative education, internships, off-campus study, and study-abroad. A complete listing of majors at COA appears in the Majors Index beginning on page 430.

The **faculty** at COA has 22 full-time members. The student-faculty ratio is 10:1.

Students of COA

The student body totals 271, of whom 269 are undergraduates. 58.7% are women and 41.3% are men. Students come from 33 states and territories and 19 other countries. 22% are from Maine. 9.7% are international students. 0.7% are African American and 0.4% Asian American. 90% returned for their sophomore year.

Facilities and Resources

Student rooms are linked to a campus network. 48 **computers** are available on campus for student use. The **library** has 35,000 books and 475 subscriptions.

Campus Life

There are 12 active organizations on campus, including a drama/theater group, newspaper, and choral group. No national or local **fraternities** or **sororities**.

This institution has no intercollegiate sports.

Campus Safety

Student safety services include late-night transport/escort service, 24-hour emergency telephone alarm devices, and 24-hour patrols by trained security personnel.

Applying

COA requires an essay, a high school transcript, and 3 recommendations, and in some cases an interview. It recommends SAT I and SAT II or ACT, an interview, and a minimum high school GPA of 3.0. Application deadline: 3/1; 2/15 priority date for financial aid. Early and deferred admission are possible.

College of the Atlantic integrates student qualities of intellectual rigor, self-motivation, independence, and passion for the environment with institutional characteristics of self-designed concentrations of study, small seminar-style classes, and an abundance of supplementary fieldwork, allowing students the opportunity to combine areas of academic interest with the interdisciplinary liberal arts exploration of human ecology. At a college where questioning ideas and seeking relationships are encouraged, faculty members work along with students as they develop individualized programs of study that enable them to address ecological problems from multiple perspectives. This personalized approach to education, combined with practical experience in problem solving, allows students to develop the important skills necessary to make meaningful contributions to society.

Getting in Last Year
233 applied
75% were accepted
69 enrolled (40%)
18% from top tenth of their h.s. class
3.53 average high school GPA
63% had SAT verbal scores over 600
49% had SAT math scores over 600
100% had ACT scores over 24
20% had SAT verbal scores over 700
9% had SAT math scores over 700
22% had ACT scores over 30
8 National Merit Scholars
4 class presidents
1 valedictorian

Graduation and After
46% graduated in 4 years
4% graduated in 5 years
6% graduated in 6 years
3% pursued further study (2% arts and sciences, 2% education, 2% law)
75% had job offers within 6 months

Financial Matters
$21,384 tuition and fees (2001–02)
$5610 room and board
89% average percent of need met
$17,425 average financial aid amount received per undergraduate

COLLEGE OF THE HOLY CROSS

SUBURBAN SETTING ■ PRIVATE ■ INDEPENDENT RELIGIOUS ■ COED
WORCESTER, MASSACHUSETTS

Web site: www.holycross.edu
Contact: Ms. Ann Bowe McDermott, Director of Admissions, 1 College
 Street, Worcester, MA 01610-2395
Telephone: 508-793-2443 or toll-free 800-442-2421
E-mail: admissions@holycross.edu

Established in 1843, the College of the Holy Cross is renowned for its mentoring-based, liberal arts education in the Jesuit tradition. With a total enrollment of 2,700 and a student/faculty ratio of 13:1, students are assured of highly personalized instruction. Professors of the exclusively undergraduate college conduct all their own classes and laboratories and students have full access to sate-of-the-art equipment and information technology. A storied sports tradition and diverse extracurricular activities round out the Holy Cross experience. Integrating faith and knowledge with an emphasis on public service, Holy Cross prepares its students for success in all aspects of life.

Getting in Last Year
4,753 applied
43% were accepted
691 enrolled (34%)
60% from top tenth of their h.s. class
71% had SAT verbal scores over 600
74% had SAT math scores over 600
17% had SAT verbal scores over 700
14% had SAT math scores over 700

Graduation and After
88% graduated in 4 years
2% graduated in 5 years
23% pursued further study (10% arts and sciences, 8% law, 3% medicine)
69% had job offers within 6 months
70 organizations recruited on campus

Financial Matters
$25,020 tuition and fees (2001–02)
$7760 room and board
100% average percent of need met
$18,419 average financial aid amount received per undergraduate

Academics
Holy Cross awards bachelor's **degrees**. Challenging opportunities include advanced placement credit, accelerated degree programs, student-designed majors, an honors program, double majors, independent study, and a senior project. Special programs include internships, off-campus study, study-abroad, and Army, Navy and Air Force ROTC.

The most frequently chosen **baccalaureate** fields are social sciences and history, English, and psychology. A complete listing of majors at Holy Cross appears in the Majors Index beginning on page 430.

The **faculty** at Holy Cross has 222 full-time members, 97% with terminal degrees. The student-faculty ratio is 12:1.

Students of Holy Cross
The student body is made up of 2,811 undergraduates. 52.4% are women and 47.6% are men. Students come from 47 states and territories and 17 other countries. 34% are from Massachusetts. 0.8% are international students. 3% are African American, 0.3% American Indian, 3.7% Asian American, and 4.7% Hispanic American. 95% returned for their sophomore year.

Facilities and Resources
Student rooms are linked to a campus network. 267 **computers** are available on campus that provide access to the Internet. The 3 **libraries** have 566,900 books and 10,139 subscriptions.

Campus Life
There are 101 active organizations on campus, including a drama/theater group, newspaper, radio station, choral group, and marching band. No national or local **fraternities** or **sororities**.

Holy Cross is a member of the NCAA (Division I). **Intercollegiate sports** (some offering scholarships) include baseball (m), basketball, crew, cross-country running, field hockey (w), football (m), golf, ice hockey, lacrosse, soccer, softball (w), swimming, tennis, track and field, volleyball (w).

Campus Safety
Student safety services include late-night transport/escort service, 24-hour emergency telephone alarm devices, 24-hour patrols by trained security personnel, and electronically operated dormitory entrances.

Applying
Holy Cross requires an essay, SAT II: Writing Test, SAT I and SAT II or ACT, a high school transcript, and 2 recommendations. It recommends an interview. Application deadline: 1/15; 2/1 for financial aid. Early and deferred admission are possible.

The College of William and Mary

SMALL-TOWN SETTING ■ PUBLIC ■ STATE-SUPPORTED ■ COED
WILLIAMSBURG, VIRGINIA

Web site: www.wm.edu
Contact: Dr. Karen R. Cottrell, Associate Provost for Enrollment, PO Box 8795, Williamsburg, VA 23187-8795
Telephone: 757-221-4223 **Fax:** 757-221-1242
E-mail: admiss@facstaff.wm.edu

Academics

William and Mary awards bachelor's, master's, doctoral, and first-professional **degrees**. Challenging opportunities include advanced placement credit, accelerated degree programs, student-designed majors, an honors program, double majors, independent study, and a senior project. Special programs include summer session for credit, study-abroad, and Army ROTC.

The most frequently chosen **baccalaureate** fields are social sciences and history, business/marketing, and English. A complete listing of majors at William and Mary appears in the Majors Index beginning on page 430.

The **faculty** at William and Mary has 577 full-time members, 91% with terminal degrees. The student-faculty ratio is 12:1.

Students of William and Mary

The student body totals 7,489, of whom 5,604 are undergraduates. 56.6% are women and 43.4% are men. Students come from 50 states and territories and 52 other countries. 65% are from Virginia. 1.2% are international students. 4.8% are African American, 0.3% American Indian, 7.1% Asian American, and 2.7% Hispanic American. 95% returned for their sophomore year.

Facilities and Resources

Student rooms are linked to a campus network. 300 **computers** are available on campus that provide access to the Internet. The 10 **libraries** have 2,043,906 books and 11,541 subscriptions.

Campus Life

There are 300 active organizations on campus, including a drama/theater group, newspaper, radio station, television station, and choral group. 30% of eligible men and 30% of eligible women are members of national **fraternities** and national **sororities**.

William and Mary is a member of the NCAA (Division I). **Intercollegiate sports** (some offering scholarships) include baseball (m), basketball, cross-country running, field hockey (w), football (m), golf, gymnastics, lacrosse (w), soccer, swimming, tennis, track and field, volleyball (w).

Campus Safety

Student safety services include late-night transport/escort service, 24-hour emergency telephone alarm devices, 24-hour patrols by trained security personnel, student patrols, and electronically operated dormitory entrances.

Applying

William and Mary requires an essay, SAT I or ACT, and a high school transcript. It recommends SAT II Subject Tests, SAT II: Writing Test, and 1 recommendation. Application deadline: 1/5; 3/15 for financial aid, with a 2/15 priority date. Early and deferred admission are possible.

Getting in Last Year

8,610 applied
37% were accepted
1,348 enrolled (42%)
83% from top tenth of their h.s. class
4.0 average high school GPA
81% had SAT verbal scores over 600
80% had SAT math scores over 600
98% had ACT scores over 24
36% had SAT verbal scores over 700
30% had SAT math scores over 700
57% had ACT scores over 30
15 National Merit Scholars
29 class presidents
121 valedictorians

Graduation and After

80% graduated in 4 years
8% graduated in 5 years
1% graduated in 6 years
20% pursued further study
47% had job offers within 6 months
150 organizations recruited on campus

Financial Matters

$4780 resident tuition and fees (2001–02)
$17,808 nonresident tuition and fees (2001–02)
$5222 room and board
88% average percent of need met
$8701 average financial aid amount received per undergraduate

THE COLLEGE OF WOOSTER

SMALL-TOWN SETTING ■ PRIVATE ■ INDEPENDENT RELIGIOUS ■ COED
WOOSTER, OHIO

Web site: www.wooster.edu
Contact: Ms. Carol D. Wheatley, Director of Admissions, 1189 Beall Avenue,
Wooster, OH 44691
Telephone: 330-263-2270 ext. 2118 or toll-free 800-877-9905 **Fax:**
330-263-2621
E-mail: admissions@wooster.edu

Wooster's curriculum provides students the breadth that is to be found in hundreds of course offerings and the depth that comes from 47 majors and programs of study. Small classes and an accessible faculty committed to teaching undergraduates ensure individual attention for every student. A First-Year Seminar in Critical Inquiry links advising with teaching in a small seminar setting, while senior-year students work one-on-one with a faculty member on an Independent Study Project, a concept that was introduced into Wooster's curriculum more than 50 years ago. Wooster is one of the very few colleges that requires independent research of every student.

Getting in Last Year
2,357 applied
72% were accepted
532 enrolled (31%)
35% from top tenth of their h.s. class
3.50 average high school GPA
52% had SAT verbal scores over 600
47% had SAT math scores over 600
66% had ACT scores over 24
13% had SAT verbal scores over 700
7% had SAT math scores over 700
13% had ACT scores over 30
18 valedictorians

Graduation and After
66% graduated in 4 years
3% graduated in 6 years
Graduates pursuing further study: 7% arts and
sciences, 7% medicine, 5% business
88% had job offers within 6 months
30 organizations recruited on campus

Financial Matters
$22,430 tuition and fees (2001–02)
$5920 room and board
100% average percent of need met
$19,821 average financial aid amount received
per undergraduate

Academics
Wooster awards bachelor's **degrees**. Challenging opportunities include advanced placement credit, student-designed majors, double majors, independent study, and a senior project. Special programs include internships, summer session for credit, off-campus study, and study-abroad.

The most frequently chosen **baccalaureate** fields are social sciences and history, English, and biological/life sciences. A complete listing of majors at Wooster appears in the Majors Index beginning on page 430.

The **faculty** at Wooster has 135 full-time members, 97% with terminal degrees. The student-faculty ratio is 12:1.

Students of Wooster
The student body is made up of 1,823 undergraduates. 52.8% are women and 47.2% are men. Students come from 45 states and territories and 35 other countries. 57% are from Ohio. 7.4% are international students. 4.9% are African American, 0.2% American Indian, 1.3% Asian American, and 0.9% Hispanic American. 88% returned for their sophomore year.

Facilities and Resources
Student rooms are linked to a campus network. 230 **computers** are available on campus that provide access to the Internet. The 4 **libraries** have 448,348 books and 5,039 subscriptions.

Campus Life
There are 102 active organizations on campus, including a drama/theater group, newspaper, radio station, choral group, and marching band. 9% of eligible men and 9% of eligible women are members of local **fraternities**, local **sororities**, and coed fraternity.

Wooster is a member of the NCAA (Division III). **Intercollegiate sports** include baseball (m), basketball, cross-country running, field hockey (w), football (m), golf (m), lacrosse, soccer, softball (w), swimming, tennis, track and field, volleyball (w).

Campus Safety
Student safety services include late-night transport/escort service, 24-hour emergency telephone alarm devices, 24-hour patrols by trained security personnel, student patrols, and electronically operated dormitory entrances.

Applying
Wooster requires an essay, SAT I or ACT, a high school transcript, and 2 recommendations. It recommends an interview. Application deadline: 2/15; 2/15 priority date for financial aid. Early and deferred admission are possible.

THE COLORADO COLLEGE

URBAN SETTING ■ PRIVATE ■ INDEPENDENT ■ COED
COLORADO SPRINGS, COLORADO

Web site: www.coloradocollege.edu
Contact: Mr. Mark Hatch, Dean of Admission and Financial Aid, 900 Block
North Cascade, West, Colorado Springs, CO 80903-3294
Telephone: 719-389-6344 or toll-free 800-542-7214 **Fax:** 719-389-6816
E-mail: admission@coloradocollege.edu

Academics

CC awards bachelor's and master's **degrees** (master's degree in education only). Challenging opportunities include advanced placement credit, student-designed majors, an honors program, double majors, independent study, and a senior project. Special programs include summer session for credit, off-campus study, study-abroad, and Army ROTC.

The most frequently chosen **baccalaureate** fields are social sciences and history, biological/life sciences, and English. A complete listing of majors at CC appears in the Majors Index beginning on page 430.

The **faculty** at CC has 168 full-time members, 96% with terminal degrees. The student-faculty ratio is 9:1.

Students of CC

The student body totals 1,952, of whom 1,934 are undergraduates. 54.6% are women and 45.4% are men. Students come from 46 states and territories and 25 other countries. 31% are from Colorado. 1.8% are international students. 2.4% are African American, 1.1% American Indian, 4.3% Asian American, and 6.3% Hispanic American. 98% returned for their sophomore year.

Facilities and Resources

Student rooms are linked to a campus network. 237 **computers** are available on campus that provide access to the Internet. The 3 **libraries** have 481,050 books and 4,010 subscriptions.

Campus Life

There are 80 active organizations on campus, including a drama/theater group, newspaper, radio station, and choral group. 16% of eligible men and 18% of eligible women are members of national **fraternities** and national **sororities**.

CC is a member of the NCAA (Division III). **Intercollegiate sports** (some offering scholarships) include basketball, cross-country running, football (m), ice hockey (m), lacrosse, soccer, softball (w), swimming, tennis, track and field, volleyball (w).

Campus Safety

Student safety services include whistle program, late-night transport/escort service, 24-hour emergency telephone alarm devices, 24-hour patrols by trained security personnel, and electronically operated dormitory entrances.

Applying

CC requires an essay, SAT I or ACT, a high school transcript, and 3 recommendations. Application deadline: 1/15; 2/15 priority date for financial aid. Deferred admission is possible.

Getting in Last Year

3,402 applied
69% were accepted
479 enrolled (20%)
50% from top tenth of their h.s. class
67% had SAT verbal scores over 600
67% had SAT math scores over 600
85% had ACT scores over 24
19% had SAT verbal scores over 700
16% had SAT math scores over 700
23% had ACT scores over 30
12 National Merit Scholars
31 valedictorians

Graduation and After

72% graduated in 4 years
6% graduated in 5 years
1% graduated in 6 years
22% pursued further study
68 organizations recruited on campus

Financial Matters

$24,893 tuition and fees (2001–02)
$6632 room and board
92% average percent of need met
$20,719 average financial aid amount received per undergraduate

COLORADO SCHOOL OF MINES

SMALL-TOWN SETTING ■ PUBLIC ■ STATE-SUPPORTED ■ COED
GOLDEN, COLORADO

Web site: www.mines.edu
Contact: Ms. Tricia Douthit, Assistant Director of Enrollment Management, 1600 Maple Street, Golden, CO 80401-1842
Telephone: 303-273-3224 or toll-free 800-446-9488 (out-of-state) **Fax:** 303-273-3509
E-mail: admit@mines.edu

Getting in Last Year
1,702 applied
82% were accepted
600 enrolled (43%)
50% from top tenth of their h.s. class
3.70 average high school GPA
45% had SAT verbal scores over 600
74% had SAT math scores over 600
84% had ACT scores over 24
9% had SAT verbal scores over 700
18% had SAT math scores over 700
19% had ACT scores over 30
77 class presidents
77 valedictorians

Graduation and After
31% graduated in 4 years
26% graduated in 5 years
4% graduated in 6 years
15% pursued further study (11% engineering, 1% arts and sciences, 1% business)
85% had job offers within 6 months
169 organizations recruited on campus

Financial Matters
$5898 resident tuition and fees (2001–02)
$17,583 nonresident tuition and fees (2001–02)
$5680 room and board
100% average percent of need met
$12,100 average financial aid amount received per undergraduate

Academics

CSM awards bachelor's, master's, doctoral, and first-professional **degrees**. Challenging opportunities include advanced placement credit, accelerated degree programs, an honors program, double majors, independent study, and a senior project. Special programs include cooperative education, internships, summer session for credit, study-abroad, and Army and Air Force ROTC.

The most frequently chosen **baccalaureate** fields are engineering/engineering technologies, mathematics, and physical sciences. A complete listing of majors at CSM appears in the Majors Index beginning on page 430.

The **faculty** at CSM has 202 full-time members, 88% with terminal degrees. The student-faculty ratio is 13:1.

Students of CSM

The student body totals 3,255, of whom 2,556 are undergraduates. 24.7% are women and 75.3% are men. Students come from 51 states and territories and 62 other countries. 79% are from Colorado. 4.2% are international students. 1.2% are African American, 0.7% American Indian, 5.4% Asian American, and 5.8% Hispanic American. 83% returned for their sophomore year.

Facilities and Resources

Student rooms are linked to a campus network. The **library** has 102,533 books and 1,840 subscriptions.

Campus Life

There are 95 active organizations on campus, including a drama/theater group, newspaper, choral group, and marching band. 19% of eligible men and 19% of eligible women are members of national **fraternities** and national **sororities**.

CSM is a member of the NCAA (Division II). **Intercollegiate sports** (some offering scholarships) include baseball (m), basketball, cross-country running, football (m), golf (m), skiing (downhill) (m), soccer (m), softball (w), swimming, tennis, track and field, volleyball (w), wrestling (m).

Campus Safety

Student safety services include 24-hour emergency telephone alarm devices and 24-hour patrols by trained security personnel.

Applying

CSM requires SAT I or ACT and a high school transcript, and in some cases an essay, an interview, and recommendations. It recommends rank in upper one-third of high school class. Application deadline: 6/1; 3/1 priority date for financial aid. Deferred admission is possible.

COLORADO STATE UNIVERSITY
URBAN SETTING ■ PUBLIC ■ STATE-SUPPORTED ■ COED
FORT COLLINS, COLORADO

Web site: www.colostate.edu
Contact: Ms. Mary Ontiveros, Director of Admissions, Spruce Hall, Fort
  Collins, CO 80523-0015
Telephone: 970-491-6909 **Fax:** 970-491-7799
E-mail: admissions@vines.colostate.edu

Academics
Colorado State awards bachelor's, master's, doctoral, and first-professional **degrees**.
Challenging opportunities include advanced placement credit, accelerated degree
programs, student-designed majors, an honors program, double majors, independent
study, and a senior project. Special programs include cooperative education, internships,
summer session for credit, off-campus study, study-abroad, and Army and Air Force
ROTC.

The most frequently chosen **baccalaureate** fields are business/marketing,
agriculture, and engineering/engineering technologies. A complete listing of majors at
Colorado State appears in the Majors Index beginning on page 430.

The **faculty** at Colorado State has 934 full-time members, 99% with terminal
degrees. The student-faculty ratio is 18:1.

Students of Colorado State
The student body totals 23,934, of whom 19,899 are undergraduates. 52.4% are women
and 47.6% are men. Students come from 55 states and territories and 57 other countries.
80% are from Colorado. 1.2% are international students. 1.9% are African American,
1.1% American Indian, 2.7% Asian American, and 5.9% Hispanic American. 81%
returned for their sophomore year.

Facilities and Resources
Student rooms are linked to a campus network. The 4 **libraries** have 1,218,636 books
and 21,208 subscriptions.

Campus Life
There are 300 active organizations on campus, including a drama/theater group,
newspaper, radio station, television station, choral group, and marching band. 8% of
eligible men and 8% of eligible women are members of national **fraternities**, national
sororities, local fraternities, and local sororities.

Colorado State is a member of the NCAA (Division I). **Intercollegiate sports** (some
offering scholarships) include basketball, cross-country running, football (m), golf,
softball (w), swimming (w), tennis (w), track and field, volleyball (w).

Campus Safety
Student safety services include late-night transport/escort service, 24-hour emergency
telephone alarm devices, 24-hour patrols by trained security personnel, student patrols,
and electronically operated dormitory entrances.

Applying
Colorado State requires SAT I or ACT and a high school transcript. It recommends an
essay and recommendations. Application deadline: 7/1; 3/1 priority date for financial aid.
Deferred admission is possible.

Colorado State's scenic
location, at the base of
the Rocky Mountain
foothills, offers the perfect
background for intellectual and
personal growth. The University
provides an academically challenging
and rigorous curriculum in a
supportive environment. Students
describe Colorado State as a place
where they can feel free to be
themselves and are encouraged to
develop their own unique talents. In
addition to nearly 150 programs of
study, students can enhance their
education through the Honors
Program, study abroad, and many
opportunities for hands-on
experience, including undergraduate
research, an extensive network of
internships, and volunteer/
community service. Colorado State
students graduate with the
confidence that their education will
lead them on an amazing journey
with the knowledge to go places.

Getting in Last Year
11,806 applied
78% were accepted
3,720 enrolled (40%)
24% from top tenth of their h.s. class
3.50 average high school GPA
27% had SAT verbal scores over 600
31% had SAT math scores over 600
53% had ACT scores over 24
4% had SAT verbal scores over 700
4% had SAT math scores over 700
7% had ACT scores over 30
5 National Merit Scholars

Graduation and After
29% graduated in 4 years
28% graduated in 5 years
5% graduated in 6 years
501 organizations recruited on campus

Financial Matters
$4252 resident tuition and fees (2001–02)
$11,694 nonresident tuition and fees (2001–
  02)
$5670 room and board
82% average percent of need met
$7288 average financial aid amount received
  per undergraduate (2000–01)

COLUMBIA COLLEGE
URBAN SETTING ■ PRIVATE ■ INDEPENDENT ■ COED
NEW YORK, NEW YORK

Web site: www.columbia.edu
Contact: Mr. Eric Furda, Director of Undergraduate Admissions, 1130 Amsterdam Avenue MC 2807, New York, NY 10027
Telephone: 212-854-2522 **Fax:** 212-854-1209
E-mail: ugrad-admiss@columbia.edu

Getting in Last Year
14,094 applied
12% were accepted
1,005 enrolled (58%)
87% from top tenth of their h.s. class
3.65 average high school GPA
90% had SAT verbal scores over 600
92% had SAT math scores over 600
95% had ACT scores over 24
61% had SAT verbal scores over 700
58% had SAT math scores over 700
55% had ACT scores over 30

Graduation and After
80% pursued further study

Financial Matters
$26,908 tuition and fees (2001–02)
$8280 room and board
100% average percent of need met
$23,266 average financial aid amount received per undergraduate

Academics
Columbia awards bachelor's **degrees**. Challenging opportunities include advanced placement credit, student-designed majors, an honors program, and a senior project. Special programs include internships, summer session for credit, off-campus study, and study-abroad. A complete listing of majors at Columbia appears in the Majors Index beginning on page 430.

The **faculty** at Columbia has 632 full-time members. The student-faculty ratio is 7:1.

Students of Columbia
The student body is made up of 4,092 undergraduates. Students come from 54 states and territories and 72 other countries. 30% are from New York. 4.7% are international students. 8.7% are African American, 0.2% American Indian, 12.7% Asian American, and 7.8% Hispanic American. 98% returned for their sophomore year.

Facilities and Resources
Student rooms are linked to a campus network. 400 **computers** are available on campus for student use. The 21 **libraries** have 6,800,000 books and 66,000 subscriptions.

Campus Life
There are 300 active organizations on campus, including a drama/theater group, newspaper, radio station, television station, choral group, and marching band. 19% of eligible men and 25% of eligible women are members of national **fraternities**, national **sororities**, and coed fraternities.

Columbia is a member of the NCAA (Division I). **Intercollegiate sports** include archery (w), baseball (m), basketball, crew, cross-country running, fencing, field hockey (w), football (m), golf (m), lacrosse (w), soccer, softball (w), swimming, tennis, track and field, volleyball (w), wrestling (m).

Campus Safety
Student safety services include 24-hour ID check at door, late-night transport/escort service, 24-hour emergency telephone alarm devices, 24-hour patrols by trained security personnel, and student patrols.

Applying
Columbia requires an essay, SAT II Subject Tests, SAT II: Writing Test, SAT I or ACT, a high school transcript, and 3 recommendations. Application deadline: 1/2; 2/10 for financial aid. Early and deferred admission are possible.

COLUMBIA UNIVERSITY, THE FU FOUNDATION SCHOOL OF ENGINEERING AND APPLIED SCIENCE

URBAN SETTING ■ PRIVATE ■ INDEPENDENT ■ COED
NEW YORK, NEW YORK

Web site: www.columbia.edu
Contact: Mr. Eric J. Furda, Director of Undergraduate Admissions, 1130 Amsterdam Avenue MC 2807, New York, NY 10027
Telephone: 212-854-2522 **Fax:** 212-854-1209
E-mail: ugrad-admiss@columbia.edu

Academics

Columbia SEAS awards bachelor's, master's, and doctoral **degrees**. Challenging opportunities include advanced placement credit, accelerated degree programs, and an honors program. Special programs include internships, summer session for credit, and study-abroad.

The most frequently chosen **baccalaureate** fields are engineering/engineering technologies, social sciences and history, and computer/information sciences. A complete listing of majors at Columbia SEAS appears in the Majors Index beginning on page 430.

The **faculty** at Columbia SEAS has 108 full-time members. The student-faculty ratio is 7:1.

Students of Columbia SEAS

The student body is made up of 1,264 undergraduates. Students come from 44 states and territories and 59 other countries. 25% are from New York. 11.6% are international students. 4.8% are African American, 33.8% Asian American, and 5.8% Hispanic American. 97% returned for their sophomore year.

Facilities and Resources

Student rooms are linked to a campus network. 400 **computers** are available on campus that provide access to the Internet. The 21 **libraries** have 6,800,000 books and 66,000 subscriptions.

Campus Life

There are 300 active organizations on campus, including a drama/theater group, newspaper, radio station, television station, choral group, and marching band. 19% of eligible men and 25% of eligible women are members of national **fraternities**, national **sororities**, and coed fraternities.

Columbia SEAS is a member of the NCAA (Division I). **Intercollegiate sports** include archery (w), baseball (m), basketball, crew, cross-country running, fencing, field hockey (w), football (m), golf (m), lacrosse (w), soccer, softball (w), swimming, tennis, track and field, volleyball (w), wrestling (m).

Campus Safety

Student safety services include 24-hour ID check at door, late-night transport/escort service, 24-hour emergency telephone alarm devices, and 24-hour patrols by trained security personnel.

Applying

Columbia SEAS requires an essay, SAT II Subject Tests, SAT II: Writing Test, SAT I or ACT, a high school transcript, and 3 recommendations. It recommends an interview. Application deadline: 1/1; 2/10 for financial aid. Early and deferred admission are possible.

Getting in Last Year
2,466 applied
26% were accepted
312 enrolled (48%)
86% from top tenth of their h.s. class
3.65 average high school GPA
89% had SAT verbal scores over 600
99% had SAT math scores over 600
100% had ACT scores over 24
41% had SAT verbal scores over 700
83% had SAT math scores over 700
47% had ACT scores over 30

Financial Matters
$26,908 tuition and fees (2001–02)
$8280 room and board
100% average percent of need met
$23,337 average financial aid amount received per undergraduate

CONCORDIA COLLEGE

SUBURBAN SETTING ■ PRIVATE ■ INDEPENDENT RELIGIOUS ■ COED
MOORHEAD, MINNESOTA

Getting in Last Year
2,326 applied
86% were accepted
773 enrolled (39%)
28% from top tenth of their h.s. class
39% had SAT verbal scores over 600
38% had SAT math scores over 600
52% had ACT scores over 24
5% had SAT verbal scores over 700
5% had SAT math scores over 700
6% had ACT scores over 30
4 National Merit Scholars

Graduation and After
57% graduated in 4 years
6% graduated in 5 years
3% graduated in 6 years
23% pursued further study (12% arts and
  sciences, 3% medicine, 2% law)
75% had job offers within 6 months
75 organizations recruited on campus

Financial Matters
$14,847 tuition and fees (2001–02)
$4110 room and board
92% average percent of need met
$12,400 average financial aid amount received
  per undergraduate

Web site: www.concordiacollege.edu
Contact: Mr. Scott E. Ellingson, Director of Admissions, 901 8th Street
  South, Moorhead, MN 56562
Telephone: 218-299-3004 or toll-free 800-699-9897 **Fax:** 218-299-3947
E-mail: admissions@cord.edu

Academics

Concordia awards bachelor's and master's **degrees**. Challenging opportunities include advanced placement credit, an honors program, double majors, independent study, and a senior project. Special programs include cooperative education, internships, summer session for credit, off-campus study, study-abroad, and Army and Air Force ROTC.

The most frequently chosen **baccalaureate** fields are education, business/marketing, and foreign language/literature. A complete listing of majors at Concordia appears in the Majors Index beginning on page 430.

The **faculty** at Concordia has 199 full-time members, 79% with terminal degrees. The student-faculty ratio is 14:1.

Students of Concordia

The student body is made up of 2,766 undergraduates. 62.1% are women and 37.9% are men. Students come from 31 states and territories and 41 other countries. 61% are from Minnesota. 5.6% are international students. 0.6% are African American, 0.5% American Indian, 1.3% Asian American, and 0.7% Hispanic American. 81% returned for their sophomore year.

Facilities and Resources

Student rooms are linked to a campus network. 185 **computers** are available on campus for student use. The **library** has 300,000 books and 1,440 subscriptions.

Campus Life

There are 80 active organizations on campus, including a drama/theater group, newspaper, radio station, television station, and choral group. 4% of eligible men and 4% of eligible women are members of local **fraternities**, local **sororities**, and local coed fraternity.

Concordia is a member of the NCAA (Division III). **Intercollegiate sports** include baseball (m), basketball, cross-country running, football (m), golf, ice hockey, soccer, softball (w), swimming (w), tennis, track and field, volleyball (w), wrestling (m).

Campus Safety

Student safety services include well-lit campus, 24-hour locked wing doors, late-night transport/escort service, 24-hour emergency telephone alarm devices, 24-hour patrols by trained security personnel, and student patrols.

Applying

Concordia requires SAT I or ACT, a high school transcript, and 2 recommendations. It recommends ACT. Application deadline: rolling admissions. Early and deferred admission are possible.

CONNECTICUT COLLEGE

SUBURBAN SETTING ■ PRIVATE ■ INDEPENDENT ■ COED
NEW LONDON, CONNECTICUT

Web site: www.connecticutcollege.edu
Contact: Ms. Martha Merrill, Dean of Admissions and Financial Aid, 270 Mohegan Avenue, New London, CT 06320-4196
Telephone: 860-439-2200 **Fax:** 860-439-4301
E-mail: admission@conncoll.edu

Academics

Connecticut awards bachelor's and master's **degrees**. Challenging opportunities include advanced placement credit, accelerated degree programs, student-designed majors, an honors program, double majors, independent study, and a senior project. Special programs include internships, summer session for credit, off-campus study, and study-abroad.

The most frequently chosen **baccalaureate** fields are social sciences and history, biological/life sciences, and psychology. A complete listing of majors at Connecticut appears in the Majors Index beginning on page 430.

The **faculty** at Connecticut has 155 full-time members, 90% with terminal degrees. The student-faculty ratio is 11:1.

Students of Connecticut

The student body totals 1,879, of whom 1,835 are undergraduates. 59.2% are women and 40.8% are men. Students come from 42 states and territories and 69 other countries. 23% are from Connecticut. 8.2% are international students. 2.7% are African American, 0.5% American Indian, 2.9% Asian American, and 2.5% Hispanic American. 93% returned for their sophomore year.

Facilities and Resources

Student rooms are linked to a campus network. 461 **computers** are available on campus that provide access to the Internet. The 2 **libraries** have 436,582 books and 2,357 subscriptions.

Campus Life

There are 60 active organizations on campus, including a drama/theater group, newspaper, radio station, and choral group. No national or local **fraternities** or **sororities**.

Connecticut is a member of the NCAA (Division III). **Intercollegiate sports** include basketball, crew, cross-country running, field hockey (w), ice hockey, lacrosse, sailing, soccer, squash, swimming, tennis, track and field, volleyball, water polo.

Campus Safety

Student safety services include late-night transport/escort service, 24-hour emergency telephone alarm devices, 24-hour patrols by trained security personnel, and electronically operated dormitory entrances.

Applying

Connecticut requires an essay, ACT or 3 SAT II Subject Tests (including SAT II: Writing Test), a high school transcript, 2 recommendations, and a minimum high school GPA of 2.0. It recommends SAT I and an interview. Application deadline: 1/1; 1/15 for financial aid. Deferred admission is possible.

Getting in Last Year

4,318 applied
34% were accepted
472 enrolled (32%)
55% from top tenth of their h.s. class
87% had SAT verbal scores over 600
84% had SAT math scores over 600
93% had ACT scores over 24
32% had SAT verbal scores over 700
18% had SAT math scores over 700
17% had ACT scores over 30

Graduation and After

75% graduated in 4 years
6% graduated in 5 years
17% pursued further study (11% arts and sciences, 2% education, 2% law)
87 organizations recruited on campus

Financial Matters

$33,585 comprehensive fee (2001–02)
100% average percent of need met
$21,943 average financial aid amount received per undergraduate

CONVERSE COLLEGE

URBAN SETTING ■ PRIVATE ■ INDEPENDENT ■ WOMEN ONLY
SPARTANBURG, SOUTH CAROLINA

Getting in Last Year
535 applied
79% were accepted
164 enrolled (39%)
34% from top tenth of their h.s. class
3.60 average high school GPA
37% had SAT verbal scores over 600
28% had SAT math scores over 600
43% had ACT scores over 24
6% had SAT verbal scores over 700
3% had SAT math scores over 700
8% had ACT scores over 30

Graduation and After
53% graduated in 4 years
1% graduated in 5 years
27% pursued further study (10% education,
  5% arts and sciences, 5% business)
60% had job offers within 6 months

Financial Matters
$16,850 tuition and fees (2001–02)
$5140 room and board
89% average percent of need met
$13,994 average financial aid amount received
  per undergraduate

Web site: www.converse.edu
Contact: Ms. Wanda McDowell, Director of Admissions, 580 East Main
  Street, Spartanburg, SC 29302-0006
Telephone: 864-596-9040 ext. 9746 or toll-free 800-766-1125 **Fax:**
  864-596-9158
E-mail: admissions@converse.edu

Academics

Converse awards bachelor's and master's **degrees** and post-master's certificates. Challenging opportunities include advanced placement credit, accelerated degree programs, an honors program, double majors, independent study, and a senior project. Special programs include internships, summer session for credit, off-campus study, study-abroad, and Army ROTC.

The most frequently chosen **baccalaureate** fields are visual/performing arts, education, and business/marketing. A complete listing of majors at Converse appears in the Majors Index beginning on page 430.

The **faculty** at Converse has 71 full-time members, 89% with terminal degrees. The student-faculty ratio is 13:1.

Students of Converse

The student body totals 1,527, of whom 732 are undergraduates. Students come from 17 states and territories and 10 other countries. 65% are from South Carolina. 1.9% are international students. 8.6% are African American, 1.5% Asian American, and 1.2% Hispanic American. 73% returned for their sophomore year.

Facilities and Resources

Student rooms are linked to a campus network. 65 **computers** are available on campus that provide access to the Internet. The **library** has 129,411 books and 1,467 subscriptions.

Campus Life

There are 30 active organizations on campus, including a drama/theater group, newspaper, and choral group. No national or local **sororities**.

Converse is a member of the NCAA (Division II). **Intercollegiate sports** (some offering scholarships) include basketball, cross-country running, soccer, tennis, volleyball.

Campus Safety

Student safety services include late-night transport/escort service, 24-hour emergency telephone alarm devices, 24-hour patrols by trained security personnel, and electronically operated dormitory entrances.

Applying

Converse requires an essay, SAT I or ACT, a high school transcript, and a minimum high school GPA of 2.00, and in some cases 1 recommendation. It recommends an interview and a minimum high school GPA of 2.50. Application deadline: 3/1; 3/1 priority date for financial aid. Early and deferred admission are possible.

COOPER UNION FOR THE ADVANCEMENT OF SCIENCE AND ART

URBAN SETTING ■ PRIVATE ■ INDEPENDENT ■ COED
NEW YORK, NEW YORK

Web site: www.cooper.edu
Contact: Mr. Richard Bory, Dean of Admissions and Records and Registrar, 30 Cooper Square, New York, NY 10003
Telephone: 212-353-4120 **Fax:** 212-353-4342
E-mail: admission@cooper.edu

Academics

Cooper Union awards bachelor's and master's **degrees**. Challenging opportunities include advanced placement credit, student-designed majors, an honors program, independent study, and a senior project. Special programs include internships, summer session for credit, off-campus study, and study-abroad. A complete listing of majors at Cooper Union appears in the Majors Index beginning on page 430.

The **faculty** at Cooper Union has 56 full-time members, 75% with terminal degrees. The student-faculty ratio is 7:1.

Students of Cooper Union

The student body totals 906, of whom 878 are undergraduates. 36.2% are women and 63.8% are men. Students come from 41 states and territories. 56% are from New York. 8.4% are international students. 5% are African American, 0.5% American Indian, 28.1% Asian American, and 6.9% Hispanic American. 92% returned for their sophomore year.

Facilities and Resources

Student rooms are linked to a campus network. 200 **computers** are available on campus that provide access to the Internet. The **library** has 97,000 books and 370 subscriptions.

Campus Life

There are 68 active organizations on campus, including a drama/theater group and newspaper. 20% of eligible men and 10% of eligible women are members of national **fraternities** and national **sororities**.

Intercollegiate sports include basketball (m), soccer (m), table tennis, tennis, volleyball.

Campus Safety

Student safety services include security guards, 24-hour emergency telephone alarm devices, and 24-hour patrols by trained security personnel.

Applying

Cooper Union requires SAT I or ACT, a high school transcript, and a minimum high school GPA of 2.0, and in some cases an essay, SAT II Subject Tests, 3 recommendations, and portfolio, home examination. It recommends a minimum high school GPA of 3.0. Application deadline: 1/1; 4/15 priority date for financial aid. Early and deferred admission are possible.

Each of Cooper Union's schools—Art, Architecture, Engineering—adheres strongly to preparation for its profession within a design-centered, problem-solving philosophy of education in a full tuition scholarship environment. A rigorous curriculum and group projects reinforce this unique atmosphere in higher education and are factors in *Money* magazine's decision to name Cooper Union "In a Class by Itself."

Getting in Last Year
2,210 applied
13% were accepted
202 enrolled (68%)
80% from top tenth of their h.s. class
3.40 average high school GPA
83% had SAT verbal scores over 600
82% had SAT math scores over 600
37% had SAT verbal scores over 700
54% had SAT math scores over 700

Graduation and After
57% graduated in 4 years
17% graduated in 5 years
3% graduated in 6 years
43% pursued further study
98% had job offers within 6 months
80 organizations recruited on campus

Financial Matters
$600 tuition and fees (2001–02)
$8000 room only
92% average percent of need met
$5709 average financial aid amount received per undergraduate (2000–01)

Cornell College

Small-town setting ■ Private ■ Independent Religious ■ Coed
Mount Vernon, Iowa

Web site: www.cornellcollege.edu
Contact: Dean of Admissions and Financial Assistance, 600 First Street West,
Mount Vernon, IA 52314-1098
Telephone: 319-895-4477 or toll-free 800-747-1112 **Fax:** 319-895-4451
E-mail: admissions@cornellcollege.edu

Getting in Last Year
1,182 applied
70% were accepted
302 enrolled (37%)
26% from top tenth of their h.s. class
3.49 average high school GPA
48% had SAT verbal scores over 600
46% had SAT math scores over 600
59% had ACT scores over 24
9% had SAT verbal scores over 700
11% had SAT math scores over 700
11% had ACT scores over 30

Graduation and After
52% graduated in 4 years
2% graduated in 5 years
1% graduated in 6 years
33% pursued further study
28 organizations recruited on campus

Financial Matters
$20,250 tuition and fees (2001–02)
$5600 room and board
90% average percent of need met
$19,500 average financial aid amount received per undergraduate

Academics

Cornell awards bachelor's **degrees**. Challenging opportunities include advanced placement credit, student-designed majors, double majors, independent study, and a senior project. Special programs include internships, off-campus study, and study-abroad.

The most frequently chosen **baccalaureate** fields are social sciences and history, biological/life sciences, and education. A complete listing of majors at Cornell appears in the Majors Index beginning on page 430.

The **faculty** at Cornell has 85 full-time members, 91% with terminal degrees. The student-faculty ratio is 11:1.

Students of Cornell

The student body is made up of 986 undergraduates. 57.7% are women and 42.3% are men. Students come from 38 states and territories and 7 other countries. 30% are from Iowa. 1.7% are international students. 2.5% are African American, 0.4% American Indian, 1.1% Asian American, and 2.2% Hispanic American. 79% returned for their sophomore year.

Facilities and Resources

Student rooms are linked to a campus network. 100 **computers** are available on campus that provide access to the Internet. The **library** has 128,098 books and 731 subscriptions.

Campus Life

There are 76 active organizations on campus, including a drama/theater group, newspaper, radio station, and choral group. 30% of eligible men and 32% of eligible women are members of local **fraternities** and local **sororities**.

Cornell is a member of the NCAA (Division III). **Intercollegiate sports** include baseball (m), basketball, cross-country running, football (m), golf, soccer, softball (w), tennis, track and field, volleyball (w), wrestling (m).

Campus Safety

Student safety services include 24-hour emergency telephone alarm devices and 24-hour patrols by trained security personnel.

Applying

Cornell requires an essay, SAT I or ACT, a high school transcript, and 1 recommendation. It recommends an interview and a minimum high school GPA of 2.80. Application deadline: 2/1; 3/1 priority date for financial aid. Early and deferred admission are possible.

Cornell University

SMALL-TOWN SETTING ■ PRIVATE ■ INDEPENDENT ■ COED
ITHACA, NEW YORK

Web site: www.cornell.edu
Contact: Ms. Wendy Schaerer, Director of Undergraduate Admissions, 410 Thurston Avenue, Ithaca, NY 14850
Telephone: 607-255-5241 **Fax:** 607-255-0659
E-mail: admissions@cornell.edu

Academics

Cornell awards bachelor's, master's, doctoral, and first-professional **degrees**. Challenging opportunities include advanced placement credit, accelerated degree programs, student-designed majors, an honors program, double majors, independent study, and a senior project. Special programs include cooperative education, internships, summer session for credit, off-campus study, study-abroad, and Army and Air Force ROTC.

The most frequently chosen **baccalaureate** fields are engineering/engineering technologies, agriculture, and business/marketing. A complete listing of majors at Cornell appears in the Majors Index beginning on page 430.

The **faculty** at Cornell has 1,627 full-time members, 89% with terminal degrees. The student-faculty ratio is 13:1.

Students of Cornell

The student body totals 19,420, of whom 13,801 are undergraduates. Students come from 55 states and territories and 82 other countries. 48% are from New York. 7.4% are international students. 4.7% are African American, 0.5% American Indian, 16.4% Asian American, and 5.5% Hispanic American. 93% returned for their sophomore year.

Facilities and Resources

Student rooms are linked to a campus network. 700 **computers** are available on campus that provide access to the Internet. The 18 **libraries** have 6,260,779 books and 61,941 subscriptions.

Campus Life

There are 400 active organizations on campus, including a drama/theater group, newspaper, radio station, choral group, and marching band. 21% of eligible men and 19% of eligible women are members of national **fraternities**, national **sororities**, and local fraternities.

Cornell is a member of the NCAA (Division I). **Intercollegiate sports** include baseball (m), basketball, crew, cross-country running, equestrian sports (w), fencing (w), field hockey (w), football (m), golf (m), gymnastics (w), ice hockey (m), lacrosse, soccer, squash, swimming, tennis, track and field, volleyball (w), wrestling (m).

Campus Safety

Student safety services include escort service, late-night transport/escort service, 24-hour emergency telephone alarm devices, 24-hour patrols by trained security personnel, and electronically operated dormitory entrances.

Applying

Cornell requires an essay, SAT I or ACT, a high school transcript, and 1 recommendation, and in some cases SAT II Subject Tests, SAT II: Writing Test, and an interview. Application deadline: 1/1; 2/11 for financial aid. Early and deferred admission are possible.

Cornell University, an Ivy League land-grant school located in central New York, is home to 13,600 undergraduates pursuing studies in more than 70 majors found in the University's 7 small to midsized undergraduate colleges: Agriculture & Life Sciences; Architecture, Art & Planning; Arts & Sciences; Engineering; Hotel Administration; Human Ecology; and Industrial & Labor Relations. Students come from all 50 states and more than 100 countries. Cornell's special features include a world-renowned faculty; an outstanding undergraduate research program; 17 libraries; superb research and teaching facilities; a large, diverse study-abroad program; more than 500 student organizations; more than 35 varsity sports; and a graduation rate close to 90%.

Getting in Last Year
21,519 applied
27% were accepted
2,988 enrolled (51%)
82% from top tenth of their h.s. class
85% had SAT verbal scores over 600
92% had SAT math scores over 600
37% had SAT verbal scores over 700
56% had SAT math scores over 700
63 National Merit Scholars

Graduation and After
30% pursued further study
90% had job offers within 6 months
900 organizations recruited on campus

Financial Matters
$26,062 tuition and fees (2001–02)
$8552 room and board
100% average percent of need met
$21,390 average financial aid amount received per undergraduate

COVENANT COLLEGE

SUBURBAN SETTING ■ PRIVATE ■ INDEPENDENT RELIGIOUS ■ COED
LOOKOUT MOUNTAIN, GEORGIA

Web site: www.covenant.edu
Contact: Ms. Leda Goodman, Regional Director, 14049 Scenic Highway, Lookout Mountain, GA 30750
Telephone: 706-419-1644 or toll-free 888-451-2683 (in-state) **Fax:** 706-820-0893
E-mail: admissions@covenant.edu

Getting in Last Year
544 applied
96% were accepted
225 enrolled (43%)
20% from top tenth of their h.s. class
3.57 average high school GPA
49% had SAT verbal scores over 600
37% had SAT math scores over 600
56% had ACT scores over 24
17% had SAT verbal scores over 700
8% had SAT math scores over 700
16% had ACT scores over 30

Graduation and After
47% graduated in 4 years
4% graduated in 5 years
1% graduated in 6 years
100 organizations recruited on campus

Financial Matters
$17,070 tuition and fees (2001–02)
$500 room and board
80% average percent of need met
$13,399 average financial aid amount received per undergraduate

Academics
Covenant awards associate, bachelor's, and master's **degrees** (master's degree in education only). Challenging opportunities include advanced placement credit, student-designed majors, double majors, independent study, and a senior project. Special programs include internships, summer session for credit, off-campus study, and study-abroad.

The most frequently chosen **baccalaureate** fields are social sciences and history, education, and biological/life sciences. A complete listing of majors at Covenant appears in the Majors Index beginning on page 430.

The **faculty** at Covenant has 55 full-time members, 82% with terminal degrees. The student-faculty ratio is 15:1.

Students of Covenant
The student body totals 1,245, of whom 1,179 are undergraduates. 61.1% are women and 38.9% are men. Students come from 47 states and territories and 8 other countries. 23% are from Georgia. 1.2% are international students. 4.3% are African American, 1.8% Asian American, and 2.5% Hispanic American. 83% returned for their sophomore year.

Facilities and Resources
135 **computers** are available on campus that provide access to the Internet. The **library** has 61,502 books and 554 subscriptions.

Campus Life
There are 48 active organizations on campus, including a drama/theater group, newspaper, and choral group. No national or local **fraternities** or **sororities**.

Covenant is a member of the NAIA. **Intercollegiate sports** (some offering scholarships) include basketball, cross-country running, soccer, volleyball (w).

Campus Safety
Student safety services include night security guards.

Applying
Covenant requires an essay, SAT I or ACT, a high school transcript, an interview, 2 recommendations, and a minimum high school GPA of 2.5. It recommends SAT I. Application deadline: rolling admissions; 3/1 priority date for financial aid. Early and deferred admission are possible.

CREIGHTON UNIVERSITY

URBAN SETTING ■ PRIVATE ■ INDEPENDENT RELIGIOUS ■ COED
OMAHA, NEBRASKA

Web site: www.creighton.edu
Contact: Mr. Dennis J. O'Driscoll, Director of Admissions, 2500 California
  Plaza, Omaha, NE 68178-0001
Telephone: 402-280-2703 or toll-free 800-282-5835 **Fax:** 402-280-2685
E-mail: admissions@creighton.edu

Academics

Creighton awards associate, bachelor's, master's, doctoral, and first-professional
degrees. Challenging opportunities include advanced placement credit, accelerated
degree programs, an honors program, double majors, independent study, and a senior
project. Special programs include internships, summer session for credit, off-campus
study, study-abroad, and Army and Air Force ROTC.

The most frequently chosen **baccalaureate** fields are health professions and related
sciences, business/marketing, and biological/life sciences. A complete listing of majors at
Creighton appears in the Majors Index beginning on page 430.

The **faculty** at Creighton has 650 full-time members. The student-faculty ratio is
14:1.

Students of Creighton

The student body totals 6,297, of whom 3,679 are undergraduates. 58.1% are women
and 41.9% are men. Students come from 41 states and territories and 64 other countries.
54% are from Nebraska. 3.2% are international students. 2.8% are African American,
1.1% American Indian, 8.8% Asian American, and 3.3% Hispanic American. 85%
returned for their sophomore year.

Facilities and Resources

Student rooms are linked to a campus network. The 3 **libraries** have 481,848 books and
1,666 subscriptions.

Campus Life

There are 140 active organizations on campus, including a drama/theater group,
newspaper, radio station, television station, and choral group. 29% of eligible men and
30% of eligible women are members of national **fraternities** and national **sororities**.

Creighton is a member of the NCAA (Division I). **Intercollegiate sports** (some offering scholarships) include baseball (m), basketball, crew (w), cross-country running,
golf, soccer, softball (w), tennis, volleyball (w).

Campus Safety

Student safety services include late-night transport/escort service, 24-hour emergency
telephone alarm devices, 24-hour patrols by trained security personnel, student patrols,
and electronically operated dormitory entrances.

Applying

Creighton requires SAT I or ACT, a high school transcript, 1 recommendation, and a
minimum high school GPA of 2.75. It recommends an essay. Application deadline: 8/1;
5/15 priority date for financial aid. Deferred admission is possible.

Getting in Last Year

2,605 applied
90% were accepted
746 enrolled (32%)
33% from top tenth of their h.s. class
3.61 average high school GPA
37% had SAT verbal scores over 600
41% had SAT math scores over 600
68% had ACT scores over 24
4% had SAT verbal scores over 700
9% had SAT math scores over 700
12% had ACT scores over 30
56 valedictorians

Graduation and After

55% graduated in 4 years
10% graduated in 5 years
2% graduated in 6 years
54 organizations recruited on campus

Financial Matters

$17,136 tuition and fees (2001–02)
$6190 room and board
88% average percent of need met
$13,695 average financial aid amount received
  per undergraduate (2000–01)

DARTMOUTH COLLEGE

RURAL SETTING ■ PRIVATE ■ INDEPENDENT ■ COED
HANOVER, NEW HAMPSHIRE

Web site: www.dartmouth.edu
Contact: Mr. Karl M. Furstenberg, Dean of Admissions and Financial Aid,
  6016 McNutt Hall, Hanover, NH 03755
Telephone: 603-646-2875
E-mail: admissions.office@dartmouth.edu

From Daniel Webster to Dr. Seuss, Dartmouth College has empowered talented individuals to explore the life of the mind, to engage the world, and to build community. Members of the tightly knit student body profess an uncommon love for their alma mater. This dynamic group of women and men find common ground in intellectual pursuits and an appreciation of diversity. Dartmouth supports these core values with university-level resources that enable exceptional undergraduates to collaborate with distinguished faculty members and to work in cutting-edge research facilities.

Getting in Last Year
9,719 applied
23% were accepted
1,135 enrolled (51%)
86% from top tenth of their h.s. class
92% had SAT verbal scores over 600
96% had SAT math scores over 600
59% had SAT verbal scores over 700
66% had SAT math scores over 700

Graduation and After
20% pursued further study
215 organizations recruited on campus

Financial Matters
$26,562 tuition and fees (2001–02)
$7896 room and board
100% average percent of need met
$24,666 average financial aid amount received
  per undergraduate (2000–01 estimated)

Academics
Dartmouth awards bachelor's, master's, doctoral, and first-professional **degrees**. Challenging opportunities include advanced placement credit, accelerated degree programs, student-designed majors, an honors program, double majors, independent study, and a senior project. Special programs include internships, summer session for credit, off-campus study, study-abroad, and Army ROTC.

The most frequently chosen **baccalaureate** fields are social sciences and history, English, and biological/life sciences. A complete listing of majors at Dartmouth appears in the Majors Index beginning on page 430.

The **faculty** at Dartmouth has 446 full-time members, 96% with terminal degrees. The student-faculty ratio is 9:1.

Students of Dartmouth
The student body totals 5,495, of whom 4,118 are undergraduates. 48.6% are women and 51.4% are men. Students come from 52 states and territories and 64 other countries. 3% are from New Hampshire. 4.5% are international students. 5.7% are African American, 2.6% American Indian, 10.6% Asian American, and 5.8% Hispanic American. 97% returned for their sophomore year.

Facilities and Resources
Student rooms are linked to a campus network. 12,000 **computers** are available on campus that provide access to the Internet. The 11 **libraries** have 2,355,700 books and 20,679 subscriptions.

Campus Life
There are 250 active organizations on campus, including a drama/theater group, newspaper, radio station, television station, choral group, and marching band. 50% of eligible men and 48% of eligible women are members of national **fraternities**, national **sororities**, local fraternities, local sororities, and coed fraternities.

Dartmouth is a member of the NCAA (Division I). **Intercollegiate sports** include baseball (m), basketball, crew, cross-country running, equestrian sports, field hockey (w), football (m), golf, ice hockey, lacrosse, sailing, skiing (cross-country), skiing (downhill), soccer, softball (w), squash, swimming, tennis, track and field, volleyball (w).

Campus Safety
Student safety services include late-night transport/escort service, 24-hour emergency telephone alarm devices, 24-hour patrols by trained security personnel, student patrols, and electronically operated dormitory entrances.

Applying
Dartmouth requires an essay, SAT I and SAT II or ACT, a high school transcript, and 3 recommendations. It recommends an interview. Application deadline: 1/1; 2/1 for financial aid. Early and deferred admission are possible.

DAVIDSON COLLEGE

SMALL-TOWN SETTING ■ PRIVATE ■ INDEPENDENT RELIGIOUS ■ COED
DAVIDSON, NORTH CAROLINA

Web site: www.davidson.edu
Contact: Dr. Nancy J. Cable, Dean of Admission and Financial Aid, Box
7156, Davidson, NC 28035-7156
Telephone: 704-894-2230 or toll-free 800-768-0380 **Fax:** 704-894-2016
E-mail: admission@davidson.edu

Academics

Davidson awards bachelor's **degrees**. Challenging opportunities include advanced placement credit, accelerated degree programs, student-designed majors, an honors program,
double majors, independent study, and a senior project. Special programs include off-
campus study, study-abroad, and Army and Air Force ROTC.

The most frequently chosen **baccalaureate** fields are social sciences and history,
English, and biological/life sciences. A complete listing of majors at Davidson appears in
the Majors Index beginning on page 430.

The **faculty** at Davidson has 154 full-time members, 97% with terminal degrees.
The student-faculty ratio is 11:1.

Students of Davidson

The student body is made up of 1,673 undergraduates. 50.8% are women and 49.2% are
men. Students come from 44 states and territories and 32 other countries. 19% are from
North Carolina. 2.8% are international students. 5.3% are African American, 0.4%
American Indian, 2.5% Asian American, and 2.8% Hispanic American. 96% returned for
their sophomore year.

Facilities and Resources

Student rooms are linked to a campus network. 118 **computers** are available on campus
that provide access to the Internet. The 2 **libraries** have 569,981 books and 2,566
subscriptions.

Campus Life

There are 100 active organizations on campus, including a drama/theater group,
newspaper, radio station, and choral group. Davidson has national **fraternities** and
women's eating houses.

Davidson is a member of the NCAA (Division I). **Intercollegiate sports** (some offering scholarships) include baseball (m), basketball, cross-country running, field hockey
(w), football (m), golf (m), lacrosse (w), soccer, swimming, tennis, track and field, volleyball (w), wrestling (m).

Campus Safety

Student safety services include late-night transport/escort service, 24-hour emergency
telephone alarm devices, 24-hour patrols by trained security personnel, and electronically operated dormitory entrances.

Applying

Davidson requires an essay, SAT I or ACT, a high school transcript, and 4 recommendations. It recommends SAT II Subject Tests, SAT II: Writing Test, and an interview. Application deadline: 1/2; 2/15 priority date for financial aid. Early and deferred admission
are possible.

Davidson College is one of
the nation's premier
academic institutions, a
college of the liberal arts and
sciences respected for its intellectual
vigor, the high quality of its faculty
and students, and the achievements
of its alumni. It is distinguished by
its strong honor system, close
interaction between professors and
students, an environment that
encourages both intellectual growth
and community service, and a
commitment to international
education. Davidson places great
value on student participation in
extracurricular activities,
intercollegiate athletics, and
intramural sports. Nearby Charlotte,
North Carolina, offers students the
cultural, international, and internship
opportunities of a major
metropolitan center.

Getting in Last Year
3,363 applied
35% were accepted
465 enrolled (40%)
75% from top tenth of their h.s. class
83% had SAT verbal scores over 600
85% had SAT math scores over 600
90% had ACT scores over 24
31% had SAT verbal scores over 700
30% had SAT math scores over 700
40% had ACT scores over 30

Graduation and After
89% graduated in 4 years
2% graduated in 5 years
25% pursued further study
69% had job offers within 6 months
243 organizations recruited on campus

Financial Matters
$23,995 tuition and fees (2001–02)
$6828 room and board
100% average percent of need met
$14,947 average financial aid amount received
per undergraduate (2000–01)

DENISON UNIVERSITY

SMALL-TOWN SETTING ■ PRIVATE ■ INDEPENDENT ■ COED
GRANVILLE, OHIO

Web site: www.denison.edu
Contact: Mollie Rodenbeck, Campus Visit Coordinator, Box H, Granville, OH 43023
Telephone: 740-587-6276 or toll-free 800-DENISON
E-mail: admissions@denison.edu

Denison University, a 4-year, highly selective, national, residential liberal arts college for men and women, located in Granville, Ohio, is known for its intellectual rigor, curricular innovation, and unique faculty-student learning partnerships. Students may choose from 43 academic majors and concentrations and 9 preprofessional programs or design their own programs of study while living on the beautiful 1,200-acre hillside campus. Founded in 1831, Denison has more than 25,500 alumni and an endowment of $430 million.

Getting in Last Year
3,336 applied
58% were accepted
553 enrolled (28%)
50% from top tenth of their h.s. class
3.5 average high school GPA
51% had SAT verbal scores over 600
55% had SAT math scores over 600
82% had ACT scores over 24
12% had SAT verbal scores over 700
10% had SAT math scores over 700
20% had ACT scores over 30
15 National Merit Scholars
21 class presidents
26 valedictorians

Graduation and After
63% graduated in 4 years
4% graduated in 5 years
1% graduated in 6 years
22% pursued further study (8% arts and sciences, 5% medicine, 4% law)
75% had job offers within 6 months
45 organizations recruited on campus

Financial Matters
$23,090 tuition and fees (2001–02)
$6550 room and board
98% average percent of need met
$20,593 average financial aid amount received per undergraduate

Academics
Denison awards bachelor's **degrees**. Challenging opportunities include advanced placement credit, student-designed majors, an honors program, double majors, independent study, and a senior project. Special programs include cooperative education, internships, off-campus study, study-abroad, and Army ROTC.

The most frequently chosen **baccalaureate** fields are social sciences and history, communications/communication technologies, and biological/life sciences. A complete listing of majors at Denison appears in the Majors Index beginning on page 430.

The **faculty** at Denison has 179 full-time members, 96% with terminal degrees. The student-faculty ratio is 11:1.

Students of Denison
The student body is made up of 2,107 undergraduates. 57.1% are women and 42.9% are men. Students come from 50 states and territories and 29 other countries. 46% are from Ohio. 4.7% are international students. 5.4% are African American, 0.1% American Indian, 2.6% Asian American, and 1.9% Hispanic American. 87% returned for their sophomore year.

Facilities and Resources
Student rooms are linked to a campus network. 410 **computers** are available on campus that provide access to the Internet. The **library** has 687,933 books and 1,212 subscriptions.

Campus Life
There are 146 active organizations on campus, including a drama/theater group, newspaper, radio station, television station, and choral group. 32% of eligible men and 44% of eligible women are members of national **fraternities** and national **sororities**.

Denison is a member of the NCAA (Division III). **Intercollegiate sports** include baseball (m), basketball, cross-country running, field hockey (w), football (m), golf (m), lacrosse, soccer, softball (w), swimming, tennis, track and field, volleyball (w).

Campus Safety
Student safety services include security lighting, escort service, late-night transport/escort service, 24-hour emergency telephone alarm devices, 24-hour patrols by trained security personnel, student patrols, and electronically operated dormitory entrances.

Applying
Denison requires an essay, SAT I or ACT, a high school transcript, and 2 recommendations. It recommends SAT II Subject Tests and an interview. Application deadline: 2/1; 2/15 priority date for financial aid. Early and deferred admission are possible.

DePauw University

SMALL-TOWN SETTING ■ PRIVATE ■ INDEPENDENT RELIGIOUS ■ COED
GREENCASTLE, INDIANA

Web site: www.depauw.edu
Contact: Director of Admission, 101 East Seminary Street, Greencastle, IN 46135-0037
Telephone: 765-658-4006 or toll-free 800-447-2495 **Fax:** 765-658-4007
E-mail: admission@depauw.edu

Academics

DePauw awards bachelor's **degrees**. Challenging opportunities include advanced placement credit, student-designed majors, an honors program, double majors, independent study, and a senior project. Special programs include internships, off-campus study, study-abroad, and Army and Air Force ROTC.

The most frequently chosen **baccalaureate** fields are communications/communication technologies, English, and computer/information sciences. A complete listing of majors at DePauw appears in the Majors Index beginning on page 430.

The **faculty** at DePauw has 208 full-time members, 92% with terminal degrees. The student-faculty ratio is 10:1.

Students of DePauw

The student body is made up of 2,219 undergraduates. 56.3% are women and 43.7% are men. Students come from 43 states and territories and 16 other countries. 54% are from Indiana. 1.2% are international students. 5.5% are African American, 0.4% American Indian, 1.8% Asian American, and 2.4% Hispanic American. 92% returned for their sophomore year.

Facilities and Resources

Student rooms are linked to a campus network. 235 **computers** are available on campus that provide access to the Internet. The 4 **libraries** have 545,736 books and 2,134 subscriptions.

Campus Life

There are 65 active organizations on campus, including a drama/theater group, newspaper, radio station, television station, and choral group. 57% of eligible men and 54% of eligible women are members of national **fraternities**, national **sororities**, and local sororities.

DePauw is a member of the NCAA (Division III). **Intercollegiate sports** include baseball (m), basketball, cross-country running, field hockey (w), football (m), golf, soccer, softball (w), swimming, tennis, track and field, volleyball (w).

Campus Safety

Student safety services include late-night transport/escort service, 24-hour emergency telephone alarm devices, 24-hour patrols by trained security personnel, and electronically operated dormitory entrances.

Applying

DePauw requires an essay, SAT I or ACT, a high school transcript, and 1 recommendation. It recommends an interview and a minimum high school GPA of 3.0. Application deadline: 2/1; 2/15 priority date for financial aid. Early and deferred admission are possible.

Nationally recognized as a top liberal arts college, DePauw University provides a traditional education in a small, residential setting. There is 1 faculty member for every 10 of DePauw's 2,200 students, keeping class sizes small. Ranked number 1 in the nation for students studying abroad, DePauw also provides extensive internship opportunities as wide-ranging as MTV, Goldman Sachs, and the PGA Tour. More than half of DePauw's students volunteer for community service each year. Honors programs are offered in management, media, science, and technology, and DePauw's School of Music is one of the oldest in America.

Getting in Last Year
3,004 applied
53% were accepted
620 enrolled (39%)
52% from top tenth of their h.s. class
3.59 average high school GPA
48% had SAT verbal scores over 600
53% had SAT math scores over 600
77% had ACT scores over 24
11% had SAT verbal scores over 700
10% had SAT math scores over 700
17% had ACT scores over 30
7 National Merit Scholars
47 valedictorians

Graduation and After
75% graduated in 4 years
4% graduated in 5 years
1% graduated in 6 years
21% pursued further study (25% law, 8% medicine, 5% arts and sciences)
94% had job offers within 6 months
52 organizations recruited on campus

Financial Matters
$21,500 tuition and fees (2001–02)
$6500 room and board
100% average percent of need met
$18,740 average financial aid amount received per undergraduate

DICKINSON COLLEGE

SUBURBAN SETTING ■ PRIVATE ■ INDEPENDENT ■ COED
CARLISLE, PENNSYLVANIA

Web site: www.dickinson.edu
Contact: Mr. Christopher Seth Allen, Director of Admissions, PO Box 1773, Carlisle, PA 17013-2896
Telephone: 717-245-1231 or toll-free 800-644-1773 **Fax:** 717-245-1231
E-mail: admit@dickinson.edu

Getting in Last Year

3,820 applied
64% were accepted
611 enrolled (25%)
47% from top tenth of their h.s. class
66% had SAT verbal scores over 600
62% had SAT math scores over 600
15% had SAT verbal scores over 700
8% had SAT math scores over 700

Graduation and After

74% graduated in 4 years
3% graduated in 5 years
1% graduated in 6 years
17% pursued further study (7% arts and sciences, 4% law, 2% education)
98% had job offers within 6 months
59 organizations recruited on campus

Financial Matters

$25,485 tuition and fees (2001–02)
$6725 room and board
98% average percent of need met
$21,229 average financial aid amount received per undergraduate

Academics

Dickinson awards bachelor's **degrees**. Challenging opportunities include advanced placement credit, accelerated degree programs, student-designed majors, double majors, independent study, and a senior project. Special programs include internships, summer session for credit, off-campus study, study-abroad, and Army ROTC.

The most frequently chosen **baccalaureate** fields are social sciences and history, foreign language/literature, and English. A complete listing of majors at Dickinson appears in the Majors Index beginning on page 430.

The **faculty** at Dickinson has 163 full-time members, 90% with terminal degrees. The student-faculty ratio is 12:1.

Students of Dickinson

The student body is made up of 2,208 undergraduates. 58.5% are women and 41.5% are men. Students come from 48 states and territories and 18 other countries. 41% are from Pennsylvania. 1.3% are international students. 1.6% are African American, 0.2% American Indian, 2.1% Asian American, and 1.7% Hispanic American. 89% returned for their sophomore year.

Facilities and Resources

Student rooms are linked to a campus network. 472 **computers** are available on campus that provide access to the Internet. The 7 **libraries** have 305,272 books and 6,163 subscriptions.

Campus Life

There are 120 active organizations on campus, including a drama/theater group, newspaper, radio station, and choral group. 25% of eligible men and 26% of eligible women are members of national **fraternities**, national **sororities**, local fraternities, and local sororities.

Dickinson is a member of the NCAA (Division III). **Intercollegiate sports** include baseball (m), basketball, cross-country running, field hockey (w), football (m), golf, lacrosse, soccer, softball (w), swimming, tennis, track and field, volleyball (w).

Campus Safety

Student safety services include late-night transport/escort service, 24-hour emergency telephone alarm devices, 24-hour patrols by trained security personnel, student patrols, and electronically operated dormitory entrances.

Applying

Dickinson requires an essay, a high school transcript, and 2 recommendations. It recommends SAT I and SAT II or ACT, an interview, and a minimum high school GPA of 3.0. Application deadline: 2/1; 2/1 priority date for financial aid. Deferred admission is possible.

DRAKE UNIVERSITY

SUBURBAN SETTING ■ PRIVATE ■ INDEPENDENT ■ COED
DES MOINES, IOWA

Web site: www.drake.edu
Contact: Mr. Thomas F. Willoughby, Dean of Admission and Financial Aid, 2507 University Avenue, Des Moines, IA 50311
Telephone: 515-271-3181 or toll-free 800-44DRAKE **Fax:** 515-271-2831
E-mail: admission@drake.edu

Academics

Drake awards bachelor's, master's, doctoral, and first-professional **degrees**. Challenging opportunities include advanced placement credit, student-designed majors, an honors program, double majors, independent study, and a senior project. Special programs include cooperative education, internships, summer session for credit, off-campus study, study-abroad, and Army and Air Force ROTC.

The most frequently chosen **baccalaureate** fields are business/marketing, communications/communication technologies, and education. A complete listing of majors at Drake appears in the Majors Index beginning on page 430.

The **faculty** at Drake has 255 full-time members, 92% with terminal degrees. The student-faculty ratio is 13:1.

Students of Drake

The student body totals 5,150, of whom 3,577 are undergraduates. 61.1% are women and 38.9% are men. Students come from 43 states and territories and 57 other countries. 40% are from Iowa. 5% are international students. 3% are African American, 0.3% American Indian, 4.6% Asian American, and 1.6% Hispanic American. 81% returned for their sophomore year.

Facilities and Resources

Student rooms are linked to a campus network. 1,081 **computers** are available on campus that provide access to the Internet. The 2 **libraries** have 559,764 books and 2,120 subscriptions.

Campus Life

There are 150 active organizations on campus, including a drama/theater group, newspaper, radio station, television station, choral group, and marching band. 32% of eligible men and 30% of eligible women are members of national **fraternities** and national **sororities**.

Drake is a member of the NCAA (Division I). **Intercollegiate sports** (some offering scholarships) include basketball, crew (w), cross-country running, football (m), golf (m), soccer, softball (w), tennis, track and field, volleyball (w).

Campus Safety

Student safety services include 24-hour desk attendants in residence halls, late-night transport/escort service, 24-hour emergency telephone alarm devices, and 24-hour patrols by trained security personnel.

Applying

Drake requires SAT I or ACT and a high school transcript, and in some cases PCAT for pharmacy transfers. It recommends an essay and an interview. Application deadline: rolling admissions; 3/1 priority date for financial aid. Early and deferred admission are possible.

Drake University maximizes the potential of its students with a unique set of advantages. It is large enough to offer more than 70 undergraduate academic programs, 160 organizations, and a community of students from around the world. Yet Drake's exceptional faculty and academic and extracurricular options are highly accessible to students beginning their first year of college. Drake's location in Des Moines, Iowa's capital, offers numerous professional internships; 70% of Drake's undergraduates have at least one. Drake is affordable; 95% of its students receive financial assistance. It is a great value, too—more than 97% of Drake's graduates obtain career positions or enter graduate school within 6 months of graduating.

Getting in Last Year
2,735 applied
87% were accepted
757 enrolled (32%)
35% from top tenth of their h.s. class
3.58 average high school GPA
47% had SAT verbal scores over 600
38% had SAT math scores over 600
67% had ACT scores over 24
11% had SAT verbal scores over 700
6% had SAT math scores over 700
16% had ACT scores over 30
4 National Merit Scholars

Graduation and After
45% graduated in 4 years
10% graduated in 5 years
8% graduated in 6 years
17% pursued further study (6% arts and sciences, 4% law, 3% business)
97.7% had job offers within 6 months
110 organizations recruited on campus

Financial Matters
$17,790 tuition and fees (2001–02)
$5040 room and board
87% average percent of need met
$15,118 average financial aid amount received per undergraduate

DREW UNIVERSITY

SUBURBAN SETTING ■ PRIVATE ■ INDEPENDENT RELIGIOUS ■ COED
MADISON, NEW JERSEY

Getting in Last Year
2,513 applied
72% were accepted
397 enrolled (22%)
39% from top tenth of their h.s. class
60% had SAT verbal scores over 600
51% had SAT math scores over 600
16% had SAT verbal scores over 700
12% had SAT math scores over 700

Graduation and After
25% pursued further study (13% arts and sciences, 6% business, 5% law)

Financial Matters
$25,122 tuition and fees (2001–02)
$7030 room and board
83% average percent of need met
$18,093 average financial aid amount received per undergraduate (2000–01)

Web site: www.drew.edu
Contact: Mr. Roberto Noya, Dean of Admissions and Financial Aid, 36 Madison Avenue, Madison, NJ 07940
Telephone: 973-408-3739 **Fax:** 973-408-3036
E-mail: cadm@drew.edu

Academics

Drew awards bachelor's, master's, doctoral, and first-professional **degrees** and post-bachelor's certificates. Challenging opportunities include advanced placement credit, accelerated degree programs, student-designed majors, double majors, independent study, and a senior project. Special programs include internships, summer session for credit, off-campus study, study-abroad, and Army and Air Force ROTC.

The most frequently chosen **baccalaureate** fields are social sciences and history, psychology, and biological/life sciences. A complete listing of majors at Drew appears in the Majors Index beginning on page 430.

The **faculty** at Drew has 120 full-time members, 96% with terminal degrees. The student-faculty ratio is 11:1.

Students of Drew

The student body totals 2,418, of whom 1,536 are undergraduates. 61.5% are women and 38.5% are men. Students come from 37 states and territories and 18 other countries. 58% are from New Jersey. 1.7% are international students. 3.8% are African American, 0.4% American Indian, 6.3% Asian American, and 4.4% Hispanic American. 85% returned for their sophomore year.

Facilities and Resources

Student rooms are linked to a campus network. 200 **computers** are available on campus that provide access to the Internet. The **library** has 487,562 books and 3,066 subscriptions.

Campus Life

There are 80 active organizations on campus, including a drama/theater group, newspaper, radio station, television station, and choral group. No national or local **fraternities** or **sororities**.

Drew is a member of the NCAA (Division III). **Intercollegiate sports** include baseball (m), basketball, cross-country running, equestrian sports, fencing, field hockey (w), lacrosse, soccer, softball (w), swimming, tennis.

Campus Safety

Student safety services include late-night transport/escort service, 24-hour emergency telephone alarm devices, 24-hour patrols by trained security personnel, and electronically operated dormitory entrances.

Applying

Drew requires an essay, SAT I or ACT, a high school transcript, and 1 recommendation. It recommends an interview and 1 recommendation. Application deadline: 2/15; 2/15 for financial aid. Early and deferred admission are possible.

DUKE UNIVERSITY

SUBURBAN SETTING ■ PRIVATE ■ INDEPENDENT RELIGIOUS ■ COED
DURHAM, NORTH CAROLINA

Web site: www.duke.edu
Contact: Mr. Christoph Guttentag, Director of Admissions, 2138 Campus
  Drive, Durham, NC 27708
Telephone: 919-684-3214 **Fax:** 919-684-8941
E-mail: askduke@admiss.duke.edu

Academics

Duke awards bachelor's, master's, doctoral, and first-professional **degrees** and post-master's certificates. Challenging opportunities include advanced placement credit, accelerated degree programs, student-designed majors, an honors program, independent study, and a senior project. Special programs include internships, summer session for credit, off-campus study, study-abroad, and Army, Navy and Air Force ROTC.

The most frequently chosen **baccalaureate** fields are social sciences and history, biological/life sciences, and engineering/engineering technologies. A complete listing of majors at Duke appears in the Majors Index beginning on page 430.

The **faculty** at Duke has 2,299 full-time members, 97% with terminal degrees. The student-faculty ratio is 11:1.

Students of Duke

The student body totals 11,794, of whom 6,071 are undergraduates. 48.5% are women and 51.5% are men. Students come from 52 states and territories and 85 other countries. 15% are from North Carolina. 4.2% are international students. 10.4% are African American, 0.4% American Indian, 11.9% Asian American, and 5.7% Hispanic American. 96% returned for their sophomore year.

Facilities and Resources

Student rooms are linked to a campus network. 600 **computers** are available on campus that provide access to the Internet. The 12 **libraries** have 4,960,746 books and 31,941 subscriptions.

Campus Life

There are 350 active organizations on campus, including a drama/theater group, newspaper, radio station, television station, choral group, and marching band. 29% of eligible men and 42% of eligible women are members of national **fraternities** and national **sororities**.

Duke is a member of the NCAA (Division I). **Intercollegiate sports** (some offering scholarships) include baseball (m), basketball, crew (w), cross-country running, fencing, field hockey (w), football (m), golf, lacrosse, soccer, swimming, tennis, track and field, volleyball (w), wrestling (m).

Campus Safety

Student safety services include late-night transport/escort service, 24-hour emergency telephone alarm devices, 24-hour patrols by trained security personnel, and electronically operated dormitory entrances.

Applying

Duke requires an essay, SAT I or ACT, a high school transcript, and 3 recommendations, and in some cases SAT II Subject Tests and SAT II: Writing Test. It recommends an interview, audition tape for applicants with outstanding dance, dramatic, or musical talent; slides of artwork, and a minimum high school GPA of 3.0. Application deadline: 1/2; 2/1 for financial aid. Early and deferred admission are possible.

Getting in Last Year
13,976 applied
26% were accepted
1,615 enrolled (44%)
86% from top tenth of their h.s. class
3.85 average high school GPA
91% had SAT verbal scores over 600
94% had SAT math scores over 600
98% had ACT scores over 24
50% had SAT verbal scores over 700
63% had SAT math scores over 700
58% had ACT scores over 30
196 valedictorians

Graduation and After
88% graduated in 4 years
5% graduated in 5 years
25% pursued further study (7% law, 6% medicine, 3% arts and sciences)
45% had job offers within 6 months
245 organizations recruited on campus

Financial Matters
$26,768 tuition and fees (2001–02)
$7628 room and board
100% average percent of need met
$22,687 average financial aid amount received per undergraduate

Duquesne University

URBAN SETTING ■ PRIVATE ■ INDEPENDENT RELIGIOUS ■ COED
PITTSBURGH, PENNSYLVANIA

Web site: www.duq.edu
Contact: Office of Admissions, 600 Forbes Avenue, Pittsburgh, PA
15282-0201
Telephone: 412-396-5000 or toll-free 800-456-0590 **Fax:** 412-396-5644
E-mail: admissions@duq.edu

Getting in Last Year
3,139 applied
96% were accepted
1,191 enrolled (39%)
22% from top tenth of their h.s. class
3.40 average high school GPA
23% had SAT verbal scores over 600
25% had SAT math scores over 600
41% had ACT scores over 24
2% had SAT verbal scores over 700
3% had SAT math scores over 700
4% had ACT scores over 30
39 valedictorians

Graduation and After
25% pursued further study
82% had job offers within 6 months
850 organizations recruited on campus

Financial Matters
$17,478 tuition and fees (2001–02)
$6764 room and board
82% average percent of need met
$13,444 average financial aid amount received
per undergraduate

Academics
Duquesne awards bachelor's, master's, doctoral, and first-professional **degrees** and post-bachelor's and post-master's certificates. Challenging opportunities include advanced placement credit, accelerated degree programs, student-designed majors, freshman honors college, an honors program, double majors, independent study, and a senior project. Special programs include cooperative education, internships, summer session for credit, off-campus study, study-abroad, and Army, Navy and Air Force ROTC.

The most frequently chosen **baccalaureate** fields are business/marketing, health professions and related sciences, and education. A complete listing of majors at Duquesne appears in the Majors Index beginning on page 430.

The **faculty** at Duquesne has 410 full-time members. The student-faculty ratio is 14:1.

Students of Duquesne
The student body totals 9,451, of whom 5,404 are undergraduates. 57.9% are women and 42.1% are men. Students come from 48 states and territories and 83 other countries. 82% are from Pennsylvania. 3% are international students. 4% are African American, 0.1% American Indian, 1.4% Asian American, and 1.8% Hispanic American. 85% returned for their sophomore year.

Facilities and Resources
Student rooms are linked to a campus network. 650 **computers** are available on campus that provide access to the Internet. The 2 **libraries** have 325,377 books and 4,135 subscriptions.

Campus Life
There are 134 active organizations on campus, including a drama/theater group, newspaper, radio station, television station, choral group, and marching band. 14% of eligible men and 14% of eligible women are members of national **fraternities**, national **sororities**, local fraternities, and local sororities.

Duquesne is a member of the NCAA (Division I). **Intercollegiate sports** (some offering scholarships) include baseball (m), basketball, crew (w), cross-country running, football (m), golf (m), lacrosse (w), riflery, soccer, swimming, tennis, track and field (w), volleyball (w), wrestling (m).

Campus Safety
Student safety services include 24-hour front desk personnel, 24-hour video monitors at residence hall entrances, surveillance cameras throughout the campus, late-night transport/escort service, 24-hour emergency telephone alarm devices, 24-hour patrols by trained security personnel, and electronically operated dormitory entrances.

Applying
Duquesne requires an essay, SAT I or ACT, and a high school transcript, and in some cases an interview and a minimum high school GPA of 2.75. It recommends 1 recommendation. Application deadline: 7/1; 5/1 for financial aid. Early and deferred admission are possible.

Earlham College

SMALL-TOWN SETTING ■ PRIVATE ■ INDEPENDENT RELIGIOUS ■ COED
RICHMOND, INDIANA

Web site: www.earlham.edu

Contact: Director of Admissions, 801 National Road West, Richmond, IN 47374

Telephone: 765-983-1200 or toll-free 800-327-5426 **Fax:** 765-983-1560

E-mail: admission@earlham.edu

Earlham College, founded in 1847 by the Society of Friends, is an independent liberal arts college. Earlham students live in a community in which learning is challenging, exciting, and cooperative. More than 50% of students study abroad, with another 15 to 20% studying off campus at locations in the U.S. In the classroom, Earlham introduces students to a learning style that encourages questions and discussion. Outside the classroom, students are encouraged to become involved in any of the more than 65 student organizations and to fully engage in the fun of college life. Earlham alumni are leaders in education, medicine, politics, and business.

Academics

Earlham awards bachelor's and master's **degrees**. Challenging opportunities include advanced placement credit, accelerated degree programs, student-designed majors, double majors, independent study, and a senior project. Special programs include internships, off-campus study, and study-abroad.

The most frequently chosen **baccalaureate** fields are social sciences and history, psychology, and biological/life sciences. A complete listing of majors at Earlham appears in the Majors Index beginning on page 430.

The **faculty** at Earlham has 92 full-time members, 97% with terminal degrees. The student-faculty ratio is 11:1.

Students of Earlham

The student body totals 1,098, of whom 1,078 are undergraduates. 55.4% are women and 44.6% are men. Students come from 48 states and territories and 30 other countries. 28% are from Indiana. 4.9% are international students. 8.1% are African American, 0.1% American Indian, 2.5% Asian American, and 2.4% Hispanic American. 89% returned for their sophomore year.

Facilities and Resources

Student rooms are linked to a campus network. 116 **computers** are available on campus that provide access to the Internet. The 2 **libraries** have 389,000 books and 1,195 subscriptions.

Campus Life

There are 66 active organizations on campus, including a drama/theater group, newspaper, radio station, and choral group. No national or local **fraternities** or **sororities**.

Earlham is a member of the NCAA (Division III). **Intercollegiate sports** include baseball (m), basketball, cross-country running, field hockey (w), football (m), lacrosse (w), soccer, tennis, track and field, volleyball (w).

Campus Safety

Student safety services include late-night transport/escort service, 24-hour emergency telephone alarm devices, 24-hour patrols by trained security personnel, student patrols, and electronically operated dormitory entrances.

Applying

Earlham requires an essay, SAT I or ACT, a high school transcript, 2 recommendations, and a minimum high school GPA of 3.0. It recommends SAT I and an interview. Application deadline: 2/15; 3/1 priority date for financial aid. Early and deferred admission are possible.

Getting in Last Year
1,153 applied
80% were accepted
267 enrolled (29%)
26% from top tenth of their h.s. class
3.35 average high school GPA
66% had SAT verbal scores over 600
46% had SAT math scores over 600
67% had ACT scores over 24
20% had SAT verbal scores over 700
11% had SAT math scores over 700
23% had ACT scores over 30
5 National Merit Scholars
8 class presidents
7 valedictorians

Graduation and After
19% pursued further study (10% arts and sciences, 2% medicine, 1% engineering)
73% had job offers within 6 months
65 organizations recruited on campus

Financial Matters
$22,308 tuition and fees (2001–02)
$5138 room and board
94% average percent of need met
$19,343 average financial aid amount received per undergraduate

ECKERD COLLEGE

SUBURBAN SETTING ■ PRIVATE ■ INDEPENDENT RELIGIOUS ■ COED
ST. PETERSBURG, FLORIDA

Web site: www.eckerd.edu
Contact: Dr. Richard R. Hallin, Dean of Admissions, 4200 54th Avenue
  South, St. Petersburg, FL 33711
Telephone: 727-864-8331 or toll-free 800-456-9009 **Fax:** 727-866-2304
E-mail: admissions@eckerd.edu

Academics

Eckerd awards bachelor's **degrees**. Challenging opportunities include advanced place-ment credit, accelerated degree programs, student-designed majors, an honors program, double majors, independent study, and a senior project. Special programs include cooperative education, internships, summer session for credit, off-campus study, study-abroad, and Army and Air Force ROTC.

The most frequently chosen **baccalaureate** fields are biological/life sciences, busi-ness/marketing, and social sciences and history. A complete listing of majors at Eckerd appears in the Majors Index beginning on page 430.

The **faculty** at Eckerd has 97 full-time members, 95% with terminal degrees. The student-faculty ratio is 14:1.

Students of Eckerd

The student body is made up of 1,582 undergraduates. 55.6% are women and 44.4% are men. Students come from 50 states and territories and 49 other countries. 27% are from Florida. 9.6% are international students. 2.2% are African American, 1.5% Asian American, and 4% Hispanic American. 77% returned for their sophomore year.

Facilities and Resources

Student rooms are linked to a campus network. 144 **computers** are available on campus that provide access to the Internet. The **library** has 113,850 books and 3,009 subscrip-tions.

Campus Life

There are 50 active organizations on campus, including a drama/theater group, newspaper, radio station, television station, and choral group. No national or local **fraternities** or **sororities**.

Eckerd is a member of the NCAA (Division II). **Intercollegiate sports** (some offer-ing scholarships) include baseball (m), basketball, cross-country running (w), golf (m), sailing, soccer, softball (w), tennis, volleyball (w).

Campus Safety

Student safety services include late-night transport/escort service, 24-hour emergency telephone alarm devices, 24-hour patrols by trained security personnel, student patrols, and electronically operated dormitory entrances.

Applying

Eckerd requires an essay, SAT I or ACT, a high school transcript, and 1 recom-mendation. It recommends SAT II Subject Tests, SAT II: Writing Test, an interview, and a minimum high school GPA of 3.0. Application deadline: rolling admissions; 4/1 prior-ity date for financial aid. Early and deferred admission are possible.

The Eckerd campus is a peaceful, tropical setting bordering Tampa Bay and the Gulf of Mexico. Students feel very secure in the suburban environment and have easy access to the cultural, social, and recreational opportunities of the Tampa Bay metropolitan area. Classes are small. Independent study and study-abroad experiences are encouraged. Almost all students live on campus, where a sense of community flourishes. Students enjoy a great deal of freedom in their social lives and in the design of their academic programs. Volunteer service is extensive, since the Eckerd Honor Code encourages students to be "givers" rather than "takers."

Getting in Last Year
1,930 applied
78% were accepted
424 enrolled (28%)
23% from top tenth of their h.s. class
3.50 average high school GPA
32% had SAT verbal scores over 600
29% had SAT math scores over 600
51% had ACT scores over 24
8% had SAT verbal scores over 700
5% had SAT math scores over 700
8% had ACT scores over 30
8 National Merit Scholars
27 class presidents
15 valedictorians

Graduation and After
55% graduated in 4 years
5% graduated in 5 years
1% graduated in 6 years
27% pursued further study
45% had job offers within 6 months
140 organizations recruited on campus

Financial Matters
$20,085 tuition and fees (2001–02)
$2550 room and board
85% average percent of need met
$17,608 average financial aid amount received
  per undergraduate

ELIZABETHTOWN COLLEGE

SMALL-TOWN SETTING ■ PRIVATE ■ INDEPENDENT RELIGIOUS ■ COED
ELIZABETHTOWN, PENNSYLVANIA

Web site: www.etown.edu
Contact: W. Kent Barnds, Director of Admissions, 1 Alpha Drive,
    Elizabethtown, PA 17022-2298
Telephone: 717-361-1400 **Fax:** 717-361-1365
E-mail: admissions@acad.etown.edu

Academics

E-town awards associate, bachelor's, and master's **degrees** and post-bachelor's certificates. Challenging opportunities include advanced placement credit, an honors program, double majors, independent study, and a senior project. Special programs include internships, summer session for credit, off-campus study, and study-abroad.

The most frequently chosen **baccalaureate** fields are business/marketing, education, and health professions and related sciences. A complete listing of majors at E-town appears in the Majors Index beginning on page 430.

The **faculty** at E-town has 110 full-time members, 85% with terminal degrees. The student-faculty ratio is 12:1.

Students of E-town

The student body is made up of 1,901 undergraduates. 62.4% are women and 37.6% are men. Students come from 30 states and territories and 30 other countries. 69% are from Pennsylvania. 3.3% are international students. 1.4% are African American, 0.2% American Indian, 1.3% Asian American, and 1.2% Hispanic American. 84% returned for their sophomore year.

Facilities and Resources

Student rooms are linked to a campus network. 175 **computers** are available on campus that provide access to e-mail, file space, personal Web page and the Internet. The 2 **libraries** have 184,052 books and 1,090 subscriptions.

Campus Life

There are 80 active organizations on campus, including a drama/theater group, newspaper, radio station, television station, and choral group. No national or local **fraternities** or **sororities**.

E-town is a member of the NCAA (Division III). **Intercollegiate sports** include baseball (m), basketball, cross-country running, field hockey (w), golf (m), lacrosse, soccer, softball (w), swimming, tennis, track and field, volleyball (w), wrestling (m).

Campus Safety

Student safety services include self-defense workshops, crime prevention program, late-night transport/escort service, 24-hour emergency telephone alarm devices, 24-hour patrols by trained security personnel, and student patrols.

Applying

E-town requires an essay, SAT I or ACT, a high school transcript, 2 recommendations, and a minimum high school GPA of 2.0, and in some cases an interview. It recommends an interview and a minimum high school GPA of 3.0. Application deadline: rolling admissions; 3/15 priority date for financial aid. Early and deferred admission are possible.

Elizabethtown College is exceeding expectations for personal attention, experiential learning, and combining the liberal arts with professional programs. The College is located in south-central Pennsylvania, near Hershey and Harrisburg, the state capital. Faculty members put student learning first and take pride in mentoring. Diverse opportunities, great facilities, collaborative research, internships, and the College's residential environment provide the perfect atmosphere for experiential learning. Athletes excel within nationally competitive programs. Musical ensembles and theater groups perform throughout the region, and students are leaders in more than 80 clubs and organizations. The College offers 40 majors and 50 minors. Elizabethtown allows graduates to distinguish themselves to employers and graduate schools.

Getting in Last Year
2,763 applied
69% were accepted
542 enrolled (29%)
31% from top tenth of their h.s. class
30% had SAT verbal scores over 600
30% had SAT math scores over 600
40% had ACT scores over 24
3% had SAT verbal scores over 700
3% had SAT math scores over 700
9% had ACT scores over 30
13 class presidents
9 valedictorians

Graduation and After
66% graduated in 4 years
4% graduated in 5 years
28% pursued further study
90% had job offers within 6 months
33 organizations recruited on campus

Financial Matters
$21,350 tuition and fees (2001–02)
$6000 room and board
89% average percent of need met
$15,714 average financial aid amount received
    per undergraduate

ELMIRA COLLEGE

SMALL-TOWN SETTING ■ PRIVATE ■ INDEPENDENT ■ COED
ELMIRA, NEW YORK

Web site: www.elmira.edu
Contact: Mr. William S. Neal, Dean of Admissions, Office of Admissions, Elmira, NY 14901
Telephone: 607-735-1724 or toll-free 800-935-6472 **Fax:** 607-735-1718
E-mail: admissions@elmira.edu

Getting in Last Year
1,691 applied
80% were accepted
370 enrolled (28%)
32% from top tenth of their h.s. class
3.50 average high school GPA
22% had SAT verbal scores over 600
17% had SAT math scores over 600
54% had ACT scores over 24
3% had SAT verbal scores over 700
1% had SAT math scores over 700
2% had ACT scores over 30
1 National Merit Scholar
38 class presidents
39 valedictorians

Graduation and After
55% graduated in 4 years
1% graduated in 5 years
41% pursued further study (18% arts and sciences, 11% business, 7% education)
50% had job offers within 6 months
58 organizations recruited on campus

Financial Matters
$23,540 tuition and fees (2001–02)
$7530 room and board
90% average percent of need met
$19,393 average financial aid amount received per undergraduate

Academics
Elmira awards bachelor's **degrees**. Challenging opportunities include advanced placement credit, accelerated degree programs, student-designed majors, and independent study. Special programs include internships, summer session for credit, off-campus study, study-abroad, and Army and Air Force ROTC.

The most frequently chosen **baccalaureate** fields are education, psychology, and business/marketing. A complete listing of majors at Elmira appears in the Majors Index beginning on page 430.

The **faculty** at Elmira has 80 full-time members, 100% with terminal degrees. The student-faculty ratio is 12:1.

Students of Elmira
The student body totals 1,941, of whom 1,584 are undergraduates. 69.1% are women and 30.9% are men. Students come from 35 states and territories and 18 other countries. 52% are from New York. 6.4% are international students. 2% are African American, 0.2% American Indian, 0.7% Asian American, and 1.5% Hispanic American. 79% returned for their sophomore year.

Facilities and Resources
Student rooms are linked to a campus network. 90 **computers** are available on campus that provide access to the Internet. The **library** has 389,036 books and 855 subscriptions.

Campus Life
There are 70 active organizations on campus, including a drama/theater group, newspaper, radio station, and choral group. No national or local **fraternities** or **sororities**.

Elmira is a member of the NCAA (Division III). **Intercollegiate sports** include basketball, field hockey (w), golf, ice hockey, lacrosse, soccer, softball (w), tennis, volleyball (w).

Campus Safety
Student safety services include 24-hour locked residence hall entrances, late-night transport/escort service, and 24-hour patrols by trained security personnel.

Applying
Elmira requires an essay, SAT I or ACT, a high school transcript, 2 recommendations, and a minimum high school GPA of 2.0, and in some cases an interview. It recommends an interview. Application deadline: 5/15; 2/1 priority date for financial aid. Early and deferred admission are possible.

EMBRY-RIDDLE AERONAUTICAL UNIVERSITY

SMALL-TOWN SETTING ■ PRIVATE ■ INDEPENDENT ■ COED, PRIMARILY MEN
PRESCOTT, ARIZONA

Web site: www.embryriddle.edu
Contact: Bill Thompson, Director of Admissions, 3200 Willow Creek Road, Prescott, AZ 86301
Telephone: 928-777-6692 or toll-free 800-888-3728 **Fax:** 928-777-6606
E-mail: admit@pc.erau.edu

Academics

Embry-Riddle awards bachelor's and master's **degrees**. Challenging opportunities include advanced placement credit, double majors, independent study, and a senior project. Special programs include cooperative education, internships, summer session for credit, study-abroad, and Army and Air Force ROTC.

The most frequently chosen **baccalaureate** fields are trade and industry, engineering/engineering technologies, and computer/information sciences. A complete listing of majors at Embry-Riddle appears in the Majors Index beginning on page 430.

The **faculty** at Embry-Riddle has 76 full-time members, 55% with terminal degrees. The student-faculty ratio is 18:1.

Students of Embry-Riddle

The student body totals 1,740, of whom 1,724 are undergraduates. 16.1% are women and 83.9% are men. Students come from 53 states and territories and 33 other countries. 22% are from Arizona. 8.8% are international students. 1.2% are African American, 1.3% American Indian, 6% Asian American, and 5.2% Hispanic American. 77% returned for their sophomore year.

Facilities and Resources

Student rooms are linked to a campus network. 200 **computers** are available on campus for student use. The **library** has 26,130 books and 575 subscriptions.

Campus Life

There are 61 active organizations on campus, including a newspaper and radio station. 85% of eligible men and 93% of eligible women are members of national **fraternities** and national **sororities**.

Embry-Riddle is a member of the NAIA. **Intercollegiate sports** (some offering scholarships) include volleyball (w), wrestling (m).

Campus Safety

Student safety services include late-night transport/escort service, 24-hour emergency telephone alarm devices, 24-hour patrols by trained security personnel, and student patrols.

Applying

Embry-Riddle requires SAT I or ACT, a high school transcript, and a minimum high school GPA of 2.0, and in some cases medical examination for flight students and a minimum high school GPA of 3.0. It recommends an essay, an interview, and recommendations. Application deadline: rolling admissions; 6/30 for financial aid, with a 4/15 priority date. Early and deferred admission are possible.

Embry-Riddle continues to integrate engineering, technology, and global education with bachelor's degrees related to careers in the aviation and aerospace industry. Embry-Riddle graduates are uniquely prepared to be leaders and global citizens with the skill-set to understand and function effectively within global relationships, political systems, cultures, and natural environments. Students enjoy small class sizes, classes related to current topics in the industry, and caring professors. Students have the opportunity to engage in international exchange programs, present design projects at national conferences, get involved in internships, and take field trips—all leading to exciting career options upon graduation.

Getting in Last Year
1,330 applied
79% were accepted
375 enrolled (36%)
14% from top tenth of their h.s. class
3.38 average high school GPA
25% had SAT verbal scores over 600
35% had SAT math scores over 600
55% had ACT scores over 24
2% had SAT verbal scores over 700
5% had SAT math scores over 700
8% had ACT scores over 30

Graduation and After
5% pursued further study
90% had job offers within 6 months
85 organizations recruited on campus

Financial Matters
$18,210 tuition and fees (2001–02)
$5040 room and board
$9736 average financial aid amount received per undergraduate (2000–01)

Emerson College

URBAN SETTING ■ PRIVATE ■ INDEPENDENT ■ COED
BOSTON, MASSACHUSETTS

Web site: www.emerson.edu
Contact: Ms. Sara Ramirez, Director of Admission, 120 Boylston Street, Boston, MA 02116-4624
Telephone: 617-824-8600 **Fax:** 617-824-8609
E-mail: admission@emerson.edu

Boston is one of the country's most popular college towns, and Emerson's campus is located on Boston Common in the heart of the city's Theatre District. WERS-FM, the 950-seat Emerson Majestic Theatre, and the award-winning literary journal, *Ploughshares,* are located here. Emerson's 2,700 students come from more than 45 states and 60 other countries and participate in more than 50 student organizations and performance groups, NCAA intercollegiate teams, student publications, and honor societies. The College also sponsors programs in Los Angeles and Kasteel Well (the Netherlands), summer film study in Prague, and course cross-registration with the 6-member Boston Pro-Arts Consortium.

Getting in Last Year
4,071 applied
47% were accepted
639 enrolled (33%)
26% from top tenth of their h.s. class
3.45 average high school GPA
61% had SAT verbal scores over 600
41% had SAT math scores over 600
74% had ACT scores over 24
14% had SAT verbal scores over 700
5% had SAT math scores over 700
12% had ACT scores over 30
10 valedictorians

Graduation and After
7% pursued further study
87% had job offers within 6 months
55 organizations recruited on campus

Financial Matters
$20,718 tuition and fees (2001–02)
$9290 room and board
68% average percent of need met
$12,500 average financial aid amount received per undergraduate (2000–01)

Academics
Emerson awards bachelor's, master's, and doctoral **degrees**. Challenging opportunities include advanced placement credit, student-designed majors, an honors program, double majors, independent study, and a senior project. Special programs include internships, summer session for credit, off-campus study, and study-abroad.

The most frequently chosen **baccalaureate** fields are communications/communication technologies, visual/performing arts, and English. A complete listing of majors at Emerson appears in the Majors Index beginning on page 430.

The **faculty** at Emerson has 124 full-time members, 79% with terminal degrees. The student-faculty ratio is 15:1.

Students of Emerson
The student body totals 4,339, of whom 3,412 are undergraduates. 60.1% are women and 39.9% are men. Students come from 51 states and territories and 3 other countries. 35% are from Massachusetts. 5.4% are international students. 1.5% are African American, 0.3% American Indian, 2.7% Asian American, and 3.7% Hispanic American. 84% returned for their sophomore year.

Facilities and Resources
Student rooms are linked to a campus network. 265 **computers** are available on campus that provide access to the Internet. The 2 **libraries** have 193,000 books and 7,430 subscriptions.

Campus Life
There are 52 active organizations on campus, including a drama/theater group, newspaper, radio station, and television station. 4% of eligible men and 4% of eligible women are members of national **fraternities**, national **sororities**, local fraternities, and local sororities.

Emerson is a member of the NCAA (Division III). **Intercollegiate sports** include baseball (m), basketball, cross-country running, lacrosse (m), soccer, softball (w), tennis, volleyball (w).

Campus Safety
Student safety services include late-night transport/escort service, 24-hour emergency telephone alarm devices, 24-hour patrols by trained security personnel, and electronically operated dormitory entrances.

Applying
Emerson requires an essay, SAT I or ACT, a high school transcript, and 2 recommendations, and in some cases an interview and audition, portfolio, or resume for performing arts applicants. Application deadline: 2/1; 3/1 priority date for financial aid. Early and deferred admission are possible.

EMORY UNIVERSITY

SUBURBAN SETTING ■ PRIVATE ■ INDEPENDENT RELIGIOUS ■ COED
ATLANTA, GEORGIA

Web site: www.emory.edu
Contact: Mr. Daniel C. Walls, Dean of Admission, Boisfeuillet Jones Center–
Office of Admissions, Atlanta, GA 30322-1100
Telephone: 404-727-6036 or toll-free 800-727-6036
E-mail: admiss@unix.cc.emory.edu

Academics

Emory awards bachelor's, master's, doctoral, and first-professional **degrees** (enrollment figures include Emory University, Oxford College; application data for main campus only). Challenging opportunities include advanced placement credit, accelerated degree programs, an honors program, double majors, and a senior project. Special programs include internships, summer session for credit, off-campus study, study-abroad, and Air Force ROTC.

The most frequently chosen **baccalaureate** fields are social sciences and history, business/marketing, and biological/life sciences. A complete listing of majors at Emory appears in the Majors Index beginning on page 430.

The **faculty** at Emory has 1,848 full-time members, 100% with terminal degrees. The student-faculty ratio is 7:1.

Students of Emory

The student body totals 11,443, of whom 6,374 are undergraduates. 55.1% are women and 44.9% are men. Students come from 52 states and territories and 59 other countries. 20% are from Georgia. 3.2% are international students. 9.6% are African American, 0.2% American Indian, 15.2% Asian American, and 3.2% Hispanic American. 94% returned for their sophomore year.

Facilities and Resources

Student rooms are linked to a campus network. 600 **computers** are available on campus that provide access to the Internet. The 8 **libraries** have 2,300,000 books and 24,687 subscriptions.

Campus Life

There are 200 active organizations on campus, including a drama/theater group, newspaper, radio station, television station, and choral group. 35% of eligible men and 35% of eligible women are members of national **fraternities** and national **sororities**.

Emory is a member of the NCAA (Division III). **Intercollegiate sports** include baseball (m), basketball, cross-country running, golf (m), soccer, softball (w), swimming, tennis, track and field, volleyball (w).

Campus Safety

Student safety services include late-night transport/escort service, 24-hour emergency telephone alarm devices, 24-hour patrols by trained security personnel, and student patrols.

Applying

Emory requires an essay, SAT I or ACT, a high school transcript, and 1 recommendation. It recommends SAT II Subject Tests and a minimum high school GPA of 3.0. Application deadline: 1/15; 4/1 for financial aid, with a 2/15 priority date. Early and deferred admission are possible.

Getting in Last Year
9,607 applied
43% were accepted
1,558 enrolled (38%)
88% from top tenth of their h.s. class
3.80 average high school GPA
83% had SAT verbal scores over 600
91% had SAT math scores over 600
100% had ACT scores over 24
21% had SAT verbal scores over 700
31% had SAT math scores over 700
40% had ACT scores over 30
56 National Merit Scholars

Graduation and After
82% graduated in 4 years
4% graduated in 5 years
1% graduated in 6 years
74% pursued further study (25% medicine, 22% law, 20% arts and sciences)
250 organizations recruited on campus

Financial Matters
$25,552 tuition and fees (2001–02)
$8240 room and board
100% average percent of need met
$22,530 average financial aid amount received per undergraduate

EUGENE LANG COLLEGE, NEW SCHOOL UNIVERSITY

URBAN SETTING ■ PRIVATE ■ INDEPENDENT ■ COED
NEW YORK, NEW YORK

Web site: www.newschool.edu
Contact: Mr. Terence Peavy, Director of Admissions, 65 West 11th Street, New York, NY 10011-8601
Telephone: 212-229-5665
E-mail: lang@newschool.edu

Eugene Lang College offers students of diverse backgrounds the opportunity to design their own program of study within one of 5 interdisciplinary liberal arts concentrations in the social sciences and the humanities. Students discuss and debate issues in small seminar courses that are never larger than 19 students. They enrich their programs with internships in a wide variety of areas, such as media and publishing, community service, and education, and they can pursue a dual degree at one of the University's 5 other divisions. The Greenwich Village location makes all the cultural treasures of the city—museums, libraries, dance, music, and theater—a distinct part of the campus.

Getting in Last Year
686 applied
65% were accepted
155 enrolled (35%)
24% from top tenth of their h.s. class
3.09 average high school GPA
66% had SAT verbal scores over 600
37% had SAT math scores over 600
22% had SAT verbal scores over 700
3% had SAT math scores over 700
5 class presidents
4 valedictorians

Graduation and After
82% had job offers within 6 months

Financial Matters
$21,980 tuition and fees (2001–02)
$9612 room and board
70% average percent of need met
$16,048 average financial aid amount received per undergraduate

Academics
Eugene Lang College awards bachelor's **degrees**. Challenging opportunities include accelerated degree programs, independent study, and a senior project. Special programs include internships, summer session for credit, off-campus study, and study-abroad.

The most frequently chosen **baccalaureate** field is liberal arts/general studies. A complete listing of majors at Eugene Lang College appears in the Majors Index beginning on page 430.

The **faculty** at Eugene Lang College has 53 full-time members. The student-faculty ratio is 10:1.

Students of Eugene Lang College
The student body is made up of 595 undergraduates. 67.9% are women and 32.1% are men. Students come from 35 states and territories and 14 other countries. 47% are from New York. 2.8% are international students. 6.4% are African American, 0.3% American Indian, 5.4% Asian American, and 9.1% Hispanic American. 73% returned for their sophomore year.

Facilities and Resources
705 **computers** are available on campus for student use. The 3 **libraries** have 368,390 books and 1,155 subscriptions.

Campus Life
There are 10 active organizations on campus, including a drama/theater group, newspaper, and choral group. No national or local **fraternities** or **sororities**.

This institution has no intercollegiate sports.

Campus Safety
Student safety services include 24-hour desk attendants in residence halls, 24-hour emergency telephone alarm devices, and electronically operated dormitory entrances.

Applying
Eugene Lang College requires an essay, SAT I, ACT, or 4 SAT II Subject Tests, a high school transcript, an interview, 2 recommendations, and a minimum high school GPA of 2.0. It recommends a minimum high school GPA of 3.0. Application deadline: 2/1; 3/1 priority date for financial aid. Early and deferred admission are possible.

FAIRFIELD UNIVERSITY

SUBURBAN SETTING ■ PRIVATE ■ INDEPENDENT RELIGIOUS ■ COED
FAIRFIELD, CONNECTICUT

Web site: www.fairfield.edu
Contact: Ms. Judith M. Dobai, Director of Admission, 1073 North Benson
Road, Fairfield, CT 06430-5195
Telephone: 203-254-4100 **Fax:** 203-254-4199
E-mail: admis@mail.fairfield.edu

Academics

Fairfield awards bachelor's and master's **degrees** and post-master's certificates. Challenging opportunities include advanced placement credit, freshman honors college, an honors program, double majors, independent study, and a senior project. Special programs include internships, summer session for credit, study-abroad, and Army ROTC.

The most frequently chosen **baccalaureate** fields are business/marketing, trade and industry, and English. A complete listing of majors at Fairfield appears in the Majors Index beginning on page 430.

The **faculty** at Fairfield has 224 full-time members, 93% with terminal degrees. The student-faculty ratio is 13:1.

Students of Fairfield

The student body totals 5,154, of whom 4,164 are undergraduates. 54.8% are women and 45.2% are men. Students come from 33 states and territories and 43 other countries. 26% are from Connecticut. 1.6% are international students. 2.7% are African American, 0.2% American Indian, 3.5% Asian American, and 5.2% Hispanic American. 90% returned for their sophomore year.

Facilities and Resources

Student rooms are linked to a campus network. 150 **computers** are available on campus that provide access to the Internet. The **library** has 293,191 books and 1,790 subscriptions.

Campus Life

There are 100 active organizations on campus, including a drama/theater group, newspaper, radio station, television station, and choral group. No national or local **fraternities** or **sororities**.

Fairfield is a member of the NCAA (Division I). **Intercollegiate sports** (some offering scholarships) include baseball (m), basketball, crew (w), cross-country running, field hockey (w), football (m), golf, ice hockey (m), lacrosse, soccer, softball (w), swimming, tennis, volleyball (w).

Campus Safety

Student safety services include bicycle patrols, late-night transport/escort service, 24-hour emergency telephone alarm devices, 24-hour patrols by trained security personnel, and electronically operated dormitory entrances.

Applying

Fairfield requires SAT I or ACT, a high school transcript, 1 recommendation, rank in upper 20% of high school class, and a minimum high school GPA of 3.0. It recommends SAT II Subject Tests and an interview. Application deadline: 2/1; 2/15 priority date for financial aid. Deferred admission is possible.

Getting in Last Year
7,128 applied
49% were accepted
832 enrolled (24%)
35% from top tenth of their h.s. class
3.6 average high school GPA
45% had SAT verbal scores over 600
52% had SAT math scores over 600
6% had SAT verbal scores over 700
5% had SAT math scores over 700
12 National Merit Scholars
33 class presidents
4 valedictorians

Graduation and After
77% graduated in 4 years
3% graduated in 5 years
18% pursued further study (5% medicine, 4% arts and sciences, 4% law)
75% had job offers within 6 months
139 organizations recruited on campus

Financial Matters
$22,885 tuition and fees (2001–02)
$8000 room and board
79% average percent of need met
$15,322 average financial aid amount received per undergraduate (2000–01 estimated)

FLORIDA INSTITUTE OF TECHNOLOGY
SMALL-TOWN SETTING ■ PRIVATE ■ INDEPENDENT ■ COED
MELBOURNE, FLORIDA

Web site: www.fit.edu
Contact: Ms. Judith Marino, Director of Undergraduate Admissions, 150 West University Boulevard, Melbourne, FL 32901-6975
Telephone: 321-674-8030 or toll-free 800-888-4348 **Fax:** 321-723-9468
E-mail: admissions@fit.edu

Florida Tech's reputation has grown tremendously in computer science and computer-related majors. More than 10 percent of undergraduates studying computer science at Florida Tech are paid to participate in real-time research for the country's leading corporations, including Microsoft, IBM, Rational Software, the U.S. Navy, Harris Corporation, Texas Instruments, and the National Science Foundation.

Getting in Last Year
2,156 applied
82% were accepted
545 enrolled (31%)
29% from top tenth of their h.s. class
3.52 average high school GPA
34% had SAT verbal scores over 600
53% had SAT math scores over 600
64% had ACT scores over 24
4% had SAT verbal scores over 700
12% had SAT math scores over 700
18% had ACT scores over 30

Graduation and After
31% graduated in 4 years
23% graduated in 5 years
2% graduated in 6 years
17% pursued further study (12% engineering, 7% arts and sciences, 2% business)
98% had job offers within 6 months
100 organizations recruited on campus

Financial Matters
$19,700 tuition and fees (2001–02)
$5550 room and board
84% average percent of need met
$16,864 average financial aid amount received per undergraduate

Academics
Florida Tech awards associate, bachelor's, master's, and doctoral **degrees** and post-master's certificates. Challenging opportunities include advanced placement credit, accelerated degree programs, and a senior project. Special programs include cooperative education, internships, summer session for credit, and Army ROTC.

The most frequently chosen **baccalaureate** fields are engineering/engineering technologies, biological/life sciences, and trade and industry. A complete listing of majors at Florida Tech appears in the Majors Index beginning on page 430.

The **faculty** at Florida Tech has 177 full-time members, 88% with terminal degrees. The student-faculty ratio is 12:1.

Students of Florida Tech
The student body totals 4,409, of whom 2,191 are undergraduates. 30% are women and 70% are men. Students come from 54 states and territories and 82 other countries. 57% are from Florida. 26.1% are international students. 4% are African American, 0.2% American Indian, 2.4% Asian American, and 4.7% Hispanic American. 77% returned for their sophomore year.

Facilities and Resources
Student rooms are linked to a campus network. 600 **computers** are available on campus that provide access to the Internet. The **library** has 138,503 books and 5,325 subscriptions.

Campus Life
There are 102 active organizations on campus, including a drama/theater group, newspaper, television station, and marching band. 17% of eligible men and 11% of eligible women are members of national **fraternities**, national **sororities**, and local sororities.

Florida Tech is a member of the NCAA (Division II). **Intercollegiate sports** (some offering scholarships) include baseball (m), basketball, crew, cross-country running, soccer (m), softball (w), volleyball (w).

Campus Safety
Student safety services include self-defense education, late-night transport/escort service, 24-hour emergency telephone alarm devices, and 24-hour patrols by trained security personnel.

Applying
Florida Tech requires SAT I or ACT, a high school transcript, and a minimum high school GPA of 2.5, and in some cases a minimum high school GPA of 3.0. It recommends an essay, an interview, and a minimum high school GPA of 2.8. Application deadline: rolling admissions; 3/15 priority date for financial aid. Early and deferred admission are possible.

FLORIDA INTERNATIONAL UNIVERSITY

URBAN SETTING ▪ PUBLIC ▪ STATE-SUPPORTED ▪ COED
MIAMI, FLORIDA

Web site: www.fiu.edu
Contact: Ms. Carmen Brown, Director of Admissions, University Park, PC
140, 11200 SW 8 Street, PC140, Miami, FL 33199
Telephone: 305-348-3675 **Fax:** 305-348-3648
E-mail: admiss@fiu.edu

Academics

FIU awards bachelor's, master's, and doctoral **degrees**. Challenging opportunities
include advanced placement credit, accelerated degree programs, freshman honors college, an honors program, double majors, independent study, and a senior project. Special
programs include cooperative education, internships, summer session for credit, off-
campus study, study-abroad, and Army and Air Force ROTC.

The most frequently chosen **baccalaureate** fields are business/marketing, education,
and health professions and related sciences. A complete listing of majors at FIU appears
in the Majors Index beginning on page 430.

The **faculty** at FIU has 877 full-time members, 77% with terminal degrees. The student-faculty ratio is 14:1.

Students of FIU

The student body totals 31,727, of whom 25,971 are undergraduates. 56.5% are women
and 43.5% are men. Students come from 52 states and territories and 115 other
countries. 95% are from Florida. 7.5% are international students. 13.9% are African
American, 0.2% American Indian, 3.8% Asian American, and 55% Hispanic American.
88% returned for their sophomore year.

Facilities and Resources

Student rooms are linked to a campus network. 600 **computers** are available on campus
that provide access to the Internet. The 3 **libraries** have 2,234,911 books and 14,978
subscriptions.

Campus Life

There are 190 active organizations on campus, including a drama/theater group,
newspaper, radio station, and choral group. 8% of eligible men and 9% of eligible
women are members of national **fraternities** and national **sororities**.

FIU is a member of the NCAA (Division I). **Intercollegiate sports** (some offering
scholarships) include baseball (m), basketball, cross-country running, golf (w), soccer,
softball (w), tennis (w), track and field, volleyball (w).

Campus Safety

Student safety services include late-night transport/escort service, 24-hour emergency
telephone alarm devices, 24-hour patrols by trained security personnel, and electronically operated dormitory entrances.

Applying

FIU requires SAT I or ACT, a high school transcript, and a minimum high school GPA
of 3.0, and in some cases 1 recommendation. Application deadline: rolling admissions;
3/1 priority date for financial aid. Early and deferred admission are possible.

Getting in Last Year
6,561 applied
47% were accepted
2,492 enrolled (81%)
42% from top tenth of their h.s. class
3.47 average high school GPA
28% had SAT verbal scores over 600
28% had SAT math scores over 600
83% had ACT scores over 24
4% had SAT verbal scores over 700
3% had SAT math scores over 700
6% had ACT scores over 30
5 National Merit Scholars
20 valedictorians

Graduation and After
18% graduated in 4 years
20% graduated in 5 years
8% graduated in 6 years
70% had job offers within 6 months
600 organizations recruited on campus

Financial Matters
$2562 resident tuition and fees (2001–02)
$10,450 nonresident tuition and fees (2001–02)
$3504 room only
61% average percent of need met

FLORIDA STATE UNIVERSITY

SUBURBAN SETTING ■ PUBLIC ■ STATE-SUPPORTED ■ COED
TALLAHASSEE, FLORIDA

Web site: www.fsu.edu
Contact: Office of Admissions, A2500 University Center, Tallahassee, FL
 32306-2400
Telephone: 850-644-6200 **Fax:** 850-644-0197
E-mail: admissions@admin.fsu.edu

Florida State University is one of the nation's most popular universities, enrolling students from all 50 states and over 100 countries. Its diverse student population participates in a Liberal Studies Program that has been nationally recognized for its effectiveness in fostering a spirit of free inquiry into humane values and for developing strong written analytical skills. Home of the National High Magnetic Field Laboratory, the Supercomputer Computations Institute, and other internationally acclaimed research centers, Florida State is one of only 88 institutions in the Research I category as classified by the Carnegie Foundation for the Advancement of Teaching. FSU invites students to explore the state of their future, Florida State University.

Getting in Last Year
28,817 applied
53% were accepted
5,763 enrolled (37%)
47% from top tenth of their h.s. class
3.63 average high school GPA
40% had SAT verbal scores over 600
43% had SAT math scores over 600
58% had ACT scores over 24
7% had SAT verbal scores over 700
6% had SAT math scores over 700
7% had ACT scores over 30
68 National Merit Scholars

Graduation and After
38% graduated in 4 years
22% graduated in 5 years
4% graduated in 6 years
35% pursued further study
942 organizations recruited on campus

Financial Matters
$2513 resident tuition and fees (2001–02)
$10,402 nonresident tuition and fees (2001–02)
$5322 room and board
38% average percent of need met
$6807 average financial aid amount received per undergraduate

Academics
Florida State awards associate, bachelor's, master's, doctoral, and first-professional **degrees** and post-bachelor's and post-master's certificates. Challenging opportunities include advanced placement credit, accelerated degree programs, an honors program, double majors, independent study, and a senior project. Special programs include cooperative education, internships, summer session for credit, off-campus study, study-abroad, and Army, Navy and Air Force ROTC.

The most frequently chosen **baccalaureate** fields are business/marketing, social sciences and history, and protective services/public administration. A complete listing of majors at Florida State appears in the Majors Index beginning on page 430.

The **faculty** at Florida State has 1,084 full-time members, 91% with terminal degrees. The student-faculty ratio is 22:1.

Students of Florida State
The student body totals 34,982, of whom 28,231 are undergraduates. 56.6% are women and 43.4% are men. Students come from 51 states and territories and 120 other countries. 81% are from Florida. 0.8% are international students. 12.2% are African American, 0.5% American Indian, 2.8% Asian American, and 8.9% Hispanic American. 85% returned for their sophomore year.

Facilities and Resources
Student rooms are linked to a campus network. 1,249 **computers** are available on campus that provide access to Web pages and the Internet. The 7 **libraries** have 2,338,492 books and 15,446 subscriptions.

Campus Life
There are 245 active organizations on campus, including a drama/theater group, newspaper, radio station, television station, choral group, and marching band. 11% of eligible men and 11% of eligible women are members of national **fraternities**, national **sororities**, local fraternities, and local sororities.

Florida State is a member of the NCAA (Division I). **Intercollegiate sports** (some offering scholarships) include baseball (m), basketball, cross-country running, football (m), golf, soccer (w), softball (w), swimming, tennis, track and field, volleyball (w).

Campus Safety
Student safety services include late-night transport/escort service, 24-hour emergency telephone alarm devices, 24-hour patrols by trained security personnel, and electronically operated dormitory entrances.

Applying
Florida State requires SAT I or ACT and a high school transcript, and in some cases audition. It recommends an essay and a minimum high school GPA of 3.0. Application deadline: 3/1; 2/15 priority date for financial aid. Early admission is possible.

FORDHAM UNIVERSITY

URBAN SETTING ■ PRIVATE ■ INDEPENDENT RELIGIOUS ■ COED
NEW YORK, NEW YORK

Web site: www.fordham.edu
Contact: Mr. John W. Buckley, Dean of Admission, Theband Hall, 441 East Fordham Road, New York, NY 10458
Telephone: 718-817-4000 or toll-free 800-FORDHAM **Fax:** 718-367-9404
E-mail: enroll@fordham.edu

Academics

Fordham awards bachelor's, master's, doctoral, and first-professional **degrees** and post-master's certificates (branch locations: an 85-acre campus at Rose Hill and an 8-acre campus at Lincoln Center). Challenging opportunities include advanced placement credit, accelerated degree programs, student-designed majors, an honors program, double majors, independent study, and a senior project. Special programs include internships, summer session for credit, off-campus study, study-abroad, and Army, Navy and Air Force ROTC.

The most frequently chosen **baccalaureate** fields are social sciences and history, business/marketing, and communications/communication technologies. A complete listing of majors at Fordham appears in the Majors Index beginning on page 430.

The **faculty** at Fordham has 594 full-time members, 16% with terminal degrees. The student-faculty ratio is 10:1.

Students of Fordham

The student body totals 13,843, of whom 7,062 are undergraduates. 59.8% are women and 40.2% are men. Students come from 53 states and territories and 40 other countries. 56% are from New York. 1.4% are international students. 5.2% are African American, 0.2% American Indian, 5.2% Asian American, and 11% Hispanic American. 89% returned for their sophomore year.

Facilities and Resources

Student rooms are linked to a campus network. 617 **computers** are available on campus that provide access to the Internet. The 4 **libraries** have 1,799,171 books and 14,094 subscriptions.

Campus Life

Active organizations on campus include a drama/theater group, newspaper, radio station, choral group, and marching band. No national or local **fraternities** or **sororities**.

Fordham is a member of the NCAA (Division I). **Intercollegiate sports** (some offering scholarships) include baseball (m), basketball, crew (w), cross-country running, football (m), golf (m), soccer, softball (w), squash (m), swimming, tennis, track and field, volleyball (w), water polo (m).

Campus Safety

Student safety services include late-night transport/escort service, 24-hour emergency telephone alarm devices, 24-hour patrols by trained security personnel, student patrols, and electronically operated dormitory entrances.

Applying

Fordham requires an essay, SAT I or ACT, a high school transcript, and 1 recommendation, and in some cases an interview. It recommends SAT II Subject Tests, an interview, and a minimum high school GPA of 3.0. Application deadline: 2/1; 2/1 priority date for financial aid. Early admission is possible.

Getting in Last Year
10,663 applied
55% were accepted
1,663 enrolled (28%)
30% from top tenth of their h.s. class
3.62 average high school GPA
43% had SAT verbal scores over 600
39% had SAT math scores over 600
64% had ACT scores over 24
7% had SAT verbal scores over 700
4% had SAT math scores over 700
11% had ACT scores over 30

Graduation and After
60% graduated in 4 years
7% graduated in 5 years
1% graduated in 6 years
25% pursued further study (7% arts and sciences, 6% law, 5% business)
90% had job offers within 6 months
632 organizations recruited on campus

Financial Matters
$22,460 tuition and fees (2001–02)
$8745 room and board
79% average percent of need met
$18,317 average financial aid amount received per undergraduate (2000–01)

Franklin and Marshall College

Suburban setting ■ Private ■ Independent ■ Coed
Lancaster, Pennsylvania

Web site: www.fandm.edu
Contact: Ms. Penny Johnston, Acting Director of Admissions, PO Box 3003, Lancaster, PA 17604-3003
Telephone: 717-291-3953 **Fax:** 717-291-4389
E-mail: admission@fandm.edu

Getting in Last Year
3,702 applied
55% were accepted
511 enrolled (25%)
55% from top tenth of their h.s. class
64% had SAT verbal scores over 600
73% had SAT math scores over 600
18% had SAT verbal scores over 700
21% had SAT math scores over 700

Graduation and After
78% graduated in 4 years
4% graduated in 5 years
1% graduated in 6 years
24% pursued further study (12% arts and sciences, 8% law, 4% medicine)
62% had job offers within 6 months
64 organizations recruited on campus

Financial Matters
$26,110 tuition and fees (2001–02)
$6300 room and board
100% average percent of need met
$18,107 average financial aid amount received per undergraduate

Academics
F&M awards bachelor's **degrees**. Challenging opportunities include advanced placement credit, accelerated degree programs, student-designed majors, an honors program, double majors, independent study, and a senior project. Special programs include internships, summer session for credit, off-campus study, and study-abroad.

The most frequently chosen **baccalaureate** fields are social sciences and history, business/marketing, and interdisciplinary studies. A complete listing of majors at F&M appears in the Majors Index beginning on page 430.

The **faculty** at F&M has 159 full-time members, 97% with terminal degrees. The student-faculty ratio is 11:1.

Students of F&M
The student body is made up of 1,887 undergraduates. 49.9% are women and 50.1% are men. Students come from 43 states and territories and 62 other countries. 36% are from Pennsylvania. 8.1% are international students. 2.5% are African American, 0.1% American Indian, 3.4% Asian American, and 2.6% Hispanic American. 87% returned for their sophomore year.

Facilities and Resources
Student rooms are linked to a campus network. 139 **computers** are available on campus that provide access to the Internet. The 2 **libraries** have 437,789 books and 2,135 subscriptions.

Campus Life
There are 120 active organizations on campus, including a drama/theater group, newspaper, radio station, television station, and choral group. No national or local **fraternities** or **sororities**.

F&M is a member of the NCAA (Division III). **Intercollegiate sports** include baseball (m), basketball, cross-country running, field hockey (w), football (m), golf, lacrosse, soccer, softball (w), squash, swimming, tennis, track and field, volleyball (w), wrestling (m).

Campus Safety
Student safety services include residence hall security, campus security connected to city police and fire company, late-night transport/escort service, 24-hour emergency telephone alarm devices, 24-hour patrols by trained security personnel, and electronically operated dormitory entrances.

Applying
F&M requires an essay, SAT II: Writing Test, SAT I and SAT II or ACT, a high school transcript, and 2 recommendations. It recommends an interview. Application deadline: 2/1; 2/1 for financial aid. Early and deferred admission are possible.

FRIENDS UNIVERSITY

URBAN SETTING ■ PRIVATE ■ INDEPENDENT ■ COED
WICHITA, KANSAS

Web site: www.friends.edu
Contact: Mr. Tony Myers, Director of Admissions, 2100 West University Street, Wichita, KS 67213
Telephone: 316-295-5100 or toll-free 800-577-2233 **Fax:** 316-262-5027
E-mail: tmyers@friends.edu

Academics

Friends University awards associate, bachelor's, and master's **degrees**. Challenging opportunities include advanced placement credit, accelerated degree programs, student-designed majors, an honors program, and a senior project. Special programs include cooperative education, internships, summer session for credit, and off-campus study. A complete listing of majors at Friends University appears in the Majors Index beginning on page 430.

The **faculty** at Friends University has 75 full-time members.

Students of Friends University

The student body totals 3,190, of whom 2,629 are undergraduates. Students come from 30 states and territories and 25 other countries. 90% are from Kansas. 63% returned for their sophomore year.

Facilities and Resources

Student rooms are linked to a campus network. 190 **computers** are available on campus for student use. The 4 **libraries** have 105,989 books and 857 subscriptions.

Campus Life

Active organizations on campus include a drama/theater group and choral group. Friends University has local **fraternities** and local **sororities**.

Friends University is a member of the NAIA. **Intercollegiate sports** (some offering scholarships) include baseball (m), basketball, cross-country running, football (m), golf (m), soccer, softball (w), tennis, track and field, volleyball (w).

Campus Safety

Student safety services include late-night transport/escort service and 24-hour patrols by trained security personnel.

Applying

Friends University requires SAT I or ACT and a high school transcript, and in some cases an essay and 1 recommendation. It recommends an interview. Application deadline: rolling admissions; 3/15 priority date for financial aid. Early admission is possible.

FURMAN UNIVERSITY
SUBURBAN SETTING ■ PRIVATE ■ INDEPENDENT ■ COED
GREENVILLE, SOUTH CAROLINA

Web site: www.furman.edu
Contact: Mr. David R. O'Cain, Director of Admissions, 3300 Poinsett
  Highway, Greenville, SC 29613
Telephone: 864-294-2034 **Fax:** 864-294-3127
E-mail: admissions@furman.edu

Getting in Last Year
3,564 applied
61% were accepted
736 enrolled (34%)
60% from top tenth of their h.s. class
3.52 average high school GPA
68% had SAT verbal scores over 600
68% had SAT math scores over 600
86% had ACT scores over 24
19% had SAT verbal scores over 700
17% had SAT math scores over 700
28% had ACT scores over 30
70 National Merit Scholars
28 class presidents
49 valedictorians

Graduation and After
36% pursued further study (11% arts and
  sciences, 6% law, 5% education)
74% had job offers within 6 months
89 organizations recruited on campus

Financial Matters
$20,076 tuition and fees (2001–02)
$5416 room and board
89% average percent of need met
$16,500 average financial aid amount received
  per undergraduate

Academics
Furman awards bachelor's and master's **degrees** and post-bachelor's certificates. Challenging opportunities include advanced placement credit, accelerated degree programs, student-designed majors, double majors, independent study, and a senior project. Special programs include internships, summer session for credit, study-abroad, and Army ROTC.

The most frequently chosen **baccalaureate** fields are trade and industry, interdisciplinary studies, and business/marketing. A complete listing of majors at Furman appears in the Majors Index beginning on page 430.

The **faculty** at Furman has 200 full-time members, 97% with terminal degrees. The student-faculty ratio is 12:1.

Students of Furman
The student body totals 3,183, of whom 2,767 are undergraduates. 55.5% are women and 44.5% are men. Students come from 48 states and territories and 20 other countries. 30% are from South Carolina. 1% are international students. 5.8% are African American, 0.1% American Indian, 1.4% Asian American, and 1.1% Hispanic American. 92% returned for their sophomore year.

Facilities and Resources
Student rooms are linked to a campus network. 340 **computers** are available on campus that provide access to the Internet. The 3 **libraries** have 445,900 books and 3,347 subscriptions.

Campus Life
There are 130 active organizations on campus, including a drama/theater group, newspaper, radio station, choral group, and marching band. 30% of eligible men and 35% of eligible women are members of national **fraternities** and national **sororities**.

Furman is a member of the NCAA (Division I). **Intercollegiate sports** (some offering scholarships) include baseball (m), basketball, cross-country running, football (m), golf, soccer, softball (w), tennis, track and field, volleyball (w).

Campus Safety
Student safety services include late-night transport/escort service, 24-hour emergency telephone alarm devices, 24-hour patrols by trained security personnel, student patrols, and electronically operated dormitory entrances.

Applying
Furman requires an essay, SAT I or ACT, and a high school transcript, and in some cases SAT II Subject Tests and SAT II: Writing Test. It recommends 2 recommendations and a minimum high school GPA of 3.0. Application deadline: 1/15; 1/15 for financial aid. Early admission is possible.

GEORGE FOX UNIVERSITY

SMALL-TOWN SETTING ■ PRIVATE ■ INDEPENDENT RELIGIOUS ■ COED
NEWBERG, OREGON

Web site: www.georgefox.edu
Contact: Mr. Dale Seipp, Director of Admissions, 414 North Meridian, Newberg, OR 97132-2697
Telephone: 503-554-2240 or toll-free 800-765-4369 **Fax:** 503-554-3110
E-mail: admissions@georgefox.edu

Academics

George Fox awards bachelor's, master's, doctoral, and first-professional **degrees**. Challenging opportunities include advanced placement credit, accelerated degree programs, student-designed majors, an honors program, double majors, independent study, and a senior project. Special programs include cooperative education, internships, off-campus study, study-abroad, and Air Force ROTC.

The most frequently chosen **baccalaureate** fields are business/marketing, education, and interdisciplinary studies. A complete listing of majors at George Fox appears in the Majors Index beginning on page 430.

The **faculty** at George Fox has 71 full-time members, 61% with terminal degrees. The student-faculty ratio is 15:1.

Students of George Fox

The student body totals 2,640, of whom 1,665 are undergraduates. 58.6% are women and 41.4% are men. Students come from 25 states and territories and 16 other countries. 61% are from Oregon. 2.7% are international students. 1% are African American, 1% American Indian, 2.2% Asian American, and 2.5% Hispanic American. 83% returned for their sophomore year.

Facilities and Resources

Student rooms are linked to a campus network. 1,300 **computers** are available on campus that provide access to the Internet. The 2 **libraries** have 123,734 books and 1,323 subscriptions.

Campus Life

There are 18 active organizations on campus, including a drama/theater group, newspaper, radio station, and choral group. No national or local **fraternities** or **sororities**.

George Fox is a member of the NAIA. **Intercollegiate sports** include baseball (m), basketball, cross-country running, soccer, softball (w), tennis, track and field, volleyball (w).

Campus Safety

Student safety services include late-night transport/escort service, 24-hour emergency telephone alarm devices, 24-hour patrols by trained security personnel, student patrols, and electronically operated dormitory entrances.

Applying

George Fox requires an essay, SAT I or ACT, a high school transcript, and 2 recommendations, and in some cases an interview. It recommends an interview. Application deadline: 6/1; 3/1 priority date for financial aid. Early and deferred admission are possible.

Getting in Last Year

824 applied
91% were accepted
318 enrolled (43%)
35% from top tenth of their h.s. class
3.59 average high school GPA
37% had SAT verbal scores over 600
33% had SAT math scores over 600
47% had ACT scores over 24
8% had SAT verbal scores over 700
5% had SAT math scores over 700
9% had ACT scores over 30

Graduation and After

53% graduated in 4 years
6% graduated in 5 years
1% graduated in 6 years
18% pursued further study (78% arts and sciences, 7% business, 7% education)
64% had job offers within 6 months
200 organizations recruited on campus

Financial Matters

$18,325 tuition and fees (2001–02)
$5770 room and board
82% average percent of need met
$12,162 average financial aid amount received per undergraduate

GEORGETOWN COLLEGE
SUBURBAN SETTING ■ PRIVATE ■ INDEPENDENT RELIGIOUS ■ COED
GEORGETOWN, KENTUCKY

Web site: www.georgetowncollege.edu
Contact: Mr. Brian Taylor, Director of Admissions, 400 East College Street, Georgetown, KY 40324
Telephone: 502-863-8009 or toll-free 800-788-9985 **Fax:** 502-868-7733
E-mail: admissions@georgetowncollege.edu

Georgetown College distinguishes itself from many other small liberal arts colleges across the nation by offering a combination of a rigorous and respected academic program, a wealth of opportunities for leadership and involvement in extracurricular activities, and a strong commitment to Christian values and principles. While there is no shortage of schools that possess any one of these characteristics, institutions that combine any two of these qualities are less common. By placing all three side by side at unique levels and combinations, Georgetown provides a special framework that fosters intellectual, social, and spiritual growth.

Getting in Last Year
827 applied
95% were accepted
357 enrolled (46%)
38% from top tenth of their h.s. class
3.56 average high school GPA
22% had SAT verbal scores over 600
22% had SAT math scores over 600
50% had ACT scores over 24
2% had SAT verbal scores over 700
2% had SAT math scores over 700
7% had ACT scores over 30
28 valedictorians

Graduation and After
38% graduated in 4 years
16% graduated in 5 years
2% graduated in 6 years
45% pursued further study
45 organizations recruited on campus

Financial Matters
$13,580 tuition and fees (2001–02)
$4820 room and board
93% average percent of need met
$14,780 average financial aid amount received per undergraduate

Academics
Georgetown awards bachelor's and master's **degrees**. Challenging opportunities include advanced placement credit, accelerated degree programs, student-designed majors, double majors, and a senior project. Special programs include cooperative education, internships, summer session for credit, off-campus study, study-abroad, and Army and Air Force ROTC.

The most frequently chosen **baccalaureate** fields are psychology, business/marketing, and visual/performing arts. A complete listing of majors at Georgetown appears in the Majors Index beginning on page 430.

The **faculty** at Georgetown has 92 full-time members, 92% with terminal degrees. The student-faculty ratio is 13:1.

Students of Georgetown
The student body totals 1,703, of whom 1,361 are undergraduates. 56.6% are women and 43.4% are men. Students come from 25 states and territories and 16 other countries. 84% are from Kentucky. 1.2% are international students. 2.3% are African American, 0.1% American Indian, 0.3% Asian American, and 0.2% Hispanic American. 79% returned for their sophomore year.

Facilities and Resources
Student rooms are linked to a campus network. 150 **computers** are available on campus that provide access to the Internet. The 2 **libraries** have 145,794 books and 833 subscriptions.

Campus Life
There are 97 active organizations on campus, including a drama/theater group, newspaper, radio station, and choral group. 28% of eligible men and 40% of eligible women are members of national **fraternities**, national **sororities**, and local fraternities.

Georgetown is a member of the NAIA. **Intercollegiate sports** (some offering scholarships) include baseball (m), basketball, cross-country running, football (m), golf, soccer, softball (w), tennis, volleyball (w).

Campus Safety
Student safety services include late-night transport/escort service and 24-hour patrols by trained security personnel.

Applying
Georgetown requires an essay, SAT I or ACT, a high school transcript, and a minimum high school GPA of 2.5, and in some cases an interview and recommendations. It recommends ACT. Application deadline: 7/1; 2/15 priority date for financial aid.

Georgetown University

Urban setting ■ Private ■ Independent Religious ■ Coed
Washington, District of Columbia

Web site: www.georgetown.edu
Contact: Mr. Charles A. Deacon, Dean of Undergraduate Admissions, 37th
and O Street, NW, Washington, DC 20057
Telephone: 202-687-3600 **Fax:** 202-687-6660

Academics

Georgetown awards bachelor's, master's, doctoral, and first-professional **degrees**. Challenging opportunities include advanced placement credit, student-designed majors, an honors program, double majors, independent study, and a senior project. Special programs include internships, summer session for credit, study-abroad, and Army, Navy and Air Force ROTC.

The most frequently chosen **baccalaureate** fields are social sciences and history, business/marketing, and English. A complete listing of majors at Georgetown appears in the Majors Index beginning on page 430.

The **faculty** at Georgetown has 639 full-time members. The student-faculty ratio is 11:1.

Students of Georgetown

The student body totals 12,688, of whom 6,422 are undergraduates. 52.6% are women and 47.4% are men. Students come from 52 states and territories and 86 other countries. 1% are from District of Columbia. 5.2% are international students. 6.5% are African American, 0.2% American Indian, 9.5% Asian American, and 5.1% Hispanic American. 98% returned for their sophomore year.

Facilities and Resources

Student rooms are linked to a campus network. 360 **computers** are available on campus that provide access to online grade reports and the Internet. The 7 **libraries** have 2,472,368 books and 28,547 subscriptions.

Campus Life

There are 111 active organizations on campus, including a drama/theater group, newspaper, radio station, and choral group. No national or local **fraternities** or **sororities**.

Georgetown is a member of the NCAA (Division I). **Intercollegiate sports** (some offering scholarships) include baseball (m), basketball, crew, cross-country running, field hockey (w), football (m), golf (m), lacrosse, sailing, soccer, swimming, tennis, track and field, volleyball (w).

Campus Safety

Student safety services include student guards at residence halls and academic facilities, late-night transport/escort service, 24-hour emergency telephone alarm devices, 24-hour patrols by trained security personnel, and electronically operated dormitory entrances.

Applying

Georgetown requires an essay, SAT I or ACT, a high school transcript, an interview, and 2 recommendations. It recommends SAT II Subject Tests and SAT II: Writing Test. Application deadline: 1/10; 2/1 priority date for financial aid. Early and deferred admission are possible.

Getting in Last Year
15,327 applied
21% were accepted
1,515 enrolled (47%)
79% from top tenth of their h.s. class
89% had SAT verbal scores over 600
91% had SAT math scores over 600
93% had ACT scores over 24
46% had SAT verbal scores over 700
47% had SAT math scores over 700
61% had ACT scores over 30
64 class presidents
149 valedictorians

Graduation and After
86% graduated in 4 years
5% graduated in 5 years
1% graduated in 6 years
28% pursued further study (12% law, 8% arts and sciences, 6% medicine)
77% had job offers within 6 months
443 organizations recruited on campus

Financial Matters
$25,425 tuition and fees (2001–02)
$9422 room and board
100% average percent of need met
$20,302 average financial aid amount received per undergraduate

The George Washington University

URBAN SETTING ■ PRIVATE ■ INDEPENDENT ■ COED
WASHINGTON, DISTRICT OF COLUMBIA

Web site: www.gwu.edu
Contact: Dr. Kathryn M. Napper, Director of Admission, 2121 I Street, NW, Suite 201, Washington, DC 20052
Telephone: 202-994-6040 or toll-free 800-447-3765 **Fax:** 202-944-0325
E-mail: gwadm@gwu.edu

Getting in Last Year
15,959 applied
48% were accepted
2,578 enrolled (33%)
42% from top tenth of their h.s. class
64% had SAT verbal scores over 600
67% had SAT math scores over 600
82% had ACT scores over 24
15% had SAT verbal scores over 700
14% had SAT math scores over 700
16% had ACT scores over 30
36 National Merit Scholars

Graduation and After
21% pursued further study (7% arts and sciences, 6% law, 4% medicine)
383 organizations recruited on campus

Financial Matters
$25,920 tuition and fees (2001–02)
$8830 room and board
94% average percent of need met
$24,000 average financial aid amount received per undergraduate

Academics

GW awards associate, bachelor's, master's, doctoral, and first-professional **degrees** and post-bachelor's and post-master's certificates. Challenging opportunities include advanced placement credit, accelerated degree programs, student-designed majors, an honors program, double majors, independent study, and a senior project. Special programs include cooperative education, internships, summer session for credit, off-campus study, study-abroad, and Army, Navy and Air Force ROTC. A complete listing of majors at GW appears in the Majors Index beginning on page 430.

The **faculty** at GW has 746 full-time members, 93% with terminal degrees. The student-faculty ratio is 13:1.

Students of GW

The student body totals 22,184, of whom 10,063 are undergraduates. 56.2% are women and 43.8% are men. Students come from 55 states and territories and 101 other countries. 6% are from District of Columbia. 5% are international students. 6.1% are African American, 0.3% American Indian, 10% Asian American, and 4.7% Hispanic American. 92% returned for their sophomore year.

Facilities and Resources

Student rooms are linked to a campus network. 550 **computers** are available on campus for student use. The 3 **libraries** have 1,841,842 books and 14,729 subscriptions.

Campus Life

There are 208 active organizations on campus, including a drama/theater group, newspaper, radio station, television station, choral group, and marching band. 16% of eligible men and 14% of eligible women are members of national **fraternities** and national **sororities**.

GW is a member of the NCAA (Division I). **Intercollegiate sports** (some offering scholarships) include baseball (m), basketball, crew, cross-country running, golf (m), gymnastics (w), soccer, swimming, tennis, volleyball (w), water polo (m).

Campus Safety

Student safety services include late-night transport/escort service, 24-hour emergency telephone alarm devices, 24-hour patrols by trained security personnel, and electronically operated dormitory entrances.

Applying

GW requires an essay, SAT I or ACT, a high school transcript, and 2 recommendations, and in some cases SAT II Subject Tests. It recommends SAT I, SAT II: Writing Test, and an interview. Application deadline: 1/15; 1/31 priority date for financial aid. Early and deferred admission are possible.

GEORGIA INSTITUTE OF TECHNOLOGY
URBAN SETTING ■ PUBLIC ■ STATE-SUPPORTED ■ COED
ATLANTA, GEORGIA

Web site: www.gatech.edu
Contact: Ms. Deborah Smith, Director of Admissions, 225 North Avenue, NW, Atlanta, GA 30332-0320
Telephone: 404-894-4154 **Fax:** 404-894-9511
E-mail: admissions@success.gatech.edu

Academics
Georgia Tech awards bachelor's, master's, and doctoral **degrees**. Challenging opportunities include advanced placement credit, accelerated degree programs, student-designed majors, an honors program, double majors, independent study, and a senior project. Special programs include cooperative education, internships, summer session for credit, off-campus study, study-abroad, and Army, Navy and Air Force ROTC.

The most frequently chosen **baccalaureate** fields are engineering/engineering technologies, business/marketing, and computer/information sciences. A complete listing of majors at Georgia Tech appears in the Majors Index beginning on page 430.

The **faculty** at Georgia Tech has 756 full-time members, 94% with terminal degrees. The student-faculty ratio is 14:1.

Students of Georgia Tech
The student body totals 15,576, of whom 11,043 are undergraduates. 28.7% are women and 71.3% are men. Students come from 55 states and territories and 87 other countries. 65% are from Georgia. 4.5% are international students. 7.9% are African American, 0.1% American Indian, 13.7% Asian American, and 2.6% Hispanic American. 90% returned for their sophomore year.

Facilities and Resources
Student rooms are linked to a campus network. 1,450 **computers** are available on campus that provide access to the Internet.

Campus Life
There are 281 active organizations on campus, including a drama/theater group, newspaper, radio station, choral group, and marching band. 29% of eligible men and 20% of eligible women are members of national **fraternities** and national **sororities**.

Georgia Tech is a member of the NCAA (Division I). **Intercollegiate sports** (some offering scholarships) include baseball (m), basketball, cross-country running, football (m), golf (m), softball (w), swimming, tennis, track and field, volleyball (w).

Campus Safety
Student safety services include late-night transport/escort service, 24-hour emergency telephone alarm devices, 24-hour patrols by trained security personnel, student patrols, and electronically operated dormitory entrances.

Applying
Georgia Tech requires an essay, SAT I or ACT, and a high school transcript, and in some cases SAT II Subject Tests. It recommends SAT I. Application deadline: 1/15; 3/1 priority date for financial aid. Early admission is possible.

Getting in Last Year
9,255 applied
56% were accepted
2,229 enrolled (43%)
60% from top tenth of their h.s. class
3.70 average high school GPA
76% had SAT verbal scores over 600
94% had SAT math scores over 600
22% had SAT verbal scores over 700
47% had SAT math scores over 700

Graduation and After
18% graduated in 4 years
39% graduated in 5 years
12% graduated in 6 years
20% pursued further study
70% had job offers within 6 months
800 organizations recruited on campus

Financial Matters
$3454 resident tuition and fees (2001–02)
$12,350 nonresident tuition and fees (2001–02)
$5574 room and board
65% average percent of need met
$7261 average financial aid amount received per undergraduate

GEORGIA STATE UNIVERSITY

URBAN SETTING ■ PUBLIC ■ STATE-SUPPORTED ■ COED
ATLANTA, GEORGIA

Web site: www.gsu.edu
Contact: Mr. Rob Sheinkopf, Dean of Admissions and Acting Dean for Enrollment Services, PO Box 4009, Atlanta, GA 30302-4009
Telephone: 404-651-2365 or toll-free 404-651-2365 (in-state) **Fax:** 404-651-4811

Undergraduate education is a strong focus at Georgia State, with small classes and opportunities for students to work with faculty members in a research setting. There are almost 1,000 faculty members in 217 fields of study. Students can live in University housing and participate in more than 100 different student organizations. Georgia State is located in the heart of Atlanta, an exciting metropolis that offers a variety of job and internship opportunities. Students can walk to such places as the State Capitol and CNN Center or take the rapid transit system to explore all that Atlanta has to offer.

Getting in Last Year
8,134 applied
53% were accepted
2,200 enrolled (51%)
3.23 average high school GPA
18% had SAT verbal scores over 600
19% had SAT math scores over 600
24% had ACT scores over 24
2% had SAT verbal scores over 700
2% had SAT math scores over 700
1% had ACT scores over 30

Graduation and After
45% had job offers within 6 months
368 organizations recruited on campus

Financial Matters
$3292 resident tuition and fees (2001–02)
$11,188 nonresident tuition and fees (2001–02)
$4500 room only

Academics

Georgia State awards bachelor's, master's, doctoral, and first-professional **degrees** and post-master's certificates. Challenging opportunities include student-designed majors, an honors program, double majors, and independent study. Special programs include cooperative education, internships, summer session for credit, off-campus study, study-abroad, and Army and Navy ROTC.

The most frequently chosen **baccalaureate** fields are business/marketing, social sciences and history, and computer/information sciences. A complete listing of majors at Georgia State appears in the Majors Index beginning on page 430.

The **faculty** at Georgia State has 981 full-time members, 86% with terminal degrees. The student-faculty ratio is 14:1.

Students of Georgia State

The student body totals 25,745, of whom 18,245 are undergraduates. 61.1% are women and 38.9% are men. Students come from 49 states and territories and 96 other countries. 96% are from Georgia. 2.6% are international students. 32.2% are African American, 0.3% American Indian, 9.7% Asian American, and 3.1% Hispanic American. 80% returned for their sophomore year.

Facilities and Resources

Student rooms are linked to a campus network. 500 **computers** are available on campus for student use. The 2 **libraries** have 12,053 subscriptions.

Campus Life

There are 162 active organizations on campus, including a drama/theater group, newspaper, radio station, television station, and choral group. 4% of eligible men and 3% of eligible women are members of national **fraternities**, national **sororities**, local fraternities, and local sororities.

Georgia State is a member of the NCAA (Division I). **Intercollegiate sports** (some offering scholarships) include baseball (m), basketball, cross-country running, golf, soccer (m), softball (w), tennis, track and field, volleyball (w).

Campus Safety

Student safety services include late-night transport/escort service, 24-hour emergency telephone alarm devices, 24-hour patrols by trained security personnel, and electronically operated dormitory entrances.

Applying

Georgia State requires SAT I or ACT and a high school transcript, and in some cases SAT II Subject Tests and an interview. It recommends an essay and a minimum high school GPA of 2.9. Application deadline: 6/1; 4/1 priority date for financial aid. Deferred admission is possible.

GETTYSBURG COLLEGE

SMALL-TOWN SETTING ■ PRIVATE ■ INDEPENDENT RELIGIOUS ■ COED
GETTYSBURG, PENNSYLVANIA

Web site: www.gettysburg.edu
Contact: Ms. Gail Sweezey, Director of Admissions, 300 North Washington
   Street, Gettysburg, PA 17325
Telephone: 717-337-6100 or toll-free 800-431-0803 **Fax:** 717-337-6145
E-mail: admiss@gettysburg.edu

Academics

Gettysburg College awards bachelor's **degrees**. Challenging opportunities include
advanced placement credit, accelerated degree programs, student-designed majors,
double majors, independent study, and a senior project. Special programs include internships, off-campus study, and study-abroad.

The most frequently chosen **baccalaureate** fields are social sciences and history,
business/marketing, and English. A complete listing of majors at Gettysburg College
appears in the Majors Index beginning on page 430.

The **faculty** at Gettysburg College has 174 full-time members, 92% with terminal
degrees. The student-faculty ratio is 11:1.

Students of Gettysburg College

The student body is made up of 2,258 undergraduates. 51.7% are women and 48.3% are
men. Students come from 70 states and territories and 35 other countries. 28% are from
Pennsylvania. 1.8% are international students. 2.4% are African American, 0.2%
American Indian, 1.3% Asian American, and 1.3% Hispanic American. 88% returned for
their sophomore year.

Facilities and Resources

Student rooms are linked to a campus network. 620 **computers** are available on campus
that provide access to the Internet. The **library** has 328,503 books and 2,331 subscriptions.

Campus Life

There are 60 active organizations on campus, including a drama/theater group,
newspaper, radio station, television station, choral group, and marching band. 46% of
eligible men and 27% of eligible women are members of national **fraternities** and
national **sororities**.

Gettysburg College is a member of the NCAA (Division III). **Intercollegiate sports**
include baseball (m), basketball, cross-country running, field hockey (w), football (m),
golf, lacrosse, soccer, softball (w), swimming, tennis, track and field, volleyball (w),
wrestling (m).

Campus Safety

Student safety services include late-night transport/escort service, 24-hour emergency
telephone alarm devices, 24-hour patrols by trained security personnel, and electronically operated dormitory entrances.

Applying

Gettysburg College requires an essay, SAT I or ACT, a high school transcript, and 2
recommendations. It recommends an interview and a minimum high school GPA of 3.0.
Application deadline: 2/15; 3/15 for financial aid, with a 2/15 priority date. Early and
deferred admission are possible.

As the 21st century dawns,
higher education faces a
new world of change and
challenge. Revolutionary advances in
technology, unprecedented access to
information, a rich diversity of
perspectives, and frequent calls to
social action demand more from a
liberal arts education than ever
before. Leading colleges must
respond with innovative programs,
appropriate resources, and
exceptional teaching. Gettysburg
College is committed to preparing
students for the opportunities of
this changing world. Its founding
principles embrace a rigorous liberal
arts education that fosters a global
perspective, a spirit of collaboration,
a dedication to public service, and
an enriching campus life. Gettysburg
believes that this approach to
education instills in students a
lifelong desire for learning, a drive
for discovery and contribution, and a
compassionate respect for others
and the world.

Getting in Last Year
4,364 applied
53% were accepted
659 enrolled (29%)
42% from top tenth of their h.s. class
47% had SAT verbal scores over 600
52% had SAT math scores over 600
5% had SAT verbal scores over 700
6% had SAT math scores over 700

Graduation and After
Graduates pursuing further study: 9% arts and
   sciences, 7% law, 6% education
170 organizations recruited on campus

Financial Matters
$25,748 tuition and fees (2001–02)
$6322 room and board
100% average percent of need met
$21,100 average financial aid amount received
   per undergraduate

GONZAGA UNIVERSITY

URBAN SETTING ■ PRIVATE ■ INDEPENDENT RELIGIOUS ■ COED
SPOKANE, WASHINGTON

Getting in Last Year
3,042 applied
82% were accepted
971 enrolled (39%)
38% from top tenth of their h.s. class
3.62 average high school GPA
40% had SAT verbal scores over 600
49% had SAT math scores over 600
73% had ACT scores over 24
9% had SAT verbal scores over 700
8% had SAT math scores over 700
15% had ACT scores over 30
15 National Merit Scholars
18 class presidents
44 valedictorians

Graduation and After
53% graduated in 4 years
10% graduated in 5 years
2% graduated in 6 years
70% had job offers within 6 months
94 organizations recruited on campus

Financial Matters
$18,541 tuition and fees (2001–02)
$5680 room and board
82% average percent of need met
$15,735 average financial aid amount received per undergraduate (2000–01)

Web site: www.gonzaga.edu
Contact: Ms. Julie McCulloh, Associate Dean of Admission, Ad Box 102, Spokane, WA 99258-0102
Telephone: 509-323-6591 or toll-free 800-322-2584 ext. 6572 **Fax:** 509-323-5780
E-mail: ballinger@gu.gonzaga.edu

Academics
Gonzaga awards bachelor's, master's, doctoral, and first-professional **degrees** and post-master's certificates. Challenging opportunities include advanced placement credit, student-designed majors, an honors program, double majors, independent study, and a senior project. Special programs include internships, summer session for credit, off-campus study, study-abroad, and Army ROTC.

The most frequently chosen **baccalaureate** fields are business/marketing, social sciences and history, and communications/communication technologies. A complete listing of majors at Gonzaga appears in the Majors Index beginning on page 430.

The **faculty** at Gonzaga has 279 full-time members, 82% with terminal degrees. The student-faculty ratio is 11:1.

Students of Gonzaga
The student body totals 5,128, of whom 3,483 are undergraduates. 54.5% are women and 45.5% are men. Students come from 34 states and territories and 35 other countries. 46% are from Washington. 2% are international students. 1% are African American, 1.3% American Indian, 5.4% Asian American, and 3.1% Hispanic American. 90% returned for their sophomore year.

Facilities and Resources
Student rooms are linked to a campus network. 340 **computers** are available on campus that provide access to the Internet. The 2 **libraries** have 351,616 books and 1,470 subscriptions.

Campus Life
There are 69 active organizations on campus, including a drama/theater group, newspaper, radio station, television station, and choral group. No national or local **fraternities** or **sororities**.

Gonzaga is a member of the NCAA (Division I). **Intercollegiate sports** (some offering scholarships) include baseball (m), basketball, cross-country running, golf, soccer, tennis, track and field, volleyball (w).

Campus Safety
Student safety services include late-night transport/escort service, 24-hour emergency telephone alarm devices, 24-hour patrols by trained security personnel, and electronically operated dormitory entrances.

Applying
Gonzaga requires an essay, SAT I or ACT, a high school transcript, 1 recommendation, and a minimum high school GPA of 3.0. It recommends an interview. Application deadline: 2/1; 2/1 priority date for financial aid. Early and deferred admission are possible.

GORDON COLLEGE

SMALL-TOWN SETTING ■ PRIVATE ■ INDEPENDENT RELIGIOUS ■ COED
WENHAM, MASSACHUSETTS

Web site: www.gordon.edu
Contact: Mr. Silvio E. Vazquez, Dean of Admissions, 255 Grapevine Road, Wenham, MA 01984-1899
Telephone: 978-927-2300 ext. 4218 or toll-free 800-343-1379 **Fax:** 978-524-3722
E-mail: admissions@hope.gordon.edu

Academics

Gordon awards bachelor's and master's **degrees**. Challenging opportunities include advanced placement credit, student-designed majors, an honors program, double majors, independent study, and a senior project. Special programs include cooperative education, internships, off-campus study, study-abroad, and Army and Air Force ROTC.

The most frequently chosen **baccalaureate** fields are philosophy, education, and social sciences and history. A complete listing of majors at Gordon appears in the Majors Index beginning on page 430.

The **faculty** at Gordon has 87 full-time members, 91% with terminal degrees. The student-faculty ratio is 15:1.

Students of Gordon

The student body totals 1,694, of whom 1,624 are undergraduates. 66.4% are women and 33.6% are men. Students come from 42 states and territories and 21 other countries. 27% are from Massachusetts. 2.2% are international students. 0.7% are African American, 0.1% American Indian, 1.3% Asian American, and 1.5% Hispanic American. 88% returned for their sophomore year.

Facilities and Resources

Student rooms are linked to a campus network. 75 **computers** are available on campus that provide access to the Internet. The **library** has 136,625 books and 563 subscriptions.

Campus Life

There are 35 active organizations on campus, including a drama/theater group, newspaper, and choral group. No national or local **fraternities** or **sororities**.

Gordon is a member of the NCAA (Division III). **Intercollegiate sports** include baseball (m), basketball, cross-country running, field hockey (w), lacrosse, soccer, softball (w), swimming (w), tennis, volleyball (w).

Campus Safety

Student safety services include late-night transport/escort service, 24-hour emergency telephone alarm devices, 24-hour patrols by trained security personnel, and electronically operated dormitory entrances.

Applying

Gordon requires an essay, SAT I or ACT, a high school transcript, an interview, 2 recommendations, and pastoral recommendation, statement of Christian faith. It recommends a minimum high school GPA of 3.0. Application deadline: rolling admissions; 3/1 priority date for financial aid. Early and deferred admission are possible.

Founded in Boston in 1889 by a small group of Christians who recognized the need for church and society to have educated leadership, Gordon is the only nondenominational Christian liberal arts college in New England. Members of its select faculty are known nationwide for research and writing that bring culture and faith together. Students interested in a top-flight education and a framework that shows them how to apply that knowledge should visit Gordon.

Getting in Last Year
1,089 applied
78% were accepted
441 enrolled (52%)
28% from top tenth of their h.s. class
3.56 average high school GPA
53% had SAT verbal scores over 600
51% had SAT math scores over 600
86% had ACT scores over 24
11% had SAT verbal scores over 700
5% had SAT math scores over 700
19% had ACT scores over 30
6 National Merit Scholars

Graduation and After
54% graduated in 4 years
13% graduated in 5 years
4% graduated in 6 years
20% pursued further study
73 organizations recruited on campus

Financial Matters
$18,134 tuition and fees (2001–02)
$5460 room and board
79% average percent of need met
$13,825 average financial aid amount received per undergraduate

GOUCHER COLLEGE
SUBURBAN SETTING ■ PRIVATE ■ INDEPENDENT ■ COED
BALTIMORE, MARYLAND

Web site: www.goucher.edu
Contact: Mr. Carlton E. Surbeck III, Director of Admissions, 1021 Dulaney
  Valley Road, Baltimore, MD 21204-2794
Telephone: 410-337-6100 or toll-free 800-GOUCHER **Fax:** 410-337-6354
E-mail: admission@goucher.edu

A strong commitment to excellence in liberal arts education has been a hallmark of Goucher since 1885. Goucher's core curriculum in the liberal arts is complemented by independent study, study abroad, and an extensive internship program. The College has played a leading role in integrating information technology in all subject areas. Goucher is located 8 miles north of Baltimore and an hour from Washington, DC.

Getting in Last Year
2,146 applied
73% were accepted
343 enrolled (22%)
31% from top tenth of their h.s. class
3.19 average high school GPA
58% had SAT verbal scores over 600
40% had SAT math scores over 600
80% had ACT scores over 24
13% had SAT verbal scores over 700
5% had SAT math scores over 700
8% had ACT scores over 30
6 valedictorians

Graduation and After
51% graduated in 4 years
6% graduated in 5 years
2% graduated in 6 years
25% pursued further study
84% had job offers within 6 months
17 organizations recruited on campus

Financial Matters
$22,300 tuition and fees (2001–02)
$7750 room and board
82% average percent of need met
$16,737 average financial aid amount received
  per undergraduate (2000–01 estimated)

Academics
Goucher awards bachelor's and master's **degrees** and post-bachelor's certificates. Challenging opportunities include advanced placement credit, accelerated degree programs, student-designed majors, an honors program, double majors, independent study, and a senior project. Special programs include internships, off-campus study, and study-abroad.

The most frequently chosen **baccalaureate** fields are psychology, visual/performing arts, and communications/communication technologies. A complete listing of majors at Goucher appears in the Majors Index beginning on page 430.

The **faculty** at Goucher has 78 full-time members, 95% with terminal degrees. The student-faculty ratio is 10:1.

Students of Goucher
The student body totals 1,996, of whom 1,221 are undergraduates. 71.6% are women and 28.4% are men. Students come from 43 states and territories and 21 other countries. 40% are from Maryland. 1.2% are international students. 6.9% are African American, 0.3% American Indian, 2.5% Asian American, and 3% Hispanic American. 83% returned for their sophomore year.

Facilities and Resources
Student rooms are linked to a campus network. 150 **computers** are available on campus that provide access to the Internet. The **library** has 295,593 books and 1,138 subscriptions.

Campus Life
There are 40 active organizations on campus, including a drama/theater group, newspaper, and choral group. No national or local **fraternities** or **sororities**.

Goucher is a member of the NCAA (Division III). **Intercollegiate sports** include basketball, cross-country running, equestrian sports, field hockey (w), lacrosse, soccer, swimming, tennis, volleyball (w).

Campus Safety
Student safety services include late-night transport/escort service, 24-hour emergency telephone alarm devices, and 24-hour patrols by trained security personnel.

Applying
Goucher requires an essay, SAT I or ACT, a high school transcript, 3 recommendations, and a minimum high school GPA of 2.0. It recommends SAT II Subject Tests, SAT II: Writing Test, an interview, and a minimum high school GPA of 3.0. Application deadline: 2/1; 2/15 priority date for financial aid. Early and deferred admission are possible.

GRINNELL COLLEGE

SMALL-TOWN SETTING ■ PRIVATE ■ INDEPENDENT ■ COED
GRINNELL, IOWA

Web site: www.grinnell.edu
Contact: Mr. James Sumner, Dean for Admission and Financial Aid, Grinnell, IA 50112-1690
Telephone: 641-269-3600 or toll-free 800-247-0113 **Fax:** 641-269-4800
E-mail: askgrin@grinnell.edu

Academics

Grinnell College awards bachelor's **degrees**. Challenging opportunities include advanced placement credit, accelerated degree programs, student-designed majors, double majors, and independent study. Special programs include internships, off-campus study, and study-abroad.

The most frequently chosen **baccalaureate** fields are social sciences and history, biological/life sciences, and English. A complete listing of majors at Grinnell College appears in the Majors Index beginning on page 430.

The **faculty** at Grinnell College has 137 full-time members, 94% with terminal degrees. The student-faculty ratio is 10:1.

Students of Grinnell College

The student body is made up of 1,338 undergraduates. 53.5% are women and 46.5% are men. Students come from 51 states and territories and 53 other countries. 14% are from Iowa. 9.6% are international students. 4% are African American, 0.5% American Indian, 4.4% Asian American, and 3.9% Hispanic American. 92% returned for their sophomore year.

Facilities and Resources

Student rooms are linked to a campus network. 240 **computers** are available on campus that provide access to e-mail and the Internet. The 3 **libraries** have 970,403 books and 3,400 subscriptions.

Campus Life

There are 145 active organizations on campus, including a drama/theater group, newspaper, radio station, and choral group. No national or local **fraternities** or **sororities**.

Grinnell College is a member of the NCAA (Division III). **Intercollegiate sports** include baseball (m), basketball, cross-country running, football (m), golf, soccer, softball (w), swimming, tennis, track and field, volleyball (w).

Campus Safety

Student safety services include late-night transport/escort service, 24-hour emergency telephone alarm devices, 24-hour patrols by trained security personnel, student patrols, and electronically operated dormitory entrances.

Applying

Grinnell College requires an essay, SAT I or ACT, a high school transcript, and 3 recommendations. It recommends an interview. Application deadline: 1/20; 2/1 for financial aid. Early and deferred admission are possible.

Getting in Last Year

1,980 applied
65% were accepted
358 enrolled (28%)
63% from top tenth of their h.s. class
86% had SAT verbal scores over 600
86% had SAT math scores over 600
92% had ACT scores over 24
43% had SAT verbal scores over 700
34% had SAT math scores over 700
54% had ACT scores over 30
28 National Merit Scholars
38 valedictorians

Graduation and After

78% graduated in 4 years
5% graduated in 5 years
1% graduated in 6 years
33% pursued further study (15% arts and sciences, 5% engineering, 5% law)
50% had job offers within 6 months
52 organizations recruited on campus

Financial Matters

$22,250 tuition and fees (2001–02)
$6050 room and board
100% average percent of need met
$18,711 average financial aid amount received per undergraduate

GROVE CITY COLLEGE

SMALL-TOWN SETTING ▪ PRIVATE ▪ INDEPENDENT RELIGIOUS ▪ COED
GROVE CITY, PENNSYLVANIA

Web site: www.gcc.edu
Contact: Mr. Jeffrey C. Mincey, Director of Admissions, 100 Campus Drive,
    Grove City, PA 16127-2104
Telephone: 724-458-2100 **Fax:** 724-458-3395
E-mail: admissions@gcc.edu

Grove City is a nationally acclaimed 4-year private Christian college of liberal arts and sciences. From its founding days, the College has endeavored to give young people the best in liberal and scientific education at the lowest possible cost and, in keeping with this historic policy, still maintain one of the lowest tuitions of an independent, high-quality college. J. Howard Pew, one of the guiding spirits in building Grove City College, stated that the College's "prime responsibility is to inculcate in the minds and hearts of youth those Christian, moral, and ethical principles without which our country cannot long endure." These principles have been part of the dynamic motivation of Grove City College.

Getting in Last Year
2,188 applied
43% were accepted
586 enrolled (63%)
62% from top tenth of their h.s. class
3.70 average high school GPA
71% had SAT verbal scores over 600
73% had SAT math scores over 600
88% had ACT scores over 24
22% had SAT verbal scores over 700
20% had SAT math scores over 700
26% had ACT scores over 30
17 National Merit Scholars
5 class presidents
92 valedictorians

Graduation and After
64% graduated in 4 years
9% graduated in 5 years
1% graduated in 6 years
18% pursued further study (11% arts and
    sciences, 2% education, 2% medicine)
94% had job offers within 6 months
140 organizations recruited on campus

Financial Matters
$7870 tuition and fees (2001–02)
$4410 room and board
66% average percent of need met
$5348 average financial aid amount received
    per undergraduate

Academics

Grove City awards bachelor's **degrees**. Challenging opportunities include advanced placement credit, student-designed majors, double majors, independent study, and a senior project. Special programs include internships, summer session for credit, study-abroad, and Army ROTC.

The most frequently chosen **baccalaureate** fields are business/marketing, education, and biological/life sciences. A complete listing of majors at Grove City appears in the Majors Index beginning on page 430.

The **faculty** at Grove City has 121 full-time members, 77% with terminal degrees. The student-faculty ratio is 19:1.

Students of Grove City

The student body totals 2,334, of whom 2,331 are undergraduates. 50.4% are women and 49.6% are men. Students come from 46 states and territories and 11 other countries. 54% are from Pennsylvania. 0.9% are international students. 0.3% are African American, 0.2% American Indian, 0.7% Asian American, and 0.2% Hispanic American. 90% returned for their sophomore year.

Facilities and Resources

Student rooms are linked to a campus network. 50 **computers** are available on campus that provide access to the Internet. The **library** has 158,467 books and 976 subscriptions.

Campus Life

There are 123 active organizations on campus, including a drama/theater group, newspaper, radio station, choral group, and marching band. 9% of eligible men and 19% of eligible women are members of local **fraternities** and local **sororities**.

Grove City is a member of the NCAA (Division III). **Intercollegiate sports** include baseball (m), basketball, cross-country running, football (m), golf, soccer, softball (w), swimming, tennis, track and field, volleyball (w), water polo.

Campus Safety

Student safety services include monitored women's residence hall entrances, late-night transport/escort service, 24-hour emergency telephone alarm devices, 24-hour patrols by trained security personnel, student patrols, and electronically operated dormitory entrances.

Applying

Grove City requires an essay, SAT I or ACT, a high school transcript, and 2 recommendations. It recommends an interview. Application deadline: 2/15; 4/15 for financial aid. Early and deferred admission are possible.

Gustavus Adolphus College

SMALL-TOWN SETTING ■ PRIVATE ■ INDEPENDENT RELIGIOUS ■ COED
ST. PETER, MINNESOTA

Web site: www.gustavus.edu
Contact: Mr. Mark H. Anderson, Dean of Admission, 800 West College
    Avenue, St. Peter, MN 56082-1498
Telephone: 507-933-7676 or toll-free 800-GUSTAVU(S) **Fax:** 507-933-7474
E-mail: admission@gac.edu

Academics

Gustavus awards bachelor's **degrees**. Challenging opportunities include advanced placement credit, accelerated degree programs, student-designed majors, an honors program,
double majors, independent study, and a senior project. Special programs include
cooperative education, internships, summer session for credit, off-campus study, study-
abroad, and Army ROTC.

The most frequently chosen **baccalaureate** fields are social sciences and history,
business/marketing, and biological/life sciences. A complete listing of majors at Gustavus
appears in the Majors Index beginning on page 430.

The **faculty** at Gustavus has 174 full-time members, 86% with terminal degrees. The
student-faculty ratio is 13:1.

Students of Gustavus

The student body is made up of 2,592 undergraduates. 57.8% are women and 42.2% are
men. Students come from 39 states and territories and 22 other countries. 78% are from
Minnesota. 1.6% are international students. 1% are African American, 0.2% American
Indian, 3.2% Asian American, and 0.9% Hispanic American. 89% returned for their
sophomore year.

Facilities and Resources

Student rooms are linked to a campus network. 441 **computers** are available on campus
that provide access to the Internet. The 5 **libraries** have 267,677 books and 1,088
subscriptions.

Campus Life

There are 110 active organizations on campus, including a drama/theater group,
newspaper, radio station, and choral group. 27% of eligible men and 22% of eligible
women are members of local **fraternities** and local **sororities**.

Gustavus is a member of the NCAA (Division III). **Intercollegiate sports** include
baseball (m), basketball, cross-country running, football (m), golf, gymnastics (w), ice
hockey, skiing (cross-country), soccer, softball (w), swimming, tennis, track and field, volleyball (w).

Campus Safety

Student safety services include late-night transport/escort service, 24-hour emergency
telephone alarm devices, 24-hour patrols by trained security personnel, and electronically operated dormitory entrances.

Applying

Gustavus requires an essay, SAT I or ACT, a high school transcript, and 2 recommendations. It recommends an interview. Application deadline: 4/1; 2/15 priority date for
financial aid. Early and deferred admission are possible.

Getting in Last Year
2,163 applied
76% were accepted
670 enrolled (41%)
39% from top tenth of their h.s. class
3.62 average high school GPA
50% had SAT verbal scores over 600
56% had SAT math scores over 600
70% had ACT scores over 24
16% had SAT verbal scores over 700
15% had SAT math scores over 700
18% had ACT scores over 30
18 National Merit Scholars
58 valedictorians

Graduation and After
72% graduated in 4 years
3% graduated in 5 years
36% pursued further study (13% arts and
    sciences, 7% business, 5% law)
92% had job offers within 6 months

Financial Matters
$19,355 tuition and fees (2001–02)
$4900 room and board
91% average percent of need met
$14,694 average financial aid amount received
    per undergraduate

HAMILTON COLLEGE

RURAL SETTING ■ PRIVATE ■ INDEPENDENT ■ COED
CLINTON, NEW YORK

Web site: www.hamilton.edu
Contact: Mr. Richard M. Fuller, Dean of Admission and Financial Aid, 198
   College Hill Road, Clinton, NY 13323-1296
Telephone: 315-859-4421 or toll-free 800-843-2655 **Fax:** 315-859-4457
E-mail: admission@hamilton.edu

Chartered in 1812, Hamilton is the third-oldest college in New York State and is named in honor of U.S. statesman Alexander Hamilton. The College is a highly selective, residential community offering students a rigorous liberal arts curriculum for the 21st century. Students are challenged to think, write, and speak critically, creatively, and analytically so that upon graduation they will distinguish themselves in both their professions and their communities. Renowned for its beautiful campus in the foothills of the Adirondack Mountains, Hamilton offers a strong sense of community; highly qualified, often internationally recognized, faculty members; and state-of-the-art facilities.

Getting in Last Year
4,601 applied
35% were accepted
465 enrolled (29%)
61% from top tenth of their h.s. class
74% had SAT verbal scores over 600
84% had SAT math scores over 600
20% had SAT verbal scores over 700
23% had SAT math scores over 700
3 National Merit Scholars
12 valedictorians

Graduation and After
30% pursued further study
90% had job offers within 6 months
33 organizations recruited on campus

Financial Matters
$27,350 tuition and fees (2001–02)
$6800 room and board
99% average percent of need met
$20,823 average financial aid amount received
  per undergraduate

Academics
Hamilton awards bachelor's **degrees**. Challenging opportunities include advanced placement credit, accelerated degree programs, student-designed majors, double majors, independent study, and a senior project. Special programs include internships, off-campus study, study-abroad, and Army and Air Force ROTC.

The most frequently chosen **baccalaureate** fields are social sciences and history, psychology, and English. A complete listing of majors at Hamilton appears in the Majors Index beginning on page 430.

The **faculty** at Hamilton has 176 full-time members, 95% with terminal degrees. The student-faculty ratio is 9:1.

Students of Hamilton
The student body is made up of 1,770 undergraduates. 51.4% are women and 48.6% are men. Students come from 43 states and territories and 29 other countries. 41% are from New York. 3% are international students. 4% are African American, 0.2% American Indian, 4.3% Asian American, and 3.9% Hispanic American. 92% returned for their sophomore year.

Facilities and Resources
Student rooms are linked to a campus network. 475 **computers** are available on campus that provide access to the Internet. The 4 **libraries** have 538,377 books and 3,585 subscriptions.

Campus Life
There are 80 active organizations on campus, including a drama/theater group, newspaper, radio station, and choral group. Hamilton has national **fraternities**, local **sororities**, and private society.

Hamilton is a member of the NCAA (Division III). **Intercollegiate sports** include baseball (m), basketball, crew, cross-country running, field hockey (w), football (m), golf (m), ice hockey, lacrosse, soccer, softball (w), squash, swimming, tennis, track and field, volleyball (w).

Campus Safety
Student safety services include student safety program, late-night transport/escort service, 24-hour emergency telephone alarm devices, 24-hour patrols by trained security personnel, and electronically operated dormitory entrances.

Applying
Hamilton requires an essay, SAT I, SAT II or ACT, a high school transcript, 1 recommendation, and sample of expository prose. It recommends an interview. Application deadline: 1/15; 2/1 for financial aid. Early and deferred admission are possible.

HAMLINE UNIVERSITY

URBAN SETTING ■ PRIVATE ■ INDEPENDENT RELIGIOUS ■ COED
ST. PAUL, MINNESOTA

Web site: www.hamline.edu
Contact: Mr. Steven Bjork, Director of Undergraduate Admission, 1536
    Hewitt Avenue C1930, St. Paul, MN 55104-1284
Telephone: 651-523-2207 or toll-free 800-753-9753 **Fax:** 651-523-2458
E-mail: cla-admis@gw.hamline.edu

Academics

Hamline awards bachelor's, master's, doctoral, and first-professional **degrees** and post-bachelor's, post-master's, and first-professional certificates. Challenging opportunities include advanced placement credit, student-designed majors, an honors program, double majors, independent study, and a senior project. Special programs include cooperative education, internships, summer session for credit, off-campus study, study-abroad, and Air Force ROTC.

The most frequently chosen **baccalaureate** fields are social sciences and history, psychology, and business/marketing. A complete listing of majors at Hamline appears in the Majors Index beginning on page 430.

The **faculty** at Hamline has 165 full-time members, 87% with terminal degrees. The student-faculty ratio is 13:1.

Students of Hamline

The student body totals 4,123, of whom 1,873 are undergraduates. 63.8% are women and 36.2% are men. Students come from 35 states and territories and 32 other countries. 66% are from Minnesota. 3.1% are international students. 3.8% are African American, 0.7% American Indian, 4% Asian American, and 1.4% Hispanic American. 81% returned for their sophomore year.

Facilities and Resources

Student rooms are linked to a campus network. 326 **computers** are available on campus that provide access to the Internet. The 2 **libraries** have 445,902 books and 3,803 subscriptions.

Campus Life

There are 75 active organizations on campus, including a drama/theater group, newspaper, and choral group. 5% of eligible women are members of local **sororities** and international dining club.

Hamline is a member of the NCAA (Division III). **Intercollegiate sports** include baseball (m), basketball, cross-country running, football (m), gymnastics (w), ice hockey (m), soccer, softball (w), swimming, tennis, track and field, volleyball (w).

Campus Safety

Student safety services include late-night transport/escort service, 24-hour emergency telephone alarm devices, 24-hour patrols by trained security personnel, student patrols, and electronically operated dormitory entrances.

Applying

Hamline requires an essay, SAT I or ACT, a high school transcript, and 2 recommendations. It recommends an interview. Application deadline: rolling admissions; 5/1 priority date for financial aid. Early and deferred admission are possible.

Getting in Last Year

1,461 applied
79% were accepted
421 enrolled (36%)
26% from top tenth of their h.s. class
3.4 average high school GPA
63% had ACT scores over 24
12% had ACT scores over 30
5 National Merit Scholars
18 valedictorians

Graduation and After

57% graduated in 4 years
6% graduated in 5 years
1% graduated in 6 years
21% pursued further study (9% arts and sciences, 3% education, 3% law)
83% had job offers within 6 months

Financial Matters

$17,602 tuition and fees (2001–02)
$5887 room and board
71% average percent of need met
$17,200 average financial aid amount received per undergraduate

HAMPSHIRE COLLEGE

RURAL SETTING ■ PRIVATE ■ INDEPENDENT ■ COED
AMHERST, MASSACHUSETTS

Web site: www.hampshire.edu
Contact: Ms. Karen S. Parker, Director of Admissions, 839 West Street, Amherst, MA 01002
Telephone: 413-559-5471 or toll-free 877-937-4267 (out-of-state) **Fax:** 413-559-5631
E-mail: admissions@hampshire.edu

Hampshire College's bold, innovative approach to the liberal arts creates an academic atmosphere that energizes students to work hard and grow tremendously, both personally and intellectually. Students have the freedom to design an individualized course of study in a graduate school–like environment, culminating in original final projects such as science or social science research, academic study, or a body of work in writing, performing, visual, or media arts. Students work closely with faculty mentors, often integrating different disciplines. Independent thinking is expected. Hampshire students and faculty members agree: if you incorporate what you love into your education, you will love your education.

Getting in Last Year
1,974 applied
59% were accepted
343 enrolled (30%)
26% from top tenth of their h.s. class
3.28 average high school GPA
76% had SAT verbal scores over 600
49% had SAT math scores over 600
88% had ACT scores over 24
30% had SAT verbal scores over 700
7% had SAT math scores over 700
24% had ACT scores over 30
7 National Merit Scholars
47 class presidents

Graduation and After
38% graduated in 4 years
16% graduated in 5 years
1% graduated in 6 years

Financial Matters
$26,871 tuition and fees (2001–02)
$7010 room and board
100% average percent of need met
$22,465 average financial aid amount received per undergraduate (2000–01)

Academics

Hampshire awards associate and bachelor's **degrees**. Challenging opportunities include advanced placement credit, accelerated degree programs, student-designed majors, double majors, independent study, and a senior project. Special programs include internships, off-campus study, study-abroad, and Army ROTC. A complete listing of majors at Hampshire appears in the Majors Index beginning on page 430.

The **faculty** at Hampshire has 103 full-time members, 87% with terminal degrees. The student-faculty ratio is 11:1.

Students of Hampshire

The student body is made up of 1,219 undergraduates. 57.9% are women and 42.1% are men. Students come from 46 states and territories and 25 other countries. 19% are from Massachusetts. 3.3% are international students. 3.7% are African American, 0.4% American Indian, 3.6% Asian American, and 4.8% Hispanic American. 77% returned for their sophomore year.

Facilities and Resources

Student rooms are linked to a campus network. 125 **computers** are available on campus for student use. The **library** has 105,809 books and 750 subscriptions.

Campus Life

There are 80 active organizations on campus, including a drama/theater group, newspaper, television station, and choral group. No national or local **fraternities** or **sororities**.

Hampshire is a member of the NSCAA. **Intercollegiate sports** include fencing.

Campus Safety

Student safety services include late-night transport/escort service, 24-hour emergency telephone alarm devices, 24-hour patrols by trained security personnel, and student patrols.

Applying

Hampshire requires an essay, a high school transcript, and 2 recommendations. It recommends an interview. Application deadline: 2/1; 2/1 priority date for financial aid. Early and deferred admission are possible.

HANOVER COLLEGE
RURAL SETTING ■ PRIVATE ■ INDEPENDENT RELIGIOUS ■ COED
HANOVER, INDIANA

Web site: www.hanover.edu
Contact: Mr. Kenneth Moyer Jr., Dean of Admissions, Box 108, Hanover, IN
47243-0108
Telephone: 812-866-7021 or toll-free 800-213-2178 **Fax:** 812-866-7098
E-mail: admissions@hanover.edu

Academics
Hanover awards bachelor's **degrees**. Challenging opportunities include advanced placement credit, accelerated degree programs, an honors program, double majors,
independent study, and a senior project. Special programs include internships, off-
campus study, and study-abroad.

The most frequently chosen **baccalaureate** fields are business/marketing, social sciences and history, and education. A complete listing of majors at Hanover appears in the
Majors Index beginning on page 430.

The **faculty** at Hanover has 94 full-time members, 90% with terminal degrees. The
student-faculty ratio is 11:1.

Students of Hanover
The student body is made up of 1,111 undergraduates. 53.8% are women and 46.2% are
men. Students come from 36 states and territories and 18 other countries. 66% are from
Indiana. 2.9% are international students. 1.7% are African American, 0.4% American
Indian, 2.1% Asian American, and 1.5% Hispanic American. 78% returned for their
sophomore year.

Facilities and Resources
Student rooms are linked to a campus network. 90 **computers** are available on campus
that provide access to the Internet. The **library** has 256,909 books and 1,743 subscriptions.

Campus Life
There are 39 active organizations on campus, including a drama/theater group,
newspaper, television station, choral group, and marching band. 37% of eligible men and
47% of eligible women are members of national **fraternities** and national **sororities**.

Hanover is a member of the NCAA (Division III). **Intercollegiate sports** include
baseball (m), basketball, cross-country running, field hockey (w), football (m), golf, soccer, softball (w), tennis, track and field, volleyball (w).

Campus Safety
Student safety services include late-night transport/escort service, 24-hour emergency
telephone alarm devices, 24-hour patrols by trained security personnel, and electronically operated dormitory entrances.

Applying
Hanover requires an essay, SAT I or ACT, a high school transcript, and 1 recom-
mendation. It recommends an interview. Application deadline: 3/1; 3/1 for financial aid.
Early and deferred admission are possible.

Getting in Last Year
1,171 applied
80% were accepted
306 enrolled (33%)
31% from top tenth of their h.s. class
33% had SAT verbal scores over 600
37% had SAT math scores over 600
57% had ACT scores over 24
5% had SAT verbal scores over 700
5% had SAT math scores over 700
15% had ACT scores over 30
18 valedictorians

Graduation and After
31% pursued further study (11% arts and
sciences, 8% law, 4% medicine)
30 organizations recruited on campus

Financial Matters
$12,370 tuition and fees (2001–02)
$5190 room and board
94% average percent of need met
$10,287 average financial aid amount received
per undergraduate (1999–2000)

HARDING UNIVERSITY

SMALL-TOWN SETTING ■ PRIVATE ■ INDEPENDENT RELIGIOUS ■ COED
SEARCY, ARKANSAS

Web site: www.harding.edu
Contact: Mr. Mike Williams, Assistant Vice President of Admissions, Box
    11255, Searcy, AR 72149-0001
Telephone: 501-279-4407 or toll-free 800-477-4407 **Fax:** 501-279-4865
E-mail: admissions@harding.edu

ocated in the beautiful foothills of the Ozark Mountains, Harding is one of America's more highly regarded private universities. At Harding, students build lifetime friendships and, upon graduation, are highly recruited. Harding's Christian environment and challenging academic program develop students who can compete and succeed. Whether on the main campus or in the international studies program in Italy, Greece, England, or Australia, students find Harding to be a caring and serving family. From Missouri flood relief to working with orphans in Haiti or farmers in Kenya, hundreds of Harding students serve others worldwide each year.

Getting in Last Year
1,967 applied
70% were accepted
1,017 enrolled (73%)
35% from top tenth of their h.s. class
3.30 average high school GPA
42% had SAT verbal scores over 600
36% had SAT math scores over 600
49% had ACT scores over 24
6% had SAT verbal scores over 700
6% had SAT math scores over 700
12% had ACT scores over 30
16 National Merit Scholars
45 valedictorians

Graduation and After
29% graduated in 4 years
21% graduated in 5 years
5% graduated in 6 years
25% pursued further study (9% education, 7% arts and sciences, 3% business)
90% had job offers within 6 months
240 organizations recruited on campus

Financial Matters
$9030 tuition and fees (2001–02)
$4498 room and board
73% average percent of need met
$9086 average financial aid amount received per undergraduate

Academics
Harding awards bachelor's and master's **degrees**. Challenging opportunities include advanced placement credit, accelerated degree programs, student-designed majors, freshman honors college, an honors program, double majors, and a senior project. Special programs include cooperative education, internships, summer session for credit, study-abroad, and Army ROTC.

The most frequently chosen **baccalaureate** fields are business/marketing, education, and health professions and related sciences. A complete listing of majors at Harding appears in the Majors Index beginning on page 430.

The **faculty** at Harding has 208 full-time members, 71% with terminal degrees. The student-faculty ratio is 16:1.

Students of Harding
The student body totals 4,677, of whom 4,078 are undergraduates. 54.4% are women and 45.6% are men. Students come from 50 states and territories and 48 other countries. 31% are from Arkansas. 5.6% are international students. 4% are African American, 1.3% American Indian, 0.5% Asian American, and 1.4% Hispanic American. 77% returned for their sophomore year.

Facilities and Resources
Student rooms are linked to a campus network. 150 **computers** are available on campus that provide access to the Internet. The 2 **libraries** have 321,928 books and 1,368 subscriptions.

Campus Life
There are 52 active organizations on campus, including a drama/theater group, newspaper, radio station, choral group, and marching band. 50% of eligible men and 39% of eligible women are members of local **fraternities** and local **sororities**.

Harding is a member of the NCAA (Division II). **Intercollegiate sports** (some offering scholarships) include baseball (m), basketball, cross-country running, football (m), golf (m), soccer, tennis, track and field, volleyball (w).

Campus Safety
Student safety services include 24-hour emergency telephone alarm devices and 24-hour patrols by trained security personnel.

Applying
Harding requires SAT I or ACT, a high school transcript, an interview, and 2 recommendations. Application deadline: 7/1. Early and deferred admission are possible.

HARVARD UNIVERSITY

URBAN SETTING ■ PRIVATE ■ INDEPENDENT ■ COED
CAMBRIDGE, MASSACHUSETTS

Web site: www.harvard.edu
Contact: Office of Admissions and Financial Aid, Byerly Hall, 8 Garden Street, Cambridge, MA 02138
Telephone: 617-495-1551
E-mail: college@harvard.edu

Academics

Harvard awards bachelor's, master's, doctoral, and first-professional **degrees**. Challenging opportunities include advanced placement credit, accelerated degree programs, student-designed majors, an honors program, double majors, independent study, and a senior project. Special programs include internships, summer session for credit, off-campus study, study-abroad, and Army, Navy and Air Force ROTC. A complete listing of majors at Harvard appears in the Majors Index beginning on page 430.

The **faculty** at Harvard has 760 members, 100% with terminal degrees. The student-faculty ratio is 8:1.

Students of Harvard

The student body totals 17,850, of whom 6,660 are undergraduates. Students come from 53 states and territories and 82 other countries. 6.9% are international students. 8% are African American, 0.7% American Indian, 17.5% Asian American, and 7.6% Hispanic American. 97% returned for their sophomore year.

Facilities and Resources

Student rooms are linked to a campus network. The 91 **libraries** have 13,400,000 books and 97,568 subscriptions.

Campus Life

There are 250 active organizations on campus, including a drama/theater group, newspaper, radio station, television station, choral group, and marching band. 99% of eligible men and 99% of eligible women are members of "House" system.

Harvard is a member of the NCAA (Division I). **Intercollegiate sports** include baseball (m), basketball, crew, cross-country running, fencing, field hockey (w), football (m), golf, ice hockey, lacrosse, sailing, skiing (cross-country), skiing (downhill), soccer, softball (w), squash, swimming, tennis, track and field, volleyball, water polo, wrestling (m).

Campus Safety

Student safety services include required and optional safety courses, late-night transport/escort service, 24-hour emergency telephone alarm devices, 24-hour patrols by trained security personnel, and electronically operated dormitory entrances.

Applying

Harvard requires an essay, SAT II Subject Tests, SAT I or ACT, a high school transcript, an interview, and 2 recommendations. Application deadline: 1/1; 2/1 priority date for financial aid. Deferred admission is possible.

Harvard College, the coeducational undergraduate college of Harvard University, offers a curriculum of 3,500 courses, the world's largest university library, a state-of-the-art Science Center, art museums, athletic facilities, and a comprehensive housing system. Excellence and diversity are hallmarks of the experience. Students come from all 50 states and many other countries and from all educational, ethnic, and economic backgrounds. Students choose from more than 40 academic fields and pursue more than 250 different extracurricular activities. The admission process is rigorous. The committee considers academic achievement, extracurricular strengths, and personal qualities. Admission is fully need-blind and financial aid is fully need-based.

Getting in Last Year
19,014 applied
11% were accepted
90% from top tenth of their h.s. class

Graduation and After
86% graduated in 4 years
9% graduated in 5 years
2% graduated in 6 years

Financial Matters
$26,019 tuition and fees (2001–02)
$8250 room and board
100% average percent of need met
$23,064 average financial aid amount received per undergraduate (2000–01)

Harvey Mudd College

Suburban setting ■ Private ■ Independent ■ Coed
Claremont, California

Web site: www.hmc.edu
Contact: Mr. Deren Finks, Vice President and Dean of Admissions and Financial Aid, 301 East 12th Street, Claremont, CA 91711
Telephone: 909-621-8011 **Fax:** 909-607-7046
E-mail: admission@hmc.edu

Getting in Last Year
1,524 applied
34% were accepted
176 enrolled (34%)
89% from top tenth of their h.s. class
96% had SAT verbal scores over 600
100% had SAT math scores over 600
62% had SAT verbal scores over 700
90% had SAT math scores over 700
37 National Merit Scholars
27 valedictorians

Graduation and After
75% graduated in 4 years
7% graduated in 5 years
1% graduated in 6 years
30% pursued further study (21% arts and sciences, 9% engineering)
90% had job offers within 6 months
72 organizations recruited on campus

Financial Matters
$25,506 tuition and fees (2001–02)
$8544 room and board
100% average percent of need met
$19,256 average financial aid amount received per undergraduate

Academics
Harvey Mudd awards bachelor's and master's **degrees**. Challenging opportunities include advanced placement credit, student-designed majors, double majors, and a senior project. Special programs include internships, off-campus study, study-abroad, and Army and Air Force ROTC.

The most frequently chosen **baccalaureate** fields are engineering/engineering technologies, physical sciences, and computer/information sciences. A complete listing of majors at Harvey Mudd appears in the Majors Index beginning on page 430.

The **faculty** at Harvey Mudd has 79 full-time members, 100% with terminal degrees. The student-faculty ratio is 9:1.

Students of Harvey Mudd
The student body totals 707, of whom 706 are undergraduates. 31.6% are women and 68.4% are men. Students come from 43 states and territories and 15 other countries. 46% are from California. 2.5% are international students. 0.7% are African American, 0.6% American Indian, 21.8% Asian American, and 4% Hispanic American. 94% returned for their sophomore year.

Facilities and Resources
Student rooms are linked to a campus network. 200 **computers** are available on campus for student use. The 2 **libraries** have 1,381,108 books and 4,321 subscriptions.

Campus Life
There are 80 active organizations on campus, including a drama/theater group, newspaper, radio station, and choral group. No national or local **fraternities** or **sororities**.

Harvey Mudd is a member of the NCAA (Division III). **Intercollegiate sports** include baseball (m), basketball, cross-country running, football (m), golf (m), soccer, softball (w), swimming, tennis, track and field, volleyball (w), water polo.

Campus Safety
Student safety services include late-night transport/escort service, 24-hour emergency telephone alarm devices, and 24-hour patrols by trained security personnel.

Applying
Harvey Mudd requires an essay, SAT I, SAT II: Writing Test, SAT II Subject Test in math, third SAT II Subject Test, a high school transcript, and 3 recommendations. It recommends an interview. Application deadline: 1/15; 2/1 for financial aid. Deferred admission is possible.

HAVERFORD COLLEGE
SUBURBAN SETTING ■ PRIVATE ■ INDEPENDENT ■ COED
HAVERFORD, PENNSYLVANIA

Web site: www.haverford.edu
Contact: Ms. Delsie Z. Phillips, Director of Admission, 370 Lancaster
  Avenue, Haverford, PA 19041-1392
Telephone: 610-896-1350 **Fax:** 610-896-1338
E-mail: admitme@haverford.edu

Academics
Haverford awards bachelor's **degrees**. Challenging opportunities include advanced placement credit, accelerated degree programs, student-designed majors, double majors, independent study, and a senior project. Special programs include internships, off-campus study, and study-abroad.

The most frequently chosen **baccalaureate** fields are social sciences and history, biological/life sciences, and English. A complete listing of majors at Haverford appears in the Majors Index beginning on page 430.

The **faculty** at Haverford has 103 full-time members, 97% with terminal degrees. The student-faculty ratio is 9:1.

Students of Haverford
The student body is made up of 1,138 undergraduates. Students come from 45 states and territories and 27 other countries. 21% are from Pennsylvania. 2.7% are international students. 5.5% are African American, 0.4% American Indian, 12.8% Asian American, and 5.4% Hispanic American. 96% returned for their sophomore year.

Facilities and Resources
Student rooms are linked to a campus network. 196 **computers** are available on campus for student use. The 6 **libraries** have 395,799 books and 3,240 subscriptions.

Campus Life
There are 50 active organizations on campus, including a drama/theater group, newspaper, radio station, and choral group. No national or local **fraternities** or **sororities**.

Haverford is a member of the NCAA (Division III). **Intercollegiate sports** include baseball (m), basketball, cross-country running, fencing, field hockey (w), lacrosse, soccer, softball (w), squash, tennis, track and field, volleyball (w).

Campus Safety
Student safety services include late-night transport/escort service, 24-hour emergency telephone alarm devices, and 24-hour patrols by trained security personnel.

Applying
Haverford requires SAT II Subject Tests, SAT II: Writing Test, SAT I or ACT, a high school transcript, and 2 recommendations. It recommends an interview. Application deadline: 1/15; 1/31 for financial aid. Early and deferred admission are possible.

Haverford is a liberal arts college of 1,100 students located 10 miles outside of Philadelphia. Academic rigor, integrity, and concern for others form the foundation of Haverford's approach to education. Aspects such as a student-run Honor Code, a sense of Quaker heritage, and a cooperative program with Bryn Mawr College, Swarthmore College, and the University of Pennsylvania mark Haverford as unique. Students thrive in part because classes are small and extracurricular commitment is expected and because the community is passionate about learning, understanding, and making sound and thoughtful judgments.

Getting in Last Year
2,574 applied
33% were accepted
296 enrolled (35%)
81% from top tenth of their h.s. class
88% had SAT verbal scores over 600
88% had SAT math scores over 600
52% had SAT verbal scores over 700
44% had SAT math scores over 700

Graduation and After
89% graduated in 4 years
3% graduated in 5 years
18% pursued further study (9% arts and sciences, 7% medicine, 2% law)
68% had job offers within 6 months
162 organizations recruited on campus

Financial Matters
$26,070 tuition and fees (2001–02)
$8230 room and board
100% average percent of need met
$22,646 average financial aid amount received per undergraduate

HEIDELBERG COLLEGE
SMALL-TOWN SETTING ■ PRIVATE ■ INDEPENDENT RELIGIOUS ■ COED
TIFFIN, OHIO

Web site: www.heidelberg.edu
Contact: Ms. Sharon Pugh, Director of Admission, 310 East Market Street,
　Tiffin, OH 44883
Telephone: 419-448-2330 or toll-free 800-434-3352 **Fax:** 419-448-2334
E-mail: adminfo@heidelberg.edu

Getting in Last Year
1,424 applied
89% were accepted
294 enrolled (23%)
20% from top tenth of their h.s. class
3.2 average high school GPA
23% had SAT verbal scores over 600
20% had SAT math scores over 600
33% had ACT scores over 24
1% had SAT verbal scores over 700
4% had ACT scores over 30
7 valedictorians

Graduation and After
38% graduated in 4 years
10% graduated in 5 years
20% pursued further study (14% arts and
　sciences, 3% medicine, 1% dentistry)
95% had job offers within 6 months
30 organizations recruited on campus

Financial Matters
$18,130 tuition and fees (2001–02)
$5747 room and board
91% average percent of need met
$16,011 average financial aid amount received
　per undergraduate

Academics
Heidelberg awards bachelor's and master's **degrees**. Challenging opportunities include advanced placement credit, accelerated degree programs, an honors program, double majors, and a senior project. Special programs include internships, summer session for credit, off-campus study, study-abroad, and Army and Air Force ROTC.

The most frequently chosen **baccalaureate** fields are business/marketing, education, and parks and recreation. A complete listing of majors at Heidelberg appears in the Majors Index beginning on page 430.

The **faculty** at Heidelberg has 74 full-time members, 73% with terminal degrees. The student-faculty ratio is 13:1.

Students of Heidelberg
The student body totals 1,517, of whom 1,288 are undergraduates. 54.4% are women and 45.6% are men. Students come from 25 states and territories and 7 other countries. 87% are from Ohio. 0.8% are international students. 2.6% are African American, 0.5% American Indian, 0.5% Asian American, and 1.4% Hispanic American. 79% returned for their sophomore year.

Facilities and Resources
Student rooms are linked to a campus network. 125 **computers** are available on campus that provide access to the Internet. The 2 **libraries** have 260,055 books and 829 subscriptions.

Campus Life
There are 60 active organizations on campus, including a drama/theater group, newspaper, radio station, and choral group. 75% of eligible men and 75% of eligible women are members of local **fraternities** and local **sororities**.

Heidelberg is a member of the NCAA (Division III). **Intercollegiate sports** include baseball (m), basketball, cross-country running, football (m), golf, soccer, softball (w), tennis, track and field, volleyball (w), wrestling (m).

Campus Safety
Student safety services include late-night transport/escort service, 24-hour emergency telephone alarm devices, student patrols, and electronically operated dormitory entrances.

Applying
Heidelberg requires SAT I or ACT, a high school transcript, and a minimum high school GPA of 2.4. It recommends an interview and 1 recommendation. Application deadline: 8/1; 3/1 priority date for financial aid. Deferred admission is possible.

HENDRIX COLLEGE

SUBURBAN SETTING ■ PRIVATE ■ INDEPENDENT RELIGIOUS ■ COED
CONWAY, ARKANSAS

Web site: www.hendrix.edu
Contact: Mr. Art Weeden, Vice President for Enrollment, 1600 Washington
  Avenue, Conway, AR 72032
Telephone: 501-450-1362 or toll-free 800-277-9017 **Fax:** 501-450-3843
E-mail: adm@hendrix.edu

Academics

Hendrix awards bachelor's and master's **degrees**. Challenging opportunities include
advanced placement credit, student-designed majors, double majors, independent study,
and a senior project. Special programs include internships, off-campus study, study-
abroad, and Army ROTC.

The most frequently chosen **baccalaureate** fields are social sciences and history,
biological/life sciences, and psychology. A complete listing of majors at Hendrix appears
in the Majors Index beginning on page 430.

The **faculty** at Hendrix has 79 full-time members, 95% with terminal degrees. The
student-faculty ratio is 13:1.

Students of Hendrix

The student body totals 1,085, of whom 1,079 are undergraduates. 53.7% are women
and 46.3% are men. Students come from 32 states and territories and 13 other countries.
69% are from Arkansas. 4.7% are African American, 1.4% American Indian, 2.1% Asian
American, and 2.3% Hispanic American. 84% returned for their sophomore year.

Facilities and Resources

Student rooms are linked to a campus network. 75 **computers** are available on campus
for student use. The **library** has 232,663 books and 731 subscriptions.

Campus Life

There are 56 active organizations on campus, including a drama/theater group,
newspaper, radio station, and choral group. No national or local **fraternities** or **sororities**.

Hendrix is a member of the NCAA (Division III). **Intercollegiate sports** include
baseball (m), basketball, cross-country running, golf, soccer, softball (w), swimming, tennis, track and field, volleyball (w).

Campus Safety

Student safety services include late-night transport/escort service, 24-hour emergency
telephone alarm devices, 24-hour patrols by trained security personnel, and electronically operated dormitory entrances.

Applying

Hendrix requires an essay, SAT I or ACT, and a high school transcript, and in some cases
an interview. It recommends 2 recommendations. Application deadline: rolling admissions; 2/15 priority date for financial aid. Deferred admission is possible.

Getting in Last Year
1,056 applied
82% were accepted
279 enrolled (32%)
41% from top tenth of their h.s. class
3.70 average high school GPA
66% had SAT verbal scores over 600
55% had SAT math scores over 600
87% had ACT scores over 24
20% had SAT verbal scores over 700
10% had SAT math scores over 700
33% had ACT scores over 30
6 National Merit Scholars
16 valedictorians

Graduation and After
55% graduated in 4 years
4% graduated in 5 years
1% graduated in 6 years
40% pursued further study (20% medicine,
  17% law, 11% business)
44% had job offers within 6 months
73 organizations recruited on campus

Financial Matters
$13,711 tuition and fees (2001–02)
$4752 room and board
87% average percent of need met
$12,451 average financial aid amount received
  per undergraduate

HILLSDALE COLLEGE

SMALL-TOWN SETTING ■ PRIVATE ■ INDEPENDENT ■ COED
HILLSDALE, MICHIGAN

Web site: www.hillsdale.edu
Contact: Mr. Jeffrey S. Lantis, Director of Admissions, 33 East College
  Street, Hillsdale, MI 49242-1298
Telephone: 517-607-2327 ext. 2327 **Fax:** 517-607-2298
E-mail: admissions@hillsdale.edu

A t Hillsdale College, our curriculum and daily campus life are guided by a set of ideals basic to the American way of life. Hillsdale's history of independence has tangible consequences in shaping how we run our school and what we teach. Our Judeo-Christian heritage and the honored truths of Western civilization form the basis for our curriculum.

Getting in Last Year
925 applied
85% were accepted
355 enrolled (45%)
42% from top tenth of their h.s. class
3.56 average high school GPA
63% had SAT verbal scores over 600
55% had SAT math scores over 600
72% had ACT scores over 24
26% had SAT verbal scores over 700
13% had SAT math scores over 700
19% had ACT scores over 30
12 National Merit Scholars
26 valedictorians

Graduation and After
53% graduated in 4 years
18% graduated in 5 years
Graduates pursuing further study: 7% arts and
  sciences, 5% business, 5% law
98% had job offers within 6 months
44 organizations recruited on campus

Financial Matters
$14,700 tuition and fees (2001–02)
$5886 room and board
77% average percent of need met
$14,000 average financial aid amount received
  per undergraduate

Academics
Hillsdale awards bachelor's **degrees**. Challenging opportunities include advanced placement credit, accelerated degree programs, an honors program, double majors, independent study, and a senior project. Special programs include internships, summer session for credit, and study-abroad.

The most frequently chosen **baccalaureate** fields are business/marketing, social sciences and history, and education. A complete listing of majors at Hillsdale appears in the Majors Index beginning on page 430.

The **faculty** at Hillsdale has 89 full-time members, 100% with terminal degrees. The student-faculty ratio is 11:1.

Students of Hillsdale
The student body is made up of 1,168 undergraduates. 51.2% are women and 48.8% are men. Students come from 47 states and territories and 10 other countries. 49% are from Michigan. 87% returned for their sophomore year.

Facilities and Resources
Student rooms are linked to a campus network. 175 **computers** are available on campus that provide access to the Internet. The 4 **libraries** have 205,000 books and 1,623 subscriptions.

Campus Life
There are 45 active organizations on campus, including a drama/theater group, newspaper, and choral group. 35% of eligible men and 45% of eligible women are members of national **fraternities** and national **sororities**.

Hillsdale is a member of the NCAA (Division II). **Intercollegiate sports** (some offering scholarships) include baseball (m), basketball, cross-country running, equestrian sports (w), football (m), golf (m), ice hockey (m), soccer, softball (w), swimming, tennis, track and field, volleyball (w).

Campus Safety
Student safety services include late-night transport/escort service, 24-hour emergency telephone alarm devices, 24-hour patrols by trained security personnel, and electronically operated dormitory entrances.

Applying
Hillsdale requires an essay, SAT I or ACT, a high school transcript, 1 recommendation, and a minimum high school GPA of 3.1, and in some cases an interview. It recommends SAT II Subject Tests, SAT II: Writing Test, and an interview. Application deadline: rolling admissions; 3/15 priority date for financial aid. Early and deferred admission are possible.

HIRAM COLLEGE

RURAL SETTING ■ PRIVATE ■ INDEPENDENT RELIGIOUS ■ COED
HIRAM, OHIO

Web site: www.hiram.edu

Contact: Mr. Ed Frato Sweeney, Director of Admission, Box 96, Hiram, OH
44234-0067

Telephone: 330-569-5169 or toll-free 800-362-5280 **Fax:** 330-569-5944

E-mail: admission@hiram.edu

Academics

Hiram awards bachelor's **degrees**. Challenging opportunities include advanced placement credit, accelerated degree programs, student-designed majors, double majors, independent study, and a senior project. Special programs include internships, summer session for credit, off-campus study, and study-abroad.

The most frequently chosen **baccalaureate** fields are business/marketing, biological/life sciences, and social sciences and history. A complete listing of majors at Hiram appears in the Majors Index beginning on page 430.

The **faculty** at Hiram has 73 full-time members, 96% with terminal degrees. The student-faculty ratio is 11:1.

Students of Hiram

The student body is made up of 1,190 undergraduates. 57.1% are women and 42.9% are men. Students come from 23 states and territories and 19 other countries. 79% are from Ohio. 3.2% are international students. 8.5% are African American, 0.3% American Indian, 1.2% Asian American, and 1.3% Hispanic American. 77% returned for their sophomore year.

Facilities and Resources

Student rooms are linked to a campus network. The **library** has 185,153 books and 4,191 subscriptions.

Campus Life

There are 60 active organizations on campus, including a drama/theater group, newspaper, radio station, television station, and choral group. 8% of eligible men and 12% of eligible women are members of local **fraternities**, local **sororities**, and vegetarian co-op.

Hiram is a member of the NCAA (Division III). **Intercollegiate sports** include baseball (m), basketball, cross-country running, football (m), golf, soccer, softball (w), swimming, tennis, track and field, volleyball (w).

Campus Safety

Student safety services include late-night transport/escort service, 24-hour emergency telephone alarm devices, 24-hour patrols by trained security personnel, and electronically operated dormitory entrances.

Applying

Hiram requires an essay, SAT I or ACT, a high school transcript, and 2 recommendations, and in some cases an interview. It recommends an interview and 3 recommendations. Application deadline: 2/1; 2/15 priority date for financial aid. Early and deferred admission are possible.

Hiram's 12-3 academic calendar is unique among colleges and universities. Each 15-week semester combines a comprehensive 12-week session of 3 courses with an intensive, 3-week immersion in a single seminar either on or off campus. Hiram supplements classroom study through career-oriented internships and an extensive and distinctive study-abroad program that takes Hiram students all over the world. More than 50% of Hiram students participate, and all courses are taught by Hiram faculty members and are a regular part of the curriculum. Hiram recently opened a new $6.2-million science hall.

Getting in Last Year
1,022 applied
79% were accepted
275 enrolled (34%)
10% from top tenth of their h.s. class
3.42 average high school GPA
41% had SAT verbal scores over 600
33% had SAT math scores over 600
49% had ACT scores over 24
10% had SAT verbal scores over 700
4% had SAT math scores over 700
6% had ACT scores over 30
11 valedictorians

Graduation and After
62% graduated in 4 years
2% graduated in 5 years
1% graduated in 6 years
52% had job offers within 6 months
70 organizations recruited on campus

Financial Matters
$19,392 tuition and fees (2001–02)
$6514 room and board
84% average percent of need met
$16,455 average financial aid amount received per undergraduate

HOBART AND WILLIAM SMITH COLLEGES

SMALL-TOWN SETTING ■ PRIVATE ■ INDEPENDENT ■ COED
GENEVA, NEW YORK

Web site: www.hws.edu
Contact: Ms. Mara O'Laughlin, Director of Admissions, 629 South Main Street, Geneva, NY 14456-3397
Telephone: 315-781-3472 or toll-free 800-245-0100 **Fax:** 315-781-5471
E-mail: admissions@hws.edu

With maximum breadth and depth of course offerings, innovative teaching methods, and small classes that foster close interaction with faculty members, Hobart and William Smith provide a true liberal arts education. In addition to learning on campus, a majority of HWS students study abroad, choosing from nearly 30 locales, or take part in internships—or both. The interdisciplinary, holistic approach at Hobart and William Smith helps students reach whatever academic and personal goals they set for themselves.

Getting in Last Year
2,928 applied
69% were accepted
548 enrolled (27%)
30% from top tenth of their h.s. class
3.21 average high school GPA
37% had SAT verbal scores over 600
36% had SAT math scores over 600
4% had SAT verbal scores over 700
3% had SAT math scores over 700
7 National Merit Scholars
11 class presidents
1 valedictorian

Graduation and After
68% graduated in 4 years
4% graduated in 5 years
1% graduated in 6 years
30% pursued further study (14% arts and sciences, 5% medicine, 4% law)
70% had job offers within 6 months
48 organizations recruited on campus

Financial Matters
$26,177 tuition and fees (2001–02)
$7018 room and board
97% average percent of need met
$22,089 average financial aid amount received per undergraduate

Academics
HWS awards bachelor's **degrees**. Challenging opportunities include advanced placement credit, accelerated degree programs, student-designed majors, an honors program, double majors, independent study, and a senior project. Special programs include internships, off-campus study, and study-abroad.

The most frequently chosen **baccalaureate** fields are social sciences and history, English, and psychology. A complete listing of majors at HWS appears in the Majors Index beginning on page 430.

The **faculty** at HWS has 148 full-time members, 91% with terminal degrees. The student-faculty ratio is 12:1.

Students of HWS
The student body is made up of 1,892 undergraduates. 55.8% are women and 44.2% are men. Students come from 38 states and territories and 18 other countries. 50% are from New York. 1.5% are international students. 4.5% are African American, 0.3% American Indian, 1.6% Asian American, and 3.9% Hispanic American. 85% returned for their sophomore year.

Facilities and Resources
Student rooms are linked to a campus network. 221 **computers** are available on campus that provide access to the Internet. The 2 **libraries** have 359,742 books and 3,289 subscriptions.

Campus Life
There are 60 active organizations on campus, including a drama/theater group, newspaper, radio station, and choral group. 15% of eligible men are members of national **fraternities**.

HWS is a member of the NCAA (Division III). **Intercollegiate sports** include basketball, crew, cross-country running, field hockey (w), football (m), golf (m), ice hockey (m), lacrosse, sailing, soccer, squash, swimming (w), tennis.

Campus Safety
Student safety services include late-night transport/escort service, 24-hour emergency telephone alarm devices, 24-hour patrols by trained security personnel, and electronically operated dormitory entrances.

Applying
HWS requires an essay, SAT I or ACT, a high school transcript, and 2 recommendations. It recommends SAT II Subject Tests and an interview. Application deadline: 2/1; 3/15 for financial aid, with a 2/15 priority date. Early and deferred admission are possible.

Hope College

SMALL-TOWN SETTING ■ PRIVATE ■ INDEPENDENT RELIGIOUS ■ COED
HOLLAND, MICHIGAN

Web site: www.hope.edu
Contact: Dr. James R. Bekkering, Vice President for Admissions, 69 East 10th Street, PO Box 9000, Holland, MI 49422-9000
Telephone: 616-395-7955 or toll-free 800-968-7850 **Fax:** 616-395-7130
E-mail: admissions@hope.edu

Academics

Hope awards bachelor's **degrees**. Challenging opportunities include advanced placement credit, student-designed majors, double majors, independent study, and a senior project. Special programs include internships, summer session for credit, off-campus study, and study-abroad.

The most frequently chosen **baccalaureate** fields are business/marketing, English, and social sciences and history. A complete listing of majors at Hope appears in the Majors Index beginning on page 430.

The **faculty** at Hope has 208 full-time members, 83% with terminal degrees. The student-faculty ratio is 14:1.

Students of Hope

The student body is made up of 2,999 undergraduates. 60.3% are women and 39.7% are men. Students come from 38 states and territories and 40 other countries. 77% are from Michigan. 1.6% are international students. 1% are African American, 0.2% American Indian, 2.4% Asian American, and 1.5% Hispanic American. 87% returned for their sophomore year.

Facilities and Resources

Student rooms are linked to a campus network. 300 **computers** are available on campus that provide access to the Internet. The 2 **libraries** have 330,408 books and 2,250 subscriptions.

Campus Life

There are 67 active organizations on campus, including a drama/theater group, newspaper, radio station, television station, and choral group. 6% of eligible men and 15% of eligible women are members of local **fraternities** and local **sororities**.

Hope is a member of the NCAA (Division III). **Intercollegiate sports** include baseball (m), basketball, cross-country running, football (m), golf, soccer, softball (w), swimming, tennis, track and field, volleyball (w).

Campus Safety

Student safety services include deputized sheriffs, late-night transport/escort service, 24-hour emergency telephone alarm devices, 24-hour patrols by trained security personnel, and electronically operated dormitory entrances.

Applying

Hope requires an essay, SAT I or ACT, and a high school transcript, and in some cases 1 recommendation. It recommends an interview. Application deadline: rolling admissions; 2/15 priority date for financial aid. Early and deferred admission are possible.

Getting in Last Year

2,110 applied
89% were accepted
763 enrolled (41%)
34% from top tenth of their h.s. class
3.69 average high school GPA
49% had SAT verbal scores over 600
57% had SAT math scores over 600
64% had ACT scores over 24
12% had SAT verbal scores over 700
16% had SAT math scores over 700
15% had ACT scores over 30
13 National Merit Scholars
17 valedictorians

Graduation and After

52% graduated in 4 years
15% graduated in 5 years
2% graduated in 6 years
27% pursued further study (9% arts and sciences, 3% education, 2% medicine)
61 organizations recruited on campus

Financial Matters

$17,448 tuition and fees (2001–02)
$5474 room and board
88% average percent of need met
$14,670 average financial aid amount received per undergraduate

HUNTINGDON COLLEGE

SUBURBAN SETTING ■ PRIVATE ■ INDEPENDENT RELIGIOUS ■ COED
MONTGOMERY, ALABAMA

Web site: www.huntingdon.edu
Contact: Mrs. Laura Huncan, Director of Admissions, 1500 East Fairview
  Avenue, Montgomery, AL 36106
Telephone: 334-833-4496 or toll-free 800-763-0313 **Fax:** 334-833-4347
E-mail: admiss@huntingdon.edu

Getting in Last Year

579 applied
82% were accepted
152 enrolled (32%)
49% from top tenth of their h.s. class
3.38 average high school GPA
47% had SAT verbal scores over 600
39% had SAT math scores over 600
48% had ACT scores over 24
8% had SAT verbal scores over 700
4% had ACT scores over 30
3 class presidents
7 valedictorians

Graduation and After

34% graduated in 4 years
13% graduated in 5 years
2% graduated in 6 years
25% pursued further study
50% had job offers within 6 months
50 organizations recruited on campus

Financial Matters

$12,420 tuition and fees (2001–02)
$5750 room and board
91% average percent of need met
$10,654 average financial aid amount received
  per undergraduate (2000–01 estimated)

Academics

Huntingdon awards associate and bachelor's **degrees**. Challenging opportunities include advanced placement credit, accelerated degree programs, student-designed majors, an honors program, double majors, independent study, and a senior project. Special programs include cooperative education, internships, summer session for credit, off-campus study, study-abroad, and Army and Air Force ROTC.

The most frequently chosen **baccalaureate** fields are business/marketing, parks and recreation, and visual/performing arts. A complete listing of majors at Huntingdon appears in the Majors Index beginning on page 430.

The **faculty** at Huntingdon has 41 full-time members, 85% with terminal degrees. The student-faculty ratio is 12:1.

Students of Huntingdon

The student body is made up of 615 undergraduates. 64.6% are women and 35.4% are men. Students come from 21 states and territories and 12 other countries. 81% are from Alabama. 3.6% are international students. 7.5% are African American, 0.8% American Indian, 1.1% Asian American, and 0.3% Hispanic American. 80% returned for their sophomore year.

Facilities and Resources

Student rooms are linked to a campus network. 75 **computers** are available on campus that provide access to personal computer given to each entering student and the Internet. The **library** has 97,436 books and 443 subscriptions.

Campus Life

There are 50 active organizations on campus, including a drama/theater group, newspaper, and choral group. 30% of eligible men and 26% of eligible women are members of national **fraternities** and national **sororities**.

Huntingdon is a member of the NCAA (Division III). **Intercollegiate sports** include baseball (m), basketball, cross-country running, golf (m), soccer, softball (w), tennis, volleyball (w).

Campus Safety

Student safety services include electronic video surveillance, late-night transport/escort service, 24-hour emergency telephone alarm devices, 24-hour patrols by trained security personnel, and electronically operated dormitory entrances.

Applying

Huntingdon requires SAT I or ACT, a high school transcript, and a minimum high school GPA of 2.25, and in some cases an essay, an interview, and 2 recommendations. It recommends 3 recommendations. Application deadline: rolling admissions; 4/15 priority date for financial aid. Early and deferred admission are possible.

Illinois College

SMALL-TOWN SETTING ■ PRIVATE ■ INDEPENDENT RELIGIOUS ■ COED
JACKSONVILLE, ILLINOIS

Web site: www.ic.edu
Contact: Mr. Rick Bystry, Director of Admission, 1101 West College, Jacksonville, IL 62650
Telephone: 217-245-3030 or toll-free 866-464-5265 **Fax:** 217-245-3034
E-mail: admissions@ic.edu

Academics

IC awards bachelor's **degrees**. Challenging opportunities include advanced placement credit, accelerated degree programs, double majors, independent study, and a senior project. Special programs include internships, summer session for credit, and study-abroad.

The most frequently chosen **baccalaureate** fields are education, business/marketing, and social sciences and history. A complete listing of majors at IC appears in the Majors Index beginning on page 430.

The **faculty** at IC has 59 full-time members, 80% with terminal degrees. The student-faculty ratio is 14:1.

Students of IC

The student body is made up of 874 undergraduates. 54.8% are women and 45.2% are men. Students come from 12 states and territories and 6 other countries. 98% are from Illinois. 0.7% are international students. 2.7% are African American, 0.2% American Indian, 0.5% Asian American, and 1.8% Hispanic American. 75% returned for their sophomore year.

Facilities and Resources

Student rooms are linked to a campus network. 97 **computers** are available on campus for student use. The **library** has 143,500 books and 620 subscriptions.

Campus Life

There are 50 active organizations on campus, including a drama/theater group, newspaper, television station, and choral group. 30% of eligible men and 30% of eligible women are members of local **fraternities** and local **sororities**.

IC is a member of the NCAA (Division III). **Intercollegiate sports** include baseball (m), cross-country running, football (m), golf, soccer, softball (w), tennis, track and field, volleyball (w), wrestling (m).

Campus Safety

Student safety services include late-night transport/escort service, 24-hour emergency telephone alarm devices, 24-hour patrols by trained security personnel, and electronically operated dormitory entrances.

Applying

IC requires SAT I or ACT, a high school transcript, and 2 recommendations, and in some cases an essay. It recommends an interview. Application deadline: 8/15; 3/15 priority date for financial aid.

Founded in 1829, Illinois College is a private liberal arts institution enrolling approximately 1,000 students. The College offers more than 45 recognized academic programs, provides an individualized educational experience, and is distinguished as a Phi Beta Kappa institution. Its one-of-a-kind Break Away program features off-campus and international adventures, internships, and more.

Getting in Last Year
919 applied
67% were accepted
205 enrolled (33%)
20% from top tenth of their h.s. class
3.25 average high school GPA
50% had SAT verbal scores over 600
36% had ACT scores over 24
8% had ACT scores over 30

Graduation and After
44% graduated in 4 years
8% graduated in 5 years
1% graduated in 6 years
27% pursued further study

Financial Matters
$11,272 tuition and fees (2001–02)
$4962 room and board
90% average percent of need met
$10,630 average financial aid amount received per undergraduate

ILLINOIS INSTITUTE OF TECHNOLOGY

URBAN SETTING ■ PRIVATE ■ INDEPENDENT ■ COED
CHICAGO, ILLINOIS

Web site: www.iit.edu
Contact: Mr. Terry Miller, Dean of Undergraduate Admission, 10 West 33rd Street PH101, Chicago, IL 60616-3793
Telephone: 312-567-3025 or toll-free 800-448-2329 (out-of-state) **Fax:** 312-567-6939
E-mail: admission@iit.edu

As a member of the Association of Independent Technological Universities, Illinois Institute of Technology (IIT) is known for its excellent programs in architecture, engineering, science, premed, and prelaw. A small undergraduate population of approximately 1,700 students results in small class size and a 12:1 student-faculty ratio. Admission is competitive and the student body is diverse. Approximately 70% of students live on campus. (Freshman on-campus housing is guaranteed.) Located in the city of Chicago, IIT offers numerous opportunities to explore a variety of cultural and recreational activities. IIT offers need-based financial aid and generous scholarship programs up to full tuition and room and board.

Academics
IIT awards bachelor's, master's, doctoral, and first-professional **degrees** and post-bachelor's certificates. Challenging opportunities include advanced placement credit, accelerated degree programs, double majors, and a senior project. Special programs include cooperative education, internships, summer session for credit, study-abroad, and Army, Navy and Air Force ROTC.

The most frequently chosen **baccalaureate** fields are engineering/engineering technologies, architecture, and computer/information sciences. A complete listing of majors at IIT appears in the Majors Index beginning on page 430.

The **faculty** at IIT has 317 full-time members, 98% with terminal degrees. The student-faculty ratio is 12:1.

Students of IIT
The student body totals 6,050, of whom 1,842 are undergraduates. 25.1% are women and 74.9% are men. Students come from 49 states and territories and 77 other countries. 54% are from Illinois. 18.7% are international students. 6.4% are African American, 0.4% American Indian, 15.6% Asian American, and 7.5% Hispanic American. 88% returned for their sophomore year.

Facilities and Resources
Student rooms are linked to a campus network. 450 **computers** are available on campus that provide access to the Internet. The 6 **libraries** have 829,386 books and 7,512 subscriptions.

Campus Life
There are 75 active organizations on campus, including a drama/theater group, newspaper, and radio station. 18% of eligible men and 9% of eligible women are members of national **fraternities**, national **sororities**, and local sororities.

IIT is a member of the NAIA. **Intercollegiate sports** (some offering scholarships) include baseball (m), basketball, cross-country running, swimming, volleyball (w).

Campus Safety
Student safety services include late-night transport/escort service, 24-hour emergency telephone alarm devices, 24-hour patrols by trained security personnel, and electronically operated dormitory entrances.

Applying
IIT requires SAT I or ACT, a high school transcript, 1 recommendation, and a minimum high school GPA of 3.0, and in some cases an essay and an interview. It recommends SAT II Subject Tests. Application deadline: rolling admissions. Deferred admission is possible.

Getting in Last Year
2,562 applied
62% were accepted
294 enrolled (19%)
53% from top tenth of their h.s. class
3.75 average high school GPA
75% had SAT verbal scores over 600
85% had SAT math scores over 600
95% had ACT scores over 24
23% had SAT verbal scores over 700
47% had SAT math scores over 700
39% had ACT scores over 30

Graduation and After
24% graduated in 4 years
20% graduated in 5 years
2% graduated in 6 years
30% pursued further study
56% had job offers within 6 months
90 organizations recruited on campus

Financial Matters
$18,760 tuition and fees (2001–02)
$5624 room and board
57% average percent of need met
$18,808 average financial aid amount received per undergraduate

Illinois Wesleyan University

Suburban setting ■ Private ■ Independent ■ Coed
Bloomington, Illinois

Web site: www.iwu.edu
Contact: Mr. James R. Ruoti, Dean of Admissions, PO Box 2900,
Bloomington, IL 61702-2900
Telephone: 309-556-3031 or toll-free 800-332-2498 **Fax:** 309-556-3411
E-mail: iwuadmit@titan.iwu.edu

Academics

IWU awards bachelor's **degrees**. Challenging opportunities include advanced placement credit, student-designed majors, an honors program, double majors, and independent study. Special programs include cooperative education, internships, summer session for credit, off-campus study, study-abroad, and Army ROTC.

The most frequently chosen **baccalaureate** fields are business/marketing, social sciences and history, and visual/performing arts. A complete listing of majors at IWU appears in the Majors Index beginning on page 430.

The **faculty** at IWU has 154 full-time members, 94% with terminal degrees. The student-faculty ratio is 12:1.

Students of IWU

The student body is made up of 2,064 undergraduates. 56.4% are women and 43.6% are men. Students come from 31 states and territories and 27 other countries. 89% are from Illinois. 2.6% are international students. 2.6% are African American, 2.8% Asian American, and 1.7% Hispanic American. 90% returned for their sophomore year.

Facilities and Resources

Student rooms are linked to a campus network. 450 **computers** are available on campus that provide access to the Internet. The **library** has 271,577 books and 11,577 subscriptions.

Campus Life

There are 130 active organizations on campus, including a drama/theater group, newspaper, radio station, television station, and choral group. 39% of eligible men and 30% of eligible women are members of national **fraternities** and national **sororities**.

IWU is a member of the NCAA (Division III). **Intercollegiate sports** include baseball (m), basketball, cross-country running, football (m), golf, soccer, softball (w), swimming, tennis, track and field, volleyball (w).

Campus Safety

Student safety services include student/administration security committee, late-night transport/escort service, 24-hour emergency telephone alarm devices, 24-hour patrols by trained security personnel, and student patrols.

Applying

IWU requires an essay, SAT I or ACT, a high school transcript, and a minimum high school GPA of 2.0. It recommends an interview, 3 recommendations, and a minimum high school GPA of 3.0. Application deadline: 3/1; 3/1 for financial aid. Early and deferred admission are possible.

Illinois Wesleyan University (IWU) students are encouraged to pursue multiple interests simultaneously—a philosophy in keeping with the spirit and value of a broad liberal arts education. A student majoring in music and biology put it this way: "At IWU, it's possible to double major and graduate in 4 years. Other campuses told me it would take 5 years." IWU is prepared for the 21st century. With the opening of the $26-million Ames Library and the $8-million Hanson Student Center in spring 2002, IWU will have invested more than $115 million in campus resources in just the last 7 years.

Getting in Last Year
2,795 applied
57% were accepted
567 enrolled (35%)
47% from top tenth of their h.s. class
67% had SAT verbal scores over 600
72% had SAT math scores over 600
99% had ACT scores over 24
21% had SAT verbal scores over 700
19% had SAT math scores over 700
28% had ACT scores over 30
8 National Merit Scholars

Graduation and After
25% pursued further study (11% arts and sciences, 5% law, 5% medicine)
68% had job offers within 6 months
76 organizations recruited on campus

Financial Matters
$21,640 tuition and fees (2001–02)
$5330 room and board
93% average percent of need met
$16,024 average financial aid amount received per undergraduate

Indiana Wesleyan University

SMALL-TOWN SETTING ■ PRIVATE ■ INDEPENDENT RELIGIOUS ■ COED
MARION, INDIANA

Web site: www.indwes.edu
Contact: Ms. Gaytha Holloway, Director of Admissions, 4201 South
  Washington Street, Marion, IN 46953
Telephone: 765-677-2138 or toll-free 800-332-6901 **Fax:** 765-677-2333
E-mail: admissions@indwes.edu

Getting in Last Year
1,702 applied
79% were accepted
3.40 average high school GPA
28% had SAT verbal scores over 600
25% had SAT math scores over 600
51% had ACT scores over 24
4% had SAT verbal scores over 700
4% had SAT math scores over 700
9% had ACT scores over 30
8 National Merit Scholars
20 valedictorians

Graduation and After
40 organizations recruited on campus

Financial Matters
$12,740 tuition and fees (2001–02)
$4940 room and board

Academics
IWU awards associate, bachelor's, and master's **degrees** and post-master's certificates
(also offers adult program with significant enrollment not reflected in profile). Challenging opportunities include advanced placement credit, accelerated degree programs, student-designed majors, freshman honors college, an honors program, double majors,
independent study, and a senior project. Special programs include internships, summer
session for credit, off-campus study, and study-abroad.

The most frequently chosen **baccalaureate** fields are business/marketing, health
professions and related sciences, and education. A complete listing of majors at IWU
appears in the Majors Index beginning on page 430.

The **faculty** at IWU has 104 full-time members, 48% with terminal degrees. The
student-faculty ratio is 17:1.

Students of IWU
The student body totals 7,933, of whom 5,725 are undergraduates. Students come from
42 states and territories and 17 other countries. 80% are from Indiana. 1% are international students. 10.4% are African American, 0.5% American Indian, 0.6% Asian
American, and 1% Hispanic American. 74% returned for their sophomore year.

Facilities and Resources
Student rooms are linked to a campus network. 163 **computers** are available on campus
that provide access to the Internet. The **library** has 106,362 books and 5,343 subscriptions.

Campus Life
There are 35 active organizations on campus, including a drama/theater group,
newspaper, radio station, television station, and choral group. No national or local
fraternities or **sororities**.

IWU is a member of the NAIA and NCCAA. **Intercollegiate sports** (some offering
scholarships) include baseball (m), basketball, cross-country running, golf (m), soccer,
softball (w), tennis, track and field, volleyball (w).

Campus Safety
Student safety services include late-night transport/escort service, 24-hour emergency
telephone alarm devices, 24-hour patrols by trained security personnel, and electronically operated dormitory entrances.

Applying
IWU requires an essay, SAT I or ACT, a high school transcript, 1 recommendation, and
a minimum high school GPA of 2.0, and in some cases an interview. Application
deadline: rolling admissions; 3/1 priority date for financial aid. Deferred admission is
possible.

Iowa State University of Science and Technology

Suburban setting ■ Public ■ State-supported ■ Coed
Ames, Iowa

Web site: www.iastate.edu
Contact: Mr. Phil Caffrey, Associate Director for Freshman Admissions, 100 Alumni Hall, Ames, IA 50011-2010
Telephone: 515-294-5836 or toll-free 800-262-3810 **Fax:** 515-294-2592
E-mail: admissions@iastate.edu

Academics
Iowa State awards bachelor's, master's, doctoral, and first-professional **degrees** and post-master's certificates. Challenging opportunities include advanced placement credit, accelerated degree programs, student-designed majors, freshman honors college, an honors program, double majors, independent study, and a senior project. Special programs include cooperative education, internships, summer session for credit, off-campus study, study-abroad, and Army, Navy and Air Force ROTC.

The most frequently chosen **baccalaureate** fields are business/marketing, engineering/engineering technologies, and agriculture. A complete listing of majors at Iowa State appears in the Majors Index beginning on page 430.

The **faculty** at Iowa State has 1,403 full-time members, 95% with terminal degrees. The student-faculty ratio is 16:1.

Students of Iowa State
The student body totals 27,823, of whom 23,060 are undergraduates. 44.4% are women and 55.6% are men. Students come from 54 states and territories and 116 other countries. 81% are from Iowa. 4.9% are international students. 2.6% are African American, 0.3% American Indian, 2.6% Asian American, and 1.8% Hispanic American. 84% returned for their sophomore year.

Facilities and Resources
Student rooms are linked to a campus network. 2,600 **computers** are available on campus that provide access to e-mail, network services. The 2 **libraries** have 2,266,061 books and 21,239 subscriptions.

Campus Life
There are 515 active organizations on campus, including a drama/theater group, newspaper, radio station, television station, choral group, and marching band. 16% of eligible men and 16% of eligible women are members of national **fraternities**, national **sororities**, local fraternities, and local sororities.

Iowa State is a member of the NCAA (Division I). **Intercollegiate sports** (some offering scholarships) include baseball (m), basketball, cross-country running, football (m), golf, gymnastics (w), soccer (w), softball (w), swimming, tennis (w), track and field, volleyball (w), wrestling (m).

Campus Safety
Student safety services include crime prevention programs, threat assessment team, motor vehicle help van, late-night transport/escort service, 24-hour emergency telephone alarm devices, 24-hour patrols by trained security personnel, student patrols, and electronically operated dormitory entrances.

Applying
Iowa State requires SAT I or ACT, a high school transcript, and rank in upper 50% of high school class. Application deadline: 8/21; 3/1 priority date for financial aid. Early and deferred admission are possible.

Iowa State has a national and international reputation for academic excellence, offering more than 100 majors in 7 undergraduate colleges. Known for technology (the first electronic digital computer and fax technology were both developed there), Iowa State was named one of the "most wired" college campuses—students have 24-hour access to more than 1,600 computer workstations, instant e-mail accounts, personal Web page space, and Internet access from every residence hall room. Out-of-class activities, leadership opportunities, and excellent job placement rates, together with a top-notch faculty and challenging in-class work, add up to an outstanding college experience.

Getting in Last Year
10,658 applied
90% were accepted
4,654 enrolled (48%)
26% from top tenth of their h.s. class
3.50 average high school GPA
46% had SAT verbal scores over 600
60% had SAT math scores over 600
57% had ACT scores over 24
17% had SAT verbal scores over 700
23% had SAT math scores over 700
12% had ACT scores over 30
113 National Merit Scholars

Graduation and After
24% graduated in 4 years
31% graduated in 5 years
7% graduated in 6 years
16% pursued further study
76% had job offers within 6 months
1000 organizations recruited on campus

Financial Matters
$3442 resident tuition and fees (2001–02)
$10,776 nonresident tuition and fees (2001–02)
$4666 room and board
100% average percent of need met
$7920 average financial aid amount received per undergraduate (1999–2000)

ITHACA COLLEGE

SMALL-TOWN SETTING ■ PRIVATE ■ INDEPENDENT ■ COED
ITHACA, NEW YORK

Web site: www.ithaca.edu
Contact: Ms. Paula J. Mitchell, Director of Admission, 100 Job Hall, Ithaca, NY 14850-7020
Telephone: 607-274-3124 or toll-free 800-429-4274 **Fax:** 607-274-1900
E-mail: admission@ithaca.edu

Getting in Last Year

10,504 applied
66% were accepted
1,755 enrolled (25%)
32% from top tenth of their h.s. class
42% had SAT verbal scores over 600
44% had SAT math scores over 600
6% had SAT verbal scores over 700
6% had SAT math scores over 700
6 National Merit Scholars
26 valedictorians

Graduation and After

33% pursued further study (26% arts and sciences, 4% education, 1% business)
310 organizations recruited on campus

Financial Matters

$20,104 tuition and fees (2001–02)
$8615 room and board
87% average percent of need met
$18,960 average financial aid amount received per undergraduate

Academics

Ithaca College awards bachelor's and master's **degrees**. Challenging opportunities include advanced placement credit, accelerated degree programs, student-designed majors, freshman honors college, an honors program, double majors, independent study, and a senior project. Special programs include internships, summer session for credit, off-campus study, study-abroad, and Army and Air Force ROTC.

The most frequently chosen **baccalaureate** fields are communications/communication technologies, visual/performing arts, and health professions and related sciences. A complete listing of majors at Ithaca College appears in the Majors Index beginning on page 430.

The **faculty** at Ithaca College has 418 full-time members, 88% with terminal degrees. The student-faculty ratio is 13:1.

Students of Ithaca College

The student body totals 6,483, of whom 6,209 are undergraduates. 55.3% are women and 44.7% are men. Students come from 48 states and territories and 77 other countries. 49% are from New York. 2.4% are international students. 2.1% are African American, 0.2% American Indian, 2.6% Asian American, and 2.7% Hispanic American. 87% returned for their sophomore year.

Facilities and Resources

Student rooms are linked to a campus network. 584 **computers** are available on campus that provide access to the Internet. The **library** has 238,613 books and 2,400 subscriptions.

Campus Life

There are 140 active organizations on campus, including a drama/theater group, newspaper, radio station, television station, and choral group. 2% of eligible women are members of local **sororities**.

Ithaca College is a member of the NCAA (Division III). **Intercollegiate sports** include baseball (m), basketball, crew, cross-country running, field hockey (w), football (m), gymnastics (w), lacrosse, soccer, softball (w), swimming, tennis, track and field, volleyball (w), wrestling (m).

Campus Safety

Student safety services include patrols by trained security personnel 11 p.m. to 7 a.m, late-night transport/escort service, 24-hour emergency telephone alarm devices, and student patrols.

Applying

Ithaca College requires an essay, SAT I or ACT, a high school transcript, and 1 recommendation, and in some cases audition for music and theater programs. It recommends an interview and a minimum high school GPA of 3.0. Application deadline: 3/1; 2/1 priority date for financial aid. Early and deferred admission are possible.

John Carroll University

SUBURBAN SETTING ■ PRIVATE ■ INDEPENDENT RELIGIOUS ■ COED
UNIVERSITY HEIGHTS, OHIO

Web site: www.jcu.edu
Contact: Mr. Thomas P. Fanning, Director of Admission, 20700 North Park
 Boulevard, University Heights, OH 44118-4581
Telephone: 216-397-4294 **Fax:** 216-397-4981
E-mail: admission@jcu.edu

John Carroll University, founded in 1886, is one of 28 Catholic colleges and universities operated in the United States by the Society of Jesus. In the Jesuit tradition of leadership, faith, and service, John Carroll provides its students with a rigorous education rooted in the liberal arts and focused on questions of moral and ethical values. John Carroll offers more than 85 student organizations, community volunteer service opportunities, and academic honor societies to foster leadership activities outside the classroom.

Academics

John Carroll awards bachelor's and master's **degrees**. Challenging opportunities include advanced placement credit, accelerated degree programs, student-designed majors, an honors program, double majors, independent study, and a senior project. Special programs include cooperative education, internships, summer session for credit, off-campus study, study-abroad, and Army ROTC.

The most frequently chosen **baccalaureate** fields are business/marketing, social sciences and history, and communications/communication technologies. A complete listing of majors at John Carroll appears in the Majors Index beginning on page 430.

The **faculty** at John Carroll has 246 full-time members, 85% with terminal degrees. The student-faculty ratio is 15:1.

Students of John Carroll

The student body totals 4,301, of whom 3,508 are undergraduates. 54.7% are women and 45.3% are men. Students come from 35 states and territories. 73% are from Ohio. 0.1% are international students. 4.4% are African American, 0.2% American Indian, 2.8% Asian American, and 2.3% Hispanic American. 86% returned for their sophomore year.

Facilities and Resources

Student rooms are linked to a campus network. 210 **computers** are available on campus that provide access to the Internet. The **library** has 620,000 books and 2,198 subscriptions.

Campus Life

There are 87 active organizations on campus, including a drama/theater group, newspaper, radio station, and choral group. 13% of eligible men and 18% of eligible women are members of national **fraternities** and national **sororities**.

John Carroll is a member of the NCAA (Division III). **Intercollegiate sports** include baseball (m), basketball, cross-country running, football (m), golf, soccer, softball (w), swimming, tennis, track and field, volleyball (w), wrestling (m).

Campus Safety

Student safety services include late-night transport/escort service, 24-hour emergency telephone alarm devices, and 24-hour patrols by trained security personnel.

Applying

John Carroll requires SAT I or ACT, a high school transcript, and 1 recommendation, and in some cases an interview. It recommends an essay and an interview. Application deadline: 2/1; 3/1 priority date for financial aid. Early and deferred admission are possible.

Getting in Last Year
2,764 applied
86% were accepted
792 enrolled (33%)
24% from top tenth of their h.s. class
3.27 average high school GPA
32% had SAT verbal scores over 600
43% had SAT math scores over 600
48% had ACT scores over 24
6% had SAT verbal scores over 700
4% had SAT math scores over 700
6% had ACT scores over 30
5 National Merit Scholars
12 valedictorians

Graduation and After
62% graduated in 4 years
12% graduated in 5 years
1% graduated in 6 years
22% pursued further study (12% arts and
 sciences, 4% law, 2% business)
64% had job offers within 6 months
332 organizations recruited on campus

Financial Matters
$17,837 tuition and fees (2001–02)
$6312 room and board
88% average percent of need met
$14,104 average financial aid amount received
 per undergraduate (2000–01 estimated)

JOHNS HOPKINS UNIVERSITY

URBAN SETTING ■ PRIVATE ■ INDEPENDENT ■ COED
BALTIMORE, MARYLAND

Web site: www.jhu.edu
Contact: Mr. John Latting, Director of Undergraduate Admissions, 140
  Garland Hall, 3400 North Charles Street, Baltimore, MD 21218-2699
Telephone: 410-516-8341 **Fax:** 410-516-6025
E-mail: gotojhu@jhu.edu

S ince its founding in 1876 as America's first great research university, Johns Hopkins University has been attracting brilliant thinkers. Johns Hopkins puts the power of education directly into the hands of students through opportunities to become engaged with professors and peers in the areas of humanities, social and behavioral sciences, engineering, and natural sciences. This, combined with a small undergraduate enrollment, affords extensive exposure to creative investigation and discovery beginning in the freshman year.

Getting in Last Year
9,127 applied
34% were accepted
1,015 enrolled (32%)
73% from top tenth of their h.s. class
3.84 average high school GPA
91% had SAT verbal scores over 600
97% had SAT math scores over 600
97% had ACT scores over 24
47% had SAT verbal scores over 700
67% had SAT math scores over 700
66% had ACT scores over 30
31 National Merit Scholars

Graduation and After
45% pursued further study (24% medicine, 21% law)
308 organizations recruited on campus

Financial Matters
$26,710 tuition and fees (2001–02)
$8506 room and board
95% average percent of need met
$24,285 average financial aid amount received per undergraduate

Academics

Johns Hopkins awards bachelor's, master's, doctoral, and first-professional **degrees** and post-bachelor's and post-master's certificates. Challenging opportunities include advanced placement credit, accelerated degree programs, student-designed majors, an honors program, double majors, independent study, and a senior project. Special programs include cooperative education, internships, summer session for credit, off-campus study, study-abroad, and Army and Air Force ROTC.

The most frequently chosen **baccalaureate** fields are health professions and related sciences, engineering/engineering technologies, and social sciences and history. A complete listing of majors at Johns Hopkins appears in the Majors Index beginning on page 430.

The **faculty** at Johns Hopkins has 404 full-time members, 90% with terminal degrees. The student-faculty ratio is 9:1.

Students of Johns Hopkins

The student body totals 5,832, of whom 3,961 are undergraduates. 40.9% are women and 59.1% are men. Students come from 55 states and territories and 53 other countries. 22% are from Maryland. 7.9% are international students. 4.3% are African American, 0.2% American Indian, 18.7% Asian American, and 2.4% Hispanic American. 96% returned for their sophomore year.

Facilities and Resources

Student rooms are linked to a campus network. 185 **computers** are available on campus that provide access to the Internet. The 7 **libraries** have 3,380,206 books and 23,043 subscriptions.

Campus Life

There are 183 active organizations on campus, including a drama/theater group, newspaper, radio station, choral group, and marching band. 18% of eligible men and 19% of eligible women are members of national **fraternities** and national **sororities**.

Johns Hopkins is a member of the NCAA (Division III). **Intercollegiate sports** (some offering scholarships) include baseball (m), basketball, crew, cross-country running, fencing, field hockey (w), football (m), lacrosse, soccer, swimming, tennis, track and field, volleyball (w), water polo (m), wrestling (m).

Campus Safety

Student safety services include late-night transport/escort service, 24-hour emergency telephone alarm devices, 24-hour patrols by trained security personnel, student patrols, and electronically operated dormitory entrances.

Applying

Johns Hopkins requires an essay, SAT II: Writing Test, SAT I and SAT II or ACT, a high school transcript, and 1 recommendation, and in some cases an interview. Application deadline: 1/1; 2/15 for financial aid, with a 2/1 priority date. Early and deferred admission are possible.

JUNIATA COLLEGE

SMALL-TOWN SETTING ■ PRIVATE ■ INDEPENDENT RELIGIOUS ■ COED
HUNTINGDON, PENNSYLVANIA

Web site: www.juniata.edu
Contact: Terry Bollman, Director of Admissions, 1700 Moore Street,
Huntingdon, PA 16652-2119
Telephone: 814-641-3424 or toll-free 877-JUNIATA **Fax:** 814-641-3100
E-mail: info@juniata.edu

Academics

Juniata awards bachelor's **degrees**. Challenging opportunities include advanced placement credit, student-designed majors, freshman honors college, an honors program, double majors, independent study, and a senior project. Special programs include internships, summer session for credit, off-campus study, and study-abroad.

The most frequently chosen **baccalaureate** fields are biological/life sciences, social sciences and history, and business/marketing. A complete listing of majors at Juniata appears in the Majors Index beginning on page 430.

The **faculty** at Juniata has 83 full-time members, 96% with terminal degrees. The student-faculty ratio is 14:1.

Students of Juniata

The student body is made up of 1,302 undergraduates. 58% are women and 42% are men. Students come from 36 states and territories and 22 other countries. 76% are from Pennsylvania. 2.5% are international students. 0.6% are African American, 0.1% American Indian, 0.4% Asian American, and 1% Hispanic American. 90% returned for their sophomore year.

Facilities and Resources

Student rooms are linked to a campus network. 250 **computers** are available on campus that provide access to the Internet. The **library** has 208,000 books and 3,500 subscriptions.

Campus Life

There are 97 active organizations on campus, including a drama/theater group, newspaper, radio station, and choral group. No national or local **fraternities** or **sororities**.

Juniata is a member of the NCAA (Division III). **Intercollegiate sports** include baseball (m), basketball, cross-country running, field hockey (w), football (m), soccer, softball (w), swimming (w), tennis (w), track and field, volleyball.

Campus Safety

Student safety services include late-night transport/escort service, 24-hour emergency telephone alarm devices, 24-hour patrols by trained security personnel, and student patrols.

Applying

Juniata requires an essay, SAT I or ACT, a high school transcript, 1 recommendation, and a minimum high school GPA of 3.0. It recommends an interview. Application deadline: 3/15; 3/1 priority date for financial aid. Early and deferred admission are possible.

Getting in Last Year

1,402 applied
79% were accepted
342 enrolled (31%)
39% from top tenth of their h.s. class
3.70 average high school GPA
41% had SAT verbal scores over 600
45% had SAT math scores over 600
6% had SAT verbal scores over 700
6% had SAT math scores over 700
10 National Merit Scholars
7 valedictorians

Graduation and After

31% pursued further study (17% arts and sciences, 4% medicine, 2% business)
65% had job offers within 6 months
72 organizations recruited on campus

Financial Matters

90% average percent of need met
$17,273 average financial aid amount received per undergraduate

KALAMAZOO COLLEGE
SUBURBAN SETTING ■ PRIVATE ■ INDEPENDENT RELIGIOUS ■ COED
KALAMAZOO, MICHIGAN

Getting in Last Year
1,328 applied
78% were accepted
341 enrolled (33%)
43% from top tenth of their h.s. class
3.67 average high school GPA
72% had SAT verbal scores over 600
68% had SAT math scores over 600
94% had ACT scores over 24
20% had SAT verbal scores over 700
16% had SAT math scores over 700
31% had ACT scores over 30
11 National Merit Scholars
21 valedictorians

Graduation and After
60% graduated in 4 years
6% graduated in 5 years
3% graduated in 6 years
35% pursued further study (6% medicine, 4% arts and sciences, 2% law)
23 organizations recruited on campus

Financial Matters
$20,652 tuition and fees (2001–02)
$6228 room and board
$17,775 average financial aid amount received per undergraduate

Web site: www.kzoo.edu
Contact: Mrs. Linda Wirgau, Records Manager, Mandelle Hall, 1200 Academy Street, Kalamazoo, MI 49006-3295
Telephone: 616-337-7166 or toll-free 800-253-3602
E-mail: admission@kzoo.edu

Academics
K-College awards bachelor's **degrees**. Challenging opportunities include advanced placement credit, double majors, independent study, and a senior project. Special programs include cooperative education, internships, off-campus study, study-abroad, and Army ROTC.

The most frequently chosen **baccalaureate** fields are social sciences and history, English, and biological/life sciences. A complete listing of majors at K-College appears in the Majors Index beginning on page 430.

The **faculty** at K-College has 97 full-time members, 90% with terminal degrees. The student-faculty ratio is 12:1.

Students of K-College
The student body is made up of 1,384 undergraduates. Students come from 42 states and territories and 16 other countries. 76% are from Michigan. 2.2% are international students. 2% are African American, 0.1% American Indian, 3.8% Asian American, and 1.5% Hispanic American. 88% returned for their sophomore year.

Facilities and Resources
Student rooms are linked to a campus network. 130 **computers** are available on campus that provide access to the Internet. The 2 **libraries** have 346,484 books and 1,331 subscriptions.

Campus Life
There are 50 active organizations on campus, including a drama/theater group, newspaper, radio station, and choral group. No national or local **fraternities** or **sororities**.

K-College is a member of the NCAA (Division III). **Intercollegiate sports** include baseball (m), basketball, cross-country running, football (m), golf, soccer, softball (w), swimming, tennis, volleyball (w).

Campus Safety
Student safety services include late-night transport/escort service, 24-hour emergency telephone alarm devices, 24-hour patrols by trained security personnel, and electronically operated dormitory entrances.

Applying
K-College requires an essay, SAT I or ACT, a high school transcript, and 2 recommendations. It recommends an interview and a minimum high school GPA of 3.0. Application deadline: 2/15; 2/15 priority date for financial aid. Deferred admission is possible.

KENYON COLLEGE

RURAL SETTING ■ PRIVATE ■ INDEPENDENT ■ COED
GAMBIER, OHIO

Web site: www.kenyon.edu
Contact: Mr. John W. Anderson, Dean of Admissions, Office of Admissions,
Gambier, OH 43022-9623
Telephone: 740-427-5776 or toll-free 800-848-2468 **Fax:** 740-427-5770
E-mail: admissions@kenyon.edu

Academics

Kenyon awards bachelor's **degrees**. Challenging opportunities include advanced placement credit, accelerated degree programs, student-designed majors, an honors program,
double majors, independent study, and a senior project. Special programs include internships, off-campus study, and study-abroad.

The most frequently chosen **baccalaureate** fields are social sciences and history,
English, and visual/performing arts. A complete listing of majors at Kenyon appears in
the Majors Index beginning on page 430.

The **faculty** at Kenyon has 142 full-time members, 97% with terminal degrees. The
student-faculty ratio is 10:1.

Students of Kenyon

The student body is made up of 1,587 undergraduates. 55% are women and 45% are
men. Students come from 49 states and territories and 28 other countries. 25% are from
Ohio. 2.6% are international students. 3.8% are African American, 2.1% Asian
American, and 2.5% Hispanic American. 92% returned for their sophomore year.

Facilities and Resources

Student rooms are linked to a campus network. 225 **computers** are available on campus
that provide access to commercial databases and the Internet. The 2 **libraries** have
858,000 books and 4,500 subscriptions.

Campus Life

There are 129 active organizations on campus, including a drama/theater group,
newspaper, radio station, and choral group. 36% of eligible men and 10% of eligible
women are members of national **fraternities**, national **sororities**, local fraternities, and
local sororities.

Kenyon is a member of the NCAA (Division III). **Intercollegiate sports** include
baseball (m), basketball, cross-country running, field hockey (w), football (m), golf (m),
lacrosse, soccer, softball (w), swimming, tennis, track and field, volleyball (w).

Campus Safety

Student safety services include late-night transport/escort service, 24-hour emergency
telephone alarm devices, 24-hour patrols by trained security personnel, and student
patrols.

Applying

Kenyon requires an essay, SAT I or ACT, a high school transcript, 1 recommendation,
and a minimum high school GPA of 2.0. It recommends an interview, 2 recommendations, and a minimum high school GPA of 3.0. Application deadline: 1/15; 2/15 priority
date for financial aid. Early and deferred admission are possible.

Getting in Last Year
2,001 applied
66% were accepted
425 enrolled (32%)
55% from top tenth of their h.s. class
3.68 average high school GPA
79% had SAT verbal scores over 600
71% had SAT math scores over 600
95% had ACT scores over 24
30% had SAT verbal scores over 700
17% had SAT math scores over 700
42% had ACT scores over 30
24 National Merit Scholars
3 class presidents
20 valedictorians

Graduation and After
80% graduated in 4 years
4% graduated in 5 years
27% pursued further study (10% arts and
sciences, 5% law, 3% medicine)
89% had job offers within 6 months
65 organizations recruited on campus

Financial Matters
$32,130 comprehensive fee (2001–02)
98% average percent of need met
$18,941 average financial aid amount received
per undergraduate

KETTERING UNIVERSITY

Suburban setting ■ Private ■ Independent ■ Coed
Flint, Michigan

Web site: www.kettering.edu
Contact: Mr. Rawlan Lillard II, Director of Admissions, 1700 West Third
Avenue, Flint, MI 48504-4898
Telephone: 810-762-7865 or toll-free 800-955-4464 ext. 7865 (in-state),
800-955-4464 (out-of-state) **Fax:** 810-762-9837
E-mail: admissions@kettering.edu

Kettering University, formerly GMI Engineering and Management Institute, provides an excellent education for the real world. Kettering University continues the long tradition of academic excellence in engineering, computers, science, math, and business management. Kettering's goal is to provide students with top-notch classroom instruction and career-directed professional co-op work experience in business and industry, giving students the opportunity for a head start in a career plus up to $65,000 in co-op earnings over the course of the program. The unique, fully cooperative education program has students alternating 11-week academic terms on campus with 12-week terms of paid work experience with a co-op employer. With a placement rate of nearly 100%, Kettering University graduates are in high demand at America's leading corporations and have the credentials for admittance into the nation's top graduate and professional schools.

Academics

Kettering/GMI awards bachelor's and master's **degrees**. Challenging opportunities include advanced placement credit, accelerated degree programs, double majors, independent study, and a senior project. Special programs include cooperative education, internships, and study-abroad.

The most frequently chosen **baccalaureate** fields are engineering/engineering technologies, business/marketing, and computer/information sciences. A complete listing of majors at Kettering/GMI appears in the Majors Index beginning on page 430.

The **faculty** at Kettering/GMI has 145 full-time members, 87% with terminal degrees. The student-faculty ratio is 9:1.

Students of Kettering/GMI

The student body totals 3,346, of whom 2,653 are undergraduates. 18.9% are women and 81.1% are men. Students come from 48 states and territories and 18 other countries. 60% are from Michigan. 3.5% are international students. 7.1% are African American, 0.3% American Indian, 4.3% Asian American, and 2.2% Hispanic American. 87% returned for their sophomore year.

Facilities and Resources

Student rooms are linked to a campus network. 300 **computers** are available on campus that provide access to the Internet. The 2 **libraries** have 100,339 books and 1,011 subscriptions.

Campus Life

There are 40 active organizations on campus, including a drama/theater group, newspaper, radio station, and choral group. 45% of eligible men and 47% of eligible women are members of national **fraternities** and national **sororities**.

This institution has no intercollegiate sports.

Campus Safety

Student safety services include late-night transport/escort service, 24-hour emergency telephone alarm devices, 24-hour patrols by trained security personnel, and electronically operated dormitory entrances.

Applying

Kettering/GMI requires SAT I or ACT and a high school transcript, and in some cases an essay. It recommends SAT II Subject Tests, an interview, and a minimum high school GPA of 3.0. Application deadline: rolling admissions; 2/14 priority date for financial aid. Deferred admission is possible.

Getting in Last Year
2,413 applied
71% were accepted
593 enrolled (35%)
33% from top tenth of their h.s. class
3.53 average high school GPA
43% had SAT verbal scores over 600
79% had SAT math scores over 600
84% had ACT scores over 24
7% had SAT verbal scores over 700
19% had SAT math scores over 700
12% had ACT scores over 30
20 valedictorians

Graduation and After
4% graduated in 4 years
48% graduated in 5 years
11% graduated in 6 years
33% pursued further study (17% business,
10% engineering, 4% arts and sciences)
98% had job offers within 6 months
550 organizations recruited on campus

Financial Matters
$18,656 tuition and fees (2001–02)
$4600 room and board
64% average percent of need met
$13,078 average financial aid amount received
per undergraduate

KNOX COLLEGE

SMALL-TOWN SETTING ■ PRIVATE ■ INDEPENDENT ■ COED
GALESBURG, ILLINOIS

Web site: www.knox.edu
Contact: Paul Steenis, Director of Admissions, Admission Office, Box K-148,
Galesburg, IL 61401
Telephone: 309-341-7100 or toll-free 800-678-KNOX **Fax:** 309-341-7070
E-mail: admission@knox.edu

Academics

Knox awards bachelor's **degrees**. Challenging opportunities include advanced placement credit, student-designed majors, an honors program, double majors, independent study, and a senior project. Special programs include internships, off-campus study, and study-abroad.

The most frequently chosen **baccalaureate** fields are social sciences and history, biological/life sciences, and English. A complete listing of majors at Knox appears in the Majors Index beginning on page 430.

The **faculty** at Knox has 92 full-time members, 92% with terminal degrees. The student-faculty ratio is 12:1.

Students of Knox

The student body is made up of 1,143 undergraduates. 55.6% are women and 44.4% are men. Students come from 48 states and territories and 37 other countries. 54% are from Illinois. 9.9% are international students. 4.5% are African American, 0.8% American Indian, 3.9% Asian American, and 3.8% Hispanic American. 88% returned for their sophomore year.

Facilities and Resources

Student rooms are linked to a campus network. 171 **computers** are available on campus that provide access to software applications and the Internet. The 3 **libraries** have 178,945 books and 1,824 subscriptions.

Campus Life

There are 75 active organizations on campus, including a drama/theater group, newspaper, radio station, and choral group. 33% of eligible men and 13% of eligible women are members of national **fraternities** and national **sororities**.

Intercollegiate sports include baseball (m), basketball, cross-country running, football (m), golf, soccer, softball (w), swimming, tennis, track and field, volleyball (w), wrestling (m).

Campus Safety

Student safety services include late-night transport/escort service, 24-hour emergency telephone alarm devices, and 24-hour patrols by trained security personnel.

Applying

Knox requires an essay, SAT I or ACT, a high school transcript, and 2 recommendations. It recommends an interview. Application deadline: 2/1; 3/1 priority date for financial aid. Early and deferred admission are possible.

Getting in Last Year

1,428 applied
72% were accepted
275 enrolled (27%)
34% from top tenth of their h.s. class
59% had SAT verbal scores over 600
58% had SAT math scores over 600
77% had ACT scores over 24
21% had SAT verbal scores over 700
9% had SAT math scores over 700
19% had ACT scores over 30
5 National Merit Scholars
10 valedictorians

Graduation and After

67% graduated in 4 years
6% graduated in 5 years
1% graduated in 6 years
35% pursued further study (23% arts and sciences, 6% law, 5% medicine)
20% had job offers within 6 months
70 organizations recruited on campus

Financial Matters

$22,620 tuition and fees (2001–02)
$5610 room and board
99% average percent of need met
$19,669 average financial aid amount received per undergraduate

LAFAYETTE COLLEGE

SUBURBAN SETTING ■ PRIVATE ■ INDEPENDENT RELIGIOUS ■ COED
EASTON, PENNSYLVANIA

Web site: www.lafayette.edu
Contact: Ms. Carol Rowlands, Director of Admissions, Easton, PA
  18042-1798
Telephone: 610-330-5100 **Fax:** 610-330-5355
E-mail: admissions@lafayette.edu

Lafayette has achieved a unique niche in American higher education: liberal arts, sciences, and engineering programs in a most academically competitive, small-college setting. Lafayette offers small classes, interdisciplinary first-year seminars, and student-faculty collaborative research on a residential campus located in eastern Pennsylvania, close to New York and Philadelphia.

Getting in Last Year
5,195 applied
39% were accepted
576 enrolled (28%)
59% from top tenth of their h.s. class
3.90 average high school GPA
58% had SAT verbal scores over 600
76% had SAT math scores over 600
82% had ACT scores over 24
11% had SAT verbal scores over 700
19% had SAT math scores over 700
16% had ACT scores over 30
5 National Merit Scholars

Graduation and After
79% graduated in 4 years
4% graduated in 5 years
1% graduated in 6 years
32% pursued further study (12% arts and
  sciences, 8% engineering, 6% law)
42% had job offers within 6 months
320 organizations recruited on campus

Financial Matters
$23,758 tuition and fees (2001–02)
$7413 room and board
96% average percent of need met
$20,593 average financial aid amount received
  per undergraduate

Academics

Lafayette awards bachelor's **degrees**. Challenging opportunities include advanced place-ment credit, accelerated degree programs, student-designed majors, and an honors program. Special programs include internships, summer session for credit, off-campus study, study-abroad, and Army ROTC. A complete listing of majors at Lafayette appears in the Majors Index beginning on page 430.

The **faculty** at Lafayette has 184 full-time members, 100% with terminal degrees. The student-faculty ratio is 11:1.

Students of Lafayette

The student body is made up of 2,330 undergraduates. 49.3% are women and 50.7% are men. Students come from 42 states and territories and 53 other countries. 29% are from Pennsylvania. 4.4% are international students. 4.2% are African American, 0.3% American Indian, 1.5% Asian American, and 1.9% Hispanic American. 95% returned for their sophomore year.

Facilities and Resources

Student rooms are linked to a campus network. 600 **computers** are available on campus that provide access to the Internet. The 2 **libraries** have 500,000 books and 2,630 subscriptions.

Campus Life

There are 250 active organizations on campus, including a drama/theater group, newspaper, radio station, and choral group. 26% of eligible men and 45% of eligible women are members of national **fraternities**, national **sororities**, and social dorms.

Lafayette is a member of the NCAA (Division I). **Intercollegiate sports** include baseball (m), basketball, cross-country running, fencing, field hockey (w), football (m), golf (m), lacrosse, soccer, softball (w), swimming, tennis, track and field, volleyball (w).

Campus Safety

Student safety services include late-night transport/escort service, 24-hour emergency telephone alarm devices, 24-hour patrols by trained security personnel, student patrols, and electronically operated dormitory entrances.

Applying

Lafayette requires an essay, SAT I, SAT II Subject Tests, a high school transcript, and 1 recommendation. It recommends SAT II: Writing Test and an interview. Application deadline: 1/1; 2/1 for financial aid. Early and deferred admission are possible.

LAKE FOREST COLLEGE

SUBURBAN SETTING ■ PRIVATE ■ INDEPENDENT ■ COED
LAKE FOREST, ILLINOIS

Web site: www.lakeforest.edu
Contact: Mr. William G. Motzer Jr., Director of Admissions, 555 North
Sheridan Road, Lake Forest, IL 60045-2399
Telephone: 847-735-5000 or toll-free 800-828-4751 **Fax:** 847-735-6271
E-mail: admissions@lakeforest.edu

Academics

Lake Forest awards bachelor's and master's **degrees**. Challenging opportunities include advanced placement credit, accelerated degree programs, student-designed majors, freshman honors college, an honors program, double majors, independent study, and a senior project. Special programs include internships, summer session for credit, off-campus study, and study-abroad.

The most frequently chosen **baccalaureate** fields are social sciences and history, business/marketing, and psychology. A complete listing of majors at Lake Forest appears in the Majors Index beginning on page 430.

The **faculty** at Lake Forest has 82 full-time members, 99% with terminal degrees. The student-faculty ratio is 12:1.

Students of Lake Forest

The student body totals 1,277, of whom 1,260 are undergraduates. 58.4% are women and 41.6% are men. Students come from 44 states and territories and 41 other countries. 50% are from Illinois. 7.9% are international students. 5.2% are African American, 0.4% American Indian, 4.4% Asian American, and 3% Hispanic American. 77% returned for their sophomore year.

Facilities and Resources

Student rooms are linked to a campus network. 120 **computers** are available on campus that provide access to the Internet. The 2 **libraries** have 268,760 books and 1,133 subscriptions.

Campus Life

There are 101 active organizations on campus, including a drama/theater group, newspaper, radio station, and choral group. 18% of eligible men and 14% of eligible women are members of national **fraternities**, local fraternities, and local **sororities**.

Lake Forest is a member of the NCAA (Division III). **Intercollegiate sports** include basketball, cross-country running, football (m), ice hockey, soccer, softball (w), swimming, tennis, volleyball (w), water polo (m).

Campus Safety

Student safety services include late-night transport/escort service, 24-hour emergency telephone alarm devices, 24-hour patrols by trained security personnel, and student patrols.

Applying

Lake Forest requires an essay, SAT I or ACT, a high school transcript, 2 recommendations, and graded paper. It recommends an interview. Application deadline: 3/1; 3/1 priority date for financial aid. Early and deferred admission are possible.

Lake Forest College is situated in the remarkably beautiful community of Lake Forest, Illinois' safest city, with a population of more than 19,000. Chicago is located just 30 miles south of the campus, and students enhance their liberal arts education through the world-renowned resources of this great city. More than 80% of Lake Forest students strengthen their education through domestic and international internships, practicums, and the College's extensive study-abroad program. On campus, the distinguished faculty offers students high-quality teaching and the unique opportunity to conduct independent research. Students enjoy the tree-lined campus near the shore of Lake Michigan.

Getting in Last Year
1,607 applied
69% were accepted
336 enrolled (30%)
22% from top tenth of their h.s. class
3.40 average high school GPA
36% had SAT verbal scores over 600
39% had SAT math scores over 600
68% had ACT scores over 24
5% had SAT verbal scores over 700
6% had SAT math scores over 700
12% had ACT scores over 30
1 National Merit Scholar
17 class presidents
6 valedictorians

Graduation and After
54% graduated in 4 years
6% graduated in 5 years
21% pursued further study
89% had job offers within 6 months
79 organizations recruited on campus

Financial Matters
$22,206 tuition and fees (2001–02)
$5254 room and board
100% average percent of need met
$19,050 average financial aid amount received per undergraduate

Lawrence Technological University

Suburban setting ■ Private ■ Independent ■ Coed
Southfield, Michigan

Web site: www.ltu.edu
Contact: Mrs. Lisa Kujawa, Director of Admissions, 2100 West 10 Mile Road, Southfield, MI 48075
Telephone: 248-204-3180 or toll-free 800-225-5588 **Fax:** 248-204-3188
E-mail: admissions@ltu.edu

Top job placement and higher starting salaries. How the real world works and why. Industry-savvy faculty members. A nurturing environment focused on success. Isn't this what students have a right to expect from their education? Growth, opportunity, personal attention, knowledge, experience, and career direction are important priorities at Lawrence Technological University, and its commitment is to prepare students for leadership through theory and practice. A remarkable 97% of recent graduates found positions matching their academic preparation within a year of graduation. Lawrence Tech ranks first among all of Michigan's independent colleges and universities as a source of recent graduates sought by leading employers in southeastern Michigan.

Getting in Last Year
2,250 applied
78% were accepted
3.50 average high school GPA
72% had ACT scores over 24
37% had ACT scores over 30
2 National Merit Scholars
25 class presidents
8 valedictorians

Graduation and After
15% pursued further study (7% business, 7% engineering, 2% arts and sciences)
98% had job offers within 6 months
100 organizations recruited on campus

Financial Matters
$12,250 tuition and fees (2001–02)
$2475 room only
95% average percent of need met

Academics
Lawrence Tech awards associate, bachelor's, and master's **degrees**. Challenging opportunities include advanced placement credit, student-designed majors, an honors program, double majors, independent study, and a senior project. Special programs include cooperative education, internships, summer session for credit, and Army and Air Force ROTC. A complete listing of majors at Lawrence Tech appears in the Majors Index beginning on page 430.

The student-faculty ratio is 12:1.

Students of Lawrence Tech
The student body totals 4,117, of whom 2,979 are undergraduates. Students come from 39 states and territories and 34 other countries. 92% are from Michigan. 75% returned for their sophomore year.

Facilities and Resources
Student rooms are linked to a campus network. 400 **computers** are available on campus for student use. The 2 **libraries** have 107,000 books and 665 subscriptions.

Campus Life
There are 40 active organizations on campus, including a drama/theater group and newspaper. 10% of eligible men and 10% of eligible women are members of national **fraternities**, national **sororities**, and local sororities.

This institution has no intercollegiate sports.

Campus Safety
Student safety services include late-night transport/escort service, 24-hour patrols by trained security personnel, and electronically operated dormitory entrances.

Applying
Lawrence Tech requires SAT I or ACT, a high school transcript, and a minimum high school GPA of 2.5, and in some cases an essay, an interview, and recommendations. It recommends an essay. Application deadline: 4/15; 8/1 priority date for financial aid. Early and deferred admission are possible.

LAWRENCE UNIVERSITY

SMALL-TOWN SETTING ■ PRIVATE ■ INDEPENDENT ■ COED
APPLETON, WISCONSIN

Web site: www.lawrence.edu
Contact: Mr. Steven T. Syverson, Dean of Admissions and Financial Aid, PO
Box 599, Appleton, WI 54912-0599
Telephone: 920-832-6500 or toll-free 800-227-0982 **Fax:** 920-832-6782
E-mail: excel@lawrence.edu

Academics

Lawrence awards bachelor's **degrees**. Challenging opportunities include advanced placement credit, student-designed majors, double majors, independent study, and a senior
project. Special programs include internships, off-campus study, and study-abroad.

The most frequently chosen **baccalaureate** fields are visual/performing arts, social
sciences and history, and biological/life sciences. A complete listing of majors at Lawrence appears in the Majors Index beginning on page 430.

The **faculty** at Lawrence has 130 full-time members, 94% with terminal degrees.
The student-faculty ratio is 11:1.

Students of Lawrence

The student body is made up of 1,323 undergraduates. 54.2% are women and 45.8% are
men. Students come from 49 states and territories and 39 other countries. 42% are from
Wisconsin. 8.9% are international students. 1.1% are African American, 0.5% American
Indian, 2.3% Asian American, and 1.8% Hispanic American. 87% returned for their
sophomore year.

Facilities and Resources

Student rooms are linked to a campus network. 140 **computers** are available on campus
for student use. The **library** has 365,612 books and 1,406 subscriptions.

Campus Life

There are 130 active organizations on campus, including a drama/theater group,
newspaper, radio station, and choral group. 35% of eligible men and 20% of eligible
women are members of national **fraternities** and national **sororities**.

Lawrence is a member of the NCAA (Division III). **Intercollegiate sports** include
baseball (m), basketball, cross-country running, fencing, football (m), golf (m), ice hockey
(m), soccer, softball (w), swimming, tennis, track and field, volleyball (w), wrestling (m).

Campus Safety

Student safety services include evening patrols by trained security personnel, late-night
transport/escort service, 24-hour emergency telephone alarm devices, student patrols,
and electronically operated dormitory entrances.

Applying

Lawrence requires an essay, SAT I or ACT, a high school transcript, 2 recommendations,
and audition for music program. It recommends an interview and a minimum high
school GPA of 3.0. Application deadline: 1/15; 3/1 priority date for financial aid. Early
and deferred admission are possible.

Lawrence University is
committed to the
development of intellect and
talent, the acquisition of knowledge
and understanding, and the
cultivation of judgment and values.
Independence and creativity are
highly prized, with more than half
of the students participating in
off-campus programs and some
90% pursuing independent study
with individual faculty members.
Music, art, and the sciences, as well
as the traditional liberal arts areas
within the humanities and social
sciences, are significant strengths
within the curriculum. Bright,
motivated, curious, and talented
students excel at Lawrence.

Getting in Last Year
1,629 applied
68% were accepted
320 enrolled (29%)
43% from top tenth of their h.s. class
3.67 average high school GPA
63% had SAT verbal scores over 600
66% had SAT math scores over 600
85% had ACT scores over 24
30% had SAT verbal scores over 700
27% had SAT math scores over 700
30% had ACT scores over 30
24 valedictorians

Graduation and After
58% graduated in 4 years
9% graduated in 5 years
1% graduated in 6 years
30% pursued further study
64% had job offers within 6 months
26 organizations recruited on campus

Financial Matters
$22,728 tuition and fees (2001–02)
$4983 room and board
100% average percent of need met
$20,530 average financial aid amount received
per undergraduate

LEBANON VALLEY COLLEGE

SMALL-TOWN SETTING ■ PRIVATE ■ INDEPENDENT RELIGIOUS ■ COED
ANNVILLE, PENNSYLVANIA

Web site: www.lvc.edu

Contact: William J. Brown, Jr., Dean of Admission and Financial Aid, 101 N. College Avenue, Annville, PA 17003-1400

Telephone: 717-867-6181 or toll-free 866-582-4236 (out-of-state) **Fax:** 717-867-6026

E-mail: admission@lvc.edu

Getting in Last Year
1,864 applied
79% were accepted
422 enrolled (29%)
33% from top tenth of their h.s. class
25% had SAT verbal scores over 600
31% had SAT math scores over 600
2% had SAT verbal scores over 700
5% had SAT math scores over 700
15 class presidents
9 valedictorians

Graduation and After
11% pursued further study

Financial Matters
$19,810 tuition and fees (2001–02)
$5890 room and board
85% average percent of need met
$14,762 average financial aid amount received per undergraduate

Academics

LVC awards associate, bachelor's, and master's **degrees** and post-bachelor's certificates (offers master of business administration degree on a part-time basis only). Challenging opportunities include advanced placement credit, student-designed majors, double majors, and independent study. Special programs include internships, summer session for credit, study-abroad, and Army ROTC.

The most frequently chosen **baccalaureate** fields are business/marketing, education, and social sciences and history. A complete listing of majors at LVC appears in the Majors Index beginning on page 430.

The **faculty** at LVC has 89 full-time members, 83% with terminal degrees. The student-faculty ratio is 14:1.

Students of LVC

The student body totals 2,117, of whom 1,920 are undergraduates. 59.8% are women and 40.2% are men. Students come from 21 states and territories and 10 other countries. 79% are from Pennsylvania. 0.8% are international students. 2% are African American, 0.1% American Indian, 1.5% Asian American, and 1.5% Hispanic American. 81% returned for their sophomore year.

Facilities and Resources

Student rooms are linked to a campus network. 194 **computers** are available on campus that provide access to the Internet. The **library** has 165,642 books and 6,160 subscriptions.

Campus Life

There are 74 active organizations on campus, including a drama/theater group, newspaper, radio station, choral group, and marching band. 14% of eligible men and 10% of eligible women are members of national **fraternities**, national **sororities**, local fraternities, and local sororities.

LVC is a member of the NCAA (Division III). **Intercollegiate sports** include baseball (m), basketball, cross-country running, field hockey (w), football (m), golf, ice hockey (m), soccer, softball (w), swimming, tennis, track and field, volleyball (w).

Campus Safety

Student safety services include dormitory entrances locked at midnight, late-night transport/escort service, 24-hour emergency telephone alarm devices, and 24-hour patrols by trained security personnel.

Applying

LVC requires SAT I or ACT and a high school transcript, and in some cases an essay and audition for music majors; interview for physical therapy program. It recommends an interview and 2 recommendations. Application deadline: rolling admissions; 3/1 priority date for financial aid. Early and deferred admission are possible.

LEHIGH UNIVERSITY
SUBURBAN SETTING ■ PRIVATE ■ INDEPENDENT ■ COED
BETHLEHEM, PENNSYLVANIA

Web site: www.lehigh.edu
Contact: Mr. J. Bruce Gardiner, Interim Dean of Admissions and Financial Aid, 27 Memorial Drive West, Bethlehem, PA 18015
Telephone: 610-758-3100 **Fax:** 610-758-4361
E-mail: admissions@lehigh.edu

Academics
Lehigh awards bachelor's, master's, and doctoral **degrees** and post-master's certificates. Challenging opportunities include advanced placement credit, accelerated degree programs, an honors program, double majors, independent study, and a senior project. Special programs include cooperative education, internships, summer session for credit, off-campus study, study-abroad, and Army ROTC.

The most frequently chosen **baccalaureate** fields are business/marketing, engineering/engineering technologies, and social sciences and history. A complete listing of majors at Lehigh appears in the Majors Index beginning on page 430.

The **faculty** at Lehigh has 393 full-time members, 99% with terminal degrees. The student-faculty ratio is 11:1.

Students of Lehigh
The student body totals 6,479, of whom 4,650 are undergraduates. 40.9% are women and 59.1% are men. Students come from 52 states and territories and 46 other countries. 32% are from Pennsylvania. 3.3% are international students. 3.3% are African American, 0.1% American Indian, 5.7% Asian American, and 3% Hispanic American. 94% returned for their sophomore year.

Facilities and Resources
Student rooms are linked to a campus network. 516 **computers** are available on campus that provide access to the Internet. The 2 **libraries** have 1,176,028 books and 6,271 subscriptions.

Campus Life
There are 130 active organizations on campus, including a drama/theater group, newspaper, radio station, choral group, and marching band. 41% of eligible men and 43% of eligible women are members of national **fraternities** and national **sororities**.

Lehigh is a member of the NCAA (Division I). **Intercollegiate sports** (some offering scholarships) include baseball (m), basketball, cross-country running, field hockey (w), football (m), golf (m), lacrosse, riflery, soccer, softball (w), swimming, tennis, track and field, volleyball (w), wrestling (m).

Campus Safety
Student safety services include late-night transport/escort service, 24-hour emergency telephone alarm devices, 24-hour patrols by trained security personnel, student patrols, and electronically operated dormitory entrances.

Applying
Lehigh requires SAT I or ACT, a high school transcript, 1 recommendation, and graded writing sample. It recommends an essay, SAT II Subject Tests, and an interview. Application deadline: 1/1; 3/1 for financial aid, with a 2/1 priority date. Early and deferred admission are possible.

Located on the East Coast, 75 miles from New York and 50 miles from Philadelphia in historic Bethlehem, Pennsylvania, Lehigh is among the nation's most selective and highly ranked private research universities. Lehigh offers the broad academic programs of a leading research university and the personal attention of a small college. Students have access to some of the world's best microscopes and compete in NCAA Division I sports, yet they also enjoy an intimate 12:1 student-faculty ratio. Four colleges offer students more than 110 majors in the liberal arts, business, education, engineering, and the sciences. Students can customize their college experience, like those who opt for a 5-year engineering program that leads to teaching. They work with renowned faculty members on hands-on projects, internships, and innovative study that crosses disciplines. For example, students from all colleges study the relationship between the environment and society in the undergraduate-operated Lehigh Earth Observatory.

Getting in Last Year
8,088 applied
47% were accepted
1,112 enrolled (29%)
52% from top tenth of their h.s. class
3.75 average high school GPA
63% had SAT verbal scores over 600
83% had SAT math scores over 600
12% had SAT verbal scores over 700
31% had SAT math scores over 700

Graduation and After
26% pursued further study
68% had job offers within 6 months
399 organizations recruited on campus

Financial Matters
$25,140 tuition and fees (2001–02)
$7150 room and board
95% average percent of need met
$18,100 average financial aid amount received per undergraduate (2000–01 estimated)

LE MOYNE COLLEGE

SUBURBAN SETTING ■ PRIVATE ■ INDEPENDENT RELIGIOUS ■ COED
SYRACUSE, NEW YORK

Web site: www.lemoyne.edu
Contact: Mr. Dennis J. Nicholson, Director of Admission, 1419 Salt Spring
   Road, Syracuse, NY 13214-1399
Telephone: 315-445-4300 or toll-free 800-333-4733 **Fax:** 315-445-4711
E-mail: admission@lemoyne.edu

Le Moyne is a coeducational, residential college founded in the Jesuit tradition of academic excellence. Offering a comprehensive program rooted in the liberal arts and sciences, Le Moyne's shared mission of learning and services stresses education of the whole person. Strong academic programs, committed faculty, a reassuring Jesuit presence, and career advisement/internship opportunities prepare Le Moyne students for leadership and service in their personal and professional lives. Le Moyne is consistently recognized for outstanding quality and value in the *U.S. News & World Report's* annual college rankings.

Getting in Last Year
2,443 applied
77% were accepted
502 enrolled (27%)
20% from top tenth of their h.s. class
3.33 average high school GPA
24% had SAT verbal scores over 600
25% had SAT math scores over 600
39% had ACT scores over 24
5% had SAT verbal scores over 700
2% had SAT math scores over 700
4% had ACT scores over 30

Graduation and After
68% graduated in 4 years
5% graduated in 5 years
2% graduated in 6 years
17% pursued further study (5% law, 4% arts
   and sciences, 4% education)
65% had job offers within 6 months
80 organizations recruited on campus

Financial Matters
$16,850 tuition and fees (2001–02)
$6990 room and board
85% average percent of need met
$12,413 average financial aid amount received
   per undergraduate (2000–01)

Academics
Le Moyne awards bachelor's and master's **degrees** and post-bachelor's certificates. Challenging opportunities include advanced placement credit, accelerated degree programs, an honors program, double majors, independent study, and a senior project. Special programs include internships, summer session for credit, off-campus study, study-abroad, and Army and Air Force ROTC.

The most frequently chosen **baccalaureate** fields are business/marketing, psychology, and social sciences and history. A complete listing of majors at Le Moyne appears in the Majors Index beginning on page 430.

The **faculty** at Le Moyne has 139 full-time members, 90% with terminal degrees. The student-faculty ratio is 13:1.

Students of Le Moyne
The student body totals 3,166, of whom 2,445 are undergraduates. 58.8% are women and 41.2% are men. Students come from 22 states and territories. 95% are from New York. 4.1% are African American, 0.8% American Indian, 1.4% Asian American, and 3.4% Hispanic American. 84% returned for their sophomore year.

Facilities and Resources
Student rooms are linked to a campus network. 225 **computers** are available on campus that provide access to the Internet. The **library** has 159,323 books and 1,308 subscriptions.

Campus Life
There are 70 active organizations on campus, including a drama/theater group, newspaper, radio station, and choral group. No national or local **fraternities** or **sororities**.

Le Moyne is a member of the NCAA (Division II). **Intercollegiate sports** (some offering scholarships) include baseball (m), basketball, cross-country running, golf (m), lacrosse, soccer, softball (w), swimming, tennis, volleyball (w).

Campus Safety
Student safety services include campus watch program, self-defense education, lighted pathways, closed circuit TV monitors, security phones, late-night transport/escort service, 24-hour emergency telephone alarm devices, 24-hour patrols by trained security personnel, and electronically operated dormitory entrances.

Applying
Le Moyne requires an essay, SAT I or ACT, a high school transcript, and 2 recommendations. It recommends an interview. Application deadline: 3/1; 2/1 priority date for financial aid. Early and deferred admission are possible.

LeTourneau University

Suburban setting ■ Private ■ Independent Religious ■ Coed
Longview, Texas

Web site: www.letu.edu
Contact: Mr. James Townsend, Director of Admissions, PO Box 7001, Longview, TX 75607
Telephone: 903-233-3400 or toll-free 800-759-8811 **Fax:** 903-233-3411
E-mail: admissions@letu.edu

Academics

LeTourneau awards associate, bachelor's, and master's **degrees**. Challenging opportunities include advanced placement credit, an honors program, double majors, independent study, and a senior project. Special programs include cooperative education, internships, summer session for credit, off-campus study, and study-abroad.

The most frequently chosen **baccalaureate** fields are engineering/engineering technologies, business/marketing, and education. A complete listing of majors at LeTourneau appears in the Majors Index beginning on page 430.

The **faculty** at LeTourneau has 69 full-time members, 72% with terminal degrees. The student-faculty ratio is 15:1.

Students of LeTourneau

The student body totals 3,098, of whom 2,807 are undergraduates. 49.6% are women and 50.4% are men. Students come from 49 states and territories and 19 other countries. 50% are from Texas. 2% are international students. 16.6% are African American, 0.6% American Indian, 1.1% Asian American, and 5.4% Hispanic American. 75% returned for their sophomore year.

Facilities and Resources

Student rooms are linked to a campus network. 120 **computers** are available on campus for student use. The **library** has 72,957 books and 459 subscriptions.

Campus Life

There are 22 active organizations on campus, including a drama/theater group, newspaper, and choral group. 8% of eligible men and 3% of eligible women are members of 3 societies for men, 1 society for women.

LeTourneau is a member of the NCAA (Division III) and NCCAA. **Intercollegiate sports** include baseball (m), basketball, cross-country running, golf, soccer, softball (w), tennis, volleyball (w).

Campus Safety

Student safety services include late-night transport/escort service, 24-hour emergency telephone alarm devices, 24-hour patrols by trained security personnel, and electronically operated dormitory entrances.

Applying

LeTourneau requires an essay, SAT I or ACT, a high school transcript, 2 recommendations, and a minimum high school GPA of 2.5, and in some cases an interview. Application deadline: 8/1; 2/15 priority date for financial aid. Deferred admission is possible.

Getting in Last Year
765 applied
85% were accepted
244 enrolled (37%)
34% from top tenth of their h.s. class
3.51 average high school GPA
45% had SAT verbal scores over 600
46% had SAT math scores over 600
68% had ACT scores over 24
13% had SAT verbal scores over 700
11% had SAT math scores over 700
19% had ACT scores over 30
6 National Merit Scholars
10 valedictorians

Graduation and After
90% had job offers within 6 months
63 organizations recruited on campus

Financial Matters
$12,840 tuition and fees (2001–02)
$5420 room and board
85% average percent of need met
$10,130 average financial aid amount received per undergraduate (2000–01 estimated)

LEWIS & CLARK COLLEGE

SUBURBAN SETTING ■ PRIVATE ■ INDEPENDENT ■ COED
PORTLAND, OREGON

Web site: www.lclark.edu
Contact: Mr. Michael Sexton, Dean of Admissions, 0615 SW Palatine Hill Road, Portland, OR 97219-7899
Telephone: 503-768-7040 or toll-free 800-444-4111 **Fax:** 503-768-7055
E-mail: admissions@lclark.edu

Getting in Last Year

3,040 applied
67% were accepted
416 enrolled (21%)
36% from top tenth of their h.s. class
3.60 average high school GPA
80% had SAT verbal scores over 600
61% had SAT math scores over 600
70% had ACT scores over 24
22% had SAT verbal scores over 700
13% had SAT math scores over 700
26% had ACT scores over 30
5 National Merit Scholars
18 valedictorians

Graduation and After

56% graduated in 4 years
9% graduated in 5 years
1% graduated in 6 years
26% pursued further study (10% arts and sciences, 4% education, 2% business)
38 organizations recruited on campus

Financial Matters

$22,810 tuition and fees (2001–02)
$6650 room and board
88% average percent of need met
$18,957 average financial aid amount received per undergraduate

Academics

L & C awards bachelor's, master's, and first-professional **degrees** and first-professional certificates. Challenging opportunities include advanced placement credit, accelerated degree programs, student-designed majors, an honors program, double majors, independent study, and a senior project. Special programs include internships, summer session for credit, off-campus study, and study-abroad.

The most frequently chosen **baccalaureate** fields are social sciences and history, biological/life sciences, and visual/performing arts. A complete listing of majors at L & C appears in the Majors Index beginning on page 430.

The **faculty** at L & C has 191 full-time members, 93% with terminal degrees. The student-faculty ratio is 12:1.

Students of L & C

The student body totals 2,947, of whom 1,682 are undergraduates. 59.6% are women and 40.4% are men. Students come from 51 states and territories and 26 other countries. 23% are from Oregon. 5.5% are international students. 1.2% are African American, 1.1% American Indian, 6.3% Asian American, and 2.7% Hispanic American. 82% returned for their sophomore year.

Facilities and Resources

Student rooms are linked to a campus network. 150 **computers** are available on campus that provide access to the Internet. The 2 **libraries** have 442,265 books and 8,326 subscriptions.

Campus Life

There are 70 active organizations on campus, including a drama/theater group, newspaper, radio station, television station, and choral group. No national or local **fraternities** or **sororities**.

L & C is a member of the NCAA (Division III) and NAIA. **Intercollegiate sports** include baseball (m), basketball, crew, cross-country running, football (m), golf, softball (w), swimming, tennis, track and field, volleyball (w).

Campus Safety

Student safety services include late-night transport/escort service, 24-hour emergency telephone alarm devices, 24-hour patrols by trained security personnel, student patrols, and electronically operated dormitory entrances.

Applying

L & C requires an essay, SAT I, ACT, or academic portfolio, a high school transcript, 2 recommendations, and a minimum high school GPA of 2.0, and in some cases 4 recommendations and portfolio applicants must submit samples of graded work. It recommends an interview and a minimum high school GPA of 3.0. Application deadline: 2/1; 3/1 priority date for financial aid. Early and deferred admission are possible.

LIPSCOMB UNIVERSITY

URBAN SETTING ■ PRIVATE ■ INDEPENDENT RELIGIOUS ■ COED
NASHVILLE, TENNESSEE

Web site: www.lipscomb.edu
Contact: Mr. Scott Gilmer, Director of Admissions, 3901 Granny White Pike,
    Nashville, TN 37204-3951
Telephone: 615-269-1776 or toll-free 800-333-4358 **Fax:** 615-269-1804
E-mail: admissions@lipscom.edu

Academics

Lipscomb University awards bachelor's, master's, and first-professional **degrees**. Challenging opportunities include advanced placement credit, accelerated degree programs, an honors program, double majors, independent study, and a senior project. Special programs include internships, summer session for credit, study-abroad, and Army and Air Force ROTC. A complete listing of majors at Lipscomb University appears in the Majors Index beginning on page 430.

The **faculty** at Lipscomb University has 115 full-time members, 77% with terminal degrees. The student-faculty ratio is 16:1.

Students of Lipscomb University

The student body totals 2,661, of whom 2,408 are undergraduates. 56.9% are women and 43.1% are men. Students come from 42 states and territories and 41 other countries. 62% are from Tennessee. 74% returned for their sophomore year.

Facilities and Resources

Student rooms are linked to a campus network. 232 **computers** are available on campus that provide access to the Internet. The 2 **libraries** have 199,400 books and 886 subscriptions.

Campus Life

There are 60 active organizations on campus, including a drama/theater group, newspaper, radio station, and choral group. 15% of eligible men and 20% of eligible women are members of local **fraternities** and local **sororities**.

Lipscomb University is a member of the NCAA (Division I). **Intercollegiate sports** (some offering scholarships) include baseball (m), basketball, cross-country running, golf, soccer, softball (w), tennis, volleyball (w).

Campus Safety

Student safety services include late-night transport/escort service, 24-hour emergency telephone alarm devices, 24-hour patrols by trained security personnel, and electronically operated dormitory entrances.

Applying

Lipscomb University requires SAT I or ACT, a high school transcript, 2 recommendations, and a minimum high school GPA of 2.25. It recommends an essay and an interview. Application deadline: rolling admissions; 2/28 priority date for financial aid. Early admission is possible.

Founded in 1891, Lipscomb is a distinctly Christian university with a sterling academic reputation. More than 100 major programs of study are offered. Lipscomb's 21st-century campuswide fiber-optic network provides PC connections in every residence hall, residence hall lobby lab, and many other locations for Internet access to resources worldwide. Lipscomb University is a beautiful, quiet place with a special atmosphere that encourages learning. Nashville is one of the most exciting cities in the South. Its wide range of cultural and career opportunities enhances the academic program and each student's potential for employment following graduation.

Getting in Last Year
1,601 applied
85% were accepted
596 enrolled (44%)
29% from top tenth of their h.s. class
3.46 average high school GPA
30% had SAT verbal scores over 600
28% had SAT math scores over 600
48% had ACT scores over 24
7% had SAT verbal scores over 700
7% had SAT math scores over 700
10% had ACT scores over 30
20 valedictorians

Graduation and After
169 organizations recruited on campus

Financial Matters
$10,828 tuition and fees (2001–02)
$5420 room and board

LIST COLLEGE, JEWISH THEOLOGICAL SEMINARY OF AMERICA

URBAN SETTING ■ PRIVATE ■ INDEPENDENT RELIGIOUS ■ COED
NEW YORK, NEW YORK

Web site: www.jtsa.edu
Contact: Ms. Reena Kamins, Assistant Director of Admissions, Room 614 Schiff, 3080 Broadway, New York, NY 10027-4649
Telephone: 212-678-8832 **Fax:** 212-678-8947
E-mail: rekamins@jtsa.edu

The Albert A. List College of Jewish Studies, the undergraduate school of the Jewish Theological Seminary, offers students a unique opportunity to pursue 2 bachelor's degrees simultaneously. Students earn a degree from List in one of a dozen areas of Jewish study and a second degree in the liberal arts field of their choice from Columbia University or Barnard College. This exciting 4-year program enables students to experience an intimate and supportive Jewish community as well as a diverse and dynamic campus life.

Getting in Last Year
118 applied
59% were accepted
51 enrolled (73%)
3.80 average high school GPA

Graduation and After
100% graduated in 4 years
60% pursued further study

Financial Matters
$9940 tuition and fees (2001–02)
$6470 room only
75% average percent of need met

Academics

List College awards bachelor's, master's, doctoral, and first-professional **degrees** (double bachelor's degree with Barnard College, Columbia University). Challenging opportunities include advanced placement credit, student-designed majors, freshman honors college, an honors program, double majors, and a senior project. Special programs include internships, summer session for credit, off-campus study, and study-abroad.

The most frequently chosen **baccalaureate** field is philosophy. A complete listing of majors at List College appears in the Majors Index beginning on page 430.

The **faculty** at List College has 115 members. The student-faculty ratio is 5:1.

Students of List College

The student body totals 585, of whom 177 are undergraduates. 50.3% are women and 49.7% are men. Students come from 21 states and territories and 3 other countries. 35% are from New York. 88% returned for their sophomore year.

Facilities and Resources

Student rooms are linked to a campus network. 20 **computers** are available on campus that provide access to the Internet. The **library** has 271,000 books and 720 subscriptions.

Campus Life

Active organizations on campus include a drama/theater group, newspaper, radio station, and choral group. No national or local **fraternities** or **sororities**.

This institution has no intercollegiate sports.

Campus Safety

Student safety services include late-night transport/escort service, 24-hour emergency telephone alarm devices, 24-hour patrols by trained security personnel, and electronically operated dormitory entrances.

Applying

List College requires an essay, SAT II: Writing Test, SAT I and SAT II or ACT, a high school transcript, and 2 recommendations. It recommends an interview and a minimum high school GPA of 3.0. Application deadline: 2/15; 3/1 for financial aid. Early and deferred admission are possible.

LOYOLA COLLEGE IN MARYLAND

URBAN SETTING ■ PRIVATE ■ INDEPENDENT RELIGIOUS ■ COED
BALTIMORE, MARYLAND

Web site: www.loyola.edu

Contact: Mr. William Bossemeyer, Dean of Admissions, 4501 North Charles Street, Baltimore, MD 21210

Telephone: 410-617-2000 ext. 2252 or toll-free 800-221-9107 Ext. 2252 (in-state) **Fax:** 410-617-2176

Academics

Loyola awards bachelor's, master's, and doctoral **degrees** and post-master's certificates. Challenging opportunities include advanced placement credit, accelerated degree programs, an honors program, double majors, independent study, and a senior project. Special programs include internships, summer session for credit, off-campus study, study-abroad, and Army and Air Force ROTC.

The most frequently chosen **baccalaureate** fields are business/marketing, social sciences and history, and communications/communication technologies. A complete listing of majors at Loyola appears in the Majors Index beginning on page 430.

The **faculty** at Loyola has 223 full-time members, 96% with terminal degrees. The student-faculty ratio is 13:1.

Students of Loyola

The student body totals 6,144, of whom 3,477 are undergraduates. 57.3% are women and 42.7% are men. Students come from 41 states and territories and 6 other countries. 23% are from Maryland. 0.2% are international students. 5.2% are African American, 1.6% Asian American, and 1.5% Hispanic American. 89% returned for their sophomore year.

Facilities and Resources

Student rooms are linked to a campus network. 292 **computers** are available on campus that provide access to the Internet. The **library** has 380,000 books and 2,100 subscriptions.

Campus Life

Active organizations on campus include a drama/theater group, newspaper, and choral group. No national or local **fraternities** or **sororities**.

Loyola is a member of the NCAA (Division I).

Campus Safety

Student safety services include late-night transport/escort service, 24-hour emergency telephone alarm devices, 24-hour patrols by trained security personnel, and electronically operated dormitory entrances.

Applying

Loyola requires an essay, SAT I, and a high school transcript. It recommends an interview. Application deadline: 1/15; 2/10 for financial aid. Early and deferred admission are possible.

Traditional academic standards are central to Jesuit education. Loyola's curriculum is rigorous, and the faculty's expectations for students are high. The aim is to challenge students and to try to develop their skills and abilities. Hard work is required for a good education, and Loyola is interested in admitting students who have been ambitious in their course selection in high school and who have shown that they can do well in academic work.

Getting in Last Year
6,577 applied
61% were accepted
884 enrolled (22%)
38% from top tenth of their h.s. class
3.40 average high school GPA
53% had SAT verbal scores over 600
60% had SAT math scores over 600
9% had SAT verbal scores over 700
9% had SAT math scores over 700

Graduation and After
72% had job offers within 6 months
269 organizations recruited on campus

Financial Matters
$23,500 tuition and fees (2001–02)
$7400 room and board
98% average percent of need met
$15,280 average financial aid amount received per undergraduate

LOYOLA UNIVERSITY CHICAGO

URBAN SETTING ■ PRIVATE ■ INDEPENDENT RELIGIOUS ■ COED
CHICAGO, ILLINOIS

Web site: www.luc.edu
Contact: Mr. Aaron Meis, Acting Director of Admissions, 820 North
   Michigan Avenue, Suite 613, Chicago, IL 60611
Telephone: 312-915-6500 or toll-free 800-262-2373 **Fax:** 312-915-7216
E-mail: admission@luc.edu

Chicago offers an ideal environment to enrich students' academic experience, with its world-class museums and performing arts; professional sports; culturally rich diversity; and international headquarters for media, commerce, medicine, and banking. Loyola's partnership with the city of Chicago adds an extra dimension—vast resources for internships, fieldwork, and independent exploration—rare in universities of Loyola's affiliation (Jesuit, Catholic), size (medium), and ranking (national research university). Extraordinary resources include a distinguished and dedicated faculty (97% with the PhD) teaching classes averaging 23 students while mentoring new students' living and learning experience on Loyola's residential lakefront campus on Chicago's north shore.

Getting in Last Year
8,746 applied
77% were accepted
1,422 enrolled (21%)
31% from top tenth of their h.s. class
42% had SAT verbal scores over 600
42% had SAT math scores over 600
61% had ACT scores over 24
7% had SAT verbal scores over 700
7% had SAT math scores over 700
10% had ACT scores over 30
12 valedictorians

Graduation and After
46% graduated in 4 years
18% graduated in 5 years
3% graduated in 6 years

Financial Matters
$19,274 tuition and fees (2001–02)
$7266 room and board
93% average percent of need met
$17,836 average financial aid amount received
   per undergraduate

Academics

Loyola awards bachelor's, master's, doctoral, and first-professional **degrees** and post-bachelor's and post-master's certificates (also offers adult part-time program with significant enrollment not reflected in profile). Challenging opportunities include advanced placement credit, accelerated degree programs, an honors program, and double majors. Special programs include internships, summer session for credit, off-campus study, study-abroad, and Army ROTC.

The most frequently chosen **baccalaureate** fields are business/marketing, social sciences and history, and psychology. A complete listing of majors at Loyola appears in the Majors Index beginning on page 430.

The **faculty** at Loyola has 940 full-time members, 100% with terminal degrees. The student-faculty ratio is 14:1.

Students of Loyola

The student body totals 13,019, of whom 7,497 are undergraduates. 65.5% are women and 34.5% are men. Students come from 50 states and territories and 60 other countries. 80% are from Illinois. 1.8% are international students. 9.2% are African American, 0.1% American Indian, 12.1% Asian American, and 9.7% Hispanic American. 85% returned for their sophomore year.

Facilities and Resources

Student rooms are linked to a campus network. 318 **computers** are available on campus that provide access to the Internet. The 4 **libraries** have 983,023 books and 110,502 subscriptions.

Campus Life

There are 136 active organizations on campus, including a drama/theater group, newspaper, radio station, and choral group. 8% of eligible men and 7% of eligible women are members of national **fraternities** and national **sororities**.

Loyola is a member of the NCAA (Division I). **Intercollegiate sports** (some offering scholarships) include basketball, cross-country running, golf, soccer, softball (w), track and field, volleyball.

Campus Safety

Student safety services include late-night transport/escort service, 24-hour emergency telephone alarm devices, 24-hour patrols by trained security personnel, and electronically operated dormitory entrances.

Applying

Loyola requires an essay, SAT I or ACT, and a high school transcript. It recommends an interview. Application deadline: 4/1; 3/1 priority date for financial aid. Early admission is possible.

LOYOLA UNIVERSITY NEW ORLEANS

URBAN SETTING ■ PRIVATE ■ INDEPENDENT RELIGIOUS ■ COED
NEW ORLEANS, LOUISIANA

Web site: www.loyno.edu

Contact: Ms. Deborah C. Stieffel, Dean of Admission and Enrollment
Management, 6363 Saint Charles Avenue, Box 18, New Orleans, LA
70118-6195

Telephone: 504-865-3240 or toll-free 800-4-LOYOLA **Fax:** 504-865-3383

E-mail: admit@loyno.edu

Academics

Loyola awards bachelor's, master's, and first-professional **degrees**. Challenging opportunities include advanced placement credit, accelerated degree programs, student-designed majors, an honors program, double majors, independent study, and a senior project. Special programs include internships, summer session for credit, off-campus study, study-abroad, and Army and Air Force ROTC.

The most frequently chosen **baccalaureate** fields are communications/communication technologies, business/marketing, and social sciences and history. A complete listing of majors at Loyola appears in the Majors Index beginning on page 430.

The **faculty** at Loyola has 263 full-time members, 92% with terminal degrees. The student-faculty ratio is 14:1.

Students of Loyola

The student body totals 5,509, of whom 3,792 are undergraduates. 64.4% are women and 35.6% are men. Students come from 50 states and territories and 44 other countries. 53% are from Louisiana. 3.3% are international students. 10.7% are African American, 0.5% American Indian, 4.2% Asian American, and 9.6% Hispanic American. 81% returned for their sophomore year.

Facilities and Resources

Student rooms are linked to a campus network. 300 **computers** are available on campus that provide access to the Internet. The 2 **libraries** have 384,774 books and 5,111 subscriptions.

Campus Life

There are 120 active organizations on campus, including a drama/theater group, newspaper, radio station, television station, and choral group. 16% of eligible men and 17% of eligible women are members of national **fraternities**, national **sororities**, and local fraternities.

Loyola is a member of the NAIA. **Intercollegiate sports** include baseball (m), basketball, cross-country running, soccer (w), track and field, volleyball (w).

Campus Safety

Student safety services include self-defense education, bicycle patrols, closed circuit TV monitors, door alarms, crime prevention programs, late-night transport/escort service, 24-hour emergency telephone alarm devices, 24-hour patrols by trained security personnel, and electronically operated dormitory entrances.

Applying

Loyola requires an essay, SAT I or ACT, a high school transcript, and 1 recommendation, and in some cases PAA and an interview. It recommends an interview. Application deadline: 1/15; 2/15 priority date for financial aid. Deferred admission is possible.

Getting in Last Year
3,419 applied
69% were accepted
872 enrolled (37%)
27% from top tenth of their h.s. class
3.54 average high school GPA
47% had SAT verbal scores over 600
35% had SAT math scores over 600
67% had ACT scores over 24
10% had SAT verbal scores over 700
3% had SAT math scores over 700
9% had ACT scores over 30
15 valedictorians

Graduation and After
24% pursued further study
62% had job offers within 6 months
168 organizations recruited on campus

Financial Matters
85% average percent of need met
$14,084 average financial aid amount received
per undergraduate

LUTHER COLLEGE

SMALL-TOWN SETTING ■ PRIVATE ■ INDEPENDENT RELIGIOUS ■ COED
DECORAH, IOWA

Web site: www.luther.edu

Contact: Mr. Jon Lund, Vice President for Enrollment and Marketing, 700 College Drive, Decorah, IA 52101

Telephone: 563-387-1287 or toll-free 800-458-8437 **Fax:** 563-387-2159

E-mail: admissions@luther.edu

Getting in Last Year

1,911 applied
83% were accepted
636 enrolled (40%)
35% from top tenth of their h.s. class
3.60 average high school GPA
62% had SAT verbal scores over 600
58% had SAT math scores over 600
65% had ACT scores over 24
15% had SAT verbal scores over 700
11% had SAT math scores over 700
16% had ACT scores over 30
11 National Merit Scholars
18 class presidents
45 valedictorians

Graduation and After

66% graduated in 4 years
7% graduated in 5 years
22% pursued further study (10% arts and sciences, 3% medicine, 2% theology)
69% had job offers within 6 months
157 organizations recruited on campus

Financial Matters

$19,325 tuition and fees (2001–02)
$3975 room and board
86% average percent of need met
$15,639 average financial aid amount received per undergraduate (2000–01)

Academics

Luther awards bachelor's **degrees**. Challenging opportunities include advanced placement credit, student-designed majors, an honors program, double majors, independent study, and a senior project. Special programs include internships, summer session for credit, off-campus study, and study-abroad.

The most frequently chosen **baccalaureate** fields are biological/life sciences, business/marketing, and education. A complete listing of majors at Luther appears in the Majors Index beginning on page 430.

The **faculty** at Luther has 181 full-time members, 81% with terminal degrees. The student-faculty ratio is 13:1.

Students of Luther

The student body is made up of 2,575 undergraduates. 60.4% are women and 39.6% are men. Students come from 39 states and territories and 44 other countries. 37% are from Iowa. 6.1% are international students. 0.6% are African American, 0.2% American Indian, 1.2% Asian American, and 0.6% Hispanic American. 84% returned for their sophomore year.

Facilities and Resources

Student rooms are linked to a campus network. 526 **computers** are available on campus that provide access to the Internet. The **library** has 345,743 books and 1,663 subscriptions.

Campus Life

There are 116 active organizations on campus, including a drama/theater group, newspaper, radio station, and choral group. 8% of eligible men and 9% of eligible women are members of national **fraternities**, local fraternities, and local **sororities**.

Luther is a member of the NCAA (Division III). **Intercollegiate sports** include baseball (m), basketball, cross-country running, football (m), golf, soccer, softball (w), swimming, tennis, track and field, volleyball (w), wrestling (m).

Campus Safety

Student safety services include late-night transport/escort service, 24-hour emergency telephone alarm devices, 24-hour patrols by trained security personnel, and electronically operated dormitory entrances.

Applying

Luther requires an essay, SAT I or ACT, a high school transcript, and 1 recommendation. It recommends an interview. Application deadline: 3/1 priority date for financial aid. Early and deferred admission are possible.

LYCOMING COLLEGE

SMALL-TOWN SETTING ■ PRIVATE ■ INDEPENDENT RELIGIOUS ■ COED
WILLIAMSPORT, PENNSYLVANIA

Web site: www.lycoming.edu
Contact: Mr. James Spencer, Dean of Admissions and Financial Aid,
Admissions House, 700 College Place, Williamsport, PA 17701
Telephone: 570-321-4026 or toll-free 800-345-3920 ext. 4026 **Fax:**
570-321-4317
E-mail: admissions@lycoming.edu

Academics

Lycoming awards bachelor's **degrees**. Challenging opportunities include advanced
placement credit, accelerated degree programs, student-designed majors, an honors
program, double majors, independent study, and a senior project. Special programs
include internships, summer session for credit, off-campus study, study-abroad, and
Army ROTC.

The most frequently chosen **baccalaureate** fields are business/marketing, biological/
life sciences, and psychology. A complete listing of majors at Lycoming appears in the
Majors Index beginning on page 430.

The **faculty** at Lycoming has 88 full-time members, 91% with terminal degrees. The
student-faculty ratio is 13:1.

Students of Lycoming

The student body is made up of 1,429 undergraduates. 54.6% are women and 45.4% are
men. Students come from 21 states and territories and 9 other countries. 79% are from
Pennsylvania. 0.8% are international students. 1.6% are African American, 0.4%
American Indian, 0.6% Asian American, and 0.7% Hispanic American. 81% returned for
their sophomore year.

Facilities and Resources

Student rooms are linked to a campus network. 140 **computers** are available on campus
that provide access to the Internet. The 2 **libraries** have 165,000 books and 950
subscriptions.

Campus Life

There are 60 active organizations on campus, including a drama/theater group,
newspaper, radio station, television station, and choral group. 9% of eligible men and
10% of eligible women are members of national **fraternities**, national **sororities**, and
local sororities.

Lycoming is a member of the NCAA (Division III). **Intercollegiate sports** include
basketball, cross-country running, football (m), golf (m), lacrosse, soccer, softball (w),
swimming, tennis, track and field, volleyball (w), wrestling (m).

Campus Safety

Student safety services include late-night transport/escort service, 24-hour emergency
telephone alarm devices, 24-hour patrols by trained security personnel, student patrols,
and electronically operated dormitory entrances.

Applying

Lycoming requires an essay, SAT I or ACT, a high school transcript, and 2 recommendations. It recommends an interview and a minimum high school GPA of 2.3. Application
deadline: 4/1; 4/15 priority date for financial aid. Early and deferred admission are possible.

Getting in Last Year
1,431 applied
80% were accepted
408 enrolled (36%)
25% from top tenth of their h.s. class
3.20 average high school GPA
23% had SAT verbal scores over 600
20% had SAT math scores over 600
2% had SAT verbal scores over 700
2% had SAT math scores over 700
18 class presidents
20 valedictorians

Graduation and After
43% graduated in 4 years
18% graduated in 5 years
1% graduated in 6 years
20% pursued further study (6% arts and sciences, 4% medicine, 3% law)
99% had job offers within 6 months
40 organizations recruited on campus

Financial Matters
$19,404 tuition and fees (2001–02)
$5376 room and board
86% average percent of need met
$16,232 average financial aid amount received
per undergraduate

LYON COLLEGE

SMALL-TOWN SETTING ■ PRIVATE ■ INDEPENDENT RELIGIOUS ■ COED
BATESVILLE, ARKANSAS

Web site: www.lyon.edu
Contact: Mr. David Wilkey, Vice President for Enrollment Services, PO Box 2317, Batesville, AR 72503-2317
Telephone: 870-698-4250 or toll-free 800-423-2542 **Fax:** 870-793-1791
E-mail: admissions@lyon.edu

Lyon's powerful sense of community, commitment to honor, and dedication to the education of the total person make it a place where students grow in remarkable ways. Located in the beautiful foothills of the Ozark Mountains, Lyon offers access to talented teacher-scholars as part of a stimulating academic community organized around a residential house system. A strong endowment supports a challenging academic program and exceptional opportunities in such areas as study abroad and student research. Lyon students are noted for their enthusiasm, involvement, and high acceptance rates into graduate and professional schools.

Academics

Lyon awards bachelor's **degrees**. Challenging opportunities include advanced placement credit, student-designed majors, double majors, independent study, and a senior project. Special programs include internships, summer session for credit, and study-abroad.

The most frequently chosen **baccalaureate** fields are social sciences and history, psychology, and business/marketing. A complete listing of majors at Lyon appears in the Majors Index beginning on page 430.

The **faculty** at Lyon has 41 full-time members, 85% with terminal degrees. The student-faculty ratio is 11:1.

Students of Lyon

The student body is made up of 526 undergraduates. 56.8% are women and 43.2% are men. Students come from 21 states and territories and 15 other countries. 83% are from Arkansas. 5.4% are international students. 3.2% are African American, 1.2% American Indian, 1.2% Asian American, and 1.6% Hispanic American. 87% returned for their sophomore year.

Facilities and Resources

Student rooms are linked to a campus network. 60 **computers** are available on campus that provide access to the Internet. The **library** has 147,893 books and 1,160 subscriptions.

Campus Life

There are 36 active organizations on campus, including a drama/theater group, newspaper, and choral group. 21% of eligible men and 31% of eligible women are members of national **fraternities**, national **sororities**, and local sororities.

Lyon is a member of the NAIA. **Intercollegiate sports** (some offering scholarships) include baseball (m), basketball, cross-country running, golf, soccer (m), tennis, volleyball (w).

Campus Safety

Student safety services include late-night transport/escort service and 24-hour patrols by trained security personnel.

Applying

Lyon requires an essay, SAT I or ACT, a high school transcript, and 1 recommendation. It recommends an interview and a minimum high school GPA of 2.5. Application deadline: rolling admissions; 4/1 priority date for financial aid. Deferred admission is possible.

Getting in Last Year
439 applied
78% were accepted
127 enrolled (37%)
46% from top tenth of their h.s. class
3.56 average high school GPA
29% had SAT verbal scores over 600
33% had SAT math scores over 600
66% had ACT scores over 24
4% had SAT math scores over 700
8% had ACT scores over 30
18 valedictorians

Graduation and After
28% pursued further study (4% arts and sciences, 2% law, 1% business)
55% had job offers within 6 months
2 organizations recruited on campus

Financial Matters
$11,375 tuition and fees (2001–02)
$5125 room and board
75% average percent of need met
$12,558 average financial aid amount received per undergraduate

MACALESTER COLLEGE

URBAN SETTING ■ PRIVATE ■ INDEPENDENT RELIGIOUS ■ COED
ST. PAUL, MINNESOTA

Web site: www.macalester.edu
Contact: Mr. Lorne T. Robinson, Dean of Admissions and Financial Aid,
   1600 Grand Avenue, St. Paul, MN 55105-1899
Telephone: 651-696-6357 or toll-free 800-231-7974 **Fax:** 651-696-6724
E-mail: admissions@macalester.edu

Academics

Mac awards bachelor's **degrees**. Challenging opportunities include student-designed
majors, an honors program, independent study, and a senior project. Special programs
include internships, off-campus study, study-abroad, and Army and Air Force ROTC.

The most frequently chosen **baccalaureate** fields are social sciences and history,
biological/life sciences, and psychology. A complete listing of majors at Mac appears in
the Majors Index beginning on page 430.

The **faculty** at Mac has 148 full-time members, 95% with terminal degrees. The student-faculty ratio is 11:1.

Students of Mac

The student body is made up of 1,822 undergraduates. 58.3% are women and 41.7% are
men. Students come from 50 states and territories and 88 other countries. 27% are from
Minnesota. 14.1% are international students. 3.4% are African American, 0.8%
American Indian, 4.6% Asian American, and 2.5% Hispanic American. 91% returned for
their sophomore year.

Facilities and Resources

Student rooms are linked to a campus network. 350 **computers** are available on campus
that provide access to the Internet. The **library** has 407,321 books and 2,459 subscriptions.

Campus Life

There are 70 active organizations on campus, including a drama/theater group,
newspaper, radio station, television station, and choral group. No national or local
fraternities or **sororities**.

Mac is a member of the NCAA (Division III). **Intercollegiate sports** include
baseball (m), basketball, cross-country running, football (m), golf, skiing (cross-country),
soccer, softball (w), swimming, tennis, track and field, volleyball (w), water polo (w).

Campus Safety

Student safety services include late-night transport/escort service, 24-hour emergency
telephone alarm devices, 24-hour patrols by trained security personnel, and electronically operated dormitory entrances.

Applying

Mac requires an essay, SAT I or ACT, a high school transcript, and 3 recommendations.
It recommends an interview. Application deadline: 1/15; 2/8 priority date for financial
aid. Early and deferred admission are possible.

Getting in Last Year
3,480 applied
50% were accepted
505 enrolled (29%)
65% from top tenth of their h.s. class
92% had SAT verbal scores over 600
83% had SAT math scores over 600
98% had ACT scores over 24
46% had SAT verbal scores over 700
31% had SAT math scores over 700
48% had ACT scores over 30
51 National Merit Scholars
44 valedictorians

Graduation and After
71% graduated in 4 years
6% graduated in 5 years
64% had job offers within 6 months
100 organizations recruited on campus

Financial Matters
$22,608 tuition and fees (2001–02)
$6206 room and board
100% average percent of need met
$18,194 average financial aid amount received
   per undergraduate

MAHARISHI UNIVERSITY OF MANAGEMENT

SMALL-TOWN SETTING ■ PRIVATE ■ INDEPENDENT ■ COED
FAIRFIELD, IOWA

Web site: www.mum.edu
Contact: Mr. Brad Mylett, Director of Admissions, 1000 North 4th Street, Fairfield, IA 52557
Telephone: 641-472-1110 **Fax:** 641-472-1179
E-mail: admissions@mum.edu

Getting in Last Year

94 applied
62% were accepted
58 enrolled (100%)
3.46 average high school GPA
58% had SAT verbal scores over 600
46% had SAT math scores over 600
67% had ACT scores over 24
8% had SAT verbal scores over 700
12% had SAT math scores over 700
19% had ACT scores over 30
3 National Merit Scholars
1 class president
2 valedictorians

Graduation and After

30% graduated in 4 years
16% graduated in 6 years
75% had job offers within 6 months
20 organizations recruited on campus

Financial Matters

$16,390 tuition and fees (2001–02)
84% average percent of need met
$20,597 average financial aid amount received per undergraduate

Academics

M.U.M. awards associate, bachelor's, master's, and doctoral **degrees**. Challenging opportunities include advanced placement credit, student-designed majors, an honors program, double majors, independent study, and a senior project. Special programs include cooperative education, internships, and study-abroad.

The most frequently chosen **baccalaureate** fields are visual/performing arts, business/marketing, and biological/life sciences. A complete listing of majors at M.U.M. appears in the Majors Index beginning on page 430.

The **faculty** at M.U.M. has 56 full-time members, 88% with terminal degrees. The student-faculty ratio is 9:1.

Students of M.U.M.

The student body totals 734, of whom 210 are undergraduates. 49% are women and 51% are men. Students come from 27 states and territories and 19 other countries. 60% are from Iowa. 36.4% are international students. 4.4% are African American, 2.9% Asian American, and 2.4% Hispanic American. 66% returned for their sophomore year.

Facilities and Resources

Student rooms are linked to a campus network. 120 **computers** are available on campus that provide access to the Internet. The 2 **libraries** have 111,022 books and 846 subscriptions.

Campus Life

There are 15 active organizations on campus, including a drama/theater group, newspaper, radio station, and choral group. No national or local **fraternities** or **sororities**.

Intercollegiate sports include basketball (m), golf (m).

Campus Safety

Student safety services include late-night transport/escort service, 24-hour emergency telephone alarm devices, 24-hour patrols by trained security personnel, and electronically operated dormitory entrances.

Applying

M.U.M. requires an essay, SAT I or ACT, a high school transcript, 2 recommendations, minimum SAT score of 950 or ACT score of 19, and a minimum high school GPA of 2.5. It recommends an interview. Application deadline: 8/1; 4/15 priority date for financial aid. Early and deferred admission are possible.

MARIETTA COLLEGE

SMALL-TOWN SETTING ■ PRIVATE ■ INDEPENDENT ■ COED
MARIETTA, OHIO

Web site: www.marietta.edu

Contact: Ms. Marke Vickers, Director of Admission, 215 Fifth Street, Marietta, OH 45750-4000

Telephone: 740-376-4600 or toll-free 800-331-7896 **Fax:** 740-376-8888

E-mail: admit@marietta.edu

Academics

Marietta awards associate, bachelor's, and master's **degrees**. Challenging opportunities include advanced placement credit, accelerated degree programs, student-designed majors, an honors program, double majors, independent study, and a senior project. Special programs include internships, summer session for credit, off-campus study, and study-abroad.

The most frequently chosen **baccalaureate** fields are business/marketing, education, and parks and recreation. A complete listing of majors at Marietta appears in the Majors Index beginning on page 430.

The **faculty** at Marietta has 128 members. The student-faculty ratio is 12:1.

Students of Marietta

The student body totals 1,278, of whom 1,205 are undergraduates. 50.4% are women and 49.6% are men. Students come from 37 states and territories and 9 other countries. 62% are from Ohio. 5.4% are international students. 2% are African American, 0.3% American Indian, 1.2% Asian American, and 1.1% Hispanic American. 76% returned for their sophomore year.

Facilities and Resources

Student rooms are linked to a campus network. 200 **computers** are available on campus that provide access to the Internet. The **library** has 250,000 books and 1,300 subscriptions.

Campus Life

There are 65 active organizations on campus, including a drama/theater group, newspaper, radio station, television station, and choral group. 20% of eligible men and 30% of eligible women are members of national **fraternities** and national **sororities**.

Marietta is a member of the NCAA (Division III). **Intercollegiate sports** include baseball (m), basketball, crew, cross-country running, football (m), golf, lacrosse (m), soccer, softball (w), tennis, track and field, volleyball (w).

Campus Safety

Student safety services include late-night transport/escort service, 24-hour emergency telephone alarm devices, 24-hour patrols by trained security personnel, student patrols, and electronically operated dormitory entrances.

Applying

Marietta requires an essay, SAT I or ACT, a high school transcript, 2 recommendations, and a minimum high school GPA of 2.0. It recommends SAT II Subject Tests, an interview, and a minimum high school GPA of 3.0. Application deadline: 4/15; 3/1 priority date for financial aid. Early and deferred admission are possible.

Founded in 1788, Marietta, Ohio, has the distinction of being the first permanent settlement of America's Northwest Territory. The College traces its beginning to 1797. Both the city and the College are rich in history, with stately homes, brick-paved streets, and antique stores. In 1860, Marietta College became only the 16th college in America to be awarded a chapter of Phi Beta Kappa. Students' academic life is enriched by the McDonough Leadership Program, the most comprehensive program in leadership studies in the country, whereby students may earn a minor, be actively involved in volunteer work, and participate in internships throughout the world.

Getting in Last Year
1,152 applied
94% were accepted
367 enrolled (34%)
19% from top tenth of their h.s. class
3.25 average high school GPA
25% had SAT verbal scores over 600
31% had SAT math scores over 600
43% had ACT scores over 24
3% had SAT verbal scores over 700
3% had SAT math scores over 700
7% had ACT scores over 30

Graduation and After
22% pursued further study (15% arts and sciences, 6% education, 3% dentistry)
85% had job offers within 6 months
32 organizations recruited on campus

Financial Matters
$19,076 tuition and fees (2001–02)
$2940 room and board
90% average percent of need met
$16,520 average financial aid amount received per undergraduate

---

MARQUETTE UNIVERSITY

URBAN SETTING ■ PRIVATE ■ INDEPENDENT RELIGIOUS ■ COED
MILWAUKEE, WISCONSIN

Web site: www.marquette.edu
Contact: Mr. Robert Blust, Dean of Undergraduate Admissions, PO Box 1881, Milwaukee, WI 53201-1881
Telephone: 414-288-7004 or toll-free 800-222-6544 **Fax:** 414-288-3764
E-mail: admissions@marquette.edu

Since 1881, Marquette University has challenged students to strive for excellence in all things. A Jesuit Catholic university, Marquette emphasizes a rigorous core curriculum, professional preparation, and the notion that "care for others" is something to be acted upon, not merely talked about. All faculty members—96% hold the highest degrees in their fields—teach, advise, and conduct research. Marquette's campus, in downtown Milwaukee, is located about 1 mile from the Lake Michigan shoreline. With grass, trees, and a diverse residential student population hailing from all 50 states and more than 80 countries, Marquette provides a unique living and learning environment in the heart of a vibrant city.

Getting in Last Year
6,743 applied
84% were accepted
1,665 enrolled (29%)
29% from top tenth of their h.s. class
42% had SAT verbal scores over 600
42% had SAT math scores over 600
68% had ACT scores over 24
7% had SAT verbal scores over 700
7% had SAT math scores over 700
11% had ACT scores over 30
13 National Merit Scholars

Graduation and After
28% pursued further study
396 organizations recruited on campus

Financial Matters
$18,482 tuition and fees (2001–02)
$6362 room and board
90% average percent of need met
$15,483 average financial aid amount received per undergraduate

Academics

Marquette awards associate, bachelor's, master's, doctoral, and first-professional **degrees** and post-bachelor's and post-master's certificates. Challenging opportunities include advanced placement credit, accelerated degree programs, an honors program, double majors, independent study, and a senior project. Special programs include cooperative education, internships, summer session for credit, off-campus study, study-abroad, and Army, Navy and Air Force ROTC.

The most frequently chosen **baccalaureate** fields are business/marketing, communications/communication technologies, and engineering/engineering technologies. A complete listing of majors at Marquette appears in the Majors Index beginning on page 430.

The **faculty** at Marquette has 596 full-time members, 79% with terminal degrees. The student-faculty ratio is 15:1.

Students of Marquette

The student body totals 10,832, of whom 7,499 are undergraduates. 55.5% are women and 44.5% are men. Students come from 54 states and territories and 54 other countries. 48% are from Wisconsin. 2% are international students. 4.7% are African American, 0.3% American Indian, 4.4% Asian American, and 4.1% Hispanic American. 89% returned for their sophomore year.

Facilities and Resources

Student rooms are linked to a campus network. 600 **computers** are available on campus that provide access to the Internet. The 3 **libraries** have 719,906 books and 9,225 subscriptions.

Campus Life

There are 150 active organizations on campus, including a drama/theater group, newspaper, radio station, television station, and choral group. 9% of eligible men and 9% of eligible women are members of national **fraternities** and national **sororities**.

Marquette is a member of the NCAA (Division I). **Intercollegiate sports** (some offering scholarships) include basketball, cross-country running, golf (m), soccer, tennis, track and field, volleyball (w).

Campus Safety

Student safety services include 24-hour desk attendants in residence halls, late-night transport/escort service, 24-hour emergency telephone alarm devices, 24-hour patrols by trained security personnel, and student patrols.

Applying

Marquette requires an essay, SAT I or ACT, a high school transcript, and a minimum high school GPA of 2.5. It recommends an interview, 1 recommendation, and a minimum high school GPA of 3.4. Application deadline: rolling admissions. Early and deferred admission are possible.

MARYVILLE COLLEGE

SUBURBAN SETTING ▪ PRIVATE ▪ INDEPENDENT RELIGIOUS ▪ COED
MARYVILLE, TENNESSEE

Web site: www.maryvillecollege.edu
Contact: Ms. Linda L. Moore, Administrative Assistant of Admissions, 502 East Lamar Alexander Parkway, Maryville, TN 37804-5907
Telephone: 865-981-8092 or toll-free 800-597-2687 **Fax:** 865-981-8005
E-mail: admissions@maryvillecollege.edu

Academics

MC awards bachelor's **degrees**. Challenging opportunities include advanced placement credit, student-designed majors, an honors program, double majors, independent study, and a senior project. Special programs include internships, summer session for credit, off-campus study, and study-abroad.

The most frequently chosen **baccalaureate** fields are business/marketing, education, and biological/life sciences. A complete listing of majors at MC appears in the Majors Index beginning on page 430.

The **faculty** at MC has 63 full-time members, 94% with terminal degrees. The student-faculty ratio is 14:1.

Students of MC

The student body is made up of 1,026 undergraduates. 57.9% are women and 42.1% are men. Students come from 29 states and territories and 19 other countries. 70% are from Tennessee. 2.9% are international students. 6% are African American, 0.6% American Indian, 1.1% Asian American, and 0.8% Hispanic American. 70% returned for their sophomore year.

Facilities and Resources

Student rooms are linked to a campus network. 62 **computers** are available on campus that provide access to the Internet. The 2 **libraries** have 83,573 books and 672 subscriptions.

Campus Life

There are 39 active organizations on campus, including a drama/theater group, newspaper, and choral group. No national or local **fraternities** or **sororities**.

MC is a member of the NCAA (Division III). **Intercollegiate sports** include baseball (m), basketball, cross-country running, equestrian sports, football (m), soccer, softball (w), tennis, volleyball (w).

Campus Safety

Student safety services include late-night transport/escort service, 24-hour emergency telephone alarm devices, 24-hour patrols by trained security personnel, and electronically operated dormitory entrances.

Applying

MC requires SAT I or ACT, a high school transcript, and a minimum high school GPA of 2.5, and in some cases an essay, an interview, and recommendations. It recommends a minimum high school GPA of 3.0. Application deadline: 3/1; 3/1 priority date for financial aid. Early and deferred admission are possible.

Maryville, one of the South's best colleges, emphasizes education for the individual. Students are guided in the development of a personal plan for intellectual, social, and spiritual growth grounded in a strong liberal arts curriculum supported by a rich array of experiential learning opportunities, including internships, study abroad, service learning, and the College's distinctive outdoor adventure program, Mountain Challenge. A Presbyterian (U.S.A.) college, Maryville is located in the foothills of east Tennessee near Great Smoky Mountain National Park.

Getting in Last Year
1,494 applied
79% were accepted
288 enrolled (25%)
33% from top tenth of their h.s. class
3.49 average high school GPA
39% had SAT verbal scores over 600
25% had SAT math scores over 600
50% had ACT scores over 24
10% had SAT verbal scores over 700
2% had SAT math scores over 700
10% had ACT scores over 30
10 valedictorians

Graduation and After
39% graduated in 4 years
11% graduated in 5 years
2% graduated in 6 years
20% pursued further study (11% arts and sciences, 3% law, 2% business)
70% had job offers within 6 months
80 organizations recruited on campus

Financial Matters
$17,560 tuition and fees (2001–02)
$5650 room and board
92% average percent of need met
$18,573 average financial aid amount received per undergraduate

MARY WASHINGTON COLLEGE

SMALL-TOWN SETTING ■ PUBLIC ■ STATE-SUPPORTED ■ COED
FREDERICKSBURG, VIRGINIA

Web site: www.mwc.edu
Contact: Dr. Jenifer Blair, Dean of Undergraduate Admissions, 1301 College Avenue, Fredericksburg, VA 22401-5358
Telephone: 540-654-2000 or toll-free 800-468-5614
E-mail: admit@mwc.edu

Getting in Last Year

4,320 applied
55% were accepted
843 enrolled (35%)
52% from top tenth of their h.s. class
3.72 average high school GPA
59% had SAT verbal scores over 600
47% had SAT math scores over 600
11% had SAT verbal scores over 700
4% had SAT math scores over 700
1 National Merit Scholar
44 valedictorians

Graduation and After

65% graduated in 4 years
9% graduated in 5 years
1% graduated in 6 years
18% pursued further study (6% arts and sciences, 3% law, 2% education)
70% had job offers within 6 months
64 organizations recruited on campus

Financial Matters

$3340 resident tuition and fees (2001–02)
$10,010 nonresident tuition and fees (2001–02)
$5692 room and board
57% average percent of need met
$5375 average financial aid amount received per undergraduate (2000–01)

Academics

Mary Washington awards bachelor's and master's **degrees**. Challenging opportunities include advanced placement credit, accelerated degree programs, student-designed majors, double majors, independent study, and a senior project. Special programs include cooperative education, internships, summer session for credit, and study-abroad.

The most frequently chosen **baccalaureate** fields are social sciences and history, business/marketing, and liberal arts/general studies. A complete listing of majors at Mary Washington appears in the Majors Index beginning on page 430.

The **faculty** at Mary Washington has 202 full-time members, 82% with terminal degrees. The student-faculty ratio is 17:1.

Students of Mary Washington

The student body totals 4,483, of whom 4,173 are undergraduates. 67.4% are women and 32.6% are men. Students come from 46 states and territories and 14 other countries. 65% are from Virginia. 0.3% are international students. 4.3% are African American, 0.3% American Indian, 4% Asian American, and 2.6% Hispanic American. 87% returned for their sophomore year.

Facilities and Resources

Student rooms are linked to a campus network. 238 **computers** are available on campus for student use. The **library** has 354,326 books and 1,713 subscriptions.

Campus Life

There are 96 active organizations on campus, including a drama/theater group, newspaper, radio station, and choral group. No national or local **fraternities** or **sororities**.

Mary Washington is a member of the NCAA (Division III). **Intercollegiate sports** include baseball (m), basketball, crew, cross-country running, equestrian sports, field hockey (w), lacrosse, soccer, softball (w), swimming, tennis, track and field, volleyball (w).

Campus Safety

Student safety services include self-defense and safety classes, late-night transport/escort service, 24-hour emergency telephone alarm devices, 24-hour patrols by trained security personnel, student patrols, and electronically operated dormitory entrances.

Applying

Mary Washington requires an essay, SAT I or ACT, and a high school transcript. It recommends SAT II Subject Tests. Application deadline: 2/1; 3/1 for financial aid. Deferred admission is possible.

MASSACHUSETTS INSTITUTE OF TECHNOLOGY

URBAN SETTING ■ PRIVATE ■ INDEPENDENT ■ COED
CAMBRIDGE, MASSACHUSETTS

Web site: web.mit.edu
Contact: Ms. Marilee Jones, Dean of Admissions, 77 Massachusetts Avenue,
    Cambridge, MA 02139-4307
Telephone: 617-253-4791

Academics

MIT awards bachelor's, master's, and doctoral **degrees**. Challenging opportunities include advanced placement credit, accelerated degree programs, student-designed majors, and a senior project. Special programs include cooperative education, internships, summer session for credit, off-campus study, and Army, Navy and Air Force ROTC.

The most frequently chosen **baccalaureate** fields are engineering/engineering technologies, computer/information sciences, and biological/life sciences. A complete listing of majors at MIT appears in the Majors Index beginning on page 430.

The **faculty** at MIT has 1,310 full-time members. The student-faculty ratio is 7:1.

Students of MIT

The student body totals 10,204, of whom 4,220 are undergraduates. 41.8% are women and 58.2% are men. Students come from 55 states and territories and 88 other countries. 10% are from Massachusetts. 8.1% are international students. 6.1% are African American, 2% American Indian, 27.8% Asian American, and 11.2% Hispanic American. 97% returned for their sophomore year.

Facilities and Resources

Student rooms are linked to a campus network. 950 **computers** are available on campus for student use. The 11 **libraries** have 2,605,490 books and 20,207 subscriptions.

Campus Life

There are 332 active organizations on campus, including a drama/theater group, newspaper, radio station, television station, choral group, and marching band. 40% of eligible men and 20% of eligible women are members of national **fraternities**, national **sororities**, and local fraternities.

MIT is a member of the NCAA (Division III). **Intercollegiate sports** include baseball (m), basketball, crew, cross-country running, fencing, field hockey (w), football (m), golf (m), gymnastics, ice hockey (w), lacrosse, riflery, sailing, skiing (cross-country), skiing (downhill), soccer, softball (w), squash (m), swimming, tennis, track and field, volleyball, water polo (m), wrestling (m).

Campus Safety

Student safety services include late-night transport/escort service, 24-hour emergency telephone alarm devices, 24-hour patrols by trained security personnel, student patrols, and electronically operated dormitory entrances.

Applying

MIT requires an essay, SAT II Subject Tests, SAT I or ACT, a high school transcript, an interview, and 2 recommendations. Application deadline: 1/1. Deferred admission is possible.

Getting in Last Year
10,490 applied
17% were accepted
1,030 enrolled (58%)
98% from top tenth of their h.s. class
95% had SAT verbal scores over 600
100% had SAT math scores over 600
99% had ACT scores over 24
63% had SAT verbal scores over 700
89% had SAT math scores over 700
80% had ACT scores over 30
251 valedictorians

Graduation and After
37% pursued further study
661 organizations recruited on campus

Financial Matters
$26,960 tuition and fees (2001–02)
$7500 room and board

McKendree College

SMALL-TOWN SETTING ■ PRIVATE ■ INDEPENDENT RELIGIOUS ■ COED
LEBANON, ILLINOIS

Web site: www.mckendree.edu

Contact: Mr. Mark Campbell, Vice President for Admissions and Financial Aid, 701 College Road, Lebanon, IL 62254

Telephone: 618-537-4481 ext. 6835 or toll-free 800-232-7228 ext. 6835 **Fax:** 618-537-6496

E-mail: mecampbell@mckendree.edu

Getting in Last Year

1,156 applied
68% were accepted
323 enrolled (41%)
25% from top tenth of their h.s. class
3.60 average high school GPA
45% had ACT scores over 24
8% had ACT scores over 30
11 class presidents
16 valedictorians

Graduation and After

38% graduated in 4 years
17% graduated in 5 years
2% graduated in 6 years
16% pursued further study (6% business, 5% arts and sciences, 3% law)
96% had job offers within 6 months
115 organizations recruited on campus

Financial Matters

$13,350 tuition and fees (2001–02)
$4950 room and board
95% average percent of need met
$10,607 average financial aid amount received per undergraduate

Academics

McKendree awards bachelor's **degrees**. Challenging opportunities include advanced placement credit, accelerated degree programs, student-designed majors, an honors program, double majors, independent study, and a senior project. Special programs include internships, summer session for credit, off-campus study, study-abroad, and Army and Air Force ROTC.

The most frequently chosen **baccalaureate** fields are business/marketing, health professions and related sciences, and education. A complete listing of majors at McKendree appears in the Majors Index beginning on page 430.

The **faculty** at McKendree has 66 full-time members, 86% with terminal degrees. The student-faculty ratio is 17:1.

Students of McKendree

The student body is made up of 2,107 undergraduates. 61.5% are women and 38.5% are men. Students come from 15 states and territories and 12 other countries. 69% are from Illinois. 4% are international students. 9.8% are African American, 0.3% American Indian, 1% Asian American, and 1.2% Hispanic American. 78% returned for their sophomore year.

Facilities and Resources

Student rooms are linked to a campus network. 450 **computers** are available on campus for student use. The **library** has 85,000 books and 450 subscriptions.

Campus Life

There are 54 active organizations on campus, including a drama/theater group, newspaper, choral group, and marching band. 8% of eligible men and 6% of eligible women are members of national **fraternities**, local fraternities, and local **sororities**.

McKendree is a member of the NAIA. **Intercollegiate sports** (some offering scholarships) include baseball (m), basketball, bowling, cross-country running, football (m), golf, soccer, softball (w), tennis, track and field, volleyball (w).

Campus Safety

Student safety services include late-night transport/escort service, 24-hour emergency telephone alarm devices, 24-hour patrols by trained security personnel, student patrols, and electronically operated dormitory entrances.

Applying

McKendree requires SAT I or ACT, a high school transcript, 1 recommendation, and a minimum high school GPA of 2.5, and in some cases an essay and an interview. Application deadline: rolling admissions; 5/31 priority date for financial aid. Deferred admission is possible.

MERCER UNIVERSITY
SUBURBAN SETTING ■ PRIVATE ■ INDEPENDENT RELIGIOUS ■ COED
MACON, GEORGIA

Web site: www.mercer.edu
Contact: Mr. Allen S. London, Associate Vice President for Freshman
Admissions, 1400 Coleman Avenue, Macon, GA 31207-0003
Telephone: 478-301-2650 or toll-free 800-840-8577 **Fax:** 478-301-2828
E-mail: admissions@mercer.edu

Academics
Mercer awards bachelor's, master's, doctoral, and first-professional **degrees** and post-bachelor's and post-master's certificates. Challenging opportunities include advanced placement credit, accelerated degree programs, student-designed majors, an honors program, double majors, independent study, and a senior project. Special programs include cooperative education, internships, summer session for credit, off-campus study, study-abroad, and Army ROTC.

The most frequently chosen **baccalaureate** fields are business/marketing, education, and social sciences and history. A complete listing of majors at Mercer appears in the Majors Index beginning on page 430.

The **faculty** at Mercer has 318 full-time members, 84% with terminal degrees. The student-faculty ratio is 15:1.

Students of Mercer
The student body totals 7,315, of whom 4,740 are undergraduates. 67.3% are women and 32.7% are men. Students come from 30 states and territories and 35 other countries. 84% are from Georgia. 4.1% are international students. 27.6% are African American, 0.7% American Indian, 3.1% Asian American, and 1.1% Hispanic American. 75% returned for their sophomore year.

Facilities and Resources
Student rooms are linked to a campus network. 140 **computers** are available on campus that provide access to the Internet. The 4 **libraries** have 439,121 books and 9,567 subscriptions.

Campus Life
There are 90 active organizations on campus, including a drama/theater group, newspaper, and choral group. 25% of eligible men and 25% of eligible women are members of national **fraternities**, national **sororities**, and local sororities.

Mercer is a member of the NCAA (Division I). **Intercollegiate sports** (some offering scholarships) include baseball (m), basketball, cross-country running, golf, riflery, soccer, softball (w), tennis, volleyball (w).

Campus Safety
Student safety services include patrols by police officers, late-night transport/escort service, 24-hour emergency telephone alarm devices, 24-hour patrols by trained security personnel, student patrols, and electronically operated dormitory entrances.

Applying
Mercer requires SAT I or ACT, a high school transcript, and a minimum high school GPA of 2.8, and in some cases an interview, 2 recommendations, counselor's evaluation, and a minimum high school GPA of 3.0. It recommends an interview and a minimum high school GPA of 3.0. Application deadline: 7/1; 4/1 priority date for financial aid. Early and deferred admission are possible.

Mercer University is a private, coeducational institution located in Macon, Georgia, just 90 miles south of Atlanta. Founded in 1833, the University is composed of 9 schools: the College of Liberal Arts, the Eugene W. Stetson School of Business and Economics, the School of Engineering, the Tift College of Education, the Walter F. George School of Law, the School of Medicine, the Southern School of Pharmacy, the James and Carolyn McAfee School of Theology, and the Georgia Baptist College of Nursing. *U.S. News & World Report* consistently ranks Mercer as one of the top regional universities in the South in its annual *America's Best Colleges.*

Getting in Last Year
2,771 applied
83% were accepted
803 enrolled (35%)
43% from top tenth of their h.s. class
3.50 average high school GPA
39% had SAT verbal scores over 600
42% had SAT math scores over 600
60% had ACT scores over 24
7% had SAT verbal scores over 700
6% had SAT math scores over 700
11% had ACT scores over 30
15 National Merit Scholars
54 valedictorians

Graduation and After
45% pursued further study
70% had job offers within 6 months
258 organizations recruited on campus

Financial Matters
$18,290 tuition and fees (2001–02)
$5840 room and board
86% average percent of need met
$18,388 average financial aid amount received per undergraduate

MESSIAH COLLEGE

SMALL-TOWN SETTING ■ PRIVATE ■ INDEPENDENT RELIGIOUS ■ COED
GRANTHAM, PENNSYLVANIA

Web site: www.messiah.edu
Contact: Mr. William G. Strausbaugh, Dean for Enrollment Management,
One College Avenue, Grantham, PA 17027
Telephone: 717-691-6000 or toll-free 800-382-1349 (in-state), 800-233-4220
(out-of-state) **Fax:** 717-796-5374
E-mail: admiss@messiah.edu

Messiah College provides an education that is both rigorously academic and unapologetically Christian. The learning process is characterized by lively student-faculty interaction that actively integrates faith issues with academic content. Messiah offers a strategically located campus, impressive academic and residence life facilities, and over 50 majors and 50 minors in the applied and liberal arts and sciences. Students pursue extracurricular interests in 18 intercollegiate sports, ministries, service learning areas, music ensembles, and scores of other activities. A multifaceted internship program provides career experience for students before they graduate. After graduation, 96% of graduates report employment/voluntary service or enrollment in graduate school within 6 months.

Academics

Messiah College awards bachelor's **degrees**. Challenging opportunities include advanced placement credit, accelerated degree programs, student-designed majors, freshman honors college, an honors program, double majors, independent study, and a senior project. Special programs include internships, summer session for credit, off-campus study, and study-abroad.

The most frequently chosen **baccalaureate** fields are education, business/marketing, and home economics/vocational home economics. A complete listing of majors at Messiah College appears in the Majors Index beginning on page 430.

The **faculty** at Messiah College has 158 full-time members, 70% with terminal degrees. The student-faculty ratio is 13:1.

Students of Messiah College

The student body is made up of 2,858 undergraduates. 61.2% are women and 38.8% are men. Students come from 38 states and territories and 25 other countries. 52% are from Pennsylvania. 2.2% are international students. 2.1% are African American, 0.2% American Indian, 1.5% Asian American, and 1.7% Hispanic American. 85% returned for their sophomore year.

Facilities and Resources

Student rooms are linked to a campus network. 479 **computers** are available on campus that provide access to the Internet. The **library** has 247,627 books and 1,260 subscriptions.

Campus Life

There are 60 active organizations on campus, including a drama/theater group, newspaper, radio station, and choral group. No national or local **fraternities** or **sororities**.

Messiah College is a member of the NCAA (Division III). **Intercollegiate sports** include baseball (m), basketball, cross-country running, field hockey (w), golf (m), lacrosse, soccer, softball (w), tennis, track and field, volleyball (w), wrestling (m).

Campus Safety

Student safety services include bicycle patrols, security lighting, self-defense classes, prevention/awareness programs, late-night transport/escort service, 24-hour emergency telephone alarm devices, 24-hour patrols by trained security personnel, student patrols, and electronically operated dormitory entrances.

Applying

Messiah College requires an essay, a high school transcript, and 2 recommendations, and in some cases SAT I or ACT. It recommends an interview and a minimum high school GPA of 3.0. Application deadline: rolling admissions; 4/1 priority date for financial aid. Early and deferred admission are possible.

Getting in Last Year
2,231 applied
78% were accepted
702 enrolled (40%)
35% from top tenth of their h.s. class
3.69 average high school GPA
46% had SAT verbal scores over 600
47% had SAT math scores over 600
70% had ACT scores over 24
11% had SAT verbal scores over 700
8% had SAT math scores over 700
17% had ACT scores over 30
16 National Merit Scholars
32 valedictorians

Graduation and After
7% pursued further study (5% arts and sciences, 1% medicine, 1% theology)
89% had job offers within 6 months
594 organizations recruited on campus

Financial Matters
$17,210 tuition and fees (2001–02)
$5970 room and board
72% average percent of need met
$12,387 average financial aid amount received per undergraduate

MIAMI UNIVERSITY
SMALL-TOWN SETTING ■ PUBLIC ■ STATE-RELATED ■ COED
OXFORD, OHIO

Web site: www.muohio.edu

Contact: Michael E. Mills, Director of Undergraduate Admissions, 301 South Campus Avenue, Campus Avenue Building, Oxford, OH 45056

Telephone: 513-529-5040 **Fax:** 513-529-1550

E-mail: admission@muohio.edu

Academics
Miami University awards bachelor's, master's, and doctoral **degrees** and post-master's certificates. Challenging opportunities include advanced placement credit, student-designed majors, an honors program, double majors, independent study, and a senior project. Special programs include cooperative education, internships, summer session for credit, off-campus study, study-abroad, and Army, Navy and Air Force ROTC.

The most frequently chosen **baccalaureate** fields are business/marketing, education, and social sciences and history. A complete listing of majors at Miami University appears in the Majors Index beginning on page 430.

The **faculty** at Miami University has 814 full-time members, 86% with terminal degrees. The student-faculty ratio is 17:1.

Students of Miami University
The student body totals 16,946, of whom 15,153 are undergraduates. 54.8% are women and 45.2% are men. Students come from 49 states and territories and 70 other countries. 73% are from Ohio. 0.5% are international students. 3.9% are African American, 0.5% American Indian, 2% Asian American, and 1.7% Hispanic American. 90% returned for their sophomore year.

Facilities and Resources
Student rooms are linked to a campus network. 1,000 **computers** are available on campus that provide access to the Internet. The 4 **libraries** have 2,663,166 books and 12,234 subscriptions.

Campus Life
There are 350 active organizations on campus, including a drama/theater group, newspaper, radio station, television station, choral group, and marching band. 24% of eligible men and 27% of eligible women are members of national **fraternities** and national **sororities**.

Miami University is a member of the NCAA (Division I). **Intercollegiate sports** (some offering scholarships) include baseball (m), basketball, cross-country running, field hockey (w), football (m), golf (m), ice hockey (m), soccer (w), softball (w), swimming, tennis (w), track and field, volleyball (w).

Campus Safety
Student safety services include late-night transport/escort service, 24-hour emergency telephone alarm devices, 24-hour patrols by trained security personnel, student patrols, and electronically operated dormitory entrances.

Applying
Miami University requires SAT I or ACT and a high school transcript. It recommends an essay and 1 recommendation. Application deadline: 1/31; 2/15 priority date for financial aid.

Miami University is acclaimed for an "unusually strong commitment to undergraduate teaching" by *U.S. News & World Report's America's Best Colleges* and is considered one of only 21 "Best Buy" public institutions, offering "remarkable educational opportunities at a relatively modest cost," by *Fiske Guide to Colleges 2001*. Also noteworthy are Miami's honors program that combines seminar-style courses, research and creative projects, community service, and an honors residence hall; its many research opportunities for undergraduates; and its high rate of students accepted at professional schools. Miami is among the top 10 U.S. universities for the number of students studying abroad.

Getting in Last Year
12,500 applied
74% were accepted
3,385 enrolled (36%)
37% from top tenth of their h.s. class
50% had SAT verbal scores over 600
66% had SAT math scores over 600
84% had ACT scores over 24
7% had SAT verbal scores over 700
12% had SAT math scores over 700
15% had ACT scores over 30
120 National Merit Scholars
180 valedictorians

Graduation and After
61% graduated in 4 years
17% graduated in 5 years
2% graduated in 6 years
Graduates pursuing further study: 14% arts and sciences, 7% law, 7% medicine
550 organizations recruited on campus

Financial Matters
$6915 resident tuition and fees (2001–02)
$14,589 nonresident tuition and fees (2001–02)
$5970 room and board
68% average percent of need met
$5762 average financial aid amount received per undergraduate (2000–01 estimated)

MICHIGAN TECHNOLOGICAL UNIVERSITY

SMALL-TOWN SETTING ■ PUBLIC ■ STATE-SUPPORTED ■ COED
HOUGHTON, MICHIGAN

Web site: www.mtu.edu
Contact: Ms. Nancy Rehling, Director of Undergraduate Admissions, 1400
  Townsend Drive, Houghton, MI 49931-1295
Telephone: 906-487-2335 **Fax:** 906-487-3343
E-mail: mtu4u@mtu.edu

Michigan Tech is more than a great engineering university. Students also learn from world-renowned experts in the sciences, business (in the only AACSB-accredited school in the region), technology, forestry (in the University's 4,000-acre forest), and communication in Michigan's beautiful Upper Peninsula. Students gain a hard-earned college degree that nearly guarantees employment (9.75 job offers per graduate) while enjoying the University's ski hill and trails, lakes and streams, golf course, and friendly downtown shops of Houghton, one of the nation's safest college towns.

Getting in Last Year
3,111 applied
94% were accepted
1,275 enrolled (43%)
31% from top tenth of their h.s. class
3.5 average high school GPA
38% had SAT verbal scores over 600
64% had SAT math scores over 600
68% had ACT scores over 24
10% had SAT verbal scores over 700
21% had SAT math scores over 700
13% had ACT scores over 30
11 National Merit Scholars
74 valedictorians

Graduation and After
22% graduated in 4 years
32% graduated in 5 years
9% graduated in 6 years
20% pursued further study
91% had job offers within 6 months
212 organizations recruited on campus

Financial Matters
$5887 resident tuition and fees (2001–02)
$13,165 nonresident tuition and fees (2001–02)
$5181 room and board
80% average percent of need met
$7451 average financial aid amount received per undergraduate

Academics

Michigan Tech awards associate, bachelor's, master's, and doctoral **degrees**. Challenging opportunities include advanced placement credit, student-designed majors, double majors, and a senior project. Special programs include cooperative education, internships, summer session for credit, off-campus study, study-abroad, and Army and Air Force ROTC. A complete listing of majors at Michigan Tech appears in the Majors Index beginning on page 430.

The **faculty** at Michigan Tech has 372 full-time members, 88% with terminal degrees. The student-faculty ratio is 12:1.

Students of Michigan Tech

The student body totals 6,336, of whom 5,666 are undergraduates. 25.6% are women and 74.4% are men. Students come from 36 states and territories and 60 other countries. 82% are from Michigan. 5% are international students. 2.2% are African American, 0.9% American Indian, 1.1% Asian American, and 0.8% Hispanic American. 82% returned for their sophomore year.

Facilities and Resources

Student rooms are linked to a campus network. 1,235 **computers** are available on campus that provide access to the Internet. The **library** has 992,197 books and 10,585 subscriptions.

Campus Life

There are 145 active organizations on campus, including a drama/theater group, newspaper, radio station, and choral group. 85% of eligible men and 15% of eligible women are members of national **fraternities**, national **sororities**, local fraternities, and local sororities.

Michigan Tech is a member of the NCAA (Division II). **Intercollegiate sports** (some offering scholarships) include basketball, cross-country running, football (m), ice hockey (m), skiing (cross-country), tennis, track and field, volleyball (w).

Campus Safety

Student safety services include late-night transport/escort service, 24-hour emergency telephone alarm devices, and 24-hour patrols by trained security personnel.

Applying

Michigan Tech requires SAT I or ACT and a high school transcript. It recommends an interview. Application deadline: rolling admissions; 2/21 priority date for financial aid. Deferred admission is possible.

MIDDLEBURY COLLEGE

SMALL-TOWN SETTING ■ PRIVATE ■ INDEPENDENT ■ COED
MIDDLEBURY, VERMONT

Web site: www.middlebury.edu
Contact: Mr. John Hanson, Director of Admissions, Emma Willard House,
Middlebury, VT 05753-6002
Telephone: 802-443-3000 **Fax:** 802-443-2056
E-mail: admissions@middlebury.edu

Academics

Middlebury awards bachelor's, master's, and doctoral **degrees**. Challenging opportunities include advanced placement credit, accelerated degree programs, student-designed majors, an honors program, double majors, and independent study. Special programs include internships, summer session for credit, off-campus study, study-abroad, and Army ROTC.

The most frequently chosen **baccalaureate** fields are social sciences and history, area/ethnic studies, and English. A complete listing of majors at Middlebury appears in the Majors Index beginning on page 430.

The **faculty** at Middlebury has 217 full-time members, 94% with terminal degrees. The student-faculty ratio is 11:1.

Students of Middlebury

The student body is made up of 2,307 undergraduates. 51.5% are women and 48.5% are men. Students come from 50 states and territories and 83 other countries. 7% are from Vermont. 7.6% are international students. 2.3% are African American, 0.6% American Indian, 5.9% Asian American, and 5.7% Hispanic American. 97% returned for their sophomore year.

Facilities and Resources

Student rooms are linked to a campus network. 225 **computers** are available on campus that provide access to computer helpline and the Internet. The 4 **libraries** have 1,500,600 books and 2,496 subscriptions.

Campus Life

There are 100 active organizations on campus, including a drama/theater group, newspaper, radio station, and choral group. 11% of eligible men and 15% of eligible women are members of social houses, commons system.

Middlebury is a member of the NCAA (Division III). **Intercollegiate sports** include baseball (m), basketball, cross-country running, field hockey (w), football (m), golf, ice hockey, lacrosse, skiing (cross-country), skiing (downhill), soccer, softball (w), squash (w), swimming, tennis, track and field, volleyball (w).

Campus Safety

Student safety services include late-night transport/escort service, 24-hour patrols by trained security personnel, and student patrols.

Getting in Last Year

5,411 applied
23% were accepted
513 enrolled (42%)
72% from top tenth of their h.s. class
94% had SAT verbal scores over 600
95% had SAT math scores over 600
57% had SAT verbal scores over 700
56% had SAT math scores over 700
67 class presidents

Graduation and After

81% graduated in 4 years
5% graduated in 5 years
1% graduated in 6 years
Graduates pursuing further study: 3% arts and sciences, 2% law, 1% medicine
80% had job offers within 6 months
80 organizations recruited on campus

Financial Matters

$34,300 comprehensive fee (2001–02)
100% average percent of need met
$26,039 average financial aid amount received per undergraduate

MILLIGAN COLLEGE

Suburban setting ■ Private ■ Independent Religious ■ Coed
Milligan College, Tennessee

Web site: www.milligan.edu
Contact: Mr. David Mee, Vice President for Enrollment Management, PO
Box 210, Milligan College, TN 37682
Telephone: 423-461-8730 or toll-free 800-262-8337 (in-state) **Fax:**
423-461-8982
E-mail: admissions@milligan.edu

Getting in Last Year
712 applied
76% were accepted
192 enrolled (35%)
3.50 average high school GPA
24% had SAT verbal scores over 600
21% had SAT math scores over 600
40% had ACT scores over 24
3% had SAT verbal scores over 700
2% had SAT math scores over 700
4% had ACT scores over 30

Graduation and After
40% graduated in 4 years
8% graduated in 5 years
1% graduated in 6 years
87% had job offers within 6 months
10 organizations recruited on campus

Financial Matters
$13,250 tuition and fees (2001–02)
$4300 room and board
84% average percent of need met
$11,182 average financial aid amount received
per undergraduate (2000–01)

Academics
Milligan awards bachelor's and master's **degrees**. Challenging opportunities include advanced placement credit, accelerated degree programs, double majors, and independent study. Special programs include cooperative education, internships, summer session for credit, off-campus study, study-abroad, and Army ROTC.

The most frequently chosen **baccalaureate** fields are business/marketing, education, and biological/life sciences. A complete listing of majors at Milligan appears in the Majors Index beginning on page 430.

The **faculty** at Milligan has 65 full-time members, 71% with terminal degrees. The student-faculty ratio is 11:1.

Students of Milligan
The student body totals 899, of whom 789 are undergraduates. 59.6% are women and 40.4% are men. Students come from 38 states and territories and 8 other countries. 41% are from Tennessee. 2.1% are international students. 1.9% are African American, 0.4% American Indian, 0.5% Asian American, and 0.8% Hispanic American. 73% returned for their sophomore year.

Facilities and Resources
Student rooms are linked to a campus network. 79 **computers** are available on campus that provide access to the Internet. The **library** has 107,464 books and 2,478 subscriptions.

Campus Life
There are 31 active organizations on campus, including a drama/theater group, newspaper, radio station, and choral group. No national or local **fraternities** or **sororities**.

Milligan is a member of the NAIA. **Intercollegiate sports** (some offering scholarships) include baseball (m), basketball, cross-country running, golf (m), soccer, softball (w), tennis, volleyball (w).

Campus Safety
Student safety services include late-night transport/escort service and 24-hour patrols by trained security personnel.

Applying
Milligan requires an essay, SAT I or ACT, a high school transcript, 2 recommendations, and a minimum high school GPA of 2.0, and in some cases an interview. It recommends a minimum high school GPA of 3.0. Application deadline: rolling admissions; 3/1 priority date for financial aid. Deferred admission is possible.

MILLSAPS COLLEGE

URBAN SETTING ■ PRIVATE ■ INDEPENDENT RELIGIOUS ■ COED
JACKSON, MISSISSIPPI

Web site: www.millsaps.edu
Contact: Mr. John Gaines, Director of Admissions, 1701 North State Street, Jackson, MS 39210-0001
Telephone: 601-974-1050 or toll-free 800-352-1050 **Fax:** 601-974-1059
E-mail: admissions@millsaps.edu

Academics

Millsaps awards bachelor's and master's **degrees**. Challenging opportunities include advanced placement credit, an honors program, double majors, and a senior project. Special programs include internships, summer session for credit, off-campus study, study-abroad, and Army ROTC.

The most frequently chosen **baccalaureate** fields are business/marketing, social sciences and history, and psychology. A complete listing of majors at Millsaps appears in the Majors Index beginning on page 430.

The **faculty** at Millsaps has 93 full-time members, 91% with terminal degrees. The student-faculty ratio is 13:1.

Students of Millsaps

The student body totals 1,330, of whom 1,221 are undergraduates. 54.5% are women and 45.5% are men. Students come from 25 states and territories and 10 other countries. 58% are from Mississippi. 0.6% are international students. 11.3% are African American, 0.3% American Indian, 2.5% Asian American, and 0.7% Hispanic American. 83% returned for their sophomore year.

Facilities and Resources

Student rooms are linked to a campus network. 117 **computers** are available on campus that provide access to the Internet. The **library** has 117,640 books and 3,087 subscriptions.

Campus Life

There are 50 active organizations on campus, including a drama/theater group, newspaper, and choral group. 60% of eligible men and 60% of eligible women are members of national **fraternities** and national **sororities**.

Millsaps is a member of the NCAA (Division III). **Intercollegiate sports** include baseball (m), basketball, cross-country running, football (m), golf, soccer, softball (w), tennis, volleyball (w).

Campus Safety

Student safety services include self-defense education, lighted pathways, late-night transport/escort service, 24-hour emergency telephone alarm devices, 24-hour patrols by trained security personnel, student patrols, and electronically operated dormitory entrances.

Applying

Millsaps requires an essay, SAT I or ACT, a high school transcript, and a minimum high school GPA of 2.5. It recommends an interview and recommendations. Application deadline: 2/1. Early and deferred admission are possible.

Millsaps College is a community founded on trust in disciplined learning as a key to a rewarding life. In keeping with its character as a liberal arts college and its historic role in the mission of the United Methodist Church, Millsaps seeks to provide a learning environment that increases knowledge, deepens understanding of faith, and inspires the development of mature citizens with the intellectual capacities, ethical principles, and sense of responsibility that are needed for leadership in all sectors of society.

Getting in Last Year
952 applied
86% were accepted
324 enrolled (40%)
46% from top tenth of their h.s. class
3.54 average high school GPA
53% had SAT verbal scores over 600
49% had SAT math scores over 600
73% had ACT scores over 24
12% had SAT verbal scores over 700
10% had SAT math scores over 700
21% had ACT scores over 30
19 valedictorians

Graduation and After
57% graduated in 4 years
10% graduated in 5 years
1% graduated in 6 years
46% pursued further study
44% had job offers within 6 months
60 organizations recruited on campus

Financial Matters
$16,546 tuition and fees (2001–02)
$6062 room and board
90% average percent of need met
$15,670 average financial aid amount received per undergraduate

MILLS COLLEGE

URBAN SETTING ■ PRIVATE ■ INDEPENDENT ■ WOMEN ONLY
OAKLAND, CALIFORNIA

Web site: www.mills.edu
Contact: Avis Hinkson, Dean of Admission, 5000 MacArthur Boulevard, Oakland, CA 94613-1000
Telephone: 510-430-2135 or toll-free 800-87-MILLS **Fax:** 510-430-3314
E-mail: admission@mills.edu

Why a women's college? "I came to college to study, and I wanted a college that was very pro-women— a college that would prepare me to do well and succeed," says Mills regional scholar Leah Hathaway. And Mills does. Even in their first year, bright students like Leah can tackle original hands-on research that most students don't experience until graduate school. Since half the professors at Mills are women (not the case in coeducational institutions), students have successful role models in every field. And all of Mills' undergraduate resources are committed to women. When women graduate from Mills, they *know* they can succeed. That confidence makes all the difference.

Getting in Last Year
498 applied
74% were accepted
113 enrolled (31%)
39% from top tenth of their h.s. class
3.47 average high school GPA
43% had SAT verbal scores over 600
29% had SAT math scores over 600
16% had SAT verbal scores over 700
2% had SAT math scores over 700

Graduation and After
51% graduated in 4 years
4% graduated in 5 years
4% graduated in 6 years
17 organizations recruited on campus

Financial Matters
$20,622 tuition and fees (2001–02)
$8000 room and board
86% average percent of need met
$18,852 average financial aid amount received per undergraduate (2000–01 estimated)

Academics

Mills awards bachelor's, master's, and doctoral **degrees**. Challenging opportunities include advanced placement credit, student-designed majors, double majors, independent study, and a senior project. Special programs include internships, off-campus study, and Army ROTC.

The most frequently chosen **baccalaureate** fields are mathematics, visual/performing arts, and social sciences and history. A complete listing of majors at Mills appears in the Majors Index beginning on page 430.

The **faculty** at Mills has 87 full-time members, 80% with terminal degrees. The student-faculty ratio is 10:1.

Students of Mills

The student body totals 1,176, of whom 742 are undergraduates. Students come from 36 states and territories and 12 other countries. 75% are from California. 9.4% are African American, 0.8% American Indian, 9.4% Asian American, and 9.2% Hispanic American. 80% returned for their sophomore year.

Facilities and Resources

Student rooms are linked to a campus network. 66 **computers** are available on campus for student use. The 2 **libraries** have 189,814 books and 2,029 subscriptions.

Campus Life

There are 30 active organizations on campus, including a drama/theater group, newspaper, and choral group. No national or local **sororities**.

Mills is a member of the NCAA (Division III). **Intercollegiate sports** include crew, cross-country running, soccer, tennis, volleyball.

Campus Safety

Student safety services include late-night transport/escort service, 24-hour emergency telephone alarm devices, 24-hour patrols by trained security personnel, and electronically operated dormitory entrances.

Applying

Mills requires SAT I or ACT, a high school transcript, 3 recommendations, and essay or graded paper. It recommends SAT II Subject Tests and an interview. Application deadline: 2/1; 2/15 priority date for financial aid. Deferred admission is possible.

MILWAUKEE SCHOOL OF ENGINEERING

URBAN SETTING ■ PRIVATE ■ INDEPENDENT ■ COED, PRIMARILY MEN
MILWAUKEE, WISCONSIN

Web site: www.msoe.edu
Contact: Mr. Tim A. Valley, Dean of Enrollment Management, 1025 North
   Broadway, Milwaukee, WI 53202-3109
Telephone: 414-277-6763 or toll-free 800-332-6763 **Fax:** 414-277-7475
E-mail: explore@msoe.edu

Academics

MSOE awards bachelor's and master's **degrees**. Challenging opportunities include
advanced placement credit, accelerated degree programs, double majors, independent
study, and a senior project. Special programs include internships, summer session for
credit, study-abroad, and Army and Air Force ROTC.

The most frequently chosen **baccalaureate** fields are engineering/engineering
technologies, business/marketing, and communications/communication technologies. A
complete listing of majors at MSOE appears in the Majors Index beginning on page 430.

The **faculty** at MSOE has 117 full-time members, 55% with terminal degrees. The
student-faculty ratio is 11:1.

Students of MSOE

The student body totals 2,563, of whom 2,246 are undergraduates. 15.4% are women
and 84.6% are men. Students come from 37 states and territories and 26 other countries.
78% are from Wisconsin. 3.7% are international students. 3.4% are African American,
0.3% American Indian, 2.8% Asian American, and 1.7% Hispanic American. 77%
returned for their sophomore year.

Facilities and Resources

Student rooms are linked to a campus network. 105 **computers** are available on campus
that provide access to e-mail and the Internet. The **library** has 45,638 books and 430
subscriptions.

Campus Life

There are 61 active organizations on campus, including a drama/theater group,
newspaper, and radio station. 9% of eligible men and 12% of eligible women are
members of national **fraternities**, national **sororities**, local fraternities, and local sororities.

MSOE is a member of the NCAA (Division III). **Intercollegiate sports** include
baseball (m), basketball, cross-country running, golf, ice hockey (m), soccer, softball (w),
tennis, track and field, volleyball, wrestling (m).

Campus Safety

Student safety services include late-night transport/escort service, 24-hour emergency
telephone alarm devices, 24-hour patrols by trained security personnel, and electronically operated dormitory entrances.

Applying

MSOE requires SAT I or ACT, a high school transcript, and a minimum high school
GPA of 2.5, and in some cases an essay and an interview. Application deadline: rolling
admissions. Deferred admission is possible.

Getting in Last Year
2,093 applied
69% were accepted
488 enrolled (34%)
28% from top tenth of their h.s. class
3.50 average high school GPA
35% had SAT verbal scores over 600
74% had SAT math scores over 600
84% had ACT scores over 24
7% had SAT verbal scores over 700
14% had SAT math scores over 700
31% had ACT scores over 30

Graduation and After
37% graduated in 4 years
13% graduated in 5 years
2% graduated in 6 years
6% pursued further study (3% engineering,
   2% business, 1% law)
99% had job offers within 6 months
170 organizations recruited on campus

Financial Matters
$20,835 tuition and fees (2001–02)
$4845 room and board
62% average percent of need met
$13,713 average financial aid amount received
   per undergraduate (2000–01)

MOREHOUSE COLLEGE
URBAN SETTING ■ PRIVATE ■ INDEPENDENT ■ MEN ONLY
ATLANTA, GEORGIA

Web site: www.morehouse.edu
Contact: Mr. Terrance Dixon, Associate Dean for Admissions and
   Recruitment, 830 Westview Drive, SW, Atlanta, GA 30314
Telephone: 404-215-2632 or toll-free 800-851-1254 **Fax:** 404-524-5635
E-mail: admissions@morehouse.edu

Morehouse College seeks to develop leaders who will be qualified and committed to solving the problems of society, with special attention given to those of African Americans. Inspired by the legacy of distinguished alumni, presidents, and professors—persons who have initiated and inspired significant social changes—the College supports and encourages programs that benefit all people and that seek to eradicate discrimination and injustice. Morehouse is firmly committed to attracting and enrolling students of high caliber from a wide variety of educational and economic backgrounds and providing them with learning and leadership development opportunities.

Academics
Morehouse College awards bachelor's **degrees**. Challenging opportunities include advanced placement credit, an honors program, double majors, and a senior project. Special programs include cooperative education, internships, summer session for credit, off-campus study, study-abroad, and Army, Navy and Air Force ROTC.

The most frequently chosen **baccalaureate** fields are business/marketing, foreign language/literature, and biological/life sciences. A complete listing of majors at Morehouse College appears in the Majors Index beginning on page 430.

The **faculty** at Morehouse College has 172 full-time members, 81% with terminal degrees. The student-faculty ratio is 15:1.

Students of Morehouse College
The student body is made up of 2,808 undergraduates. Students come from 43 states and territories and 23 other countries. 33% are from Georgia. 5.3% are international students. 93.3% are African American, 0.1% Asian American, and 0.1% Hispanic American. 85% returned for their sophomore year.

Facilities and Resources
Student rooms are linked to a campus network. 325 **computers** are available on campus that provide access to the Internet. The **library** has 560,000 books and 1,000 subscriptions.

Campus Life
There are 34 active organizations on campus, including a drama/theater group, newspaper, choral group, and marching band. 7% of eligible undergraduates are members of national **fraternities**.

Morehouse College is a member of the NCAA (Division II). **Intercollegiate sports** (some offering scholarships) include basketball, cross-country running, football, tennis, track and field.

Campus Safety
Student safety services include late-night transport/escort service, 24-hour emergency telephone alarm devices, and 24-hour patrols by trained security personnel.

Applying
Morehouse College requires an essay, SAT I or ACT, a high school transcript, recommendations, and a minimum high school GPA of 2.8. It recommends an interview and a minimum high school GPA of 3.0. Application deadline: 2/15; 4/1 priority date for financial aid. Early and deferred admission are possible.

Getting in Last Year
2,094 applied
76% were accepted
656 enrolled (41%)
42% from top tenth of their h.s. class
3.08 average high school GPA
21% had SAT verbal scores over 600
19% had SAT math scores over 600
24% had ACT scores over 24
3% had SAT verbal scores over 700
2% had SAT math scores over 700
3% had ACT scores over 30

Graduation and After
27% graduated in 4 years
25% graduated in 5 years
9% graduated in 6 years
Graduates pursuing further study: 14% arts and sciences, 5% law, 4% medicine
51% had job offers within 6 months
55 organizations recruited on campus

Financial Matters
$12,432 tuition and fees (2001–02)
$7382 room and board

MOUNT HOLYOKE COLLEGE
SMALL-TOWN SETTING ■ PRIVATE ■ INDEPENDENT ■ WOMEN ONLY
SOUTH HADLEY, MASSACHUSETTS

Web site: www.mtholyoke.edu
Contact: Ms. Diane Anci, Dean of Admission, 50 College Street, South
Hadley, MA 01075
Telephone: 413-538-2023 **Fax:** 413-538-2409
E-mail: admission@mtholyoke.edu

Academics
Mount Holyoke awards bachelor's and master's **degrees** and post-bachelor's certificates.
Challenging opportunities include advanced placement credit, student-designed majors,
an honors program, double majors, independent study, and a senior project. Special
programs include internships, off-campus study, study-abroad, and Army and Air Force
ROTC.

The most frequently chosen **baccalaureate** fields are social sciences and history,
psychology, and English. A complete listing of majors at Mount Holyoke appears in the
Majors Index beginning on page 430.

The **faculty** at Mount Holyoke has 190 full-time members, 95% with terminal
degrees. The student-faculty ratio is 10:1.

Students of Mount Holyoke
The student body totals 2,038, of whom 2,037 are undergraduates. Students come from
47 states and territories and 77 other countries. 25% are from Massachusetts. 17.1% are
international students. 4.6% are African American, 0.5% American Indian, 9.7% Asian
American, and 4.2% Hispanic American. 97% returned for their sophomore year.

Facilities and Resources
Student rooms are linked to a campus network. 245 **computers** are available on campus
that provide access to personal Web pages and the Internet. The 2 **libraries** have
724,634 books and 3,189 subscriptions.

Campus Life
There are 125 active organizations on campus, including a drama/theater group,
newspaper, radio station, and choral group. No national or local **sororities**.

Mount Holyoke is a member of the NCAA (Division III). **Intercollegiate sports**
include basketball, crew, cross-country running, equestrian sports, field hockey, golf,
lacrosse, soccer, softball, squash, swimming, tennis, track and field, volleyball.

Campus Safety
Student safety services include police officers on-campus, late-night transport/escort
service, 24-hour emergency telephone alarm devices, 24-hour patrols by trained security
personnel, student patrols, and electronically operated dormitory entrances.

Applying
Mount Holyoke requires an essay, a high school transcript, and 2 recommendations. It
recommends an interview. Application deadline: 1/15; 2/1 for financial aid. Early and
deferred admission are possible.

Mount Holyoke is a highly
selective,
nondenominational,
residential, liberal arts college for
women located in South Hadley,
Massachusetts. Founded in 1837 by
revolutionary educator, Mary Lyon,
the College is recognized worldwide
for its rigorous and innovative
academic program, its global
community, its legacy of women
leaders, and its commitment to
connecting the work of the academy
to the concerns of the world.
Students benefit from membership in
the Five College Consortium with
Amherst, Hampshire, and Smith
Colleges and the University of
Massachusetts.

Getting in Last Year
2,881 applied
49% were accepted
488 enrolled (34%)
51% from top tenth of their h.s. class
3.65 average high school GPA
77% had SAT verbal scores over 600
65% had SAT math scores over 600
86% had ACT scores over 24
22% had SAT verbal scores over 700
13% had SAT math scores over 700
26% had ACT scores over 30
12 National Merit Scholars
15 valedictorians

Graduation and After
75% graduated in 4 years
4% graduated in 5 years
27% pursued further study
60 organizations recruited on campus

Financial Matters
$26,408 tuition and fees (2001–02)
$7720 room and board
100% average percent of need met
$22,800 average financial aid amount received
per undergraduate

MOUNT ST. MARY'S COLLEGE

SUBURBAN SETTING ■ PRIVATE ■ INDEPENDENT RELIGIOUS ■ COED, PRIMARILY WOMEN

LOS ANGELES, CALIFORNIA

Web site: www.msmc.la.edu

Contact: Ms. Katy Murphy, Executive Director of Admissions and Financial Aid, 12001 Chalon Road, Los Angeles, CA 90049-1599

Telephone: 310-954-4252 or toll-free 800-999-9893

E-mail: admissions@msmc.la.edu

Getting in Last Year
420 applied
54% were accepted
343 enrolled (150%)
33% from top tenth of their h.s. class
3.50 average high school GPA
17% had SAT verbal scores over 600
12% had SAT math scores over 600
4% had SAT verbal scores over 700

Graduation and After
30% pursued further study
65% had job offers within 6 months

Financial Matters
$18,588 tuition and fees (2001–02)
$7459 room and board

Academics
Mount St. Mary's awards associate, bachelor's, and master's **degrees** and post-bachelor's certificates. Challenging opportunities include advanced placement credit, accelerated degree programs, student-designed majors, freshman honors college, an honors program, double majors, independent study, and a senior project. Special programs include internships, summer session for credit, off-campus study, study-abroad, and Army, Navy and Air Force ROTC. A complete listing of majors at Mount St. Mary's appears in the Majors Index beginning on page 430.

The **faculty** at Mount St. Mary's has 82 full-time members, 55% with terminal degrees. The student-faculty ratio is 16:1.

Students of Mount St. Mary's
The student body totals 1,965, of whom 1,694 are undergraduates. 95.1% are women and 4.9% are men. Students come from 21 states and territories. 97% are from California. 0.1% are international students. 11.5% are African American, 0.3% American Indian, 15.4% Asian American, and 44.9% Hispanic American. 85% returned for their sophomore year.

Facilities and Resources
Student rooms are linked to a campus network. 85 **computers** are available on campus for student use. The **library** has 140,000 books and 750 subscriptions.

Campus Life
There are 29 active organizations on campus, including a drama/theater group, newspaper, and choral group. 6% of eligible women are members of national **sororities** and local sororities.

This institution has no intercollegiate sports.

Campus Safety
Student safety services include 24-hour patrols by trained security personnel and electronically operated dormitory entrances.

Applying
Mount St. Mary's requires an essay, SAT I or ACT, a high school transcript, 1 recommendation, and a minimum high school GPA of 2.0. It recommends SAT I, an interview, and a minimum high school GPA of 3.0. Application deadline: rolling admissions. Deferred admission is possible.

MOUNT UNION COLLEGE

SUBURBAN SETTING ■ PRIVATE ■ INDEPENDENT RELIGIOUS ■ COED
ALLIANCE, OHIO

Web site: www.muc.edu
Contact: Ms. Amy Tomko, Vice President of Enrollment Services, 1972 Clark
  Avenue, Alliance, OH 44601
Telephone: 330-823-2590 or toll-free 800-334-6682 (in-state), 800-992-6682
  (out-of-state) **Fax:** 330-823-3487
E-mail: admissn@muc.edu

Academics

Mount Union awards bachelor's **degrees**. Challenging opportunities include advanced
placement credit, accelerated degree programs, student-designed majors, an honors
program, double majors, independent study, and a senior project. Special programs
include cooperative education, internships, summer session for credit, off-campus study,
study-abroad, and Army and Air Force ROTC.

The most frequently chosen **baccalaureate** fields are business/marketing, education,
and parks and recreation. A complete listing of majors at Mount Union appears in the
Majors Index beginning on page 430.

The **faculty** at Mount Union has 118 full-time members, 73% with terminal degrees.
The student-faculty ratio is 14:1.

Students of Mount Union

The student body is made up of 2,368 undergraduates. 57.9% are women and 42.1% are
men. Students come from 20 states and territories and 15 other countries. 92% are from
Ohio. 1.4% are international students. 3.8% are African American, 0.3% American
Indian, 0.3% Asian American, and 0.6% Hispanic American. 74% returned for their
sophomore year.

Facilities and Resources

Student rooms are linked to a campus network. 200 **computers** are available on campus
that provide access to the Internet. The 3 **libraries** have 228,850 books and 972
subscriptions.

Campus Life

There are 74 active organizations on campus, including a drama/theater group,
newspaper, radio station, choral group, and marching band. 26% of eligible men and
30% of eligible women are members of national **fraternities**, national **sororities**, and
local sororities.

Mount Union is a member of the NCAA (Division III). **Intercollegiate sports**
include baseball (m), basketball, cross-country running, football (m), golf, soccer, swimming, tennis, track and field, volleyball (w), wrestling (m).

Campus Safety

Student safety services include 24-hour locked residence hall entrances, outside phones,
24-hour emergency telephone alarm devices, and 24-hour patrols by trained security
personnel.

Applying

Mount Union requires an essay, SAT I or ACT, a high school transcript, 1 recommendation, and a minimum high school GPA of 2.0. It recommends an interview. Application deadline: rolling admissions. Early and deferred admission are possible.

Mount Union College has
established a reputation
for producing successful
graduates in a wide array of
occupations. The College affirms the
importance of reason, open inquiry,
living faith, and individual worth.
Mount Union's mission is to prepare
students for meaningful work,
fulfilling lives, and responsible
citizenship. Mount Union strives to
provide the best education possible
for each of its students so that its
graduates develop communication
skills, critical thinking, a sensitivity
to social responsibility, and a
concern for human needs.

Getting in Last Year
2,026 applied
81% were accepted
608 enrolled (37%)
19% from top tenth of their h.s. class
3.23 average high school GPA
33% had ACT scores over 24
2% had ACT scores over 30
18 valedictorians

Graduation and After
47% graduated in 4 years
12% graduated in 5 years
2% graduated in 6 years
16% pursued further study
90% had job offers within 6 months
53 organizations recruited on campus

Financial Matters
$16,310 tuition and fees (2001–02)
$4810 room and board
85% average percent of need met
$13,422 average financial aid amount received
  per undergraduate

MUHLENBERG COLLEGE
SUBURBAN SETTING ■ PRIVATE ■ INDEPENDENT RELIGIOUS ■ COED
ALLENTOWN, PENNSYLVANIA

Web site: www.muhlenberg.edu
Contact: Mr. Christopher Hooker-Haring, Dean of Admissions, 2400 Chew Street, Allentown, PA 18104-5586
Telephone: 484-664-3245 **Fax:** 484-664-3234
E-mail: adm@muhlenberg.edu

L ocated in a beautiful campus setting on the outskirts of a small city, Muhlenberg offers its students an active, highly participatory educational experience within the context of a friendly, very supportive community. Local internships, field study, study abroad, and a Washington semester all supplement the traditional classroom experience. Every year, large numbers of Muhlenberg students go on to law and medical school as well as into a variety of competitive entry-level career positions. They take with them an ability to analyze and think critically as well as an ability to express themselves effectively in person and in writing. These are the most prized outcomes of a Muhlenberg education.

Getting in Last Year
3,892 applied
35% were accepted
573 enrolled (42%)
37% from top tenth of their h.s. class
3.69 average high school GPA
50% had SAT verbal scores over 600
54% had SAT math scores over 600
8% had SAT verbal scores over 700
9% had SAT math scores over 700
16 class presidents
7 valedictorians

Graduation and After
79% graduated in 4 years
2% graduated in 5 years
1% graduated in 6 years
25% pursued further study (9% arts and sciences, 6% law, 5% medicine)
67% had job offers within 6 months
78 organizations recruited on campus

Financial Matters
$22,210 tuition and fees (2001–02)
$5960 room and board

Academics
Muhlenberg awards bachelor's **degrees**. Challenging opportunities include advanced placement credit, accelerated degree programs, student-designed majors, an honors program, double majors, independent study, and a senior project. Special programs include internships, summer session for credit, off-campus study, study-abroad, and Army ROTC.

The most frequently chosen **baccalaureate** fields are business/marketing, social sciences and history, and communications/communication technologies. A complete listing of majors at Muhlenberg appears in the Majors Index beginning on page 430.

The **faculty** at Muhlenberg has 146 full-time members, 85% with terminal degrees. The student-faculty ratio is 13:1.

Students of Muhlenberg
The student body is made up of 2,629 undergraduates. 57.2% are women and 42.8% are men. Students come from 34 states and territories and 6 other countries. 34% are from Pennsylvania. 2.2% are African American, 0.3% American Indian, 3.3% Asian American, and 2.6% Hispanic American. 93% returned for their sophomore year.

Facilities and Resources
Student rooms are linked to a campus network. 150 **computers** are available on campus that provide access to microcomputer network and the Internet. The **library** has 270,700 books and 1,700 subscriptions.

Campus Life
There are 104 active organizations on campus, including a drama/theater group, newspaper, radio station, television station, and choral group. 27% of eligible men and 28% of eligible women are members of national **fraternities** and national **sororities**.

Muhlenberg is a member of the NCAA (Division III). **Intercollegiate sports** include baseball (m), basketball, cross-country running, field hockey (w), football (m), golf, lacrosse, soccer, softball (w), tennis, track and field, volleyball (w), wrestling (m).

Campus Safety
Student safety services include late-night transport/escort service, 24-hour emergency telephone alarm devices, 24-hour patrols by trained security personnel, and electronically operated dormitory entrances.

Applying
Muhlenberg requires an essay, a high school transcript, and 2 recommendations, and in some cases SAT I or ACT and an interview. It recommends an interview. Application deadline: 2/15; 2/15 for financial aid. Early and deferred admission are possible.

NAZARETH COLLEGE OF ROCHESTER
SUBURBAN SETTING ■ PRIVATE ■ INDEPENDENT ■ COED
ROCHESTER, NEW YORK

Web site: www.naz.edu

Contact: Mr. Thomas K. DaRin, Vice President for Enrollment Management, 4245 East Avenue, Rochester, NY 14618-3790

Telephone: 585-389-2860 or toll-free 800-462-3944 (in-state) **Fax:** 585-389-2826

E-mail: admissions@naz.edu

Academics
Nazareth College awards bachelor's and master's **degrees**. Challenging opportunities include advanced placement credit, an honors program, double majors, independent study, and a senior project. Special programs include cooperative education, internships, summer session for credit, off-campus study, study-abroad, and Air Force ROTC.

The most frequently chosen **baccalaureate** fields are education, health professions and related sciences, and business/marketing. A complete listing of majors at Nazareth College appears in the Majors Index beginning on page 430.

The **faculty** at Nazareth College has 135 full-time members, 94% with terminal degrees. The student-faculty ratio is 12:1.

Students of Nazareth College
The student body totals 3,107, of whom 1,898 are undergraduates. 75.7% are women and 24.3% are men. Students come from 20 states and territories and 12 other countries. 96% are from New York. 0.2% are international students. 3.3% are African American, 0.2% American Indian, 1.6% Asian American, and 2% Hispanic American. 84% returned for their sophomore year.

Facilities and Resources
Student rooms are linked to a campus network. 190 **computers** are available on campus that provide access to the Internet. The **library** has 283,810 books and 1,959 subscriptions.

Campus Life
There are 33 active organizations on campus, including a drama/theater group, newspaper, radio station, and choral group. No national or local **fraternities** or **sororities**.

Nazareth College is a member of the NCAA (Division III). **Intercollegiate sports** include basketball, equestrian sports, field hockey (w), golf, lacrosse, soccer, swimming, tennis, volleyball (w).

Campus Safety
Student safety services include alarm system, security beeper, lighted pathways, late-night transport/escort service, 24-hour emergency telephone alarm devices, 24-hour patrols by trained security personnel, student patrols, and electronically operated dormitory entrances.

Applying
Nazareth College requires an essay, SAT I or ACT, a high school transcript, and 1 recommendation. It recommends an interview and 2 recommendations. Application deadline: 2/15; 2/15 priority date for financial aid. Early and deferred admission are possible.

Getting in Last Year
1,750 applied
76% were accepted
361 enrolled (27%)
41% from top tenth of their h.s. class
3.40 average high school GPA
34% had SAT verbal scores over 600
32% had SAT math scores over 600
62% had ACT scores over 24
3% had SAT verbal scores over 700
5% had SAT math scores over 700
6% had ACT scores over 30

Graduation and After
54% graduated in 4 years
10% graduated in 5 years
1% graduated in 6 years
39% pursued further study
74% had job offers within 6 months
18 organizations recruited on campus

Financial Matters
$15,384 tuition and fees (2001–02)
$6660 room and board
90% average percent of need met
$14,539 average financial aid amount received per undergraduate

NEW COLLEGE OF FLORIDA

SUBURBAN SETTING ■ PUBLIC ■ STATE-SUPPORTED ■ COED
SARASOTA, FLORIDA

Web site: www.ncf.edu
Contact: Mr. Joel Bauman, Dean of Admissions and Financial Aid, 5700
    North Tamiami Trail, Sarasota, FL 34243-2197
Telephone: 941-359-4269 **Fax:** 941-359-4435
E-mail: admissions@ncf.edu

New College offers an innovative, rigorous approach to the liberal arts and sciences. Students choose courses through discussion with their faculty sponsor (instead of following a list of mandatory general requirements), create credited courses of study through individualized research projects and tutorials, and receive written narrative evaluations instead of grades. Located on the beautiful Gulf of Mexico in Sarasota, Florida, New College is the public honors college of Florida and is designed for independent and motivated students who are eager to take responsibility for their own education. Novo Collegians are a diverse group, with active alumni ranging from a Fields Medal winner in mathematics to the first woman chair of the Florida Fish and Wildlife Commission.

Getting in Last Year
490 applied
61% were accepted
150 enrolled (50%)
56% from top tenth of their h.s. class
3.90 average high school GPA
93% had SAT verbal scores over 600
73% had SAT math scores over 600
94% had ACT scores over 24
60% had SAT verbal scores over 700
19% had SAT math scores over 700
33% had ACT scores over 30
12 National Merit Scholars
4 valedictorians

Financial Matters
$2885 resident tuition and fees (2001–02)
$12,350 nonresident tuition and fees (2001–02)
$5120 room and board
89% average percent of need met
$8192 average financial aid amount received per undergraduate

Academics

New College of Florida awards bachelor's **degrees**. Challenging opportunities include accelerated degree programs, student-designed majors, an honors program, double majors, independent study, and a senior project. Special programs include internships, off-campus study, study-abroad, and Army and Air Force ROTC.

The most frequently chosen **baccalaureate** field is liberal arts/general studies. A complete listing of majors at New College of Florida appears in the Majors Index beginning on page 430.

The **faculty** at New College of Florida has 58 full-time members, 98% with terminal degrees. The student-faculty ratio is 11:1.

Students of New College of Florida

The student body is made up of 634 undergraduates. 75% are from Florida. 1.6% are international students. 1.7% are African American, 0.2% American Indian, 3.5% Asian American, and 6.2% Hispanic American. 81% returned for their sophomore year.

Facilities and Resources

Student rooms are linked to a campus network. 34 **computers** are available on campus that provide access to the Internet. The **library** has 251,940 books and 1,852 subscriptions.

Campus Life

There are 42 active organizations on campus, including a drama/theater group, newspaper, radio station, and choral group. No national or local **fraternities** or **sororities**.

This institution has no intercollegiate sports.

Campus Safety

Student safety services include late-night transport/escort service, 24-hour emergency telephone alarm devices, and 24-hour patrols by trained security personnel.

Applying

New College of Florida requires an essay, SAT I or ACT, a high school transcript, and 2 recommendations, and in some cases an interview. It recommends an interview, graded writing sample, and a minimum high school GPA of 3.0. Application deadline: 5/1; 3/1 priority date for financial aid. Early and deferred admission are possible.

NEW JERSEY INSTITUTE OF TECHNOLOGY

URBAN SETTING ■ PUBLIC ■ STATE-SUPPORTED ■ COED
NEWARK, NEW JERSEY

Web site: www.njit.edu

Contact: Ms. Kathy Kelly, Director of Admissions, University Heights, Newark, NJ 07102-1982

Telephone: 973-596-3300 or toll-free 800-925-NJIT **Fax:** 973-596-3461

E-mail: admissions@njit.edu

Academics

NJIT awards bachelor's, master's, and doctoral **degrees**. Challenging opportunities include advanced placement credit, accelerated degree programs, freshman honors college, an honors program, double majors, independent study, and a senior project. Special programs include cooperative education, internships, summer session for credit, off-campus study, study-abroad, and Air Force ROTC.

The most frequently chosen **baccalaureate** fields are engineering/engineering technologies, computer/information sciences, and business/marketing. A complete listing of majors at NJIT appears in the Majors Index beginning on page 430.

The **faculty** at NJIT has 418 full-time members, 100% with terminal degrees. The student-faculty ratio is 14:1.

Students of NJIT

The student body totals 8,862, of whom 5,698 are undergraduates. 22.1% are women and 77.9% are men. Students come from 25 states and territories and 69 other countries. 95% are from New Jersey. 6.1% are international students. 11% are African American, 0.2% American Indian, 23.1% Asian American, and 10.9% Hispanic American. 80% returned for their sophomore year.

Facilities and Resources

Student rooms are linked to a campus network. 4,500 **computers** are available on campus for student use. The 2 **libraries** have 160,000 books and 1,100 subscriptions.

Campus Life

There are 70 active organizations on campus, including a drama/theater group, newspaper, and radio station. 12% of eligible men and 9% of eligible women are members of national **fraternities**, national **sororities**, local fraternities, and local sororities.

NJIT is a member of the NCAA (Division II). **Intercollegiate sports** include baseball (m), basketball, cross-country running, fencing (m), golf (m), soccer (m), softball (w), swimming (w), tennis, track and field (w), volleyball.

Campus Safety

Student safety services include bicycle patrols, sexual assault response team, late-night transport/escort service, 24-hour emergency telephone alarm devices, 24-hour patrols by trained security personnel, and electronically operated dormitory entrances.

Applying

NJIT requires SAT I or ACT and a high school transcript, and in some cases an essay, SAT II Subject Tests, and an interview. It recommends 1 recommendation. Application deadline: 4/1; 5/15 for financial aid, with a 3/15 priority date. Early and deferred admission are possible.

Getting in Last Year

2,227 applied
65% were accepted
716 enrolled (49%)
23% from top tenth of their h.s. class
23% had SAT verbal scores over 600
51% had SAT math scores over 600
3% had SAT verbal scores over 700
10% had SAT math scores over 700

Graduation and After

7% graduated in 4 years
24% graduated in 5 years
14% graduated in 6 years
22% pursued further study
85% had job offers within 6 months
400 organizations recruited on campus

Financial Matters

$7200 resident tuition and fees (2001–02)
$11,852 nonresident tuition and fees (2001–02)
$7490 room and board
84% average percent of need met
$9986 average financial aid amount received per undergraduate (1999–2000)

New Mexico Institute of Mining and Technology

SMALL-TOWN SETTING ■ PUBLIC ■ STATE-SUPPORTED ■ COED
SOCORRO, NEW MEXICO

Web site: www.nmt.edu
Contact: Ms. Melissa Jaramillo-Fleming, Director of Admissions, 801 Leroy
    Place, Socorro, NM 87801
Telephone: 505-835-5424 or toll-free 800-428-TECH **Fax:** 505-835-5989
E-mail: admission@admin.nmt.edu

Getting in Last Year
343 applied
84% were accepted
218 enrolled (75%)
23% from top tenth of their h.s. class
3.50 average high school GPA
52% had SAT verbal scores over 600
60% had SAT math scores over 600
72% had ACT scores over 24
12% had SAT verbal scores over 700
17% had SAT math scores over 700
18% had ACT scores over 30

Graduation and After
15% graduated in 4 years
17% graduated in 5 years
5% graduated in 6 years
26% pursued further study (14% arts and
    sciences, 9% engineering, 2% education)
75% had job offers within 6 months
22 organizations recruited on campus

Financial Matters
$2722 resident tuition and fees (2001–02)
$8419 nonresident tuition and fees (2001–02)
$4430 room and board
90% average percent of need met
$7103 average financial aid amount received
    per undergraduate (1999–2000)

Academics

New Mexico Tech awards associate, bachelor's, master's, and doctoral **degrees**. Challenging opportunities include advanced placement credit, accelerated degree programs, student-designed majors, double majors, independent study, and a senior project. Special programs include cooperative education, internships, summer session for credit, and study-abroad.

The most frequently chosen **baccalaureate** fields are engineering/engineering technologies, physical sciences, and computer/information sciences. A complete listing of majors at New Mexico Tech appears in the Majors Index beginning on page 430.

The **faculty** at New Mexico Tech has 110 full-time members, 100% with terminal degrees. The student-faculty ratio is 12:1.

Students of New Mexico Tech

The student body totals 1,588, of whom 1,256 are undergraduates. 37.8% are women and 62.2% are men. Students come from 52 states and territories and 14 other countries. 83% are from New Mexico. 2.9% are international students. 0.7% are African American, 4.3% American Indian, 3% Asian American, and 19.9% Hispanic American. 74% returned for their sophomore year.

Facilities and Resources

Student rooms are linked to a campus network. 225 **computers** are available on campus that provide access to the Internet. The 2 **libraries** have 89,725 books and 766 subscriptions.

Campus Life

There are 55 active organizations on campus, including a drama/theater group, newspaper, radio station, and choral group. No national or local **fraternities** or **sororities**.

This institution has no intercollegiate sports.

Campus Safety

Student safety services include late-night transport/escort service, 24-hour emergency telephone alarm devices, and 24-hour patrols by trained security personnel.

Applying

New Mexico Tech requires SAT I or ACT, a high school transcript, and a minimum high school GPA of 2.5, and in some cases 2 recommendations. It recommends an interview. Application deadline: 8/1; 3/1 priority date for financial aid. Deferred admission is possible.

NEW YORK UNIVERSITY

URBAN SETTING ■ PRIVATE ■ INDEPENDENT ■ COED
NEW YORK, NEW YORK

Web site: www.nyu.edu
Contact: Mr. Richard A. Avisable, Assistant Vice President for Enrollment Services, 22 Washington Square North, New York, NY 10011
Telephone: 212-998-4500 **Fax:** 212-995-4902

Academics

NYU awards associate, bachelor's, master's, doctoral, and first-professional **degrees** and post-bachelor's, post-master's, and first-professional certificates. Challenging opportunities include advanced placement credit, accelerated degree programs, student-designed majors, freshman honors college, an honors program, double majors, independent study, and a senior project. Special programs include internships, summer session for credit, off-campus study, and study-abroad. A complete listing of majors at NYU appears in the Majors Index beginning on page 430.

The **faculty** at NYU has 1,705 full-time members. The student-faculty ratio is 12:1.

Students of NYU

The student body totals 37,134, of whom 19,028 are undergraduates. 60% are women and 40% are men. Students come from 52 states and territories and 137 other countries. 48% are from New York. 4.6% are international students. 6.2% are African American, 0.1% American Indian, 14.3% Asian American, and 6.9% Hispanic American. 91% returned for their sophomore year.

Facilities and Resources

Student rooms are linked to a campus network. 1,400 **computers** are available on campus that provide access to the Internet. The 12 **libraries** have 4,459,879 books and 32,766 subscriptions.

Campus Life

There are 250 active organizations on campus, including a drama/theater group, newspaper, radio station, television station, and choral group. 5% of eligible men and 2% of eligible women are members of national **fraternities**, national **sororities**, local fraternities, and local sororities.

NYU is a member of the NCAA (Division III). **Intercollegiate sports** include basketball, cross-country running, fencing, golf (m), soccer, swimming, tennis, track and field, volleyball, wrestling (m).

Campus Safety

Student safety services include 24-hour security in residence halls, late-night transport/escort service, 24-hour emergency telephone alarm devices, 24-hour patrols by trained security personnel, student patrols, and electronically operated dormitory entrances.

Applying

NYU requires an essay, SAT I or ACT, a high school transcript, 2 recommendations, and a minimum high school GPA of 3.0, and in some cases SAT II Subject Tests, an interview, and audition, portfolio. It recommends SAT II Subject Tests and SAT II: Writing Test. Application deadline: 1/15; 2/15 priority date for financial aid. Deferred admission is possible.

Getting in Last Year
30,533 applied
28% were accepted
4,009 enrolled (46%)
72% from top tenth of their h.s. class
3.70 average high school GPA
88% had SAT verbal scores over 600
87% had SAT math scores over 600
96% had ACT scores over 24
35% had SAT verbal scores over 700
37% had SAT math scores over 700
51% had ACT scores over 30
132 National Merit Scholars

Graduation and After
65% graduated in 4 years
7% graduated in 5 years
2% graduated in 6 years
84% had job offers within 6 months
650 organizations recruited on campus

Financial Matters
$25,380 tuition and fees (2001–02)
$9820 room and board
73% average percent of need met
$17,413 average financial aid amount received per undergraduate

NORTH CAROLINA STATE UNIVERSITY

SUBURBAN SETTING ■ PUBLIC ■ STATE-SUPPORTED ■ COED
RALEIGH, NORTH CAROLINA

Web site: www.ncsu.edu
Contact: Dr. George R. Dixon, Vice Provost and Director of Admissions, Box 7103, 112 Peele Hall, Raleigh, NC 27695
Telephone: 919-515-2434
E-mail: undergrad_admissions@ncsu.edu

Getting in Last Year
11,835 applied
66% were accepted
3,893 enrolled (50%)
35% from top tenth of their h.s. class
3.94 average high school GPA
37% had SAT verbal scores over 600
53% had SAT math scores over 600
71% had ACT scores over 24
6% had SAT verbal scores over 700
12% had SAT math scores over 700
14% had ACT scores over 30
43 National Merit Scholars
99 valedictorians

Graduation and After
25% graduated in 4 years
28% graduated in 5 years
7% graduated in 6 years
20% pursued further study
92% had job offers within 6 months
722 organizations recruited on campus

Financial Matters
85% average percent of need met
$6725 average financial aid amount received per undergraduate

Academics
NC State awards associate, bachelor's, master's, doctoral, and first-professional **degrees** and first-professional certificates. Challenging opportunities include advanced placement credit, accelerated degree programs, student-designed majors, freshman honors college, an honors program, double majors, independent study, and a senior project. Special programs include cooperative education, internships, summer session for credit, off-campus study, study-abroad, and Army, Navy and Air Force ROTC.

The most frequently chosen **baccalaureate** fields are engineering/engineering technologies, business/marketing, and biological/life sciences. A complete listing of majors at NC State appears in the Majors Index beginning on page 430.

The **faculty** at NC State has 1,592 full-time members, 92% with terminal degrees. The student-faculty ratio is 13:1.

Students of NC State
The student body totals 29,286, of whom 22,418 are undergraduates. 41.9% are women and 58.1% are men. Students come from 51 states and territories and 65 other countries. 92% are from North Carolina. 1.1% are international students. 10.3% are African American, 0.7% American Indian, 4.7% Asian American, and 1.9% Hispanic American. 89% returned for their sophomore year.

Facilities and Resources
Student rooms are linked to a campus network. 4,600 **computers** are available on campus that provide access to the Internet. The 5 **libraries** have 951,788 books and 35,882 subscriptions.

Campus Life
There are 300 active organizations on campus, including a drama/theater group, newspaper, radio station, television station, choral group, and marching band. 11% of eligible men and 11% of eligible women are members of national **fraternities**, national **sororities**, and local sororities.

NC State is a member of the NCAA (Division I). **Intercollegiate sports** (some offering scholarships) include baseball (m), basketball, cross-country running, fencing, football (m), golf, gymnastics, riflery, soccer, swimming, tennis, track and field, volleyball (w), wrestling (m).

Campus Safety
Student safety services include late-night transport/escort service, 24-hour emergency telephone alarm devices, 24-hour patrols by trained security personnel, student patrols, and electronically operated dormitory entrances.

Applying
NC State requires SAT I or ACT and a high school transcript, and in some cases an interview and 1 recommendation. It recommends an essay and a minimum high school GPA of 3.0. Application deadline: 2/1; 3/1 priority date for financial aid. Early and deferred admission are possible.

NORTH CENTRAL COLLEGE
SUBURBAN SETTING ■ PRIVATE ■ INDEPENDENT RELIGIOUS ■ COED
NAPERVILLE, ILLINOIS

Web site: www.noctrl.edu
Contact: Mr. Stephen Potts, Coordinator of Freshman Admission, 30 North
  Brainard Street, PO Box 3063, Naperville, IL 60566-7063
Telephone: 630-637-5815 or toll-free 800-411-1861 **Fax:** 630-637-5819
E-mail: ncadm@noctrl.edu

Academics
North Central awards bachelor's and master's **degrees**. Challenging opportunities
include advanced placement credit, accelerated degree programs, student-designed
majors, an honors program, double majors, independent study, and a senior project.
Special programs include cooperative education, internships, summer session for credit,
off-campus study, study-abroad, and Army and Air Force ROTC.

The most frequently chosen **baccalaureate** fields are business/marketing, social sciences and history, and education. A complete listing of majors at North Central appears
in the Majors Index beginning on page 430.

The **faculty** at North Central has 119 full-time members, 84% with terminal
degrees. The student-faculty ratio is 14:1.

Students of North Central
The student body totals 2,605, of whom 2,162 are undergraduates. 57.3% are women
and 42.7% are men. Students come from 26 states and territories and 18 other countries.
89% are from Illinois. 1.4% are international students. 4.2% are African American, 0.2%
American Indian, 1.9% Asian American, and 3.2% Hispanic American. 81% returned for
their sophomore year.

Facilities and Resources
Student rooms are linked to a campus network. 200 **computers** are available on campus
that provide access to software packages and the Internet. The **library** has 132,322 books
and 736 subscriptions.

Campus Life
There are 42 active organizations on campus, including a drama/theater group,
newspaper, radio station, and choral group. No national or local **fraternities** or **sororities**.

North Central is a member of the NCAA (Division III). **Intercollegiate sports**
include baseball (m), basketball, cross-country running, football (m), golf, soccer, softball
(w), swimming, tennis, track and field, volleyball (w), wrestling (m).

Campus Safety
Student safety services include late-night transport/escort service, 24-hour emergency
telephone alarm devices, and 24-hour patrols by trained security personnel.

Applying
North Central requires SAT I or ACT, a high school transcript, and a minimum high
school GPA of 2.0, and in some cases an interview. It recommends an essay, ACT, and 1
recommendation. Application deadline: rolling admissions. Early and deferred admission
are possible.

North Central College is a
community of learners
dedicated to preparing
informed, involved, principled, and
productive citizens and leaders over
a lifetime. This mission is grounded
in the liberal arts, with a balanced
curriculum emphasizing leadership,
ethics, and values. North Central
College is committed to
undergraduate teaching and to
sustaining its strong residential
college tradition. The College offers
more than 50 academic areas of
concentration in business, science,
education, communications, liberal
arts, and preprofessional programs.
Cocurricular opportunities include
Division III intercollegiate athletics, a
nationally recognized student radio
station, a Model UN, forensics,
community volunteering, and campus
ministry. More than 90 percent of
the freshman class receives financial
assistance.

Getting in Last Year
1,457 applied
78% were accepted
444 enrolled (39%)
20% from top tenth of their h.s. class
3.40 average high school GPA
30% had SAT verbal scores over 600
39% had SAT math scores over 600
58% had ACT scores over 24
3% had SAT verbal scores over 700
8% had SAT math scores over 700
9% had ACT scores over 30
1 National Merit Scholar
6 valedictorians

Graduation and After
10% pursued further study (6% arts and sciences, 2% business, 1% education)
77% had job offers within 6 months
60 organizations recruited on campus

Financial Matters
$17,175 tuition and fees (2001–02)
$5724 room and board
75% average percent of need met
$13,913 average financial aid amount received
  per undergraduate (2000–01)

NORTHWESTERN COLLEGE
SUBURBAN SETTING ■ PRIVATE ■ INDEPENDENT RELIGIOUS ■ COED
ST. PAUL, MINNESOTA

Getting in Last Year
742 applied
99% were accepted
431 enrolled (59%)
23% from top tenth of their h.s. class
3.48 average high school GPA
53% had SAT verbal scores over 600
35% had SAT math scores over 600
50% had ACT scores over 24
12% had SAT verbal scores over 700
19% had SAT math scores over 700
6% had ACT scores over 30
9 valedictorians

Graduation and After
38% graduated in 4 years
9% graduated in 5 years
1% graduated in 6 years
4% pursued further study (1% arts and sciences, 1% business, 1% education)
77% had job offers within 6 months
147 organizations recruited on campus

Financial Matters
$15,600 tuition and fees (2001–02)
$5050 room and board
76% average percent of need met
$12,025 average financial aid amount received per undergraduate (2000–01)

Web site: www.nwc.edu
Contact: Mr. Kenneth K. Faffler, Director of Recruitment, 3003 Snelling Avenue North, Nazareth Hall, Room 229, St. Paul, MN 55113-1598
Telephone: 651-631-5209 or toll-free 800-827-6827 **Fax:** 651-631-5680
E-mail: admissions@nwc.edu

Academics
Northwestern awards associate and bachelor's **degrees**. Challenging opportunities include advanced placement credit, double majors, independent study, and a senior project. Special programs include internships, summer session for credit, off-campus study, study-abroad, and Army and Air Force ROTC.

The most frequently chosen **baccalaureate** fields are education, philosophy, and business/marketing. A complete listing of majors at Northwestern appears in the Majors Index beginning on page 430.

The **faculty** at Northwestern has 68 full-time members, 76% with terminal degrees. The student-faculty ratio is 15:1.

Students of Northwestern
The student body is made up of 2,278 undergraduates. 62.7% are women and 37.3% are men. Students come from 32 states and territories and 27 other countries. 63% are from Minnesota. 0.6% are international students. 3.2% are African American, 0.2% American Indian, 1.9% Asian American, and 1.2% Hispanic American. 78% returned for their sophomore year.

Facilities and Resources
130 **computers** are available on campus that provide access to the Internet. The **library** has 74,857 books and 1,695 subscriptions.

Campus Life
There are 25 active organizations on campus, including a drama/theater group, newspaper, radio station, and choral group. No national or local **fraternities** or **sororities**.

Northwestern is a member of the NAIA and NCCAA. **Intercollegiate sports** include baseball (m), basketball, cross-country running, football (m), golf, soccer, softball (w), tennis, track and field, volleyball (w).

Campus Safety
Student safety services include late-night transport/escort service, 24-hour patrols by trained security personnel, and electronically operated dormitory entrances.

Applying
Northwestern requires an essay, SAT I or ACT, a high school transcript, 2 recommendations, lifestyle agreement, statement of Christian faith, and a minimum high school GPA of 2.0, and in some cases an interview. It recommends an interview and a minimum high school GPA of 3.0. Application deadline: 8/1; 7/1 for financial aid, with a 3/1 priority date. Early and deferred admission are possible.

NORTHWESTERN UNIVERSITY
SUBURBAN SETTING ■ PRIVATE ■ INDEPENDENT ■ COED
EVANSTON, ILLINOIS

Web site: www.northwestern.edu
Contact: Ms. Carol Lunkenheimer, Director of Admissions, PO Box 3060,
   Evanston, IL 60204-3060
Telephone: 847-491-7271
E-mail: ug-admission@northwestern.edu

Academics
Northwestern awards bachelor's, master's, doctoral, and first-professional **degrees**. Challenging opportunities include advanced placement credit, accelerated degree programs, student-designed majors, an honors program, double majors, independent study, and a senior project. Special programs include cooperative education, internships, summer session for credit, off-campus study, study-abroad, and Army, Navy and Air Force ROTC.

The most frequently chosen **baccalaureate** fields are social sciences and history, engineering/engineering technologies, and communications/communication technologies. A complete listing of majors at Northwestern appears in the Majors Index beginning on page 430.

The **faculty** at Northwestern has 918 full-time members, 100% with terminal degrees. The student-faculty ratio is 7:1.

Students of Northwestern
The student body totals 15,649, of whom 7,816 are undergraduates. 52.7% are women and 47.3% are men. Students come from 50 states and territories and 98 other countries. 23% are from Illinois. 4% are international students. 6% are African American, 0.2% American Indian, 16.6% Asian American, and 4.5% Hispanic American. 96% returned for their sophomore year.

Facilities and Resources
Student rooms are linked to a campus network. 661 **computers** are available on campus that provide access to the Internet. The 7 **libraries** have 4,082,737 books and 37,467 subscriptions.

Campus Life
There are 250 active organizations on campus, including a drama/theater group, newspaper, radio station, television station, choral group, and marching band. 30% of eligible men and 39% of eligible women are members of national **fraternities** and national **sororities**.

Northwestern is a member of the NCAA (Division I). **Intercollegiate sports** (some offering scholarships) include baseball (m), basketball, cross-country running (w), fencing (w), field hockey (w), football (m), golf, soccer, softball (w), swimming, tennis, volleyball (w), wrestling (m).

Campus Safety
Student safety services include late-night transport/escort service, 24-hour emergency telephone alarm devices, 24-hour patrols by trained security personnel, and electronically operated dormitory entrances.

Applying
Northwestern requires an essay, SAT I or ACT, a high school transcript, and 1 recommendation, and in some cases SAT II Subject Tests and audition for music program. It recommends SAT II Subject Tests and an interview. Application deadline: 1/1; 2/1 priority date for financial aid. Early and deferred admission are possible.

Getting in Last Year
13,988 applied
34% were accepted
1,952 enrolled (41%)
82% from top tenth of their h.s. class
90% had SAT verbal scores over 600
94% had SAT math scores over 600
97% had ACT scores over 24
44% had SAT verbal scores over 700
58% had SAT math scores over 700
68% had ACT scores over 30
139 National Merit Scholars
186 valedictorians

Graduation and After
83% graduated in 4 years
9% graduated in 5 years
510 organizations recruited on campus

Financial Matters
$25,839 tuition and fees (2001–02)
$7776 room and board
100% average percent of need met
$21,314 average financial aid amount received
   per undergraduate

OBERLIN COLLEGE

SMALL-TOWN SETTING ■ PRIVATE ■ INDEPENDENT ■ COED
OBERLIN, OHIO

Web site: www.oberlin.edu
Contact: Ms. Debra Chermonte, Dean of Admissions and Financial Aid, Admissions Office, Carnegie Building, Oberlin, OH 44074-1090
Telephone: 440-775-8411 or toll-free 800-622-OBIE **Fax:** 440-775-6905
E-mail: ad_mail@oberlin.edu

From its founding, Oberlin has been a pioneering college. Oberlin was the first coeducational school in the United States and a historic leader in educating African-American students. Among primarily undergraduate institutions, Oberlin ranks first for the number of students going on to earn PhD degrees. Oberlin alumni include 3 Nobel laureates and leaders in law, scientific and scholarly research, medicine, the arts, theology, communication, business, and government. Oberlin has more students, programs, and facilities than most small colleges, including a 5-year double-degree program, combining studies at the Conservatory of Music and the College of Arts and Sciences.

Getting in Last Year
5,548 applied
36% were accepted
767 enrolled (39%)
59% from top tenth of their h.s. class
3.50 average high school GPA
84% had SAT verbal scores over 600
79% had SAT math scores over 600
91% had ACT scores over 24
45% had SAT verbal scores over 700
27% had SAT math scores over 700
48% had ACT scores over 30
51 National Merit Scholars
39 valedictorians

Graduation and After
30% pursued further study
70% had job offers within 6 months
43 organizations recruited on campus

Financial Matters
$26,580 tuition and fees (2001–02)
$6560 room and board
100% average percent of need met
$23,851 average financial aid amount received per undergraduate

Academics

Oberlin awards bachelor's and master's **degrees** and post-bachelor's certificates. Challenging opportunities include advanced placement credit, accelerated degree programs, student-designed majors, an honors program, double majors, independent study, and a senior project. Special programs include internships, off-campus study, and study-abroad.

The most frequently chosen **baccalaureate** fields are visual/performing arts, social sciences and history, and biological/life sciences. A complete listing of majors at Oberlin appears in the Majors Index beginning on page 430.

The **faculty** at Oberlin has 263 full-time members, 94% with terminal degrees. The student-faculty ratio is 10:1.

Students of Oberlin

The student body totals 2,863, of whom 2,840 are undergraduates. 57.3% are women and 42.7% are men. Students come from 55 states and territories and 26 other countries. 11% are from Ohio. 6.4% are international students. 8% are African American, 0.7% American Indian, 6.3% Asian American, and 3.6% Hispanic American. 90% returned for their sophomore year.

Facilities and Resources

Student rooms are linked to a campus network. 275 **computers** are available on campus for student use. The 4 **libraries** have 1,541,260 books and 4,560 subscriptions.

Campus Life

There are 120 active organizations on campus, including a drama/theater group, newspaper, radio station, and choral group. No national or local **fraternities** or **sororities**.

Oberlin is a member of the NCAA (Division III). **Intercollegiate sports** include baseball (m), basketball, cross-country running, field hockey (w), football (m), golf (m), lacrosse, soccer, swimming, tennis, track and field, volleyball (w).

Campus Safety

Student safety services include crime prevention programs, late-night transport/escort service, 24-hour emergency telephone alarm devices, 24-hour patrols by trained security personnel, and electronically operated dormitory entrances.

Applying

Oberlin requires an essay, SAT I or ACT, a high school transcript, and 2 recommendations, and in some cases an interview. It recommends SAT II Subject Tests. Application deadline: 1/15; 1/15 for financial aid. Early and deferred admission are possible.

OCCIDENTAL COLLEGE

URBAN SETTING ■ PRIVATE ■ INDEPENDENT ■ COED
LOS ANGELES, CALIFORNIA

Web site: www.oxy.edu

Contact: Mr. Vince Cuseo, Director of Admission, 1600 Campus Road, Los Angeles, CA 90041-3314

Telephone: 323-259-2700 or toll-free 800-825-5262 **Fax:** 323-341-4875

E-mail: admission@oxy.edu

Academics

OXY awards bachelor's and master's **degrees**. Challenging opportunities include advanced placement credit, accelerated degree programs, student-designed majors, an honors program, double majors, independent study, and a senior project. Special programs include internships, summer session for credit, off-campus study, study-abroad, and Army, Navy and Air Force ROTC.

The most frequently chosen **baccalaureate** field is visual/performing arts. A complete listing of majors at OXY appears in the Majors Index beginning on page 430.

The **faculty** at OXY has 133 full-time members, 93% with terminal degrees. The student-faculty ratio is 12:1.

Students of OXY

The student body totals 1,796, of whom 1,770 are undergraduates. Students come from 46 states and territories and 34 other countries. 68% are from California. 92% returned for their sophomore year.

Facilities and Resources

Student rooms are linked to a campus network. 131 **computers** are available on campus that provide access to the Internet. The 3 **libraries** have 481,822 books and 1,135 subscriptions.

Campus Life

There are 90 active organizations on campus, including a drama/theater group, newspaper, radio station, and choral group. 11% of eligible men and 6% of eligible women are members of national **fraternities** and local **sororities**.

OXY is a member of the NCAA (Division III). **Intercollegiate sports** include baseball (m), basketball, cross-country running, football (m), golf, soccer, softball (w), swimming, tennis, track and field, volleyball (w), water polo.

Campus Safety

Student safety services include community police services, late-night transport/escort service, 24-hour emergency telephone alarm devices, 24-hour patrols by trained security personnel, student patrols, and electronically operated dormitory entrances.

Applying

OXY requires an essay, SAT I or ACT, a high school transcript, and 2 recommendations. It recommends SAT II Subject Tests, SAT II: Writing Test, and an interview. Application deadline: 1/15; 2/1 priority date for financial aid. Early and deferred admission are possible.

Getting in Last Year
3,636 applied
48% were accepted
58% from top tenth of their h.s. class
56% had SAT verbal scores over 600
53% had SAT math scores over 600
13% had SAT verbal scores over 700
10% had SAT math scores over 700
13 valedictorians

Graduation and After
30% pursued further study (23% arts and sciences, 3% law, 3% medicine)
62 organizations recruited on campus

Financial Matters
$25,420 tuition and fees (2001–02)
$7100 room and board
93% average percent of need met
$25,810 average financial aid amount received per undergraduate

OGLETHORPE UNIVERSITY

SUBURBAN SETTING ■ PRIVATE ■ INDEPENDENT ■ COED
ATLANTA, GEORGIA

Web site: www.oglethorpe.edu
Contact: Mr. Dennis T. Matthews, Associate Dean for Enrollment
   Management, 4484 Peachtree Road, NE, Atlanta, GA 30319-2797
Telephone: 404-364-8307 or toll-free 800-428-4484 **Fax:** 404-364-8500
E-mail: admission@oglethorpe.edu

I t's not just the rigorous core curriculum, the small class discussions, and the motivating professors that make Oglethorpe different. It's the location—near the center of one of the country's most exciting, dynamic, and international cities, Atlanta. A distinctive honors program and a dynamic Rich Foundation Urban Leadership Program are gaining much recognition from city leaders as Oglethorpe helps connect students to the rich resources of Atlanta. Internships are available in every major and are very popular among the student body.

Getting in Last Year
761 applied
70% were accepted
192 enrolled (36%)
36% from top tenth of their h.s. class
3.65 average high school GPA
55% had SAT verbal scores over 600
43% had SAT math scores over 600
76% had ACT scores over 24
14% had SAT verbal scores over 700
7% had SAT math scores over 700
20% had ACT scores over 30

Graduation and After
62% graduated in 4 years
7% graduated in 5 years
1% graduated in 6 years
34% pursued further study (14% business, 11% arts and sciences, 4% medicine)
70% had job offers within 6 months

Financial Matters
$19,100 tuition and fees (2001–02)
$6060 room and board
89% average percent of need met
$15,010 average financial aid amount received per undergraduate (2000–01 estimated)

Academics
Oglethorpe awards bachelor's and master's **degrees**. Challenging opportunities include advanced placement credit, accelerated degree programs, student-designed majors, an honors program, double majors, independent study, and a senior project. Special programs include cooperative education, internships, summer session for credit, off-campus study, and study-abroad. A complete listing of majors at Oglethorpe appears in the Majors Index beginning on page 430.

The **faculty** at Oglethorpe has 53 full-time members, 96% with terminal degrees. The student-faculty ratio is 13:1.

Students of Oglethorpe
The student body totals 1,267, of whom 1,169 are undergraduates. 66.8% are women and 33.2% are men. 2.3% are international students. 18.5% are African American, 0.1% American Indian, 3.9% Asian American, and 2.3% Hispanic American. 81% returned for their sophomore year.

Facilities and Resources
Student rooms are linked to a campus network. 60 **computers** are available on campus for student use. The **library** has 135,000 books and 950 subscriptions.

Campus Life
There are 52 active organizations on campus, including a drama/theater group, newspaper, radio station, and choral group. 33% of eligible men and 28% of eligible women are members of national **fraternities** and national **sororities**.

Oglethorpe is a member of the NCAA (Division III). **Intercollegiate sports** include baseball (m), basketball, cross-country running, golf (m), soccer, tennis, track and field, volleyball (w).

Campus Safety
Student safety services include late-night transport/escort service, 24-hour emergency telephone alarm devices, 24-hour patrols by trained security personnel, student patrols, and electronically operated dormitory entrances.

Applying
Oglethorpe requires an essay, SAT I or ACT, a high school transcript, and 1 recommendation, and in some cases an interview. It recommends an interview and a minimum high school GPA of 2.5. Application deadline: rolling admissions. Deferred admission is possible.

OHIO NORTHERN UNIVERSITY

SMALL-TOWN SETTING ■ PRIVATE ■ INDEPENDENT RELIGIOUS ■ COED
ADA, OHIO

Web site: www.onu.edu

Contact: Ms. Karen Condeni, Vice President of Admissions and Financial Aid,
525 South Main, Ada, OH 45810-1599

Telephone: 419-772-2260 or toll-free 888-408-4ONU **Fax:** 419-772-2313

E-mail: admissions-ug@onu.edu

Academics

Ohio Northern awards bachelor's and first-professional **degrees**. Challenging opportunities include advanced placement credit, an honors program, double majors, and a senior project. Special programs include cooperative education, internships, summer session for credit, study-abroad, and Army and Air Force ROTC.

The most frequently chosen **baccalaureate** fields are engineering/engineering technologies, business/marketing, and health professions and related sciences. A complete listing of majors at Ohio Northern appears in the Majors Index beginning on page 430.

The **faculty** at Ohio Northern has 187 full-time members, 82% with terminal degrees. The student-faculty ratio is 13:1.

Students of Ohio Northern

The student body totals 3,345, of whom 2,366 are undergraduates. 47.3% are women and 52.7% are men. Students come from 42 states and territories and 17 other countries. 86% are from Ohio. 82% returned for their sophomore year.

Facilities and Resources

Student rooms are linked to a campus network. 461 **computers** are available on campus that provide access to the Internet. The 2 **libraries** have 246,103 books and 1,038 subscriptions.

Campus Life

There are 170 active organizations on campus, including a drama/theater group, newspaper, radio station, television station, choral group, and marching band. 25% of eligible men and 22% of eligible women are members of national **fraternities** and national **sororities**.

Ohio Northern is a member of the NCAA (Division III). **Intercollegiate sports** include baseball (m), basketball, cross-country running, football (m), golf, soccer, softball (w), swimming, tennis, track and field, volleyball (w), wrestling (m).

Campus Safety

Student safety services include late-night transport/escort service, 24-hour emergency telephone alarm devices, 24-hour patrols by trained security personnel, and electronically operated dormitory entrances.

Applying

Ohio Northern requires SAT I or ACT and a high school transcript. It recommends an essay, an interview, and a minimum high school GPA of 2.5. Application deadline: 8/15; 6/1 for financial aid, with a 4/15 priority date. Early and deferred admission are possible.

National recognition, smaller classes, excellent facilities, and outstanding faculty members are just a few of the features that set Ohio Northern apart from other universities in the Midwest. The unique and dynamic partnership of the arts and sciences with professional programs is rich in cross-learning opportunities. But what makes ONU truly special is its students. They are scholars reflecting the values of service and leadership, which are the products of the individual attention and encouragement they receive from the faculty and staff of ONU.

Getting in Last Year
2,358 applied
91% were accepted
483 enrolled (23%)
39% from top tenth of their h.s. class
3.74 average high school GPA
36% had SAT verbal scores over 600
44% had SAT math scores over 600
61% had ACT scores over 24
5% had SAT verbal scores over 700
7% had SAT math scores over 700
11% had ACT scores over 30
82 valedictorians

Graduation and After
30% graduated in 4 years
29% graduated in 5 years
7% graduated in 6 years
16% pursued further study
88% had job offers within 6 months
232 organizations recruited on campus

Financial Matters
$22,275 tuition and fees (2001–02)
$5490 room and board
89% average percent of need met

THE OHIO STATE UNIVERSITY

URBAN SETTING ■ PUBLIC ■ STATE-SUPPORTED ■ COED
COLUMBUS, OHIO

Web site: www.osu.edu

Contact: Dr. Mabel G. Freeman, Director of Undergraduate Admissions and Vice President for First-Year Experience, 3rd Floor, Lincoln Tower, 1800 Cannon Drive, Columbus, OH 43210

Telephone: 614-292-3974 **Fax:** 614-292-4818

E-mail: askabuckeye@osu.edu

Getting in Last Year
19,968 applied
73% were accepted
5,996 enrolled (41%)
33% from top tenth of their h.s. class
41% had SAT verbal scores over 600
50% had SAT math scores over 600
69% had ACT scores over 24
9% had SAT verbal scores over 700
12% had SAT math scores over 700
13% had ACT scores over 30
104 National Merit Scholars
239 valedictorians

Graduation and After
10% pursued further study

Financial Matters
$4788 resident tuition and fees (2001–02)
$13,554 nonresident tuition and fees (2001–02)
$6031 room and board
76% average percent of need met
$7747 average financial aid amount received per undergraduate

Academics

Ohio State awards bachelor's, master's, doctoral, and first-professional **degrees** and post-master's certificates. Challenging opportunities include advanced placement credit, accelerated degree programs, student-designed majors, freshman honors college, an honors program, double majors, independent study, and a senior project. Special programs include cooperative education, internships, summer session for credit, off-campus study, study-abroad, and Army and Air Force ROTC.

The most frequently chosen **baccalaureate** fields are business/marketing, social sciences and history, and home economics/vocational home economics. A complete listing of majors at Ohio State appears in the Majors Index beginning on page 430.

The **faculty** at Ohio State has 2,713 full-time members, 99% with terminal degrees. The student-faculty ratio is 13:1.

Students of Ohio State

The student body totals 48,477, of whom 36,049 are undergraduates. 48.3% are women and 51.7% are men. Students come from 53 states and territories and 89 other countries. 89% are from Ohio. 3.9% are international students. 8% are African American, 0.4% American Indian, 5.5% Asian American, and 2.1% Hispanic American. 86% returned for their sophomore year.

Facilities and Resources

Student rooms are linked to a campus network. 1,000 **computers** are available on campus that provide access to the Internet. The 13 **libraries** have 5,394,140 books and 42,707 subscriptions.

Campus Life

There are 550 active organizations on campus, including a drama/theater group, newspaper, radio station, television station, choral group, and marching band. 5% of eligible men and 6% of eligible women are members of national **fraternities** and national **sororities**.

Ohio State is a member of the NCAA (Division I). **Intercollegiate sports** (some offering scholarships) include baseball (m), basketball, cross-country running, fencing, field hockey (w), football (m), golf, gymnastics, ice hockey, lacrosse, riflery, soccer, softball (w), swimming, tennis, track and field, volleyball, wrestling (m).

Campus Safety

Student safety services include dorm entrances locked after 9 p.m, late-night transport/escort service, 24-hour emergency telephone alarm devices, 24-hour patrols by trained security personnel, student patrols, and electronically operated dormitory entrances.

Applying

Ohio State requires SAT I or ACT and a high school transcript. Application deadline: 2/15; 2/15 priority date for financial aid.

OHIO WESLEYAN UNIVERSITY

SMALL-TOWN SETTING ■ PRIVATE ■ INDEPENDENT RELIGIOUS ■ COED
DELAWARE, OHIO

Web site: web.owu.edu

Contact: Ms. Margaret L. Drugovich, Vice President of Admission and
Financial Aid, 61 South Sandusky Street, Delaware, OH 43015

Telephone: 740-368-3020 or toll-free 800-922-8953 **Fax:** 740-368-3314

E-mail: owuadmit@owu.edu

Academics

Ohio Wesleyan awards bachelor's **degrees**. Challenging opportunities include advanced placement credit, student-designed majors, freshman honors college, an honors program, double majors, independent study, and a senior project. Special programs include internships, summer session for credit, off-campus study, study-abroad, and Army ROTC.

The most frequently chosen **baccalaureate** fields are social sciences and history, business/marketing, and biological/life sciences. A complete listing of majors at Ohio Wesleyan appears in the Majors Index beginning on page 430.

The **faculty** at Ohio Wesleyan has 127 full-time members, 100% with terminal degrees. The student-faculty ratio is 13:1.

Students of Ohio Wesleyan

The student body is made up of 1,886 undergraduates. 52.1% are women and 47.9% are men. Students come from 42 states and territories and 52 other countries. 53% are from Ohio. 12.4% are international students. 4.6% are African American, 0.2% American Indian, 1.9% Asian American, and 1.5% Hispanic American. 79% returned for their sophomore year.

Facilities and Resources

Student rooms are linked to a campus network. 275 **computers** are available on campus that provide access to the Internet. The 4 **libraries** have 348,952 books and 2,829 subscriptions.

Campus Life

There are 100 active organizations on campus, including a drama/theater group, newspaper, radio station, and choral group. 44% of eligible men and 34% of eligible women are members of national **fraternities** and national **sororities**.

Ohio Wesleyan is a member of the NCAA (Division III). **Intercollegiate sports** include baseball (m), basketball, cross-country running, field hockey (w), football (m), golf (m), lacrosse, soccer, softball (w), swimming, tennis, track and field, volleyball (w).

Campus Safety

Student safety services include late-night transport/escort service, 24-hour emergency telephone alarm devices, 24-hour patrols by trained security personnel, and electronically operated dormitory entrances.

Applying

Ohio Wesleyan requires an essay, SAT I or ACT, a high school transcript, and 2 recommendations. It recommends SAT II Subject Tests, an interview, and a minimum high school GPA of 2.5. Application deadline: 3/15; 3/15 priority date for financial aid. Early and deferred admission are possible.

Ohio Wesleyan is one of the nation's most balanced selective liberal arts colleges. Students praise the faculty for its dedication to teaching and active encouragement in the classroom. Students balance their academic experience with strong participation in community service, athletics, and student government. Loren Pope, author of *Beyond the Ivy League* and *Colleges That Change Lives*, says, "Ohio Wesleyan has a much more diverse, cosmopolitan, and friendly student body than a lot of the selective east and west coast schools." OWU has been recognized repeatedly by The John Templeton Foundation as a "college that encourages character development."

Getting in Last Year
2,227 applied
78% were accepted
582 enrolled (33%)
32% from top tenth of their h.s. class
3.35 average high school GPA
57% had SAT verbal scores over 600
59% had SAT math scores over 600
73% had ACT scores over 24
12% had SAT verbal scores over 700
14% had SAT math scores over 700
23% had ACT scores over 30
33 valedictorians

Graduation and After
34% pursued further study (14% arts and sciences, 7% medicine, 5% law)
28 organizations recruited on campus

Financial Matters
$22,860 tuition and fees (2001–02)
$6810 room and board
91% average percent of need met
$20,422 average financial aid amount received per undergraduate

Oklahoma Baptist University

Small-town setting ■ Private ■ Independent Religious ■ Coed
Shawnee, Oklahoma

Web site: www.okbu.edu
Contact: Mr. Michael Cappo, Dean of Admissions, Box 61174, Shawnee, OK 74804
Telephone: 405-878-2033 or toll-free 800-654-3285 **Fax:** 405-878-2046
E-mail: admissions@mail.okbu.edu

Getting in Last Year
871 applied
86% were accepted
436 enrolled (58%)
34% from top tenth of their h.s. class
3.65 average high school GPA
38% had SAT verbal scores over 600
34% had SAT math scores over 600
53% had ACT scores over 24
12% had SAT verbal scores over 700
7% had SAT math scores over 700
11% had ACT scores over 30
6 National Merit Scholars
36 valedictorians

Graduation and After
35% graduated in 4 years
14% graduated in 5 years
4% graduated in 6 years
Graduates pursuing further study: 16% theology, 12% arts and sciences, 5% business
45 organizations recruited on campus

Financial Matters
$10,338 tuition and fees (2001–02)
$3470 room and board
75% average percent of need met
$3412 average financial aid amount received per undergraduate (2000–01 estimated)

Academics
OBU awards bachelor's and master's **degrees**. Challenging opportunities include advanced placement credit, student-designed majors, an honors program, double majors, independent study, and a senior project. Special programs include cooperative education, internships, summer session for credit, off-campus study, study-abroad, and Air Force ROTC. A complete listing of majors at OBU appears in the Majors Index beginning on page 430.

The **faculty** at OBU has 115 full-time members, 70% with terminal degrees. The student-faculty ratio is 14:1.

Students of OBU
The student body totals 2,017, of whom 1,993 are undergraduates. 55.7% are women and 44.3% are men. Students come from 42 states and territories and 19 other countries. 61% are from Oklahoma. 1.1% are international students. 3% are African American, 5.1% American Indian, 1.9% Asian American, and 1.6% Hispanic American. 74% returned for their sophomore year.

Facilities and Resources
Student rooms are linked to a campus network. 170 **computers** are available on campus that provide access to the Internet. The **library** has 230,000 books and 1,800 subscriptions.

Campus Life
There are 50 active organizations on campus, including a drama/theater group, newspaper, television station, and choral group. 10% of eligible men and 10% of eligible women are members of local **fraternities** and local **sororities**.

OBU is a member of the NAIA. **Intercollegiate sports** (some offering scholarships) include baseball (m), basketball, cross-country running, golf, softball (w), tennis, track and field.

Campus Safety
Student safety services include late-night transport/escort service, 24-hour emergency telephone alarm devices, 24-hour patrols by trained security personnel, and electronically operated dormitory entrances.

Applying
OBU requires SAT I or ACT, a high school transcript, and a minimum high school GPA of 2.5, and in some cases an essay, an interview, and recommendations. Application deadline: 8/1; 3/1 priority date for financial aid. Early and deferred admission are possible.

OKLAHOMA CHRISTIAN UNIVERSITY

SUBURBAN SETTING ■ PRIVATE ■ INDEPENDENT RELIGIOUS ■ COED
OKLAHOMA CITY, OKLAHOMA

Web site: www.oc.edu
Contact: Mr. Kyle Ray, Director of Admissions, Box 11000, Oklahoma City, OK 73136-1100
Telephone: 405-425-5050 or toll-free 800-877-5010 (in-state) **Fax:** 405-425-5208
E-mail: info@oc.edu

Academics

Oklahoma Christian awards bachelor's and master's **degrees**. Challenging opportunities include advanced placement credit, accelerated degree programs, an honors program, and a senior project. Special programs include internships, summer session for credit, off-campus study, study-abroad, and Army and Air Force ROTC.

The most frequently chosen **baccalaureate** fields are business/marketing, education, and biological/life sciences. A complete listing of majors at Oklahoma Christian appears in the Majors Index beginning on page 430.

The **faculty** at Oklahoma Christian has 87 full-time members, 67% with terminal degrees. The student-faculty ratio is 16:1.

Students of Oklahoma Christian

The student body totals 1,811, of whom 1,714 are undergraduates. 49.6% are women and 50.4% are men. Students come from 59 states and territories. 47% are from Oklahoma. 5% are African American, 3% American Indian, 2% Asian American, and 3% Hispanic American. 67% returned for their sophomore year.

Facilities and Resources

Student rooms are linked to a campus network. 135 **computers** are available on campus that provide access to the Internet. The **library** has 95,789 books and 415 subscriptions.

Campus Life

There are 19 active organizations on campus, including a drama/theater group, newspaper, radio station, and choral group. No national or local **fraternities** or **sororities**.

Oklahoma Christian is a member of the NAIA. **Intercollegiate sports** (some offering scholarships) include basketball, cross-country running, golf (m), soccer, softball (w), tennis, track and field.

Campus Safety

Student safety services include late-night transport/escort service, 24-hour emergency telephone alarm devices, and 24-hour patrols by trained security personnel.

Applying

Oklahoma Christian requires SAT I or ACT and a high school transcript. Application deadline: rolling admissions; 8/31 for financial aid, with a 3/15 priority date. Early and deferred admission are possible.

Getting in Last Year

1,350 applied
82% were accepted
28% had SAT verbal scores over 600
39% had SAT math scores over 600
51% had ACT scores over 24
1% had SAT verbal scores over 700
8% had SAT math scores over 700
12% had ACT scores over 30

Graduation and After

14% graduated in 4 years
19% graduated in 5 years
2% graduated in 6 years
82% had job offers within 6 months
75 organizations recruited on campus

Financial Matters

$12,100 tuition and fees (2001–02)
$4400 room and board
88% average percent of need met

OKLAHOMA CITY UNIVERSITY

URBAN SETTING ■ PRIVATE ■ INDEPENDENT RELIGIOUS ■ COED
OKLAHOMA CITY, OKLAHOMA

Web site: www.okcu.edu

Contact: Ms. Stacy Messinger, Director of Admissions, 2501 North
Blackwelder, Oklahoma City, OK 73106-1402

Telephone: 405-521-5050 or toll-free 800-633-7242 (in-state) **Fax:**
405-521-5916

E-mail: uadmissions@okcu.edu

Getting in Last Year
1,381 applied
70% were accepted
291 enrolled (30%)
30% from top tenth of their h.s. class
3.52 average high school GPA
26% had SAT verbal scores over 600
26% had SAT math scores over 600
43% had ACT scores over 24
3% had SAT verbal scores over 700
5% had SAT math scores over 700
2% had ACT scores over 30

Graduation and After
33% graduated in 4 years
15% graduated in 5 years
2% graduated in 6 years
64 organizations recruited on campus

Financial Matters
$10,880 tuition and fees (2001–02)
$4590 room and board
$7591 average financial aid amount received
per undergraduate (2000–01)

Academics

OCU awards bachelor's, master's, and first-professional **degrees**. Challenging opportunities include advanced placement credit, accelerated degree programs, student-designed majors, an honors program, double majors, independent study, and a senior project. Special programs include cooperative education, internships, summer session for credit, off-campus study, study-abroad, and Army and Air Force ROTC.

The most frequently chosen **baccalaureate** fields are liberal arts/general studies, visual/performing arts, and business/marketing. A complete listing of majors at OCU appears in the Majors Index beginning on page 430.

The **faculty** at OCU has 157 full-time members, 75% with terminal degrees. The student-faculty ratio is 14:1.

Students of OCU

The student body totals 3,705, of whom 1,861 are undergraduates. 58.6% are women and 41.4% are men. Students come from 49 states and territories and 75 other countries. 83% are from Oklahoma. 24.6% are international students. 5.2% are African American, 3.7% American Indian, 2.5% Asian American, and 2.7% Hispanic American. 70% returned for their sophomore year.

Facilities and Resources

Student rooms are linked to a campus network. 264 **computers** are available on campus that provide access to the Internet. The 2 **libraries** have 280,457 books and 5,699 subscriptions.

Campus Life

There are 35 active organizations on campus, including a drama/theater group, newspaper, television station, and choral group. 11% of eligible men and 15% of eligible women are members of national **fraternities** and national **sororities**.

OCU is a member of the NAIA. **Intercollegiate sports** (some offering scholarships) include baseball (m), basketball, golf, soccer, softball (w), tennis.

Campus Safety

Student safety services include Operation ID, late-night transport/escort service, 24-hour emergency telephone alarm devices, 24-hour patrols by trained security personnel, and student patrols.

Applying

OCU requires SAT I or ACT, a high school transcript, and a minimum high school GPA of 2.5, and in some cases an interview and audition for music and dance programs. Application deadline: 8/22. Deferred admission is possible.

OKLAHOMA STATE UNIVERSITY

SMALL-TOWN SETTING ■ PUBLIC ■ STATE-SUPPORTED ■ COED
STILLWATER, OKLAHOMA

Web site: www.okstate.edu
Contact: Ms. Paulette Cundiff, Coordinator of Admissions Processing,
    Stillwater, OK 74078
Telephone: 405-744-6858 or toll-free 800-233-5019 (in-state), 800-852-1255
    (out-of-state) **Fax:** 405-744-5285
E-mail: admit@okstate.edu

Academics

OSU awards bachelor's, master's, doctoral, and first-professional **degrees**. Challenging
opportunities include advanced placement credit, accelerated degree programs, student-
designed majors, freshman honors college, an honors program, double majors,
independent study, and a senior project. Special programs include cooperative education,
internships, summer session for credit, off-campus study, study-abroad, and Army and
Air Force ROTC.

The most frequently chosen **baccalaureate** fields are business/marketing, engineer-
ing/engineering technologies, and agriculture. A complete listing of majors at OSU appears in the Majors Index beginning on page 430.

The **faculty** at OSU has 944 full-time members, 90% with terminal degrees. The
student-faculty ratio is 18:1.

Students of OSU

The student body totals 21,872, of whom 17,211 are undergraduates. 47.9% are women
and 52.1% are men. Students come from 50 states and territories and 114 other
countries. 88% are from Oklahoma. 4.7% are international students. 3.1% are African
American, 8.4% American Indian, 1.7% Asian American, and 1.9% Hispanic American.
82% returned for their sophomore year.

Facilities and Resources

Student rooms are linked to a campus network. 2,000 **computers** are available on
campus that provide access to the Internet. The 5 **libraries** have 2,090,643 books and
35,698 subscriptions.

Campus Life

There are 374 active organizations on campus, including a drama/theater group,
newspaper, radio station, television station, choral group, and marching band. 18% of
eligible men and 24% of eligible women are members of national **fraternities** and
national **sororities**.

OSU is a member of the NCAA (Division I). **Intercollegiate sports** (some offering
scholarships) include baseball (m), basketball, cross-country running, equestrian sports
(w), football (m), golf, soccer (w), softball (w), tennis, track and field, wrestling (m).

Campus Safety

Student safety services include 24-hour emergency telephone alarm devices, 24-hour
patrols by trained security personnel, student patrols, and electronically operated dormitory entrances.

Applying

OSU requires SAT I or ACT, a high school transcript, class rank, and a minimum high
school GPA of 3.0, and in some cases an interview. It recommends ACT. Application
deadline: rolling admissions. Early admission is possible.

Getting in Last Year
5,591 applied
91% were accepted
3,165 enrolled (62%)
28% from top tenth of their h.s. class
3.50 average high school GPA
32% had SAT verbal scores over 600
39% had SAT math scores over 600
49% had ACT scores over 24
5% had SAT verbal scores over 700
8% had SAT math scores over 700
9% had ACT scores over 30
23 National Merit Scholars
312 valedictorians

Graduation and After
70% had job offers within 6 months
400 organizations recruited on campus

Financial Matters
$2794 resident tuition and fees (2001–02)
$7518 nonresident tuition and fees (2001–02)
$4856 room and board
80% average percent of need met
$7208 average financial aid amount received
    per undergraduate (2000–01)

Oklahoma Wesleyan University

SMALL-TOWN SETTING ■ PRIVATE ■ INDEPENDENT RELIGIOUS ■ COED
BARTLESVILLE, OKLAHOMA

Web site: www.okwu.edu

Contact: Mr. Marty Carver, Director of Enrollment Services, 2201 Silver Lake Road, Bartlesville, OK 74006-6299

Telephone: 918-335-6219 or toll-free 800-468-6292 (in-state) **Fax:** 918-335-6229

E-mail: admissions@okwu.edu

Getting in Last Year
427 applied
60% were accepted
31% from top tenth of their h.s. class
3.37 average high school GPA
32% had SAT verbal scores over 600
19% had SAT math scores over 600
2% had SAT verbal scores over 700
4% had SAT math scores over 700
2 National Merit Scholars
9 valedictorians

Graduation and After
10% pursued further study (6% theology, 2% arts and sciences, 1% business)

Financial Matters
58% average percent of need met
$6466 average financial aid amount received per undergraduate

Academics

Oklahoma Wesleyan University awards associate, bachelor's, and master's **degrees**. Challenging opportunities include advanced placement credit, student-designed majors, independent study, and a senior project. Special programs include cooperative education, internships, summer session for credit, and off-campus study. A complete listing of majors at Oklahoma Wesleyan University appears in the Majors Index beginning on page 430.

The **faculty** at Oklahoma Wesleyan University has 37 members. The student-faculty ratio is 14:1.

Students of Oklahoma Wesleyan University

The student body is made up of 834 undergraduates. Students come from 26 states and territories and 8 other countries. 54% are from Oklahoma. 2.9% are international students. 5.5% are African American, 7% American Indian, 1.9% Asian American, and 1.9% Hispanic American. 70% returned for their sophomore year.

Facilities and Resources

Student rooms are linked to a campus network. 30 **computers** are available on campus for student use. The **library** has 124,722 books and 300 subscriptions.

Campus Life

There are 10 active organizations on campus, including a newspaper and choral group. No national or local **fraternities** or **sororities**.

Oklahoma Wesleyan University is a member of the NAIA and NCCAA. **Intercollegiate sports** (some offering scholarships) include baseball (m), basketball, golf (m), soccer, softball (w), volleyball (w).

Campus Safety

Student safety services include 24-hour emergency telephone alarm devices, 24-hour patrols by trained security personnel, and electronically operated dormitory entrances.

Applying

Oklahoma Wesleyan University requires SAT I or ACT, a high school transcript, recommendations, and ACT/SAT Min. ACT of 18 or SAT 860. It recommends a minimum high school GPA of 2.0. Application deadline: rolling admissions; 3/31 priority date for financial aid. Early and deferred admission are possible.

PACIFIC LUTHERAN UNIVERSITY

SUBURBAN SETTING ■ PRIVATE ■ INDEPENDENT RELIGIOUS ■ COED
TACOMA, WASHINGTON

Web site: www.plu.edu
Contact: Office of Admissions, Tacoma, WA 98447
Telephone: 253-535-7151 or toll-free 800-274-6758 **Fax:** 253-536-5136
E-mail: admissions@plu.edu

Academics

PLU awards bachelor's and master's **degrees** and post-bachelor's certificates. Challenging opportunities include advanced placement credit, accelerated degree programs, student-designed majors, freshman honors college, an honors program, double majors, independent study, and a senior project. Special programs include cooperative education, internships, summer session for credit, study-abroad, and Army ROTC.

The most frequently chosen **baccalaureate** fields are business/marketing, education, and social sciences and history. A complete listing of majors at PLU appears in the Majors Index beginning on page 430.

The **faculty** at PLU has 227 full-time members, 85% with terminal degrees. The student-faculty ratio is 13:1.

Students of PLU

The student body totals 3,425, of whom 3,144 are undergraduates. 61.1% are women and 38.9% are men. Students come from 40 states and territories and 26 other countries. 74% are from Washington. 7.6% are international students. 2.1% are African American, 0.6% American Indian, 5.5% Asian American, and 1.8% Hispanic American. 82% returned for their sophomore year.

Facilities and Resources

Student rooms are linked to a campus network. 200 **computers** are available on campus that provide access to the Internet. The **library** has 365,021 books and 2,186 subscriptions.

Campus Life

There are 45 active organizations on campus, including a drama/theater group, newspaper, radio station, television station, and choral group. No national or local **fraternities** or **sororities**.

PLU is a member of the NCAA (Division III). **Intercollegiate sports** include baseball (m), basketball, crew, cross-country running, football (m), golf, soccer, softball (w), swimming, tennis, track and field, volleyball (w), wrestling (m).

Campus Safety

Student safety services include late-night transport/escort service, 24-hour emergency telephone alarm devices, 24-hour patrols by trained security personnel, and student patrols.

Applying

PLU requires an essay, SAT I or ACT, a high school transcript, 1 recommendation, and a minimum high school GPA of 2.5, and in some cases an interview. Application deadline: rolling admissions; 3/1 priority date for financial aid. Early and deferred admission are possible.

Getting in Last Year

1,808 applied
80% were accepted
581 enrolled (40%)
36% from top tenth of their h.s. class
3.60 average high school GPA
31% had SAT verbal scores over 600
29% had SAT math scores over 600
58% had ACT scores over 24
4% had SAT verbal scores over 700
5% had SAT math scores over 700
8% had ACT scores over 30
4 National Merit Scholars
22 valedictorians

Graduation and After

42% graduated in 4 years
20% graduated in 5 years
4% graduated in 6 years
13% pursued further study
69% had job offers within 6 months
70 organizations recruited on campus

Financial Matters

$17,728 tuition and fees (2001–02)
$5590 room and board
92% average percent of need met
$15,168 average financial aid amount received per undergraduate (2000–01)

PACIFIC UNIVERSITY

SMALL-TOWN SETTING ■ PRIVATE ■ INDEPENDENT ■ COED
FOREST GROVE, OREGON

Web site: www.pacificu.edu
Contact: Mr. Ian Symmonds, Executive Director of Admissions, 2043 College
Way, Forest Grove, OR 97116-1797
Telephone: 503-359-2218 or toll-free 800-677-6712 **Fax:** 503-359-2975
E-mail: admissions@pacificu.edu

Getting in Last Year

1,176 applied
82% were accepted
315 enrolled (33%)
23% from top tenth of their h.s. class
3.52 average high school GPA
30% had SAT verbal scores over 600
29% had SAT math scores over 600
53% had ACT scores over 24
6% had SAT verbal scores over 700
4% had SAT math scores over 700
9% had ACT scores over 30
11 valedictorians

Graduation and After

34% graduated in 4 years
8% graduated in 5 years
1% graduated in 6 years
40% pursued further study
150 organizations recruited on campus

Financial Matters

$18,545 tuition and fees (2001–02)
$5123 room and board
95% average percent of need met
$15,699 average financial aid amount received
per undergraduate (2000–01 estimated)

Academics

Pacific awards bachelor's, master's, doctoral, and first-professional **degrees**. Challenging opportunities include advanced placement credit, accelerated degree programs, an honors program, double majors, independent study, and a senior project. Special programs include cooperative education, internships, summer session for credit, off-campus study, study-abroad, and Army and Air Force ROTC.

The most frequently chosen **baccalaureate** fields are business/marketing, biological/life sciences, and physical sciences. A complete listing of majors at Pacific appears in the Majors Index beginning on page 430.

The **faculty** at Pacific has 157 full-time members. The student-faculty ratio is 11:1.

Students of Pacific

The student body totals 2,293, of whom 1,169 are undergraduates. 63.2% are women and 36.8% are men. Students come from 19 states and territories and 3 other countries. 45% are from Oregon. 0.7% are international students. 0.4% are African American, 1.6% American Indian, 18.4% Asian American, and 2% Hispanic American. 78% returned for their sophomore year.

Facilities and Resources

Student rooms are linked to a campus network. 150 **computers** are available on campus that provide access to the Internet. The **library** has 1,052 subscriptions.

Campus Life

There are 65 active organizations on campus, including a drama/theater group, newspaper, radio station, and choral group. 10% of eligible men and 17% of eligible women are members of local **fraternities** and local **sororities**.

Pacific is a member of the NCAA (Division III). **Intercollegiate sports** include baseball (m), basketball, cross-country running, golf, soccer, softball (w), tennis, track and field, volleyball (w), wrestling (m).

Campus Safety

Student safety services include late-night transport/escort service, 24-hour emergency telephone alarm devices, and 24-hour patrols by trained security personnel.

Applying

Pacific requires an essay, SAT I or ACT, a high school transcript, 1 recommendation, and a minimum high school GPA of 3.0. It recommends an interview. Application deadline: 8/15. Deferred admission is possible.

THE PENNSYLVANIA STATE UNIVERSITY
UNIVERSITY PARK CAMPUS
SMALL-TOWN SETTING ■ PUBLIC ■ STATE-RELATED ■ COED
UNIVERSITY PARK, PENNSYLVANIA

Web site: www.psu.edu
Contact: Undergraduate Admissions Office, 201 Old Main, University Park, PA 16802
Telephone: 814-865-5471 **Fax:** 814-863-7590
E-mail: admissions@psu.edu

Academics
Penn State awards associate, bachelor's, master's, and doctoral **degrees** and post-bachelor's certificates. Challenging opportunities include advanced placement credit, student-designed majors, freshman honors college, an honors program, double majors, independent study, and a senior project. Special programs include cooperative education, internships, summer session for credit, study-abroad, and Army, Navy and Air Force ROTC.

The most frequently chosen **baccalaureate** fields are business/marketing, engineering/engineering technologies, and education. A complete listing of majors at Penn State appears in the Majors Index beginning on page 430.

The **faculty** at Penn State has 2,085 full-time members, 77% with terminal degrees. The student-faculty ratio is 18:1.

Students of Penn State
The student body totals 40,828, of whom 34,539 are undergraduates. 46.7% are women and 53.3% are men. Students come from 54 states and territories. 77% are from Pennsylvania. 1.7% are international students. 4% are African American, 0.1% American Indian, 5% Asian American, and 3.1% Hispanic American. 92% returned for their sophomore year.

Facilities and Resources
Student rooms are linked to a campus network. 3,589 **computers** are available on campus that provide access to the Internet. The 8 **libraries** have 2,836,144 books and 22,879 subscriptions.

Campus Life
There are 400 active organizations on campus, including a drama/theater group, newspaper, radio station, television station, choral group, and marching band. 14% of eligible men and 11% of eligible women are members of national **fraternities** and national **sororities**.

Penn State is a member of the NCAA (Division I). **Intercollegiate sports** (some offering scholarships) include baseball (m), basketball, cross-country running, fencing, field hockey (w), football (m), golf, gymnastics, lacrosse, soccer, softball (w), swimming, tennis, track and field, volleyball, wrestling (m).

Campus Safety
Student safety services include late-night transport/escort service, 24-hour emergency telephone alarm devices, 24-hour patrols by trained security personnel, student patrols, and electronically operated dormitory entrances.

Applying
Penn State requires SAT I or ACT, a high school transcript, and a minimum high school GPA of 2.0, and in some cases an interview and 1 recommendation. It recommends an essay. Application deadline: rolling admissions. Early and deferred admission are possible.

Getting in Last Year
27,899 applied
57% were accepted
6,122 enrolled (38%)
42% from top tenth of their h.s. class
3.57 average high school GPA
42% had SAT verbal scores over 600
59% had SAT math scores over 600
8% had SAT verbal scores over 700
15% had SAT math scores over 700

Graduation and After
43% graduated in 4 years
33% graduated in 5 years
5% graduated in 6 years
70% had job offers within 6 months
970 organizations recruited on campus

Financial Matters
$7396 resident tuition and fees (2001–02)
$15,522 nonresident tuition and fees (2001–02)
$5310 room and board
69% average percent of need met
$10,032 average financial aid amount received per undergraduate (2000–01)

PEPPERDINE UNIVERSITY

SMALL-TOWN SETTING ■ PRIVATE ■ INDEPENDENT RELIGIOUS ■ COED
MALIBU, CALIFORNIA

Web site: www.pepperdine.edu
Contact: Mr. Paul A. Long, Dean of Admission, 24255 Pacific Coast
  Highway, Malibu, CA 90263-0002
Telephone: 310-456-4392 **Fax:** 310-456-4861
E-mail: admission-seaver@pepperdine.edu

Getting in Last Year
5,105 applied
35% were accepted
3.79 average high school GPA
65% had SAT verbal scores over 600
68% had SAT math scores over 600
87% had ACT scores over 24
16% had SAT verbal scores over 700
18% had SAT math scores over 700
39% had ACT scores over 30

Graduation and After
63% pursued further study
40% had job offers within 6 months
78 organizations recruited on campus

Financial Matters
$25,250 tuition and fees (2001–02)
$7580 room and board
93% average percent of need met
$21,970 average financial aid amount received
  per undergraduate (1999–2000)

Academics

Pepperdine awards bachelor's, master's, doctoral, and first-professional **degrees** (the university is organized into five colleges: Seaver, the School of Law, the School of Business and Management, the School of Public Policy, and the Graduate School of Education and Psychology. Seaver College is the undergraduate, residential, liberal arts school of the University and is committed to providing education of outstanding academic quality with particular attention to Christian values). Challenging opportunities include advanced placement credit, accelerated degree programs, student-designed majors, an honors program, double majors, independent study, and a senior project. Special programs include internships, summer session for credit, study-abroad, and Army, Navy and Air Force ROTC. A complete listing of majors at Pepperdine appears in the Majors Index beginning on page 430.

The **faculty** at Pepperdine has 174 full-time members, 100% with terminal degrees. The student-faculty ratio is 13:1.

Students of Pepperdine

The student body totals 7,317, of whom 2,849 are undergraduates. 59.4% are women and 40.6% are men. Students come from 51 states and territories and 70 other countries. 50% are from California. 88% returned for their sophomore year.

Facilities and Resources

Student rooms are linked to a campus network. 292 **computers** are available on campus for student use. The 3 **libraries** have 515,238 books and 3,882 subscriptions.

Campus Life

There are 50 active organizations on campus, including a drama/theater group, newspaper, radio station, television station, and choral group. 25% of eligible men and 25% of eligible women are members of national **fraternities** and national **sororities**.

Pepperdine is a member of the NCAA (Division I). **Intercollegiate sports** (some offering scholarships) include baseball (m), basketball, cross-country running, golf, soccer (w), swimming (w), tennis, volleyball, water polo (m).

Campus Safety

Student safety services include front gate security, 24-hour security in residence halls, controlled access, crime prevention programs, late-night transport/escort service, 24-hour emergency telephone alarm devices, 24-hour patrols by trained security personnel, and student patrols.

Applying

Pepperdine requires an essay, SAT I or ACT, a high school transcript, and 2 recommendations. It recommends an interview. Application deadline: 1/15; 4/1 for financial aid, with a 2/15 priority date.

Pitzer College

Suburban setting ■ Private ■ Independent ■ Coed
Claremont, California

Web site: www.pitzer.edu
Contact: Dr. Arnaldo Rodriguez, Vice President for Admission and Financial
Aid, 1050 North Mills Avenue, Claremont, CA 91711-6101
Telephone: 909-621-8129 or toll-free 800-748-9371 **Fax:** 909-621-8770
E-mail: admission@pitzer.edu

Academics

Pitzer awards bachelor's **degrees**. Challenging opportunities include advanced placement credit, student-designed majors, an honors program, double majors, independent study, and a senior project. Special programs include cooperative education, internships, off-campus study, and study-abroad.

The most frequently chosen **baccalaureate** fields are social sciences and history, psychology, and visual/performing arts. A complete listing of majors at Pitzer appears in the Majors Index beginning on page 430.

The **faculty** at Pitzer has 56 full-time members, 98% with terminal degrees. The student-faculty ratio is 12:1.

Students of Pitzer

The student body is made up of 921 undergraduates. 62.4% are women and 37.6% are men. Students come from 44 states and territories and 14 other countries. 54% are from California. 3.5% are international students. 6% are African American, 0.9% American Indian, 10.3% Asian American, and 14.4% Hispanic American. 82% returned for their sophomore year.

Facilities and Resources

Student rooms are linked to a campus network. 96 **computers** are available on campus that provide access to the Internet. The 4 **libraries** have 2,000,000 books and 6,000 subscriptions.

Campus Life

There are 75 active organizations on campus, including a drama/theater group, newspaper, radio station, and choral group. No national or local **fraternities** or **sororities**.

Pitzer is a member of the NCAA (Division III). **Intercollegiate sports** include baseball (m), basketball, cross-country running, football (m), golf (m), soccer, softball (w), swimming, tennis, track and field, volleyball (w), water polo, wrestling (m).

Campus Safety

Student safety services include late-night transport/escort service, 24-hour emergency telephone alarm devices, 24-hour patrols by trained security personnel, and electronically operated dormitory entrances.

Applying

Pitzer requires an essay, SAT I or ACT, a high school transcript, and 3 recommendations. It recommends SAT II Subject Tests, SAT II: Writing Test, and an interview. Application deadline: 1/15; 2/1 for financial aid. Early and deferred admission are possible.

Pitzer, a liberal arts and sciences college, offers students membership in a closely knit academic community and access to the resources of a midsized university through its partnership with the Claremont Colleges. Pitzer's distinctive curriculum encourages students to discover the relationship among different academic subjects (interdisciplinary learning), gives students a chance to see issues and events from different cultural perspectives (intercultural understanding), and shows students how to take responsibility for making the world a better place (social responsibility). Pitzer believes that students should have the freedom and responsibility for selecting what courses to take. Therefore, required general education courses are few.

Getting in Last Year
2,282 applied
54% were accepted
224 enrolled (18%)
32% from top tenth of their h.s. class
3.53 average high school GPA
64% had SAT verbal scores over 600
53% had SAT math scores over 600
82% had ACT scores over 24
16% had SAT verbal scores over 700
5% had SAT math scores over 700
23% had ACT scores over 30

Graduation and After
55% graduated in 4 years
9% graduated in 5 years
1% graduated in 6 years
61% had job offers within 6 months
23 organizations recruited on campus

Financial Matters
$27,030 tuition and fees (2001–02)
$6900 room and board
100% average percent of need met
$25,375 average financial aid amount received
  per undergraduate

POINT LOMA NAZARENE UNIVERSITY

SUBURBAN SETTING ■ PRIVATE ■ INDEPENDENT RELIGIOUS ■ COED
SAN DIEGO, CALIFORNIA

Getting in Last Year

1,365 applied
76% were accepted
474 enrolled (46%)
25% from top tenth of their h.s. class
3.62 average high school GPA
28% had SAT verbal scores over 600
31% had SAT math scores over 600
45% had ACT scores over 24
4% had SAT verbal scores over 700
3% had SAT math scores over 700
6% had ACT scores over 30
18 valedictorians

Graduation and After

28% graduated in 4 years
12% graduated in 5 years
2% graduated in 6 years
100 organizations recruited on campus

Financial Matters

$15,300 tuition and fees (2001–02)
$6320 room and board
76% average percent of need met
$11,493 average financial aid amount received
per undergraduate (1999–2000)

Web site: www.ptloma.edu

Contact: Mr. Scott Shoemaker, Director of Admissions, 3900 Lomaland
Drive, San Diego, CA 92106-2899

Telephone: 619-849-2273 or toll-free 800-733-7770 (out-of-state) **Fax:**
619-849-2601

E-mail: admissions@ptloma.edu

Academics

PLNU awards bachelor's and master's **degrees** and post-bachelor's and post-master's
certificates. Challenging opportunities include advanced placement credit, double
majors, and a senior project. Special programs include internships, summer session for
credit, off-campus study, study-abroad, and Army, Navy and Air Force ROTC.

The most frequently chosen **baccalaureate** fields are business/marketing, liberal
arts/general studies, and health professions and related sciences. A complete listing of
majors at PLNU appears in the Majors Index beginning on page 430.

The **faculty** at PLNU has 137 full-time members, 61% with terminal degrees. The
student-faculty ratio is 16:1.

Students of PLNU

The student body totals 2,881, of whom 2,353 are undergraduates. 59.5% are women
and 40.5% are men. Students come from 36 states and territories and 14 other countries.
78% are from California. 1.5% are international students. 0.8% are African American,
0.7% American Indian, 4.2% Asian American, and 6.9% Hispanic American. 79%
returned for their sophomore year.

Facilities and Resources

Student rooms are linked to a campus network. 125 **computers** are available on campus
for student use. The **library** has 120,991 books and 637 subscriptions.

Campus Life

There are 30 active organizations on campus, including a drama/theater group,
newspaper, radio station, and choral group. 3% of eligible men and 5% of eligible
women are members of national **sororities**, local **fraternities**, and local sororities.

PLNU is a member of the NAIA. **Intercollegiate sports** (some offering scholarships) include baseball (m), basketball, cross-country running, golf (m), soccer (m),
softball (w), tennis, track and field, volleyball (w).

Campus Safety

Student safety services include late-night transport/escort service, 24-hour patrols by
trained security personnel, and student patrols.

Applying

PLNU requires an essay, SAT I or ACT, a high school transcript, 2 recommendations,
and a minimum high school GPA of 2.8, and in some cases an interview. It recommends
SAT I. Application deadline: 3/1; 3/15 priority date for financial aid. Deferred admission
is possible.

POLYTECHNIC UNIVERSITY, BROOKLYN CAMPUS

URBAN SETTING ■ PRIVATE ■ INDEPENDENT ■ COED
BROOKLYN, NEW YORK

Web site: www.poly.edu
Contact: Mr. John S. Kerge, Dean of Admissions, Six Metrotech Center,
  Brooklyn, NY 11201-2990
Telephone: 718-260-3100 or toll-free 800-POLYTECH **Fax:** 718-260-3446
E-mail: admitme@poly.edu

Academics

Polytechnic awards bachelor's, master's, and doctoral **degrees** (all information given is for both Brooklyn and Farmingdale campuses). Challenging opportunities include advanced placement credit, accelerated degree programs, an honors program, double majors, and a senior project. Special programs include cooperative education, internships, summer session for credit, and Air Force ROTC.

The most frequently chosen **baccalaureate** fields are engineering/engineering technologies, computer/information sciences, and liberal arts/general studies. A complete listing of majors at Polytechnic appears in the Majors Index beginning on page 430.

The **faculty** at Polytechnic has 169 full-time members, 86% with terminal degrees. The student-faculty ratio is 12:1.

Students of Polytechnic

The student body totals 3,051, of whom 1,709 are undergraduates. 20.2% are women and 79.8% are men. Students come from 10 states and territories and 6 other countries. 97% are from New York. 5.9% are international students. 9.8% are African American, 0.2% American Indian, 40.5% Asian American, and 6.1% Hispanic American. 81% returned for their sophomore year.

Facilities and Resources

350 **computers** are available on campus that provide access to the Internet. The **library** has 148,000 books and 613 subscriptions.

Campus Life

There are 50 active organizations on campus, including a newspaper and radio station. 6% of eligible men and 3% of eligible women are members of national **fraternities**, national **sororities**, local fraternities, and a coed fraternity.

Polytechnic is a member of the NCAA (Division III). **Intercollegiate sports** include baseball (m), basketball, cross-country running, soccer (m), softball (w), tennis, track and field, volleyball.

Campus Safety

Student safety services include 24-hour patrols by trained security personnel.

Applying

Polytechnic requires an essay, SAT I or ACT, a high school transcript, and 2 recommendations. It recommends SAT II Subject Tests, SAT II: Writing Test, and an interview. Application deadline: rolling admissions. Deferred admission is possible.

Polytechnic University is the second-oldest engineering, science, and technology university in the country and is rated consistently high by the Gourman Report for all undergraduate programs. The location of Polytechnic's campuses puts students at the center of the world's greatest laboratory—the New York metro area—where access to cooperative education and internship opportunities in engineering, the sciences, communications, computer science, medicine, law, business, finance, and education abounds. Poly students have access to co-op or internship opportunities at more than 250 companies in the metropolitan area. In addition, the University has begun a $100-million campus expansion, adding new classrooms, labs, academic buildings, and a 400-bed dormitory. Polytechnic's 36,000 alumni include patent holders, Nobel Prize winners, and hundreds of chief executive officers at major U.S. firms in the metropolitan New York area and around the country.

Getting in Last Year
1,573 applied
69% were accepted
454 enrolled (42%)
3.40 average high school GPA
39% had SAT verbal scores over 600
87% had SAT math scores over 600
4% had SAT verbal scores over 700
25% had SAT math scores over 700

Graduation and After
39% graduated in 4 years
15% graduated in 5 years
4% graduated in 6 years
5% pursued further study
91% had job offers within 6 months
120 organizations recruited on campus

Financial Matters
$22,940 tuition and fees (2001–02)
$5250 room and board
86% average percent of need met
$18,024 average financial aid amount received per undergraduate (2000–01)

POMONA COLLEGE

SUBURBAN SETTING ■ PRIVATE ■ INDEPENDENT ■ COED
CLAREMONT, CALIFORNIA

Web site: www.pomona.edu
Contact: Mr. Bruce Poch, Vice President and Dean of Admissions, 333 North College Way, Claremont, CA 91711
Telephone: 909-621-8134 **Fax:** 909-621-8952
E-mail: admissions@pomona.edu

Pomona College is located in Claremont, California, 35 miles east of Los Angeles, and is the founding member of the Claremont Colleges. Recognized as one of the nation's premier liberal arts colleges, Pomona offers a comprehensive undergraduate curriculum and enrolls students from around the nation and across class and ethnicity. With financial resources among the strongest of any national liberal arts college, Pomona offers a broad range of resources and opportunities, including an extensive study-abroad program. The community enjoys academic, cultural, and extracurricular activities usually found only at large universities, with all of the benefits and advantages of a small college.

Getting in Last Year
3,712 applied
29% were accepted
393 enrolled (36%)
84% from top tenth of their h.s. class
3.90 average high school GPA
96% had SAT verbal scores over 600
95% had SAT math scores over 600
99% had ACT scores over 24
66% had SAT verbal scores over 700
69% had SAT math scores over 700
67% had ACT scores over 30
45 National Merit Scholars
6 class presidents
47 valedictorians

Graduation and After
83% graduated in 4 years
5% graduated in 5 years
1% graduated in 6 years
33% pursued further study (17% arts and sciences, 9% law, 9% medicine)
60% had job offers within 6 months
143 organizations recruited on campus

Financial Matters
$25,010 tuition and fees (2001–02)
$8950 room and board
100% average percent of need met
$24,200 average financial aid amount received per undergraduate

Academics
Pomona awards bachelor's **degrees**. Challenging opportunities include advanced placement credit, student-designed majors, double majors, independent study, and a senior project. Special programs include internships, off-campus study, and study-abroad. A complete listing of majors at Pomona appears in the Majors Index beginning on page 430.

The **faculty** at Pomona has 172 full-time members, 100% with terminal degrees. The student-faculty ratio is 9:1.

Students of Pomona
The student body is made up of 1,577 undergraduates. 49% are women and 51% are men. Students come from 49 states and territories. 33% are from California. 1.8% are international students. 5.6% are African American, 0.3% American Indian, 15.7% Asian American, and 8.9% Hispanic American. 98% returned for their sophomore year.

Facilities and Resources
Student rooms are linked to a campus network. 180 **computers** are available on campus that provide access to the Internet. The 4 **libraries** have 2,088,471 books and 5,733 subscriptions.

Campus Life
There are 280 active organizations on campus, including a drama/theater group, newspaper, radio station, and choral group. 6% of eligible men are members of local **fraternities** and local coed fraternities.

Pomona is a member of the NCAA (Division III). **Intercollegiate sports** include baseball (m), basketball, cross-country running, football (m), golf, soccer, softball (w), swimming, tennis, track and field, volleyball (w), water polo.

Campus Safety
Student safety services include late-night transport/escort service, 24-hour emergency telephone alarm devices, 24-hour patrols by trained security personnel, and electronically operated dormitory entrances.

Applying
Pomona requires an essay, SAT I or ACT, 3 SAT II Subject Tests (including SAT II: Writing Test), a high school transcript, and 2 recommendations. It recommends an interview, portfolio or tapes for art and performing arts programs, and a minimum high school GPA of 3.0. Application deadline: 1/2; 2/1 for financial aid. Early and deferred admission are possible.

PRESBYTERIAN COLLEGE

SMALL-TOWN SETTING ■ PRIVATE ■ INDEPENDENT RELIGIOUS ■ COED
CLINTON, SOUTH CAROLINA

Web site: www.presby.edu

Contact: Mr. Richard Dana Paul, Vice President of Enrollment and Dean of
  Admissions, South Broad Street, Clinton, SC 29325

Telephone: 864-833-8229 or toll-free 800-476-7272 **Fax:** 864-833-8481

E-mail: rdpaul@admin.presby.edu

Academics

Presbyterian College awards bachelor's **degrees**. Challenging opportunities include
advanced placement credit, freshman honors college, an honors program, double majors,
independent study, and a senior project. Special programs include internships, summer
session for credit, off-campus study, study-abroad, and Army ROTC.

The most frequently chosen **baccalaureate** fields are business/marketing, biological/
life sciences, and psychology. A complete listing of majors at Presbyterian College appears in the Majors Index beginning on page 430.

The **faculty** at Presbyterian College has 79 full-time members, 90% with terminal
degrees. The student-faculty ratio is 13:1.

Students of Presbyterian College

The student body is made up of 1,202 undergraduates. 56.1% are women and 43.9% are
men. Students come from 26 states and territories and 7 other countries. 60% are from
South Carolina. 4.6% are African American, 0.8% Asian American, and 0.9% Hispanic
American. 86% returned for their sophomore year.

Facilities and Resources

Student rooms are linked to a campus network. 130 **computers** are available on campus
that provide access to the Internet. The **library** has 149,273 books and 797 subscriptions.

Campus Life

There are 60 active organizations on campus, including a drama/theater group,
newspaper, radio station, and choral group. 44% of eligible men and 41% of eligible
women are members of national **fraternities** and national **sororities**.

Presbyterian College is a member of the NCAA (Division II). **Intercollegiate sports**
(some offering scholarships) include baseball (m), basketball, cross-country running,
football (m), golf (m), riflery, soccer, softball (w), tennis, volleyball (w).

Campus Safety

Student safety services include late-night transport/escort service, 24-hour emergency
telephone alarm devices, 24-hour patrols by trained security personnel, and electronically operated dormitory entrances.

Applying

Presbyterian College requires an essay, SAT I or ACT, a high school transcript, and 1
recommendation. It recommends an interview. Application deadline: 4/1; 3/1 priority
date for financial aid. Deferred admission is possible.

Presbyterian College—with
51 national and
international scholarship
recipients in recent years—provides
an environment that nurtures the
best and brightest. Students respect
and live by a strong Honor Code,
and nearly half volunteer for
community service. Students may
also participate in a comprehensive
Honors Program or study abroad in
locations around the world. To
prepare for graduate school and the
job market, students may intern or
conduct research with professors. A
scholarship program for outstanding
students is supported by one of the
largest per-student endowments in
the region.

Getting in Last Year

951 applied
78% were accepted
322 enrolled (43%)
29% from top tenth of their h.s. class
3.3 average high school GPA
30% had SAT verbal scores over 600
37% had SAT math scores over 600
44% had ACT scores over 24
4% had SAT verbal scores over 700
5% had SAT math scores over 700
6% had ACT scores over 30

Graduation and After

81% graduated in 4 years
10% graduated in 5 years
2% graduated in 6 years
Graduates pursuing further study: 4% arts and
  sciences, 3% law, 2% education
76% had job offers within 6 months
45 organizations recruited on campus

Financial Matters

$18,200 tuition and fees (2001–02)
$5156 room and board
83% average percent of need met
$16,358 average financial aid amount received
  per undergraduate (2000–01 estimated)

PRINCETON UNIVERSITY

SUBURBAN SETTING ■ PRIVATE ■ INDEPENDENT ■ COED
PRINCETON, NEW JERSEY

Web site: www.princeton.edu
Contact: Mr. Fred A. Hargadon, Dean of Admission, PO Box 430, Princeton, NJ 08544
Telephone: 609-258-3062 **Fax:** 609-258-6743

The 4th-oldest college in the country, Princeton was chartered in 1746. Any list of the most frequently cited strengths of Princeton would doubtless include the following: the quality of its academic programs, its relatively small size combined with the resources of one of the world's major research universities, and the emphasis it has always placed on undergraduate education. Distinctive features of Princeton also include its focus on independent work in a student's junior and senior years and the highly participatory nature of the student body.

Getting in Last Year
14,288 applied
12% were accepted
1,185 enrolled (71%)
93% from top tenth of their h.s. class
3.83 average high school GPA
96% had SAT verbal scores over 600
97% had SAT math scores over 600
67% had SAT verbal scores over 700
73% had SAT math scores over 700

Graduation and After
91% graduated in 4 years
5% graduated in 5 years
1% graduated in 6 years
47.1% had job offers within 6 months
300 organizations recruited on campus

Financial Matters
$26,160 tuition and fees (2001–02)
$7453 room and board
100% average percent of need met
$21,909 average financial aid amount received per undergraduate (2000–01)

Academics

Princeton awards bachelor's, master's, and doctoral **degrees**. Challenging opportunities include advanced placement credit, accelerated degree programs, student-designed majors, an honors program, independent study, and a senior project. Special programs include cooperative education, internships, off-campus study, study-abroad, and Army and Air Force ROTC.

The most frequently chosen **baccalaureate** fields are social sciences and history, engineering/engineering technologies, and biological/life sciences. A complete listing of majors at Princeton appears in the Majors Index beginning on page 430.

The **faculty** at Princeton has 781 full-time members, 95% with terminal degrees. The student-faculty ratio is 6:1.

Students of Princeton

The student body totals 6,668, of whom 4,744 are undergraduates. 48.2% are women and 51.8% are men. Students come from 53 states and territories and 66 other countries. 14% are from New Jersey. 6.9% are international students. 7.9% are African American, 0.5% American Indian, 12.1% Asian American, and 6.4% Hispanic American. 97% returned for their sophomore year.

Facilities and Resources

Student rooms are linked to a campus network. 500 **computers** are available on campus for student use. The 23 **libraries** have 5,095,379 books and 34,348 subscriptions.

Campus Life

There are 174 active organizations on campus, including a drama/theater group, newspaper, radio station, choral group, and marching band. 70% of eligible men and 70% of eligible women are members of eating clubs.

Princeton is a member of the NCAA (Division I). **Intercollegiate sports** include baseball (m), basketball, crew, cross-country running, fencing, field hockey (w), football (m), golf, ice hockey, lacrosse, soccer, softball (w), squash, swimming, tennis, track and field, volleyball, water polo, wrestling (m).

Campus Safety

Student safety services include late-night transport/escort service, 24-hour emergency telephone alarm devices, 24-hour patrols by trained security personnel, student patrols, and electronically operated dormitory entrances.

Applying

Princeton requires an essay, SAT II Subject Tests, SAT I or ACT, a high school transcript, and 3 recommendations. It recommends an interview. Application deadline: 1/1; 2/1 priority date for financial aid. Early and deferred admission are possible.

PROVIDENCE COLLEGE

SUBURBAN SETTING ■ PRIVATE ■ INDEPENDENT RELIGIOUS ■ COED
PROVIDENCE, RHODE ISLAND

Web site: www.providence.edu
Contact: Mr. Christopher Lydon, Dean of Enrollment Management, River Avenue and Eaton Street, Providence, RI 02918
Telephone: 401-865-2535 or toll-free 800-721-6444 **Fax:** 401-865-2826
E-mail: pcadmiss@providence.edu

Academics

PC awards associate, bachelor's, and master's **degrees**. Challenging opportunities include advanced placement credit, student-designed majors, an honors program, double majors, independent study, and a senior project. Special programs include cooperative education, internships, summer session for credit, study-abroad, and Army ROTC.

The most frequently chosen **baccalaureate** fields are business/marketing, social sciences and history, and education. A complete listing of majors at PC appears in the Majors Index beginning on page 430.

The **faculty** at PC has 259 full-time members, 80% with terminal degrees. The student-faculty ratio is 13:1.

Students of PC

The student body totals 5,308, of whom 4,389 are undergraduates. 57.5% are women and 42.5% are men. Students come from 43 states and territories and 16 other countries. 25% are from Rhode Island. 1% are international students. 1.5% are African American, 1.4% Asian American, and 4.1% Hispanic American. 92% returned for their sophomore year.

Facilities and Resources

Student rooms are linked to a campus network. 150 **computers** are available on campus that provide access to the Internet. The **library** has 383,396 books and 1,812 subscriptions.

Campus Life

There are 94 active organizations on campus, including a drama/theater group, newspaper, radio station, television station, and choral group. No national or local **fraternities** or **sororities**.

PC is a member of the NCAA (Division I). **Intercollegiate sports** (some offering scholarships) include basketball, cross-country running, field hockey (w), ice hockey, lacrosse (m), soccer, softball (w), swimming, tennis (w), track and field, volleyball (w).

Campus Safety

Student safety services include late-night transport/escort service, 24-hour emergency telephone alarm devices, 24-hour patrols by trained security personnel, student patrols, and electronically operated dormitory entrances.

Applying

PC requires an essay, SAT I or ACT, a high school transcript, and 2 recommendations. It recommends SAT II Subject Tests, SAT II: Writing Test, an interview, and a minimum high school GPA of 3.25. Application deadline: 1/15; 2/1 for financial aid. Early and deferred admission are possible.

Providence College (PC) is the only liberal arts college in the U.S. that was founded and administered by the Dominican Friars, a Catholic teaching order whose heritage spans nearly 800 years. The College is not only concerned with the rigors of intellectual life but also recognizes the importance of students' experiences outside the classroom, including service to others. Scholarship, service, and the exuberant PC spirit—these are the qualities that shape the character of Providence College. The 105-acre campus of Providence College, situated in Rhode Island's capital city, is removed from the traffic and noise of the metropolitan area but still remains close to the many cultural and educational offerings of Providence, a city that is enjoying a lively urban renaissance. The city is located only an hour's drive from Boston and just a few hours' drive from New York City. Interstate bus, train, and air transportation are conveniently available.

Getting in Last Year
5,440 applied
57% were accepted
934 enrolled (30%)
37% from top tenth of their h.s. class
3.37 average high school GPA
45% had SAT verbal scores over 600
48% had SAT math scores over 600
65% had ACT scores over 24
8% had SAT verbal scores over 700
5% had SAT math scores over 700
9% had ACT scores over 30
29 National Merit Scholars
38 class presidents
14 valedictorians

Graduation and After
81% graduated in 4 years
2% graduated in 5 years
1% graduated in 6 years
80% had job offers within 6 months
130 organizations recruited on campus

Financial Matters
$19,695 tuition and fees (2001–02)
$7925 room and board
85% average percent of need met
$15,500 average financial aid amount received per undergraduate

QUEEN'S UNIVERSITY AT KINGSTON

URBAN SETTING ■ PUBLIC ■ COED
KINGSTON, ONTARIO

Web site: www.queensu.ca
Contact: Mr. Nicholas Snider, Manager of Student Recruitment, Kingston,
ON K7L 3N6 Canada
Telephone: 613-533-2217 **Fax:** 613-533-6810
E-mail: admissn@post.queensu.ca

Getting in Last Year
21,779 applied
57% were accepted
3.48 average high school GPA
43% had SAT verbal scores over 600
50% had SAT math scores over 600
14% had SAT verbal scores over 700
17% had SAT math scores over 700

Graduation and After
96.7% had job offers within 6 months
325 organizations recruited on campus

Financial Matters
$4728 nonresident tuition and fees (2001–02)
$4711 room and board

Academics

Queen's awards bachelor's, master's, and doctoral **degrees**. Challenging opportunities include accelerated degree programs, student-designed majors, an honors program, and double majors. Special programs include cooperative education, internships, summer session for credit, and study-abroad. A complete listing of majors at Queen's appears in the Majors Index beginning on page 430.

The **faculty** at Queen's has 973 full-time members. The student-faculty ratio is 12:1.

Students of Queen's

The student body totals 18,548, of whom 14,546 are undergraduates. Students come from 13 states and territories and 80 other countries. 89% are from Ontario.

Facilities and Resources

Student rooms are linked to a campus network. 400 **computers** are available on campus for student use. The 8 **libraries** have 3,193,739 books and 10,825 subscriptions.

Campus Life

There are 235 active organizations on campus, including a drama/theater group, newspaper, radio station, choral group, and marching band. No national or local **fraternities** or **sororities**.

Intercollegiate sports include badminton, basketball, crew, cross-country running, fencing, field hockey (w), football (m), golf (m), ice hockey, rugby, skiing (cross-country), soccer, squash, swimming, tennis, track and field, volleyball, water polo, wrestling.

Campus Safety

Student safety services include late-night transport/escort service, 24-hour emergency telephone alarm devices, 24-hour patrols by trained security personnel, student patrols, and electronically operated dormitory entrances.

Applying

Queen's requires SAT I, a high school transcript, and a minimum high school GPA of 2.0, and in some cases an essay, SAT II Subject Tests, an interview, and 1 recommendation. Application deadline: 3/31. Deferred admission is possible.

Quincy University

Small-town setting ■ Private ■ Independent Religious ■ Coed
Quincy, Illinois

Web site: www.quincy.edu
Contact: Mr. Kevin A. Brown, Director of Admissions, 1800 College Avenue,
  Quincy, IL 62301-2699
Telephone: 217-222-8020 ext. 5215 or toll-free 800-688-4295
E-mail: admissions@quincy.edu

Academics

Quincy University awards associate, bachelor's, and master's **degrees**. Challenging opportunities include advanced placement credit, accelerated degree programs, student-designed majors, an honors program, double majors, independent study, and a senior project. Special programs include internships, summer session for credit, and study-abroad.

The most frequently chosen **baccalaureate** fields are business/marketing, education, and protective services/public administration. A complete listing of majors at Quincy University appears in the Majors Index beginning on page 430.

The **faculty** at Quincy University has 62 full-time members, 84% with terminal degrees. The student-faculty ratio is 14:1.

Students of Quincy University

The student body totals 1,319, of whom 1,147 are undergraduates. 56.4% are women and 43.6% are men. Students come from 30 states and territories and 14 other countries. 75% are from Illinois. 1% are international students. 5.7% are African American, 0.2% American Indian, 0.6% Asian American, and 2.1% Hispanic American. 74% returned for their sophomore year.

Facilities and Resources

Student rooms are linked to a campus network. 200 **computers** are available on campus that provide access to the Internet. The **library** has 239,983 books and 814 subscriptions.

Campus Life

There are 41 active organizations on campus, including a drama/theater group, newspaper, radio station, and choral group. 21% of eligible men and 16% of eligible women are members of national **fraternities** and national **sororities**.

Quincy University is a member of the NCAA (Division II). **Intercollegiate sports** (some offering scholarships) include baseball (m), basketball, football (m), golf, soccer, softball (w), tennis, track and field, volleyball.

Campus Safety

Student safety services include late-night transport/escort service, 24-hour emergency telephone alarm devices, 24-hour patrols by trained security personnel, student patrols, and electronically operated dormitory entrances.

Applying

Quincy University requires SAT I or ACT and a high school transcript. It recommends an interview and a minimum high school GPA of 2.0. Application deadline: rolling admissions; 4/15 priority date for financial aid. Early and deferred admission are possible.

> **Q**uincy University (QU) is a dynamic community located in the heart of Quincy, Illinois. The liberal arts–based curriculum and extensive internship program prepare students for their chosen fields; the numerous opportunities for leadership outside the classroom help prepare students to take an active role in society. Strong scholarship opportunities enable students from all walks of life to experience the Quincy advantage. While many things make Quincy unique, most important are the people who make up the University community. QU's Franciscan heritage of complete respect for all individuals and their unique gifts is at the heart of University life.

Getting in Last Year
898 applied
96% were accepted
231 enrolled (27%)
10% from top tenth of their h.s. class
3.14 average high school GPA
20% had SAT verbal scores over 600
20% had SAT math scores over 600
34% had ACT scores over 24
4% had ACT scores over 30
4 valedictorians

Graduation and After
18% pursued further study (9% arts and sciences, 3% law, 2% business)
80% had job offers within 6 months
41 organizations recruited on campus

Financial Matters
$15,430 tuition and fees (2001–02)
$5020 room and board
$13,455 average financial aid amount received per undergraduate (1999–2000)

QUINNIPIAC UNIVERSITY

SUBURBAN SETTING ■ PRIVATE ■ INDEPENDENT ■ COED
HAMDEN, CONNECTICUT

Web site: www.quinnipiac.edu
Contact: Ms. Joan Isaac Mohr, Vice President and Dean of Admissions, 275
Mount Carmel Avenue, Hamden, CT 06518-1940
Telephone: 203-582-8600 or toll-free 800-462-1944 (out-of-state) **Fax:**
203-582-8906
E-mail: admissions@quinnipiac.edu

L ocated on 300 acres,
Quinnipiac is home to 4,600
undergraduate and 2,000
graduate and law students. The
heart of the University is the Arnold
Bernhard Library, with automated
library systems and more than 100
personal computers, which provide
access to electronic resources as
well as the University's own print
collections. With more than 70% of
undergraduates coming from out of
state and 90% of freshmen residing
on campus, there is an active
campus life in an attractive setting
adjacent to the 1,700-acre Sleeping
Giant State Park, an excellent spot
for hiking and walking. Internships,
study-abroad programs, clinical
placements, and career services
prepare students for graduate study
and careers, while clubs, activities,
community service, athletics, and
recreation prepare students for a
productive lifestyle.

Getting in Last Year
7,281 applied
74% were accepted
1,187 enrolled (22%)
21% from top tenth of their h.s. class
3.20 average high school GPA
15% had SAT verbal scores over 600
21% had SAT math scores over 600
50% had ACT scores over 24
2% had SAT verbal scores over 700
2% had SAT math scores over 700
6% had ACT scores over 30
28 valedictorians

Graduation and After
65% graduated in 4 years
4% graduated in 5 years
2% graduated in 6 years
23% pursued further study (7% business, 4%
education, 4% medicine)
84% had job offers within 6 months
125 organizations recruited on campus

Financial Matters
$18,840 tuition and fees (2001–02)
$8530 room and board
70% average percent of need met
$12,195 average financial aid amount received
per undergraduate

Academics

Quinnipiac awards bachelor's, master's, and first-professional **degrees** and post-
bachelor's certificates. Challenging opportunities include advanced placement credit,
student-designed majors, an honors program, double majors, independent study, and a
senior project. Special programs include internships, summer session for credit, study-
abroad, and Army and Air Force ROTC.

The most frequently chosen **baccalaureate** fields are health professions and related
sciences, business/marketing, and liberal arts/general studies. A complete listing of
majors at Quinnipiac appears in the Majors Index beginning on page 430.

The **faculty** at Quinnipiac has 265 full-time members, 78% with terminal degrees.
The student-faculty ratio is 16:1.

Students of Quinnipiac

The student body totals 6,675, of whom 5,056 are undergraduates. 63.1% are women
and 36.9% are men. Students come from 26 states and territories and 15 other countries.
28% are from Connecticut. 0.3% are international students. 2.1% are African American,
0.3% American Indian, 1.8% Asian American, and 3.8% Hispanic American. 83%
returned for their sophomore year.

Facilities and Resources

Student rooms are linked to a campus network. 200 **computers** are available on campus
that provide access to the Internet. The 2 **libraries** have 285,000 books and 4,400
subscriptions.

Campus Life

There are 75 active organizations on campus, including a drama/theater group,
newspaper, radio station, television station, and choral group. 5% of eligible men and 7%
of eligible women are members of national **fraternities**, national **sororities**, and local
sororities.

Quinnipiac is a member of the NCAA. **Intercollegiate sports** (some offering
scholarships) include baseball (m), basketball, cross-country running, field hockey (w),
golf (m), ice hockey, lacrosse, soccer, softball (w), tennis, track and field, volleyball (w).

Campus Safety

Student safety services include late-night transport/escort service, 24-hour emergency
telephone alarm devices, 24-hour patrols by trained security personnel, and electronically operated dormitory entrances.

Applying

Quinnipiac requires an essay, SAT I or ACT, a high school transcript, and 1 recommendation, and in some cases a minimum high school GPA of 3.0. It recommends an
interview and a minimum high school GPA of 2.5. Application deadline: 2/15; 3/1 priority date for financial aid. Early and deferred admission are possible.

RANDOLPH-MACON WOMAN'S COLLEGE

SUBURBAN SETTING ■ PRIVATE ■ INDEPENDENT RELIGIOUS ■ WOMEN ONLY
LYNCHBURG, VIRGINIA

Web site: www.rmwc.edu
Contact: Pat LeDonne, Director of Admissions, 2500 Rivermont Avenue,
Lynchburg, VA 24503-1526
Telephone: 434-947-8100 or toll-free 800-745-7692 **Fax:** 434-947-8996
E-mail: admissions@rmwc.edu

Academics

R-MWC awards bachelor's **degrees**. Challenging opportunities include advanced placement credit, accelerated degree programs, student-designed majors, an honors program,
double majors, independent study, and a senior project. Special programs include internships, off-campus study, and study-abroad.

The most frequently chosen **baccalaureate** fields are social sciences and history,
biological/life sciences, and English. A complete listing of majors at R-MWC appears in
the Majors Index beginning on page 430.

The **faculty** at R-MWC has 72 full-time members, 92% with terminal degrees. The
student-faculty ratio is 9:1.

Students of R-MWC

The student body is made up of 721 undergraduates. Students come from 47 states and
territories and 44 other countries. 50% are from Virginia. 10.8% are international
students. 7% are African American, 0.6% American Indian, 3.1% Asian American, and
3.5% Hispanic American. 76% returned for their sophomore year.

Facilities and Resources

Student rooms are linked to a campus network. 154 **computers** are available on campus
that provide access to the Internet. The **library** has 123,500 books and 1,200 subscriptions.

Campus Life

There are 37 active organizations on campus, including a drama/theater group,
newspaper, radio station, and choral group. No national or local **sororities**.

R-MWC is a member of the NCAA (Division III). **Intercollegiate sports** include
basketball, equestrian sports, field hockey, lacrosse, soccer, softball, swimming, tennis,
volleyball.

Campus Safety

Student safety services include late-night transport/escort service, 24-hour emergency
telephone alarm devices, and 24-hour patrols by trained security personnel.

Applying

R-MWC requires an essay, SAT I or ACT, a high school transcript, and 2 recommendations. It recommends an interview. Application deadline: 3/1; 3/1 priority date for
financial aid. Early and deferred admission are possible.

Individualized education,
self-awareness, and
involvement—these are the
priorities at Randolph-Macon
Woman's College. Students seize
opportunities to study abroad,
participate in internships, conduct
original research with faculty
members, coordinate programs, hold
leadership positions in campus
organizations, and volunteer in the
community. The exciting and
engaging atmosphere fosters
academic excellence and helps
develop leadership potential. Since
class size is small (70% of all
classes have 15 or fewer students),
students have easy access to their
professors. Contemporary facilities
and advanced technology afford
women a competitive edge for
career prospects or advanced study.
The College provides a setting for
learning and living that prepares
women for meaningful personal and
professional lives.

Getting in Last Year
718 applied
87% were accepted
189 enrolled (30%)
43% from top tenth of their h.s. class
3.44 average high school GPA
56% had SAT verbal scores over 600
34% had SAT math scores over 600
70% had ACT scores over 24
19% had SAT verbal scores over 700
3% had SAT math scores over 700
21% had ACT scores over 30
1 National Merit Scholar
3 class presidents
11 valedictorians

Graduation and After
64% graduated in 4 years
1% graduated in 5 years
31% pursued further study (19% arts and
 sciences, 5% education, 2% law)
60% had job offers within 6 months
12 organizations recruited on campus

Financial Matters
$18,470 tuition and fees (2001–02)
$7350 room and board
91% average percent of need met
$18,268 average financial aid amount received
 per undergraduate

REED COLLEGE

SUBURBAN SETTING ■ PRIVATE ■ INDEPENDENT ■ COED
PORTLAND, OREGON

Web site: www.reed.edu
Contact: Mr. Paul Marthers, Dean of Admission, 3203 Southeast Woodstock Boulevard, Portland, OR 97202-8199
Telephone: 503-777-7511 or toll-free 800-547-4750 (out-of-state) **Fax:** 503-777-7553
E-mail: admission@reed.edu

Reed's uniqueness lies in the uncompromising rigor of its academic program and the self-discipline and intellectual curiosity of its students. Ranked first among national undergraduate institutions in percentage of graduates earning PhD's and second in the number of Rhodes Scholars, Reed has long been known as a socially progressive and intellectually dynamic school. The Reed campus features Tudor Gothic brick buildings, state-of-the-art research facilities, and plentiful greenspace, while Portland offers all the advantages of a major city. Reed graduates are leaders in the fields of science and technology, entrepreneurship, social reform, and academia and carry on the school's tradition of scholarship, service, ingenuity, and responsibility.

Getting in Last Year
1,731 applied
71% were accepted
352 enrolled (29%)
51% from top tenth of their h.s. class
3.7 average high school GPA
91% had SAT verbal scores over 600
83% had SAT math scores over 600
98% had ACT scores over 24
49% had SAT verbal scores over 700
24% had SAT math scores over 700
55% had ACT scores over 30
6 National Merit Scholars
18 valedictorians

Graduation and After
Graduates pursuing further study: 36% arts and sciences, 7% law, 5% business
24 organizations recruited on campus

Financial Matters
$26,260 tuition and fees (2001–02)
$7090 room and board
100% average percent of need met
$18,740 average financial aid amount received per undergraduate (2000–01 estimated)

Academics
Reed awards bachelor's and master's **degrees**. Challenging opportunities include advanced placement credit, accelerated degree programs, student-designed majors, double majors, independent study, and a senior project. Special programs include off-campus study, study-abroad, and Army ROTC.

The most frequently chosen **baccalaureate** fields are social sciences and history, psychology, and biological/life sciences. A complete listing of majors at Reed appears in the Majors Index beginning on page 430.

The **faculty** at Reed has 115 full-time members, 87% with terminal degrees. The student-faculty ratio is 10:1.

Students of Reed
The student body totals 1,420, of whom 1,396 are undergraduates. 54.2% are women and 45.8% are men. Students come from 52 states and territories and 31 other countries. 15% are from Oregon. 3.7% are international students. 0.8% are African American, 1.1% American Indian, 4.9% Asian American, and 3.4% Hispanic American. 87% returned for their sophomore year.

Facilities and Resources
Student rooms are linked to a campus network. 190 **computers** are available on campus that provide access to the Internet. The 2 **libraries** have 470,000 books and 1,858 subscriptions.

Campus Life
There are 59 active organizations on campus, including a drama/theater group, newspaper, radio station, and choral group. No national or local **fraternities** or **sororities**.

This institution has no intercollegiate sports.

Campus Safety
Student safety services include 24-hour emergency dispatch, late-night transport/escort service, 24-hour emergency telephone alarm devices, 24-hour patrols by trained security personnel, student patrols, and electronically operated dormitory entrances.

Applying
Reed requires an essay, SAT I or ACT, a high school transcript, and 2 recommendations. It recommends SAT II Subject Tests, SAT II: Writing Test, an interview, and a minimum high school GPA of 3.0. Application deadline: 1/15; 1/15 for financial aid. Early and deferred admission are possible.

REGIS UNIVERSITY

SUBURBAN SETTING ■ PRIVATE ■ INDEPENDENT RELIGIOUS ■ COED
DENVER, COLORADO

Web site: www.regis.edu
Contact: Mr. Vic Davolt, Director of Admissions, 3333 Regis Boulevard, Denver, CO 80221-1099
Telephone: 303-458-4905 or toll-free 800-388-2366 ext. 4900 **Fax:** 303-964-5534
E-mail: regisadm@regis.edu

Academics

Regis University awards bachelor's and master's **degrees**. Challenging opportunities include advanced placement credit, accelerated degree programs, student-designed majors, freshman honors college, an honors program, double majors, independent study, and a senior project. Special programs include cooperative education, internships, summer session for credit, off-campus study, study-abroad, and Army, Navy and Air Force ROTC. A complete listing of majors at Regis University appears in the Majors Index beginning on page 430.

The **faculty** at Regis University has 151 full-time members, 72% with terminal degrees. The student-faculty ratio is 14:1.

Students of Regis University

The student body totals 13,547, of whom 7,450 are undergraduates. Students come from 40 states and territories and 11 other countries. 61% are from Colorado. 0.6% are international students. 3.9% are African American, 0.8% American Indian, 2.5% Asian American, and 8% Hispanic American. 79% returned for their sophomore year.

Facilities and Resources

Student rooms are linked to a campus network. 300 **computers** are available on campus for student use. The **library** has 430,514 books and 7,850 subscriptions.

Campus Life

There are 30 active organizations on campus, including a drama/theater group, newspaper, radio station, and choral group. No national or local **fraternities** or **sororities**.

Regis University is a member of the NCAA (Division II). **Intercollegiate sports** (some offering scholarships) include baseball (m), basketball, golf (m), lacrosse, soccer, softball (w), volleyball (w).

Campus Safety

Student safety services include late-night transport/escort service, 24-hour emergency telephone alarm devices, 24-hour patrols by trained security personnel, student patrols, and electronically operated dormitory entrances.

Applying

Regis University requires an essay, SAT I or ACT, a high school transcript, 1 recommendation, and a minimum high school GPA of 2.2, and in some cases an interview and 2 recommendations. It recommends SAT II Subject Tests. Application deadline: 8/15; 3/5 priority date for financial aid. Deferred admission is possible.

Getting in Last Year
1,245 applied
86% were accepted
16% from top tenth of their h.s. class
3.24 average high school GPA
26% had SAT verbal scores over 600
27% had SAT math scores over 600
46% had ACT scores over 24
6% had SAT verbal scores over 700
5% had SAT math scores over 700
7% had ACT scores over 30
3 class presidents
8 valedictorians

Graduation and After
29% graduated in 4 years
13% graduated in 5 years
2% graduated in 6 years
15% pursued further study
90% had job offers within 6 months
50 organizations recruited on campus

Financial Matters
$18,570 tuition and fees (2001–02)
$7150 room and board
83% average percent of need met
$14,594 average financial aid amount received per undergraduate (1999–2000)

RENSSELAER POLYTECHNIC INSTITUTE
SUBURBAN SETTING ■ PRIVATE ■ INDEPENDENT ■ COED
TROY, NEW YORK

Web site: www.rpi.edu
Contact: Ms. Teresa Duffy, Dean of Enrollment Management, 110 8th Street, Troy, NY 12180-3590
Telephone: 518-276-6216 or toll-free 800-448-6562 **Fax:** 518-276-4072
E-mail: admissions@rpi.edu

Rensselaer celebrates discovery and prepares leaders for the technologically based marketplace. Students are challenged by a rigorous curriculum and taught through new interactive learning methods pioneered at Rensselaer. These methods have earned Rensselaer 3 prestigious awards: the Hesburgh Award, the Boeing Excellence in Education Award, and the Pew Charitable Trust Award for innovation in undergraduate education. Undergraduates have numerous opportunities to conduct research through the university-funded Undergraduate Research Program and to gain valuable job experience in the Cooperative Education Program. Among successful Rensselaer graduates are Washington Roebling, chief engineer of the Brooklyn Bridge; Nancy Fitzroy, the first woman president of the American Society of Mechanical Engineers; and Ray Tomlinson, inventor of e-mail.

Getting in Last Year
5,542 applied
68% were accepted
1,112 enrolled (30%)
61% from top tenth of their h.s. class
67% had SAT verbal scores over 600
93% had SAT math scores over 600
76% had ACT scores over 24
17% had SAT verbal scores over 700
43% had SAT math scores over 700
11% had ACT scores over 30
26 National Merit Scholars
137 valedictorians

Graduation and After
48% graduated in 4 years
25% graduated in 5 years
3% graduated in 6 years
21% pursued further study
80% had job offers within 6 months
377 organizations recruited on campus

Financial Matters
$25,555 tuition and fees (2001–02)
$8308 room and board
90% average percent of need met
$22,727 average financial aid amount received per undergraduate

Academics
Rensselaer awards bachelor's, master's, and doctoral **degrees**. Challenging opportunities include advanced placement credit, accelerated degree programs, student-designed majors, an honors program, double majors, independent study, and a senior project. Special programs include cooperative education, internships, summer session for credit, off-campus study, study-abroad, and Army, Navy and Air Force ROTC.

The most frequently chosen **baccalaureate** fields are engineering/engineering technologies, business/marketing, and computer/information sciences. A complete listing of majors at Rensselaer appears in the Majors Index beginning on page 430.

The **faculty** at Rensselaer has 356 full-time members, 96% with terminal degrees. The student-faculty ratio is 16:1.

Students of Rensselaer
The student body totals 8,106, of whom 5,272 are undergraduates. 24.4% are women and 75.6% are men. Students come from 53 states and territories and 81 other countries. 51% are from New York. 4.6% are international students. 3.8% are African American, 0.4% American Indian, 12.2% Asian American, and 4.6% Hispanic American. 91% returned for their sophomore year.

Facilities and Resources
Student rooms are linked to a campus network. 500 **computers** are available on campus that provide access to the Internet. The 2 **libraries** have 309,171 books and 10,210 subscriptions.

Campus Life
There are 130 active organizations on campus, including a drama/theater group, newspaper, radio station, and choral group. 30% of eligible men and 20% of eligible women are members of national **fraternities**, national **sororities**, local fraternities, and local sororities.

Rensselaer is a member of the NCAA (Division III). **Intercollegiate sports** include baseball (m), basketball, cross-country running, field hockey (w), football (m), golf (m), ice hockey, lacrosse, soccer, softball (w), swimming, tennis, track and field, volleyball (w).

Campus Safety
Student safety services include campus foot patrols at night, late-night transport/escort service, 24-hour emergency telephone alarm devices, 24-hour patrols by trained security personnel, and electronically operated dormitory entrances.

Applying
Rensselaer requires an essay, SAT I or ACT, a high school transcript, and 1 recommendation, and in some cases SAT II Subject Tests and portfolio for architecture and electronic arts programs. Application deadline: 1/1; 2/15 priority date for financial aid. Early and deferred admission are possible.

RHODES COLLEGE

SUBURBAN SETTING ■ PRIVATE ■ INDEPENDENT RELIGIOUS ■ COED
MEMPHIS, TENNESSEE

Web site: www.rhodes.edu
Contact: Mr. David J. Wottle, Dean of Admissions and Financial Aid, 2000 North Parkway, Memphis, TN 38112
Telephone: 901-843-3700 or toll-free 800-844-5969 (out-of-state) **Fax:** 901-843-3631
E-mail: adminfo@rhodes.edu

Academics

Rhodes awards bachelor's and master's **degrees** (master's degree in accounting only). Challenging opportunities include advanced placement credit, accelerated degree programs, student-designed majors, an honors program, double majors, independent study, and a senior project. Special programs include internships, summer session for credit, off-campus study, study-abroad, and Army and Air Force ROTC.

The most frequently chosen **baccalaureate** fields are social sciences and history, business/marketing, and biological/life sciences. A complete listing of majors at Rhodes appears in the Majors Index beginning on page 430.

The **faculty** at Rhodes has 120 full-time members, 92% with terminal degrees. The student-faculty ratio is 12:1.

Students of Rhodes

The student body totals 1,551, of whom 1,535 are undergraduates. 56.8% are women and 43.2% are men. Students come from 43 states and territories. 27% are from Tennessee. 0.5% are international students. 4% are African American, 0.1% American Indian, 2.6% Asian American, and 2% Hispanic American. 89% returned for their sophomore year.

Facilities and Resources

Student rooms are linked to a campus network. 125 **computers** are available on campus for student use. The 4 **libraries** have 263,000 books and 1,200 subscriptions.

Campus Life

There are 44 active organizations on campus, including a drama/theater group, newspaper, and choral group. 55% of eligible men and 58% of eligible women are members of national **fraternities** and national **sororities**.

Rhodes is a member of the NCAA (Division III). **Intercollegiate sports** include baseball (m), basketball, cross-country running, field hockey (w), football (m), golf, soccer, softball (w), swimming, tennis, track and field, volleyball (w).

Campus Safety

Student safety services include 24-hour monitored security cameras in parking areas, fenced campus with monitored access at night, late-night transport/escort service, 24-hour emergency telephone alarm devices, 24-hour patrols by trained security personnel, and student patrols.

Applying

Rhodes requires an essay, SAT I or ACT, a high school transcript, and 2 recommendations. It recommends an interview. Application deadline: 2/1; 3/1 priority date for financial aid. Early and deferred admission are possible.

Getting in Last Year

2,426 applied
64% were accepted
417 enrolled (27%)
53% from top tenth of their h.s. class
3.60 average high school GPA
76% had SAT verbal scores over 600
79% had SAT math scores over 600
96% had ACT scores over 24
26% had SAT verbal scores over 700
17% had SAT math scores over 700
33% had ACT scores over 30
25 National Merit Scholars
29 class presidents
34 valedictorians

Graduation and After

33% pursued further study (15% arts and sciences, 6% law, 5% medicine)
69 organizations recruited on campus

Financial Matters

$20,536 tuition and fees (2001–02)
$5900 room and board
94% average percent of need met
$18,123 average financial aid amount received per undergraduate

RICE UNIVERSITY
URBAN SETTING ■ PRIVATE ■ INDEPENDENT ■ COED
HOUSTON, TEXAS

Web site: www.rice.edu
Contact: Ms. Julie M. Browning, Dean for Undergraduate Admission, PO Box 1892, MS 17, Houston, TX 77251-1892
Telephone: 713-348-RICE or toll-free 800-527-OWLS
E-mail: admission@rice.edu

Getting in Last Year
6,740 applied
23% were accepted
657 enrolled (42%)
85% from top tenth of their h.s. class
88% had SAT verbal scores over 600
92% had SAT math scores over 600
97% had ACT scores over 24
57% had SAT verbal scores over 700
63% had SAT math scores over 700
70% had ACT scores over 30
163 National Merit Scholars
9 class presidents
96 valedictorians

Graduation and After
68% graduated in 4 years
19% graduated in 5 years
3% graduated in 6 years
34% pursued further study
275 organizations recruited on campus

Financial Matters
$17,135 tuition and fees (2001–02)
$7200 room and board
100% average percent of need met
$15,919 average financial aid amount received per undergraduate (2000–01 estimated)

Academics
Rice awards bachelor's, master's, and doctoral **degrees**. Challenging opportunities include advanced placement credit, accelerated degree programs, student-designed majors, an honors program, double majors, independent study, and a senior project. Special programs include internships, summer session for credit, off-campus study, study-abroad, and Army and Navy ROTC.

The most frequently chosen **baccalaureate** fields are social sciences and history, engineering/engineering technologies, and biological/life sciences. A complete listing of majors at Rice appears in the Majors Index beginning on page 430.

The **faculty** at Rice has 471 full-time members, 98% with terminal degrees. The student-faculty ratio is 5:1.

Students of Rice
The student body totals 4,534, of whom 2,890 are undergraduates. 48.2% are women and 51.8% are men. Students come from 52 states and territories and 32 other countries. 54% are from Texas. 2.8% are international students. 6.6% are African American, 0.5% American Indian, 13.6% Asian American, and 10.2% Hispanic American. 96% returned for their sophomore year.

Facilities and Resources
Student rooms are linked to a campus network. 600 **computers** are available on campus that provide access to the Internet. The **library** has 2,000,000 books and 14,000 subscriptions.

Campus Life
There are 197 active organizations on campus, including a drama/theater group, newspaper, radio station, television station, choral group, and marching band. No national or local **fraternities** or **sororities**.

Rice is a member of the NCAA (Division I). **Intercollegiate sports** (some offering scholarships) include baseball (m), basketball, cross-country running, football (m), golf (m), soccer (w), swimming (w), tennis, track and field, volleyball (w).

Campus Safety
Student safety services include late-night transport/escort service, 24-hour emergency telephone alarm devices, 24-hour patrols by trained security personnel, and electronically operated dormitory entrances.

Applying
Rice requires an essay, SAT II Subject Tests, SAT II: Writing Test, SAT I or ACT, a high school transcript, and 2 recommendations. It recommends an interview. Application deadline: 1/2; 3/1 priority date for financial aid. Early and deferred admission are possible.

RIPON COLLEGE

SMALL-TOWN SETTING ■ PRIVATE ■ INDEPENDENT ■ COED
RIPON, WISCONSIN

Web site: www.ripon.edu
Contact: Mr. Scott J. Goplin, Vice President and Dean of Admission and Financial Aid, 300 Seward Street, PO Box 248, Ripon, WI 54971
Telephone: 920-748-8185 or toll-free 800-947-4766 **Fax:** 920-748-8335
E-mail: adminfo@ripon.edu

Academics

Ripon awards bachelor's **degrees**. Challenging opportunities include advanced placement credit, accelerated degree programs, student-designed majors, double majors, and a senior project. Special programs include internships, off-campus study, study-abroad, and Army ROTC.

The most frequently chosen **baccalaureate** fields are trade and industry, English, and education. A complete listing of majors at Ripon appears in the Majors Index beginning on page 430.

The **faculty** at Ripon has 57 full-time members, 96% with terminal degrees. The student-faculty ratio is 15:1.

Students of Ripon

The student body is made up of 903 undergraduates. 52.9% are women and 47.1% are men. Students come from 33 states and territories and 17 other countries. 70% are from Wisconsin. 1.5% are international students. 2.3% are African American, 0.5% American Indian, 1.5% Asian American, and 3.6% Hispanic American. 88% returned for their sophomore year.

Facilities and Resources

Student rooms are linked to a campus network. 150 **computers** are available on campus that provide access to the Internet. The **library** has 164,232 books and 794 subscriptions.

Campus Life

There are 45 active organizations on campus, including a drama/theater group, newspaper, radio station, and choral group. 55% of eligible men and 21% of eligible women are members of national **fraternities**, national **sororities**, local fraternities, and local sororities.

Ripon is a member of the NCAA (Division III). **Intercollegiate sports** include baseball (m), basketball, cross-country running, football (m), golf, soccer, softball (w), swimming, tennis, track and field, volleyball (w).

Campus Safety

Student safety services include late-night transport/escort service, 24-hour emergency telephone alarm devices, 24-hour patrols by trained security personnel, student patrols, and electronically operated dormitory entrances.

Applying

Ripon requires SAT I or ACT, a high school transcript, 1 recommendation, and a minimum high school GPA of 2.0. It recommends an essay and an interview. Application deadline: rolling admissions; 3/1 priority date for financial aid. Deferred admission is possible.

Founded in 1851, Ripon College continues in its steadfast belief that mastery of the liberal arts and sciences is the key to a life of both professional and personal success. Ripon graduates have the abilities, the attitudes, and the values for a contributing and productive life. Each student works closely with faculty and staff members and fellow students to develop the fundamental analytical and communicative skills demanded for success, and all students and staff and faculty members work collaboratively to build a better future for themselves, their country, and the world.

Getting in Last Year
847 applied
84% were accepted
201 enrolled (28%)
21% from top tenth of their h.s. class
3.42 average high school GPA
48% had SAT verbal scores over 600
56% had SAT math scores over 600
50% had ACT scores over 24
4% had SAT verbal scores over 700
12% had SAT math scores over 700
7% had ACT scores over 30

Graduation and After
50% graduated in 4 years
7% graduated in 5 years
1% graduated in 6 years
30% pursued further study (17% arts and sciences, 7% law, 2% medicine)
92% had job offers within 6 months
21 organizations recruited on campus

Financial Matters
$19,500 tuition and fees (2001–02)
$4680 room and board
98% average percent of need met
$16,158 average financial aid amount received per undergraduate

ROCHESTER INSTITUTE OF TECHNOLOGY

SUBURBAN SETTING ■ PRIVATE ■ INDEPENDENT ■ COED
ROCHESTER, NEW YORK

Web site: www.rit.edu
Contact: Mr. Daniel Shelley, Director of Admissions, 60 Lomb Memorial Drive, Rochester, NY 14623-5604
Telephone: 585-475-6631 **Fax:** 585-475-7424
E-mail: admissons@rit.edu

Respected internationally as a leader in career-oriented education, RIT has been an innovative pacesetter since 1829. RIT offers outstanding teaching, a strong foundation in the liberal arts and sciences, modern classroom facilities, and work experience gained through the university's cooperative education program. Innovative programs include microelectronic engineering, imaging science, film/video, biotechnology, international business, and the programs of RIT's National Technical Institute for the Deaf (NTID). RIT draws students from every state and 85 other countries.

Getting in Last Year
8,493 applied
70% were accepted
2,245 enrolled (38%)
32% from top tenth of their h.s. class
3.70 average high school GPA
45% had SAT verbal scores over 600
63% had SAT math scores over 600
74% had ACT scores over 24
8% had SAT verbal scores over 700
15% had SAT math scores over 700
17% had ACT scores over 30
18 National Merit Scholars
40 valedictorians

Graduation and After
10% pursued further study
92% had job offers within 6 months
600 organizations recruited on campus

Financial Matters
$18,966 tuition and fees (2001–02)
$7266 room and board
90% average percent of need met
$14,800 average financial aid amount received per undergraduate (2000–01)

Academics

RIT awards associate, bachelor's, master's, and doctoral **degrees** and post-bachelor's and post-master's certificates. Challenging opportunities include advanced placement credit, accelerated degree programs, student-designed majors, an honors program, independent study, and a senior project. Special programs include cooperative education, internships, summer session for credit, off-campus study, study-abroad, and Army, Navy and Air Force ROTC.

The most frequently chosen **baccalaureate** fields are engineering/engineering technologies, visual/performing arts, and computer/information sciences. A complete listing of majors at RIT appears in the Majors Index beginning on page 430.

The **faculty** at RIT has 655 full-time members, 80% with terminal degrees. The student-faculty ratio is 14:1.

Students of RIT

The student body totals 14,430, of whom 12,029 are undergraduates. 31.8% are women and 68.2% are men. Students come from 50 states and territories and 85 other countries. 57% are from New York. 4.9% are international students. 4.7% are African American, 0.4% American Indian, 6.3% Asian American, and 3.1% Hispanic American. 87% returned for their sophomore year.

Facilities and Resources

Student rooms are linked to a campus network. 2,500 **computers** are available on campus that provide access to student account information and the Internet. The **library** has 350,000 books and 4,305 subscriptions.

Campus Life

There are 170 active organizations on campus, including a drama/theater group, newspaper, radio station, and choral group. 7% of eligible men and 5% of eligible women are members of national **fraternities**, national **sororities**, local fraternities, and local sororities.

RIT is a member of the NCAA (Division III). **Intercollegiate sports** include baseball (m), basketball, crew, cross-country running, ice hockey, lacrosse, soccer, softball (w), swimming, tennis, track and field, volleyball (w), wrestling (m).

Campus Safety

Student safety services include late-night transport/escort service, 24-hour emergency telephone alarm devices, 24-hour patrols by trained security personnel, and student patrols.

Applying

RIT requires an essay, SAT I or ACT, and a high school transcript, and in some cases portfolio for art program. It recommends an interview, 1 recommendation, and a minimum high school GPA of 3.0. Application deadline: 3/15; 3/1 priority date for financial aid. Early and deferred admission are possible.

ROCKHURST UNIVERSITY

URBAN SETTING ■ PRIVATE ■ INDEPENDENT RELIGIOUS ■ COED
KANSAS CITY, MISSOURI

Web site: www.rockhurst.edu
Contact: Mr. Phillip Gebauer, Director of Undergraduate Admissions, 1100 Rockhurst Road, Kansas City, MO 64110-2561
Telephone: 816-501-4100 or toll-free 800-842-6776 **Fax:** 816-501-4142
E-mail: admission@rockhurst.edu

R ockhurst University's mission is best defined as "Learning, Leadership and Service in the Jesuit Tradition." Rockhurst prides itself on teaching students not what to think but how to think. A Rockhurst education is education for citizenship: graduates are successful leaders who serve their communities and the world.

Academics

Rockhurst awards bachelor's and master's **degrees** and post-bachelor's certificates. Challenging opportunities include advanced placement credit, accelerated degree programs, freshman honors college, an honors program, double majors, independent study, and a senior project. Special programs include cooperative education, internships, summer session for credit, off-campus study, study-abroad, and Army ROTC.

The most frequently chosen **baccalaureate** fields are business/marketing, health professions and related sciences, and psychology. A complete listing of majors at Rockhurst appears in the Majors Index beginning on page 430.

The **faculty** at Rockhurst has 131 full-time members, 76% with terminal degrees. The student-faculty ratio is 11:1.

Students of Rockhurst

The student body totals 2,730, of whom 2,011 are undergraduates. 55.9% are women and 44.1% are men. Students come from 24 states and territories and 19 other countries. 67% are from Missouri. 2.3% are international students. 8.5% are African American, 0.7% American Indian, 2.4% Asian American, and 5.4% Hispanic American. 79% returned for their sophomore year.

Facilities and Resources

Student rooms are linked to a campus network. 500 **computers** are available on campus that provide access to the Internet. The **library** has 53,720 books and 100 subscriptions.

Campus Life

There are 54 active organizations on campus, including a drama/theater group, newspaper, radio station, and choral group. 45% of eligible men and 55% of eligible women are members of national **fraternities** and national **sororities**.

Rockhurst is a member of the NCAA (Division II). **Intercollegiate sports** (some offering scholarships) include baseball (m), basketball, golf, soccer, tennis, volleyball (w).

Campus Safety

Student safety services include closed circuit TV monitors, late-night transport/escort service, 24-hour emergency telephone alarm devices, 24-hour patrols by trained security personnel, student patrols, and electronically operated dormitory entrances.

Applying

Rockhurst requires SAT I or ACT, a high school transcript, 1 recommendation, and a minimum high school GPA of 2.0, and in some cases an essay and an interview. Application deadline: 6/30. Early and deferred admission are possible.

Getting in Last Year
973 applied
87% were accepted
298 enrolled (35%)
20% from top tenth of their h.s. class
3.24 average high school GPA
24% had SAT verbal scores over 600
18% had SAT math scores over 600
46% had ACT scores over 24
2% had SAT verbal scores over 700
4% had SAT math scores over 700
6% had ACT scores over 30
4 valedictorians

Graduation and After
26% pursued further study
63% had job offers within 6 months
65 organizations recruited on campus

Financial Matters
$15,140 tuition and fees (2001–02)
$4920 room and board
81% average percent of need met
$14,467 average financial aid amount received per undergraduate

ROLLINS COLLEGE

SUBURBAN SETTING ■ PRIVATE ■ INDEPENDENT ■ COED
WINTER PARK, FLORIDA

Web site: www.rollins.edu
Contact: Mr. David Erdmann, Dean of Admissions and Student Financial
Planning, 1000 Holt Avenue, Winter Park, FL 32789-4499
Telephone: 407-646-2161 **Fax:** 407-646-1502
E-mail: admission@rollins.edu

Getting in Last Year

2,138 applied
65% were accepted
472 enrolled (34%)
40% from top tenth of their h.s. class
3.40 average high school GPA
40% had SAT verbal scores over 600
40% had SAT math scores over 600
60% had ACT scores over 24
5% had SAT verbal scores over 700
5% had SAT math scores over 700
15% had ACT scores over 30

Graduation and After

49% graduated in 4 years
7% graduated in 5 years
2% graduated in 6 years
29% pursued further study (17% arts and
sciences, 6% law, 2% business)
65% had job offers within 6 months
25 organizations recruited on campus

Financial Matters

$23,882 tuition and fees (2001–02)
$7341 room and board
93% average percent of need met
$23,243 average financial aid amount received
per undergraduate

Academics

Rollins awards bachelor's and master's **degrees**. Challenging opportunities include advanced placement credit, accelerated degree programs, student-designed majors, an honors program, double majors, independent study, and a senior project. Special programs include internships, off-campus study, and study-abroad.

The most frequently chosen **baccalaureate** fields are social sciences and history, visual/performing arts, and psychology. A complete listing of majors at Rollins appears in the Majors Index beginning on page 430.

The **faculty** at Rollins has 168 full-time members, 89% with terminal degrees. The student-faculty ratio is 12:1.

Students of Rollins

The student body totals 2,421, of whom 1,676 are undergraduates. 60.7% are women and 39.3% are men. Students come from 52 states and territories and 25 other countries. 53% are from Florida. 3.6% are international students. 3.5% are African American, 0.6% American Indian, 2.9% Asian American, and 7.3% Hispanic American. 84% returned for their sophomore year.

Facilities and Resources

Student rooms are linked to a campus network. 200 **computers** are available on campus that provide access to the Internet. The **library** has 237,333 books and 6,259 subscriptions.

Campus Life

There are 54 active organizations on campus, including a drama/theater group, newspaper, radio station, and choral group. 33% of eligible men and 33% of eligible women are members of national **fraternities**, national **sororities**, local fraternities, and local sororities.

Rollins is a member of the NCAA (Division II). **Intercollegiate sports** (some offering scholarships) include baseball (m), basketball, crew, cross-country running, golf, soccer (m), softball (w), tennis, volleyball (w).

Campus Safety

Student safety services include late-night transport/escort service, 24-hour emergency telephone alarm devices, 24-hour patrols by trained security personnel, and electronically operated dormitory entrances.

Applying

Rollins requires an essay, SAT I or ACT, a high school transcript, and 1 recommendation. It recommends SAT II Subject Tests and an interview. Application deadline: 2/15; 2/15 priority date for financial aid. Early and deferred admission are possible.

ROSE-HULMAN INSTITUTE OF TECHNOLOGY

RURAL SETTING ■ PRIVATE ■ INDEPENDENT ■ COED, PRIMARILY MEN
TERRE HAUTE, INDIANA

Web site: www.rose-hulman.edu
Contact: Mr. Charles G. Howard, Dean of Admissions/Vice President, 5500
Wabash Avenue, Terre Haute, IN 47803-3920
Telephone: 812-877-8213 or toll-free 800-552-0725 (in-state), 800-248-7448
(out-of-state) **Fax:** 812-877-8941
E-mail: admis.ofc@rose-hulman.edu

Academics
Rose-Hulman awards bachelor's and master's **degrees**. Challenging opportunities
include advanced placement credit, an honors program, double majors, independent
study, and a senior project. Special programs include cooperative education, internships,
summer session for credit, off-campus study, study-abroad, and Army and Air Force
ROTC.

The most frequently chosen **baccalaureate** fields are engineering/engineering
technologies, computer/information sciences, and physical sciences. A complete listing of
majors at Rose-Hulman appears in the Majors Index beginning on page 430.

The **faculty** at Rose-Hulman has 123 full-time members, 98% with terminal
degrees. The student-faculty ratio is 13:1.

Students of Rose-Hulman
The student body totals 1,749, of whom 1,573 are undergraduates. 18.4% are women
and 81.6% are men. Students come from 51 states and territories and 3 other countries.
50% are from Indiana. 1.2% are international students. 1.3% are African American,
0.1% American Indian, 2.7% Asian American, and 1.1% Hispanic American. 93%
returned for their sophomore year.

Facilities and Resources
Student rooms are linked to a campus network. 100 **computers** are available on campus
that provide access to the Internet. The **library** has 74,525 books and 589 subscriptions.

Campus Life
There are 60 active organizations on campus, including a drama/theater group,
newspaper, radio station, and choral group. 40% of eligible men and 50% of eligible
women are members of national **fraternities** and national **sororities**.

Rose-Hulman is a member of the NCAA (Division III). **Intercollegiate sports**
include baseball (m), basketball, cross-country running, football (m), golf (m), riflery,
soccer, softball (w), swimming, tennis, track and field, volleyball (w), wrestling (m).

Campus Safety
Student safety services include late-night transport/escort service, 24-hour emergency
telephone alarm devices, 24-hour patrols by trained security personnel, and electronically operated dormitory entrances.

Applying
Rose-Hulman requires SAT I or ACT, a high school transcript, and 1 recommendation.
It recommends an essay and an interview. Application deadline: 3/1; 3/1 priority date for
financial aid. Deferred admission is possible.

Getting in Last Year
3,034 applied
67% were accepted
404 enrolled (20%)
70% from top tenth of their h.s. class
60% had SAT verbal scores over 600
88% had SAT math scores over 600
91% had ACT scores over 24
14% had SAT verbal scores over 700
40% had SAT math scores over 700
35% had ACT scores over 30
27 National Merit Scholars
45 valedictorians

Graduation and After
58% graduated in 4 years
13% graduated in 5 years
1% graduated in 6 years
14% pursued further study
100% had job offers within 6 months
310 organizations recruited on campus

Financial Matters
$21,668 tuition and fees (2001–02)
$6039 room and board
73% average percent of need met
$14,839 average financial aid amount received
per undergraduate (2000–01)

RUTGERS, THE STATE UNIVERSITY OF NEW JERSEY, NEW BRUNSWICK

PUBLIC ■ STATE-SUPPORTED ■ COED
NEW BRUNSWICK, NEW JERSEY

Web site: www.rutgers.edu
Contact: Ms. Diane Williams Harris, Associate Director of University
  Undergraduate Admissions, 65 Davidson Road, Piscataway, NJ 08854-8097
Telephone: 732-932-4636 **Fax:** 732-445-0237
E-mail: admissions@sb-ugadm.rutgers.edu

Getting in Last Year
27,074 applied
60% were accepted
5,321 enrolled (33%)
36% from top tenth of their h.s. class
38% had SAT verbal scores over 600
53% had SAT math scores over 600
7% had SAT verbal scores over 700
14% had SAT math scores over 700

Graduation and After
80% had job offers within 6 months
500 organizations recruited on campus

Financial Matters
$6422 resident tuition and fees (2001–02)
$11,860 nonresident tuition and fees (2001–02)
$6676 room and board
85% average percent of need met

Academics
Rutgers, The State University of New Jersey, New Brunswick awards bachelor's, master's, doctoral, and first-professional **degrees**. Challenging opportunities include advanced placement credit, accelerated degree programs, student-designed majors, an honors program, double majors, independent study, and a senior project. Special programs include cooperative education, study-abroad, and Army and Air Force ROTC.

The most frequently chosen **baccalaureate** fields are social sciences and history, psychology, and biological/life sciences. A complete listing of majors at Rutgers, The State University of New Jersey, New Brunswick appears in the Majors Index beginning on page 430.

The **faculty** at Rutgers, The State University of New Jersey, New Brunswick has 1,473 full-time members, 98% with terminal degrees. The student-faculty ratio is 17:1.

Students of Rutgers, The State University of New Jersey, New Brunswick
The student body totals 35,237, of whom 27,939 are undergraduates. 53.3% are women and 46.7% are men. 92% are from New Jersey. 2.9% are international students. 8.2% are African American, 0.2% American Indian, 18.6% Asian American, and 7.6% Hispanic American.

Facilities and Resources
Student rooms are linked to a campus network. 1,450 **computers** are available on campus that provide access to online grade reports and the Internet. The 15 **libraries** have 3,777,538 books and 28,760 subscriptions.

Campus Life
Active organizations on campus include a drama/theater group, newspaper, radio station, television station, choral group, and marching band. Rutgers, The State University of New Jersey, New Brunswick has national **fraternities** and national **sororities**.

Rutgers, The State University of New Jersey, New Brunswick is a member of the NCAA (Division I). **Intercollegiate sports** include baseball (m), basketball, crew, cross-country running, fencing, football (m), golf, gymnastics (w), lacrosse, soccer, softball (w), swimming, tennis, track and field, volleyball (w), wrestling (m).

Applying
Rutgers, The State University of New Jersey, New Brunswick requires SAT I or ACT and a high school transcript, and in some cases SAT II: Writing Test. Application deadline: rolling admissions; 3/15 priority date for financial aid. Early admission is possible.

SAINT FRANCIS UNIVERSITY

RURAL SETTING ■ PRIVATE ■ INDEPENDENT RELIGIOUS ■ COED
LORETTO, PENNSYLVANIA

Web site: www.sfcpa.edu
Contact: Evan E. Lipp, Dean for Enrollment Management, PO Box 600,
Loretto, PA 15940-0600
Telephone: 814-472-3000 or toll-free 800-342-5732 **Fax:** 814-472-3335
E-mail: admission@sfcpa.edu

Academics

Saint Francis awards associate, bachelor's, and master's **degrees**. Challenging opportunities include advanced placement credit, accelerated degree programs, student-designed majors, freshman honors college, an honors program, double majors, and a senior project. Special programs include internships, summer session for credit, off-campus study, study-abroad, and Army ROTC. A complete listing of majors at Saint Francis appears in the Majors Index beginning on page 430.

The **faculty** at Saint Francis has 87 full-time members, 71% with terminal degrees. The student-faculty ratio is 11:1.

Students of Saint Francis

The student body totals 2,027, of whom 1,416 are undergraduates. 61.2% are women and 38.8% are men. Students come from 22 states and territories and 12 other countries. 85% are from Pennsylvania. 0.9% are international students. 5.4% are African American, 0.3% American Indian, 0.4% Asian American, and 0.7% Hispanic American. 75% returned for their sophomore year.

Facilities and Resources

Student rooms are linked to a campus network. 60 **computers** are available on campus for student use. The **library** has 155,143 books and 975 subscriptions.

Campus Life

There are 63 active organizations on campus, including a drama/theater group, newspaper, radio station, television station, and choral group. 17% of eligible men and 12% of eligible women are members of national **fraternities**, national **sororities**, and local sororities.

Saint Francis is a member of the NCAA (Division I). **Intercollegiate sports** (some offering scholarships) include basketball, cross-country running, football (m), golf, soccer, softball (w), swimming (w), tennis, track and field, volleyball.

Campus Safety

Student safety services include late-night transport/escort service, 24-hour emergency telephone alarm devices, 24-hour patrols by trained security personnel, and electronically operated dormitory entrances.

Applying

Saint Francis requires SAT I or ACT, a high school transcript, and 1 recommendation, and in some cases an interview and 3 recommendations. It recommends an essay and an interview. Application deadline: rolling admissions. Deferred admission is possible.

Getting in Last Year
1,251 applied
86% were accepted
342 enrolled (32%)
20% from top tenth of their h.s. class
3.38 average high school GPA
12% had SAT verbal scores over 600
13% had SAT math scores over 600
34% had ACT scores over 24
1% had SAT verbal scores over 700
1% had SAT math scores over 700
3% had ACT scores over 30

Graduation and After
41% graduated in 4 years
21% graduated in 5 years
1% graduated in 6 years
39% pursued further study (6% arts and sciences, 4% education, 2% law)
60% had job offers within 6 months
73 organizations recruited on campus

Financial Matters
$17,512 tuition and fees (2001–02)
$6974 room and board
82% average percent of need met
$15,098 average financial aid amount received per undergraduate

ST. JOHN'S COLLEGE

SMALL-TOWN SETTING ■ PRIVATE ■ INDEPENDENT ■ COED
ANNAPOLIS, MARYLAND

Web site: www.sjca.edu
Contact: Mr. John Christensen, Director of Admissions, PO Box 2800, 60 College Avenue, Annapolis, MD 21404
Telephone: 410-626-2522 or toll-free 800-727-9238 **Fax:** 410-269-7916
E-mail: admissions@sjca.edu

Getting in Last Year
464 applied
78% were accepted
112 enrolled (31%)
34% from top tenth of their h.s. class
89% had SAT verbal scores over 600
71% had SAT math scores over 600
54% had SAT verbal scores over 700
18% had SAT math scores over 700
4 National Merit Scholars

Graduation and After
63% graduated in 4 years
6% graduated in 5 years
2% graduated in 6 years
Graduates pursuing further study: 37% arts and sciences, 10% law, 7% business
50% had job offers within 6 months
9 organizations recruited on campus

Financial Matters
$25,990 tuition and fees (2001–02)
$6770 room and board
90% average percent of need met
$21,512 average financial aid amount received per undergraduate

Academics

St. John's awards bachelor's and master's **degrees**. A senior project is a challenging opportunity. Special programs include internships and off-campus study.

The most frequently chosen **baccalaureate** field is liberal arts/general studies. A complete listing of majors at St. John's appears in the Majors Index beginning on page 430.

The **faculty** at St. John's has 66 full-time members, 73% with terminal degrees. The student-faculty ratio is 8:1.

Students of St. John's

The student body totals 543, of whom 477 are undergraduates. 45.3% are women and 54.7% are men. Students come from 47 states and territories and 8 other countries. 15% are from Maryland. 2.3% are international students. 0.4% are African American, 0.4% American Indian, 2.9% Asian American, and 2.7% Hispanic American. 81% returned for their sophomore year.

Facilities and Resources

16 **computers** are available on campus that provide access to the Internet. The 2 **libraries** have 92,806 books and 114 subscriptions.

Campus Life

There are 35 active organizations on campus, including a drama/theater group, newspaper, and choral group. No national or local **fraternities** or **sororities**.

This institution has no intercollegiate sports.

Campus Safety

Student safety services include late-night transport/escort service, 24-hour emergency telephone alarm devices, 24-hour patrols by trained security personnel, and electronically operated dormitory entrances.

Applying

St. John's requires an essay, a high school transcript, and 2 recommendations, and in some cases SAT I or ACT. It recommends SAT I or ACT and an interview. Application deadline: rolling admissions; 2/15 priority date for financial aid. Early and deferred admission are possible.

St. John's College

Small-town setting ■ Private ■ Independent ■ Coed
Santa Fe, New Mexico

Web site: www.sjcsf.edu
Contact: Mr. Larry Clendenin, Director of Admissions, 1160 Camino Cruz
 Blanca, Santa Fe, NM 87501
Telephone: 505-984-6060 or toll-free 800-331-5232 **Fax:** 505-984-6162
E-mail: admissions@mail.sjcsf.edu

Academics

St. John's awards bachelor's and master's **degrees**. A senior project is a challenging opportunity. Special programs include summer session for credit and off-campus study. A complete listing of majors at St. John's appears in the Majors Index beginning on page 430.

 The **faculty** at St. John's has 63 full-time members, 90% with terminal degrees. The student-faculty ratio is 8:1.

Students of St. John's

The student body totals 528, of whom 445 are undergraduates. Students come from 43 states and territories and 6 other countries. 8% are from New Mexico. 0.9% are international students. 0.2% are African American, 1.4% American Indian, 2.7% Asian American, and 5% Hispanic American. 73% returned for their sophomore year.

Facilities and Resources

20 **computers** are available on campus for student use. The **library** has 40,103 books and 135 subscriptions.

Campus Life

There are 17 active organizations on campus, including a drama/theater group, newspaper, and choral group. No national or local **fraternities** or **sororities**.

 Intercollegiate sports include fencing.

Campus Safety

Student safety services include late-night transport/escort service, 24-hour emergency telephone alarm devices, 24-hour patrols by trained security personnel, and student patrols.

Applying

St. John's requires an essay, a high school transcript, and 2 recommendations, and in some cases SAT I or ACT and an interview. It recommends an interview and 3 recommendations. Application deadline: rolling admissions; 2/15 priority date for financial aid. Early and deferred admission are possible.

St. John's appeals to students who value good books, love to read, and are passionate about discourse. There are no lectures and virtually no tests or electives. Instead, there are discussion-based classes of 17–21 students where professors are as likely as students to be asked to defend their points of view. Great Books provide the direction, context, and stimulus for conversation. The entire student body adheres to the same all-required arts and sciences curriculum. Seventy-five percent of the College's alumni obtain graduate and professional degrees in law, medicine, humanities, natural sciences, business, journalism, fine and performing arts, or architecture.

Getting in Last Year
360 applied
86% were accepted
24% from top tenth of their h.s. class
82% had SAT verbal scores over 600
59% had SAT math scores over 600
94% had ACT scores over 24
46% had SAT verbal scores over 700
18% had SAT math scores over 700
38% had ACT scores over 30
3 National Merit Scholars
3 class presidents
2 valedictorians

Graduation and After
39% graduated in 4 years
13% graduated in 5 years
3% graduated in 6 years
75% pursued further study (37% arts and
 sciences, 10% law, 7% business)
25% had job offers within 6 months
10 organizations recruited on campus

Financial Matters
$25,990 tuition and fees (2001–02)
$6770 room and board
99% average percent of need met
$21,734 average financial aid amount received
 per undergraduate (2000–01 estimated)

SAINT JOHN'S UNIVERSITY
COORDINATE WITH COLLEGE OF SAINT BENEDICT
RURAL SETTING ■ PRIVATE ■ INDEPENDENT RELIGIOUS ■ MEN ONLY
COLLEGEVILLE, MINNESOTA

Web site: www.csbsju.edu
Contact: Ms. Mary Milbert, Dean of Admissions, PO Box 7155, Collegeville, MN 56321-7155
Telephone: 320-363-2196 or toll-free 800-24JOHNS **Fax:** 320-363-3206
E-mail: admissions@csbsju.edu

Through a partnership of 2 national liberal arts colleges, the College of Saint Benedict (for women) and Saint John's University (for men) come together to offer one exceptional education. Enriched by a Catholic and Benedictine tradition, the colleges promote an integrated learning experience that combines a challenging academic program with extensive opportunities for international study, leadership, service, spiritual growth, and cultural and athletic involvement. The colleges' residential campuses, set amid the woods and lakes of central Minnesota, are excellent places for active students to become fully immersed in their college education.

Getting in Last Year
1,115 applied
85% were accepted
502 enrolled (53%)
23% from top tenth of their h.s. class
3.53 average high school GPA
42% had SAT verbal scores over 600
56% had SAT math scores over 600
68% had ACT scores over 24
9% had SAT verbal scores over 700
17% had SAT math scores over 700
11% had ACT scores over 30
3 National Merit Scholars

Graduation and After
67% graduated in 4 years
6% graduated in 5 years
1% graduated in 6 years
22% pursued further study
79% had job offers within 6 months
85 organizations recruited on campus

Financial Matters
$18,325 tuition and fees (2001–02)
$5606 room and board
80% average percent of need met
$16,168 average financial aid amount received per undergraduate

Academics
St. John's awards bachelor's, master's, and first-professional **degrees**. Challenging opportunities include advanced placement credit, accelerated degree programs, student-designed majors, an honors program, double majors, independent study, and a senior project. Special programs include internships, off-campus study, study-abroad, and Army ROTC.

The most frequently chosen **baccalaureate** fields are business/marketing, social sciences and history, and English. A complete listing of majors at St. John's appears in the Majors Index beginning on page 430.

The **faculty** at St. John's has 157 full-time members, 85% with terminal degrees. The student-faculty ratio is 11:1.

Students of St. John's
The student body totals 2,039, of whom 1,888 are undergraduates. Students come from 31 states and territories and 21 other countries. 86% are from Minnesota. 2.5% are international students. 0.2% are African American, 0.3% American Indian, 1.7% Asian American, and 1.1% Hispanic American. 92% returned for their sophomore year.

Facilities and Resources
Student rooms are linked to a campus network. 350 **computers** are available on campus that provide access to the Internet. The 3 **libraries** have 726,844 books and 8,564 subscriptions.

Campus Life
There are 80 active organizations on campus, including a drama/theater group, newspaper, radio station, and choral group. No national or local **fraternities**.

St. John's is a member of the NCAA (Division III). **Intercollegiate sports** include baseball, basketball, cross-country running, football, golf, ice hockey, skiing (cross-country), soccer, swimming, tennis, track and field, wrestling.

Campus Safety
Student safety services include well-lit pathways, 911 center on campus, closed circuit TV monitors, late-night transport/escort service, 24-hour emergency telephone alarm devices, and 24-hour patrols by trained security personnel.

Applying
St. John's requires an essay, SAT I or ACT, and a high school transcript, and in some cases 3 recommendations. It recommends an interview and a minimum high school GPA of 3.0. Application deadline: rolling admissions; 3/15 priority date for financial aid. Early and deferred admission are possible.

SAINT JOSEPH'S UNIVERSITY

SUBURBAN SETTING ■ PRIVATE ■ INDEPENDENT RELIGIOUS ■ COED
PHILADELPHIA, PENNSYLVANIA

Web site: www.sju.edu
Contact: Mr. David Conway, Assistant Vice President of Enrollment
Management, 5600 City Avenue, Philadelphia, PA 19131-1395
Telephone: 610-660-1300 or toll-free 888-BEAHAWK (in-state) **Fax:**
610-660-1314
E-mail: admi@sju.edu

Academics

St. Joseph's awards associate, bachelor's, master's, and doctoral **degrees** and post-master's certificates. Challenging opportunities include advanced placement credit, accelerated degree programs, student-designed majors, an honors program, double majors, independent study, and a senior project. Special programs include cooperative education, internships, summer session for credit, off-campus study, study-abroad, and Army and Air Force ROTC.

The most frequently chosen **baccalaureate** fields are business/marketing, social sciences and history, and education. A complete listing of majors at St. Joseph's appears in the Majors Index beginning on page 430.

The **faculty** at St. Joseph's has 229 full-time members, 93% with terminal degrees. The student-faculty ratio is 13:1.

Students of St. Joseph's

The student body totals 7,313, of whom 4,590 are undergraduates. 53.7% are women and 46.3% are men. 51% are from Pennsylvania. 1.5% are international students. 7.3% are African American, 0.1% American Indian, 2.2% Asian American, and 2.1% Hispanic American. 86% returned for their sophomore year.

Facilities and Resources

Student rooms are linked to a campus network. 180 **computers** are available on campus that provide access to the Internet. The 2 **libraries** have 197,788 books and 4,900 subscriptions.

Campus Life

There are 73 active organizations on campus, including a drama/theater group, newspaper, radio station, and choral group. 9% of eligible men and 12% of eligible women are members of national **fraternities** and national **sororities**.

St. Joseph's is a member of the NCAA (Division I). **Intercollegiate sports** (some offering scholarships) include baseball (m), basketball, cross-country running, field hockey (w), golf (m), lacrosse, soccer, softball (w), tennis, track and field.

Campus Safety

Student safety services include 24-hour shuttle/escort service, bicycle patrols, late-night transport/escort service, 24-hour emergency telephone alarm devices, 24-hour patrols by trained security personnel, and electronically operated dormitory entrances.

Applying

St. Joseph's requires an essay, SAT I or ACT, a high school transcript, and 1 recommendation. It recommends SAT II Subject Tests and a minimum high school GPA of 3.0. Application deadline: 2/15 priority date for financial aid. Early and deferred admission are possible.

Saint Joseph's, Philadelphia's Jesuit university, is located on a beautiful 65-acre suburban campus on the western edge of the city and offers its students a vital relationship with the educational opportunities and rich cultural resources of both the suburban and metropolitan Philadelphia areas. Distinguished by its comprehensive academic opportunities, respected teaching faculty, personal size, and highly successful students and alumni, Saint Joseph's draws top students from across the country and around the world while remaining dedicated to its tradition of service to others. Included in Saint Joseph's list of offerings are four 5-year programs (student earns both a BS and MS) in criminal justice, elementary education, international marketing, and psychology.

Getting in Last Year
5,866 applied
57% were accepted
960 enrolled (29%)
3.14 average high school GPA

Graduation and After
25% pursued further study
72% had job offers within 6 months
120 organizations recruited on campus

Financial Matters
$21,270 tuition and fees (2001–02)
$8445 room and board
$11,150 average financial aid amount received per undergraduate (1999–2000 estimated)

St. Lawrence University

SMALL-TOWN SETTING ■ PRIVATE ■ INDEPENDENT ■ COED
CANTON, NEW YORK

Web site: www.stlawu.edu
Contact: Ms. Terry Cowdrey, Dean of Admissions and Financial Aid, Canton, NY 13617-1455
Telephone: 315-229-5261 or toll-free 800-285-1856 **Fax:** 315-229-5818
E-mail: admissions@stlawu.edu

With more than 30 majors and minors from which to choose, St. Lawrence students can sample from a variety of disciplines and specialize in those areas that are most intriguing to them. The diverse options for cocurricular activities, including 32 varsity sports, encourage students to further develop their abilities and interests outside of the classroom. The University's location provides students with a residential community while providing access to the Adirondack Mountains as well as to Ottawa and Montreal. St. Lawrence alumni successfully pursue careers and graduate study, consistently achieving placement rates higher than 95% within one year of graduation.

Academics

St. Lawrence awards bachelor's and master's **degrees** and post-master's certificates. Challenging opportunities include advanced placement credit, student-designed majors, double majors, independent study, and a senior project. Special programs include internships, summer session for credit, off-campus study, study-abroad, and Army and Air Force ROTC.

The most frequently chosen **baccalaureate** fields are social sciences and history, biological/life sciences, and psychology. A complete listing of majors at St. Lawrence appears in the Majors Index beginning on page 430.

The **faculty** at St. Lawrence has 160 full-time members, 98% with terminal degrees. The student-faculty ratio is 11:1.

Students of St. Lawrence

The student body totals 2,097, of whom 1,968 are undergraduates. 52.9% are women and 47.1% are men. Students come from 37 states and territories and 19 other countries. 55% are from New York. 3.6% are international students. 1.8% are African American, 0.4% American Indian, 0.7% Asian American, and 2.2% Hispanic American. 84% returned for their sophomore year.

Facilities and Resources

Student rooms are linked to a campus network. 600 **computers** are available on campus that provide access to internships, shadowing programs and the Internet. The 2 **libraries** have 509,348 books and 2,014 subscriptions.

Campus Life

There are 100 active organizations on campus, including a drama/theater group, newspaper, radio station, television station, and choral group. 14% of eligible men and 25% of eligible women are members of national **fraternities**, national **sororities**, and local sororities.

St. Lawrence is a member of the NCAA (Division III). **Intercollegiate sports** (some offering scholarships) include baseball (m), basketball, crew, cross-country running, equestrian sports, field hockey (w), football (m), golf, ice hockey, lacrosse, skiing (crosscountry), skiing (downhill), soccer, softball (w), squash, swimming, tennis, track and field, volleyball (w).

Campus Safety

Student safety services include late-night transport/escort service, 24-hour emergency telephone alarm devices, 24-hour patrols by trained security personnel, student patrols, and electronically operated dormitory entrances.

Applying

St. Lawrence requires an essay, SAT I or ACT, a high school transcript, and 2 recommendations. It recommends SAT II Subject Tests, an interview, and a minimum high school GPA of 2.0. Application deadline: 2/15; 2/15 priority date for financial aid. Deferred admission is possible.

Getting in Last Year
2,745 applied
61% were accepted
510 enrolled (30%)
36% from top tenth of their h.s. class
3.35 average high school GPA
37% had SAT verbal scores over 600
38% had SAT math scores over 600
65% had ACT scores over 24
6% had SAT verbal scores over 700
4% had SAT math scores over 700
12% had ACT scores over 30
15 valedictorians

Graduation and After
67% graduated in 4 years
4% graduated in 5 years
1% graduated in 6 years
15% pursued further study (5% arts and sciences, 5% education, 3% medicine)
77.7% had job offers within 6 months
13 organizations recruited on campus

Financial Matters
$24,850 tuition and fees (2001–02)
$7755 room and board
92% average percent of need met
$24,726 average financial aid amount received per undergraduate

St. Louis College of Pharmacy

Urban setting ■ Private ■ Independent ■ Coed
St. Louis, Missouri

Web site: www.stlcop.edu
Contact: Ms. Penny Bryant, Director of Admissions/Registrar, 4588 Parkview Place, St. Louis, MO 63110-1088
Telephone: 314-367-8700 ext. 1067 or toll-free 800-278-5267 (in-state) **Fax:** 314-367-2784
E-mail: pbryant@stlcop.edu

Academics

St. Louis College of Pharmacy awards bachelor's, master's, and first-professional **degrees** (BS Degree program in pharmaceutical studies cannot be applied to directly; students have the option to transfer in after their second year in the PharmD program. Bachelor's degree candidates are not eligible to take the pharmacist's licensing exam). Challenging opportunities include advanced placement credit and a senior project. Special programs include internships and summer session for credit.

The most frequently chosen **baccalaureate** field is health professions and related sciences. A complete listing of majors at St. Louis College of Pharmacy appears in the Majors Index beginning on page 430.

The **faculty** at St. Louis College of Pharmacy has 64 full-time members, 92% with terminal degrees. The student-faculty ratio is 13:1.

Students of St. Louis College of Pharmacy

The student body totals 885, of whom 814 are undergraduates. 65.6% are women and 34.4% are men. Students come from 26 states and territories. 50% are from Missouri. 0.1% are international students. 4.8% are African American, 13.1% Asian American, and 1% Hispanic American. 89% returned for their sophomore year.

Facilities and Resources

Student rooms are linked to a campus network. 80 **computers** are available on campus that provide access to the Internet. The **library** has 56,636 books and 282 subscriptions.

Campus Life

There are 15 active organizations on campus, including a drama/theater group, newspaper, and choral group. 70% of eligible men and 65% of eligible women are members of national **fraternities** and national **sororities**.

St. Louis College of Pharmacy is a member of the NAIA. **Intercollegiate sports** include basketball (m), cross-country running, volleyball (w).

Campus Safety

Student safety services include late-night transport/escort service, 24-hour emergency telephone alarm devices, 24-hour patrols by trained security personnel, and electronically operated dormitory entrances.

Applying

St. Louis College of Pharmacy requires an essay, SAT I or ACT, a high school transcript, recommendations, and a minimum high school GPA of 2.5, and in some cases an interview. It recommends a minimum high school GPA of 3.0. Application deadline: rolling admissions; 11/15 for financial aid, with a 4/1 priority date.

Getting in Last Year
432 applied
66% were accepted
170 enrolled (59%)
3.56 average high school GPA
62% had ACT scores over 24
6% had ACT scores over 30

Graduation and After
6% pursued further study (2% arts and sciences, 2% business, 1% law)

Financial Matters
$13,775 tuition and fees (2001–02)
$5364 room and board
31% average percent of need met
$11,324 average financial aid amount received per undergraduate (2000–01 estimated)

SAINT LOUIS UNIVERSITY

URBAN SETTING ■ PRIVATE ■ INDEPENDENT RELIGIOUS ■ COED
ST. LOUIS, MISSOURI

Web site: imagine.slu.edu
Contact: Dr. Edwin Harris, Associate Provost, 221 North Grand Boulevard, St. Louis, MO 63103-2097
Telephone: 314-977-2500 or toll-free 800-758-3678 (out-of-state) **Fax:** 314-977-7136
E-mail: admitme@slu.edu

Founded in 1818 as the second Jesuit university in the nation, Saint Louis University offers more than 2600 courses each semester with an average class size of 22. Along with its recognition as a national research university, the University's academic rigor and wide variety of programs draw students from all 50 states. SLU is committed to developing the whole person intellectually, spiritually, physically, and socially.

Getting in Last Year
5,547 applied
69% were accepted
1,479 enrolled (39%)
33% from top tenth of their h.s. class
3.47 average high school GPA
50% had SAT verbal scores over 600
55% had SAT math scores over 600
78% had ACT scores over 24
8% had SAT verbal scores over 700
12% had SAT math scores over 700
23% had ACT scores over 30
17 National Merit Scholars

Graduation and After
52% graduated in 4 years
13% graduated in 5 years
2% graduated in 6 years
21% pursued further study
65% had job offers within 6 months
140 organizations recruited on campus

Financial Matters
$19,830 tuition and fees (2001–02)
$6760 room and board
69% average percent of need met
$19,526 average financial aid amount received per undergraduate

Academics

SLU awards bachelor's, master's, doctoral, and first-professional **degrees** and post-bachelor's and post-master's certificates. Challenging opportunities include advanced placement credit, accelerated degree programs, student-designed majors, freshman honors college, an honors program, double majors, independent study, and a senior project. Special programs include cooperative education, internships, summer session for credit, off-campus study, study-abroad, and Army and Air Force ROTC.

The most frequently chosen **baccalaureate** fields are business/marketing, health professions and related sciences, and communications/communication technologies. A complete listing of majors at SLU appears in the Majors Index beginning on page 430.

The **faculty** at SLU has 572 full-time members, 94% with terminal degrees. The student-faculty ratio is 12:1.

Students of SLU

The student body totals 11,145, of whom 7,228 are undergraduates. 54.6% are women and 45.4% are men. Students come from 50 states and territories and 80 other countries. 52% are from Missouri. 3.9% are international students. 7.6% are African American, 0.3% American Indian, 4.3% Asian American, and 2.2% Hispanic American. 86% returned for their sophomore year.

Facilities and Resources

Student rooms are linked to a campus network. 6,500 **computers** are available on campus that provide access to the Internet. The 4 **libraries** have 1,286,375 books and 14,724 subscriptions.

Campus Life

There are 100 active organizations on campus, including a drama/theater group, newspaper, radio station, television station, and choral group. 17% of eligible men and 20% of eligible women are members of national **fraternities** and national **sororities**.

SLU is a member of the NCAA (Division I). **Intercollegiate sports** (some offering scholarships) include baseball (m), basketball, cross-country running, field hockey (w), golf (m), riflery, softball (w), swimming, tennis.

Campus Safety

Student safety services include crime prevention program, bicycle patrols, late-night transport/escort service, 24-hour emergency telephone alarm devices, 24-hour patrols by trained security personnel, student patrols, and electronically operated dormitory entrances.

Applying

SLU requires an essay, SAT I or ACT, a high school transcript, and secondary school report form. It recommends an interview and 2 recommendations. Application deadline: 8/1; 3/1 priority date for financial aid. Early and deferred admission are possible.

Saint Mary's College of California

Suburban setting ■ Private ■ Independent Religious ■ Coed
Moraga, California

Web site: www.stmarys-ca.edu
Contact: Ms. Dorothy Benjamin, Dean of Admissions, PO Box 4800, Moraga,
CA 94556-4800
Telephone: 925-631-4224 or toll-free 800-800-4SMC **Fax:** 925-376-7193
E-mail: smcadmit@stmarys-ca.edu

Academics

Saint Mary's awards bachelor's, master's, and doctoral **degrees**. Challenging opportunities include advanced placement credit, student-designed majors, an honors program, double majors, independent study, and a senior project. Special programs include internships, off-campus study, study-abroad, and Army and Air Force ROTC.

The most frequently chosen **baccalaureate** fields are business/marketing, psychology, and social sciences and history. A complete listing of majors at Saint Mary's appears in the Majors Index beginning on page 430.

The **faculty** at Saint Mary's has 182 full-time members, 97% with terminal degrees. The student-faculty ratio is 13:1.

Students of Saint Mary's

The student body totals 4,127, of whom 3,061 are undergraduates. 61.5% are women and 38.5% are men. Students come from 29 states and territories and 33 other countries. 89% are from California. 2.2% are international students. 6.5% are African American, 0.8% American Indian, 8.3% Asian American, and 14.4% Hispanic American. 82% returned for their sophomore year.

Facilities and Resources

Student rooms are linked to a campus network. 250 **computers** are available on campus that provide access to the Internet. The 2 **libraries** have 153,576 books and 1,066 subscriptions.

Campus Life

There are 45 active organizations on campus, including a drama/theater group, newspaper, radio station, television station, and choral group. No national or local **fraternities** or **sororities**.

Saint Mary's is a member of the NCAA (Division I). **Intercollegiate sports** (some offering scholarships) include baseball (m), basketball, crew (w), cross-country running, football (m), golf (m), lacrosse (w), soccer, softball (w), tennis, volleyball (w).

Campus Safety

Student safety services include late-night transport/escort service, 24-hour emergency telephone alarm devices, and 24-hour patrols by trained security personnel.

Applying

Saint Mary's requires an essay, SAT I or ACT, a high school transcript, 1 recommendation, and a minimum high school GPA of 2.0, and in some cases an interview and a minimum high school GPA of 3.0. It recommends a minimum high school GPA of 3.0. Application deadline: 2/1; 3/2 priority date for financial aid. Deferred admission is possible.

It has been said that Saint Mary's College is "a classic example of a school committed to teaching students *how* to think rather than *what* to think." It is home to some of the "happiest students in the nation," has a safe and beautiful campus, and is a "good buy." Saint Mary's intimate academic community of 2,400 undergraduates is located 20 miles east of San Francisco. Operated and owned by the Christian Brothers, the College is committed to providing students with a comprehensive liberal arts education that includes reading and discussing the Great Books.

Getting in Last Year
3,230 applied
77% were accepted
609 enrolled (24%)
3.38 average high school GPA
25% had SAT verbal scores over 600
23% had SAT math scores over 600
36% had ACT scores over 24
2% had SAT verbal scores over 700
3% had SAT math scores over 700
5% had ACT scores over 30

Graduation and After
63% graduated in 4 years
3% graduated in 5 years
1% graduated in 6 years
32% pursued further study
48% had job offers within 6 months
110 organizations recruited on campus

Financial Matters
$19,525 tuition and fees (2001–02)
$8050 room and board
88% average percent of need met
$14,578 average financial aid amount received
per undergraduate (2000–01)

ST. MARY'S COLLEGE OF MARYLAND

RURAL SETTING ■ PUBLIC ■ STATE-SUPPORTED ■ COED
ST. MARY'S CITY, MARYLAND

Web site: www.smcm.edu
Contact: Mr. Richard J. Edgar, Director of Admissions, 18952 East Fisher Road, St. Mary's City, MD 20686-3001
Telephone: 240-895-5000 or toll-free 800-492-7181 **Fax:** 240-895-5001
E-mail: admissions@smcm.edu

St. Mary's College of Maryland, with its distinctive identity as Maryland's "Public Honors College," has emerged as one of the finest liberal arts colleges in the country. A lively academic atmosphere combines with the serene yet stunning natural beauty of a riverfront campus to create a challenging and memorable college experience. Construction during the past year includes the completion of a new campus center, a baseball complex, and suite-style residence halls. Construction has begun on extensive renovations to the athletics facility, including an Olympic-size pool, racquetball courts, and a state-of-the-art fitness room.

Getting in Last Year
1,447 applied
71% were accepted
456 enrolled (44%)
45% from top tenth of their h.s. class
3.48 average high school GPA
65% had SAT verbal scores over 600
54% had SAT math scores over 600
18% had SAT verbal scores over 700
8% had SAT math scores over 700
25 valedictorians

Graduation and After
58% graduated in 4 years
9% graduated in 5 years
1% graduated in 6 years
29% pursued further study (11% arts and sciences, 6% education, 6% law)
72.9% had job offers within 6 months
73 organizations recruited on campus

Financial Matters
$7549 resident tuition and fees (2001–02)
$12,534 nonresident tuition and fees (2001–02)
$6555 room and board
69% average percent of need met
$6908 average financial aid amount received per undergraduate (2000–01)

Academics
St. Mary's awards bachelor's **degrees**. Challenging opportunities include advanced placement credit, student-designed majors, freshman honors college, an honors program, double majors, independent study, and a senior project. Special programs include cooperative education, internships, summer session for credit, off-campus study, and study-abroad.

The most frequently chosen **baccalaureate** fields are social sciences and history, biological/life sciences, and psychology. A complete listing of majors at St. Mary's appears in the Majors Index beginning on page 430.

The **faculty** at St. Mary's has 120 full-time members, 90% with terminal degrees. The student-faculty ratio is 11:1.

Students of St. Mary's
The student body is made up of 1,688 undergraduates. 61.1% are women and 38.9% are men. Students come from 31 states and territories and 24 other countries. 86% are from Maryland. 0.8% are international students. 7.3% are African American, 0.5% American Indian, 3.8% Asian American, and 2.4% Hispanic American. 87% returned for their sophomore year.

Facilities and Resources
Student rooms are linked to a campus network. 165 **computers** are available on campus that provide access to e-mail and the Internet. The **library** has 116,267 books and 7,286 subscriptions.

Campus Life
There are 69 active organizations on campus, including a drama/theater group, newspaper, radio station, television station, and choral group. No national or local **fraternities** or **sororities**.

St. Mary's is a member of the NCAA (Division III). **Intercollegiate sports** include baseball (m), basketball, field hockey (w), lacrosse, sailing, soccer, swimming, tennis, volleyball (w).

Campus Safety
Student safety services include late-night transport/escort service, 24-hour emergency telephone alarm devices, 24-hour patrols by trained security personnel, student patrols, and electronically operated dormitory entrances.

Applying
St. Mary's requires an essay, SAT I or ACT, a high school transcript, and a minimum high school GPA of 2.0. It recommends an interview and 2 recommendations. Application deadline: 1/15; 2/15 for financial aid. Early admission is possible.

St. Norbert College

Suburban setting ■ Private ■ Independent Religious ■ Coed
De Pere, Wisconsin

Web site: www.snc.edu
Contact: Mr. Daniel L. Meyer, Dean of Admission and Enrollment
Management, 100 Grant Street, De Pere, WI 54115-2099
Telephone: 920-403-3005 or toll-free 800-236-4878 **Fax:** 920-403-4072
E-mail: admit@mail.snc.edu

Academics

St. Norbert awards bachelor's and master's **degrees**. Challenging opportunities include advanced placement credit, accelerated degree programs, student-designed majors, an honors program, double majors, independent study, and a senior project. Special programs include cooperative education, internships, summer session for credit, off-campus study, study-abroad, and Army ROTC.

The most frequently chosen **baccalaureate** fields are business/marketing, social sciences and history, and communications/communication technologies. A complete listing of majors at St. Norbert appears in the Majors Index beginning on page 430.

The **faculty** at St. Norbert has 115 full-time members, 92% with terminal degrees. The student-faculty ratio is 14:1.

Students of St. Norbert

The student body totals 2,131, of whom 2,059 are undergraduates. 57.4% are women and 42.6% are men. Students come from 27 states and territories and 27 other countries. 72% are from Wisconsin. 2.5% are international students. 1% are African American, 0.9% American Indian, 1.5% Asian American, and 1.3% Hispanic American. 82% returned for their sophomore year.

Facilities and Resources

Student rooms are linked to a campus network. 179 **computers** are available on campus that provide access to the Internet. The **library** has 140,514 books and 10,000 subscriptions.

Campus Life

There are 60 active organizations on campus, including a drama/theater group, newspaper, radio station, television station, and choral group. 30% of eligible men and 15% of eligible women are members of national **fraternities**, national **sororities**, local fraternities, and local sororities.

St. Norbert is a member of the NCAA (Division III). **Intercollegiate sports** include baseball (m), basketball, cross-country running, football (m), golf, ice hockey (m), soccer, softball (w), swimming (w), tennis, track and field, volleyball (w).

Campus Safety

Student safety services include crime prevention programs, late-night transport/escort service, 24-hour emergency telephone alarm devices, 24-hour patrols by trained security personnel, student patrols, and electronically operated dormitory entrances.

Applying

St. Norbert requires an essay, SAT I or ACT, a high school transcript, and 1 recommendation. It recommends an interview. Application deadline: rolling admissions; 3/1 priority date for financial aid. Deferred admission is possible.

Getting in Last Year
1,603 applied
84% were accepted
558 enrolled (41%)
31% from top tenth of their h.s. class
3.29 average high school GPA
56% had ACT scores over 24
6% had ACT scores over 30
3 National Merit Scholars
24 class presidents
35 valedictorians

Graduation and After
78% had job offers within 6 months
52 organizations recruited on campus

Financial Matters
$18,007 tuition and fees (2001–02)
$5162 room and board
88% average percent of need met
$13,971 average financial aid amount received per undergraduate

St. Olaf College

Small-town setting ■ Private ■ Independent Religious ■ Coed
Northfield, Minnesota

Web site: www.stolaf.edu

Contact: Jeff McLaughlin, Acting Director of Admissions, 1520 St. Olaf Avenue, Northfield, MN 55057

Telephone: 507-646-3025 or toll-free 800-800-3025 **Fax:** 507-646-3832

E-mail: admiss@stolaf.edu

Getting in Last Year

2,463 applied
76% were accepted
745 enrolled (40%)
49% from top tenth of their h.s. class
3.71 average high school GPA
66% had SAT verbal scores over 600
64% had SAT math scores over 600
85% had ACT scores over 24
19% had SAT verbal scores over 700
16% had SAT math scores over 700
24% had ACT scores over 30
32 National Merit Scholars
11 class presidents
59 valedictorians

Graduation and After

71% graduated in 4 years
4% graduated in 5 years
25% pursued further study (12% arts and sciences, 4% medicine, 2% law)
68.1% had job offers within 6 months
162 organizations recruited on campus

Financial Matters

$21,280 tuition and fees (2001–02)
$4600 room and board
100% average percent of need met
$16,354 average financial aid amount received per undergraduate

Academics

St. Olaf awards bachelor's **degrees**. Challenging opportunities include advanced placement credit, accelerated degree programs, student-designed majors, double majors, independent study, and a senior project. Special programs include internships, summer session for credit, off-campus study, and study-abroad.

The most frequently chosen **baccalaureate** fields are social sciences and history, biological/life sciences, and visual/performing arts. A complete listing of majors at St. Olaf appears in the Majors Index beginning on page 430.

The **faculty** at St. Olaf has 195 full-time members, 89% with terminal degrees. The student-faculty ratio is 13:1.

Students of St. Olaf

The student body is made up of 3,011 undergraduates. 58.2% are women and 41.8% are men. Students come from 47 states and territories and 20 other countries. 54% are from Minnesota. 1.2% are international students. 1% are African American, 0.2% American Indian, 2.9% Asian American, and 1.3% Hispanic American. 93% returned for their sophomore year.

Facilities and Resources

Student rooms are linked to a campus network. 1,100 **computers** are available on campus that provide access to the Internet. The 4 **libraries** have 521,383 books and 1,805 subscriptions.

Campus Life

There are 96 active organizations on campus, including a drama/theater group, newspaper, radio station, and choral group. No national or local **fraternities** or **sororities**.

St. Olaf is a member of the NCAA (Division III). **Intercollegiate sports** include baseball (m), basketball, cross-country running, football (m), golf, ice hockey, skiing (cross-country), skiing (downhill), soccer, softball (w), swimming, tennis, track and field, volleyball (w), wrestling (m).

Campus Safety

Student safety services include late-night transport/escort service, 24-hour emergency telephone alarm devices, 24-hour patrols by trained security personnel, and electronically operated dormitory entrances.

Applying

St. Olaf requires an essay, SAT I or ACT, a high school transcript, 2 recommendations, and a minimum high school GPA of 3.0. It recommends an interview. Application deadline: rolling admissions; 2/15 priority date for financial aid. Deferred admission is possible.

Salem College

Urban setting ■ Private ■ Independent Religious ■ Women Only
Winston-Salem, North Carolina

Web site: www.salem.edu
Contact: Ms. Dana E. Evans, Dean of Admissions and Financial Aid, PO Box
   10548, Shober House, Winston-Salem, NC 27108
Telephone: 336-721-2621 or toll-free 800-327-2536 **Fax:** 336-724-7102
E-mail: admissions@salem.edu

Academics

Salem awards bachelor's and master's **degrees** (only students 23 or over are eligible to enroll part-time; men may attend evening program only). Challenging opportunities include advanced placement credit, student-designed majors, an honors program, double majors, independent study, and a senior project. Special programs include internships, summer session for credit, off-campus study, study-abroad, and Army ROTC.

The most frequently chosen **baccalaureate** fields are social sciences and history, English, and business/marketing. A complete listing of majors at Salem appears in the Majors Index beginning on page 430.

The **faculty** at Salem has 52 full-time members, 87% with terminal degrees. The student-faculty ratio is 13:1.

Students of Salem

The student body totals 1,074, of whom 926 are undergraduates. Students come from 24 states and territories and 16 other countries. 52% are from North Carolina. 3.6% are international students. 18.1% are African American, 0.9% American Indian, 1.7% Asian American, and 2.1% Hispanic American. 79% returned for their sophomore year.

Facilities and Resources

Student rooms are linked to a campus network. 54 **computers** are available on campus that provide access to e-mail and the Internet. The 2 **libraries** have 125,858 books and 3,607 subscriptions.

Campus Life

There are 42 active organizations on campus, including a drama/theater group, newspaper, choral group, and marching band. No national or local **sororities**.

Intercollegiate sports include cross-country running, equestrian sports, field hockey, soccer, softball, swimming, tennis, volleyball.

Campus Safety

Student safety services include late-night transport/escort service, 24-hour emergency telephone alarm devices, 24-hour patrols by trained security personnel, and electronically operated dormitory entrances.

Applying

Salem requires an essay, SAT I or ACT, a high school transcript, and 2 recommendations. It recommends an interview. Application deadline: rolling admissions; 3/1 priority date for financial aid. Early and deferred admission are possible.

Getting in Last Year
480 applied
76% were accepted
192 enrolled (53%)
28% from top tenth of their h.s. class
3.57 average high school GPA
39% had SAT verbal scores over 600
18% had SAT math scores over 600
62% had ACT scores over 24
6% had SAT verbal scores over 700
1% had SAT math scores over 700
9% had ACT scores over 30
3 valedictorians

Graduation and After
61% graduated in 4 years
3% graduated in 5 years
20% pursued further study (13% arts and
   sciences, 3% education, 1% business)
77% had job offers within 6 months

Financial Matters
$14,495 tuition and fees (2001–02)
$8570 room and board
$12,300 average financial aid amount received
   per undergraduate (1998–99)

SAMFORD UNIVERSITY

SUBURBAN SETTING ■ PRIVATE ■ INDEPENDENT RELIGIOUS ■ COED
BIRMINGHAM, ALABAMA

Web site: www.samford.edu
Contact: Dr. Phil Kimrey, Dean of Admissions and Financial Aid, 800
  Lakeshore Drive, Samford Hall, Birmingham, AL 35229-0002
Telephone: 205-726-3673 or toll-free 800-888-7218 **Fax:** 205-726-2171
E-mail: seberry@samford.edu

Samford University is the largest private accredited university in Alabama, yet, with 4,500 students, it is an ideal size. More than half the undergraduates reside on campus. Students from 39 states and territories and 25 other countries enjoy a beautiful setting characterized by Georgian-Colonial architecture. The institution takes seriously its Christian heritage and is consistently listed in rankings of Southeastern institutions. Faculty members have earned degrees from more than 160 colleges and universities, with more than 80% holding the terminal degree in their field. Excellent opportunities to "stretch" academically, socially, physically, and spiritually are provided, as are special opportunities in computer competency, international experiences, and externships.

Getting in Last Year
1,903 applied
88% were accepted
663 enrolled (40%)
37% from top tenth of their h.s. class
3.60 average high school GPA
39% had SAT verbal scores over 600
34% had SAT math scores over 600
61% had ACT scores over 24
11% had SAT verbal scores over 700
7% had SAT math scores over 700
14% had ACT scores over 30
9 National Merit Scholars
21 class presidents
29 valedictorians

Graduation and After
57 organizations recruited on campus

Financial Matters
$11,490 tuition and fees (2001–02)
$4850 room and board
86% average percent of need met
$10,690 average financial aid amount received
  per undergraduate (2000–01 estimated)

Academics
Samford awards associate, bachelor's, master's, doctoral, and first-professional **degrees** and post-bachelor's and post-master's certificates. Challenging opportunities include advanced placement credit, accelerated degree programs, student-designed majors, an honors program, double majors, and a senior project. Special programs include cooperative education, internships, summer session for credit, off-campus study, study-abroad, and Army and Air Force ROTC.

The most frequently chosen **baccalaureate** fields are business/marketing, education, and social sciences and history. A complete listing of majors at Samford appears in the Majors Index beginning on page 430.

The **faculty** at Samford has 252 full-time members, 81% with terminal degrees. The student-faculty ratio is 13:1.

Students of Samford
The student body totals 4,377, of whom 2,890 are undergraduates. 63.3% are women and 36.7% are men. Students come from 42 states and territories and 22 other countries. 47% are from Alabama. 0.5% are international students. 6.1% are African American, 0.5% American Indian, 0.7% Asian American, and 0.8% Hispanic American. 84% returned for their sophomore year.

Facilities and Resources
Student rooms are linked to a campus network. 350 **computers** are available on campus for student use. The 4 **libraries** have 428,432 books and 11,117 subscriptions.

Campus Life
There are 133 active organizations on campus, including a drama/theater group, newspaper, radio station, television station, choral group, and marching band. 37% of eligible men and 44% of eligible women are members of national **fraternities** and national **sororities**.

Samford is a member of the NCAA (Division I). **Intercollegiate sports** (some offering scholarships) include baseball (m), basketball, cross-country running, football (m), golf, soccer (w), softball (w), tennis, track and field, volleyball (w).

Campus Safety
Student safety services include late-night transport/escort service, 24-hour emergency telephone alarm devices, 24-hour patrols by trained security personnel, and student patrols.

Applying
Samford requires an essay, SAT I or ACT, a high school transcript, and 1 recommendation. It recommends an interview. Application deadline: 8/1; 3/1 priority date for financial aid. Early and deferred admission are possible.

Santa Clara University

Suburban setting ■ Private ■ Independent Religious ■ Coed
Santa Clara, California

Web site: www.scu.edu
Contact: Ms. Sandra Hayes, Dean of Undergraduate Admissions, 500 El Camino Real, Santa Clara, CA 95053
Telephone: 408-554-4700 **Fax:** 408-554-5255
E-mail: ugadmissions@scu.edu

Academics

Santa Clara awards bachelor's, master's, doctoral, and first-professional **degrees** and post-bachelor's and post-master's certificates. Challenging opportunities include advanced placement credit, student-designed majors, an honors program, double majors, independent study, and a senior project. Special programs include cooperative education, internships, summer session for credit, study-abroad, and Army and Air Force ROTC.

The most frequently chosen **baccalaureate** fields are business/marketing, social sciences and history, and engineering/engineering technologies. A complete listing of majors at Santa Clara appears in the Majors Index beginning on page 430.

The **faculty** at Santa Clara has 410 full-time members, 91% with terminal degrees. The student-faculty ratio is 12:1.

Students of Santa Clara

The student body totals 7,368, of whom 4,279 are undergraduates. 53.7% are women and 46.3% are men. Students come from 48 states and territories and 54 other countries. 69% are from California. 2.9% are international students. 2% are African American, 0.4% American Indian, 19% Asian American, and 13.9% Hispanic American. 92% returned for their sophomore year.

Facilities and Resources

Student rooms are linked to a campus network. 535 **computers** are available on campus for student use. The 2 **libraries** have 454,470 books and 8,919 subscriptions.

Campus Life

There are 55 active organizations on campus, including a drama/theater group, newspaper, radio station, television station, and choral group. No national or local **fraternities** or **sororities**.

Santa Clara is a member of the NCAA (Division I). **Intercollegiate sports** (some offering scholarships) include baseball (m), basketball, crew, cross-country running, golf, soccer, softball (w), tennis, volleyball (w), water polo (m).

Campus Safety

Student safety services include late-night transport/escort service, 24-hour emergency telephone alarm devices, 24-hour patrols by trained security personnel, and electronically operated dormitory entrances.

Applying

Santa Clara requires an essay, SAT I or ACT, a high school transcript, and 1 recommendation. It recommends an interview. Application deadline: 1/15; 2/1 priority date for financial aid. Deferred admission is possible.

Getting in Last Year
6,048 applied
63% were accepted
1,018 enrolled (27%)
40% from top tenth of their h.s. class
3.38 average high school GPA
47% had SAT verbal scores over 600
62% had SAT math scores over 600
81% had ACT scores over 24
8% had SAT verbal scores over 700
14% had SAT math scores over 700
15% had ACT scores over 30
54 National Merit Scholars
44 valedictorians

Graduation and After
75% graduated in 4 years
6% graduated in 5 years
2% graduated in 6 years
20% pursued further study (4% arts and sciences, 4% medicine, 3% education)
400 organizations recruited on campus

Financial Matters
$22,572 tuition and fees (2001–02)
$8436 room and board
79% average percent of need met
$16,715 average financial aid amount received per undergraduate (2000–01)

Sarah Lawrence College

SUBURBAN SETTING ■ PRIVATE ■ INDEPENDENT ■ COED
BRONXVILLE, NEW YORK

Web site: www.slc.edu
Contact: Ms. Thyra L. Briggs, Dean of Admission, 1 Mead Way, Bronxville, NY 10708-5999
Telephone: 914-395-2510 or toll-free 800-888-2858 **Fax:** 914-395-2515
E-mail: slcadmit@slc.edu

Sarah Lawrence, a private, coeducational liberal arts college founded in 1926, is a lively community of students, scholars, and artists just 30 minutes from midtown Manhattan. In its distinctive seminar/conference system, each course consists of two parts: the seminar, limited to 15 students, and the conference, a private biweekly meeting with the seminar professor. In conference, student and teacher create a project that extends the seminar material and connects it to the student's academic goals. To prepare for this rigorous work, all first-year students enroll in a First-Year Studies Seminar. This seminar teacher will be the student's don, or adviser, throughout his or her Sarah Lawrence years.

Academics

Sarah Lawrence awards bachelor's and master's **degrees**. Challenging opportunities include advanced placement credit, student-designed majors, double majors, and independent study. Special programs include internships, off-campus study, and study-abroad.

The most frequently chosen **baccalaureate** field is liberal arts/general studies. A complete listing of majors at Sarah Lawrence appears in the Majors Index beginning on page 430.

The **faculty** at Sarah Lawrence has 176 full-time members. The student-faculty ratio is 6:1.

Students of Sarah Lawrence

The student body totals 1,553, of whom 1,214 are undergraduates. 73.1% are women and 26.9% are men. Students come from 50 states and territories and 27 other countries. 22% are from New York. 3.9% are international students. 5% are African American, 0.4% American Indian, 4.7% Asian American, and 4.2% Hispanic American. 94% returned for their sophomore year.

Facilities and Resources

Student rooms are linked to a campus network. 110 **computers** are available on campus that provide access to the Internet. The 3 **libraries** have 194,090 books and 877 subscriptions.

Campus Life

There are 30 active organizations on campus, including a drama/theater group, newspaper, radio station, and choral group. No national or local **fraternities** or **sororities**.

Intercollegiate sports include crew, cross-country running, equestrian sports, tennis, volleyball (w).

Campus Safety

Student safety services include late-night transport/escort service, 24-hour emergency telephone alarm devices, 24-hour patrols by trained security personnel, student patrols, and electronically operated dormitory entrances.

Applying

Sarah Lawrence requires an essay, SAT I, ACT, or any 3 SAT II Subject Tests, a high school transcript, and 3 recommendations. It recommends an interview and a minimum high school GPA of 3.0. Application deadline: 1/15; 2/1 for financial aid. Early and deferred admission are possible.

Getting in Last Year
2,782 applied
37% were accepted
323 enrolled (31%)
34% from top tenth of their h.s. class
3.60 average high school GPA
79% had SAT verbal scores over 600
50% had SAT math scores over 600
83% had ACT scores over 24
31% had SAT verbal scores over 700
7% had SAT math scores over 700
30% had ACT scores over 30
6 National Merit Scholars
5 valedictorians

Graduation and After
51% graduated in 4 years
11% graduated in 5 years
4% graduated in 6 years
30% pursued further study (10% arts and sciences, 10% law, 5% education)
65% had job offers within 6 months
58 organizations recruited on campus

Financial Matters
$27,982 tuition and fees (2001–02)
$9534 room and board
92% average percent of need met
$24,803 average financial aid amount received per undergraduate

SCRIPPS COLLEGE

SUBURBAN SETTING ■ PRIVATE ■ INDEPENDENT ■ WOMEN ONLY
CLAREMONT, CALIFORNIA

Web site: www.scrippscol.edu
Contact: Ms. Patricia F. Goldsmith, Dean of Admission and Financial Aid,
    1030 Columbia Avenue, Claremont, CA 91711-3948
Telephone: 909-621-8149 or toll-free 800-770-1333 **Fax:** 909-607-7508
E-mail: admission@scrippscol.edu

Academics
Scripps awards bachelor's **degrees** and post-bachelor's certificates. Challenging opportunities include advanced placement credit, accelerated degree programs, student-designed majors, an honors program, double majors, independent study, and a senior project. Special programs include internships, off-campus study, study-abroad, and Army and Air Force ROTC.

The most frequently chosen **baccalaureate** fields are social sciences and history, visual/performing arts, and biological/life sciences. A complete listing of majors at Scripps appears in the Majors Index beginning on page 430.

The **faculty** at Scripps has 61 full-time members, 97% with terminal degrees. The student-faculty ratio is 11:1.

Students of Scripps
The student body totals 816, of whom 798 are undergraduates. Students come from 41 states and territories and 15 other countries. 48% are from California. 2.3% are international students. 3.5% are African American, 0.5% American Indian, 13.4% Asian American, and 5.9% Hispanic American. 77% returned for their sophomore year.

Facilities and Resources
Student rooms are linked to a campus network. 72 **computers** are available on campus that provide access to the Internet. The 5 **libraries** have 1,381,108 books and 4,321 subscriptions.

Campus Life
There are 200 active organizations on campus, including a drama/theater group, newspaper, radio station, and choral group. No national or local **sororities**.

Scripps is a member of the NCAA (Division III). **Intercollegiate sports** include basketball, cross-country running, golf, soccer, softball, swimming, tennis, track and field, volleyball, water polo.

Campus Safety
Student safety services include late-night transport/escort service, 24-hour emergency telephone alarm devices, 24-hour patrols by trained security personnel, and electronically operated dormitory entrances.

Applying
Scripps requires an essay, SAT I or ACT, a high school transcript, 3 recommendations, and graded writing sample. It recommends an interview and a minimum high school GPA of 3.0. Application deadline: 2/1; 2/1 priority date for financial aid. Deferred admission is possible.

Getting in Last Year
1,200 applied
64% were accepted
201 enrolled (26%)
45% from top tenth of their h.s. class
3.70 average high school GPA
80% had SAT verbal scores over 600
64% had SAT math scores over 600
90% had ACT scores over 24
27% had SAT verbal scores over 700
14% had SAT math scores over 700
30% had ACT scores over 30
15 National Merit Scholars
9 valedictorians

Graduation and After
30% pursued further study
300 organizations recruited on campus

Financial Matters
$24,400 tuition and fees (2001–02)
$8100 room and board
100% average percent of need met
$21,731 average financial aid amount received
    per undergraduate

Seattle Pacific University

Urban setting ■ Private ■ Independent Religious ■ Coed
Seattle, Washington

Web site: www.spu.edu
Contact: Mrs. Jennifer Feddern Kenney, Director of Admissions, 3307 Third Avenue West, Seattle, WA 98119-1997
Telephone: 206-281-2517 or toll-free 800-366-3344 **Fax:** 206-281-2669
E-mail: admissions@spu.edu

Getting in Last Year

1,769 applied
83% were accepted
647 enrolled (44%)
40% from top tenth of their h.s. class
3.58 average high school GPA
38% had SAT verbal scores over 600
36% had SAT math scores over 600
55% had ACT scores over 24
8% had SAT verbal scores over 700
5% had SAT math scores over 700
13% had ACT scores over 30
8 National Merit Scholars
41 valedictorians

Graduation and After

12% pursued further study
86% had job offers within 6 months
56 organizations recruited on campus

Financial Matters

$16,425 tuition and fees (2001–02)
$6249 room and board
78% average percent of need met
$12,845 average financial aid amount received per undergraduate

Academics

SPU awards bachelor's, master's, and doctoral **degrees** and post-master's certificates. Challenging opportunities include advanced placement credit, student-designed majors, an honors program, double majors, independent study, and a senior project. Special programs include cooperative education, internships, summer session for credit, off-campus study, study-abroad, and Army, Navy and Air Force ROTC.

The most frequently chosen **baccalaureate** fields are business/marketing, social sciences and history, and health professions and related sciences. A complete listing of majors at SPU appears in the Majors Index beginning on page 430.

The **faculty** at SPU has 173 full-time members, 87% with terminal degrees. The student-faculty ratio is 16:1.

Students of SPU

The student body totals 3,615, of whom 2,828 are undergraduates. 65.7% are women and 34.3% are men. Students come from 39 states and territories and 34 other countries. 65% are from Washington. 1.6% are international students. 1.6% are African American, 0.8% American Indian, 5.3% Asian American, and 1.6% Hispanic American. 80% returned for their sophomore year.

Facilities and Resources

Student rooms are linked to a campus network. 150 **computers** are available on campus that provide access to the Internet. The **library** has 141,712 books and 1,192 subscriptions.

Campus Life

There are 50 active organizations on campus, including a drama/theater group, newspaper, radio station, and choral group. No national or local **fraternities** or **sororities**.

SPU is a member of the NCAA (Division II). **Intercollegiate sports** (some offering scholarships) include basketball, crew, cross-country running, gymnastics (w), soccer, track and field, volleyball (w).

Campus Safety

Student safety services include closed circuit TV monitors, late-night transport/escort service, 24-hour emergency telephone alarm devices, 24-hour patrols by trained security personnel, and student patrols.

Applying

SPU requires an essay, SAT I or ACT, a high school transcript, 2 recommendations, and a minimum high school GPA of 2.5. It recommends SAT I. Application deadline: 6/1; 3/1 priority date for financial aid. Early and deferred admission are possible.

SEATTLE UNIVERSITY

URBAN SETTING ■ PRIVATE ■ INDEPENDENT RELIGIOUS ■ COED
SEATTLE, WASHINGTON

Web site: www.seattleu.edu
Contact: Mr. Michael K. McKeon, Dean of Admissions, 900 Broadway, Seattle, WA 98122-4340
Telephone: 206-296-2000 or toll-free 800-542-0833 (in-state), 800-426-7123 (out-of-state) **Fax:** 206-296-5656
E-mail: admissions@seattleu.edu

Academics

Seattle U awards bachelor's, master's, doctoral, and first-professional **degrees** and post-bachelor's and post-master's certificates. Challenging opportunities include advanced placement credit, accelerated degree programs, student-designed majors, freshman honors college, an honors program, double majors, independent study, and a senior project. Special programs include internships, summer session for credit, off-campus study, study-abroad, and Army, Navy and Air Force ROTC.

The most frequently chosen **baccalaureate** fields are business/marketing, health professions and related sciences, and engineering/engineering technologies. A complete listing of majors at Seattle U appears in the Majors Index beginning on page 430.

The **faculty** at Seattle U has 331 full-time members, 90% with terminal degrees. The student-faculty ratio is 12:1.

Students of Seattle U

The student body totals 5,981, of whom 3,352 are undergraduates. 61.3% are women and 38.7% are men. Students come from 58 states and territories and 69 other countries. 83% are from Washington. 8.9% are international students. 4.4% are African American, 1.2% American Indian, 20.8% Asian American, and 5.7% Hispanic American. 83% returned for their sophomore year.

Facilities and Resources

Student rooms are linked to a campus network. 401 **computers** are available on campus for student use. The 2 **libraries** have 502,438 books and 6,504 subscriptions.

Campus Life

There are 78 active organizations on campus, including a drama/theater group, newspaper, radio station, and choral group. No national or local **fraternities** or **sororities**.

Seattle U is a member of the NCAA (Division II) and NAIA. **Intercollegiate sports** include basketball, cross-country running, soccer, softball (w), swimming, tennis, volleyball (w).

Campus Safety

Student safety services include bicycle patrols, late-night transport/escort service, 24-hour emergency telephone alarm devices, 24-hour patrols by trained security personnel, and electronically operated dormitory entrances.

Applying

Seattle U requires an essay, SAT I or ACT, a high school transcript, 2 recommendations, and a minimum high school GPA of 2.5. Application deadline: 7/1; 2/1 priority date for financial aid. Early and deferred admission are possible.

Seattle University is the Pacific Northwest's only truly urban institution. Seattle is used as an extension of the classroom, complementing the academic foundation provided on campus. This strategic location ensures a multitude of internship and part-time employment opportunities for all students. Seattle's holistic Jesuit educational philosophy, which emphasizes preparation for leadership and service, coupled with a concern for social justice, results in graduates who are competitive in seeking employment or admission to graduate programs. In addition, within the past 14 years, campus facilities have been enhanced by $123 million in both new construction and renovation.

Getting in Last Year
2,634 applied
80% were accepted
643 enrolled (30%)
33% from top tenth of their h.s. class
3.50 average high school GPA
40% had SAT verbal scores over 600
36% had SAT math scores over 600
65% had ACT scores over 24
6% had SAT verbal scores over 700
4% had SAT math scores over 700
11% had ACT scores over 30

Graduation and After
220 organizations recruited on campus

Financial Matters
$17,865 tuition and fees (2001–02)
$6318 room and board
81% average percent of need met
$15,506 average financial aid amount received per undergraduate

SIENA COLLEGE

SUBURBAN SETTING ■ PRIVATE ■ INDEPENDENT RELIGIOUS ■ COED
LOUDONVILLE, NEW YORK

Web site: www.siena.edu
Contact: Mr. Edward Jones, Director of Admissions, 515 Loudon Road,
   Loudonville, NY 12211-1462
Telephone: 518-783-2423 or toll-free 888-ATSIENA **Fax:** 518-783-2436
E-mail: admit@siena.edu

One of the Northeast's premier small, private liberal arts colleges, Siena offers a broad, time-tested liberal arts curriculum that is a journey taken with mentoring, thoughtful faculty members, friars, and friends. It is a journey that empowers students with competence, confidence, and compassion, buttressing classwork with real-world experience. The curriculum includes 25 majors in business, liberal arts, and sciences. In addition, there are more than 15 preprofessional and special academic programs. Siena's 152-acre campus is located in Loudonville, a suburb of Albany, New York, the state capital.

Getting in Last Year
3,346 applied
69% were accepted
712 enrolled (31%)
22% from top tenth of their h.s. class
22% had SAT verbal scores over 600
29% had SAT math scores over 600
50% had ACT scores over 24
1% had SAT verbal scores over 700
2% had SAT math scores over 700
4% had ACT scores over 30

Graduation and After
Graduates pursuing further study: 4% education, 4% medicine, 3% law
75% had job offers within 6 months
180 organizations recruited on campus

Financial Matters
$15,870 tuition and fees (2001–02)
$6815 room and board
75% average percent of need met
$10,501 average financial aid amount received per undergraduate (2000–01)

Academics

Siena awards bachelor's and master's **degrees**. Challenging opportunities include advanced placement credit, an honors program, double majors, independent study, and a senior project. Special programs include internships, summer session for credit, off-campus study, study-abroad, and Army and Air Force ROTC.

The most frequently chosen **baccalaureate** fields are business/marketing, social sciences and history, and psychology. A complete listing of majors at Siena appears in the Majors Index beginning on page 430.

The **faculty** at Siena has 163 full-time members, 84% with terminal degrees. The student-faculty ratio is 14:1.

Students of Siena

The student body totals 3,384, of whom 3,379 are undergraduates. 53.7% are women and 46.3% are men. Students come from 27 states and territories. 85% are from New York. 0.3% are international students. 1.8% are African American, 0.2% American Indian, 2.1% Asian American, and 2.4% Hispanic American. 88% returned for their sophomore year.

Facilities and Resources

Student rooms are linked to a campus network. 650 **computers** are available on campus that provide access to the Internet. The **library** has 299,918 books and 1,243 subscriptions.

Campus Life

There are 78 active organizations on campus, including a drama/theater group, newspaper, radio station, and choral group. No national or local **fraternities** or **sororities**.

Siena is a member of the NCAA (Division I). **Intercollegiate sports** (some offering scholarships) include baseball (m), basketball, cross-country running, field hockey (w), football (m), golf, lacrosse, soccer, softball (w), swimming (w), tennis, volleyball (w).

Campus Safety

Student safety services include call boxes in parking lots and on roadways, late-night transport/escort service, 24-hour emergency telephone alarm devices, 24-hour patrols by trained security personnel, and electronically operated dormitory entrances.

Applying

Siena requires an essay, SAT I or ACT, a high school transcript, and 1 recommendation, and in some cases an interview. Application deadline: 3/1; 2/1 priority date for financial aid. Early and deferred admission are possible.

SIMON'S ROCK COLLEGE OF BARD

RURAL SETTING ■ PRIVATE ■ INDEPENDENT ■ COED
GREAT BARRINGTON, MASSACHUSETTS

Web site: www.simons-rock.edu
Contact: Ms. Mary King Austin, Director of Admissions, 84 Alford Road,
  Great Barrington, MA 01230-9702
Telephone: 413-528-7317 or toll-free 800-235-7186 **Fax:** 413-528-7334
E-mail: admit@simons-rock.edu

Academics

Simon's Rock awards associate and bachelor's **degrees**. Challenging opportunities include student-designed majors, double majors, independent study, and a senior project. Special programs include internships, off-campus study, and study-abroad.

The most frequently chosen **baccalaureate** fields are visual/performing arts, English, and social sciences and history. A complete listing of majors at Simon's Rock appears in the Majors Index beginning on page 430.

The **faculty** at Simon's Rock has 36 full-time members, 94% with terminal degrees. The student-faculty ratio is 9:1.

Students of Simon's Rock

The student body is made up of 414 undergraduates. 57% are women and 43% are men. Students come from 28 states and territories and 3 other countries. 15% are from Massachusetts. 1.2% are international students. 3.5% are African American, 0.7% American Indian, 7% Asian American, and 2.7% Hispanic American. 81% returned for their sophomore year.

Facilities and Resources

Student rooms are linked to a campus network. 25 **computers** are available on campus that provide access to the Internet. The **library** has 71,000 books and 380 subscriptions.

Campus Life

There are 21 active organizations on campus, including a drama/theater group, newspaper, radio station, and choral group. No national or local **fraternities** or **sororities**.

Intercollegiate sports include basketball, soccer, tennis.

Campus Safety

Student safety services include 24-hour weekend patrols by trained security personnel, late-night transport/escort service, 24-hour emergency telephone alarm devices, and electronically operated dormitory entrances.

Applying

Simon's Rock requires an essay, SAT I, PSAT, a high school transcript, an interview, 2 recommendations, parent application, and a minimum high school GPA of 2.0. It recommends ACT and a minimum high school GPA of 3.0. Application deadline: 6/15. Early and deferred admission are possible.

S imon's Rock College of Bard is a selective, private, coeducational college specifically designed to offer highly motivated students the opportunity to begin college after the 10th or 11th grade. The academic and social programs are designed to meet the needs of younger scholars. The AA program combines a substantial core curriculum in the liberal arts and sciences with opportunities to pursue individual interests. The BA program includes advanced course work, tutorials, independent study, and a yearlong thesis project in one of 34 areas of concentration. The Acceleration to Excellence Program, a scholarship competition for high school sophomores, covers the full cost of attending the College for 2 years.

Getting in Last Year
562 applied
42% were accepted
162 enrolled (69%)
63% had SAT verbal scores over 600
40% had SAT math scores over 600
50% had ACT scores over 24
24% had SAT verbal scores over 700
10% had SAT math scores over 700
10% had ACT scores over 30

Graduation and After
70% graduated in 4 years
19% graduated in 5 years
4% graduated in 6 years
Graduates pursuing further study: 16% arts and sciences, 8% medicine, 4% education
62% had job offers within 6 months

Financial Matters
$25,610 tuition and fees (2001–02)
$6840 room and board
71% average percent of need met
$14,775 average financial aid amount received per undergraduate

SIMPSON COLLEGE

SMALL-TOWN SETTING ■ PRIVATE ■ INDEPENDENT RELIGIOUS ■ COED
INDIANOLA, IOWA

Web site: www.simpson.edu
Contact: Ms. Deborah Tierney, Vice President for Enrollment, 701 North C
   Street, Indianola, IA 50125-1297
Telephone: 515-961-1624 or toll-free 800-362-2454 **Fax:** 515-961-1870
E-mail: admiss@simpson.edu

Simpson College combines the best of a liberal arts education with outstanding career preparation and extracurricular programs. Activities range from an award-winning music program to nationally recognized NCAA Division III teams. Located 12 miles from Des Moines, Simpson offers the friendliness of a small town and the advantages of a metropolitan area. Outstanding facilities have been enhanced with multimillion-dollar expansions and renovations, including the state-of-the-art Carver Science Center, named after Simpson's most distinguished alumnus, George Washington Carver. The 4-4-1 academic calendar includes a May Term that provides students with unique learning opportunities. Simpson's beautiful 73-acre, tree-lined campus provides a setting that nurtures creativity, energy, and productivity.

Academics

Simpson awards bachelor's **degrees**. Challenging opportunities include advanced placement credit, accelerated degree programs, student-designed majors, freshman honors college, an honors program, double majors, independent study, and a senior project. Special programs include cooperative education, internships, summer session for credit, off-campus study, and study-abroad.

The most frequently chosen **baccalaureate** fields are business/marketing, communications/communication technologies, and education. A complete listing of majors at Simpson appears in the Majors Index beginning on page 430.

The **faculty** at Simpson has 84 full-time members, 90% with terminal degrees. The student-faculty ratio is 14:1.

Students of Simpson

The student body is made up of 1,816 undergraduates. 58.1% are women and 41.9% are men. Students come from 27 states and territories and 11 other countries. 88% are from Iowa. 1.4% are international students. 0.8% are African American, 0.6% American Indian, 0.7% Asian American, and 0.9% Hispanic American. 82% returned for their sophomore year.

Facilities and Resources

Student rooms are linked to a campus network. 265 **computers** are available on campus that provide access to the Internet. The 2 **libraries** have 174,739 books and 722 subscriptions.

Campus Life

There are 81 active organizations on campus, including a drama/theater group, newspaper, radio station, and choral group. 28% of eligible men and 28% of eligible women are members of national **fraternities**, national **sororities**, and local fraternities.

Simpson is a member of the NCAA (Division III). **Intercollegiate sports** include baseball (m), basketball, cross-country running, football (m), golf, soccer, softball (w), swimming (w), tennis, track and field, volleyball (w), wrestling (m).

Campus Safety

Student safety services include late-night transport/escort service, 24-hour emergency telephone alarm devices, 24-hour patrols by trained security personnel, student patrols, and electronically operated dormitory entrances.

Applying

Simpson requires SAT I or ACT, a high school transcript, and 1 recommendation. It recommends an interview and rank in upper 50% of high school class. Application deadline: 8/15. Early and deferred admission are possible.

Getting in Last Year
1,185 applied
86% were accepted
299 enrolled (29%)
23% from top tenth of their h.s. class
51% had ACT scores over 24
6% had ACT scores over 30
12 valedictorians

Graduation and After
56% graduated in 4 years
11% graduated in 5 years
11% pursued further study (17% arts and sciences, 17% medicine, 7% business)
85% had job offers within 6 months
154 organizations recruited on campus

Financial Matters
$15,908 tuition and fees (2001–02)
$5292 room and board
88% average percent of need met
$16,147 average financial aid amount received per undergraduate

SKIDMORE COLLEGE

SMALL-TOWN SETTING ■ PRIVATE ■ INDEPENDENT ■ COED
SARATOGA SPRINGS, NEW YORK

Web site: www.skidmore.edu
Contact: Ms. Mary Lou W. Bates, Director of Admissions, 815 North
   Broadway, Saratoga Springs, NY 12866-1632
Telephone: 518-580-5570 or toll-free 800-867-6007 **Fax:** 518-580-5584
E-mail: admissions@skidmore.edu

Academics

Skidmore awards bachelor's and master's **degrees**. Challenging opportunities include
advanced placement credit, accelerated degree programs, student-designed majors, an
honors program, double majors, independent study, and a senior project. Special
programs include internships, summer session for credit, off-campus study, study-abroad,
and Army and Air Force ROTC.

The most frequently chosen **baccalaureate** fields are social sciences and history,
business/marketing, and visual/performing arts. A complete listing of majors at Skidmore
appears in the Majors Index beginning on page 430.

The **faculty** at Skidmore has 196 full-time members, 84% with terminal degrees.
The student-faculty ratio is 11:1.

Students of Skidmore

The student body totals 2,544, of whom 2,488 are undergraduates. 59.8% are women
and 40.2% are men. Students come from 46 states and territories and 19 other countries.
29% are from New York. 1.1% are international students. 2.4% are African American,
0.4% American Indian, 4.2% Asian American, and 4.8% Hispanic American. 93%
returned for their sophomore year.

Facilities and Resources

Student rooms are linked to a campus network. 173 **computers** are available on campus
that provide access to the Internet. The **library** has 477,658 books and 2,164 subscriptions.

Campus Life

There are 80 active organizations on campus, including a drama/theater group,
newspaper, radio station, television station, and choral group. No national or local
fraternities or **sororities**.

Skidmore is a member of the NCAA (Division III). **Intercollegiate sports** include
baseball (m), basketball, crew, equestrian sports, field hockey (w), golf (m), ice hockey
(m), lacrosse, soccer, softball (w), swimming, tennis, volleyball (w).

Campus Safety

Student safety services include well-lit campus, late-night transport/escort service, 24-
hour emergency telephone alarm devices, 24-hour patrols by trained security personnel,
and electronically operated dormitory entrances.

Applying

Skidmore requires an essay, SAT I or ACT, a high school transcript, and 2 recommendations. It recommends an interview. Application deadline: 1/15; 1/15 for financial aid.
Early and deferred admission are possible.

Skidmore College, located on a beautiful 850-acre campus, is a liberal arts college with a history of innovation and imagination. An interdisciplinary liberal studies curriculum challenges students to explore broadly. A rich cocurricular program provides further opportunities for personal growth and leadership. Among the largest majors are business, studio art, English, psychology, government, and biology/chemistry. Students from 43 states and territories and 25 countries live and learn in Skidmore's lively intellectual climate and beautiful campus surroundings.

Getting in Last Year
5,633 applied
42% were accepted
599 enrolled (25%)
36% from top tenth of their h.s. class
3.40 average high school GPA
63% had SAT verbal scores over 600
63% had SAT math scores over 600
81% had ACT scores over 24
13% had SAT verbal scores over 700
9% had SAT math scores over 700
11% had ACT scores over 30

Graduation and After
13% pursued further study (5% arts and sciences, 2% education, 2% law)
89% had job offers within 6 months
212 organizations recruited on campus

Financial Matters
$26,676 tuition and fees (2001–02)
$7525 room and board
97% average percent of need met
$22,095 average financial aid amount received
   per undergraduate

Smith College

URBAN SETTING ■ PRIVATE ■ INDEPENDENT ■ WOMEN ONLY
NORTHAMPTON, MASSACHUSETTS

Web site: www.smith.edu
Contact: Ms. Audrey Y. Smith, Director of Admissions, 7 College Lane, Northampton, MA 01063
Telephone: 413-585-2500 **Fax:** 413-585-2527
E-mail: admission@smith.edu

S tudents choose Smith because of its outstanding academic reputation. From its founding in 1871, the College has been committed to providing women with countless opportunities for personal and intellectual growth. The open curriculum allows each student, with the assistance of a faculty adviser, to plan an individualized course of study outside the major. Superb facilities, a beautiful New England campus, and a diverse student body complement the rigorous academic program. New initiatives include the first engineering science major at a women's college and the guarantee that all students will receive funding for an internship related to career and academic goals.

Getting in Last Year
2,869 applied
54% were accepted
660 enrolled (42%)
59% from top tenth of their h.s. class
3.80 average high school GPA
74% had SAT verbal scores over 600
61% had SAT math scores over 600
88% had ACT scores over 24
28% had SAT verbal scores over 700
15% had SAT math scores over 700
35% had ACT scores over 30

Graduation and After
15% pursued further study (7% arts and sciences, 3% law, 1% education)
55 organizations recruited on campus

Financial Matters
$24,550 tuition and fees (2001–02)
$8560 room and board
100% average percent of need met
$23,172 average financial aid amount received per undergraduate

Academics
Smith awards bachelor's, master's, and doctoral **degrees** and post-bachelor's and post-master's certificates. Challenging opportunities include advanced placement credit, accelerated degree programs, student-designed majors, an honors program, double majors, independent study, and a senior project. Special programs include internships, off-campus study, study-abroad, and Army and Air Force ROTC.

The most frequently chosen **baccalaureate** fields are social sciences and history, biological/life sciences, and visual/performing arts. A complete listing of majors at Smith appears in the Majors Index beginning on page 430.

The **faculty** at Smith has 280 full-time members, 96% with terminal degrees. The student-faculty ratio is 9:1.

Students of Smith
The student body totals 3,113, of whom 2,665 are undergraduates. Students come from 53 states and territories and 53 other countries. 24% are from Massachusetts. 6.4% are international students. 5.4% are African American, 0.9% American Indian, 8.6% Asian American, and 5.2% Hispanic American. 91% returned for their sophomore year.

Facilities and Resources
Student rooms are linked to a campus network. 550 **computers** are available on campus that provide access to e-mail and the Internet. The 4 **libraries** have 1,246,348 books and 5,119 subscriptions.

Campus Life
There are 112 active organizations on campus, including a drama/theater group, newspaper, radio station, and choral group. No national or local **sororities**.

Smith is a member of the NCAA (Division III). **Intercollegiate sports** include basketball, crew, cross-country running, equestrian sports, field hockey, lacrosse, skiing (downhill), soccer, softball, squash, swimming, tennis, track and field, volleyball.

Campus Safety
Student safety services include self-defense workshops, emergency telephones, programs in crime and sexual assault prevention, late-night transport/escort service, 24-hour emergency telephone alarm devices, and 24-hour patrols by trained security personnel.

Applying
Smith requires an essay, SAT I or ACT, a high school transcript, and 3 recommendations. It recommends SAT II Subject Tests, SAT II: Writing Test, and an interview. Application deadline: 1/15; 2/1 for financial aid. Early and deferred admission are possible.

SOUTHERN METHODIST UNIVERSITY

SUBURBAN SETTING ■ PRIVATE ■ INDEPENDENT RELIGIOUS ■ COED
DALLAS, TEXAS

Web site: www. smu.edu
Contact: Mr. Ron W. Moss, Director of Admission and Enrollment
Management, PO Box 750181, Dallas, TX 75275-0181
Telephone: 214-768-2058 or toll-free 800-323-0672 **Fax:** 214-768-0103
E-mail: enrol_serv@mail.smu.edu

Academics

SMU awards bachelor's, master's, doctoral, and first-professional **degrees** and post-bachelor's certificates. Challenging opportunities include advanced placement credit, accelerated degree programs, student-designed majors, an honors program, double majors, and independent study. Special programs include cooperative education, internships, summer session for credit, study-abroad, and Army and Air Force ROTC.

The most frequently chosen **baccalaureate** fields are business/marketing, trade and industry, and communications/communication technologies. A complete listing of majors at SMU appears in the Majors Index beginning on page 430.

The **faculty** at SMU has 520 full-time members, 87% with terminal degrees. The student-faculty ratio is 12:1.

Students of SMU

The student body totals 10,266, of whom 5,836 are undergraduates. 54.3% are women and 45.7% are men. Students come from 48 states and territories and 54 other countries. 65% are from Texas. 4.2% are international students. 5.6% are African American, 0.7% American Indian, 6% Asian American, and 8.1% Hispanic American. 86% returned for their sophomore year.

Facilities and Resources

Student rooms are linked to a campus network. 409 **computers** are available on campus for student use. The 8 **libraries** have 3,130,179 books and 11,216 subscriptions.

Campus Life

There are 152 active organizations on campus, including a drama/theater group, newspaper, radio station, choral group, and marching band. 35% of eligible men and 38% of eligible women are members of national **fraternities** and national **sororities**.

SMU is a member of the NCAA (Division I). **Intercollegiate sports** (some offering scholarships) include basketball, crew (w), cross-country running, football (m), golf, soccer, swimming, tennis, track and field, volleyball (w).

Campus Safety

Student safety services include late-night transport/escort service, 24-hour emergency telephone alarm devices, 24-hour patrols by trained security personnel, and electronically operated dormitory entrances.

Applying

SMU requires an essay, SAT I or ACT, a high school transcript, and 1 recommendation, and in some cases SAT II Subject Tests. Application deadline: 1/15; 2/1 priority date for financial aid. Early and deferred admission are possible.

Getting in Last Year
5,322 applied
75% were accepted
1,353 enrolled (34%)
32% from top tenth of their h.s. class
3.33 average high school GPA
39% had SAT verbal scores over 600
47% had SAT math scores over 600
69% had ACT scores over 24
7% had SAT verbal scores over 700
9% had SAT math scores over 700
10% had ACT scores over 30
16 National Merit Scholars

Graduation and After
16% pursued further study (5% arts and sciences, 4% engineering, 3% law)
80% had job offers within 6 months
210 organizations recruited on campus

Financial Matters
$20,796 tuition and fees (2001–02)
$7553 room and board
94% average percent of need met
$20,604 average financial aid amount received per undergraduate

SOUTHWESTERN UNIVERSITY

SUBURBAN SETTING ■ PRIVATE ■ INDEPENDENT RELIGIOUS ■ COED
GEORGETOWN, TEXAS

Web site: www.southwestern.edu
Contact: Mr. John W. Lind, Vice President for Enrollment Management,
    1001 East University Avenue, Georgetown, TX 78626
Telephone: 512-863-1200 or toll-free 800-252-3166 **Fax:** 512-863-9601
E-mail: admission@southwestern.edu

Southwestern University (SU) is a selective national liberal arts college recognized for a high-quality undergraduate academic program, professor-scholars who are dedicated to teaching, superior facilities, and a price that is lower than comparable institutions. Located just north of vibrant Austin, Texas, SU offers its 1,290 students a values-centered educational experience through a broad-based curriculum, preprofessional programs, and extensive extracurricular opportunities, such as internships, study abroad, and NCAA Division III competition. SU's facilities are exemplary among schools of its type. In the past 6 years, SU has built a campus center, a recreational activities complex, a technology-enriched academic building, a science hall addition, residence halls, on-campus apartments, playing fields, and a fine arts expansion.

Academics

SU awards bachelor's **degrees**. Challenging opportunities include advanced placement credit, accelerated degree programs, student-designed majors, freshman honors college, an honors program, double majors, independent study, and a senior project. Special programs include internships, summer session for credit, off-campus study, and study-abroad. A complete listing of majors at SU appears in the Majors Index beginning on page 430.

The **faculty** at SU has 110 full-time members, 96% with terminal degrees. The student-faculty ratio is 11:1.

Students of SU

The student body is made up of 1,320 undergraduates. 56.6% are women and 43.4% are men. Students come from 31 states and territories and 7 other countries. 92% are from Texas. 0.1% are international students. 3% are African American, 0.5% American Indian, 2.3% Asian American, and 12.3% Hispanic American. 88% returned for their sophomore year.

Facilities and Resources

Student rooms are linked to a campus network. 223 **computers** are available on campus that provide access to the Internet. The **library** has 303,017 books and 1,425 subscriptions.

Campus Life

There are 81 active organizations on campus, including a drama/theater group, newspaper, television station, and choral group. 31% of eligible men and 32% of eligible women are members of national **fraternities** and national **sororities**.

SU is a member of the NCAA (Division III). **Intercollegiate sports** include baseball (m), basketball, cross-country running, golf, soccer, swimming, tennis, volleyball (w).

Campus Safety

Student safety services include late-night transport/escort service, 24-hour emergency telephone alarm devices, 24-hour patrols by trained security personnel, student patrols, and electronically operated dormitory entrances.

Applying

SU requires an essay, SAT I or ACT, a high school transcript, and 1 recommendation, and in some cases an interview. It recommends an interview. Application deadline: 2/15; 3/1 for financial aid. Early and deferred admission are possible.

Getting in Last Year
1,561 applied
59% were accepted
325 enrolled (35%)
52% from top tenth of their h.s. class
3.5 average high school GPA
63% had SAT verbal scores over 600
62% had SAT math scores over 600
75% had ACT scores over 24
14% had SAT verbal scores over 700
12% had SAT math scores over 700
19% had ACT scores over 30
2 National Merit Scholars
72 class presidents
9 valedictorians

Graduation and After
57% graduated in 4 years
11% graduated in 5 years
1% graduated in 6 years
23% pursued further study (8% medicine, 7% arts and sciences, 7% law)
63% had job offers within 6 months
23 organizations recruited on campus

Financial Matters
$16,650 tuition and fees (2001–02)
$5900 room and board
98% average percent of need met
$14,613 average financial aid amount received per undergraduate

SOUTHWEST MISSOURI STATE UNIVERSITY

SUBURBAN SETTING ■ PUBLIC ■ STATE-SUPPORTED ■ COED
SPRINGFIELD, MISSOURI

Web site: www.smsu.edu
Contact: Ms. Jill Duncan, Associate Director of Admissions, 901 South
  National, Springfield, MO 65804-0094
Telephone: 417-836-5517 or toll-free 800-492-7900 **Fax:** 417-836-6334
E-mail: smsuinfo@smsu.edu

Academics

SMSU awards bachelor's and master's **degrees** and post-bachelor's certificates. Challenging opportunities include advanced placement credit, accelerated degree programs, student-designed majors, freshman honors college, an honors program, double majors, independent study, and a senior project. Special programs include cooperative education, internships, summer session for credit, off-campus study, study-abroad, and Army ROTC.

The most frequently chosen **baccalaureate** fields are business/marketing, education, and communications/communication technologies. A complete listing of majors at SMSU appears in the Majors Index beginning on page 430.

The **faculty** at SMSU has 719 full-time members, 75% with terminal degrees. The student-faculty ratio is 18:1.

Students of SMSU

The student body totals 18,252, of whom 15,147 are undergraduates. 54.4% are women and 45.6% are men. Students come from 48 states and territories and 85 other countries. 91% are from Missouri. 2.1% are international students. 2.5% are African American, 1.1% American Indian, 1.2% Asian American, and 1.1% Hispanic American. 73% returned for their sophomore year.

Facilities and Resources

Student rooms are linked to a campus network. 3,500 **computers** are available on campus for student use. The 4 **libraries** have 771,382 books and 891,319 subscriptions.

Campus Life

There are 232 active organizations on campus, including a drama/theater group, newspaper, radio station, choral group, and marching band. 12% of eligible men and 10% of eligible women are members of national **fraternities** and national **sororities**.

SMSU is a member of the NCAA (Division I). **Intercollegiate sports** (some offering scholarships) include baseball (m), basketball, cross-country running, field hockey (w), football (m), golf, soccer, softball (w), swimming, tennis, track and field, volleyball (w).

Campus Safety

Student safety services include on-campus police substation, late-night transport/escort service, 24-hour emergency telephone alarm devices, 24-hour patrols by trained security personnel, and electronically operated dormitory entrances.

Applying

SMSU requires SAT I or ACT and a high school transcript, and in some cases an essay and an interview. It recommends ACT. Application deadline: 8/1. Deferred admission is possible.

Southwest Missouri State University is Missouri's second-largest university, with more than 18,000 students from 49 states and 80 countries. As Missouri's public affairs university, SMSU offers 140 undergraduate programs, 40 graduate programs, an Honors College, one of the largest cooperative education programs in the Midwest, NCAA Division I athletics, 250 student organizations, and much more. The compact SMSU campus, with a comfortable blend of traditional and modern buildings and outstanding residence halls, is in Springfield, Missouri's third-largest city. Springfield and the surrounding Ozarks region offer abundant opportunities for recreation, entertainment, and employment.

Getting in Last Year
5,786 applied
86% were accepted
2,570 enrolled (52%)
21% from top tenth of their h.s. class
3.50 average high school GPA
47% had ACT scores over 24
7% had ACT scores over 30
6 National Merit Scholars
83 valedictorians

Graduation and After
20% pursued further study (6% business, 4% arts and sciences, 4% education)
72% had job offers within 6 months
365 organizations recruited on campus

Financial Matters
$3748 resident tuition and fees (2001–02)
$7078 nonresident tuition and fees (2001–02)
$4284 room and board
87% average percent of need met
$7147 average financial aid amount received per undergraduate (2000–01)

STANFORD UNIVERSITY
Suburban setting ■ Private ■ Independent ■ Coed
Stanford, California

Getting in Last Year
19,052 applied
13% were accepted
1,615 enrolled (67%)
84% from top tenth of their h.s. class
3.86 average high school GPA
94% had SAT verbal scores over 600
96% had SAT math scores over 600
98% had ACT scores over 24
67% had SAT verbal scores over 700
71% had SAT math scores over 700
67% had ACT scores over 30

Graduation and After
92% had job offers within 6 months
425 organizations recruited on campus

Financial Matters
$25,917 tuition and fees (2001–02)
$8305 room and board
98% average percent of need met
$22,819 average financial aid amount received per undergraduate (2000–01)

Web site: www.stanford.edu
Contact: Ms. Robin G. Mamlet, Dean of Undergraduate Admissions and Financial Aid, Old Union 232, Old Union, 520 Lasuen Mall, Stanford, CA 94305
Telephone: 650-723-2091 **Fax:** 650-723-6050
E-mail: undergrad.admissions@forsythe.stanford.edu

Academics
Stanford awards bachelor's, master's, doctoral, and first-professional **degrees**. Challenging opportunities include advanced placement credit, student-designed majors, an honors program, double majors, independent study, and a senior project. Special programs include internships, summer session for credit, off-campus study, study-abroad, and Army, Navy and Air Force ROTC.

The most frequently chosen **baccalaureate** fields are social sciences and history, engineering/engineering technologies, and interdisciplinary studies. A complete listing of majors at Stanford appears in the Majors Index beginning on page 430.

The **faculty** at Stanford has 1,671 full-time members, 98% with terminal degrees. The student-faculty ratio is 7:1.

Students of Stanford
The student body totals 17,540, of whom 7,279 are undergraduates. 50.6% are women and 49.4% are men. Students come from 52 states and territories and 58 other countries. 49% are from California. 5.2% are international students. 8.6% are African American, 1.7% American Indian, 24.7% Asian American, and 10.6% Hispanic American. 98% returned for their sophomore year.

Facilities and Resources
Student rooms are linked to a campus network. 1,000 **computers** are available on campus that provide access to the Internet. The 19 **libraries** have 7,000,000 books and 44,504 subscriptions.

Campus Life
There are 500 active organizations on campus, including a drama/theater group, newspaper, radio station, television station, choral group, and marching band. Stanford has national **fraternities**, national **sororities**, and eating clubs.

Stanford is a member of the NCAA (Division I) and NAIA. **Intercollegiate sports** (some offering scholarships) include baseball (m), basketball, crew, cross-country running, fencing, field hockey (w), football (m), golf, gymnastics, lacrosse (w), sailing (w), soccer, softball (w), swimming, tennis, track and field, volleyball, water polo, wrestling (m).

Campus Safety
Student safety services include late-night transport/escort service, 24-hour emergency telephone alarm devices, 24-hour patrols by trained security personnel, and electronically operated dormitory entrances.

Applying
Stanford requires an essay, SAT I or ACT, a high school transcript, and 2 recommendations. It recommends SAT II Subject Tests and SAT II: Writing Test. Application deadline: 12/15; 2/1 priority date for financial aid. Early and deferred admission are possible.

State University of New York at Binghamton

Suburban setting ■ Public ■ State-supported ■ Coed
Binghamton, New York

Web site: www.binghamton.edu
Contact: Cheryl S. Brown, Acting Director of Admissions, PO Box 6001, Binghamton, NY 13902-6001
Telephone: 607-777-2000 **Fax:** 607-777-4445
E-mail: admit@binghamton.edu

Academics

Binghamton University awards bachelor's, master's, and doctoral **degrees** and post-master's certificates. Challenging opportunities include advanced placement credit, accelerated degree programs, student-designed majors, an honors program, double majors, independent study, and a senior project. Special programs include internships, summer session for credit, off-campus study, study-abroad, and Air Force ROTC.

The most frequently chosen **baccalaureate** fields are social sciences and history, business/marketing, and psychology. A complete listing of majors at Binghamton University appears in the Majors Index beginning on page 430.

The **faculty** at Binghamton University has 498 full-time members, 94% with terminal degrees. The student-faculty ratio is 19:1.

Students of Binghamton University

The student body totals 12,820, of whom 10,167 are undergraduates. 53.7% are women and 46.3% are men. Students come from 32 states and territories and 48 other countries. 96% are from New York. 2.1% are international students. 5.8% are African American, 0.2% American Indian, 17.2% Asian American, and 5.4% Hispanic American. 91% returned for their sophomore year.

Facilities and Resources

Student rooms are linked to a campus network. 5,300 **computers** are available on campus that provide access to the Internet. The 2 **libraries** have 1,704,466 books and 9,196 subscriptions.

Campus Life

There are 156 active organizations on campus, including a drama/theater group, newspaper, radio station, television station, and choral group. 10% of eligible men and 12% of eligible women are members of national **fraternities**, national **sororities**, local fraternities, and local sororities.

Binghamton University is a member of the NCAA Division I. **Intercollegiate sports** (some offering scholarships) include baseball (m), basketball, cross-country running, golf (m), lacrosse, soccer, softball (w), swimming, tennis, track and field, volleyball (w), wrestling (m).

Campus Safety

Student safety services include safety awareness programs, well-lit campus, self-defense education, secured campus entrance 12 a.m. to 5 a.m., emergency telephones, late-night transport/escort service, 24-hour emergency telephone alarm devices, 24-hour patrols by trained security personnel, student patrols, and electronically operated dormitory entrances.

Applying

Binghamton University requires an essay, SAT I or ACT, and a high school transcript, and in some cases 1 recommendation and portfolio, audition. Application deadline: rolling admissions; 3/1 priority date for financial aid. Early and deferred admission are possible.

Binghamton University has earned a stellar reputation for exceptional academic programs and an outstanding educational environment. Located in scenic central New York State, Binghamton offers over 80 major degree programs across 5 academic divisions. Recognized as "the Ivy of the SUNY's," Binghamton is the most selective and prestigious university in the SUNY system and one of the most selective colleges and universities in the country. Opportunities for students include internships, study abroad, more than 150 student organizations, an honors program, NCAA athletics, and spacious and attractive housing that rates highly for student satisfaction. Binghamton University offers a high degree of excellence in education while remaining affordable and is cited as an exceptional educational value by a number of national publications.

Getting in Last Year
17,381 applied
45% were accepted
2,227 enrolled (29%)
3.38 average high school GPA
48% had SAT verbal scores over 600
66% had SAT math scores over 600
79% had ACT scores over 24
7% had SAT verbal scores over 700
16% had SAT math scores over 700
17% had ACT scores over 30
17 valedictorians

Graduation and After
38% pursued further study (9% medicine, 7% education, 7% law)
200 organizations recruited on campus

Financial Matters
$4551 resident tuition and fees (2001–02)
$9451 nonresident tuition and fees (2001–02)
$6102 room and board
100% average percent of need met
$9814 average financial aid amount received per undergraduate

State University of New York College at Geneseo

Small-town setting ■ Public ■ State-supported ■ Coed
Geneseo, New York

Web site: www.geneseo.edu
Contact: Kris Shay, Associate Director of Admissions, 1 College Circle, Geneseo, NY 14454-1401
Telephone: 585-245-5571 or toll-free 866-245-5211 (in-state) **Fax:** 585-245-5550
E-mail: admissions@geneseo.edu

Getting in Last Year
7,794 applied
52% were accepted
1,145 enrolled (28%)
47% from top tenth of their h.s. class
3.62 average high school GPA
55% had SAT verbal scores over 600
60% had SAT math scores over 600
81% had ACT scores over 24
7% had SAT verbal scores over 700
7% had SAT math scores over 700
10% had ACT scores over 30

Graduation and After
67% graduated in 4 years
11% graduated in 5 years
2% graduated in 6 years
27% pursued further study
60% had job offers within 6 months
62 organizations recruited on campus

Financial Matters
$4310 resident tuition and fees (2001–02)
$9210 nonresident tuition and fees (2001–02)
$5660 room and board
85% average percent of need met
$7421 average financial aid amount received per undergraduate

Academics

Geneseo College awards bachelor's and master's **degrees**. Challenging opportunities include advanced placement credit, an honors program, double majors, independent study, and a senior project. Special programs include internships, summer session for credit, off-campus study, study-abroad, and Army and Air Force ROTC.

The most frequently chosen **baccalaureate** fields are education, social sciences and history, and business/marketing. A complete listing of majors at Geneseo College appears in the Majors Index beginning on page 430.

The **faculty** at Geneseo College has 251 full-time members, 94% with terminal degrees. The student-faculty ratio is 19:1.

Students of Geneseo College

The student body totals 5,649, of whom 5,371 are undergraduates. 64.9% are women and 35.1% are men. Students come from 19 states and territories and 19 other countries. 99% are from New York. 0.8% are international students. 2% are African American, 0.2% American Indian, 5.2% Asian American, and 2.7% Hispanic American. 91% returned for their sophomore year.

Facilities and Resources

Student rooms are linked to a campus network. 800 **computers** are available on campus that provide access to the Internet. The 2 **libraries** have 502,537 books and 2,284 subscriptions.

Campus Life

There are 164 active organizations on campus, including a drama/theater group, newspaper, radio station, television station, and choral group. 12% of eligible men and 9% of eligible women are members of national **fraternities**, national **sororities**, local fraternities, and local sororities.

Geneseo College is a member of the NCAA (Division III). **Intercollegiate sports** include basketball, cross-country running, field hockey (w), ice hockey (m), lacrosse, soccer, softball (w), swimming, tennis (w), track and field, volleyball.

Campus Safety

Student safety services include late-night transport/escort service, 24-hour emergency telephone alarm devices, 24-hour patrols by trained security personnel, student patrols, and electronically operated dormitory entrances.

Applying

Geneseo College requires an essay, SAT I or ACT, and a high school transcript. It recommends an interview and recommendations. Application deadline: 2/15; 2/15 priority date for financial aid. Early and deferred admission are possible.

STATE UNIVERSITY OF NEW YORK COLLEGE OF ENVIRONMENTAL SCIENCE AND FORESTRY

URBAN SETTING ■ PUBLIC ■ STATE-SUPPORTED ■ COED
SYRACUSE, NEW YORK

Web site: www.esf.edu
Contact: Ms. Susan Sanford, Director of Admissions, 1 Forestry Drive,
Syracuse, NY 13210-2779
Telephone: 315-470-6600 or toll-free 800-777-7373 **Fax:** 315-470-6933
E-mail: esfinfo@esf.edu

Academics

ESF awards associate, bachelor's, master's, and doctoral **degrees**. Challenging opportunities include advanced placement credit, accelerated degree programs, freshman honors college, an honors program, double majors, independent study, and a senior project. Special programs include cooperative education, internships, off-campus study, study-abroad, and Army and Air Force ROTC.

The most frequently chosen **baccalaureate** fields are biological/life sciences, natural resources/environmental science, and architecture. A complete listing of majors at ESF appears in the Majors Index beginning on page 430.

The **faculty** at ESF has 122 full-time members, 80% with terminal degrees. The student-faculty ratio is 12:1.

Students of ESF

The student body totals 1,971, of whom 1,263 are undergraduates. 39% are women and 61% are men. Students come from 23 states and territories and 2 other countries. 91% are from New York. 0.6% are international students. 3.3% are African American, 0.4% American Indian, 1.8% Asian American, and 3.4% Hispanic American. 81% returned for their sophomore year.

Facilities and Resources

Student rooms are linked to a campus network. 150 **computers** are available on campus that provide access to the Internet. The 2 **libraries** have 130,305 books and 2,001 subscriptions.

Campus Life

There are 300 active organizations on campus, including a drama/theater group, newspaper, radio station, choral group, and marching band. 33% of eligible men and 33% of eligible women are members of national **fraternities** and national **sororities**.

This institution has no intercollegiate sports.

Campus Safety

Student safety services include late-night transport/escort service, 24-hour emergency telephone alarm devices, 24-hour patrols by trained security personnel, and electronically operated dormitory entrances.

Applying

ESF requires an essay, SAT I or ACT, a high school transcript, inventory of courses-in-progress form, and a minimum high school GPA of 3.3. It recommends an interview and 3 recommendations. Application deadline: rolling admissions; 3/1 priority date for financial aid. Early and deferred admission are possible.

Getting in Last Year
694 applied
57% were accepted
202 enrolled (51%)
18% from top tenth of their h.s. class
3.50 average high school GPA
33% had SAT verbal scores over 600
36% had SAT math scores over 600
55% had ACT scores over 24
4% had SAT verbal scores over 700
4% had SAT math scores over 700
2% had ACT scores over 30
1 National Merit Scholar
2 valedictorians

Graduation and After
51% graduated in 4 years
19% graduated in 5 years
3% graduated in 6 years
20% pursued further study (9% arts and sciences, 4% engineering, 3% education)
73% had job offers within 6 months
25 organizations recruited on campus

Financial Matters
$3776 resident tuition and fees (2001–02)
$8676 nonresident tuition and fees (2001–02)
$8670 room and board
85% average percent of need met
$8500 average financial aid amount received per undergraduate

STEVENS INSTITUTE OF TECHNOLOGY
URBAN SETTING ■ PRIVATE ■ INDEPENDENT ■ COED
HOBOKEN, NEW JERSEY

Web site: www.stevens-tech.edu
Contact: Mr. Daniel Gallagher, Dean of Undergraduate Admissions, Castle Point on Hudson, Hoboken, NJ 07030
Telephone: 201-216-5197 or toll-free 800-458-5323 **Fax:** 201-216-8348
E-mail: admissions@stevens-tech.edu

Stevens ranks in the top 5% among the nation's technological universities as it continues to educate leaders and innovators. Each undergraduate program—business, engineering, the sciences, computer science, and the humanities—follows a broad-based course curriculum taught by distinguished faculty members. The 9:1 student-faculty ratio enables personal attention and growth. All students combine their classroom and laboratory experience with cooperative education, summer internships, and/or research opportunities to enhance their prestigious Stevens education. Located in Hoboken, one of America's most desirable towns, Stevens is just minutes from New York City and all of the educational, cultural, and extracurricular opportunities it offers.

Getting in Last Year
2,622 applied
49% were accepted
3.80 average high school GPA
56% had SAT verbal scores over 600
93% had SAT math scores over 600
12% had SAT verbal scores over 700
36% had SAT math scores over 700

Graduation and After
18% pursued further study
90% had job offers within 6 months
350 organizations recruited on campus

Financial Matters
$23,150 tuition and fees (2001–02)
$7730 room and board
92% average percent of need met
$18,973 average financial aid amount received per undergraduate

Academics
Stevens awards bachelor's, master's, and doctoral **degrees** and post-bachelor's certificates. Challenging opportunities include advanced placement credit, accelerated degree programs, an honors program, double majors, independent study, and a senior project. Special programs include cooperative education, internships, summer session for credit, off-campus study, study-abroad, and Army and Air Force ROTC.

The most frequently chosen **baccalaureate** fields are engineering/engineering technologies, computer/information sciences, and business/marketing. A complete listing of majors at Stevens appears in the Majors Index beginning on page 430.

The **faculty** at Stevens has 102 full-time members, 100% with terminal degrees. The student-faculty ratio is 9:1.

Students of Stevens
The student body totals 4,263, of whom 1,646 are undergraduates. Students come from 40 states and territories and 68 other countries. 65% are from New Jersey. 89% returned for their sophomore year.

Facilities and Resources
Student rooms are linked to a campus network. 1,700 **computers** are available on campus that provide access to online grade and account information and the Internet. The **library** has 59,489 books and 162 subscriptions.

Campus Life
There are 70 active organizations on campus, including a drama/theater group, newspaper, radio station, television station, and choral group. 30% of eligible men and 33% of eligible women are members of national **fraternities**, national **sororities**, and local sororities.

Stevens is a member of the NCAA (Division III). **Intercollegiate sports** include baseball (m), basketball, cross-country running, fencing, lacrosse, soccer, swimming (w), tennis, track and field, volleyball.

Campus Safety
Student safety services include late-night transport/escort service, 24-hour emergency telephone alarm devices, 24-hour patrols by trained security personnel, and electronically operated dormitory entrances.

Applying
Stevens requires SAT I or ACT, a high school transcript, and an interview, and in some cases SAT II Subject Tests, SAT II: Writing Test, and SAT I and SAT II or ACT. It recommends an essay, SAT II Subject Tests, SAT II: Writing Test, and recommendations. Application deadline: 2/15; 2/15 priority date for financial aid. Early and deferred admission are possible.

SUSQUEHANNA UNIVERSITY

SMALL-TOWN SETTING ■ PRIVATE ■ INDEPENDENT RELIGIOUS ■ COED
SELINSGROVE, PENNSYLVANIA

Web site: www.susqu.edu
Contact: Mr. Chris Markle, Director of Admissions, 514 University Avenue,
    Selinsgrove, PA 17870-1040
Telephone: 570-372-4260 or toll-free 800-326-9672 **Fax:** 570-372-2722
E-mail: suadmiss@susqu.edu

Academics

Susquehanna awards bachelor's **degrees** (also offers associate degree through evening
program to local students). Challenging opportunities include advanced placement
credit, accelerated degree programs, student-designed majors, an honors program,
double majors, independent study, and a senior project. Special programs include internships, summer session for credit, off-campus study, study-abroad, and Army ROTC.

   The most frequently chosen **baccalaureate** fields are business/marketing, com-
munications/communication technologies, and education. A complete listing of majors at
Susquehanna appears in the Majors Index beginning on page 430.

   The **faculty** at Susquehanna has 106 full-time members, 88% with terminal degrees.
The student-faculty ratio is 14:1.

Students of Susquehanna

The student body is made up of 1,949 undergraduates. 57.1% are women and 42.9% are
men. Students come from 26 states and territories and 13 other countries. 64% are from
Pennsylvania. 0.6% are international students. 1.9% are African American, 0.3%
American Indian, 1.9% Asian American, and 1.9% Hispanic American. 90% returned for
their sophomore year.

Facilities and Resources

Student rooms are linked to a campus network. 287 **computers** are available on campus
that provide access to e-mail, online class listings and course assignments and the Internet. The **library** has 243,937 books and 2,408 subscriptions.

Campus Life

There are 100 active organizations on campus, including a drama/theater group,
newspaper, radio station, and choral group. 25% of eligible men and 25% of eligible
women are members of national **fraternities** and national **sororities**.

   Susquehanna is a member of the NCAA (Division III). **Intercollegiate sports**
include baseball (m), basketball, cross-country running, field hockey (w), football (m),
golf (m), lacrosse, soccer, softball (w), swimming, tennis, track and field, volleyball (w).

Campus Safety

Student safety services include late-night transport/escort service, 24-hour patrols by
trained security personnel, and electronically operated dormitory entrances.

Applying

Susquehanna requires an essay, a high school transcript, 1 recommendation, and a
minimum high school GPA of 2.5, and in some cases SAT I or ACT and writing
portfolio, auditions for music programs. It recommends SAT II Subject Tests, SAT II:
Writing Test, an interview, and a minimum high school GPA of 3.0. Application
deadline: 3/1; 3/1 priority date for financial aid. Early and deferred admission are possible.

With the qualities of both a residential college and a challenging university, Susquehanna offers a liberal arts curriculum that builds a broad base of knowledge to help students become educated citizens of the world. It also offers the in-depth preparation students need to succeed in graduate and professional schools and jobs. Faculty members have excellent credentials and are accessible. Thoughtful advising helps students discover their interests and strengths, and the academic program develops students' intellectual skills and self-confidence. Students benefit from professional experiences in joint research programs with faculty members, extensive internship opportunities, study abroad, award-winning community service programs, and leadership opportunities in all areas of the University. The campus is fully wired, with Internet access from every residence hall room.

Getting in Last Year
2,299 applied
76% were accepted
574 enrolled (33%)
29% from top tenth of their h.s. class
32% had SAT verbal scores over 600
38% had SAT math scores over 600
4% had SAT verbal scores over 700
4% had SAT math scores over 700
1 National Merit Scholar
29 class presidents
16 valedictorians

Graduation and After
73% graduated in 4 years
2% graduated in 5 years
17% pursued further study (9% arts and sci-
    ences, 3% law, 2% medicine)
79% had job offers within 6 months
40 organizations recruited on campus

Financial Matters
$21,270 tuition and fees (2001–02)
$6000 room and board
84% average percent of need met
$15,535 average financial aid amount received
    per undergraduate (2000–01 estimated)

SWARTHMORE COLLEGE

SUBURBAN SETTING ■ PRIVATE ■ INDEPENDENT ■ COED
SWARTHMORE, PENNSYLVANIA

Web site: www.swarthmore.edu
Contact: Office of Admissions, 500 College Avenue, Swarthmore, PA
 19081-1397
Telephone: 610-328-8300 or toll-free 800-667-3110 **Fax:** 610-328-8580
E-mail: admissions@swarthmore.edu

S warthmore is a highly selective college of liberal arts and engineering, located 11 miles southwest of Philadelphia. Founded as a coeducational institution in 1864, it is nonsectarian but reflects many traditions and values of its Quaker founders and attracts students who are engaged in the community as well as the classroom. Swarthmore's Honors Program provides an option to study in small seminars during the junior and senior years. A small school by deliberate policy, its enrollment is about 1,400, with a student-faculty ratio of 8:1. It attracts students from 50 states and 58 other countries.

Getting in Last Year
3,504 applied
26% were accepted
381 enrolled (42%)
88% from top tenth of their h.s. class
94% had SAT verbal scores over 600
95% had SAT math scores over 600
72% had SAT verbal scores over 700
67% had SAT math scores over 700
39 National Merit Scholars
52 valedictorians

Graduation and After
19% pursued further study
100 organizations recruited on campus

Financial Matters
$26,376 tuition and fees (2001–02)
$8162 room and board
100% average percent of need met
$24,474 average financial aid amount received
 per undergraduate

Academics

Swarthmore awards bachelor's **degrees**. Challenging opportunities include advanced placement credit, student-designed majors, an honors program, double majors, independent study, and a senior project. Special programs include internships, off-campus study, study-abroad, and Army, Navy and Air Force ROTC.

The most frequently chosen **baccalaureate** fields are social sciences and history, biological/life sciences, and English. A complete listing of majors at Swarthmore appears in the Majors Index beginning on page 430.

The **faculty** at Swarthmore has 160 full-time members, 99% with terminal degrees. The student-faculty ratio is 8:1.

Students of Swarthmore

The student body is made up of 1,473 undergraduates. 53% are women and 47% are men. Students come from 47 states and territories and 42 other countries. 18% are from Pennsylvania. 6.4% are international students. 7.7% are African American, 0.8% American Indian, 15.8% Asian American, and 8.1% Hispanic American. 95% returned for their sophomore year.

Facilities and Resources

Student rooms are linked to a campus network. 125 **computers** are available on campus that provide access to the Internet. The 4 **libraries** have 558,508 books and 8,202 subscriptions.

Campus Life

There are 100 active organizations on campus, including a drama/theater group, newspaper, radio station, and choral group. 6% of eligible men are members of national **fraternities** and local fraternities.

Swarthmore is a member of the NCAA (Division III). **Intercollegiate sports** include badminton (w), baseball (m), basketball, cross-country running, field hockey (w), golf (m), lacrosse, soccer, softball (w), swimming, tennis, track and field, volleyball (w).

Campus Safety

Student safety services include late-night transport/escort service, 24-hour emergency telephone alarm devices, 24-hour patrols by trained security personnel, and student patrols.

Applying

Swarthmore requires an essay, SAT II Subject Tests, SAT II: Writing Test, SAT I or ACT, a high school transcript, and 2 recommendations, and in some cases SAT II Subject Test in math. It recommends an interview. Application deadline: 1/1; 2/15 priority date for financial aid. Early and deferred admission are possible.

SWEET BRIAR COLLEGE

RURAL SETTING ■ PRIVATE ■ INDEPENDENT ■ WOMEN ONLY
SWEET BRIAR, VIRGINIA

Web site: www.sbc.edu
Contact: Ms. Margaret Williams Blount, Director of Admissions, PO Box B, Sweet Briar, VA 24595
Telephone: 434-381-6142 or toll-free 800-381-6142 **Fax:** 434-381-6152
E-mail: admissions@sbc.edu

Academics

Sweet Briar awards bachelor's **degrees**. Challenging opportunities include advanced placement credit, accelerated degree programs, student-designed majors, an honors program, double majors, independent study, and a senior project. Special programs include internships, summer session for credit, off-campus study, and study-abroad.

The most frequently chosen **baccalaureate** fields are social sciences and history, mathematics, and psychology. A complete listing of majors at Sweet Briar appears in the Majors Index beginning on page 430.

The **faculty** at Sweet Briar has 71 full-time members, 94% with terminal degrees. The student-faculty ratio is 7:1.

Students of Sweet Briar

The student body is made up of 738 undergraduates. Students come from 44 states and territories and 11 other countries. 40% are from Virginia. 2.5% are international students. 4.4% are African American, 0.7% American Indian, 2% Asian American, and 3% Hispanic American. 82% returned for their sophomore year.

Facilities and Resources

Student rooms are linked to a campus network. 117 **computers** are available on campus that provide access to the Internet. The 4 **libraries** have 474,818 books and 9,792 subscriptions.

Campus Life

There are 43 active organizations on campus, including a drama/theater group, newspaper, radio station, television station, and choral group. No national or local **sororities**.

Sweet Briar is a member of the NCAA (Division III). **Intercollegiate sports** include field hockey, lacrosse, soccer, swimming, tennis, volleyball.

Campus Safety

Student safety services include front gate security, late-night transport/escort service, 24-hour emergency telephone alarm devices, 24-hour patrols by trained security personnel, and electronically operated dormitory entrances.

Applying

Sweet Briar requires an essay, SAT I or ACT, a high school transcript, and 2 recommendations, and in some cases an interview. It recommends SAT II Subject Tests. Application deadline: 2/1; 3/1 priority date for financial aid. Early and deferred admission are possible.

Sweet Briar women are intellectually adventurous, willing to explore new fields and challenge boundaries. This attitude helps graduates compete confidently in graduate school and in the corporate world as scientists and writers, lawyers and judges, and dancers and art historians. Sweet Briar attracts women who enjoy being involved not only in a first-rate academic program but also in meaningful activities outside the classroom. A hands-on, one-on-one approach to the sciences; strong prelaw, international affairs, environmental studies, and fine arts programs; and superior study-abroad programs encourage bright students to excel. Sweet Briar students are taken seriously, and professors take an interest in their intellectual development and personal growth.

Getting in Last Year

440 applied
81% were accepted
159 enrolled (44%)
33% from top tenth of their h.s. class
3.43 average high school GPA
40% had SAT verbal scores over 600
28% had SAT math scores over 600
54% had ACT scores over 24
5% had SAT verbal scores over 700
2% had SAT math scores over 700
9% had ACT scores over 30
1 National Merit Scholar
1 class president
7 valedictorians

Graduation and After

70% graduated in 4 years
2% graduated in 5 years
1% graduated in 6 years
20% pursued further study (10% arts and sciences, 1% business, 1% law)
50% had job offers within 6 months
14 organizations recruited on campus

Financial Matters

$18,010 tuition and fees (2001–02)
$7300 room and board
92% average percent of need met
$16,690 average financial aid amount received per undergraduate

SYRACUSE UNIVERSITY

URBAN SETTING ■ PRIVATE ■ INDEPENDENT ■ COED
SYRACUSE, NEW YORK

Web site: www.syracuse.edu
Contact: Office of Admissions, 201 Tolley Administration Building, Syracuse, NY 13244-1100
Telephone: 315-443-3611
E-mail: orange@syr.edu

As a leading student-centered research university, Syracuse University is committed to giving students the very best education available. Faculty members encourage interaction through small classes and integrate research into teaching. A continued commitment to the liberal arts complements professional teaching in all colleges. Students' individual needs are met through the University's enhanced system of orientation and advising, expanded use of introductory courses, and an increased selection of interdisciplinary majors and minors. Syracuse students augment their course work with internships, study-abroad opportunities, and a wide variety of extracurricular activities.

Getting in Last Year
14,514 applied
64% were accepted
2,627 enrolled (28%)
40% from top tenth of their h.s. class
3.50 average high school GPA
50% had SAT verbal scores over 600
61% had SAT math scores over 600
9% had SAT verbal scores over 700
13% had SAT math scores over 700
41 valedictorians

Graduation and After
61% graduated in 4 years
11% graduated in 5 years
2% graduated in 6 years
14% pursued further study (3% law, 2% arts and sciences, 2% education)
82% had job offers within 6 months
256 organizations recruited on campus

Financial Matters
$21,960 tuition and fees (2001–02)
$8750 room and board
80% average percent of need met
$17,000 average financial aid amount received per undergraduate

Academics
SU awards bachelor's, master's, doctoral, and first-professional **degrees** and post-master's certificates. Challenging opportunities include advanced placement credit, accelerated degree programs, student-designed majors, an honors program, double majors, independent study, and a senior project. Special programs include cooperative education, internships, summer session for credit, off-campus study, study-abroad, and Army and Air Force ROTC.

The most frequently chosen **baccalaureate** fields are communications/communication technologies, business/marketing, and social sciences and history. A complete listing of majors at SU appears in the Majors Index beginning on page 430.

The **faculty** at SU has 832 full-time members, 86% with terminal degrees. The student-faculty ratio is 12:1.

Students of SU
The student body totals 14,421, of whom 10,702 are undergraduates. 54.7% are women and 45.3% are men. Students come from 52 states and territories and 61 other countries. 45% are from New York. 3.4% are international students. 7.2% are African American, 0.2% American Indian, 5.2% Asian American, and 4.4% Hispanic American. 90% returned for their sophomore year.

Facilities and Resources
Student rooms are linked to a campus network. 1,200 **computers** are available on campus that provide access to online services, networked client and server computing and the Internet. The 7 **libraries** have 3,000,000 books and 12,000 subscriptions.

Campus Life
There are 250 active organizations on campus, including a drama/theater group, newspaper, radio station, television station, choral group, and marching band. 8% of eligible men and 13% of eligible women are members of national **fraternities**, national **sororities**, and local fraternities.

SU is a member of the NCAA (Division I). **Intercollegiate sports** (some offering scholarships) include basketball, crew, cross-country running, field hockey (w), football (m), lacrosse, soccer, softball (w), swimming, tennis (w), track and field, volleyball (w).

Campus Safety
Student safety services include crime prevention and neighborhood outreach programs, late-night transport/escort service, 24-hour emergency telephone alarm devices, 24-hour patrols by trained security personnel, and electronically operated dormitory entrances.

Applying
SU requires an essay, SAT I or ACT, a high school transcript, and 2 recommendations, and in some cases audition for drama and music programs, portfolio for art and architecture programs. It recommends an interview. Application deadline: 1/1; 2/1 priority date for financial aid. Early and deferred admission are possible.

TAYLOR UNIVERSITY
RURAL SETTING ■ PRIVATE ■ INDEPENDENT RELIGIOUS ■ COED
UPLAND, INDIANA

Web site: www.tayloru.edu
Contact: Mr. Stephen R. Mortland, Director of Admissions, 236 West Reade
   Avenue, Upland, IN 46989-1001
Telephone: 765-998-5134 or toll-free 800-882-3456 **Fax:** 765-998-4925
E-mail: admissions_u@tayloru.edu

Academics
Taylor awards associate and bachelor's **degrees**. Challenging opportunities include advanced placement credit, accelerated degree programs, student-designed majors, an honors program, double majors, independent study, and a senior project. Special programs include internships, summer session for credit, off-campus study, and study-abroad.

The most frequently chosen **baccalaureate** fields are education, business/marketing, and philosophy. A complete listing of majors at Taylor appears in the Majors Index beginning on page 430.

The **faculty** at Taylor has 134 full-time members, 70% with terminal degrees. The student-faculty ratio is 15:1.

Students of Taylor
The student body is made up of 1,861 undergraduates. 52.2% are women and 47.8% are men. Students come from 48 states and territories and 17 other countries. 31% are from Indiana. 89% returned for their sophomore year.

Facilities and Resources
Student rooms are linked to a campus network. 235 **computers** are available on campus for student use. The **library** has 188,000 books and 737 subscriptions.

Campus Life
There are 30 active organizations on campus, including a drama/theater group, newspaper, radio station, television station, and choral group. No national or local **fraternities** or **sororities**.

Taylor is a member of the NAIA and NCCAA. **Intercollegiate sports** (some offering scholarships) include baseball (m), basketball, cross-country running, football (m), golf (m), soccer, softball (w), tennis, track and field, volleyball (w).

Campus Safety
Student safety services include late-night transport/escort service, 24-hour patrols by trained security personnel, and student patrols.

Applying
Taylor requires an essay, SAT I or ACT, a high school transcript, an interview, and 2 recommendations. It recommends a minimum high school GPA of 2.8. Application deadline: rolling admissions; 3/1 for financial aid. Deferred admission is possible.

Getting in Last Year
1,389 applied
78% were accepted
492 enrolled (46%)
43% from top tenth of their h.s. class
3.70 average high school GPA
56% had SAT verbal scores over 600
55% had SAT math scores over 600
78% had ACT scores over 24
9% had SAT verbal scores over 700
11% had SAT math scores over 700
16% had ACT scores over 30
8 National Merit Scholars
37 valedictorians

Graduation and After
71% graduated in 4 years
3% graduated in 5 years
1% graduated in 6 years
13% pursued further study
48% had job offers within 6 months
125 organizations recruited on campus

Financial Matters
$16,572 tuition and fees (2001–02)
$4990 room and board
81% average percent of need met
$11,835 average financial aid amount received
   per undergraduate

Texas A&M University

SUBURBAN SETTING ■ PUBLIC ■ STATE-SUPPORTED ■ COED
COLLEGE STATION, TEXAS

Web site: www.tamu.edu
Contact: Dr. Frank Ashley, Director of Admissions, 217 John J. Koldus Building, College Station, TX 77843-1265
Telephone: 979-845-3741 **Fax:** 979-845-8737
E-mail: admissions@tamu.edu

Getting in Last Year
16,685 applied
69% were accepted
6,760 enrolled (59%)
55% from top tenth of their h.s. class
40% had SAT verbal scores over 600
50% had SAT math scores over 600
65% had ACT scores over 24
7% had SAT verbal scores over 700
13% had SAT math scores over 700
15% had ACT scores over 30
149 National Merit Scholars
237 valedictorians

Graduation and After
27% graduated in 4 years
35% graduated in 5 years
6% graduated in 6 years
17% pursued further study
52% had job offers within 6 months
1501 organizations recruited on campus

Financial Matters
$3722 resident tuition and fees (2001–02)
$10,052 nonresident tuition and fees (2001–02)
$5266 room and board

Academics
Texas A&M awards bachelor's, master's, doctoral, and first-professional **degrees** and post-bachelor's certificates. Challenging opportunities include advanced placement credit, an honors program, double majors, independent study, and a senior project. Special programs include cooperative education, internships, summer session for credit, off-campus study, study-abroad, and Army, Navy and Air Force ROTC.

The most frequently chosen **baccalaureate** fields are business/marketing, engineering/engineering technologies, and agriculture. A complete listing of majors at Texas A&M appears in the Majors Index beginning on page 430.

The **faculty** at Texas A&M has 1,879 full-time members, 92% with terminal degrees. The student-faculty ratio is 22:1.

Students of Texas A&M
The student body totals 44,618, of whom 36,603 are undergraduates. 48.8% are women and 51.2% are men. Students come from 52 states and territories and 111 other countries. 96% are from Texas. 1.3% are international students. 2.4% are African American, 0.5% American Indian, 3.3% Asian American, and 9% Hispanic American. 88% returned for their sophomore year.

Facilities and Resources
Student rooms are linked to a campus network. 1,500 **computers** are available on campus for student use. The 5 **libraries** have 1,506,107 books and 26,625 subscriptions.

Campus Life
There are 700 active organizations on campus, including a drama/theater group, newspaper, radio station, television station, choral group, and marching band. 3% of eligible men and 7% of eligible women are members of national **fraternities**, national **sororities**, local fraternities, and local sororities.

Texas A&M is a member of the NCAA (Division I). **Intercollegiate sports** (some offering scholarships) include archery (w), baseball (m), basketball, cross-country running, equestrian sports (w), football (m), golf, soccer (w), softball (w), swimming, tennis, track and field, volleyball (w).

Campus Safety
Student safety services include student escorts, late-night transport/escort service, 24-hour emergency telephone alarm devices, 24-hour patrols by trained security personnel, and electronically operated dormitory entrances.

Applying
Texas A&M requires an essay, SAT I or ACT, and a high school transcript. Application deadline: 2/15.

Texas Christian University

Suburban setting ■ Private ■ Independent Religious ■ Coed
Fort Worth, Texas

Web site: www.tcu.edu
Contact: Mr. Ray Brown, Dean of Admissions, TCU Box 297013, Fort
  Worth, TX 76129-0002
Telephone: 817-257-7490 or toll-free 800-828-3764 **Fax:** 817-257-7268
E-mail: frogmail@tcu.edu

Academics

TCU awards bachelor's, master's, doctoral, and first-professional **degrees**. Challenging opportunities include advanced placement credit, accelerated degree programs, student-designed majors, an honors program, double majors, independent study, and a senior project. Special programs include internships, summer session for credit, study-abroad, and Army and Air Force ROTC.

The most frequently chosen **baccalaureate** fields are business/marketing, communications/communication technologies, and education. A complete listing of majors at TCU appears in the Majors Index beginning on page 430.

The **faculty** at TCU has 392 full-time members, 92% with terminal degrees. The student-faculty ratio is 15:1.

Students of TCU

The student body totals 8,054, of whom 6,885 are undergraduates. 57.5% are women and 42.5% are men. Students come from 50 states and territories and 75 other countries. 78% are from Texas. 4.4% are international students. 4.5% are African American, 0.5% American Indian, 1.9% Asian American, and 5.8% Hispanic American. 82% returned for their sophomore year.

Facilities and Resources

Student rooms are linked to a campus network. 4,225 **computers** are available on campus that provide access to the Internet. The **library** has 1,284,100 books and 4,734 subscriptions.

Campus Life

There are 195 active organizations on campus, including a drama/theater group, newspaper, radio station, television station, choral group, and marching band. TCU has national **fraternities**, national **sororities**, local fraternities, local sororities, and local coed music fraternities.

TCU is a member of the NCAA (Division I). **Intercollegiate sports** (some offering scholarships) include baseball (m), basketball, cross-country running, football (m), golf, riflery (w), soccer, swimming, tennis, track and field, volleyball (w).

Campus Safety

Student safety services include emergency call boxes, video camera surveillance in parking lots, late-night transport/escort service, 24-hour emergency telephone alarm devices, 24-hour patrols by trained security personnel, student patrols, and electronically operated dormitory entrances.

Applying

TCU requires an essay, SAT I or ACT, a high school transcript, 2 recommendations, and a minimum high school GPA of 2.0. It recommends SAT II Subject Tests, SAT II: Writing Test, an interview, and a minimum high school GPA of 3.0. Application deadline: 2/15; 5/1 priority date for financial aid. Deferred admission is possible.

TCU's mission—*to educate individuals to think and act as ethical leaders and responsible citizens in the global community*—influences every area of this person-centered, private university. TCU ranks among the top 6 universities in the nation in percentage of students who study abroad. Our degree programs offer internships as part of the education. The Freshman Commitment provides the opportunities students need to succeed, from writing enhancement to Internet connections in every residence room. A Division I-A teaching and research university, TCU provides the personal attention crucial to every student's success. The final grade? TCU students earn more than degrees that will improve their lives. They learn to change their world.

Getting in Last Year
5,822 applied
72% were accepted
1,514 enrolled (36%)
32% from top tenth of their h.s. class
3.0 average high school GPA

Graduation and After
275 organizations recruited on campus

Financial Matters
$15,040 tuition and fees (2001–02)
$4870 room and board
94% average percent of need met
$10,828 average financial aid amount received
  per undergraduate

Texas Tech University

URBAN SETTING ■ PUBLIC ■ STATE-SUPPORTED ■ COED
LUBBOCK, TEXAS

Web site: www.ttu.edu
Contact: Mrs. Marty Grassel, Director Admissions and School Relations, Box 45005, Lubbock, TX 79409-5005
Telephone: 806-742-1482 **Fax:** 806-742-0980
E-mail: martyg@ttu.edu

Texas Tech University is a residential, state-assisted university with more than 25,000 students. This major research institution offers 150 undergraduate degree programs through its 9 academic colleges. The University's newest addition is the College of Visual and Performing Arts, which combines the School of Art, the School of Music, and the Department of Theatre and Dance, formerly a part of the Arts and Sciences College. The University also offers the colleges of Agricultural Sciences and Natural Resources, Architecture, Arts and Sciences, Business Administration, Education, Engineering, Human Sciences, and the Honors College. Students enrolled in any college can take classes within the Honors College, which offers highly motivated and academically talented students an opportunity to maximize their college education. The ultimate objectives of an Honors College education are to provide a breadth of education, development of critical-thinking abilities, acquisition of needed life skills, and encouragement of intellectual independence.

Getting in Last Year
12,008 applied
74% were accepted
4,257 enrolled (48%)
22% from top tenth of their h.s. class
22% had SAT verbal scores over 600
29% had SAT math scores over 600
47% had ACT scores over 24
3% had SAT verbal scores over 700
4% had SAT math scores over 700
6% had ACT scores over 30
22 National Merit Scholars
103 valedictorians

Graduation and After
22% graduated in 4 years
22% graduated in 5 years
7% graduated in 6 years
80% had job offers within 6 months
850 organizations recruited on campus

Financial Matters
$3489 resident tuition and fees (2001–02)
$9819 nonresident tuition and fees (2001–02)
$5337 room and board
62% average percent of need met
$5441 average financial aid amount received per undergraduate

Academics
Texas Tech awards bachelor's, master's, doctoral, and first-professional **degrees**. Challenging opportunities include advanced placement credit, accelerated degree programs, student-designed majors, freshman honors college, an honors program, double majors, independent study, and a senior project. Special programs include cooperative education, internships, summer session for credit, off-campus study, study-abroad, and Army and Air Force ROTC.

The most frequently chosen **baccalaureate** fields are business/marketing, engineering/engineering technologies, and communications/communication technologies. A complete listing of majors at Texas Tech appears in the Majors Index beginning on page 430.

The **faculty** at Texas Tech has 902 full-time members, 93% with terminal degrees. The student-faculty ratio is 20:1.

Students of Texas Tech
The student body totals 25,573, of whom 21,269 are undergraduates. 46.3% are women and 53.7% are men. Students come from 53 states and territories and 79 other countries. 95% are from Texas. 0.7% are international students. 3% are African American, 0.5% American Indian, 2.2% Asian American, and 10.2% Hispanic American. 81% returned for their sophomore year.

Facilities and Resources
Student rooms are linked to a campus network. 2,000 **computers** are available on campus that provide access to the Internet. The 4 **libraries** have 4,245,818 books and 27,054 subscriptions.

Campus Life
There are 388 active organizations on campus, including a drama/theater group, newspaper, radio station, choral group, and marching band. 12% of eligible men and 19% of eligible women are members of national **fraternities**, national **sororities**, local fraternities, and local sororities.

Texas Tech is a member of the NCAA (Division I). **Intercollegiate sports** (some offering scholarships) include baseball (m), basketball, cross-country running, football (m), golf, soccer (w), softball (w), tennis, track and field, volleyball (w).

Campus Safety
Student safety services include late-night transport/escort service, 24-hour emergency telephone alarm devices, 24-hour patrols by trained security personnel, and electronically operated dormitory entrances.

Applying
Texas Tech requires SAT I or ACT, a high school transcript, and a minimum high school GPA of 2.0, and in some cases an essay. Application deadline: rolling admissions; 5/1 priority date for financial aid. Early and deferred admission are possible.

Thomas Aquinas College

Rural setting ■ Private ■ Independent Religious ■ Coed
Santa Paula, California

Web site: www.thomasaquinas.edu
Contact: Mr. Thomas J. Susanka Jr., Director of Admissions, 10000 North Ojai Road, Santa Paula, CA 93060-9980
Telephone: 805-525-4417 ext. 361 or toll-free 800-634-9797 **Fax:** 805-525-9342
E-mail: admissions@thomasaquinas.edu

Academics

TAC awards bachelor's **degrees**. A senior project is a challenging opportunity.

The most frequently chosen **baccalaureate** field is liberal arts/general studies. A complete listing of majors at TAC appears in the Majors Index beginning on page 430.

The **faculty** at TAC has 27 full-time members, 67% with terminal degrees. The student-faculty ratio is 11:1.

Students of TAC

The student body is made up of 301 undergraduates. Students come from 36 states and territories and 3 other countries. 49% are from California. 7.3% are international students. 0.7% are African American, 0.3% American Indian, 3% Asian American, and 8.3% Hispanic American. 88% returned for their sophomore year.

Facilities and Resources

10 **computers** are available on campus that provide access to e-mail. The **library** has 45,000 books and 130 subscriptions.

Campus Life

There are 5 active organizations on campus, including a drama/theater group and choral group. No national or local **fraternities** or **sororities**.

This institution has no intercollegiate sports.

Campus Safety

Student safety services include daily security daytime patrol, 24-hour emergency telephone alarm devices, and student patrols.

Applying

TAC requires an essay, SAT I or ACT, a high school transcript, and 3 recommendations, and in some cases an interview. It recommends a minimum high school GPA of 2.0. Application deadline: rolling admissions. Early and deferred admission are possible.

Getting in Last Year

124 applied
87% were accepted
64 enrolled (59%)
35% from top tenth of their h.s. class
3.70 average high school GPA
77% had SAT verbal scores over 600
60% had SAT math scores over 600
90% had ACT scores over 24
26% had SAT verbal scores over 700
6% had SAT math scores over 700
30% had ACT scores over 30

Graduation and After

65% graduated in 4 years
3% graduated in 5 years
9% pursued further study
62% had job offers within 6 months
4 organizations recruited on campus

Financial Matters

$15,900 tuition and fees (2001–02)
$4600 room and board
100% average percent of need met
$13,559 average financial aid amount received per undergraduate

TRANSYLVANIA UNIVERSITY

URBAN SETTING ■ PRIVATE ■ INDEPENDENT RELIGIOUS ■ COED
LEXINGTON, KENTUCKY

Web site: www.transy.edu
Contact: Ms. Sarah Coen, Director of Admissions, 300 North Broadway, Lexington, KY 40508-1797
Telephone: 859-233-8242 or toll-free 800-872-6798 **Fax:** 859-233-8797
E-mail: admissions@transy.edu

Founded in 1780 as the nation's 16th college, Transylvania is known for its ongoing legacy of academic excellence. It is consistently ranked among the nation's best liberal arts colleges and is considered an exceptional value in education. Students benefit from an innovative teacher-recognition program, the first in the nation to attract and reward outstanding teaching on a substantial scale. Small classes and individual attention from faculty members prepare students well for highly selective graduate and professional schools, especially in law and medicine. Transylvania's location in a historic district near downtown Lexington, Kentucky, provides opportunities for internships, jobs, and cultural activities.

Getting in Last Year
1,092 applied
88% were accepted
306 enrolled (32%)
54% from top tenth of their h.s. class
3.60 average high school GPA
49% had SAT verbal scores over 600
51% had SAT math scores over 600
73% had ACT scores over 24
15% had SAT verbal scores over 700
11% had SAT math scores over 700
18% had ACT scores over 30
4 National Merit Scholars
33 valedictorians

Graduation and After
59% graduated in 4 years
4% graduated in 5 years
1% graduated in 6 years
44% pursued further study (22% arts and sciences, 11% medicine, 6% law)
55% had job offers within 6 months
86 organizations recruited on campus

Financial Matters
$16,010 tuition and fees (2001–02)
$5770 room and board
89% average percent of need met
$14,071 average financial aid amount received per undergraduate

Academics

Transylvania awards bachelor's **degrees**. Challenging opportunities include advanced placement credit, student-designed majors, double majors, and independent study. Special programs include internships, summer session for credit, off-campus study, study-abroad, and Army and Air Force ROTC.

The most frequently chosen **baccalaureate** fields are business/marketing, biological/life sciences, and psychology. A complete listing of majors at Transylvania appears in the Majors Index beginning on page 430.

The **faculty** at Transylvania has 76 full-time members, 97% with terminal degrees. The student-faculty ratio is 13:1.

Students of Transylvania

The student body is made up of 1,052 undergraduates. 56.6% are women and 43.4% are men. Students come from 30 states and territories and 2 other countries. 82% are from Kentucky. 0.5% are international students. 2.7% are African American, 0.3% American Indian, 1.9% Asian American, and 1% Hispanic American. 80% returned for their sophomore year.

Facilities and Resources

Student rooms are linked to a campus network. 240 **computers** are available on campus that provide access to the Internet. The **library** has 93,019 books and 500 subscriptions.

Campus Life

There are 51 active organizations on campus, including a drama/theater group, newspaper, radio station, and choral group. 60% of eligible men and 60% of eligible women are members of national **fraternities** and national **sororities**.

Transylvania is a member of the NCAA (Division III). **Intercollegiate sports** include baseball (m), basketball, cross-country running, field hockey (w), golf, soccer, softball (w), swimming, tennis, volleyball (w).

Campus Safety

Student safety services include late-night transport/escort service, 24-hour emergency telephone alarm devices, and 24-hour patrols by trained security personnel.

Applying

Transylvania requires an essay, SAT I or ACT, a high school transcript, 2 recommendations, and a minimum high school GPA of 2.75, and in some cases an interview. It recommends an interview. Application deadline: 2/1; 3/1 priority date for financial aid. Early and deferred admission are possible.

Trinity College

URBAN SETTING ■ PRIVATE ■ INDEPENDENT ■ COED
HARTFORD, CONNECTICUT

Web site: www.trincoll.edu
Contact: Mr. Larry Dow, Dean of Admissions and Financial Aid, 300 Summit Street, Hartford, CT 06106-3100
Telephone: 860-297-2180 **Fax:** 860-297-2287
E-mail: admissions.office@trincoll.edu

Academics

Trinity College awards bachelor's and master's **degrees**. Challenging opportunities include advanced placement credit, accelerated degree programs, student-designed majors, an honors program, double majors, independent study, and a senior project. Special programs include internships, summer session for credit, off-campus study, study-abroad, and Army ROTC.

The most frequently chosen **baccalaureate** fields are social sciences and history, area/ethnic studies, and English. A complete listing of majors at Trinity College appears in the Majors Index beginning on page 430.

The **faculty** at Trinity College has 196 full-time members, 91% with terminal degrees. The student-faculty ratio is 9:1.

Students of Trinity College

The student body totals 2,256, of whom 2,074 are undergraduates. 51.3% are women and 48.7% are men. Students come from 46 states and territories and 41 other countries. 21% are from Connecticut. 3.6% are international students. 6.1% are African American, 0.1% American Indian, 5.5% Asian American, and 4.8% Hispanic American. 91% returned for their sophomore year.

Facilities and Resources

Student rooms are linked to a campus network. 315 **computers** are available on campus that provide access to e-mail, Web pages and the Internet. The 3 **libraries** have 962,703 books and 3,492 subscriptions.

Campus Life

There are 112 active organizations on campus, including a drama/theater group, newspaper, radio station, television station, and choral group. 27% of eligible men and 22% of eligible women are members of coed fraternities.

Trinity College is a member of the NCAA (Division III). **Intercollegiate sports** include baseball (m), basketball, crew, cross-country running, field hockey (w), football (m), golf (m), ice hockey, lacrosse, soccer, softball (w), squash, swimming, tennis, track and field, volleyball (w), wrestling (m).

Campus Safety

Student safety services include late-night transport/escort service, 24-hour emergency telephone alarm devices, 24-hour patrols by trained security personnel, and electronically operated dormitory entrances.

Applying

Trinity College requires an essay, SAT II: Writing Test, SAT I and SAT II or ACT, a high school transcript, and 3 recommendations. It recommends an interview. Application deadline: 1/15; 3/1 for financial aid, with a 2/1 priority date. Early and deferred admission are possible.

F ounded in 1823, Trinity College in Hartford is one of the oldest and finest liberal arts colleges in the nation. Its rigorous curriculum includes the traditional liberal arts disciplines as well as outstanding science, engineering, and interdisciplinary programs. As a residential college in the heart of the city, Trinity offers unique opportunities for combining challenging, personalized classroom instruction with applied, experiential learning in the urban environment. Two thirds of the students take part in internships, and more than half study abroad at global learning sites and participate in community service. Whether they choose to study further or go on to rewarding careers, Trinity graduates have learned to make a difference in the world.

Getting in Last Year

5,476 applied
30% were accepted
493 enrolled (30%)
48% from top tenth of their h.s. class
73% had SAT verbal scores over 600
76% had SAT math scores over 600
77% had ACT scores over 24
20% had SAT verbal scores over 700
20% had SAT math scores over 700
23% had ACT scores over 30

Graduation and After

75% had job offers within 6 months
261 organizations recruited on campus

Financial Matters

$26,786 tuition and fees (2001–02)
$7514 room and board
100% average percent of need met
$22,860 average financial aid amount received per undergraduate

TRINITY UNIVERSITY
URBAN SETTING ■ PRIVATE ■ INDEPENDENT RELIGIOUS ■ COED
SAN ANTONIO, TEXAS

Web site: www.trinity.edu
Contact: Christopher Ellertson, Dean of Admissions and Financial Aid, 715 Stadium Drive, San Antonio, TX 78212-7200
Telephone: 210-999-7207 or toll-free 800-TRINITY **Fax:** 210-999-8164
E-mail: admissions@trinity.edu

Trinity University is a highly selective liberal arts and sciences institution that also offers several professional programs that are nationally cited as models in their fields. Trinity offers its students a unique undergraduate experience. Class sizes are small, research labs and other facilities equal to those of moderate-sized Ph.D.-granting institutions are devoted exclusively to undergraduates, and contact with professors is frequent and personal. (Trinity employs no graduate assistants and few part-time faculty members.) The 117-acre campus is known for its beauty and for its skyline view of downtown San Antonio, one of America's most interesting multicultural cities.

Getting in Last Year
2,683 applied
75% were accepted
630 enrolled (31%)
46% from top tenth of their h.s. class
3.80 average high school GPA
66% had SAT verbal scores over 600
74% had SAT math scores over 600
95% had ACT scores over 24
18% had SAT verbal scores over 700
17% had SAT math scores over 700
40% had ACT scores over 30

Graduation and After
65% graduated in 4 years
8% graduated in 5 years
1% graduated in 6 years
31% pursued further study (8% arts and sciences, 5% education, 4% dentistry)
43% had job offers within 6 months
28 organizations recruited on campus

Financial Matters
$16,554 tuition and fees (2001–02)
$6560 room and board
100% average percent of need met
$15,529 average financial aid amount received per undergraduate (2000–01 estimated)

Academics
Trinity awards bachelor's and master's **degrees**. Challenging opportunities include advanced placement credit, accelerated degree programs, an honors program, double majors, independent study, and a senior project. Special programs include internships, summer session for credit, study-abroad, and Air Force ROTC.

The most frequently chosen **baccalaureate** fields are business/marketing, social sciences and history, and English. A complete listing of majors at Trinity appears in the Majors Index beginning on page 430.

The **faculty** at Trinity has 211 full-time members, 100% with terminal degrees. The student-faculty ratio is 11:1.

Students of Trinity
The student body totals 2,592, of whom 2,386 are undergraduates. 51.5% are women and 48.5% are men. Students come from 51 states and territories and 18 other countries. 71% are from Texas. 1.7% are international students. 2.1% are African American, 0.6% American Indian, 6.7% Asian American, and 10.2% Hispanic American. 86% returned for their sophomore year.

Facilities and Resources
Student rooms are linked to a campus network. 100 **computers** are available on campus that provide access to the Internet. The **library** has 871,081 books and 3,450 subscriptions.

Campus Life
Active organizations on campus include a drama/theater group, newspaper, radio station, television station, and choral group. 26% of eligible men and 28% of eligible women are members of local **fraternities** and local **sororities**.

Trinity is a member of the NCAA (Division III). **Intercollegiate sports** include baseball (m), basketball, cross-country running, football (m), golf, soccer, softball (w), swimming, tennis, track and field, volleyball (w).

Campus Safety
Student safety services include late-night transport/escort service, 24-hour emergency telephone alarm devices, 24-hour patrols by trained security personnel, and electronically operated dormitory entrances.

Applying
Trinity requires an essay, SAT I or ACT, a high school transcript, and 2 recommendations. It recommends an interview. Application deadline: 2/1; 2/1 priority date for financial aid. Deferred admission is possible.

Truman State University

Small-town setting ■ Public ■ State-supported ■ Coed
Kirksville, Missouri

Web site: www.truman.edu
Contact: Mr. Brad Chambers, Co-Director of Admissions, 205 McClain Hall, Kirksville, MO 63501-4221
Telephone: 660-785-4114 or toll-free 800-892-7792 (in-state) **Fax:** 660-785-7456
E-mail: admissions@truman.edu

Academics

Truman awards bachelor's and master's **degrees**. Challenging opportunities include advanced placement credit, accelerated degree programs, an honors program, double majors, and a senior project. Special programs include internships, summer session for credit, off-campus study, study-abroad, and Army ROTC.

The most frequently chosen **baccalaureate** fields are business/marketing, biological/life sciences, and English. A complete listing of majors at Truman appears in the Majors Index beginning on page 430.

The **faculty** at Truman has 370 full-time members, 78% with terminal degrees. The student-faculty ratio is 15:1.

Students of Truman

The student body totals 5,919, of whom 5,685 are undergraduates. 57.9% are women and 42.1% are men. Students come from 43 states and territories and 50 other countries. 76% are from Missouri. 3.9% are international students. 3.3% are African American, 0.4% American Indian, 1.8% Asian American, and 1.6% Hispanic American.

Facilities and Resources

Student rooms are linked to a campus network. 769 **computers** are available on campus that provide access to the Internet. The 2 **libraries** have 472,652 books and 3,665 subscriptions.

Campus Life

There are 221 active organizations on campus, including a drama/theater group, newspaper, radio station, television station, choral group, and marching band. 30% of eligible men and 20% of eligible women are members of national **fraternities**, national **sororities**, and local sororities.

Truman is a member of the NCAA (Division II). **Intercollegiate sports** (some offering scholarships) include baseball (m), basketball, cross-country running, football (m), golf, soccer, softball (w), swimming, tennis, track and field, volleyball (w), wrestling (m).

Campus Safety

Student safety services include patrols by commissioned officers, late-night transport/escort service, 24-hour emergency telephone alarm devices, 24-hour patrols by trained security personnel, and student patrols.

Applying

Truman requires an essay, SAT I or ACT, and a high school transcript. It recommends ACT, an interview, and a minimum high school GPA of 3.0. Application deadline: 3/1; 4/1 priority date for financial aid. Early and deferred admission are possible.

Getting in Last Year
5,002 applied
82% were accepted
1,459 enrolled (36%)
46% from top tenth of their h.s. class
3.73 average high school GPA
55% had SAT verbal scores over 600
50% had SAT math scores over 600
84% had ACT scores over 24
17% had SAT verbal scores over 700
10% had SAT math scores over 700
27% had ACT scores over 30
12 National Merit Scholars
131 valedictorians

Graduation and After
39% graduated in 4 years
21% graduated in 5 years
2% graduated in 6 years
35% pursued further study (11% arts and sciences, 9% education, 5% medicine)
60.1% had job offers within 6 months
228 organizations recruited on campus

Financial Matters
$3832 resident tuition and fees (2001–02)
$6960 nonresident tuition and fees (2001–02)
$4736 room and board
83% average percent of need met
$4782 average financial aid amount received per undergraduate (2000–01)

Tufts University

Suburban setting ■ Private ■ Independent ■ Coed
Medford, Massachusetts

Web site: www.tufts.edu
Contact: Mr. David D. Cuttino, Dean of Undergraduate Admissions,
  Bendetson Hall, Medford, MA 02155
Telephone: 617-627-3170 **Fax:** 617-627-3860
E-mail: admissions.inquiry@ase.tufts.edu

Getting in Last Year
13,700 applied
23% were accepted
1,161 enrolled (37%)
66% from top tenth of their h.s. class
75% had SAT verbal scores over 600
86% had SAT math scores over 600
89% had ACT scores over 24
26% had SAT verbal scores over 700
39% had SAT math scores over 700
37% had ACT scores over 30

Graduation and After
30% pursued further study (11% law, 9% medicine, 8% business)
211 organizations recruited on campus

Financial Matters
$26,892 tuition and fees (2001–02)
$7987 room and board
100% average percent of need met
$22,109 average financial aid amount received per undergraduate

Academics
Tufts awards bachelor's, master's, doctoral, and first-professional **degrees** and post-master's certificates. Challenging opportunities include advanced placement credit, student-designed majors, an honors program, double majors, independent study, and a senior project. Special programs include internships, summer session for credit, off-campus study, study-abroad, and Army, Navy and Air Force ROTC.

The most frequently chosen **baccalaureate** fields are social sciences and history, engineering/engineering technologies, and visual/performing arts. A complete listing of majors at Tufts appears in the Majors Index beginning on page 430.

The **faculty** at Tufts has 679 full-time members. The student-faculty ratio is 9:1.

Students of Tufts
The student body totals 9,031, of whom 4,755 are undergraduates. 54% are women and 46% are men. Students come from 52 states and territories and 70 other countries. 23% are from Massachusetts. 7% are international students. 7.5% are African American, 0.2% American Indian, 13.3% Asian American, and 8.2% Hispanic American. 96% returned for their sophomore year.

Facilities and Resources
Student rooms are linked to a campus network. 254 **computers** are available on campus that provide access to the Internet. The 2 **libraries** have 1,552,500 books and 5,329 subscriptions.

Campus Life
There are 160 active organizations on campus, including a drama/theater group, newspaper, radio station, television station, choral group, and marching band. 15% of eligible men and 4% of eligible women are members of national **fraternities** and national **sororities**.

Tufts is a member of the NCAA (Division III). **Intercollegiate sports** include baseball (m), basketball, crew, cross-country running, fencing (w), field hockey (w), football (m), golf (m), ice hockey (m), lacrosse, sailing, soccer, softball (w), squash, swimming, tennis, track and field, volleyball (w).

Campus Safety
Student safety services include security lighting, call boxes to campus police, late-night transport/escort service, 24-hour emergency telephone alarm devices, 24-hour patrols by trained security personnel, and electronically operated dormitory entrances.

Applying
Tufts requires an essay, SAT I and SAT II or ACT, a high school transcript, and 1 recommendation, and in some cases SAT II: Writing Test. It recommends an interview. Application deadline: 1/1; 2/15 for financial aid, with a 2/1 priority date. Early and deferred admission are possible.

Tulane University

Urban setting ■ Private ■ Independent ■ Coed
New Orleans, Louisiana

Web site: www.tulane.edu

Contact: Mr. Richard Whiteside, Vice President of Enrollment Management and Institutional Research, 6823 St Charles Avenue, New Orleans, LA 70118-5669

Telephone: 504-865-5731 or toll-free 800-873-9283 **Fax:** 504-862-8715

E-mail: undergrad.admission@tulane.edu

Academics

Tulane awards associate, bachelor's, master's, doctoral, and first-professional **degrees** and post-bachelor's certificates. Challenging opportunities include advanced placement credit, accelerated degree programs, student-designed majors, freshman honors college, an honors program, double majors, independent study, and a senior project. Special programs include cooperative education, internships, summer session for credit, off-campus study, study-abroad, and Army, Navy and Air Force ROTC.

The most frequently chosen **baccalaureate** fields are business/marketing, social sciences and history, and engineering/engineering technologies. A complete listing of majors at Tulane appears in the Majors Index beginning on page 430.

The **faculty** at Tulane has 538 full-time members, 90% with terminal degrees. The student-faculty ratio is 12:1.

Students of Tulane

The student body totals 12,373, of whom 7,522 are undergraduates. 53.2% are women and 46.8% are men. Students come from 59 states and territories and 108 other countries. 36% are from Louisiana. 3.2% are international students. 8.7% are African American, 0.3% American Indian, 5.2% Asian American, and 3.5% Hispanic American. 83% returned for their sophomore year.

Facilities and Resources

Student rooms are linked to a campus network. The 9 **libraries** have 1,300,050 books and 15,286 subscriptions.

Campus Life

There are 200 active organizations on campus, including a drama/theater group, newspaper, radio station, television station, and choral group. 16% of eligible men and 19% of eligible women are members of national **fraternities** and national **sororities**.

Tulane is a member of the NCAA (Division I). **Intercollegiate sports** (some offering scholarships) include baseball (m), basketball, cross-country running, football (m), golf, soccer (w), tennis, track and field, volleyball (w).

Campus Safety

Student safety services include on and off-campus shuttle service, crime prevention programs, late-night transport/escort service, 24-hour emergency telephone alarm devices, 24-hour patrols by trained security personnel, student patrols, and electronically operated dormitory entrances.

Applying

Tulane requires an essay, SAT I, SAT I or ACT, a high school transcript, and 1 recommendation, and in some cases SAT II Subject Tests. It recommends SAT II Subject Tests. Application deadline: 1/15; 2/1 for financial aid, with a 1/15 priority date. Early and deferred admission are possible.

Among national universities, Tulane is known for its emphasis on undergraduate teaching and its accomplishments in research. The same senior faculty members who do research regularly teach freshmen and sophomores. With 7,100 students in 5 divisions, Tulane gives each student the personal attention and teaching excellence typically associated with smaller colleges, while providing the state-of-the-art facilities and interdisciplinary resources usually found only at major universities. Tulane students play active roles in more than 200 campus organizations and have numerous internship opportunities in the exciting city of New Orleans. Close student-teacher relationships pay off—graduates frequently win prestigious fellowships, and many go on to earn advanced degrees in their chosen field of study.

Getting in Last Year
10,862 applied
61% were accepted
1,517 enrolled (23%)
65% from top tenth of their h.s. class
85% had SAT verbal scores over 600
78% had SAT math scores over 600
33% had SAT verbal scores over 700
24% had SAT math scores over 700

Graduation and After
56% graduated in 4 years
12% graduated in 5 years
2% graduated in 6 years
31% pursued further study (5% engineering)
557 organizations recruited on campus

Financial Matters
$26,886 tuition and fees (2001–02)
$7128 room and board
94% average percent of need met
$22,948 average financial aid amount received per undergraduate (1999–2000)

UNION COLLEGE

SUBURBAN SETTING ■ PRIVATE ■ INDEPENDENT ■ COED
SCHENECTADY, NEW YORK

Web site: www.union.edu
Contact: Mr. Daniel Lundquist, Vice President for Admissions and Financial Aid, Grant Hall, Schenectady, NY 12308
Telephone: 518-388-6112 or toll-free 888-843-6688 (in-state) **Fax:** 518-388-6986
E-mail: admissions@union.edu

Union College, one of the oldest nondenominational colleges in America, is located in the small city of Schenectady, about 3 hours north of New York City. Its distinctive curriculum combines the traditional liberal arts with engineering study. Three basic tenets undergird a Union education: commitments to lifelong learning, the liberal arts, and a close working relationship between students and faculty members. People from many different backgrounds come to Union, attracted by these values and the opportunities they imply: small classes, excellent access to superb facilities, a caring and committed faculty, and an academic program of depth and diversity.

Getting in Last Year
3,910 applied
41% were accepted
522 enrolled (32%)
55% from top tenth of their h.s. class
3.40 average high school GPA
52% had SAT verbal scores over 600
68% had SAT math scores over 600
7% had SAT verbal scores over 700
15% had SAT math scores over 700

Graduation and After
75% graduated in 4 years
5% graduated in 5 years
1% graduated in 6 years
31% pursued further study (7% arts and sciences, 6% law, 6% medicine)
67% had job offers within 6 months
57 organizations recruited on campus

Financial Matters
$26,007 tuition and fees (2001–02)
$6639 room and board
97% average percent of need met
$21,580 average financial aid amount received per undergraduate (2000–01)

Academics

Union College awards bachelor's and master's **degrees**. Challenging opportunities include advanced placement credit, accelerated degree programs, student-designed majors, an honors program, double majors, independent study, and a senior project. Special programs include cooperative education, internships, summer session for credit, off-campus study, study-abroad, and Army, Navy and Air Force ROTC.

The most frequently chosen **baccalaureate** fields are social sciences and history, business/marketing, and engineering/engineering technologies. A complete listing of majors at Union College appears in the Majors Index beginning on page 430.

The **faculty** at Union College has 195 full-time members, 92% with terminal degrees. The student-faculty ratio is 11:1.

Students of Union College

The student body totals 2,427, of whom 2,118 are undergraduates. 48.1% are women and 51.9% are men. Students come from 33 states and territories and 22 other countries. 47% are from New York. 2.5% are international students. 4.1% are African American, 0.1% American Indian, 4.7% Asian American, and 4.1% Hispanic American. 92% returned for their sophomore year.

Facilities and Resources

Student rooms are linked to a campus network. 320 **computers** are available on campus that provide access to microcomputer network and the Internet. The **library** has 287,293 books and 6,826 subscriptions.

Campus Life

There are 95 active organizations on campus, including a drama/theater group, newspaper, radio station, and choral group. 22% of eligible men and 19% of eligible women are members of national **fraternities**, national **sororities**, local fraternities, local sororities, and theme houses.

Union College is a member of the NCAA (Division III). **Intercollegiate sports** include baseball (m), basketball, crew, cross-country running, field hockey (w), football (m), ice hockey, lacrosse, soccer, softball (w), swimming, tennis, track and field, volleyball (w).

Campus Safety

Student safety services include awareness programs, bicycle patrol, shuttle service, late-night transport/escort service, 24-hour emergency telephone alarm devices, 24-hour patrols by trained security personnel, student patrols, and electronically operated dormitory entrances.

Applying

Union College requires an essay, SAT I, ACT, or 3 SAT II Subject Tests (including SAT II: Writing Test), a high school transcript, and 2 recommendations. It recommends an interview. Application deadline: 1/15; 2/1 priority date for financial aid. Early and deferred admission are possible.

UNION UNIVERSITY

SMALL-TOWN SETTING ■ PRIVATE ■ INDEPENDENT RELIGIOUS ■ COED
JACKSON, TENNESSEE

Web site: www.uu.edu
Contact: Mr. Robbie Graves, Director of Enrollment Services, 1050 Union University Drive, Jackson, TN 38305-3697
Telephone: 731-661-5008 or toll-free 800-33-UNION **Fax:** 731-661-5017
E-mail: info@uu.edu

Academics

Union awards associate, bachelor's, and master's **degrees** and post-master's certificates. Challenging opportunities include advanced placement credit, accelerated degree programs, an honors program, double majors, independent study, and a senior project. Special programs include internships, summer session for credit, off-campus study, and study-abroad.

The most frequently chosen **baccalaureate** fields are business/marketing, health professions and related sciences, and education. A complete listing of majors at Union appears in the Majors Index beginning on page 430.

The **faculty** at Union has 147 full-time members, 61% with terminal degrees. The student-faculty ratio is 12:1.

Students of Union

The student body totals 2,544, of whom 1,965 are undergraduates. 59.2% are women and 40.8% are men. Students come from 40 states and territories and 28 other countries. 73% are from Tennessee. 2.2% are international students. 6.4% are African American, 0.2% American Indian, 0.8% Asian American, and 0.6% Hispanic American. 93% returned for their sophomore year.

Facilities and Resources

Student rooms are linked to a campus network. 236 **computers** are available on campus that provide access to the Internet. The **library** has 135,877 books and 4,655 subscriptions.

Campus Life

There are 52 active organizations on campus, including a drama/theater group, newspaper, and choral group. 27% of eligible men and 25% of eligible women are members of national **fraternities** and national **sororities**.

Union is a member of the NAIA and NCCAA. **Intercollegiate sports** (some offering scholarships) include baseball (m), basketball, cross-country running, golf (m), soccer (m), softball (w), tennis, volleyball (w).

Campus Safety

Student safety services include late-night transport/escort service, 24-hour emergency telephone alarm devices, 24-hour patrols by trained security personnel, and student patrols.

Applying

Union requires SAT I or ACT, a high school transcript, and a minimum high school GPA of 2.5, and in some cases recommendations. It recommends an essay and an interview. Application deadline: rolling admissions; 2/15 priority date for financial aid. Early admission is possible.

Conscious of the changing global atmosphere awaiting the next generation of students, Union University is preparing leaders and change agents for the coming century. High-quality classroom teaching is a University trademark, as students are challenged to become influential players in their chosen field of study. Union's vision and goals of excellence in liberal arts education are shaped by an enduring faith in God and an unfaltering commitment to Christian values. Union is a place where students grow both in faith and vision, fulfilling their dreams and changing the world.

Getting in Last Year

1,042 applied
86% were accepted
430 enrolled (48%)
29% from top tenth of their h.s. class
3.52 average high school GPA
42% had SAT verbal scores over 600
35% had SAT math scores over 600
53% had ACT scores over 24
10% had SAT verbal scores over 700
13% had SAT math scores over 700
14% had ACT scores over 30
3 National Merit Scholars
39 valedictorians

Graduation and After

33% graduated in 4 years
11% graduated in 5 years
3% graduated in 6 years
40% pursued further study (13% education, 13% theology, 4% arts and sciences)
83% had job offers within 6 months
85 organizations recruited on campus

Financial Matters

$12,670 tuition and fees (2001–02)
$4110 room and board

UNITED STATES AIR FORCE ACADEMY

SUBURBAN SETTING ■ PUBLIC ■ FEDERALLY SUPPORTED ■ COED, PRIMARILY MEN
USAF ACADEMY, COLORADO

Web site: www.usafa.edu/rr
Contact: Mr. Rolland Stoneman, Associate Director of Admissions/Selections, HQ USAFA/RR 2304 Cadet Drive, Suite 200, USAF Academy, CO 80840-5025
Telephone: 719-333-2520 or toll-free 800-443-9266 **Fax:** 719-333-3012
E-mail: rr_webmail@usafa.af.mil

The Air Force Academy challenge requires a well-rounded academic, physical, and leadership background. Cadets must accept discipline, be competitive, and have a desire to serve others with a sense of duty and integrity. Applicants should prepare early to meet the admissions requirements, competition, and demands they will face at the Academy.

Getting in Last Year
9,552 applied
17% were accepted
1,202 enrolled (74%)
57% from top tenth of their h.s. class
3.80 average high school GPA
66% had SAT verbal scores over 600
79% had SAT math scores over 600
15% had SAT verbal scores over 700
25% had SAT math scores over 700
195 National Merit Scholars
140 class presidents
104 valedictorians

Graduation and After
76% graduated in 4 years
1% graduated in 5 years
1% graduated in 6 years
9% pursued further study (3% arts and sciences, 2% medicine, 2% engineering)
100% had job offers within 6 months
1 organization recruited on campus

Academics

USAFA awards bachelor's **degrees**. Challenging opportunities include advanced placement credit, student-designed majors, double majors, independent study, and a senior project. Special programs include internships, summer session for credit, off-campus study, and study-abroad.

The most frequently chosen **baccalaureate** fields are engineering/engineering technologies, social sciences and history, and business/marketing. A complete listing of majors at USAFA appears in the Majors Index beginning on page 430.

The **faculty** at USAFA has 531 full-time members, 55% with terminal degrees. The student-faculty ratio is 8:1.

Students of USAFA

The student body is made up of 4,365 undergraduates. Students come from 54 states and territories and 22 other countries. 5% are from Colorado. 0.8% are international students. 5.7% are African American, 1.3% American Indian, 4.3% Asian American, and 6.4% Hispanic American. 90% returned for their sophomore year.

Facilities and Resources

Student rooms are linked to a campus network. The 3 **libraries** have 445,379 books and 1,693 subscriptions.

Campus Life

There are 100 active organizations on campus, including a drama/theater group, newspaper, radio station, choral group, and marching band. No national or local **fraternities** or **sororities**.

USAFA is a member of the NCAA (Division I). **Intercollegiate sports** include baseball (m), basketball, cross-country running, fencing, football (m), golf (m), gymnastics, ice hockey (m), lacrosse (m), riflery, soccer, swimming, tennis, track and field, volleyball (w), water polo (m), wrestling (m).

Campus Safety

Student safety services include self-defense education, well-lit campus, late-night transport/escort service, 24-hour emergency telephone alarm devices, and 24-hour patrols by trained security personnel.

Applying

USAFA requires an essay, SAT I or ACT, a high school transcript, an interview, authorized nomination, and a minimum high school GPA of 2.0. Application deadline: 1/31.

United States Coast Guard Academy

Suburban setting ■ Public ■ Federally supported ■ Coed
New London, Connecticut

Web site: www.cga.edu
Contact: Capt. Susan D. Bibeau, Director of Admissions, 31 Mohegan
   Avenue, New London, CT 06320-4195
Telephone: 860-444-8500 or toll-free 800-883-8724 **Fax:** 860-701-6700
E-mail: admissions@cga.uscg.mil

Academics

USCGA awards bachelor's **degrees**. Challenging opportunities include double majors, independent study, and a senior project. Special programs include internships, summer session for credit, and off-campus study.

The most frequently chosen **baccalaureate** fields are engineering/engineering technologies, social sciences and history, and law/legal studies. A complete listing of majors at USCGA appears in the Majors Index beginning on page 430.

The **faculty** at USCGA has 110 full-time members, 41% with terminal degrees. The student-faculty ratio is 8:1.

Students of USCGA

The student body is made up of 917 undergraduates. 28.2% are women and 71.8% are men. Students come from 50 states and territories and 8 other countries. 6% are from Connecticut. 1.9% are international students. 5.5% are African American, 0.9% American Indian, 4.9% Asian American, and 6.2% Hispanic American. 84% returned for their sophomore year.

Facilities and Resources

Student rooms are linked to a campus network. 120 **computers** are available on campus that provide access to laptop for each student and the Internet. The **library** has 150,000 books and 1,690 subscriptions.

Campus Life

Active organizations on campus include a drama/theater group, choral group, and marching band. No national or local **fraternities** or **sororities**.

USCGA is a member of the NCAA (Division III). **Intercollegiate sports** include baseball (m), basketball, crew, cross-country running, football (m), riflery, sailing, soccer, softball (w), swimming, tennis (m), track and field, volleyball (w), wrestling (m).

Campus Safety

Student safety services include 24-hour patrols by trained security personnel and student patrols.

Applying

USCGA requires an essay, SAT I or ACT, a high school transcript, and 3 recommendations, and in some cases an interview. Application deadline: 12/15.

Getting in Last Year
5,621 applied
7% were accepted
282 enrolled (70%)
61% from top tenth of their h.s. class
63% had SAT verbal scores over 600
78% had SAT math scores over 600
91% had ACT scores over 24
12% had SAT verbal scores over 700
21% had SAT math scores over 700
30% had ACT scores over 30
22 class presidents
13 valedictorians

Graduation and After
64% graduated in 4 years
1% graduated in 5 years

UNITED STATES MERCHANT MARINE ACADEMY

SUBURBAN SETTING ■ PUBLIC ■ FEDERALLY SUPPORTED ■ COED
KINGS POINT, NEW YORK

Web site: www.usmma.edu
Contact: Capt. James M. Skinner, Director of Admissions, 300 Steamboat
Road, Wiley Hall, Kings Point, NY 11024-1699
Telephone: 516-773-5391 or toll-free 800-732-6267 (out-of-state) **Fax:**
516-773-5390
E-mail: admissions@usmma.edu

The United States Merchant Marine Academy is a 4-year federal service academy dedicated to educating and training young men and women as officers in America's merchant marine and U.S. Naval Reserve and as future leaders of the maritime and transportation industries. The Academy, in Kings Point, Long Island, offers accredited programs in marine transportation and engineering leading to a BS degree, a U.S. merchant marine officer's license, and a Naval Reserve commission. Students spend 3 trimesters at sea aboard U.S. merchant ships as part of their training.

Getting in Last Year
1,586 applied
18% were accepted
16% from top tenth of their h.s. class
3.50 average high school GPA
47% had SAT verbal scores over 600
59% had SAT math scores over 600
10% had SAT verbal scores over 700
5% had SAT math scores over 700

Graduation and After
2% pursued further study (1% business, 1% engineering)
96% had job offers within 6 months
34 organizations recruited on campus

Academics

United States Merchant Marine Academy awards bachelor's **degrees**. Challenging opportunities include an honors program and a senior project. Special programs include cooperative education and internships.

The most frequently chosen **baccalaureate** field is engineering/engineering technologies. A complete listing of majors at United States Merchant Marine Academy appears in the Majors Index beginning on page 430.

The **faculty** at United States Merchant Marine Academy has 80 full-time members. The student-faculty ratio is 12:1.

Students of United States Merchant Marine Academy

The student body is made up of 931 undergraduates. Students come from 53 states and territories and 4 other countries. 92% returned for their sophomore year.

Facilities and Resources

Student rooms are linked to a campus network. 1,200 **computers** are available on campus that provide access to engineering and economics software. The **library** has 232,576 books and 985 subscriptions.

Campus Life

There are 45 active organizations on campus, including a drama/theater group, newspaper, choral group, and marching band. No national or local **fraternities** or **sororities**.

United States Merchant Marine Academy is a member of the NCAA (Division III). **Intercollegiate sports** include baseball (m), basketball, crew, cross-country running, football (m), golf, lacrosse (m), riflery, sailing, soccer (m), softball (w), swimming, tennis, track and field, volleyball, water polo (m), wrestling (m).

Campus Safety

Student safety services include 24-hour patrols by trained security personnel.

Applying

United States Merchant Marine Academy requires an essay, SAT I or ACT, a high school transcript, and 3 recommendations. It recommends an interview. Application deadline: 3/1.

UNITED STATES MILITARY ACADEMY

SMALL-TOWN SETTING ■ PUBLIC ■ FEDERALLY SUPPORTED ■ COED, PRIMARILY MEN
WEST POINT, NEW YORK

Web site: www.usma.edu
Contact: Col. Michael C. Jones, Director of Admissions, United States
Military Academy, West Point, NY 10996
Telephone: 845-938-4041
E-mail: 8dad@sunams.usma.army.mil

Academics

West Point awards bachelor's **degrees**. Challenging opportunities include advanced placement credit and double majors. Special programs include summer session for credit and off-campus study.

The most frequently chosen **baccalaureate** fields are engineering/engineering technologies, social sciences and history, and physical sciences. A complete listing of majors at West Point appears in the Majors Index beginning on page 430.

The **faculty** at West Point has 588 full-time members, 56% with terminal degrees. The student-faculty ratio is 7:1.

Students of West Point

The student body is made up of 4,394 undergraduates. Students come from 53 states and territories and 18 other countries. 8% are from New York. 0.7% are international students. 7.8% are African American, 0.7% American Indian, 5.8% Asian American, and 6.1% Hispanic American. 92% returned for their sophomore year.

Facilities and Resources

Student rooms are linked to a campus network. 5,500 **computers** are available on campus for student use. The 2 **libraries** have 457,340 books and 2,220 subscriptions.

Campus Life

There are 114 active organizations on campus, including a drama/theater group, radio station, and choral group. No national or local **fraternities** or **sororities**.

West Point is a member of the NCAA (Division I). **Intercollegiate sports** include baseball (m), basketball, cross-country running, football (m), golf (m), gymnastics (m), ice hockey (m), lacrosse (m), soccer, softball (w), swimming, tennis, track and field, volleyball (w), wrestling (m).

Campus Safety

Student safety services include late-night transport/escort service, 24-hour emergency telephone alarm devices, 24-hour patrols by trained security personnel, and student patrols.

Applying

West Point requires an essay, SAT I or ACT, a high school transcript, 4 recommendations, and medical examination, authorized nomination. It recommends an interview. Application deadline: 3/21.

West Point is about leadership. If you want to lead, then choose the right path. Choose West Point. It offers a prestigious academic program, challenging military leadership skills, and memorable life experiences. West Point builds a foundation for career success as an Army officer, developing your leadership skills to motivate and guide young and promising soldiers. West Point is tough, but it is worth the challenge. One cadet may have said it best: "The person I have become is so much better than the person who first came here."

Getting in Last Year
9,893 applied
15% were accepted
47% from top tenth of their h.s. class
65% had SAT verbal scores over 600
76% had SAT math scores over 600
96% had ACT scores over 24
18% had SAT verbal scores over 700
22% had SAT math scores over 700
34% had ACT scores over 30
227 National Merit Scholars
208 class presidents
82 valedictorians

Graduation and After
80% graduated in 4 years
2% graduated in 5 years
1% graduated in 6 years
2% pursued further study (2% medicine)
100% had job offers within 6 months

UNITED STATES NAVAL ACADEMY

SMALL-TOWN SETTING ■ PUBLIC ■ FEDERALLY SUPPORTED ■ COED
ANNAPOLIS, MARYLAND

Web site: www.usna.edu
Contact: Col. David A. Vetter, Dean of Admissions, 117 Decatur Road,
  Annapolis, MD 21402-5000
Telephone: 410-293-4361 **Fax:** 410-293-4348
E-mail: webmail@gwmail.usna.edu

Getting in Last Year
11,558 applied
13% were accepted
1,182 enrolled (80%)
56% from top tenth of their h.s. class
77% had SAT verbal scores over 600
88% had SAT math scores over 600
22% had SAT verbal scores over 700
30% had SAT math scores over 700
135 class presidents

Graduation and After
84% graduated in 4 years
1% graduated in 5 years
1% graduated in 6 years
2% pursued further study (1% medicine)
100% had job offers within 6 months
2 organizations recruited on campus

Academics
Naval Academy awards bachelor's **degrees**. Challenging opportunities include advanced placement credit, an honors program, double majors, and independent study. Summer session for credit is a special program.

The most frequently chosen **baccalaureate** fields are social sciences and history, engineering/engineering technologies, and physical sciences. A complete listing of majors at Naval Academy appears in the Majors Index beginning on page 430.

The **faculty** at Naval Academy has 554 full-time members, 58% with terminal degrees. The student-faculty ratio is 7:1.

Students of Naval Academy
The student body is made up of 4,297 undergraduates. Students come from 54 states and territories and 17 other countries. 4% are from Maryland. 0.7% are international students. 6.1% are African American, 1% American Indian, 4.1% Asian American, and 7.7% Hispanic American. 96% returned for their sophomore year.

Facilities and Resources
Student rooms are linked to a campus network. 6,100 **computers** are available on campus that provide access to the Internet. The 2 **libraries** have 800,000 books and 1,892 subscriptions.

Campus Life
There are 75 active organizations on campus, including a drama/theater group, radio station, choral group, and marching band. No national or local **fraternities** or **sororities**.

Naval Academy is a member of the NCAA (Division I). **Intercollegiate sports** include baseball (m), basketball, crew, cross-country running, football (m), golf (m), gymnastics (m), lacrosse (m), riflery, sailing, soccer, squash (m), swimming, tennis (m), track and field, volleyball (w), water polo (m), wrestling (m).

Campus Safety
Student safety services include front gate security, 24-hour emergency telephone alarm devices, 24-hour patrols by trained security personnel, and student patrols.

Applying
Naval Academy requires an essay, SAT I or ACT, a high school transcript, an interview, 2 recommendations, authorized nomination, and a minimum high school GPA of 2.0. Application deadline: 2/15.

University at Buffalo, The State University of New York

Suburban setting ■ Public ■ State-supported ■ Coed
Buffalo, New York

Web site: www.buffalo.edu
Contact: Ms. Regina Toomey, Director of Admissions, Capen Hall, Room 17, North Campus, Buffalo, NY 14260-1660
Telephone: 716-645-6900 or toll-free 888-UB-ADMIT **Fax:** 716-645-6411
E-mail: ubadmissions@admissions.buffalo.edu

Academics

UB awards bachelor's, master's, doctoral, and first-professional **degrees** and post-master's and first-professional certificates. Challenging opportunities include advanced placement credit, student-designed majors, freshman honors college, an honors program, double majors, independent study, and a senior project. Special programs include internships, summer session for credit, off-campus study, study-abroad, and Army ROTC.

The most frequently chosen **baccalaureate** fields are business/marketing, social sciences and history, and engineering/engineering technologies. A complete listing of majors at UB appears in the Majors Index beginning on page 430.

The **faculty** at UB has 1,236 full-time members, 98% with terminal degrees. The student-faculty ratio is 14:1.

Students of UB

The student body totals 25,838, of whom 17,290 are undergraduates. 45.8% are women and 54.2% are men. Students come from 44 states and territories and 71 other countries. 98% are from New York. 5% are international students. 8.3% are African American, 0.4% American Indian, 9.3% Asian American, and 3.6% Hispanic American. 85% returned for their sophomore year.

Facilities and Resources

Student rooms are linked to a campus network. 1,800 **computers** are available on campus that provide access to the Internet. The 8 **libraries** have 3,213,870 books and 26,444 subscriptions.

Campus Life

There are 200 active organizations on campus, including a drama/theater group, newspaper, radio station, television station, choral group, and marching band. 5% of eligible men and 5% of eligible women are members of national **fraternities**, national **sororities**, local fraternities, and local sororities.

UB is a member of the NCAA (Division I). **Intercollegiate sports** (some offering scholarships) include baseball (m), basketball, crew (w), cross-country running, football (m), soccer, softball (w), swimming, tennis, track and field, volleyball (w), wrestling (m).

Campus Safety

Student safety services include self-defense and awareness programs, late-night transport/escort service, 24-hour emergency telephone alarm devices, 24-hour patrols by trained security personnel, student patrols, and electronically operated dormitory entrances.

Applying

UB requires SAT I or ACT and a high school transcript, and in some cases recommendations and portfolio, audition. Application deadline: rolling admissions; 3/1 priority date for financial aid. Early admission is possible.

T he University at Buffalo (UB) is New York's premier public research university—an academic community in which undergraduates work side by side with faculty members who are on the cutting edge of their fields. UB offers the most comprehensive scholarship programs in the State University of New York System and more undergraduate degree programs than any other public university in New York and New England. In a true community of scholars, students are encouraged to explore the possibilities among extensive programs in architecture, arts and letters, engineering, health sciences, informatics, management, medicine and biomedical sciences, natural sciences and mathematics, nursing, pharmacy, and social sciences.

Getting in Last Year
16,016 applied
63% were accepted
3,020 enrolled (30%)
21% from top tenth of their h.s. class
3.70 average high school GPA
28% had SAT verbal scores over 600
40% had SAT math scores over 600
57% had ACT scores over 24
4% had SAT verbal scores over 700
7% had SAT math scores over 700
10% had ACT scores over 30
3 National Merit Scholars
15 valedictorians

Graduation and After
32% graduated in 4 years
20% graduated in 5 years
4% graduated in 6 years
30% pursued further study

Financial Matters
$4790 resident tuition and fees (2001–02)
$9690 nonresident tuition and fees (2001–02)
$6318 room and board
70% average percent of need met
$7491 average financial aid amount received per undergraduate

THE UNIVERSITY OF ALABAMA IN HUNTSVILLE
SUBURBAN SETTING ■ PUBLIC ■ STATE-SUPPORTED ■ COED
HUNTSVILLE, ALABAMA

Web site: www.uah.edu
Contact: Ms. Sabrina Williams, Associate Director of Admissions, 301
   Sparkman Drive, Huntsville, AL 35899
Telephone: 256-824-6070 or toll-free 800-UAH-CALL **Fax:** 256-824-6073
E-mail: admitme@email.uah.edu

The University of Alabama in Huntsville (UAH) is strategically located in the 2nd-largest research park in America. UAH is a partner with more than 100 high-tech industries as well as major federal laboratories, such as NASA's Marshall Space Flight Center and the U.S. Army. Its unique location makes possible many co-op opportunities for students to earn much of their college costs and to maximize their employment potential. Huntsville is an international university: 7,000 students hail from 93 countries. Students have many opportunities to work with some of the top scientists in the country. Some of their research has flown aboard the space shuttle, while others have helped solve human problems and improve business management.

Getting in Last Year
1,198 applied
84% were accepted
628 enrolled (63%)
28% from top tenth of their h.s. class
3.36 average high school GPA
32% had SAT verbal scores over 600
39% had SAT math scores over 600
57% had ACT scores over 24
7% had SAT verbal scores over 700
10% had SAT math scores over 700
9% had ACT scores over 30

Graduation and After
10% graduated in 4 years
19% graduated in 5 years
10% graduated in 6 years
15% pursued further study (9% arts and sciences, 3% engineering, 2% business)
73% had job offers within 6 months
350 organizations recruited on campus

Financial Matters
$3536 resident tuition and fees (2001–02)
$7430 nonresident tuition and fees (2001–02)
$4380 room and board
70% average percent of need met
$6612 average financial aid amount received per undergraduate

Academics
UAH awards bachelor's, master's, and doctoral **degrees** and post-bachelor's and post-master's certificates. Challenging opportunities include advanced placement credit, accelerated degree programs, an honors program, double majors, independent study, and a senior project. Special programs include cooperative education, internships, summer session for credit, off-campus study, and Army ROTC.

The most frequently chosen **baccalaureate** fields are engineering/engineering technologies, business/marketing, and health professions and related sciences. A complete listing of majors at UAH appears in the Majors Index beginning on page 430.

The **faculty** at UAH has 277 full-time members, 91% with terminal degrees. The student-faculty ratio is 14:1.

Students of UAH
The student body totals 6,754, of whom 5,466 are undergraduates. 50.3% are women and 49.7% are men. Students come from 45 states and territories and 66 other countries. 89% are from Alabama. 4% are international students. 14.4% are African American, 2.2% American Indian, 3.7% Asian American, and 1.9% Hispanic American. 71% returned for their sophomore year.

Facilities and Resources
Student rooms are linked to a campus network. 520 **computers** are available on campus that provide access to the Internet. The **library** has 627,132 books and 1,668 subscriptions.

Campus Life
There are 111 active organizations on campus, including a drama/theater group, newspaper, and choral group. 6% of eligible men and 5% of eligible women are members of national **fraternities** and national **sororities**.

UAH is a member of the NCAA (Division II). **Intercollegiate sports** (some offering scholarships) include baseball (m), basketball, cross-country running, ice hockey (m), soccer, softball (w), tennis, volleyball (w).

Campus Safety
Student safety services include late-night transport/escort service, 24-hour emergency telephone alarm devices, 24-hour patrols by trained security personnel, and electronically operated dormitory entrances.

Applying
UAH requires SAT I or ACT and a high school transcript. Application deadline: 8/15; 4/1 priority date for financial aid. Early and deferred admission are possible.

THE UNIVERSITY OF ARIZONA

URBAN SETTING ■ PUBLIC ■ STATE-SUPPORTED ■ COED
TUCSON, ARIZONA

Web site: www.arizona.edu
Contact: Ms. Lori Goldman, Director of Admissions, PO Box 210040,
   Tucson, AZ 85721-0040
Telephone: 520-621-3237 **Fax:** 520-621-9799
E-mail: appinfo@arizona.edu

Academics

UA awards bachelor's, master's, doctoral, and first-professional **degrees** and post-master's certificates. Challenging opportunities include advanced placement credit, freshman honors college, an honors program, double majors, independent study, and a senior project. Special programs include internships, summer session for credit, study-abroad, and Army and Air Force ROTC.

The most frequently chosen **baccalaureate** fields are business/marketing, social sciences and history, and biological/life sciences. A complete listing of majors at UA appears in the Majors Index beginning on page 430.

The **faculty** at UA has 1,380 full-time members, 98% with terminal degrees. The student-faculty ratio is 18:1.

Students of UA

The student body totals 35,747, of whom 27,532 are undergraduates. 52.7% are women and 47.3% are men. Students come from 55 states and territories and 130 other countries. 73% are from Arizona. 4.4% are international students. 2.8% are African American, 2% American Indian, 5.8% Asian American, and 14.5% Hispanic American.

Facilities and Resources

Student rooms are linked to a campus network. 1,750 **computers** are available on campus that provide access to the Internet. The 6 **libraries** have 4,721,975 books and 26,908 subscriptions.

Campus Life

There are 280 active organizations on campus, including a drama/theater group, newspaper, radio station, television station, choral group, and marching band. 15% of eligible men and 15% of eligible women are members of national **fraternities**, national **sororities**, local fraternities, and local sororities.

UA is a member of the NCAA (Division I). **Intercollegiate sports** (some offering scholarships) include baseball (m), basketball, cross-country running, football (m), golf, gymnastics (w), soccer (w), softball (w), swimming, tennis, track and field, volleyball (w).

Campus Safety

Student safety services include emergency telephones, late-night transport/escort service, 24-hour patrols by trained security personnel, and student patrols.

Applying

UA requires SAT I or ACT and a high school transcript, and in some cases an interview, recommendations, and a minimum high school GPA of 3.0. Application deadline: 4/1; 3/1 priority date for financial aid. Early admission is possible.

The University of Arizona offers a top-drawer education in a resort-like setting. Some of the nation's highest-ranked departments make their homes here. Tucson's clear skies provide an ideal setting for one of the country's best astronomy programs. Anthropology, nursing, management information systems, and optical sciences are also nationally ranked. The University balances a strong research component with an emphasis on teaching, including the recent completion of a learning/advising/computing center for freshmen.

Getting in Last Year
19,719 applied
84% were accepted
5,949 enrolled (36%)
31% from top tenth of their h.s. class
3.35 average high school GPA
29% had SAT verbal scores over 600
35% had SAT math scores over 600
51% had ACT scores over 24
5% had SAT verbal scores over 700
6% had SAT math scores over 700
9% had ACT scores over 30
50 National Merit Scholars

Graduation and After
280 organizations recruited on campus

Financial Matters
$2490 resident tuition and fees (2001–02)
$10,356 nonresident tuition and fees (2001–02)
$6124 room and board
$9228 average financial aid amount received per undergraduate (2000–01)

UNIVERSITY OF ARKANSAS

SUBURBAN SETTING ■ PUBLIC ■ STATE-SUPPORTED ■ COED
FAYETTEVILLE, ARKANSAS

Web site: www.uark.edu
Contact: Ms. Maxine Jones, Interim Director, 200 Silas H. Hunt Hall,
  Fayetteville, AR 72701-1201
Telephone: 479-575-5346 or toll-free 800-377-8632 **Fax:** 479-575-7515
E-mail: uafadmis@uark.edu

Getting in Last Year
4,470 applied
89% were accepted
2,330 enrolled (58%)
35% from top tenth of their h.s. class
3.52 average high school GPA
37% had SAT verbal scores over 600
42% had SAT math scores over 600
58% had ACT scores over 24
8% had SAT verbal scores over 700
9% had SAT math scores over 700
16% had ACT scores over 30
29 National Merit Scholars
177 valedictorians

Graduation and After
20% graduated in 4 years
20% graduated in 5 years
5% graduated in 6 years
Graduates pursuing further study: 10% arts and sciences, 10% business, 10% engineering
36% had job offers within 6 months
700 organizations recruited on campus

Financial Matters
$3880 resident tuition and fees (2001–02)
$9438 nonresident tuition and fees (2001–02)
$4454 room and board
78% average percent of need met
$7690 average financial aid amount received per undergraduate (2000–01 estimated)

Academics
Arkansas awards bachelor's, master's, doctoral, and first-professional **degrees**. Challenging opportunities include advanced placement credit, an honors program, double majors, independent study, and a senior project. Special programs include cooperative education, internships, summer session for credit, off-campus study, study-abroad, and Army and Air Force ROTC.

The most frequently chosen **baccalaureate** fields are business/marketing, engineering/engineering technologies, and education. A complete listing of majors at Arkansas appears in the Majors Index beginning on page 430.

The **faculty** at Arkansas has 800 full-time members. The student-faculty ratio is 16:1.

Students of Arkansas
The student body totals 15,752, of whom 12,818 are undergraduates. 48.4% are women and 51.6% are men. Students come from 49 states and territories and 109 other countries. 91% are from Arkansas. 3.2% are international students. 6.1% are African American, 2% American Indian, 2.7% Asian American, and 1.5% Hispanic American. 82% returned for their sophomore year.

Facilities and Resources
Student rooms are linked to a campus network. 1,415 **computers** are available on campus that provide access to the Internet. The 6 **libraries** have 643,468 books and 15,431 subscriptions.

Campus Life
There are 260 active organizations on campus, including a drama/theater group, newspaper, radio station, television station, choral group, and marching band. 15% of eligible men and 20% of eligible women are members of national **fraternities** and national **sororities**.

Arkansas is a member of the NCAA (Division I). **Intercollegiate sports** (some offering scholarships) include baseball (m), basketball, cross-country running, football (m), golf, gymnastics (w), soccer (w), softball (w), swimming (w), tennis, track and field, volleyball (w).

Campus Safety
Student safety services include RAD (Rape Aggression Defense program), late-night transport/escort service, 24-hour emergency telephone alarm devices, 24-hour patrols by trained security personnel, student patrols, and electronically operated dormitory entrances.

Applying
Arkansas requires SAT I or ACT and a high school transcript, and in some cases recommendations. It recommends an essay, 1 recommendation, and a minimum high school GPA of 3.0. Application deadline: 8/15. Early and deferred admission are possible.

University of California, Berkeley

URBAN SETTING ■ PUBLIC ■ STATE-SUPPORTED ■ COED
BERKELEY, CALIFORNIA

Web site: www.berkeley.edu
Contact: Pre-Admission Advising, Office of Undergraduate Admission and Relations With Schools, Berkeley, CA 94720-1500
Telephone: 510-642-3175 **Fax:** 510-642-7333
E-mail: ouars@uclink.berkeley.edu

Academics

Cal awards bachelor's, master's, doctoral, and first-professional **degrees**. Challenging opportunities include advanced placement credit, accelerated degree programs, student-designed majors, an honors program, double majors, independent study, and a senior project. Special programs include internships, summer session for credit, off-campus study, study-abroad, and Army ROTC.

The most frequently chosen **baccalaureate** fields are social sciences and history, biological/life sciences, and engineering/engineering technologies. A complete listing of majors at Cal appears in the Majors Index beginning on page 430.

The **faculty** at Cal has 1,444 full-time members, 98% with terminal degrees. The student-faculty ratio is 17:1.

Students of Cal

The student body totals 31,276, of whom 22,677 are undergraduates. 52.3% are women and 47.7% are men. Students come from 53 states and territories and 100 other countries. 86% are from California. 3.7% are international students. 4.3% are African American, 0.6% American Indian, 40.2% Asian American, and 9.6% Hispanic American. 95% returned for their sophomore year.

Facilities and Resources

Student rooms are linked to a campus network. 600 **computers** are available on campus that provide access to the Internet. The 31 **libraries** have 12,281,792 books and 139,455 subscriptions.

Campus Life

There are 400 active organizations on campus, including a drama/theater group, newspaper, radio station, television station, choral group, and marching band. 11% of eligible men and 10% of eligible women are members of national **fraternities**, national **sororities**, local fraternities, and local sororities.

Cal is a member of the NCAA (Division I). **Intercollegiate sports** (some offering scholarships) include baseball (m), basketball, crew, cross-country running, field hockey (w), football (m), golf, gymnastics, lacrosse (w), rugby (m), soccer, softball (w), swimming, tennis, track and field, volleyball (w), water polo.

Campus Safety

Student safety services include Office of Emergency Preparedness, late-night transport/escort service, 24-hour emergency telephone alarm devices, 24-hour patrols by trained security personnel, and electronically operated dormitory entrances.

Applying

Cal requires an essay, SAT II Subject Tests, SAT II: Writing Test, SAT I or ACT, a high school transcript, and minimum 2.8 GPA for California residents; 3.4 for all others. Application deadline: 11/30; 3/2 priority date for financial aid.

Getting in Last Year
32,963 applied
26% were accepted
3,748 enrolled (43%)
98% from top tenth of their h.s. class
3.76 average high school GPA
68% had SAT verbal scores over 600
82% had SAT math scores over 600
30% had SAT verbal scores over 700
46% had SAT math scores over 700
245 National Merit Scholars

Graduation and After
48% graduated in 4 years
30% graduated in 5 years
5% graduated in 6 years
606 organizations recruited on campus

Financial Matters
$4122 resident tuition and fees (2001–02)
$14,826 nonresident tuition and fees (2001–02)
$10,047 room and board
92% average percent of need met
$10,906 average financial aid amount received per undergraduate (2000–01 estimated)

UNIVERSITY OF CALIFORNIA, DAVIS

SUBURBAN SETTING ■ PUBLIC ■ STATE-SUPPORTED ■ COED
DAVIS, CALIFORNIA

Web site: www.ucdavis.edu
Contact: Dr. Gary Tudor, Director of Undergraduate Admissions,
Undergraduate Admission and Outreach Services, 175 Mrak Hall, Davis,
CA 95616
Telephone: 530-752-2971 **Fax:** 530-752-1280
E-mail: thinkucd@ucdavis.edu

Getting in Last Year
27,937 applied
63% were accepted
4,408 enrolled (25%)
3.71 average high school GPA
36% had SAT verbal scores over 600
58% had SAT math scores over 600
59% had ACT scores over 24
6% had SAT verbal scores over 700
13% had SAT math scores over 700
9% had ACT scores over 30
92 National Merit Scholars

Graduation and After
28% graduated in 4 years
37% graduated in 5 years
10% graduated in 6 years
38% pursued further study (15% arts and
sciences, 9% education, 7% medicine)
91% had job offers within 6 months

Financial Matters
$4594 resident tuition and fees (2001–02)
$15,298 nonresident tuition and fees (2001–
02)
$6982 room and board
81% average percent of need met
$8179 average financial aid amount received
per undergraduate (2000–01 estimated)

Academics
UC Davis awards bachelor's, master's, doctoral, and first-professional **degrees** and post-bachelor's certificates. Challenging opportunities include advanced placement credit, student-designed majors, freshman honors college, an honors program, double majors, independent study, and a senior project. Special programs include internships, summer session for credit, study-abroad, and Army and Air Force ROTC.

The most frequently chosen **baccalaureate** fields are social sciences and history, biological/life sciences, and engineering/engineering technologies. A complete listing of majors at UC Davis appears in the Majors Index beginning on page 430.

The **faculty** at UC Davis has 1,620 full-time members, 98% with terminal degrees. The student-faculty ratio is 19:1.

Students of UC Davis
The student body totals 26,513, of whom 21,294 are undergraduates. 56.5% are women and 43.5% are men. Students come from 49 states and territories and 113 other countries. 96% are from California. 1.4% are international students. 2.7% are African American, 0.8% American Indian, 35.5% Asian American, and 9.9% Hispanic American. 99% returned for their sophomore year.

Facilities and Resources
Student rooms are linked to a campus network. 600 **computers** are available on campus that provide access to software packages and the Internet. The 6 **libraries** have 2,879,533 books and 45,665 subscriptions.

Campus Life
There are 320 active organizations on campus, including a drama/theater group, newspaper, radio station, choral group, and marching band. 9% of eligible men and 9% of eligible women are members of national **fraternities**, national **sororities**, and state fraternities and sororities.

UC Davis is a member of the NCAA (Division II). **Intercollegiate sports** include baseball (m), basketball, cross-country running, football (m), golf (m), gymnastics (w), soccer, softball (w), swimming, tennis, track and field, volleyball (w), water polo (m), wrestling (m).

Campus Safety
Student safety services include rape prevention programs, late-night transport/escort service, 24-hour emergency telephone alarm devices, 24-hour patrols by trained security personnel, student patrols, and electronically operated dormitory entrances.

Applying
UC Davis requires an essay, SAT II: Writing Test, SAT I and SAT II or ACT, and a high school transcript. Application deadline: 11/30.

University of California, Irvine
Suburban setting ■ Public ■ State-supported ■ Coed
Irvine, California

Web site: www.uci.edu
Contact: Dr. Susan Wilbur, Director of Admissions, 204 Administration, Irvine, CA 92697-1075
Telephone: 949-824-6701

Academics

UCI awards bachelor's, master's, and doctoral **degrees**. Challenging opportunities include advanced placement credit, an honors program, double majors, independent study, and a senior project. Special programs include cooperative education, internships, summer session for credit, off-campus study, study-abroad, and Army and Air Force ROTC. A complete listing of majors at UCI appears in the Majors Index beginning on page 430.

The **faculty** at UCI has 753 full-time members, 95% with terminal degrees. The student-faculty ratio is 18:1.

Students of UCI

The student body totals 21,885, of whom 17,723 are undergraduates. 51.7% are women and 48.3% are men. Students come from 35 states and territories and 39 other countries. 98% are from California. 91% returned for their sophomore year.

Facilities and Resources

Student rooms are linked to a campus network. 500 **computers** are available on campus that provide access to the Internet. The 2 **libraries** have 2,392,709 books and 19,287 subscriptions.

Campus Life

There are 275 active organizations on campus, including a drama/theater group, newspaper, radio station, and choral group. 8% of eligible men and 8% of eligible women are members of national **fraternities**, national **sororities**, local fraternities, and local sororities.

UCI is a member of the NCAA (Division I). **Intercollegiate sports** (some offering scholarships) include basketball, crew, cross-country running, golf (m), sailing, soccer, swimming, tennis, track and field (w), volleyball, water polo (m).

Campus Safety

Student safety services include late-night transport/escort service, 24-hour emergency telephone alarm devices, and 24-hour patrols by trained security personnel.

Applying

UCI requires an essay, SAT II Subject Tests, SAT II: Writing Test, SAT I or ACT, a high school transcript, and a minimum high school GPA of 2.0. Application deadline: 11/30; 3/2 priority date for financial aid.

Getting in Last Year
29,178 applied
59% were accepted
4,042 enrolled (24%)
90% from top tenth of their h.s. class
3.66 average high school GPA
33% had SAT verbal scores over 600
56% had SAT math scores over 600
5% had SAT verbal scores over 700
13% had SAT math scores over 700

Graduation and After
34% graduated in 4 years
32% graduated in 5 years
6% graduated in 6 years
303 organizations recruited on campus

Financial Matters
$4556 resident tuition and fees (2001–02)
$20,186 nonresident tuition and fees (2001–02)
$7098 room and board
86% average percent of need met
$9481 average financial aid amount received per undergraduate (2000–01)

UNIVERSITY OF CALIFORNIA, LOS ANGELES

URBAN SETTING ■ PUBLIC ■ STATE-SUPPORTED ■ COED
LOS ANGELES, CALIFORNIA

Web site: www.ucla.edu
Contact: Dr. Rae Lee Siporin, Director of Undergraduate Admissions, 405
    Hilgard Avenue, Los Angeles, CA 90095
Telephone: 310-825-3101
E-mail: ugadm@saonet.ucla.edu

Getting in Last Year
40,739 applied
27% were accepted
4,246 enrolled (39%)
97% from top tenth of their h.s. class
63% had SAT verbal scores over 600
77% had SAT math scores over 600
72% had ACT scores over 24
19% had SAT verbal scores over 700
36% had SAT math scores over 700
24% had ACT scores over 30
73 National Merit Scholars

Graduation and After
40% graduated in 4 years
36% graduated in 5 years
5% graduated in 6 years
33% pursued further study
1400 organizations recruited on campus

Financial Matters
$4236 resident tuition and fees (2001–02)
$15,310 nonresident tuition and fees (2001–02)
$8991 room and board
83% average percent of need met
$9827 average financial aid amount received per undergraduate (2000–01 estimated)

Academics
UCLA awards bachelor's, master's, doctoral, and first-professional **degrees**. Challenging opportunities include advanced placement credit, student-designed majors, an honors program, double majors, and independent study. Special programs include internships, summer session for credit, off-campus study, study-abroad, and Army, Navy and Air Force ROTC.

The most frequently chosen **baccalaureate** fields are social sciences and history, psychology, and biological/life sciences. A complete listing of majors at UCLA appears in the Majors Index beginning on page 430.

The **faculty** at UCLA has 1,760 full-time members, 98% with terminal degrees. The student-faculty ratio is 17:1.

Students of UCLA
The student body totals 37,494, of whom 25,328 are undergraduates. 55.1% are women and 44.9% are men. Students come from 50 states and territories and 100 other countries. 97% are from California. 2.9% are international students. 3.7% are African American, 0.5% American Indian, 37.5% Asian American, and 14% Hispanic American. 97% returned for their sophomore year.

Facilities and Resources
Student rooms are linked to a campus network. The 14 **libraries** have 7,517,303 books and 93,854 subscriptions.

Campus Life
Active organizations on campus include a drama/theater group, newspaper, radio station, choral group, and marching band. 11% of eligible men and 9% of eligible women are members of national **fraternities**, national **sororities**, local fraternities, and local sororities.

UCLA is a member of the NCAA (Division I). **Intercollegiate sports** (some offering scholarships) include baseball (m), basketball, cross-country running, football (m), golf, gymnastics (w), soccer, softball (w), swimming (w), tennis, track and field, volleyball, water polo.

Campus Safety
Student safety services include late-night transport/escort service, 24-hour emergency telephone alarm devices, and student patrols.

Applying
UCLA requires an essay, SAT II: Writing Test, SAT I or ACT, SAT II Subject Test in math, third SAT II Subject Test, and a high school transcript. It recommends a minimum high school GPA of 3.5. Application deadline: 11/30; 3/1 priority date for financial aid.

University of California, Riverside

Urban setting ■ Public ■ State-supported ■ Coed
Riverside, California

Web site: www.ucr.edu
Contact: Ms. Laurie Nelson, Director of Undergraduate Admission, 1138 Hinderaker Hall, Riverside, CA 92521
Telephone: 909-787-3411 **Fax:** 909-787-6344
E-mail: discover@pop.ucr.edu

Academics

UCR awards bachelor's, master's, and doctoral **degrees**. Challenging opportunities include advanced placement credit, accelerated degree programs, student-designed majors, freshman honors college, an honors program, double majors, independent study, and a senior project. Special programs include cooperative education, internships, summer session for credit, off-campus study, study-abroad, and Army and Air Force ROTC.

The most frequently chosen **baccalaureate** fields are business/marketing, social sciences and history, and biological/life sciences. A complete listing of majors at UCR appears in the Majors Index beginning on page 430.

The **faculty** at UCR has 591 full-time members, 98% with terminal degrees. The student-faculty ratio is 19:1.

Students of UCR

The student body totals 14,429, of whom 12,714 are undergraduates. 53.6% are women and 46.4% are men. Students come from 35 states and territories and 22 other countries. 99% are from California. 2% are international students. 5.6% are African American, 0.5% American Indian, 42.3% Asian American, and 21.8% Hispanic American. 84% returned for their sophomore year.

Facilities and Resources

Student rooms are linked to a campus network. 600 **computers** are available on campus that provide access to the Internet. The 7 **libraries** have 2,018,284 books and 19,294 subscriptions.

Campus Life

There are 200 active organizations on campus, including a drama/theater group, newspaper, radio station, and choral group. 7% of eligible men and 7% of eligible women are members of national **fraternities**, national **sororities**, local fraternities, local sororities, and coed fraternities.

UCR is a member of the NCAA (Division II). **Intercollegiate sports** (some offering scholarships) include baseball (m), basketball, cross-country running, softball (w), tennis, track and field, volleyball (w).

Campus Safety

Student safety services include late-night transport/escort service, 24-hour emergency telephone alarm devices, 24-hour patrols by trained security personnel, student patrols, and electronically operated dormitory entrances.

Applying

UCR requires an essay, SAT II: Writing Test, SAT I or ACT, a high school transcript, and a minimum high school GPA of 2.82. Application deadline: 11/30; 3/2 priority date for financial aid. Early admission is possible.

Getting in Last Year

20,980 applied
85% were accepted
3,273 enrolled (18%)
94% from top tenth of their h.s. class
3.47 average high school GPA
17% had SAT verbal scores over 600
34% had SAT math scores over 600
27% had ACT scores over 24
2% had SAT verbal scores over 700
7% had SAT math scores over 700
3% had ACT scores over 30

Graduation and After

39% graduated in 4 years
22% graduated in 5 years
4% graduated in 6 years
37% pursued further study
136 organizations recruited on campus

Financial Matters

$4379 resident tuition and fees (2001–02)
$15,083 nonresident tuition and fees (2001–02)
$7200 room and board
88% average percent of need met
$9190 average financial aid amount received per undergraduate (2000–01 estimated)

UNIVERSITY OF CALIFORNIA, SAN DIEGO

SUBURBAN SETTING ■ PUBLIC ■ STATE-SUPPORTED ■ COED
LA JOLLA, CALIFORNIA

Web site: www.ucsd.edu

Contact: Associate Director of Admissions and Relations with Schools, 9500 Gilman Drive, 0021, La Jolla, CA 92093-0021

Telephone: 858-534-4831

E-mail: admissionsinfo@ucsd.edu

Getting in Last Year

38,051 applied
43% were accepted
3,982 enrolled (24%)
95% from top tenth of their h.s. class
3.99 average high school GPA
59% had SAT verbal scores over 600
81% had SAT math scores over 600
94% had ACT scores over 24
14% had SAT verbal scores over 700
33% had SAT math scores over 700
40% had ACT scores over 30
49 National Merit Scholars

Graduation and After

43% graduated in 4 years
29% graduated in 5 years
6% graduated in 6 years
35% pursued further study
85% had job offers within 6 months
4249 organizations recruited on campus

Financial Matters

$3863 resident tuition and fees (2001–02)
$18,430 nonresident tuition and fees (2001–02)
$7510 room and board
99% average percent of need met
$9341 average financial aid amount received per undergraduate (2000–01 estimated)

Academics

UCSD awards bachelor's, master's, doctoral, and first-professional **degrees**. Challenging opportunities include accelerated degree programs, student-designed majors, freshman honors college, an honors program, double majors, independent study, and a senior project. Special programs include cooperative education, internships, summer session for credit, off-campus study, and study-abroad. A complete listing of majors at UCSD appears in the Majors Index beginning on page 430.

The **faculty** at UCSD has 880 full-time members, 98% with terminal degrees. The student-faculty ratio is 19:1.

Students of UCSD

The student body totals 21,560, of whom 17,506 are undergraduates. 52% are women and 48% are men. 97% are from California. 2% are international students. 1.2% are African American, 0.5% American Indian, 35.3% Asian American, and 9.6% Hispanic American. 93% returned for their sophomore year.

Facilities and Resources

Student rooms are linked to a campus network. 1,020 **computers** are available on campus that provide access to e-mail and the Internet. The 8 **libraries** have 2,616,776 books and 25,000 subscriptions.

Campus Life

There are 350 active organizations on campus, including a drama/theater group, newspaper, radio station, television station, and choral group. 10% of eligible men and 10% of eligible women are members of national **fraternities** and national **sororities**.

UCSD is a member of the NCAA (Division II). **Intercollegiate sports** include baseball (m), basketball, crew, cross-country running, fencing, golf (m), soccer, softball (w), swimming, tennis, track and field, volleyball, water polo.

Campus Safety

Student safety services include crime prevention programs, late-night transport/escort service, 24-hour emergency telephone alarm devices, and 24-hour patrols by trained security personnel.

Applying

UCSD requires an essay, SAT I or ACT, 3 SAT II Subject Tests (including SAT II: Writing Test), a high school transcript, and a minimum high school GPA of 2.8, and in some cases a minimum high school GPA of 3.4. Application deadline: 11/30; 3/2 priority date for financial aid.

UNIVERSITY OF CALIFORNIA, SANTA BARBARA

SUBURBAN SETTING ■ PUBLIC ■ STATE-SUPPORTED ■ COED
SANTA BARBARA, CALIFORNIA

Web site: www.ucsb.edu
Contact: Mr. William Villa, Director of Admissions/Relations with Schools,
    Santa Barbara, CA 93106
Telephone: 805-893-2485 **Fax:** 805-893-2676
E-mail: appinfo@sa.ucsb.edu

Academics
UCSB awards bachelor's, master's, and doctoral **degrees**. Challenging opportunities include advanced placement credit, accelerated degree programs, student-designed majors, freshman honors college, an honors program, independent study, and a senior project. Special programs include internships, summer session for credit, off-campus study, and Army ROTC.

The most frequently chosen **baccalaureate** fields are social sciences and history, business/marketing, and biological/life sciences. A complete listing of majors at UCSB appears in the Majors Index beginning on page 430.

The **faculty** at UCSB has 792 full-time members. The student-faculty ratio is 19:1.

Students of UCSB
The student body totals 20,373, of whom 17,724 are undergraduates. 53.9% are women and 46.1% are men. Students come from 48 states and territories and 35 other countries. 95% are from California. 1.2% are international students. 2.5% are African American, 0.9% American Indian, 14.3% Asian American, and 14.7% Hispanic American. 91% returned for their sophomore year.

Facilities and Resources
3,000 **computers** are available on campus for student use. The **library** has 2,621,000 books and 18,155 subscriptions.

Campus Life
There are 250 active organizations on campus, including a drama/theater group, newspaper, radio station, and choral group. 8% of eligible men and 10% of eligible women are members of national **fraternities**, national **sororities**, local fraternities, and local sororities.

UCSB is a member of the NCAA (Division I). **Intercollegiate sports** (some offering scholarships) include baseball (m), basketball, cross-country running, golf (m), gymnastics, soccer, softball (w), swimming, tennis, track and field, volleyball, water polo.

Campus Safety
Student safety services include late-night transport/escort service and 24-hour emergency telephone alarm devices.

Applying
UCSB requires an essay, SAT II Subject Tests, SAT I or ACT, and a high school transcript, and in some cases an interview. Application deadline: 11/30; 3/2 priority date for financial aid. Early admission is possible.

Getting in Last Year
33,986 applied
50% were accepted
3,649 enrolled (21%)
3.73 average high school GPA
45% had SAT verbal scores over 600
60% had SAT math scores over 600
8% had SAT verbal scores over 700
15% had SAT math scores over 700

Graduation and After
1% graduated in 4 years
2% graduated in 5 years
24% pursued further study
56% had job offers within 6 months

Financial Matters
$3841 resident tuition and fees (2001–02)
$14,915 nonresident tuition and fees (2001–02)
$7891 room and board
87% average percent of need met
$8851 average financial aid amount received per undergraduate (1999–2000)

UNIVERSITY OF CALIFORNIA, SANTA CRUZ

SMALL-TOWN SETTING ■ PUBLIC ■ STATE-SUPPORTED ■ COED
SANTA CRUZ, CALIFORNIA

Web site: www.ucsc.edu

Contact: Mr. Kevin M. Browne, Executive Director of Admissions and University Registrar, Admissions Office, Cook House, Santa Cruz, CA 95064

Telephone: 831-459-5779 **Fax:** 831-459-4452

E-mail: admissions@cats.ucsc.edu

Getting in Last Year
19,578 applied
81% were accepted
3,023 enrolled (19%)
3.47 average high school GPA
40% had SAT verbal scores over 600
41% had SAT math scores over 600
53% had ACT scores over 24
8% had SAT verbal scores over 700
7% had SAT math scores over 700
8% had ACT scores over 30

Graduation and After
237 organizations recruited on campus

Financial Matters
$4300 resident tuition and fees (2001–02)
$15,374 nonresident tuition and fees (2001–02)
$8661 room and board
96% average percent of need met
$10,036 average financial aid amount received per undergraduate (1999–2000)

Academics
UCSC awards bachelor's, master's, and doctoral **degrees**. Challenging opportunities include advanced placement credit, student-designed majors, freshman honors college, an honors program, double majors, independent study, and a senior project. Special programs include cooperative education, internships, summer session for credit, off-campus study, study-abroad, and Army, Navy and Air Force ROTC.

The most frequently chosen **baccalaureate** fields are biological/life sciences, visual/performing arts, and psychology. A complete listing of majors at UCSC appears in the Majors Index beginning on page 430.

The **faculty** at UCSC has 485 full-time members. The student-faculty ratio is 19:1.

Students of UCSC
The student body totals 13,170, of whom 12,034 are undergraduates. 56.6% are women and 43.4% are men. 94% are from California. 1.1% are international students. 2.3% are African American, 0.9% American Indian, 15.8% Asian American, and 13.3% Hispanic American. 87% returned for their sophomore year.

Facilities and Resources
Student rooms are linked to a campus network. 200 **computers** are available on campus that provide access to the Internet. The 10 **libraries** have 1,200,000 books and 10,004 subscriptions.

Campus Life
There are 100 active organizations on campus, including a drama/theater group, newspaper, radio station, and choral group. 1% of eligible men and 1% of eligible women are members of national **fraternities**, national **sororities**, local fraternities, and local sororities.

UCSC is a member of the NCAA (Division III). **Intercollegiate sports** include basketball, rugby (m), soccer (m), swimming, tennis, volleyball, water polo.

Campus Safety
Student safety services include evening main gate security, campus police force and fire station, late-night transport/escort service, 24-hour emergency telephone alarm devices, 24-hour patrols by trained security personnel, and electronically operated dormitory entrances.

Applying
UCSC requires an essay, SAT I or ACT, and a high school transcript. Application deadline: 11/30; 3/2 priority date for financial aid.

University of Central Florida

Suburban setting ■ Public ■ State-supported ■ Coed
Orlando, Florida

Web site: www.ucf.edu
Contact: Undergraduate Admissions Office, PO Box 160111, Orlando, FL 32816
Telephone: 407-823-2000 **Fax:** 407-823-5625
E-mail: admission@mail.ucf.edu

Academics

UCF awards associate, bachelor's, master's, and doctoral **degrees**. Challenging opportunities include advanced placement credit, accelerated degree programs, freshman honors college, an honors program, double majors, independent study, and a senior project. Special programs include cooperative education, internships, summer session for credit, off-campus study, study-abroad, and Army and Air Force ROTC.

The most frequently chosen **baccalaureate** fields are business/marketing, education, and health professions and related sciences. A complete listing of majors at UCF appears in the Majors Index beginning on page 430.

The **faculty** at UCF has 976 full-time members, 81% with terminal degrees. The student-faculty ratio is 25:1.

Students of UCF

The student body totals 35,927, of whom 30,036 are undergraduates. 54.8% are women and 45.2% are men. Students come from 52 states and territories and 107 other countries. 97% are from Florida. 1.5% are international students. 7.9% are African American, 0.7% American Indian, 5% Asian American, and 10.9% Hispanic American. 79% returned for their sophomore year.

Facilities and Resources

Student rooms are linked to a campus network. 1,191 **computers** are available on campus that provide access to the Internet. The **library** has 865,527 books and 7,423 subscriptions.

Campus Life

There are 221 active organizations on campus, including a drama/theater group, newspaper, radio station, choral group, and marching band. 14% of eligible men and 13% of eligible women are members of national **fraternities** and national **sororities**.

UCF is a member of the NCAA (Division I). **Intercollegiate sports** (some offering scholarships) include baseball (m), basketball, crew (w), cross-country running, football (m), golf, soccer, tennis, track and field (w), volleyball (w).

Campus Safety

Student safety services include late-night transport/escort service, 24-hour emergency telephone alarm devices, 24-hour patrols by trained security personnel, and electronically operated dormitory entrances.

Applying

UCF requires SAT I or ACT, a high school transcript, and a minimum high school GPA of 2.0, and in some cases 1 recommendation. It recommends an essay. Application deadline: 5/15; 6/30 for financial aid, with a 3/1 priority date. Early admission is possible.

Getting in Last Year

17,043 applied
65% were accepted
5,246 enrolled (47%)
33% from top tenth of their h.s. class
3.6 average high school GPA
29% had SAT verbal scores over 600
33% had SAT math scores over 600
52% had ACT scores over 24
3% had SAT verbal scores over 700
4% had SAT math scores over 700
5% had ACT scores over 30
25 National Merit Scholars

Graduation and After

25% graduated in 4 years
18% graduated in 5 years
6% graduated in 6 years
98% had job offers within 6 months
3538 organizations recruited on campus

Financial Matters

$2582 resident tuition and fees (2001–02)
$10,469 nonresident tuition and fees (2001–02)
$5670 room and board
78% average percent of need met
$7029 average financial aid amount received per undergraduate

University of Chicago

Urban setting ■ Private ■ Independent ■ Coed
Chicago, Illinois

Web site: www.uchicago.edu

Contact: Mr. Theodore O'Neill, Dean of Admissions, 1116 East 59th Street, Chicago, IL 60637-1513

Telephone: 773-702-8650 **Fax:** 773-702-4199

Getting in Last Year
7,454 applied
44% were accepted
1,081 enrolled (33%)
80% from top tenth of their h.s. class
91% had SAT verbal scores over 600
92% had SAT math scores over 600
96% had ACT scores over 24
58% had SAT verbal scores over 700
53% had SAT math scores over 700
65% had ACT scores over 30
183 National Merit Scholars

Graduation and After
Graduates pursuing further study: 17% arts and sciences, 8% law, 8% medicine

Financial Matters
$26,475 tuition and fees (2001–02)
$8312 room and board

Academics

Chicago awards bachelor's, master's, doctoral, and first-professional **degrees**. Challenging opportunities include advanced placement credit, accelerated degree programs, student-designed majors, double majors, independent study, and a senior project. Special programs include internships, summer session for credit, off-campus study, study-abroad, and Army and Air Force ROTC.

The most frequently chosen **baccalaureate** fields are social sciences and history, biological/life sciences, and English. A complete listing of majors at Chicago appears in the Majors Index beginning on page 430.

The **faculty** at Chicago has 1,595 full-time members. The student-faculty ratio is 4:1.

Students of Chicago

The student body totals 12,561, of whom 4,072 are undergraduates. 50.5% are women and 49.5% are men. Students come from 52 states and territories and 49 other countries. 22% are from Illinois. 95% returned for their sophomore year.

Facilities and Resources

Student rooms are linked to a campus network. 1,000 **computers** are available on campus for student use. The 9 **libraries** have 5,800,000 books and 47,000 subscriptions.

Campus Life

There are 300 active organizations on campus, including a drama/theater group, newspaper, radio station, and choral group. 12% of eligible men and 5% of eligible women are members of national **fraternities** and national **sororities**.

Chicago is a member of the NCAA (Division III). **Intercollegiate sports** include baseball (m), basketball, cross-country running, football (m), soccer, softball (w), swimming, tennis, track and field, volleyball (w), wrestling (m).

Campus Safety

Student safety services include late-night transport/escort service, 24-hour emergency telephone alarm devices, 24-hour patrols by trained security personnel, and electronically operated dormitory entrances.

Applying

Chicago requires an essay, SAT I or ACT, a high school transcript, and 3 recommendations. It recommends an interview. Application deadline: 1/1; 2/1 priority date for financial aid. Early and deferred admission are possible.

University of Colorado at Boulder

Suburban setting ■ Public ■ State-supported ■ Coed
Boulder, Colorado

Web site: www.colorado.edu
Contact: Mr. Kevin MacLennan, Associate Director, 552 UCB, Boulder, CO 80309-0552
Telephone: 303-492-1394 **Fax:** 303-492-7115
E-mail: apply@colorado.edu

Academics

CU-Boulder awards bachelor's, master's, doctoral, and first-professional **degrees**. Challenging opportunities include advanced placement credit, accelerated degree programs, student-designed majors, freshman honors college, an honors program, double majors, independent study, and a senior project. Special programs include cooperative education, internships, summer session for credit, off-campus study, study-abroad, and Army, Navy and Air Force ROTC.

The most frequently chosen **baccalaureate** fields are social sciences and history, business/marketing, and communications/communication technologies. A complete listing of majors at CU-Boulder appears in the Majors Index beginning on page 430.

The **faculty** at CU-Boulder has 1,263 full-time members, 82% with terminal degrees. The student-faculty ratio is 15:1.

Students of CU-Boulder

The student body totals 29,609, of whom 23,998 are undergraduates. 47.5% are women and 52.5% are men. Students come from 53 states and territories and 113 other countries. 67% are from Colorado. 1.3% are international students. 1.7% are African American, 0.7% American Indian, 5.6% Asian American, and 5.6% Hispanic American. 82% returned for their sophomore year.

Facilities and Resources

Student rooms are linked to a campus network. 1,700 **computers** are available on campus that provide access to standard and academic software, student government voting and the Internet. The 6 **libraries** have 2,651,667 books and 14,772 subscriptions.

Campus Life

There are 150 active organizations on campus, including a drama/theater group, newspaper, radio station, television station, choral group, and marching band. 8% of eligible men and 12% of eligible women are members of national **fraternities**, national **sororities**, and local sororities.

CU-Boulder is a member of the NCAA (Division I). **Intercollegiate sports** (some offering scholarships) include basketball, cross-country running, football (m), golf, skiing (cross-country), skiing (downhill), soccer (w), tennis, track and field, volleyball (w).

Campus Safety

Student safety services include university police department, late-night transport/escort service, 24-hour emergency telephone alarm devices, 24-hour patrols by trained security personnel, and student patrols.

Applying

CU-Boulder requires an essay, SAT I or ACT, a high school transcript, and a minimum high school GPA of 2.0, and in some cases audition for music program. It recommends recommendations and a minimum high school GPA of 3.0. Application deadline: 2/15; 4/1 priority date for financial aid. Deferred admission is possible.

The University of Colorado at Boulder, a major research and teaching university, is located in one of the most spectacular environments in the country at the foot of the Rocky Mountains. Ranking 10th among all public universities in federally funded research, the University offers tremendous academic diversity, with faculty members committed to bringing their research into the classroom. Students may participate in honors programs, an undergraduate research program, and several academic residential programs.

Getting in Last Year
18,486 applied
79% were accepted
5,020 enrolled (34%)
22% from top tenth of their h.s. class
3.48 average high school GPA
37% had SAT verbal scores over 600
47% had SAT math scores over 600
65% had ACT scores over 24
5% had SAT verbal scores over 700
8% had SAT math scores over 700
10% had ACT scores over 30
13 National Merit Scholars
151 valedictorians

Graduation and After
18% pursued further study (6% arts and sciences, 5% medicine, 3% engineering)
79% had job offers within 6 months
389 organizations recruited on campus

Financial Matters
$3357 resident tuition and fees (2001–02)
$17,367 nonresident tuition and fees (2001–02)
$5898 room and board
75% average percent of need met
$9434 average financial aid amount received per undergraduate

University of Dallas

Suburban setting ■ Private ■ Independent Religious ■ Coed
Irving, Texas

Getting in Last Year
1,410 applied
85% were accepted
311 enrolled (26%)
47% from top tenth of their h.s. class
3.80 average high school GPA
58% had SAT verbal scores over 600
51% had SAT math scores over 600
70% had ACT scores over 24
19% had SAT verbal scores over 700
11% had SAT math scores over 700
20% had ACT scores over 30
17 National Merit Scholars
19 valedictorians

Graduation and After
50% graduated in 4 years
8% graduated in 5 years
3% graduated in 6 years
Graduates pursuing further study: 20% arts
 and sciences, 14% business, 10% medicine
50 organizations recruited on campus

Financial Matters
$16,084 tuition and fees (2001–02)
$5950 room and board
80% average percent of need met
$13,365 average financial aid amount received
 per undergraduate (2000–01 estimated)

Web site: www.udallas.edu
Contact: Mr. Larry Webb, Director of Enrollment, 1845 East Northgate
 Drive, Irving, TX 75062-4799
Telephone: 972-721-5266 or toll-free 800-628-6999 **Fax:** 972-721-5017
E-mail: ugadmis@mailadmin.udallas.edu

Academics
UD awards bachelor's, master's, and doctoral **degrees**. Challenging opportunities
include advanced placement credit, accelerated degree programs, student-designed
majors, double majors, independent study, and a senior project. Special programs include
internships, summer session for credit, off-campus study, study-abroad, and Army and
Air Force ROTC.

The most frequently chosen **baccalaureate** fields are social sciences and history,
philosophy, and biological/life sciences. A complete listing of majors at UD appears in
the Majors Index beginning on page 430.

The **faculty** at UD has 129 full-time members, 87% with terminal degrees. The student-faculty ratio is 11:1.

Students of UD
The student body totals 3,518, of whom 1,255 are undergraduates. 58.2% are women
and 41.8% are men. Students come from 48 states and territories and 21 other countries.
60% are from Texas. 2.2% are international students. 2% are African American, 0.7%
American Indian, 6.5% Asian American, and 14.3% Hispanic American. 78% returned
for their sophomore year.

Facilities and Resources
Student rooms are linked to a campus network. 70 **computers** are available on campus
for student use. The **library** has 192,468 books and 1,819 subscriptions.

Campus Life
There are 30 active organizations on campus, including a drama/theater group,
newspaper, and choral group. No national or local **fraternities** or **sororities**.

UD is a member of the NCAA (Division III). **Intercollegiate sports** include baseball
(m), basketball, cross-country running, golf, soccer, softball (w), tennis, track and field,
volleyball (w).

Campus Safety
Student safety services include late-night transport/escort service, 24-hour emergency
telephone alarm devices, 24-hour patrols by trained security personnel, and electronically operated dormitory entrances.

Applying
UD requires an essay, SAT I or ACT, a high school transcript, and 1 recommendation,
and in some cases an interview. It recommends an interview. Application deadline: 2/15;
3/1 priority date for financial aid. Early and deferred admission are possible.

University of Dayton

Suburban setting ■ Private ■ Independent Religious ■ Coed
Dayton, Ohio

Web site: www.udayton.edu
Contact: Mr. Robert F. Durkle, Director of Admission, 300 College Park,
  Dayton, OH 45469-1300
Telephone: 937-229-4411 or toll-free 800-837-7433 **Fax:** 937-229-4729
E-mail: admission@udayton.edu

Academics

UD awards bachelor's, master's, doctoral, and first-professional **degrees**. Challenging
opportunities include advanced placement credit, accelerated degree programs, an
honors program, double majors, independent study, and a senior project. Special
programs include cooperative education, internships, summer session for credit, off-
campus study, study-abroad, and Army and Air Force ROTC.

The most frequently chosen **baccalaureate** fields are business/marketing, education,
and engineering/engineering technologies. A complete listing of majors at UD appears
in the Majors Index beginning on page 430.

The **faculty** at UD has 388 full-time members, 94% with terminal degrees. The student-faculty ratio is 15:1.

Students of UD

The student body totals 10,252, of whom 7,168 are undergraduates. 51% are women and
49% are men. Students come from 48 states and territories and 48 other countries. 66%
are from Ohio. 1% are international students. 3.4% are African American, 0.1%
American Indian, 1.1% Asian American, and 2.2% Hispanic American.

Facilities and Resources

Student rooms are linked to a campus network. 550 **computers** are available on campus
that provide access to the Internet. The 2 **libraries** have 948,677 books and 4,196
subscriptions.

Campus Life

There are 160 active organizations on campus, including a drama/theater group,
newspaper, radio station, television station, choral group, and marching band. 18% of
eligible men and 22% of eligible women are members of national **fraternities**, national
sororities, local fraternities, and local sororities.

UD is a member of the NCAA (Division I). **Intercollegiate sports** (some offering
scholarships) include baseball (m), basketball, crew (w), cross-country running, football
(m), golf, soccer, softball (w), tennis, track and field (w), volleyball (w).

Campus Safety

Student safety services include late-night transport/escort service, 24-hour emergency
telephone alarm devices, 24-hour patrols by trained security personnel, student patrols,
and electronically operated dormitory entrances.

Applying

UD requires SAT I or ACT, a high school transcript, and 1 recommendation, and in
some cases an essay. It recommends an interview. Application deadline: rolling admissions; 3/31 priority date for financial aid. Early and deferred admission are possible.

The University of Dayton is
Ohio's largest private
university and a national
leader in Catholic higher education.
Competence, character, and
commitment are hallmarks of the
85,000 alumni around the world
who have called Dayton their alma
mater, including four-time Super
Bowl winner Chuck Noll, ESPN
anchor Dan Patrick, television star
Mystro Clark, and the late humorist
Erma Bombeck. University of Dayton
students are encouraged to look
critically at the world's problems
and to become part of the
solution—from joining efforts to
rebuild the Balkans to boosting
literacy and building housing in our
own backyard. The
technology-enhanced learning
environment is preparing students to
lead well into the 21st century. The
University of Dayton is a place
where the mind and heart serve the
human community.

Getting in Last Year
7,339 applied
80% were accepted
23% from top tenth of their h.s. class
39% had SAT verbal scores over 600
46% had SAT math scores over 600
64% had ACT scores over 24
7% had SAT verbal scores over 700
11% had SAT math scores over 700
14% had ACT scores over 30
15 National Merit Scholars
42 valedictorians

Graduation and After
81% had job offers within 6 months
230 organizations recruited on campus

Financial Matters
$16,850 tuition and fees (2001–02)
$5280 room and board
75% average percent of need met
$13,776 average financial aid amount received
  per undergraduate

University of Delaware

Small-town setting ■ Public ■ State-related ■ Coed
Newark, Delaware

Web site: www.udel.edu
Contact: Mr. Larry Griffith, Director of Admissions, 116 Hullihen Hall, Newark, DE 19716
Telephone: 302-831-8123 **Fax:** 302-831-6905
E-mail: admissions@udel.edu

Getting in Last Year
18,209 applied
53% were accepted
3,320 enrolled (35%)
29% from top tenth of their h.s. class
3.45 average high school GPA
34% had SAT verbal scores over 600
47% had SAT math scores over 600
55% had ACT scores over 24
4% had SAT verbal scores over 700
7% had SAT math scores over 700
9% had ACT scores over 30

Graduation and After
54% graduated in 4 years
16% graduated in 5 years
2% graduated in 6 years
18% pursued further study (10% arts and sciences, 4% law, 3% business)
72.8% had job offers within 6 months
330 organizations recruited on campus

Financial Matters
$5290 resident tuition and fees (2001–02)
$14,380 nonresident tuition and fees (2001–02)
$5534 room and board
84% average percent of need met
$9277 average financial aid amount received per undergraduate

Academics
Delaware awards associate, bachelor's, master's, and doctoral **degrees** (enrollment data for undergraduate students does not include non-degree-seeking students). Challenging opportunities include advanced placement credit, accelerated degree programs, student-designed majors, an honors program, double majors, independent study, and a senior project. Special programs include cooperative education, internships, summer session for credit, study-abroad, and Army and Air Force ROTC.

The most frequently chosen **baccalaureate** fields are business/marketing, social sciences and history, and education. A complete listing of majors at Delaware appears in the Majors Index beginning on page 430.

The **faculty** at Delaware has 1,098 full-time members, 85% with terminal degrees. The student-faculty ratio is 13:1.

Students of Delaware
The student body totals 18,673, of whom 15,731 are undergraduates. 64.7% are women and 35.3% are men. Students come from 50 states and territories and 100 other countries. 41% are from Delaware. 1% are international students. 5.5% are African American, 0.2% American Indian, 2.7% Asian American, and 2.5% Hispanic American. 88% returned for their sophomore year.

Facilities and Resources
Student rooms are linked to a campus network. 900 **computers** are available on campus for student use. The 4 **libraries** have 2,402,535 books and 12,633 subscriptions.

Campus Life
There are 200 active organizations on campus, including a drama/theater group, newspaper, radio station, television station, choral group, and marching band. 15% of eligible men and 15% of eligible women are members of national **fraternities**, national **sororities**, local fraternities, and local sororities.

Delaware is a member of the NCAA (Division I). **Intercollegiate sports** (some offering scholarships) include baseball (m), basketball, crew (w), cross-country running, field hockey (w), football (m), golf (m), lacrosse, soccer, softball (w), swimming, tennis, track and field, volleyball (w).

Campus Safety
Student safety services include late-night transport/escort service, 24-hour emergency telephone alarm devices, 24-hour patrols by trained security personnel, student patrols, and electronically operated dormitory entrances.

Applying
Delaware requires an essay, SAT I or ACT, a high school transcript, and 1 recommendation. It recommends SAT II Subject Tests and SAT II: Writing Test. Application deadline: 2/15; 3/15 for financial aid, with a 2/1 priority date. Early and deferred admission are possible.

University of Denver

Suburban setting ■ Private ■ Independent ■ Coed
Denver, Colorado

Web site: www.du.edu
Contact: Ms. Colleen Hillmeyer, Director of New Student Programs,
University Park, Denver, CO 80208
Telephone: 303-871-2782 or toll-free 800-525-9495 (out-of-state) **Fax:**
303-871-3301
E-mail: admission@du.edu

Academics

DU awards bachelor's, master's, doctoral, and first-professional **degrees**. Challenging opportunities include advanced placement credit, accelerated degree programs, student-designed majors, freshman honors college, an honors program, double majors, independent study, and a senior project. Special programs include cooperative education, internships, summer session for credit, study-abroad, and Army and Air Force ROTC.

The most frequently chosen **baccalaureate** fields are business/marketing, communications/communication technologies, and social sciences and history. A complete listing of majors at DU appears in the Majors Index beginning on page 430.

The **faculty** at DU has 425 full-time members, 88% with terminal degrees. The student-faculty ratio is 9:1.

Students of DU

The student body totals 9,385, of whom 4,110 are undergraduates. 57% are women and 43% are men. Students come from 52 states and territories and 54 other countries. 50% are from Colorado. 4.9% are international students. 4% are African American, 1.2% American Indian, 4.9% Asian American, and 6.5% Hispanic American. 86% returned for their sophomore year.

Facilities and Resources

Student rooms are linked to a campus network. 750 **computers** are available on campus for student use. The **library** has 1,268,928 books and 5,788 subscriptions.

Campus Life

There are 82 active organizations on campus, including a drama/theater group, newspaper, and choral group. 31% of eligible men and 22% of eligible women are members of national **fraternities** and national **sororities**.

DU is a member of the NCAA (Division I). **Intercollegiate sports** (some offering scholarships) include basketball, cross-country running, golf, gymnastics (w), ice hockey (m), lacrosse, skiing (cross-country), skiing (downhill), soccer, swimming, tennis, volleyball (w).

Campus Safety

Student safety services include 24-hour locked residence hall entrances, late-night transport/escort service, 24-hour emergency telephone alarm devices, 24-hour patrols by trained security personnel, and electronically operated dormitory entrances.

Applying

DU requires an essay, SAT I or ACT, a high school transcript, and 2 recommendations, and in some cases a minimum high school GPA of 2.0. It recommends a minimum high school GPA of 2.7. Application deadline: 2/1; 2/15 priority date for financial aid. Early and deferred admission are possible.

Getting in Last Year

4,275 applied
72% were accepted
964 enrolled (31%)
35% from top tenth of their h.s. class
3.40 average high school GPA
32% had SAT verbal scores over 600
39% had SAT math scores over 600
61% had ACT scores over 24
6% had SAT verbal scores over 700
5% had SAT math scores over 700
12% had ACT scores over 30

Graduation and After

57% graduated in 4 years
11% graduated in 5 years
1% graduated in 6 years
24% pursued further study
67% had job offers within 6 months
242 organizations recruited on campus

Financial Matters

$22,035 tuition and fees (2001–02)
$6747 room and board
90% average percent of need met
$18,247 average financial aid amount received per undergraduate

University of Evansville

Suburban setting ■ Private ■ Independent Religious ■ Coed
Evansville, Indiana

Web site: www.evansville.edu
Contact: Mr. Tom Bear, Dean of Admission, 1800 Lincoln Avenue, Evansville,
IN 47722-0002
Telephone: 812-479-2468 or toll-free 800-992-5877 (in-state), 800-423-8633
(out-of-state) **Fax:** 812-474-4076
E-mail: admission@evansville.edu

Getting in Last Year
1,870 applied
91% were accepted
513 enrolled (30%)
30% from top tenth of their h.s. class
3.58 average high school GPA
33% had SAT verbal scores over 600
34% had SAT math scores over 600
70% had ACT scores over 24
6% had SAT verbal scores over 700
5% had SAT math scores over 700
15% had ACT scores over 30
25 National Merit Scholars
34 valedictorians

Graduation and After
50% graduated in 4 years
17% graduated in 5 years
1% graduated in 6 years
16% pursued further study (5% business, 4% arts and sciences, 2% medicine)
60% had job offers within 6 months
95 organizations recruited on campus

Financial Matters
$17,395 tuition and fees (2001–02)
$5470 room and board
87% average percent of need met
$14,836 average financial aid amount received per undergraduate

Academics

UE awards associate, bachelor's, and master's **degrees**. Challenging opportunities include advanced placement credit, freshman honors college, an honors program, and a senior project. Special programs include cooperative education, internships, summer session for credit, and study-abroad.

The most frequently chosen **baccalaureate** fields are education, business/marketing, and health professions and related sciences. A complete listing of majors at UE appears in the Majors Index beginning on page 430.

The **faculty** at UE has 173 full-time members, 86% with terminal degrees. The student-faculty ratio is 13:1.

Students of UE

The student body totals 2,687, of whom 2,674 are undergraduates. 60.5% are women and 39.5% are men. Students come from 46 states and territories and 42 other countries. 66% are from Indiana. 6% are international students. 2.2% are African American, 0.2% American Indian, 0.6% Asian American, and 0.7% Hispanic American. 81% returned for their sophomore year.

Facilities and Resources

Student rooms are linked to a campus network. 360 **computers** are available on campus for student use. The 2 **libraries** have 268,402 books and 1,352 subscriptions.

Campus Life

There are 130 active organizations on campus, including a drama/theater group, newspaper, radio station, and choral group. 30% of eligible men and 20% of eligible women are members of national **fraternities** and national **sororities**.

UE is a member of the NCAA (Division I). **Intercollegiate sports** (some offering scholarships) include baseball (m), basketball, cross-country running, football (m), golf (m), soccer, softball (w), swimming, tennis, volleyball (w).

Campus Safety

Student safety services include late-night transport/escort service, 24-hour emergency telephone alarm devices, and 24-hour patrols by trained security personnel.

Applying

UE requires SAT I or ACT, a high school transcript, 1 recommendation, and a minimum high school GPA of 2.0, and in some cases an essay and an interview. It recommends an interview and a minimum high school GPA of 3.0. Application deadline: 2/15; 3/1 priority date for financial aid. Early and deferred admission are possible.

University of Florida

Suburban setting ■ Public ■ State-supported ■ Coed
Gainesville, Florida

Web site: www.ufl.edu
Contact: Office of Admissions, PO Box 114000, Gainesville, FL 32611-4000
Telephone: 352-392-1365
E-mail: freshmen@ufl.edu

Academics

UF awards associate, bachelor's, master's, doctoral, and first-professional **degrees**. Challenging opportunities include advanced placement credit, accelerated degree programs, student-designed majors, an honors program, double majors, independent study, and a senior project. Special programs include cooperative education, internships, summer session for credit, off-campus study, study-abroad, and Army, Navy and Air Force ROTC.

The most frequently chosen **baccalaureate** fields are business/marketing, engineering/engineering technologies, and trade and industry. A complete listing of majors at UF appears in the Majors Index beginning on page 430.

The **faculty** at UF has 1,601 full-time members, 96% with terminal degrees. The student-faculty ratio is 20:1.

Students of UF

The student body totals 46,515, of whom 33,639 are undergraduates. 52.6% are women and 47.4% are men. Students come from 52 states and territories and 114 other countries. 96% are from Florida. 1.1% are international students. 8% are African American, 0.5% American Indian, 6.8% Asian American, and 10.7% Hispanic American. 92% returned for their sophomore year.

Facilities and Resources

Student rooms are linked to a campus network. 447 **computers** are available on campus for student use. The 16 **libraries** have 5,024,637 books and 28,103 subscriptions.

Campus Life

There are 525 active organizations on campus, including a drama/theater group, newspaper, choral group, and marching band. 15% of eligible men and 15% of eligible women are members of national **fraternities** and national **sororities**.

UF is a member of the NCAA (Division I). **Intercollegiate sports** (some offering scholarships) include baseball (m), basketball, cross-country running, football (m), golf, gymnastics (w), soccer (w), softball (w), swimming, tennis, track and field, volleyball (w).

Campus Safety

Student safety services include crime and rape prevention programs, late-night transport/escort service, 24-hour emergency telephone alarm devices, 24-hour patrols by trained security personnel, student patrols, and electronically operated dormitory entrances.

Applying

UF requires SAT I or ACT and a high school transcript. Application deadline: 1/16; 3/15 priority date for financial aid. Early admission is possible.

Getting in Last Year

18,625 applied
60% were accepted
6,337 enrolled (57%)
66% from top tenth of their h.s. class
3.50 average high school GPA
55% had SAT verbal scores over 600
60% had SAT math scores over 600
66% had ACT scores over 24
12% had SAT verbal scores over 700
16% had SAT math scores over 700
16% had ACT scores over 30
130 National Merit Scholars

Graduation and After

38% graduated in 4 years
26% graduated in 5 years
6% graduated in 6 years
22% pursued further study
920 organizations recruited on campus

Financial Matters

$2444 resident tuition and fees (2001–02)
$10,332 nonresident tuition and fees (2001–02)
$5430 room and board
82% average percent of need met
$8527 average financial aid amount received per undergraduate (2000–01)

University of Georgia

Suburban setting ■ Public ■ State-supported ■ Coed
Athens, Georgia

Web site: www.uga.edu
Contact: Dr. John Albright, Associate Director of Admissions, Athens, GA 30602
Telephone: 706-542-3000
E-mail: undergrad@admissions.uga.edu

ocated in the quintessential college town of Athens, the University of Georgia (UGA) is ranked among the top public research universities nationally and recognized widely as an outstanding value because of its competitive costs, exceptional undergraduate instruction and research opportunities, and enviable student satisfaction record. Through its programs and practices, UGA seeks to foster the understanding of and respect for cultural differences necessary for an enlightened and educated citizenry. UGA's Honors Program, one of the oldest and largest in the nation, provides an enhanced liberal arts foundation for superior undergraduates, along with faculty-guided individual research and progress into graduate-level work.

Getting in Last Year
13,393 applied
62% were accepted
3.64 average high school GPA
51% had SAT verbal scores over 600
52% had SAT math scores over 600
77% had ACT scores over 24
9% had SAT verbal scores over 700
8% had SAT math scores over 700
18% had ACT scores over 30
49 National Merit Scholars

Graduation and After
46% graduated in 4 years
16% graduated in 5 years
4% graduated in 6 years
Graduates pursuing further study: 7% business, 5% arts and sciences, 4% law
91.9% had job offers within 6 months
430 organizations recruited on campus

Financial Matters
$3418 resident tuition and fees (2001–02)
$11,314 nonresident tuition and fees (2001–02)
$5388 room and board
73% average percent of need met
$6451 average financial aid amount received per undergraduate

Academics
UGA awards associate, bachelor's, master's, doctoral, and first-professional **degrees**. Challenging opportunities include advanced placement credit, accelerated degree programs, student-designed majors, an honors program, double majors, independent study, and a senior project. Special programs include cooperative education, internships, summer session for credit, off-campus study, study-abroad, and Army and Air Force ROTC.

The most frequently chosen **baccalaureate** fields are business/marketing, education, and social sciences and history. A complete listing of majors at UGA appears in the Majors Index beginning on page 430.

The **faculty** at UGA has 1,815 full-time members, 95% with terminal degrees. The student-faculty ratio is 12:1.

Students of UGA
The student body totals 32,317, of whom 24,395 are undergraduates. Students come from 53 states and territories and 131 other countries. 91% are from Georgia. 0.9% are international students. 5.8% are African American, 0.2% American Indian, 3.2% Asian American, and 1.4% Hispanic American. 90% returned for their sophomore year.

Facilities and Resources
Student rooms are linked to a campus network. 2,500 **computers** are available on campus that provide access to e-mail, Web pages and the Internet. The 3 **libraries** have 3,788,521 books and 54,366 subscriptions.

Campus Life
There are 430 active organizations on campus, including a drama/theater group, newspaper, radio station, choral group, and marching band. 16% of eligible men and 21% of eligible women are members of national **fraternities**, national **sororities**, local fraternities, and local sororities.

UGA is a member of the NCAA (Division I). **Intercollegiate sports** (some offering scholarships) include baseball (m), basketball, cross-country running, football (m), golf, gymnastics (w), soccer (w), swimming, tennis, track and field, volleyball (w).

Campus Safety
Student safety services include late-night transport/escort service, 24-hour emergency telephone alarm devices, 24-hour patrols by trained security personnel, and electronically operated dormitory entrances.

Applying
UGA requires SAT I or ACT and a high school transcript. It recommends an essay. Application deadline: 1/15; 3/1 priority date for financial aid. Early and deferred admission are possible.

University of Illinois at Chicago

Urban setting ■ Public ■ State-supported ■ Coed
Chicago, Illinois

Web site: www.uic.edu
Contact: Mr. Rob Sheinkopf, Executive Director of Admissions, Box 5220, Chicago, IL 60680-5220
Telephone: 312-996-4350 **Fax:** 312-413-7628
E-mail: uic.admit@uic.edu

Academics

UIC awards bachelor's, master's, doctoral, and first-professional **degrees** and first-professional certificates. Challenging opportunities include advanced placement credit, accelerated degree programs, student-designed majors, an honors program, double majors, independent study, and a senior project. Special programs include cooperative education, internships, summer session for credit, off-campus study, study-abroad, and Army, Navy and Air Force ROTC.

The most frequently chosen **baccalaureate** fields are business/marketing, psychology, and engineering/engineering technologies. A complete listing of majors at UIC appears in the Majors Index beginning on page 430.

The **faculty** at UIC has 1,249 full-time members, 88% with terminal degrees. The student-faculty ratio is 14:1.

Students of UIC

The student body totals 24,955, of whom 15,887 are undergraduates. 55% are women and 45% are men. Students come from 52 states and territories and 81 other countries. 97% are from Illinois. 1.8% are international students. 9.5% are African American, 0.3% American Indian, 23.5% Asian American, and 17% Hispanic American. 79% returned for their sophomore year.

Facilities and Resources

Student rooms are linked to a campus network. 600 **computers** are available on campus for student use. The 9 **libraries** have 2,072,288 books and 20,875 subscriptions.

Campus Life

There are 200 active organizations on campus, including a drama/theater group, newspaper, radio station, and choral group. 4% of eligible men and 3% of eligible women are members of national **fraternities**, national **sororities**, local fraternities, and local sororities.

UIC is a member of the NCAA (Division I). **Intercollegiate sports** (some offering scholarships) include baseball (m), basketball, cross-country running, gymnastics, soccer (m), softball (w), swimming, tennis, track and field, volleyball (w).

Campus Safety

Student safety services include housing ID stickers, guest escort policy, 24-hour closed circuit videos for exits and entrances, security screen for first floor, late-night transport/escort service, 24-hour emergency telephone alarm devices, 24-hour patrols by trained security personnel, student patrols, and electronically operated dormitory entrances.

Applying

UIC requires SAT I or ACT and a high school transcript, and in some cases an essay and an interview. Application deadline: 2/28; 3/1 priority date for financial aid. Early admission is possible.

UIC is one of the nation's top 100 research universities. Faculty members include MacArthur "genius grant" winners, discoverers of the "fountain of youth" gene, and 5 scholars in the *Norton Anthology of Theory and Criticism.* Students win Rhodes, Fulbright, and Truman scholarships. UIC students have conducted archeological digs in Alabama, performed *Our Town* in Moscow, and studied urban issues in London and Beijing. Chicago, one of the world's great cities, provides students with opportunities to do research at the Field Museum, intern with a senator, or showcase their ethanol-powered vehicles at the auto show. For further information, students should visit http://www.uic.edu.

Getting in Last Year
9,512 applied
64% were accepted
2,692 enrolled (45%)
24% from top tenth of their h.s. class
44% had ACT scores over 24
6% had ACT scores over 30

Graduation and After
9% graduated in 4 years
19% graduated in 5 years
8% graduated in 6 years
Graduates pursuing further study: 10% arts and sciences, 5% business, 3% law
92% had job offers within 6 months
917 organizations recruited on campus

Financial Matters
$4944 resident tuition and fees (2001–02)
$11,604 nonresident tuition and fees (2001–02)
$6058 room and board
86% average percent of need met
$11,800 average financial aid amount received per undergraduate (2000–01)

UNIVERSITY OF ILLINOIS AT URBANA–CHAMPAIGN

SMALL-TOWN SETTING ■ PUBLIC ■ STATE-SUPPORTED ■ COED
CHAMPAIGN, ILLINOIS

Web site: www.uiuc.edu
Contact: Mr. Abel Mandujano, Assistant Director of Admissions, 901 West Illinois, Urbana, IL 61801
Telephone: 217-333-0302
E-mail: admissions@oar.uiuc.edu

The University of Illinois at Urbana-Champaign is the state's premier public university, attracting top-notch students from across Illinois, the nation, and the world. Founded in 1867 as a land-grant institution, the University has grown to offer more than 4,000 courses in 150 undergraduate programs. The opportunities are endless for the 28,000 undergraduate students. From student organizations to study-abroad programs and research projects, few Illinois students can claim boredom as a problem. As one undergraduate describes her college selection process, "I wanted the education and diversity that a Big Ten university had to offer. I never expected the experience and education that I got here. It has been remarkable."

Getting in Last Year
19,930 applied
62% were accepted
6,247 enrolled (51%)
57% had SAT verbal scores over 600
78% had SAT math scores over 600
84% had ACT scores over 24
12% had SAT verbal scores over 700
32% had SAT math scores over 700
29% had ACT scores over 30

Graduation and After
52% graduated in 4 years
22% graduated in 5 years
3% graduated in 6 years
56% pursued further study (10% law, 9% medicine, 5% business)
87.1% had job offers within 6 months
1842 organizations recruited on campus

Financial Matters
$5794 resident tuition and fees (2001–02)
$13,614 nonresident tuition and fees (2001–02)
$6090 room and board
89% average percent of need met
$8419 average financial aid amount received per undergraduate (2000–01)

Academics

Illinois awards bachelor's, master's, doctoral, and first-professional **degrees**. Challenging opportunities include advanced placement credit, accelerated degree programs, student-designed majors, an honors program, double majors, and a senior project. Special programs include cooperative education, internships, summer session for credit, off-campus study, study-abroad, and Army and Air Force ROTC.

The most frequently chosen **baccalaureate** fields are business/marketing, engineering/engineering technologies, and social sciences and history. A complete listing of majors at Illinois appears in the Majors Index beginning on page 430.

The **faculty** at Illinois has 2,240 full-time members, 89% with terminal degrees. The student-faculty ratio is 15:1.

Students of Illinois

The student body totals 38,759, of whom 28,746 are undergraduates. 47.5% are women and 52.5% are men. Students come from 50 states and territories and 121 other countries. 93% are from Illinois. 2.3% are international students. 7% are African American, 0.2% American Indian, 13.3% Asian American, and 5.9% Hispanic American. 93% returned for their sophomore year.

Facilities and Resources

Student rooms are linked to a campus network. 3,000 **computers** are available on campus that provide access to the Internet. The 41 **libraries** have 9,469,620 books and 90,962 subscriptions.

Campus Life

There are 850 active organizations on campus, including a drama/theater group, newspaper, radio station, television station, choral group, and marching band. 22% of eligible men and 22% of eligible women are members of national **fraternities**, national **sororities**, local fraternities, and local sororities.

Illinois is a member of the NCAA (Division I). **Intercollegiate sports** (some offering scholarships) include baseball (m), basketball, cross-country running, football (m), golf, gymnastics, soccer (w), swimming (w), tennis, track and field, volleyball (w), wrestling (m).

Campus Safety

Student safety services include safety training classes, ID cards with safety numbers, late-night transport/escort service, 24-hour emergency telephone alarm devices, 24-hour patrols by trained security personnel, student patrols, and electronically operated dormitory entrances.

Applying

Illinois requires an essay, SAT I or ACT, and a high school transcript, and in some cases audition, statement of professional interest. Application deadline: 1/1; 3/15 priority date for financial aid. Deferred admission is possible.

The University of Iowa

Small-town setting ■ Public ■ State-supported ■ Coed
Iowa City, Iowa

Web site: www.uiowa.edu
Contact: Mr. Michael Barron, Director of Admissions, 107 Calvin Hall, Iowa City, IA 52242
Telephone: 319-335-3847 or toll-free 800-553-4692 **Fax:** 319-335-1535
E-mail: admissions@uiowa.edu

Academics

Iowa awards bachelor's, master's, doctoral, and first-professional **degrees**. Challenging opportunities include advanced placement credit, accelerated degree programs, student-designed majors, an honors program, double majors, independent study, and a senior project. Special programs include cooperative education, internships, summer session for credit, off-campus study, study-abroad, and Army and Air Force ROTC.

The most frequently chosen **baccalaureate** fields are business/marketing, social sciences and history, and communications/communication technologies. A complete listing of majors at Iowa appears in the Majors Index beginning on page 430.

The **faculty** at Iowa has 1,630 full-time members. The student-faculty ratio is 14:1.

Students of Iowa

The student body totals 28,768, of whom 19,603 are undergraduates. 54.6% are women and 45.4% are men. Students come from 52 states and territories and 70 other countries. 69% are from Iowa. 1.8% are international students. 2.3% are African American, 0.4% American Indian, 3.3% Asian American, and 2.3% Hispanic American. 82% returned for their sophomore year.

Facilities and Resources

Student rooms are linked to a campus network. 1,200 **computers** are available on campus that provide access to online degree process, grades, financial aid summary and the Internet. The 13 **libraries** have 4,027,546 books and 44,644 subscriptions.

Campus Life

There are 363 active organizations on campus, including a drama/theater group, newspaper, radio station, choral group, and marching band. 11% of eligible men and 12% of eligible women are members of national **fraternities** and national **sororities**.

Iowa is a member of the NCAA (Division I). **Intercollegiate sports** (some offering scholarships) include baseball (m), basketball, crew (w), cross-country running, field hockey (w), football (m), golf, gymnastics, soccer (w), softball (w), swimming, tennis, track and field, volleyball (w), wrestling (m).

Campus Safety

Student safety services include late-night transport/escort service, 24-hour emergency telephone alarm devices, 24-hour patrols by trained security personnel, and electronically operated dormitory entrances.

Applying

Iowa requires SAT I or ACT and a high school transcript. Application deadline: 5/15. Early and deferred admission are possible.

Traditionally a liberal arts university, Iowa is also strong in business, engineering, health sciences, and the fine arts. Outstanding facilities include the University of Iowa Hospitals and Clinics, one of the largest university-owned teaching hospitals in the United States, and Hancher Auditorium, which regularly attracts nationally famous cultural events. Iowa is home to the world-renowned Writers' Workshop, International Writing Program, and Playwrights' Workshop. Iowa offers more than 100 undergraduate areas of study, primarily through the Colleges of Liberal Arts and Sciences, Business, Education, Engineering, Nursing, and Pharmacy. A University-wide Honors Program is dedicated to advancing Iowa's best students.

Getting in Last Year
11,836 applied
85% were accepted
21% from top tenth of their h.s. class
3.49 average high school GPA
49% had SAT verbal scores over 600
54% had SAT math scores over 600
58% had ACT scores over 24
13% had SAT verbal scores over 700
15% had SAT math scores over 700
10% had ACT scores over 30
34 National Merit Scholars
183 valedictorians

Graduation and After
34% graduated in 4 years
25% graduated in 5 years
4% graduated in 6 years
320 organizations recruited on campus

Financial Matters
$3522 resident tuition and fees (2001–02)
$11,950 nonresident tuition and fees (2001–02)
$4870 room and board
99% average percent of need met
$6020 average financial aid amount received per undergraduate (2000–01)

University of Maryland, Baltimore County

Suburban setting ■ Public ■ State-supported ■ Coed
Baltimore, Maryland

Web site: www.umbc.edu
Contact: Ms. Yvette Mozie-Ross, Director of Admissions, 1000 Hilltop Circle, Baltimore, MD 21250-5398
Telephone: 410-455-3799 or toll-free 800-UMBC-4U2 (in-state), 800-862-2402 (out-of-state) **Fax:** 410-455-1094
E-mail: admissions@umbc.edu

Getting in Last Year

5,282 applied
66% were accepted
1,309 enrolled (38%)
31% from top tenth of their h.s. class
3.44 average high school GPA
46% had SAT verbal scores over 600
58% had SAT math scores over 600
50% had ACT scores over 24
9% had SAT verbal scores over 700
14% had SAT math scores over 700
10% had ACT scores over 30
3 National Merit Scholars

Graduation and After

35% pursued further study (25% arts and sciences, 2% business, 2% law)
87% had job offers within 6 months
843 organizations recruited on campus

Financial Matters

$5910 resident tuition and fees (2001–02)
$11,290 nonresident tuition and fees (2001–02)
$6280 room and board
62% average percent of need met
$6214 average financial aid amount received per undergraduate (2000–01)

Academics

UMBC awards bachelor's, master's, and doctoral **degrees** and post-bachelor's certificates. Challenging opportunities include advanced placement credit, student-designed majors, freshman honors college, an honors program, double majors, independent study, and a senior project. Special programs include cooperative education, internships, summer session for credit, off-campus study, study-abroad, and Army and Air Force ROTC.

The most frequently chosen **baccalaureate** fields are computer/information sciences, social sciences and history, and visual/performing arts. A complete listing of majors at UMBC appears in the Majors Index beginning on page 430.

The **faculty** at UMBC has 446 full-time members, 86% with terminal degrees. The student-faculty ratio is 17:1.

Students of UMBC

The student body totals 11,237, of whom 9,328 are undergraduates. 49.7% are women and 50.3% are men. Students come from 39 states and territories and 91 other countries. 92% are from Maryland. 4.6% are international students. 16.2% are African American, 0.5% American Indian, 18.1% Asian American, and 2.6% Hispanic American. 82% returned for their sophomore year.

Facilities and Resources

Student rooms are linked to a campus network. 500 **computers** are available on campus that provide access to student account and grade information and the Internet. The 2 **libraries** have 4,508 subscriptions.

Campus Life

There are 170 active organizations on campus, including a drama/theater group, newspaper, radio station, television station, choral group, and marching band. 3% of eligible men and 3% of eligible women are members of national **fraternities** and national **sororities**.

UMBC is a member of the NCAA (Division I). **Intercollegiate sports** (some offering scholarships) include baseball (m), basketball, cross-country running, golf, lacrosse, soccer, softball (w), swimming, tennis, track and field, volleyball (w).

Campus Safety

Student safety services include late-night transport/escort service, 24-hour emergency telephone alarm devices, and 24-hour patrols by trained security personnel.

Applying

UMBC requires an essay, SAT I or ACT, a high school transcript, and a minimum high school GPA of 2.0. It recommends SAT I. Application deadline: 3/15; 3/1 priority date for financial aid. Early and deferred admission are possible.

University of Maryland, College Park

Suburban setting ■ Public ■ State-supported ■ Coed
College Park, Maryland

Web site: www.maryland.edu
Contact: Barbara Gill, Director of Undergraduate Admissions, Mitchell Building, College Park, MD 20742-5235
Telephone: 301-314-8385 or toll-free 800-422-5867 **Fax:** 301-314-9693
E-mail: um-admit@uga.umd.edu

Academics

University of Maryland, College Park awards bachelor's, master's, doctoral, and first-professional **degrees** and post-bachelor's and post-master's certificates. Challenging opportunities include advanced placement credit, accelerated degree programs, student-designed majors, an honors program, double majors, independent study, and a senior project. Special programs include cooperative education, internships, summer session for credit, off-campus study, study-abroad, and Army, Navy and Air Force ROTC.

The most frequently chosen **baccalaureate** fields are business/marketing, social sciences and history, and biological/life sciences. A complete listing of majors at University of Maryland, College Park appears in the Majors Index beginning on page 430.

The **faculty** at University of Maryland, College Park has 1,537 full-time members, 88% with terminal degrees. The student-faculty ratio is 13:1.

Students of University of Maryland, College Park

The student body totals 34,160, of whom 25,099 are undergraduates. 48.6% are women and 51.4% are men. Students come from 53 states and territories and 154 other countries. 75% are from Maryland. 2.7% are international students. 13.1% are African American, 0.2% American Indian, 13.8% Asian American, and 5.1% Hispanic American. 91% returned for their sophomore year.

Facilities and Resources

Student rooms are linked to a campus network. 899 **computers** are available on campus that provide access to student account information, financial aid summary and the Internet. The 7 **libraries** have 2,850,285 books and 32,290 subscriptions.

Campus Life

There are 364 active organizations on campus, including a drama/theater group, newspaper, radio station, television station, choral group, and marching band. 9% of eligible men and 9% of eligible women are members of national **fraternities** and national **sororities**.

University of Maryland, College Park is a member of the NCAA (Division I). **Intercollegiate sports** (some offering scholarships) include baseball (m), basketball, cross-country running, field hockey (w), football (m), golf, gymnastics (w), lacrosse, soccer, softball (w), swimming, tennis, track and field, volleyball (w), wrestling (m).

Campus Safety

Student safety services include campus police, video camera surveillance, late-night transport/escort service, 24-hour emergency telephone alarm devices, 24-hour patrols by trained security personnel, student patrols, and electronically operated dormitory entrances.

Applying

University of Maryland, College Park requires an essay, SAT I or ACT, a high school transcript, and 1 recommendation, and in some cases an interview. It recommends 2 recommendations and resume of activities, auditions. Application deadline: 2/15; 2/15 priority date for financial aid. Early admission is possible.

> **T**he University of Maryland is among the nation's most distinguished public research universities, attracting top students and renowned faculty members from around the world. Maryland takes the lead in teaching undergraduates, providing more than 100 innovative and challenging academic programs, many nationally recognized for their exceptional quality. Opportunities for research, internships, leadership, recreation, and creativity abound with its suburban location near Washington, DC. Close-knit residence communities, distinctive programs for academically talented students, and a proud multicultural community make for an outstanding education.

Getting in Last Year
19,647 applied
55% were accepted
4,374 enrolled (40%)
83% from top tenth of their h.s. class
3.76 average high school GPA
59% had SAT verbal scores over 600
74% had SAT math scores over 600
14% had SAT verbal scores over 700
22% had SAT math scores over 700
41 National Merit Scholars

Graduation and After
33% graduated in 4 years
25% graduated in 5 years
5% graduated in 6 years
42% pursued further study (9% law, 4% medicine, 2% business)
95% had job offers within 6 months
68 organizations recruited on campus

Financial Matters
$5341 resident tuition and fees (2001–02)
$13,413 nonresident tuition and fees (2001–02)
$6618 room and board
67% average percent of need met
$7740 average financial aid amount received per undergraduate (2000–01)

University of Massachusetts Amherst

SMALL-TOWN SETTING ■ PUBLIC ■ STATE-SUPPORTED ■ COED
AMHERST, MASSACHUSETTS

Web site: www.umass.edu
Contact: Mr. Joseph Marshall, Assistant Dean for Enrollment Services, 37
Mather Drive, Amherst, MA 01003-9291
Telephone: 413-545-0222 **Fax:** 413-545-4312
E-mail: mail@admissions.umass.edu

Getting in Last Year
18,625 applied
73% were accepted
4,199 enrolled (31%)
19% from top tenth of their h.s. class
3.35 average high school GPA
31% had SAT verbal scores over 600
36% had SAT math scores over 600
5% had SAT verbal scores over 700
7% had SAT math scores over 700
52 valedictorians

Graduation and After
13% pursued further study
48% had job offers within 6 months
570 organizations recruited on campus

Financial Matters
$5880 resident tuition and fees (2001–02)
$14,103 nonresident tuition and fees (2001–02)
$5115 room and board
90% average percent of need met
$8167 average financial aid amount received per undergraduate (2000–01)

Academics

UMass Amherst awards associate, bachelor's, master's, and doctoral **degrees** and post-master's certificates. Challenging opportunities include advanced placement credit, student-designed majors, freshman honors college, an honors program, double majors, independent study, and a senior project. Special programs include cooperative education, internships, summer session for credit, off-campus study, study-abroad, and Army and Air Force ROTC.

The most frequently chosen **baccalaureate** fields are business/marketing, social sciences and history, and communications/communication technologies. A complete listing of majors at UMass Amherst appears in the Majors Index beginning on page 430.

The **faculty** at UMass Amherst has 1,151 full-time members, 94% with terminal degrees. The student-faculty ratio is 18:1.

Students of UMass Amherst

The student body totals 24,678, of whom 19,368 are undergraduates. 51.4% are women and 48.6% are men. Students come from 50 states and territories and 70 other countries. 76% are from Massachusetts. 1.9% are international students. 4.5% are African American, 0.4% American Indian, 6.5% Asian American, and 3.5% Hispanic American. 84% returned for their sophomore year.

Facilities and Resources

Student rooms are linked to a campus network. The 4 **libraries** have 2,991,397 books and 15,362 subscriptions.

Campus Life

There are 200 active organizations on campus, including a drama/theater group, newspaper, radio station, television station, choral group, and marching band. 6% of eligible men and 5% of eligible women are members of national **fraternities**, national **sororities**, local fraternities, and local sororities.

UMass Amherst is a member of the NCAA (Division I). **Intercollegiate sports** (some offering scholarships) include baseball (m), basketball, crew (w), cross-country running, field hockey (w), football (m), gymnastics, ice hockey (m), lacrosse, skiing (downhill), soccer, softball (w), swimming, tennis, track and field, volleyball (w), water polo.

Campus Safety

Student safety services include residence halls locked nights and weekends, late-night transport/escort service, 24-hour emergency telephone alarm devices, 24-hour patrols by trained security personnel, student patrols, and electronically operated dormitory entrances.

Applying

UMass Amherst requires an essay, SAT I or ACT, and a high school transcript. It recommends recommendations and a minimum high school GPA of 3.0. Application deadline: 2/1; 3/1 priority date for financial aid. Early and deferred admission are possible.

UNIVERSITY OF MIAMI

SUBURBAN SETTING ■ PRIVATE ■ INDEPENDENT ■ COED
CORAL GABLES, FLORIDA

Web site: www.miami.edu

Contact: Mr. Edward M. Gillis, Associate Dean of Enrollment and Director of Admission, PO Box 248025, Ashe Building Room 132, 1252 Memorial Drive, Coral Gables, FL 33146-4616

Telephone: 305-284-4323 **Fax:** 305-284-2507

E-mail: admission@miami.edu

Academics

UM awards bachelor's, master's, doctoral, and first-professional **degrees** and post-bachelor's and post-master's certificates. Challenging opportunities include advanced placement credit, accelerated degree programs, student-designed majors, an honors program, double majors, independent study, and a senior project. Special programs include internships, summer session for credit, study-abroad, and Army and Air Force ROTC.

The most frequently chosen **baccalaureate** fields are business/marketing, visual/performing arts, and engineering/engineering technologies. A complete listing of majors at UM appears in the Majors Index beginning on page 430.

The **faculty** at UM has 810 full-time members, 84% with terminal degrees. The student-faculty ratio is 13:1.

Students of UM

The student body totals 14,436, of whom 9,359 are undergraduates. 56.5% are women and 43.5% are men. Students come from 52 states and territories and 99 other countries. 56% are from Florida. 7.8% are international students. 10% are African American, 0.3% American Indian, 5.1% Asian American, and 25.1% Hispanic American. 82% returned for their sophomore year.

Facilities and Resources

Student rooms are linked to a campus network. 2,000 **computers** are available on campus that provide access to online student account and grade information and the Internet. The 7 **libraries** have 1,324,952 books and 17,155 subscriptions.

Campus Life

There are 175 active organizations on campus, including a drama/theater group, newspaper, radio station, television station, choral group, and marching band. 13% of eligible men and 12% of eligible women are members of national **fraternities** and national **sororities**.

UM is a member of the NCAA (Division I). **Intercollegiate sports** (some offering scholarships) include baseball (m), basketball, crew (w), cross-country running, football (m), golf (w), soccer (w), swimming (w), tennis, track and field, volleyball (w).

Campus Safety

Student safety services include crime prevention and safety workshops, residential college crime watch, late-night transport/escort service, 24-hour emergency telephone alarm devices, 24-hour patrols by trained security personnel, student patrols, and electronically operated dormitory entrances.

Applying

UM requires an essay, SAT I or ACT, a high school transcript, and 1 recommendation, and in some cases SAT II Subject Tests and an interview. It recommends a minimum high school GPA of 3.0. Application deadline: 2/15; 2/15 priority date for financial aid. Early and deferred admission are possible.

Getting in Last Year

14,724 applied
46% were accepted
2,164 enrolled (32%)
51% from top tenth of their h.s. class
3.97 average high school GPA
48% had SAT verbal scores over 600
53% had SAT math scores over 600
71% had ACT scores over 24
9% had SAT verbal scores over 700
11% had SAT math scores over 700
13% had ACT scores over 30

Graduation and After

47% graduated in 4 years
12% graduated in 5 years
3% graduated in 6 years
41% pursued further study (8% business, 7% law, 6% medicine)
93% had job offers within 6 months
201 organizations recruited on campus

Financial Matters

$23,647 tuition and fees (2001–02)
$7948 room and board
88% average percent of need met
$21,805 average financial aid amount received per undergraduate

UNIVERSITY OF MICHIGAN

SUBURBAN SETTING ■ PUBLIC ■ STATE-SUPPORTED ■ COED
ANN ARBOR, MICHIGAN

Web site: www.umich.edu
Contact: Mr. Ted Spencer, Director of Undergraduate Admissions, Ann Arbor, MI 48109
Telephone: 734-764-7433 **Fax:** 734-936-0740
E-mail: ugadmiss@umich.edu

The University of Michigan, Ann Arbor, is one of the nation's top-ranked public universities and is consistently rated among the top 25 academic institutions in the country. Nearly every one of the University's 19 academic schools and colleges is rated among the top in its field. Students and faculty members come from 134 different countries and all 50 states. The academic and personal growth achieved by students is unique and diverse, and Michigan graduates are prepared to face the challenges the 21st century has to offer. A friendly and beautiful campus, extensive resources, dedicated faculty members, and exceptional students—this is the Wolverine Spirit, the Michigan tradition.

Academics

Michigan awards bachelor's, master's, doctoral, and first-professional **degrees** and post-master's certificates. Challenging opportunities include advanced placement credit, accelerated degree programs, student-designed majors, an honors program, double majors, independent study, and a senior project. Special programs include cooperative education, internships, summer session for credit, off-campus study, study-abroad, and Army, Navy and Air Force ROTC.

The most frequently chosen **baccalaureate** fields are engineering/engineering technologies, social sciences and history, and psychology. A complete listing of majors at Michigan appears in the Majors Index beginning on page 430.

The **faculty** at Michigan has 2,127 full-time members, 92% with terminal degrees. The student-faculty ratio is 16:1.

Students of Michigan

The student body totals 38,248, of whom 24,547 are undergraduates. 50.5% are women and 49.5% are men. Students come from 54 states and territories and 87 other countries. 68% are from Michigan. 4.2% are international students. 7.8% are African American, 0.7% American Indian, 12.4% Asian American, and 4.2% Hispanic American. 95% returned for their sophomore year.

Facilities and Resources

Student rooms are linked to a campus network. The 21 **libraries** have 7,195,095 books and 68,798 subscriptions.

Campus Life

There are 900 active organizations on campus, including a drama/theater group, newspaper, radio station, television station, choral group, and marching band. 17% of eligible men and 17% of eligible women are members of national **fraternities**, national **sororities**, local fraternities, and local sororities.

Michigan is a member of the NCAA (Division I). **Intercollegiate sports** (some offering scholarships) include baseball (m), basketball (m), crew (w), cross-country running, field hockey (w), football (m), golf, gymnastics, ice hockey (m), soccer (w), softball (w), swimming, tennis, track and field, volleyball (w), water polo (w), wrestling (m).

Campus Safety

Student safety services include bicycle patrols, late-night transport/escort service, 24-hour emergency telephone alarm devices, 24-hour patrols by trained security personnel, student patrols, and electronically operated dormitory entrances.

Applying

Michigan requires an essay, SAT I or ACT, and a high school transcript, and in some cases SAT II Subject Tests, SAT II: Writing Test, an interview, and recommendations. Application deadline: 2/1; 2/15 priority date for financial aid. Deferred admission is possible.

Getting in Last Year
24,141 applied
52% were accepted
5,540 enrolled (44%)
69% from top tenth of their h.s. class
3.80 average high school GPA
64% had SAT verbal scores over 600
81% had SAT math scores over 600
88% had ACT scores over 24
17% had SAT verbal scores over 700
33% had SAT math scores over 700
31% had ACT scores over 30
76 National Merit Scholars

Graduation and After
61% graduated in 4 years
19% graduated in 5 years
2% graduated in 6 years
34% pursued further study (11% arts and sciences, 5% law, 5% medicine)
76% had job offers within 6 months
1481 organizations recruited on campus

Financial Matters
$6935 resident tuition and fees (2001–02)
$21,645 nonresident tuition and fees (2001–02)
$6068 room and board
90% average percent of need met
$10,969 average financial aid amount received per undergraduate

UNIVERSITY OF MINNESOTA, MORRIS

SMALL-TOWN SETTING ■ PUBLIC ■ STATE-SUPPORTED ■ COED
MORRIS, MINNESOTA

Web site: www.mrs.umn.edu
Contact: Mr. Scott K. Hagg, Acting Director of Admissions, 600 East 4th
   Street, Morris, MN 56267-2199
Telephone: 320-539-6035 or toll-free 800-992-8863 **Fax:** 320-589-1673
E-mail: admissions@mrs.umn.edu

Academics

UMM awards bachelor's **degrees**. Challenging opportunities include advanced placement credit, accelerated degree programs, student-designed majors, freshman honors
college, an honors program, double majors, and a senior project. Special programs
include internships, summer session for credit, off-campus study, and study-abroad.

The most frequently chosen **baccalaureate** fields are social sciences and history,
English, and biological/life sciences. A complete listing of majors at UMM appears in the
Majors Index beginning on page 430.

The **faculty** at UMM has 120 full-time members, 138% with terminal degrees. The
student-faculty ratio is 14:1.

Students of UMM

The student body is made up of 1,924 undergraduates. 59.3% are women and 40.7% are
men. Students come from 32 states and territories and 15 other countries. 79% are from
Minnesota. 5.1% are African American, 6.7% American Indian, 3.1% Asian American,
and 1.5% Hispanic American. 84% returned for their sophomore year.

Facilities and Resources

Student rooms are linked to a campus network. 190 **computers** are available on campus
for student use. The 2 **libraries** have 1,100 subscriptions.

Campus Life

There are 84 active organizations on campus, including a drama/theater group,
newspaper, radio station, and choral group. 1% of eligible men are members of local
fraternities.

UMM is a member of the NCAA (Division II). **Intercollegiate sports** include
baseball (m), basketball, cross-country running (w), football (m), golf, soccer (w), softball
(w), tennis, track and field, volleyball (w), wrestling.

Campus Safety

Student safety services include late-night transport/escort service, 24-hour emergency
telephone alarm devices, 24-hour patrols by trained security personnel, and electronically operated dormitory entrances.

Applying

UMM requires an essay, SAT I or ACT, and a high school transcript, and in some cases
an interview. It recommends a minimum high school GPA of 3.0. Application deadline:
3/15; 4/1 priority date for financial aid. Early and deferred admission are possible.

Getting in Last Year
1,268 applied
84% were accepted
480 enrolled (45%)
43% from top tenth of their h.s. class
44% had SAT verbal scores over 600
34% had SAT math scores over 600
63% had ACT scores over 24
12% had SAT verbal scores over 700
8% had SAT math scores over 700
15% had ACT scores over 30
4 National Merit Scholars
15 class presidents
45 valedictorians

Graduation and After
50% graduated in 4 years
17% graduated in 5 years
9% graduated in 6 years
30% pursued further study (16% arts and
   sciences, 3% business, 3% law)
90% had job offers within 6 months
84 organizations recruited on campus

Financial Matters
$6246 resident tuition and fees (2001–02)
$10,763 nonresident tuition and fees (2001–
   02)
$4470 room and board
$7763 average financial aid amount received
   per undergraduate

UNIVERSITY OF MINNESOTA, TWIN CITIES CAMPUS

URBAN SETTING ■ PUBLIC ■ STATE-SUPPORTED ■ COED
MINNEAPOLIS, MINNESOTA

Web site: www.umn.edu/tc
Contact: Ms. Patricia Jones Whyte, Associate Director of Admissions, 240 Williamson Hall, Minneapolis, MN 55455-0115
Telephone: 612-625-2008 or toll-free 800-752-1000 **Fax:** 612-626-1693
E-mail: admissions@tc.umn.edu

O n this beautiful Big Ten campus in the heart of the Twin Cities of Minneapolis and St. Paul, the hallmarks are quality and opportunity. The quality of a U of M–Twin Cities education is a matter of record. So are the opportunities—more than 150 undergraduate majors, many nationally ranked; an Undergraduate Research Opportunities Program that is a national model; one of the largest study-abroad programs in the country; more than 400 student organizations; the fourteenth-largest university library system in the country; and extraordinary opportunities for internships, employment, and personal enrichment in the culturally rich and thriving Twin Cities area.

Getting in Last Year
15,436 applied
76% were accepted
5,344 enrolled (46%)
29% from top tenth of their h.s. class
50% had SAT verbal scores over 600
61% had SAT math scores over 600
61% had ACT scores over 24
12% had SAT verbal scores over 700
20% had SAT math scores over 700
11% had ACT scores over 30
223 valedictorians

Financial Matters
$5536 resident tuition and fees (2001–02)
$15,002 nonresident tuition and fees (2001–02)
$5582 room and board
79% average percent of need met
$7893 average financial aid amount received per undergraduate (2000–01)

Academics
U of M-Twin Cities Campus awards bachelor's, master's, doctoral, and first-professional **degrees** and post-bachelor's and post-master's certificates. Challenging opportunities include advanced placement credit, accelerated degree programs, student-designed majors, freshman honors college, an honors program, double majors, independent study, and a senior project. Special programs include cooperative education, internships, summer session for credit, off-campus study, study-abroad, and Army, Navy and Air Force ROTC.

The most frequently chosen **baccalaureate** fields are social sciences and history, engineering/engineering technologies, and business/marketing. A complete listing of majors at U of M-Twin Cities Campus appears in the Majors Index beginning on page 430.

The **faculty** at U of M-Twin Cities Campus has 2,711 full-time members, 96% with terminal degrees.

Students of U of M-Twin Cities Campus
The student body totals 46,597, of whom 32,136 are undergraduates. 52.6% are women and 47.4% are men. Students come from 55 states and territories and 85 other countries. 74% are from Minnesota. 2.3% are international students. 4% are African American, 0.7% American Indian, 8.3% Asian American, and 1.9% Hispanic American. 82% returned for their sophomore year.

Facilities and Resources
Student rooms are linked to a campus network. The 18 **libraries** have 5,613,171 books and 46,989 subscriptions.

Campus Life
There are 350 active organizations on campus, including a drama/theater group, newspaper, radio station, television station, choral group, and marching band. 3% of eligible men and 3% of eligible women are members of national **fraternities**, national **sororities**, and local sororities.

U of M-Twin Cities Campus is a member of the NCAA (Division I). **Intercollegiate sports** (some offering scholarships) include baseball (m), basketball, cross-country running, football (m), golf, gymnastics, ice hockey, soccer (w), softball (w), swimming, tennis, track and field, volleyball (w), wrestling (m).

Campus Safety
Student safety services include safety/security orientation, security lighting, late-night transport/escort service, 24-hour emergency telephone alarm devices, 24-hour patrols by trained security personnel, student patrols, and electronically operated dormitory entrances.

Applying
U of M-Twin Cities Campus requires SAT I or ACT and a high school transcript. It recommends a minimum high school GPA of 2.0. Application deadline: rolling admissions; 1/15 priority date for financial aid. Early and deferred admission are possible.

University of Missouri–Columbia

Small-town setting ■ Public ■ State-supported ■ Coed
Columbia, Missouri

Web site: www.missouri.edu
Contact: Ms. Georgeanne Porter, Director of Admissions, 225 Jesse Hall, Columbia, MO 65211
Telephone: 573-882-7786 or toll-free 800-225-6075 (in-state) **Fax:** 573-882-7887
E-mail: mu4u@missouri.edu

Academics

MU awards bachelor's, master's, doctoral, and first-professional **degrees** and post-master's certificates. Challenging opportunities include advanced placement credit, accelerated degree programs, student-designed majors, freshman honors college, an honors program, double majors, independent study, and a senior project. Special programs include cooperative education, internships, summer session for credit, off-campus study, study-abroad, and Army, Navy and Air Force ROTC.

The most frequently chosen **baccalaureate** fields are business/marketing, communications/communication technologies, and engineering/engineering technologies. A complete listing of majors at MU appears in the Majors Index beginning on page 430.

The **faculty** at MU has 1,688 full-time members, 87% with terminal degrees. The student-faculty ratio is 18:1.

Students of MU

The student body totals 23,667, of whom 18,431 are undergraduates. 52.2% are women and 47.8% are men. Students come from 51 states and territories and 99 other countries. 88% are from Missouri. 1.4% are international students. 5.7% are African American, 0.5% American Indian, 2.6% Asian American, and 1.5% Hispanic American. 85% returned for their sophomore year.

Facilities and Resources

Student rooms are linked to a campus network. 1,150 **computers** are available on campus that provide access to telephone registration and the Internet. The 12 **libraries** have 4,723,296 books and 20,524 subscriptions.

Campus Life

There are 418 active organizations on campus, including a drama/theater group, newspaper, radio station, television station, choral group, and marching band. 23% of eligible men and 27% of eligible women are members of national **fraternities** and national **sororities**.

MU is a member of the NCAA (Division I). **Intercollegiate sports** (some offering scholarships) include baseball (m), basketball, cross-country running, football (m), golf, gymnastics (w), soccer (w), softball (w), swimming, tennis (w), track and field, volleyball (w), wrestling (m).

Campus Safety

Student safety services include late-night transport/escort service, 24-hour emergency telephone alarm devices, 24-hour patrols by trained security personnel, and electronically operated dormitory entrances.

Applying

MU requires ACT, a high school transcript, and specific high school curriculum. Application deadline: rolling admissions; 3/1 priority date for financial aid. Deferred admission is possible.

Getting in Last Year
9,678 applied
64% were accepted
4,166 enrolled (67%)
31% from top tenth of their h.s. class
70% had ACT scores over 24
18% had ACT scores over 30
33 National Merit Scholars
133 valedictorians

Graduation and After
32% graduated in 4 years
28% graduated in 5 years
5% graduated in 6 years
1400 organizations recruited on campus

Financial Matters
$3985 resident tuition and fees (2001–02)
$10,407 nonresident tuition and fees (2001–02)
$5043 room and board
86% average percent of need met
$6216 average financial aid amount received per undergraduate

University of Missouri–Kansas City
Urban setting ■ Public ■ State-supported ■ Coed
Kansas City, Missouri

Web site: www.umkc.edu
Contact: Mr. Melvin C. Tyler, Director of Admissions, 5100 Rockhill Road, Kansas City, MO 64110-2499
Telephone: 816-235-1111 **Fax:** 816-235-5544
E-mail: admit@umkc.edu

Getting in Last Year
2,523 applied
73% were accepted
773 enrolled (42%)
31% from top tenth of their h.s. class
58% had ACT scores over 24
16% had ACT scores over 30

Graduation and After
85% had job offers within 6 months
390 organizations recruited on campus

Financial Matters
$5050 resident tuition and fees (2001–02)
$13,495 nonresident tuition and fees (2001–02)
$4950 room and board
66% average percent of need met
$10,674 average financial aid amount received per undergraduate

Academics
UMKC awards bachelor's, master's, doctoral, and first-professional **degrees** and first-professional certificates. Challenging opportunities include advanced placement credit, accelerated degree programs, student-designed majors, an honors program, and a senior project. Special programs include cooperative education, internships, summer session for credit, off-campus study, study-abroad, and Army ROTC.

The most frequently chosen **baccalaureate** fields are liberal arts/general studies, business/marketing, and education. A complete listing of majors at UMKC appears in the Majors Index beginning on page 430.

The **faculty** at UMKC has 520 full-time members, 91% with terminal degrees. The student-faculty ratio is 8:1.

Students of UMKC
The student body totals 12,969, of whom 8,299 are undergraduates. 58.5% are women and 41.5% are men. Students come from 47 states and territories and 118 other countries. 88% are from Missouri. 5.2% are international students. 13.3% are African American, 0.9% American Indian, 6.2% Asian American, and 4.1% Hispanic American. 72% returned for their sophomore year.

Facilities and Resources
Student rooms are linked to a campus network. 400 **computers** are available on campus that provide access to the Internet. The 4 **libraries** have 1,617,725 books and 12,472 subscriptions.

Campus Life
There are 75 active organizations on campus, including a drama/theater group, newspaper, and choral group. 18% of eligible men and 18% of eligible women are members of national **fraternities**, national **sororities**, and local sororities.

UMKC is a member of the NCAA (Division I). **Intercollegiate sports** (some offering scholarships) include basketball, cross-country running, golf, riflery, soccer (m), softball (w), tennis, track and field, volleyball (w).

Campus Safety
Student safety services include late-night transport/escort service, 24-hour emergency telephone alarm devices, 24-hour patrols by trained security personnel, and electronically operated dormitory entrances.

Applying
UMKC requires ACT and a high school transcript. Application deadline: rolling admissions; 3/1 priority date for financial aid.

UNIVERSITY OF MISSOURI–ROLLA

SMALL-TOWN SETTING ■ PUBLIC ■ STATE-SUPPORTED ■ COED
ROLLA, MISSOURI

Web site: www.umr.edu
Contact: Mr. Jay W. Goff, Acting Director of Admission and Dean of
   Enrollment Management, 106 Parker Hall, Rolla, MO 65409
Telephone: 573-341-4164 or toll-free 800-522-0938 **Fax:** 573-341-4082
E-mail: umrolla@umr.edu

Academics

UMR awards bachelor's, master's, and doctoral **degrees**. Challenging opportunities
include advanced placement credit, accelerated degree programs, freshman honors college, an honors program, double majors, independent study, and a senior project. Special
programs include cooperative education, internships, summer session for credit, off-
campus study, study-abroad, and Army and Air Force ROTC.

The most frequently chosen **baccalaureate** fields are engineering/engineering
technologies, computer/information sciences, and physical sciences. A complete listing of
majors at UMR appears in the Majors Index beginning on page 430.

The **faculty** at UMR has 298 full-time members, 90% with terminal degrees. The
student-faculty ratio is 14:1.

Students of UMR

The student body totals 4,883, of whom 3,756 are undergraduates. 23.1% are women
and 76.9% are men. Students come from 47 states and territories and 38 other countries.
78% are from Missouri. 3.4% are international students. 4.8% are African American,
0.7% American Indian, 2.8% Asian American, and 1.4% Hispanic American. 83%
returned for their sophomore year.

Facilities and Resources

Student rooms are linked to a campus network. 800 **computers** are available on campus
that provide access to the Internet. The **library** has 255,768 books and 1,495 subscriptions.

Campus Life

There are 197 active organizations on campus, including a drama/theater group,
newspaper, radio station, choral group, and marching band. 27% of eligible men and
24% of eligible women are members of national **fraternities**, national **sororities**, and
local sororities.

UMR is a member of the NCAA (Division II). **Intercollegiate sports** (some offering
scholarships) include baseball (m), basketball, cross-country running, football (m), golf
(m), soccer, softball (w), swimming (m), tennis (m), track and field.

Campus Safety

Student safety services include crime prevention programs, late-night transport/escort
service, 24-hour emergency telephone alarm devices, 24-hour patrols by trained security
personnel, student patrols, and electronically operated dormitory entrances.

Applying

UMR requires SAT I or ACT and a high school transcript. Application deadline: 7/1;
3/1 priority date for financial aid. Early and deferred admission are possible.

Getting in Last Year
1,789 applied
96% were accepted
702 enrolled (41%)
39% from top tenth of their h.s. class
3.46 average high school GPA
80% had ACT scores over 24
30% had ACT scores over 30
44 National Merit Scholars
26 valedictorians

Graduation and After
10% graduated in 4 years
30% graduated in 5 years
12% graduated in 6 years
17% pursued further study
82% had job offers within 6 months
480 organizations recruited on campus

Financial Matters
$4974 resident tuition and fees (2001–02)
$13,419 nonresident tuition and fees (2001–02)
$5060 room and board
86% average percent of need met
$8330 average financial aid amount received per undergraduate (2000–01)

THE UNIVERSITY OF NORTH CAROLINA AT ASHEVILLE

SUBURBAN SETTING ■ PUBLIC ■ STATE-SUPPORTED ■ COED
ASHEVILLE, NORTH CAROLINA

Web site: www.unca.edu
Contact: Ms. Fran Barrett, Director of Admissions, 117 Lipinsky Hall, CPO 2210, One University Heights, Asheville, NC 28804-8510
Telephone: 828-251-6481 or toll-free 800-531-9842 **Fax:** 828-251-6482
E-mail: admissions@unca.edu

Getting in Last Year
2,020 applied
59% were accepted
455 enrolled (38%)
24% from top tenth of their h.s. class
3.77 average high school GPA
41% had SAT verbal scores over 600
39% had SAT math scores over 600
47% had ACT scores over 24
8% had SAT verbal scores over 700
5% had SAT math scores over 700
3% had ACT scores over 30
1 National Merit Scholar
7 valedictorians

Graduation and After
18% pursued further study
75% had job offers within 6 months
190 organizations recruited on campus

Financial Matters
$2496 resident tuition and fees (2001–02)
$9958 nonresident tuition and fees (2001–02)
$4400 room and board
85% average percent of need met
$6796 average financial aid amount received per undergraduate (2000–01)

Academics
UNC Asheville awards bachelor's and master's **degrees**. Challenging opportunities include advanced placement credit, student-designed majors, an honors program, double majors, independent study, and a senior project. Special programs include internships, summer session for credit, off-campus study, and study-abroad.

The most frequently chosen **baccalaureate** fields are psychology, business/marketing, and social sciences and history. A complete listing of majors at UNC Asheville appears in the Majors Index beginning on page 430.

The **faculty** at UNC Asheville has 174 full-time members, 84% with terminal degrees. The student-faculty ratio is 13:1.

Students of UNC Asheville
The student body totals 3,247, of whom 3,211 are undergraduates. 58.1% are women and 41.9% are men. Students come from 37 states and territories and 20 other countries. 89% are from North Carolina. 1.1% are international students. 2.6% are African American, 0.5% American Indian, 1.3% Asian American, and 1.4% Hispanic American. 80% returned for their sophomore year.

Facilities and Resources
Student rooms are linked to a campus network. 300 **computers** are available on campus that provide access to online grade reports and the Internet. The **library** has 252,601 books and 2,313 subscriptions.

Campus Life
There are 80 active organizations on campus, including a drama/theater group, newspaper, and choral group. 5% of eligible men and 3% of eligible women are members of national **fraternities** and national **sororities**.

UNC Asheville is a member of the NCAA (Division I). **Intercollegiate sports** (some offering scholarships) include baseball (m), basketball, cross-country running, soccer, tennis, track and field, volleyball (w).

Campus Safety
Student safety services include dorm entrances secured at night, late-night transport/escort service, and 24-hour patrols by trained security personnel.

Applying
UNC Asheville requires SAT I or ACT and a high school transcript, and in some cases an interview. It recommends an essay and a minimum high school GPA of 3.0. Application deadline: 3/15; 3/1 priority date for financial aid. Deferred admission is possible.

THE UNIVERSITY OF NORTH CAROLINA AT CHAPEL HILL

SUBURBAN SETTING ■ PUBLIC ■ STATE-SUPPORTED ■ COED
CHAPEL HILL, NORTH CAROLINA

Web site: www.unc.edu

Contact: Mr. Jerome A. Lucido, Vice Provost and Director of Undergraduate Admissions, Office of Undergraduate Admissions, Jackson Hall 153A, Campus Box 2200, Chapel Hill, NC 27599-2200

Telephone: 919-966-3621 **Fax:** 919-962-3045

E-mail: uadm@email.unc.edu

Academics

UNC Chapel Hill awards bachelor's, master's, doctoral, and first-professional **degrees** and post-master's certificates. Challenging opportunities include advanced placement credit, student-designed majors, freshman honors college, an honors program, double majors, and independent study. Special programs include internships, summer session for credit, off-campus study, study-abroad, and Army, Navy and Air Force ROTC.

The most frequently chosen **baccalaureate** fields are communications/communication technologies, social sciences and history, and business/marketing. A complete listing of majors at UNC Chapel Hill appears in the Majors Index beginning on page 430.

The **faculty** at UNC Chapel Hill has 2,375 full-time members.

Students of UNC Chapel Hill

The student body totals 25,494, of whom 15,844 are undergraduates. 60.3% are women and 39.7% are men. Students come from 52 states and territories and 100 other countries. 82% are from North Carolina. 1% are international students. 11.2% are African American, 0.8% American Indian, 5.4% Asian American, and 1.8% Hispanic American. 95% returned for their sophomore year.

Facilities and Resources

Student rooms are linked to a campus network. 540 **computers** are available on campus that provide access to on-line grade reports and the Internet. The 15 **libraries** have 4,928,026 books and 44,023 subscriptions.

Campus Life

There are 234 active organizations on campus, including a drama/theater group, newspaper, radio station, television station, choral group, and marching band. 19% of eligible men and 19% of eligible women are members of national **fraternities**, national **sororities**, local fraternities, and local sororities.

UNC Chapel Hill is a member of the NCAA (Division I). **Intercollegiate sports** (some offering scholarships) include baseball (m), basketball, crew (w), cross-country running, fencing, field hockey (w), football (m), golf, gymnastics (w), lacrosse, soccer, softball (w), swimming, tennis, track and field, volleyball (w), wrestling (m).

Campus Safety

Student safety services include crime prevention programs, late-night transport/escort service, 24-hour emergency telephone alarm devices, 24-hour patrols by trained security personnel, student patrols, and electronically operated dormitory entrances.

Applying

UNC Chapel Hill requires an essay, SAT I or ACT, a high school transcript, and recommendations. Application deadline: 1/15; 3/1 priority date for financial aid. Deferred admission is possible.

Getting in Last Year

15,947 applied
40% were accepted
3,687 enrolled (58%)
64% from top tenth of their h.s. class
65% had SAT verbal scores over 600
70% had SAT math scores over 600
78% had ACT scores over 24
18% had SAT verbal scores over 700
22% had SAT math scores over 700
26% had ACT scores over 30
137 National Merit Scholars
191 valedictorians

Graduation and After

65% graduated in 4 years
12% graduated in 5 years
1% graduated in 6 years
24% pursued further study
72.1% had job offers within 6 months
512 organizations recruited on campus

Financial Matters

$3277 resident tuition and fees (2001–02)
$13,269 nonresident tuition and fees (2001–02)
$5570 room and board
86% average percent of need met
$7129 average financial aid amount received per undergraduate (2000–01)

UNIVERSITY OF NOTRE DAME

SUBURBAN SETTING ■ PRIVATE ■ INDEPENDENT RELIGIOUS ■ COED
NOTRE DAME, INDIANA

Web site: www.nd.edu
Contact: Mr. Daniel J. Saracino, Assistant Provost for Enrollment, 220 Main
   Building, Notre Dame, IN 46556-5612
Telephone: 574-631-7505 **Fax:** 574-631-8865
E-mail: admissions.admissio.1@nd.edu

Getting in Last Year
9,385 applied
36% were accepted
2,036 enrolled (61%)
84% from top tenth of their h.s. class
84% had SAT verbal scores over 600
90% had SAT math scores over 600
98% had ACT scores over 24
37% had SAT verbal scores over 700
48% had SAT math scores over 700
79% had ACT scores over 30
45 National Merit Scholars
142 class presidents
291 valedictorians

Graduation and After
32% pursued further study (13% arts and
   sciences, 8% medicine, 7% law)
75% had job offers within 6 months
758 organizations recruited on campus

Financial Matters
$24,497 tuition and fees (2001–02)
$6210 room and board
100% average percent of need met
$22,031 average financial aid amount received
   per undergraduate

Academics
Notre Dame awards bachelor's, master's, doctoral, and first-professional **degrees**. Challenging opportunities include advanced placement credit, student-designed majors, an honors program, double majors, independent study, and a senior project. Special programs include cooperative education, internships, summer session for credit, off-campus study, study-abroad, and Army, Navy and Air Force ROTC.

The most frequently chosen **baccalaureate** fields are business/marketing, social sciences and history, and health professions and related sciences. A complete listing of majors at Notre Dame appears in the Majors Index beginning on page 430.

Students of Notre Dame
The student body totals 11,054, of whom 8,208 are undergraduates. 46.3% are women and 53.7% are men. Students come from 55 states and territories and 64 other countries. 12% are from Indiana. 2.6% are international students. 3.2% are African American, 0.5% American Indian, 4% Asian American, and 7.4% Hispanic American.

Facilities and Resources
Student rooms are linked to a campus network. 880 **computers** are available on campus that provide access to the Internet. The 9 **libraries** have 2,598,379 books and 19,100 subscriptions.

Campus Life
There are 269 active organizations on campus, including a drama/theater group, newspaper, radio station, choral group, and marching band. No national or local **fraternities** or **sororities**.

Notre Dame is a member of the NCAA (Division I). **Intercollegiate sports** (some offering scholarships) include baseball (m), basketball, crew (w), cross-country running, fencing, football (m), golf, ice hockey (m), lacrosse, soccer, softball (w), swimming, tennis, track and field, volleyball (w).

Campus Safety
Student safety services include late-night transport/escort service, 24-hour emergency telephone alarm devices, 24-hour patrols by trained security personnel, and electronically operated dormitory entrances.

Applying
Notre Dame requires an essay, SAT I or ACT, a high school transcript, and 1 recommendation. Application deadline: 1/9; 2/15 for financial aid. Deferred admission is possible.

University of Oklahoma

SUBURBAN SETTING ■ PUBLIC ■ STATE-SUPPORTED ■ COED
NORMAN, OKLAHOMA

Web site: www.ou.edu
Contact: Karen Renfroe, Executive Director of Recruitment Services, 1000 Asp Avenue, Norman, OK 73019
Telephone: 405-325-2151 or toll-free 800-234-6868 **Fax:** 405-325-7124
E-mail: admrec@ouwww.ou.edu

Academics

OU awards bachelor's, master's, doctoral, and first-professional **degrees** and post-master's certificates. Challenging opportunities include advanced placement credit, accelerated degree programs, student-designed majors, freshman honors college, an honors program, double majors, independent study, and a senior project. Special programs include cooperative education, internships, summer session for credit, off-campus study, study-abroad, and Army, Navy and Air Force ROTC.

The most frequently chosen **baccalaureate** fields are business/marketing, social sciences and history, and engineering/engineering technologies. A complete listing of majors at OU appears in the Majors Index beginning on page 430.

The **faculty** at OU has 938 full-time members, 87% with terminal degrees. The student-faculty ratio is 19:1.

Students of OU

The student body totals 22,646, of whom 18,660 are undergraduates. 48.8% are women and 51.2% are men. Students come from 48 states and territories and 87 other countries. 82% are from Oklahoma. 3.3% are international students. 6.7% are African American, 7.8% American Indian, 5.5% Asian American, and 3.8% Hispanic American. 83% returned for their sophomore year.

Facilities and Resources

Student rooms are linked to a campus network. 600 **computers** are available on campus that provide access to the Internet. The 8 **libraries** have 3,714,070 books and 15,833 subscriptions.

Campus Life

There are 235 active organizations on campus, including a drama/theater group, newspaper, radio station, television station, choral group, and marching band. 18% of eligible men and 24% of eligible women are members of national **fraternities**, national **sororities**, and international social clubs.

OU is a member of the NCAA (Division I). **Intercollegiate sports** (some offering scholarships) include baseball (m), basketball, cross-country running, football (m), golf, gymnastics, soccer (w), softball (w), tennis, track and field, volleyball (w), wrestling (m).

Campus Safety

Student safety services include crime prevention programs, police bicycle patrols, self-defense classes, late-night transport/escort service, 24-hour emergency telephone alarm devices, 24-hour patrols by trained security personnel, student patrols, and electronically operated dormitory entrances.

Applying

OU requires SAT I or ACT, a high school transcript, and a minimum high school GPA of 3.0, and in some cases an essay. Application deadline: 6/1; 6/1 for financial aid, with a 3/1 priority date.

Getting in Last Year
6,943 applied
93% were accepted
3,748 enrolled (58%)
32% from top tenth of their h.s. class
3.57 average high school GPA
66% had ACT scores over 24
14% had ACT scores over 30
110 National Merit Scholars
273 valedictorians

Graduation and After
19% graduated in 4 years
25% graduated in 5 years
7% graduated in 6 years
381 organizations recruited on campus

Financial Matters
$2713 resident tuition and fees (2001–02)
$7437 nonresident tuition and fees (2001–02)
$4903 room and board
89% average percent of need met
$5548 average financial aid amount received per undergraduate (1999–2000)

University of Pennsylvania

Urban setting ■ Private ■ Independent ■ Coed
Philadelphia, Pennsylvania

Web site: www.upenn.edu
Contact: Mr. Willis J. Stetson Jr., Dean of Admissions, 1 College Hall, Levy Park, Philadelphia, PA 19104
Telephone: 215-898-7507

Getting in Last Year

19,153 applied
22% were accepted
2,362 enrolled (57%)
92% from top tenth of their h.s. class
3.85 average high school GPA
90% had SAT verbal scores over 600
96% had SAT math scores over 600
98% had ACT scores over 24
47% had SAT verbal scores over 700
63% had SAT math scores over 700
62% had ACT scores over 30
68 National Merit Scholars
63 class presidents
235 valedictorians

Graduation and After

83% graduated in 4 years
7% graduated in 5 years
1% graduated in 6 years
20% pursued further study (7% law, 5% arts and sciences, 5% medicine)
77% had job offers within 6 months
575 organizations recruited on campus

Financial Matters

$26,630 tuition and fees (2001–02)
$7984 room and board
100% average percent of need met
$22,208 average financial aid amount received per undergraduate (1999–2000)

Academics

Penn awards associate, bachelor's, master's, doctoral, and first-professional **degrees** and post-master's certificates (also offers evening program with significant enrollment not reflected in profile). Challenging opportunities include advanced placement credit, accelerated degree programs, student-designed majors, an honors program, double majors, independent study, and a senior project. Special programs include internships, summer session for credit, off-campus study, study-abroad, and Army, Navy and Air Force ROTC.

The most frequently chosen **baccalaureate** fields are social sciences and history, business/marketing, and engineering/engineering technologies. A complete listing of majors at Penn appears in the Majors Index beginning on page 430.

The **faculty** at Penn has 1,286 full-time members, 100% with terminal degrees. The student-faculty ratio is 7:1.

Students of Penn

The student body totals 20,013, of whom 9,730 are undergraduates. 48.5% are women and 51.5% are men. Students come from 54 states and territories. 19% are from Pennsylvania. 8.3% are international students. 5.7% are African American, 0.2% American Indian, 19.6% Asian American, and 5.2% Hispanic American. 96% returned for their sophomore year.

Facilities and Resources

Student rooms are linked to a campus network. 1,000 **computers** are available on campus that provide access to the Internet. The 14 **libraries** have 4,914,244 books and 35,543 subscriptions.

Campus Life

There are 350 active organizations on campus, including a drama/theater group, newspaper, radio station, choral group, and marching band. Penn has national **fraternities**, national **sororities**, and local fraternities.

Penn is a member of the NCAA (Division I). **Intercollegiate sports** include baseball (m), basketball, crew, cross-country running, fencing, field hockey (w), football (m), golf (m), gymnastics (w), lacrosse, soccer, softball (w), squash, swimming, tennis, track and field, volleyball (w), wrestling (m).

Campus Safety

Student safety services include late-night transport/escort service, 24-hour emergency telephone alarm devices, 24-hour patrols by trained security personnel, and student patrols.

Applying

Penn requires an essay, SAT II: Writing Test, SAT I and SAT II or ACT, a high school transcript, and 2 recommendations. It recommends an interview. Application deadline: 1/1; 2/15 priority date for financial aid. Early and deferred admission are possible.

University of Pittsburgh

Urban setting ■ Public ■ State-related ■ Coed
Pittsburgh, Pennsylvania

Web site: www.pitt.edu
Contact: Dr. Betsy A. Porter, Director of Office of Admissions and Financial
   Aid, 4227 Fifth Avenue, First Floor, Masonic Temple, Pittsburgh, PA 15213
Telephone: 412-624-7488 **Fax:** 412-648-8815
E-mail: oafa+@pitt.edu

Academics

Pitt awards bachelor's, master's, doctoral, and first-professional **degrees** and post-bachelor's and post-master's certificates. Challenging opportunities include advanced placement credit, student-designed majors, freshman honors college, an honors program, double majors, independent study, and a senior project. Special programs include cooperative education, internships, summer session for credit, off-campus study, study-abroad, and Army, Navy and Air Force ROTC.

The most frequently chosen **baccalaureate** fields are social sciences and history, business/marketing, and English. A complete listing of majors at Pitt appears in the Majors Index beginning on page 430.

The **faculty** at Pitt has 1,285 full-time members, 88% with terminal degrees. The student-faculty ratio is 17:1.

Students of Pitt

The student body totals 26,710, of whom 17,798 are undergraduates. 52.8% are women and 47.2% are men. Students come from 53 states and territories and 54 other countries. 87% are from Pennsylvania. 0.9% are international students. 9.3% are African American, 0.2% American Indian, 4% Asian American, and 1.2% Hispanic American. 85% returned for their sophomore year.

Facilities and Resources

Student rooms are linked to a campus network. 600 **computers** are available on campus that provide access to on-line class listings and the Internet. The 27 **libraries** have 3,551,548 books and 22,058 subscriptions.

Campus Life

There are 500 active organizations on campus, including a drama/theater group, newspaper, radio station, television station, choral group, and marching band. Pitt has national **fraternities** and national **sororities**.

Pitt is a member of the NCAA (Division I). **Intercollegiate sports** (some offering scholarships) include baseball (m), basketball, cross-country running, football (m), gymnastics (w), soccer, softball (w), swimming, tennis (w), track and field, volleyball (w), wrestling (m).

Campus Safety

Student safety services include on-call van transportation, late-night transport/escort service, 24-hour emergency telephone alarm devices, 24-hour patrols by trained security personnel, and electronically operated dormitory entrances.

Applying

Pitt requires SAT I or ACT and a high school transcript. It recommends an essay, SAT I, an interview, and recommendations. Application deadline: rolling admissions; 3/1 priority date for financial aid. Early and deferred admission are possible.

Getting in Last Year
15,438 applied
60% were accepted
3,296 enrolled (36%)
34% from top tenth of their h.s. class
41% had SAT verbal scores over 600
47% had SAT math scores over 600
66% had ACT scores over 24
8% had SAT verbal scores over 700
8% had SAT math scores over 700
14% had ACT scores over 30
16 National Merit Scholars
72 valedictorians

Graduation and After
35% graduated in 4 years
21% graduated in 5 years
4% graduated in 6 years
40% pursued further study (8% education, 6% arts and sciences, 5% business)
400 organizations recruited on campus

Financial Matters
$7482 resident tuition and fees (2001–02)
$15,740 nonresident tuition and fees (2001–02)
$6110 room and board
76% average percent of need met
$7284 average financial aid amount received per undergraduate

UNIVERSITY OF PUGET SOUND

SUBURBAN SETTING ■ PRIVATE ■ INDEPENDENT ■ COED
TACOMA, WASHINGTON

Web site: www.ups.edu
Contact: Dr. George H. Mills Jr., Vice President for Enrollment, 1500 North Warner Street, Tacoma, WA 98416-0005
Telephone: 253-879-3211 or toll-free 800-396-7191 **Fax:** 253-879-3993
E-mail: admission@ups.edu

Getting in Last Year

4,377 applied
67% were accepted
703 enrolled (24%)
45% from top tenth of their h.s. class
3.59 average high school GPA
70% had SAT verbal scores over 600
64% had SAT math scores over 600
83% had ACT scores over 24
16% had SAT verbal scores over 700
11% had SAT math scores over 700
21% had ACT scores over 30
73 National Merit Scholars
56 valedictorians

Graduation and After

60% graduated in 4 years
10% graduated in 5 years
1% graduated in 6 years
31% pursued further study (12% arts and sciences, 7% education, 2% business)
70% had job offers within 6 months
150 organizations recruited on campus

Financial Matters

$22,505 tuition and fees (2001–02)
$5780 room and board
90% average percent of need met
$18,401 average financial aid amount received per undergraduate

Academics

Puget Sound awards bachelor's, master's, and doctoral **degrees**. Challenging opportunities include advanced placement credit, student-designed majors, an honors program, double majors, independent study, and a senior project. Special programs include cooperative education, internships, summer session for credit, study-abroad, and Army ROTC.

The most frequently chosen **baccalaureate** fields are social sciences and history, business/marketing, and English. A complete listing of majors at Puget Sound appears in the Majors Index beginning on page 430.

The **faculty** at Puget Sound has 214 full-time members, 86% with terminal degrees. The student-faculty ratio is 11:1.

Students of Puget Sound

The student body totals 2,848, of whom 2,604 are undergraduates. 60.8% are women and 39.2% are men. Students come from 48 states and territories and 20 other countries. 31% are from Washington. 1.5% are international students. 2.2% are African American, 1.3% American Indian, 10.6% Asian American, and 2.6% Hispanic American. 84% returned for their sophomore year.

Facilities and Resources

Student rooms are linked to a campus network. 180 **computers** are available on campus that provide access to the Internet. The **library** has 326,438 books and 4,510 subscriptions.

Campus Life

There are 40 active organizations on campus, including a drama/theater group, newspaper, radio station, and choral group. 23% of eligible men and 32% of eligible women are members of national **fraternities**, national **sororities**, and theme houses.

Puget Sound is a member of the NCAA (Division III). **Intercollegiate sports** include baseball (m), basketball, crew, cross-country running, football (m), golf, lacrosse (w), skiing (downhill), soccer, softball (w), swimming, tennis, track and field, volleyball (w).

Campus Safety

Student safety services include 24-hour locked residence hall entrances, late-night transport/escort service, 24-hour emergency telephone alarm devices, 24-hour patrols by trained security personnel, student patrols, and electronically operated dormitory entrances.

Applying

Puget Sound requires an essay, SAT I or ACT, a high school transcript, and 2 recommendations. It recommends an interview and a minimum high school GPA of 3.0. Application deadline: 2/1; 2/1 priority date for financial aid. Early and deferred admission are possible.

UNIVERSITY OF REDLANDS
SMALL-TOWN SETTING ■ PRIVATE ■ INDEPENDENT ■ COED
REDLANDS, CALIFORNIA

Web site: www.redlands.edu
Contact: Mr. Paul Driscoll, Dean of Admissions, PO Box 3080, Redlands, CA 92373-0999
Telephone: 909-335-4074 or toll-free 800-455-5064 **Fax:** 909-335-4089
E-mail: admissions@uor.edu

Academics
Redlands awards bachelor's and master's **degrees** and post-bachelor's and post-master's certificates. Challenging opportunities include advanced placement credit, student-designed majors, freshman honors college, an honors program, double majors, independent study, and a senior project. Special programs include internships, off-campus study, study-abroad, and Army and Air Force ROTC.

The most frequently chosen **baccalaureate** fields are liberal arts/general studies, social sciences and history, and business/marketing. A complete listing of majors at Redlands appears in the Majors Index beginning on page 430.

The **faculty** at Redlands has 132 full-time members, 86% with terminal degrees. The student-faculty ratio is 12:1.

Students of Redlands
The student body totals 2,017, of whom 1,946 are undergraduates. 58.1% are women and 41.9% are men. Students come from 42 states and territories and 18 other countries. 73% are from California. 0.8% are international students. 3% are African American, 0.7% American Indian, 5.9% Asian American, and 11.4% Hispanic American. 81% returned for their sophomore year.

Facilities and Resources
Student rooms are linked to a campus network. 277 **computers** are available on campus that provide access to the Internet. The **library** has 246,725 books and 1,876 subscriptions.

Campus Life
There are 95 active organizations on campus, including a drama/theater group, newspaper, and choral group. 18% of eligible men and 20% of eligible women are members of local **fraternities** and local **sororities**.

Redlands is a member of the NCAA (Division III). **Intercollegiate sports** include baseball (m), basketball, cross-country running, football (m), golf (m), lacrosse (w), soccer, softball (w), swimming, tennis, track and field, volleyball (w), water polo.

Campus Safety
Student safety services include safety whistles, late-night transport/escort service, 24-hour emergency telephone alarm devices, 24-hour patrols by trained security personnel, student patrols, and electronically operated dormitory entrances.

Applying
Redlands requires an essay, SAT I or ACT, a high school transcript, and 2 recommendations. It recommends an interview. Application deadline: 7/1; 2/15 priority date for financial aid. Early and deferred admission are possible.

At the University of Redlands, students explore connections, blurring the barriers often artificially imposed between academic disciplines, between the classroom and the real world, and between their own views and the way others see things. Academics are combined with a community-based residential life and a range of opportunities to gain firsthand experience through internships, international study, and original faculty-directed research. Students take ownership of their education with the active support of professors who are truly committed to student participation in the learning process; they coax, challenge, captivate, support, nourish, and actively engage students in an exchange of stimulating and provocative ideas.

Getting in Last Year
2,478 applied
77% were accepted
614 enrolled (32%)
28% from top tenth of their h.s. class
3.50 average high school GPA
31% had SAT verbal scores over 600
32% had SAT math scores over 600
44% had ACT scores over 24
5% had SAT verbal scores over 700
3% had SAT math scores over 700
4% had ACT scores over 30
4 National Merit Scholars

Graduation and After
57% graduated in 4 years
4% graduated in 5 years
1% graduated in 6 years
Graduates pursuing further study: 4% arts and sciences, 3% education, 0% law
50% had job offers within 6 months
20 organizations recruited on campus

Financial Matters
$21,406 tuition and fees (2001–02)
$7840 room and board
74% average percent of need met
$21,440 average financial aid amount received per undergraduate

UNIVERSITY OF RHODE ISLAND
SMALL-TOWN SETTING ■ PUBLIC ■ STATE-SUPPORTED ■ COED
KINGSTON, RHODE ISLAND

Web site: www.uri.edu
Contact: Ms. Catherine Zeiser, Assistant Dean of Admissions, 8 Ranger Road, Suite 1, Kingston, RI 02881-2020
Telephone: 401-874-7100 **Fax:** 401-874-5523
E-mail: uriadmit@uri.edu

O utstanding freshman candidates with strong academic credentials are eligible to be considered for a Centennial Scholarship, ranging up to full tuition. These scholarships are based on the student's total academic profile, including rank in class and standardized test scores. They are renewable each semester if the student maintains continuous full-time enrollment and a minimum 3.0 average. Eligibility requires a completed admissions application received by the December 14 early action deadline. Applications and information received after that date are not considered.

Getting in Last Year
10,794 applied
67% were accepted
2,129 enrolled (30%)
20% from top tenth of their h.s. class
3.40 average high school GPA
25% had SAT verbal scores over 600
29% had SAT math scores over 600
3% had SAT verbal scores over 700
3% had SAT math scores over 700

Graduation and After
155 organizations recruited on campus

Financial Matters
$5386 resident tuition and fees (2001–02)
$14,164 nonresident tuition and fees (2001–02)
$7028 room and board
84% average percent of need met
$8940 average financial aid amount received per undergraduate (2000–01)

Academics
Rhode Island awards bachelor's, master's, doctoral, and first-professional **degrees** and post-bachelor's certificates. Challenging opportunities include advanced placement credit, accelerated degree programs, student-designed majors, an honors program, double majors, independent study, and a senior project. Special programs include cooperative education, internships, summer session for credit, off-campus study, study-abroad, and Army ROTC.

The most frequently chosen **baccalaureate** fields are business/marketing, health professions and related sciences, and communications/communication technologies. A complete listing of majors at Rhode Island appears in the Majors Index beginning on page 430.

The **faculty** at Rhode Island has 672 full-time members, 91% with terminal degrees. The student-faculty ratio is 18:1.

Students of Rhode Island
The student body totals 14,264, of whom 10,579 are undergraduates. 56.3% are women and 43.7% are men. Students come from 38 states and territories and 47 other countries. 62% are from Rhode Island. 0.4% are international students. 4% are African American, 0.4% American Indian, 3.4% Asian American, and 4% Hispanic American. 79% returned for their sophomore year.

Facilities and Resources
552 **computers** are available on campus for student use. The 2 **libraries** have 783,237 books and 7,966 subscriptions.

Campus Life
There are 85 active organizations on campus, including a drama/theater group, newspaper, radio station, choral group, and marching band. 10% of eligible men and 13% of eligible women are members of national **fraternities**, national **sororities**, and local sororities.

Rhode Island is a member of the NCAA (Division I). **Intercollegiate sports** (some offering scholarships) include baseball (m), basketball, crew (w), cross-country running, field hockey (w), football (m), golf (m), gymnastics (w), soccer, softball (w), swimming, tennis, track and field, volleyball (w).

Campus Safety
Student safety services include late-night transport/escort service, 24-hour emergency telephone alarm devices, 24-hour patrols by trained security personnel, student patrols, and electronically operated dormitory entrances.

Applying
Rhode Island requires SAT I or ACT and a high school transcript, and in some cases a minimum high school GPA of 3.0. It recommends an interview, recommendations, and a minimum high school GPA of 3.0. Application deadline: 3/1; 3/1 priority date for financial aid. Early admission is possible.

UNIVERSITY OF RICHMOND

SUBURBAN SETTING ■ PRIVATE ■ INDEPENDENT ■ COED
UNIVERSITY OF RICHMOND, VIRGINIA

Web site: www.richmond.edu
Contact: Ms. Pamela Spence, Dean of Admission, 28 Westhampton Way,
  University of Richmond, VA 23173
Telephone: 804-289-8640 or toll-free 800-700-1662 **Fax:** 804-287-6003

Academics

University of Richmond awards associate, bachelor's, master's, and first-professional
degrees and post-bachelor's certificates. Challenging opportunities include advanced
placement credit, accelerated degree programs, student-designed majors, an honors
program, double majors, independent study, and a senior project. Special programs
include cooperative education, internships, summer session for credit, off-campus study,
study-abroad, and Army ROTC.

The most frequently chosen **baccalaureate** fields are business/marketing, social sciences and history, and biological/life sciences. A complete listing of majors at University
of Richmond appears in the Majors Index beginning on page 430.

The **faculty** at University of Richmond has 268 full-time members, 87% with
terminal degrees. The student-faculty ratio is 10:1.

Students of University of Richmond

The student body totals 3,727, of whom 3,021 are undergraduates. 51.8% are women
and 48.2% are men. Students come from 49 states and territories and 72 other countries.
15% are from Virginia. 3.6% are international students. 4.8% are African American,
0.1% American Indian, 2.9% Asian American, and 1.6% Hispanic American. 89%
returned for their sophomore year.

Facilities and Resources

Student rooms are linked to a campus network. 500 **computers** are available on campus
for student use. The 5 **libraries** have 716,677 books and 3,579 subscriptions.

Campus Life

There are 225 active organizations on campus, including a drama/theater group,
newspaper, radio station, television station, and choral group. 39% of eligible men and
49% of eligible women are members of national **fraternities** and national **sororities**.

University of Richmond is a member of the NCAA (Division I). **Intercollegiate
sports** (some offering scholarships) include baseball (m), basketball, cross-country running, field hockey (w), football (m), golf (m), lacrosse (w), soccer, swimming (w), tennis,
track and field.

Campus Safety

Student safety services include campus police, late-night transport/escort service, 24-
hour emergency telephone alarm devices, 24-hour patrols by trained security personnel,
and electronically operated dormitory entrances.

Applying

University of Richmond requires an essay, SAT II: Writing Test, SAT I and SAT II or
ACT, SAT II Subject Test in math, a high school transcript, 1 recommendation, signed
character statement, and a minimum high school GPA of 2.0. Application deadline: 1/15;
2/25 for financial aid. Early and deferred admission are possible.

Getting in Last Year

5,622 applied
44% were accepted
792 enrolled (32%)
53% from top tenth of their h.s. class
74% had SAT verbal scores over 600
84% had SAT math scores over 600
95% had ACT scores over 24
18% had SAT verbal scores over 700
20% had SAT math scores over 700
35% had ACT scores over 30
27 National Merit Scholars
23 valedictorians

Graduation and After

28% pursued further study (15% arts and
  sciences, 7% law, 6% medicine)
280 organizations recruited on campus

Financial Matters

$22,570 tuition and fees (2001–02)
$4730 room and board
96% average percent of need met
$16,134 average financial aid amount received
  per undergraduate

UNIVERSITY OF ROCHESTER

SUBURBAN SETTING ■ PRIVATE ■ INDEPENDENT ■ COED
ROCHESTER, NEW YORK

Web site: www.rochester.edu
Contact: Mr. Jamie Hobba, Director of Admissions, PO Box 270251,
 Rochester, NY 14627
Telephone: 585-275-3221 or toll-free 888-822-2256 **Fax:** 585-461-4595
E-mail: admit@admissions.rochester.edu

Founded in 1850, the University of Rochester is one of the leading private universities in the country. The University of Rochester balances the choices and intellectual excitement of a major research university with the intimacy and opportunities for personal involvement of a small liberal arts college. Programs are available in 6 divisions, including the College (Arts and Sciences and Engineering), Nursing, Education, Business, Medicine, and the Eastman School of Music. Special undergraduate opportunities include the Take Five program (fifth-year tuition free), an 8-year bachelor's/medical degree, and seminar-style Quest courses for first-year students.

Getting in Last Year
10,080 applied
50% were accepted
51% from top tenth of their h.s. class
3.63 average high school GPA
79% had SAT verbal scores over 600
87% had SAT math scores over 600
87% had ACT scores over 24
25% had SAT verbal scores over 700
35% had SAT math scores over 700
36% had ACT scores over 30
25 National Merit Scholars
69 valedictorians

Graduation and After
65% graduated in 4 years
8% graduated in 5 years
3% graduated in 6 years
50% pursued further study (20% arts and
 sciences, 10% law, 9% medicine)
57% had job offers within 6 months
127 organizations recruited on campus

Financial Matters
$24,754 tuition and fees (2001–02)
$8585 room and board
100% average percent of need met
$21,627 average financial aid amount received
 per undergraduate

Academics
University of Rochester awards bachelor's, master's, doctoral, and first-professional **degrees**. Challenging opportunities include advanced placement credit, student-designed majors, double majors, and independent study. Special programs include internships, summer session for credit, off-campus study, study-abroad, and Army, Navy and Air Force ROTC.

The most frequently chosen **baccalaureate** field is law/legal studies. A complete listing of majors at University of Rochester appears in the Majors Index beginning on page 430.

The **faculty** at University of Rochester has 1,010 full-time members. The student-faculty ratio is 12:1.

Students of University of Rochester
The student body totals 7,355, of whom 3,715 are undergraduates. Students come from 52 states and territories and 45 other countries. 93% returned for their sophomore year.

Facilities and Resources
Student rooms are linked to a campus network. 260 **computers** are available on campus for student use. The 6 **libraries** have 2,992,204 books and 11,254 subscriptions.

Campus Life
There are 150 active organizations on campus, including a drama/theater group, newspaper, radio station, and choral group. 20% of eligible men and 15% of eligible women are members of national **fraternities** and national **sororities**.

University of Rochester is a member of the NCAA (Division III). **Intercollegiate sports** include baseball (m), basketball, cross-country running, field hockey (w), football (m), golf, lacrosse (w), soccer, softball (w), squash (m), swimming, tennis, track and field, volleyball (w).

Campus Safety
Student safety services include late-night transport/escort service, 24-hour emergency telephone alarm devices, 24-hour patrols by trained security personnel, and electronically operated dormitory entrances.

Applying
University of Rochester requires an essay, SAT I or ACT, a high school transcript, and 1 recommendation, and in some cases audition, portfolio. It recommends SAT II Subject Tests and 2 recommendations. Application deadline: 1/15; 2/1 priority date for financial aid. Early and deferred admission are possible.

University of St. Thomas

Urban setting ■ Private ■ Independent Religious ■ Coed
St. Paul, Minnesota

Web site: www.stthomas.edu
Contact: Ms. Marla Friederichs, Associate Vice President of Enrollment
  Management, Mail #32F-1, 2115 Summit Avenue, St. Paul, MN
  55105-1096
Telephone: 651-962-6150 or toll-free 800-328-6819 ext. 26150 **Fax:**
  651-962-6160
E-mail: admissions@stthomas.edu

Academics

St. Thomas awards bachelor's, master's, doctoral, and first-professional **degrees** and
post-bachelor's and post-master's certificates. Challenging opportunities include
advanced placement credit, student-designed majors, an honors program, double majors,
independent study, and a senior project. Special programs include internships, summer
session for credit, off-campus study, study-abroad, and Army, Navy and Air Force
ROTC.

The most frequently chosen **baccalaureate** fields are business/marketing, com-
munications/communication technologies, and social sciences and history. A complete
listing of majors at St. Thomas appears in the Majors Index beginning on page 430.

The **faculty** at St. Thomas has 386 full-time members, 84% with terminal degrees.
The student-faculty ratio is 14:1.

Students of St. Thomas

The student body totals 11,473, of whom 5,416 are undergraduates. 52.7% are women
and 47.3% are men. Students come from 42 states and territories and 48 other countries.
82% are from Minnesota. 1.2% are international students. 1.9% are African American,
0.7% American Indian, 5.5% Asian American, and 2.1% Hispanic American. 84%
returned for their sophomore year.

Facilities and Resources

Student rooms are linked to a campus network. 843 **computers** are available on campus
that provide access to the Internet. The 3 **libraries** have 312,092 books and 2,528
subscriptions.

Campus Life

There are 94 active organizations on campus, including a drama/theater group,
newspaper, and choral group. No national or local **fraternities** or **sororities**.

St. Thomas is a member of the NCAA (Division III). **Intercollegiate sports** include
baseball (m), basketball, cross-country running, football (m), golf, ice hockey, soccer,
softball (w), swimming, tennis, track and field, volleyball (w).

Campus Safety

Student safety services include late-night transport/escort service, 24-hour emergency
telephone alarm devices, 24-hour patrols by trained security personnel, and electronically operated dormitory entrances.

Applying

St. Thomas requires an essay, SAT I or ACT, and a high school transcript. It recommends ACT, an interview, and recommendations. Application deadline: rolling admissions; 4/1 priority date for financial aid. Deferred admission is possible.

Getting in Last Year
3,257 applied
81% were accepted
1,083 enrolled (41%)
30% from top tenth of their h.s. class
3.55 average high school GPA
40% had SAT verbal scores over 600
50% had SAT math scores over 600
64% had ACT scores over 24
9% had SAT verbal scores over 700
6% had SAT math scores over 700
10% had ACT scores over 30
8 National Merit Scholars
43 valedictorians

Graduation and After
15% pursued further study (4% law, 3%
  education, 3% veterinary medicine)
122 organizations recruited on campus

Financial Matters
$18,421 tuition and fees (2001–02)
$5623 room and board
84% average percent of need met
$14,266 average financial aid amount received
  per undergraduate

UNIVERSITY OF ST. THOMAS

URBAN SETTING ■ PRIVATE ■ INDEPENDENT RELIGIOUS ■ COED
HOUSTON, TEXAS

Web site: www.stthom.edu
Contact: Mr. Gerald E. Warren, Assistant Director of Admissions, 3800
  Montrose Boulevard, Houston, TX 77006-4696
Telephone: 713-525-3500 or toll-free 800-856-8565 **Fax:** 713-525-3558
E-mail: admissions@stthom.edu

Getting in Last Year
768 applied
78% were accepted
284 enrolled (47%)
34% from top tenth of their h.s. class
3.63 average high school GPA
31% had SAT verbal scores over 600
37% had SAT math scores over 600
65% had ACT scores over 24
2% had SAT verbal scores over 700
7% had SAT math scores over 700
11% had ACT scores over 30

Graduation and After
32% graduated in 4 years
12% graduated in 5 years
3% graduated in 6 years
6 organizations recruited on campus

Financial Matters
$13,162 tuition and fees (2001–02)
$5920 room and board
62% average percent of need met
$10,275 average financial aid amount received
  per undergraduate

Academics
St. Thomas awards bachelor's, master's, doctoral, and first-professional **degrees**. Challenging opportunities include advanced placement credit, accelerated degree programs, student-designed majors, an honors program, double majors, independent study, and a senior project. Special programs include cooperative education, internships, summer session for credit, off-campus study, study-abroad, and Army ROTC.

The most frequently chosen **baccalaureate** fields are business/marketing, liberal arts/general studies, and education. A complete listing of majors at St. Thomas appears in the Majors Index beginning on page 430.

The **faculty** at St. Thomas has 112 full-time members, 87% with terminal degrees. The student-faculty ratio is 14:1.

Students of St. Thomas
The student body totals 4,310, of whom 1,851 are undergraduates. 64.8% are women and 35.2% are men. Students come from 23 states and territories and 46 other countries. 97% are from Texas. 5% are international students. 5.7% are African American, 0.7% American Indian, 12.6% Asian American, and 29.6% Hispanic American. 76% returned for their sophomore year.

Facilities and Resources
Student rooms are linked to a campus network. 143 **computers** are available on campus that provide access to the Internet. The 2 **libraries** have 226,593 books and 3,400 subscriptions.

Campus Life
There are 48 active organizations on campus, including a drama/theater group, newspaper, and choral group. No national or local **fraternities** or **sororities**.

This institution has no intercollegiate sports.

Campus Safety
Student safety services include late-night transport/escort service, 24-hour emergency telephone alarm devices, and 24-hour patrols by trained security personnel.

Applying
St. Thomas requires SAT I or ACT, a high school transcript, and a minimum high school GPA of 2.25, and in some cases an essay, an interview, and 2 recommendations. Application deadline: rolling admissions; 3/1 priority date for financial aid. Deferred admission is possible.

UNIVERSITY OF SAN DIEGO
URBAN SETTING ■ PRIVATE ■ INDEPENDENT RELIGIOUS ■ COED
SAN DIEGO, CALIFORNIA

Web site: www.sandiego.edu
Contact: Mr. Stephen Pultz, Director of Undergraduate Admissions, 5998 Alcala Park, San Diego, CA 92110
Telephone: 619-260-4506 or toll-free 800-248-4873 **Fax:** 619-260-6836
E-mail: admissions@sandiego.edu

Academics
USD awards bachelor's, master's, doctoral, and first-professional **degrees**. Challenging opportunities include advanced placement credit, an honors program, double majors, independent study, and a senior project. Special programs include internships, summer session for credit, off-campus study, study-abroad, and Army, Navy and Air Force ROTC.

The most frequently chosen **baccalaureate** fields are business/marketing, social sciences and history, and communications/communication technologies. A complete listing of majors at USD appears in the Majors Index beginning on page 430.

The **faculty** at USD has 315 full-time members, 98% with terminal degrees. The student-faculty ratio is 16:1.

Students of USD
The student body totals 7,062, of whom 4,809 are undergraduates. 59.6% are women and 40.4% are men. Students come from 50 states and territories and 67 other countries. 55% are from California. 2.9% are international students. 2.1% are African American, 1.1% American Indian, 6.6% Asian American, and 14.2% Hispanic American. 88% returned for their sophomore year.

Facilities and Resources
Student rooms are linked to a campus network. 260 **computers** are available on campus that provide access to the Internet. The 2 **libraries** have 500,000 books and 2,600 subscriptions.

Campus Life
There are 75 active organizations on campus, including a drama/theater group, newspaper, television station, and choral group. 25% of eligible men and 25% of eligible women are members of national **fraternities** and national **sororities**.

USD is a member of the NCAA (Division I). **Intercollegiate sports** (some offering scholarships) include baseball (m), basketball, crew, cross-country running, football (m), golf (m), soccer, softball (w), swimming (w), tennis, volleyball (w).

Campus Safety
Student safety services include escort service, late-night transport/escort service, 24-hour emergency telephone alarm devices, 24-hour patrols by trained security personnel, student patrols, and electronically operated dormitory entrances.

Applying
USD requires an essay, SAT I or ACT, a high school transcript, and 1 recommendation. It recommends SAT II: Writing Test. Application deadline: 1/5; 2/20 priority date for financial aid. Early and deferred admission are possible.

Getting in Last Year
6,702 applied
50% were accepted
1,004 enrolled (30%)
50% from top tenth of their h.s. class
3.75 average high school GPA
40% had SAT verbal scores over 600
48% had SAT math scores over 600
64% had ACT scores over 24
5% had SAT verbal scores over 700
5% had SAT math scores over 700
8% had ACT scores over 30
31 valedictorians

Graduation and After
40% pursued further study
96% had job offers within 6 months
105 organizations recruited on campus

Financial Matters
$20,458 tuition and fees (2001–02)
$8440 room and board
93% average percent of need met
$17,965 average financial aid amount received per undergraduate (2000–01)

THE UNIVERSITY OF SCRANTON

URBAN SETTING ■ PRIVATE ■ INDEPENDENT RELIGIOUS ■ COED
SCRANTON, PENNSYLVANIA

Web site: www.scranton.edu
Contact: Mr. Joseph Roback, Director of Admissions, Scranton, PA 18510
Telephone: 570-941-7540 or toll-free 888-SCRANTON **Fax:** 570-941-4370
E-mail: admissions@uofs.edu

The University of Scranton is known for its outstanding academic programs, well-equipped campus, state-of-the-art technology, strong sense of community, and, most of all, the remarkable success of its graduates. In 2001, for example, medical schools accepted 91% of Scranton applicants, and law schools accepted 90%. Scranton students also earned 6 Fulbrights, 3 Freeman Awards, 2 NCAA Post-Graduate Scholarships, and 2 Rotary Ambassadorial Scholarships. Scranton graduates tend to become leaders in whatever fields they choose. They have benefited from something few schools can offer: a Jesuit education that provides the rock-solid confidence to make it in the real world from day one.

Getting in Last Year
3,820 applied
88% were accepted
1,028 enrolled (31%)
23% from top tenth of their h.s. class
3.27 average high school GPA
28% had SAT verbal scores over 600
32% had SAT math scores over 600
4% had SAT verbal scores over 700
4% had SAT math scores over 700
22 National Merit Scholars
17 class presidents
16 valedictorians

Graduation and After
65% graduated in 4 years
14% graduated in 5 years
1% graduated in 6 years
Graduates pursuing further study: 16% arts and sciences, 5% medicine, 4% law
69% had job offers within 6 months
61 organizations recruited on campus

Financial Matters
$19,530 tuition and fees (2001–02)
$8434 room and board
78% average percent of need met
$13,585 average financial aid amount received per undergraduate (2000–01 estimated)

Academics

Scranton awards associate, bachelor's, and master's **degrees** and post-bachelor's and post-master's certificates. Challenging opportunities include advanced placement credit, student-designed majors, freshman honors college, an honors program, double majors, independent study, and a senior project. Special programs include internships, summer session for credit, off-campus study, and Army and Air Force ROTC.

The most frequently chosen **baccalaureate** fields are business/marketing, health professions and related sciences, and education. A complete listing of majors at Scranton appears in the Majors Index beginning on page 430.

The **faculty** at Scranton has 244 full-time members, 86% with terminal degrees. The student-faculty ratio is 13:1.

Students of Scranton

The student body totals 4,658, of whom 4,060 are undergraduates. 57.2% are women and 42.8% are men. Students come from 30 states and territories and 12 other countries. 52% are from Pennsylvania. 0.6% are international students. 1% are African American, 0.2% American Indian, 2% Asian American, and 2.5% Hispanic American. 90% returned for their sophomore year.

Facilities and Resources

Student rooms are linked to a campus network. 777 **computers** are available on campus that provide access to the Internet. The 2 **libraries** have 433,900 books and 7,553 subscriptions.

Campus Life

There are 80 active organizations on campus, including a drama/theater group, newspaper, radio station, and choral group. No national or local **fraternities** or **sororities**.

Scranton is a member of the NCAA (Division III). **Intercollegiate sports** include baseball (m), basketball, cross-country running, field hockey (w), golf (m), ice hockey (m), lacrosse (m), soccer, softball (w), swimming, tennis, volleyball (w), wrestling (m).

Campus Safety

Student safety services include late-night transport/escort service, 24-hour emergency telephone alarm devices, 24-hour patrols by trained security personnel, student patrols, and electronically operated dormitory entrances.

Applying

Scranton requires SAT I or ACT and a high school transcript, and in some cases an interview and 2 recommendations. It recommends an essay. Application deadline: 3/1; 2/15 priority date for financial aid. Early and deferred admission are possible.

University of South Carolina

Urban setting ■ Public ■ State-supported ■ Coed
Columbia, South Carolina

Web site: www.sc.edu
Contact: Ms. Terry L. Davis, Director of Undergraduate Admissions, Columbia, SC 29208
Telephone: 803-777-7700 or toll-free 800-868-5872 (in-state) **Fax:** 803-777-0101
E-mail: admissions-ugrad@sc.edu

Academics

Carolina awards associate, bachelor's, master's, doctoral, and first-professional **degrees** and post-bachelor's and post-master's certificates. Challenging opportunities include advanced placement credit, accelerated degree programs, student-designed majors, freshman honors college, an honors program, double majors, independent study, and a senior project. Special programs include cooperative education, internships, summer session for credit, study-abroad, and Army, Navy and Air Force ROTC.

The most frequently chosen **baccalaureate** fields are business/marketing, social sciences and history, and psychology. A complete listing of majors at Carolina appears in the Majors Index beginning on page 430.

The **faculty** at Carolina has 1,006 full-time members, 88% with terminal degrees. The student-faculty ratio is 14:1.

Students of Carolina

The student body totals 23,000, of whom 15,506 are undergraduates. 54.3% are women and 45.7% are men. Students come from 51 states and territories and 84 other countries. 87% are from South Carolina. 1.8% are international students. 18% are African American, 0.3% American Indian, 2.9% Asian American, and 1.4% Hispanic American. 81% returned for their sophomore year.

Facilities and Resources

Student rooms are linked to a campus network. 11,000 **computers** are available on campus that provide access to the Internet. The 8 **libraries** have 3,222,033 books and 20,468 subscriptions.

Campus Life

There are 245 active organizations on campus, including a drama/theater group, newspaper, radio station, choral group, and marching band. 17% of eligible men and 17% of eligible women are members of national **fraternities** and national **sororities**.

Carolina is a member of the NCAA (Division I). **Intercollegiate sports** (some offering scholarships) include baseball (m), basketball, cross-country running (w), equestrian sports (w), football (m), golf, soccer, softball (w), swimming, tennis, track and field, volleyball (w).

Campus Safety

Student safety services include Division of Law Enforcement and Safety, late-night transport/escort service, 24-hour emergency telephone alarm devices, 24-hour patrols by trained security personnel, student patrols, and electronically operated dormitory entrances.

Applying

Carolina requires SAT I or ACT and a high school transcript. Application deadline: 5/15; 4/15 priority date for financial aid.

Chartered in 1801, the University of South Carolina rapidly achieved a reputation for academic excellence and became one of the most distinguished colleges in the country. The University is composed of 14 schools and colleges, including the Honors College, Graduate School, School of Medicine, and School of Law, and offers more than 70 majors and 350 degree programs. More than 85% of faculty members hold a terminal degree.

Getting in Last Year

11,176 applied
70% were accepted
3,287 enrolled (42%)
25% from top tenth of their h.s. class
3.59 average high school GPA
26% had SAT verbal scores over 600
30% had SAT math scores over 600
40% had ACT scores over 24
5% had SAT verbal scores over 700
6% had SAT math scores over 700
8% had ACT scores over 30
42 National Merit Scholars
93 valedictorians

Graduation and After

31% graduated in 4 years
22% graduated in 5 years
5% graduated in 6 years
80% had job offers within 6 months
17334 organizations recruited on campus

Financial Matters

$4064 resident tuition and fees (2001–02)
$11,004 nonresident tuition and fees (2001–02)
$4684 room and board
65% average percent of need met
$3200 average financial aid amount received per undergraduate (2000–01)

UNIVERSITY OF SOUTHERN CALIFORNIA

URBAN SETTING ■ PRIVATE ■ INDEPENDENT ■ COED
LOS ANGELES, CALIFORNIA

Web site: www.usc.edu
Contact: Ms. Laurel Baker-Tew, Director of Admission, University Park
Campus, Los Angeles, CA 90089
Telephone: 213-740-1111 **Fax:** 213-740-6364
E-mail: admapp@enroll1.usc.edu

One of the country's leading private research universities, USC provides outstanding teachers, excellent facilities, and a wide array of academic offerings, including interdisciplinary programs and undergraduate research opportunities. With a student-faculty ratio of 11:1 and small classes, students work with world-acclaimed professors in every discipline as participants, not spectators. USC offers bachelor's degrees in 79 majors and 101 minors, spanning 18 professional schools in addition to the College of Letters, Arts and Sciences.

Getting in Last Year
26,294 applied
32% were accepted
2,780 enrolled (33%)
80% from top tenth of their h.s. class
3.93 average high school GPA
77% had SAT verbal scores over 600
86% had SAT math scores over 600
99% had ACT scores over 24
25% had SAT verbal scores over 700
36% had SAT math scores over 700
48% had ACT scores over 30
153 National Merit Scholars

Graduation and After
51% graduated in 4 years
18% graduated in 5 years
5% graduated in 6 years
664 organizations recruited on campus

Financial Matters
$25,533 tuition and fees (2001–02)
$8114 room and board
99% average percent of need met
$23,961 average financial aid amount received per undergraduate (2000–01)

Academics
USC awards bachelor's, master's, doctoral, and first-professional **degrees** and post-bachelor's, post-master's, and first-professional certificates. Challenging opportunities include advanced placement credit, accelerated degree programs, student-designed majors, freshman honors college, an honors program, double majors, independent study, and a senior project. Special programs include cooperative education, internships, summer session for credit, off-campus study, study-abroad, and Army, Navy and Air Force ROTC.

The most frequently chosen **baccalaureate** fields are business/marketing, social sciences and history, and visual/performing arts. A complete listing of majors at USC appears in the Majors Index beginning on page 430.

The **faculty** at USC has 1,351 full-time members, 85% with terminal degrees. The student-faculty ratio is 11:1.

Students of USC
The student body totals 29,813, of whom 16,020 are undergraduates. 49.8% are women and 50.2% are men. Students come from 52 states and territories and 100 other countries. 69% are from California. 7.2% are international students. 6.5% are African American, 0.8% American Indian, 21.7% Asian American, and 13.7% Hispanic American. 94% returned for their sophomore year.

Facilities and Resources
Student rooms are linked to a campus network. 2,300 **computers** are available on campus that provide access to on-line degree progress, grades, financial aid summary and the Internet. The 23 **libraries** have 3,459,636 books and 28,661 subscriptions.

Campus Life
There are 450 active organizations on campus, including a drama/theater group, newspaper, radio station, television station, choral group, and marching band. 20% of eligible men and 20% of eligible women are members of national **fraternities**, national **sororities**, local fraternities, and local sororities.

USC is a member of the NCAA (Division I). **Intercollegiate sports** (some offering scholarships) include baseball (m), basketball, crew (w), cross-country running (w), football (m), golf, sailing, soccer (w), swimming, tennis, track and field, volleyball, water polo.

Campus Safety
Student safety services include late-night transport/escort service, 24-hour emergency telephone alarm devices, 24-hour patrols by trained security personnel, student patrols, and electronically operated dormitory entrances.

Applying
USC requires an essay, SAT I or ACT, and a high school transcript, and in some cases SAT II Subject Tests and recommendations. It recommends an interview and recommendations. Application deadline: 1/10; 1/22 priority date for financial aid. Early and deferred admission are possible.

THE UNIVERSITY OF TEXAS AT AUSTIN

URBAN SETTING ■ PUBLIC ■ STATE-SUPPORTED ■ COED
AUSTIN, TEXAS

Web site: www.utexas.edu
Contact: Freshman Admissions Center, John Hargis Hall, Campus Mail Code D0700, Austin, TX 78712-1111
Telephone: 512-475-7440 **Fax:** 512-475-7475
E-mail: frmn@uts.cc.utexas.edu

Academics

UT Austin awards bachelor's, master's, doctoral, and first-professional **degrees**. Challenging opportunities include advanced placement credit, accelerated degree programs, student-designed majors, an honors program, double majors, independent study, and a senior project. Special programs include cooperative education, internships, summer session for credit, study-abroad, and Army, Navy and Air Force ROTC.

The most frequently chosen **baccalaureate** fields are social sciences and history, business/marketing, and communications/communication technologies. A complete listing of majors at UT Austin appears in the Majors Index beginning on page 430.

The **faculty** at UT Austin has 2,394 full-time members, 92% with terminal degrees. The student-faculty ratio is 19:1.

Students of UT Austin

The student body totals 50,616, of whom 38,609 are undergraduates. 50.5% are women and 49.5% are men. Students come from 54 states and territories and 118 other countries. 96% are from Texas. 3.4% are international students. 3.5% are African American, 0.4% American Indian, 16% Asian American, and 13.6% Hispanic American. 92% returned for their sophomore year.

Facilities and Resources

Student rooms are linked to a campus network. 4,000 **computers** are available on campus that provide access to e-mail and the Internet. The 19 **libraries** have 4,250,947 books and 50,165 subscriptions.

Campus Life

There are 750 active organizations on campus, including a drama/theater group, newspaper, radio station, television station, choral group, and marching band. 10% of eligible men and 13% of eligible women are members of national **fraternities** and national **sororities**.

UT Austin is a member of the NCAA (Division I). **Intercollegiate sports** (some offering scholarships) include baseball (m), basketball, crew (w), cross-country running, football (m), golf, soccer (w), softball (w), swimming, tennis, track and field, volleyball (w).

Campus Safety

Student safety services include late-night transport/escort service, 24-hour emergency telephone alarm devices, 24-hour patrols by trained security personnel, student patrols, and electronically operated dormitory entrances.

Applying

UT Austin requires SAT I or ACT and a high school transcript, and in some cases an essay. Application deadline: 2/1. Deferred admission is possible.

Getting in Last Year

20,954 applied
64% were accepted
7,337 enrolled (55%)
50% from top tenth of their h.s. class
50% had SAT verbal scores over 600
63% had SAT math scores over 600
69% had ACT scores over 24
12% had SAT verbal scores over 700
20% had SAT math scores over 700
14% had ACT scores over 30
231 National Merit Scholars

Financial Matters

$3766 resident tuition and fees (2001–02)
$10,096 nonresident tuition and fees (2001–02)
$5671 room and board
95% average percent of need met
$7320 average financial aid amount received per undergraduate (2000–01)

THE UNIVERSITY OF TEXAS AT DALLAS

SUBURBAN SETTING ■ PUBLIC ■ STATE-SUPPORTED ■ COED
RICHARDSON, TEXAS

Web site: www.utdallas.edu

Contact: Admissions Office, PO Box 830688 Mail Station MC11, Richardson, TX 75083-0688

Telephone: 972-883-2342 or toll-free 800-889-2443 **Fax:** 972-883-2599

E-mail: ugrad-admissions@utdallas.edu

Getting in Last Year

4,105 applied
56% were accepted
1,010 enrolled (44%)
31% from top tenth of their h.s. class
3.40 average high school GPA
38% had SAT verbal scores over 600
52% had SAT math scores over 600
56% had ACT scores over 24
8% had SAT verbal scores over 700
14% had SAT math scores over 700
12% had ACT scores over 30
39 National Merit Scholars
25 valedictorians

Graduation and After

13% pursued further study
71% had job offers within 6 months
348 organizations recruited on campus

Financial Matters

$3658 resident tuition and fees (2001–02)
$9988 nonresident tuition and fees (2001–02)
$5914 room and board
80% average percent of need met
$7940 average financial aid amount received per undergraduate

Academics

U.T. Dallas awards bachelor's, master's, and doctoral **degrees**. Challenging opportunities include advanced placement credit, accelerated degree programs, student-designed majors, an honors program, double majors, independent study, and a senior project. Special programs include cooperative education, internships, summer session for credit, study-abroad, and Army and Air Force ROTC.

The most frequently chosen **baccalaureate** fields are business/marketing, computer/information sciences, and interdisciplinary studies. A complete listing of majors at U.T. Dallas appears in the Majors Index beginning on page 430.

The **faculty** at U.T. Dallas has 339 full-time members, 97% with terminal degrees. The student-faculty ratio is 19:1.

Students of U.T. Dallas

The student body totals 12,455, of whom 7,491 are undergraduates. 48% are women and 52% are men. Students come from 35 states and territories and 129 other countries. 90% are from Texas. 4.4% are international students. 7.4% are African American, 0.5% American Indian, 21.2% Asian American, and 8.5% Hispanic American. 78% returned for their sophomore year.

Facilities and Resources

Student rooms are linked to a campus network. 428 **computers** are available on campus that provide access to the Internet. The 3 **libraries** have 447,496 books and 3,831 subscriptions.

Campus Life

There are 88 active organizations on campus, including a drama/theater group and newspaper. 4% of eligible men and 3% of eligible women are members of national **fraternities**, national **sororities**, and local sororities.

U.T. Dallas is a member of the NCAA (Division III). **Intercollegiate sports** include baseball (m), basketball, cross-country running, golf, soccer, softball (w), tennis.

Campus Safety

Student safety services include late-night transport/escort service, 24-hour emergency telephone alarm devices, and 24-hour patrols by trained security personnel.

Applying

U.T. Dallas requires an essay, SAT I or ACT, and a high school transcript, and in some cases TASP and an interview. It recommends SAT II: Writing Test and 3 recommendations. Application deadline: 8/1; 3/12 priority date for financial aid. Deferred admission is possible.

University of the Pacific

Suburban setting ■ Private ■ Independent ■ Coed
Stockton, California

Web site: www.uop.edu
Contact: Mr. Marc McGee, Director of Admissions, 3601 Pacific Avenue, Stockton, CA 95211-0197
Telephone: 209-946-2211 or toll-free 800-959-2867 **Fax:** 209-946-2413
E-mail: admissions@uop.edu

Academics

UOP awards bachelor's, master's, doctoral, and first-professional **degrees**. Challenging opportunities include advanced placement credit, accelerated degree programs, student-designed majors, an honors program, double majors, independent study, and a senior project. Special programs include cooperative education, internships, summer session for credit, study-abroad, and Air Force ROTC.

The most frequently chosen **baccalaureate** fields are business/marketing, social sciences and history, and biological/life sciences. A complete listing of majors at UOP appears in the Majors Index beginning on page 430.

The **faculty** at UOP has 363 full-time members, 90% with terminal degrees. The student-faculty ratio is 13:1.

Students of UOP

The student body totals 5,697, of whom 3,185 are undergraduates. 58% are women and 42% are men. Students come from 37 states and territories and 14 other countries. 80% are from California. 3.5% are international students. 3.1% are African American, 0.9% American Indian, 25.7% Asian American, and 10.3% Hispanic American. 87% returned for their sophomore year.

Facilities and Resources

Student rooms are linked to a campus network. 274 **computers** are available on campus that provide access to the Internet. The 2 **libraries** have 689,733 books and 3,747 subscriptions.

Campus Life

There are 90 active organizations on campus, including a drama/theater group, newspaper, radio station, and choral group. 18% of eligible men and 22% of eligible women are members of national **fraternities**, national **sororities**, and local fraternities.

UOP is a member of the NCAA (Division I). **Intercollegiate sports** (some offering scholarships) include baseball (m), basketball, cross-country running (w), field hockey (w), golf (m), soccer (w), softball (w), swimming, tennis, volleyball, water polo.

Campus Safety

Student safety services include late-night transport/escort service, 24-hour emergency telephone alarm devices, 24-hour patrols by trained security personnel, and electronically operated dormitory entrances.

Applying

UOP requires an essay, SAT I or ACT, a high school transcript, 1 recommendation, and a minimum high school GPA of 2.5, and in some cases audition for music program. It recommends an interview and a minimum high school GPA of 3.0. Application deadline: 2/15; 2/15 priority date for financial aid. Early and deferred admission are possible.

Getting in Last Year
3,162 applied
78% were accepted
732 enrolled (30%)
38% from top tenth of their h.s. class
3.42 average high school GPA
28% had SAT verbal scores over 600
41% had SAT math scores over 600
50% had ACT scores over 24
4% had SAT verbal scores over 700
8% had SAT math scores over 700
6% had ACT scores over 30

Graduation and After
30% pursued further study
80 organizations recruited on campus

Financial Matters
$21,525 tuition and fees (2001–02)
$6730 room and board
$23,877 average financial aid amount received per undergraduate

UNIVERSITY OF THE SCIENCES IN PHILADELPHIA

URBAN SETTING ■ PRIVATE ■ INDEPENDENT ■ COED
PHILADELPHIA, PENNSYLVANIA

Web site: www.usip.edu

Contact: Mr. Louis L. Hegyes, Director of Admission, 600 South 43rd Street, Philadelphia, PA 19104-4495

Telephone: 215-596-8810 or toll-free 888-996-8747 (in-state) **Fax:** 215-596-8821

E-mail: admit@usip.edu

Getting in Last Year

1,301 applied
74% were accepted
304 enrolled (32%)
36% from top tenth of their h.s. class
3.40 average high school GPA
24% had SAT verbal scores over 600
29% had SAT math scores over 600
82% had ACT scores over 24
2% had SAT verbal scores over 700
3% had SAT math scores over 700
21% had ACT scores over 30

Graduation and After

15% pursued further study (8% medicine, 3% arts and sciences, 2% business)
95% had job offers within 6 months
30 organizations recruited on campus

Financial Matters

$18,062 tuition and fees (2001–02)
$7450 room and board

Academics

USP awards bachelor's, master's, doctoral, and first-professional **degrees**. Challenging opportunities include advanced placement credit, an honors program, double majors, and a senior project. Special programs include cooperative education, internships, summer session for credit, off-campus study, and Army ROTC.

The most frequently chosen **baccalaureate** fields are health professions and related sciences, biological/life sciences, and physical sciences. A complete listing of majors at USP appears in the Majors Index beginning on page 430.

The **faculty** at USP has 134 full-time members, 87% with terminal degrees. The student-faculty ratio is 15:1.

Students of USP

The student body totals 2,400, of whom 957 are undergraduates. 68.9% are women and 31.1% are men. Students come from 35 states and territories and 28 other countries. 53% are from Pennsylvania. 2% are international students. 6.8% are African American, 0.3% American Indian, 29% Asian American, and 2.7% Hispanic American. 87% returned for their sophomore year.

Facilities and Resources

Student rooms are linked to a campus network. 105 **computers** are available on campus that provide access to the Internet. The **library** has 76,000 books and 809 subscriptions.

Campus Life

There are 54 active organizations on campus, including a drama/theater group, newspaper, and choral group. 18% of eligible men and 12% of eligible women are members of national **fraternities**, national **sororities**, local fraternities, and local sororities.

USP is a member of the NCAA (Division II). **Intercollegiate sports** (some offering scholarships) include baseball (m), basketball, cross-country running, golf, riflery, softball (w), tennis, volleyball (w).

Campus Safety

Student safety services include late-night transport/escort service, 24-hour emergency telephone alarm devices, 24-hour patrols by trained security personnel, and electronically operated dormitory entrances.

Applying

USP requires SAT I or ACT and a high school transcript. It recommends SAT I and a minimum high school GPA of 3.0. Application deadline: rolling admissions; 3/15 priority date for financial aid. Early and deferred admission are possible.

University of the South

SMALL-TOWN SETTING ■ PRIVATE ■ INDEPENDENT RELIGIOUS ■ COED
SEWANEE, TENNESSEE

Web site: www.sewanee.edu
Contact: Mr. David Lesesne, Dean of Admission, 735 University Avenue, Sewanee, TN 37383
Telephone: 931-598-1238 or toll-free 800-522-2234 **Fax:** 931-598-3248
E-mail: admiss@sewanee.edu

Academics

Sewanee awards bachelor's, master's, doctoral, and first-professional **degrees**. Challenging opportunities include advanced placement credit, student-designed majors, double majors, independent study, and a senior project. Special programs include internships, summer session for credit, and study-abroad.

The most frequently chosen **baccalaureate** fields are social sciences and history, English, and visual/performing arts. A complete listing of majors at Sewanee appears in the Majors Index beginning on page 430.

The **faculty** at Sewanee has 127 full-time members, 96% with terminal degrees. The student-faculty ratio is 10:1.

Students of Sewanee

The student body totals 1,442, of whom 1,329 are undergraduates. 53% are women and 47% are men. Students come from 44 states and territories. 25% are from Tennessee. 1.2% are international students. 4.4% are African American, 0.2% American Indian, 1.2% Asian American, and 0.7% Hispanic American. 85% returned for their sophomore year.

Facilities and Resources

Student rooms are linked to a campus network. 92 **computers** are available on campus for student use. The **library** has 457,526 books and 6,495 subscriptions.

Campus Life

There are 110 active organizations on campus, including a drama/theater group, newspaper, radio station, and choral group. 65% of eligible men and 55% of eligible women are members of national **fraternities** and local **sororities**.

Sewanee is a member of the NCAA (Division III). **Intercollegiate sports** include baseball (m), basketball, cross-country running, field hockey (w), football (m), golf, soccer, swimming, tennis, track and field, volleyball (w).

Campus Safety

Student safety services include security lighting, late-night transport/escort service, 24-hour emergency telephone alarm devices, and 24-hour patrols by trained security personnel.

Applying

Sewanee requires an essay, SAT I or ACT, a high school transcript, and 2 recommendations. It recommends SAT II Subject Tests and an interview. Application deadline: 2/1; 3/1 priority date for financial aid. Early and deferred admission are possible.

Getting in Last Year
1,620 applied
74% were accepted
355 enrolled (30%)
43% from top tenth of their h.s. class
3.46 average high school GPA
61% had SAT verbal scores over 600
59% had SAT math scores over 600
78% had ACT scores over 24
13% had SAT verbal scores over 700
8% had SAT math scores over 700
17% had ACT scores over 30
13 National Merit Scholars

Graduation and After
38% pursued further study (14% arts and sciences, 6% law, 4% business)
74% had job offers within 6 months
17 organizations recruited on campus

Financial Matters
$21,340 tuition and fees (2001–02)
$5950 room and board
100% average percent of need met
$21,067 average financial aid amount received per undergraduate

University of Tulsa

Urban setting ■ Private ■ Independent Religious ■ Coed
Tulsa, Oklahoma

Web site: www.utulsa.edu
Contact: Mr. John C. Corso, Associate Vice President for Administration/ Dean of Admission, Office of Admission, The University of Tulsa, 600 South College Avenue, Tulsa, OK 74104
Telephone: 918-631-2307 or toll-free 800-331-3050 **Fax:** 918-631-5003
E-mail: admission@utulsa.edu

Getting in Last Year
2,235 applied
67% were accepted
498 enrolled (33%)
58% from top tenth of their h.s. class
3.70 average high school GPA
62% had SAT verbal scores over 600
60% had SAT math scores over 600
75% had ACT scores over 24
21% had SAT verbal scores over 700
20% had SAT math scores over 700
23% had ACT scores over 30
25 National Merit Scholars

Graduation and After
29% pursued further study (8% arts and sciences, 6% medicine, 5% business)
85% had job offers within 6 months
215 organizations recruited on campus

Financial Matters
$14,280 tuition and fees (2001–02)
$4810 room and board
80% average percent of need met
$13,275 average financial aid amount received per undergraduate

Academics

TU awards bachelor's, master's, doctoral, and first-professional **degrees** and first-professional certificates. Challenging opportunities include advanced placement credit, accelerated degree programs, student-designed majors, an honors program, double majors, independent study, and a senior project. Special programs include internships, summer session for credit, study-abroad, and Air Force ROTC.

The most frequently chosen **baccalaureate** fields are business/marketing, engineering/engineering technologies, and visual/performing arts. A complete listing of majors at TU appears in the Majors Index beginning on page 430.

The **faculty** at TU has 299 full-time members, 96% with terminal degrees. The student-faculty ratio is 11:1.

Students of TU

The student body totals 4,119, of whom 2,769 are undergraduates. 52.3% are women and 47.7% are men. Students come from 39 states and territories and 57 other countries. 77% are from Oklahoma. 11.1% are international students. 8% are African American, 5.5% American Indian, 2% Asian American, and 3.2% Hispanic American. 77% returned for their sophomore year.

Facilities and Resources

Student rooms are linked to a campus network. 718 **computers** are available on campus that provide access to the Internet. The 2 **libraries** have 900,000 books and 9,100 subscriptions.

Campus Life

There are 272 active organizations on campus, including a drama/theater group, newspaper, radio station, television station, choral group, and marching band. 21% of eligible men and 23% of eligible women are members of national **fraternities** and national **sororities**.

TU is a member of the NCAA (Division I). **Intercollegiate sports** (some offering scholarships) include basketball, crew (w), cross-country running, football (m), golf, soccer, softball (w), tennis, track and field, volleyball (w).

Campus Safety

Student safety services include late-night transport/escort service, 24-hour emergency telephone alarm devices, 24-hour patrols by trained security personnel, and electronically operated dormitory entrances.

Applying

TU requires SAT I or ACT, a high school transcript, and 1 recommendation. It recommends an essay, an interview, and a minimum high school GPA of 3.0. Application deadline: 4/1 priority date for financial aid. Early and deferred admission are possible.

UNIVERSITY OF VIRGINIA

SUBURBAN SETTING ■ PUBLIC ■ STATE-SUPPORTED ■ COED
CHARLOTTESVILLE, VIRGINIA

Web site: www.virginia.edu
Contact: Mr. John A. Blackburn, Dean of Admission, PO Box 400160,
Charlottesville, VA 22904-4160
Telephone: 434-982-3200 **Fax:** 434-924-3587
E-mail: undergrad-admission@virginia.edu

Academics

UVA awards bachelor's, master's, doctoral, and first-professional **degrees** and post-master's certificates. Challenging opportunities include advanced placement credit, accelerated degree programs, student-designed majors, an honors program, double majors, independent study, and a senior project. Special programs include cooperative education, internships, summer session for credit, study-abroad, and Army, Navy and Air Force ROTC.

The most frequently chosen **baccalaureate** fields are social sciences and history, engineering/engineering technologies, and business/marketing. A complete listing of majors at UVA appears in the Majors Index beginning on page 430.

The **faculty** at UVA has 1,093 full-time members, 92% with terminal degrees. The student-faculty ratio is 16:1.

Students of UVA

The student body totals 22,739, of whom 13,764 are undergraduates. 54.2% are women and 45.8% are men. Students come from 51 states and territories and 101 other countries. 71% are from Virginia. 4.4% are international students. 9.3% are African American, 0.4% American Indian, 10.8% Asian American, and 2.6% Hispanic American. 96% returned for their sophomore year.

Facilities and Resources

Student rooms are linked to a campus network. 1,859 **computers** are available on campus that provide access to the Internet. The 15 **libraries** have 3,258,758 books and 51,237 subscriptions.

Campus Life

There are 300 active organizations on campus, including a drama/theater group, newspaper, radio station, television station, and choral group. 30% of eligible men and 30% of eligible women are members of national **fraternities**, national **sororities**, and local fraternities.

UVA is a member of the NCAA (Division I). **Intercollegiate sports** (some offering scholarships) include baseball (m), basketball, crew (w), cross-country running, field hockey (w), football (m), golf (m), lacrosse, soccer, softball (w), swimming, tennis, track and field, volleyball (w), wrestling (m).

Campus Safety

Student safety services include late-night transport/escort service, 24-hour emergency telephone alarm devices, 24-hour patrols by trained security personnel, and electronically operated dormitory entrances.

Applying

UVA requires an essay, SAT II Subject Tests, SAT II: Writing Test, SAT I or ACT, a high school transcript, and 1 recommendation. Application deadline: 1/2; 3/1 priority date for financial aid. Deferred admission is possible.

Getting in Last Year

14,739 applied
38% were accepted
2,980 enrolled (54%)
82% from top tenth of their h.s. class
3.97 average high school GPA
77% had SAT verbal scores over 600
82% had SAT math scores over 600
83% had ACT scores over 24
30% had SAT verbal scores over 700
37% had SAT math scores over 700
44% had ACT scores over 30
177 valedictorians

Graduation and After

81% graduated in 4 years
9% graduated in 5 years
1% graduated in 6 years
32% pursued further study
450 organizations recruited on campus

Financial Matters

$4421 resident tuition and fees (2001–02)
$18,453 nonresident tuition and fees (2001–02)
$4970 room and board
92% average percent of need met
$10,774 average financial aid amount received per undergraduate

University of Washington

Urban setting ■ Public ■ State-supported ■ Coed
Seattle, Washington

Web site: www.washington.edu
Contact: Ms. Stephanie Preston, Assistant Director of Admissions, Seattle,
  WA 98195
Telephone: 206-543-9686
E-mail: askuwadm@u.washington.edu

Getting in Last Year
14,666 applied
79% were accepted
5,210 enrolled (45%)
43% from top tenth of their h.s. class
3.67 average high school GPA
37% had SAT verbal scores over 600
48% had SAT math scores over 600
14% had ACT scores over 24
7% had SAT verbal scores over 700
11% had SAT math scores over 700
3% had ACT scores over 30

Graduation and After
450 organizations recruited on campus

Financial Matters
$3983 resident tuition and fees (2001–02)
$13,258 nonresident tuition and fees (2001–02)
$6378 room and board
88% average percent of need met
$9815 average financial aid amount received per undergraduate

Academics

UW awards bachelor's, master's, doctoral, and first-professional **degrees**. Challenging opportunities include advanced placement credit, accelerated degree programs, student-designed majors, an honors program, double majors, independent study, and a senior project. Special programs include cooperative education, internships, summer session for credit, study-abroad, and Army, Navy and Air Force ROTC.

The most frequently chosen **baccalaureate** fields are social sciences and history, business/marketing, and biological/life sciences. A complete listing of majors at UW appears in the Majors Index beginning on page 430.

The **faculty** at UW has 2,662 full-time members, 90% with terminal degrees. The student-faculty ratio is 11:1.

Students of UW

The student body totals 37,412, of whom 26,860 are undergraduates. 51.4% are women and 48.6% are men. Students come from 52 states and territories and 59 other countries. 89% are from Washington. 2.9% are international students. 2.6% are African American, 1.1% American Indian, 23.3% Asian American, and 3.6% Hispanic American. 90% returned for their sophomore year.

Facilities and Resources

Student rooms are linked to a campus network. 285 **computers** are available on campus for student use. The 22 **libraries** have 5,820,229 books and 50,245 subscriptions.

Campus Life

There are 300 active organizations on campus, including a drama/theater group, newspaper, radio station, television station, choral group, and marching band. 12% of eligible men and 11% of eligible women are members of national **fraternities** and national **sororities**.

UW is a member of the NCAA (Division I). **Intercollegiate sports** (some offering scholarships) include baseball (m), basketball, crew, cross-country running, football (m), golf, gymnastics (w), soccer, softball (w), swimming, tennis, track and field, volleyball (w).

Campus Safety

Student safety services include late-night transport/escort service, 24-hour emergency telephone alarm devices, 24-hour patrols by trained security personnel, and electronically operated dormitory entrances.

Applying

UW requires an essay, SAT I or ACT, a high school transcript, and a minimum high school GPA of 2.0. Application deadline: 1/15; 2/28 priority date for financial aid. Early admission is possible.

University of Waterloo

Suburban setting ■ Public ■ Coed
Waterloo, Ontario

Web site: www.uwaterloo.ca
Contact: Mr. P. Burroughs, Director of Admissions, 200 University Avenue
West, Waterloo, ON N2L 3G1 Canada
Telephone: 519-888-4567 ext. 2265 **Fax:** 519-746-8088 ext. 3614
E-mail: watquest@uwaterloo.ca

Getting in Last Year
23,557 applied
61% were accepted
3.50 average high school GPA

Financial Matters
$4545 nonresident tuition and fees (2001–02)
$5950 room and board

Academics

University of Waterloo awards bachelor's, master's, doctoral, and first-professional **degrees**. Challenging opportunities include accelerated degree programs, student-designed majors, an honors program, double majors, independent study, and a senior project. Special programs include cooperative education, internships, summer session for credit, off-campus study, and study-abroad.

The most frequently chosen **baccalaureate** fields are engineering/engineering technologies, computer/information sciences, and social sciences and history. A complete listing of majors at University of Waterloo appears in the Majors Index beginning on page 430.

The **faculty** at University of Waterloo has 769 full-time members. The student-faculty ratio is 15:1.

Students of University of Waterloo

The student body totals 22,127, of whom 20,064 are undergraduates. 47.9% are women and 52.1% are men. Students come from 12 states and territories and 73 other countries. 99% are from Ontario. 85% returned for their sophomore year.

Facilities and Resources

Student rooms are linked to a campus network. 6,000 **computers** are available on campus that provide access to e-mail and the Internet. The 8 **libraries** have 2,850,000 books and 13,228 subscriptions.

Campus Life

There are 65 active organizations on campus, including a drama/theater group, newspaper, radio station, and choral group. 1% of eligible men and 1% of eligible women are members of national **fraternities** and national **sororities**.

Intercollegiate sports include badminton, baseball (m), basketball, cross-country running, field hockey (w), football (m), golf (m), ice hockey, rugby, skiing (downhill), soccer, squash (m), swimming, tennis, track and field, volleyball.

Campus Safety

Student safety services include late-night transport/escort service, 24-hour emergency telephone alarm devices, 24-hour patrols by trained security personnel, and student patrols.

Applying

University of Waterloo requires a high school transcript, and in some cases an essay, SAT II Subject Tests, SAT I or ACT, an interview, recommendations, and a minimum high school GPA of 3.0. Application deadline: 7/1 priority date for financial aid. Early admission is possible.

UNIVERSITY OF WISCONSIN–MADISON

URBAN SETTING ■ PUBLIC ■ STATE-SUPPORTED ■ COED
MADISON, WISCONSIN

Web site: www.wisc.edu
Contact: Mr. Keith White, Office of Admissions, 716 Langdon Street, Madison, WI 53706-1400
Telephone: 608-262-3961 **Fax:** 608-262-7706
E-mail: on.wisconsin@mail.admin.wisc.edu

Getting in Last Year

20,330 applied
57% were accepted
50% from top tenth of their h.s. class
3.80 average high school GPA
69% had SAT verbal scores over 600
76% had SAT math scores over 600
86% had ACT scores over 24
25% had SAT verbal scores over 700
23% had SAT math scores over 700
35% had ACT scores over 30
182 National Merit Scholars
595 valedictorians

Graduation and After

69% pursued further study

Financial Matters

$4086 resident tuition and fees (2001–02)
$15,972 nonresident tuition and fees (2001–02)
$5700 room and board
$7926 average financial aid amount received per undergraduate (2000–01)

Academics

Wisconsin awards bachelor's, master's, doctoral, and first-professional **degrees**. Challenging opportunities include advanced placement credit, accelerated degree programs, student-designed majors, freshman honors college, an honors program, double majors, independent study, and a senior project. Special programs include cooperative education, internships, summer session for credit, study-abroad, and Army, Navy and Air Force ROTC. A complete listing of majors at Wisconsin appears in the Majors Index beginning on page 430.

The **faculty** at Wisconsin has 2,219 full-time members, 99% with terminal degrees. The student-faculty ratio is 14:1.

Students of Wisconsin

The student body totals 41,552, of whom 28,788 are undergraduates. Students come from 52 states and territories and 116 other countries. 61% are from Wisconsin. 4.2% are international students. 2.2% are African American, 0.5% American Indian, 4.2% Asian American, and 2.2% Hispanic American. 96% returned for their sophomore year.

Facilities and Resources

Student rooms are linked to a campus network. 2,800 **computers** are available on campus that provide access to the Internet. The 41 **libraries** have 6,100,000 books and 66,000 subscriptions.

Campus Life

There are 690 active organizations on campus, including a drama/theater group, newspaper, radio station, choral group, and marching band. 20% of eligible men and 20% of eligible women are members of national **fraternities**, national **sororities**, and eating clubs.

Wisconsin is a member of the NCAA (Division I). **Intercollegiate sports** (some offering scholarships) include basketball, crew, cross-country running, football (m), golf, ice hockey, lacrosse (w), soccer, softball (w), swimming, tennis, track and field, volleyball (w), wrestling (m).

Campus Safety

Student safety services include free cab rides throughout city, late-night transport/escort service, 24-hour emergency telephone alarm devices, 24-hour patrols by trained security personnel, and electronically operated dormitory entrances.

Applying

Wisconsin requires an essay, SAT I or ACT, and a high school transcript, and in some cases SAT II Subject Tests. It recommends SAT II Subject Tests. Application deadline: 2/1. Early and deferred admission are possible.

URSINUS COLLEGE

SUBURBAN SETTING ■ PRIVATE ■ INDEPENDENT RELIGIOUS ■ COED
COLLEGEVILLE, PENNSYLVANIA

Web site: www.ursinus.edu
Contact: Mr. Paul M. Cramer, Director of Admissions, Box 1000,
  Collegeville, PA 19426
Telephone: 610-409-3200 **Fax:** 610-409-3662
E-mail: admissions@ursinus.edu

Academics

Ursinus awards bachelor's **degrees**. Challenging opportunities include advanced placement credit, student-designed majors, an honors program, double majors, independent study, and a senior project. Special programs include internships, off-campus study, and study-abroad. A complete listing of majors at Ursinus appears in the Majors Index beginning on page 430.

The **faculty** at Ursinus has 97 full-time members, 87% with terminal degrees. The student-faculty ratio is 11:1.

Students of Ursinus

The student body is made up of 1,340 undergraduates. 57% are women and 43% are men. Students come from 25 states and territories and 19 other countries. 72% are from Pennsylvania. 3.4% are international students. 7.4% are African American, 0.1% American Indian, 3.4% Asian American, and 1.9% Hispanic American. 94% returned for their sophomore year.

Facilities and Resources

Student rooms are linked to a campus network. 350 **computers** are available on campus that provide access to class of 2004, all freshmen receive a laptop computer and the Internet. The 3 **libraries** have 200,000 books and 900 subscriptions.

Campus Life

There are 116 active organizations on campus, including a drama/theater group, newspaper, radio station, television station, and choral group. 30% of eligible men and 25% of eligible women are members of national **fraternities**, local fraternities, and local **sororities**.

Ursinus is a member of the NCAA (Division III). **Intercollegiate sports** include baseball (m), basketball, cross-country running, field hockey (w), football (m), golf, gymnastics (w), lacrosse, soccer, softball (w), swimming, tennis, track and field, volleyball (w), wrestling (m).

Campus Safety

Student safety services include late-night transport/escort service, 24-hour emergency telephone alarm devices, and 24-hour patrols by trained security personnel.

Applying

Ursinus requires an essay, SAT I or ACT, a high school transcript, 2 recommendations, and graded paper. It recommends SAT II Subject Tests and an interview. Application deadline: 2/15; 2/15 priority date for financial aid. Early and deferred admission are possible.

Getting in Last Year

1,562 applied
78% were accepted
392 enrolled (32%)
40% from top tenth of their h.s. class
3.5 average high school GPA
53% had SAT verbal scores over 600
57% had SAT math scores over 600
13% had SAT verbal scores over 700
7% had SAT math scores over 700
2 National Merit Scholars
8 class presidents
7 valedictorians

Graduation and After

70% graduated in 4 years
4% graduated in 5 years
32% pursued further study (21% arts and sciences, 8% medicine, 2% law)
60% had job offers within 6 months
50 organizations recruited on campus

Financial Matters

$24,850 tuition and fees (2001–02)
$6500 room and board
90% average percent of need met
$21,080 average financial aid amount received per undergraduate

VALPARAISO UNIVERSITY

SMALL-TOWN SETTING ■ PRIVATE ■ INDEPENDENT RELIGIOUS ■ COED
VALPARAISO, INDIANA

Web site: www.valpo.edu
Contact: Ms. Karen Foust, Director of Admissions, 651 South College
Avenue, Valparaiso, IN 46383-6493
Telephone: 219-464-5011 or toll-free 888-GO-VALPO (out-of-state) **Fax:**
219-464-6898
E-mail: undergrad.admissions@valpo.edu

Valparaiso University is home to 3,600 students seeking academic excellence in the Colleges of Arts & Sciences, Business Administration, Engineering, and Nursing and Christ College—The Honors College. Nestled in a residential community of 26,000, the University offers 60 major areas of study in the liberal arts within a Christian atmosphere. America's only independent Lutheran university, "Valpo" is consistently ranked by *U.S. News & World Report* as a top regional university and best value. A low student-faculty ratio strengthens mentoring relationships. The required interdisciplinary freshman curriculum, Valpo Core, fosters a sense of true community. A nonbinding early action admission option allows applicants to submit applications to Valpo no later than November 1.

Academics

Valpo awards associate, bachelor's, master's, and first-professional **degrees** and post-master's certificates. Challenging opportunities include advanced placement credit, accelerated degree programs, student-designed majors, freshman honors college, an honors program, double majors, independent study, and a senior project. Special programs include cooperative education, internships, summer session for credit, off-campus study, study-abroad, and Air Force ROTC.

The most frequently chosen **baccalaureate** fields are business/marketing, education, and engineering/engineering technologies. A complete listing of majors at Valpo appears in the Majors Index beginning on page 430.

The **faculty** at Valpo has 215 full-time members, 88% with terminal degrees. The student-faculty ratio is 13:1.

Students of Valpo

The student body totals 3,533, of whom 2,873 are undergraduates. 53.1% are women and 46.9% are men. Students come from 47 states and territories and 48 other countries. 35% are from Indiana. 3.5% are international students. 2.8% are African American, 0.5% American Indian, 1.8% Asian American, and 2.6% Hispanic American. 86% returned for their sophomore year.

Facilities and Resources

Student rooms are linked to a campus network. 580 **computers** are available on campus that provide access to the Internet. The 2 **libraries** have 714,657 books and 16,158 subscriptions.

Campus Life

There are 100 active organizations on campus, including a drama/theater group, newspaper, radio station, and choral group. 30% of eligible men and 30% of eligible women are members of national **fraternities** and local **sororities**.

Valpo is a member of the NCAA (Division I). **Intercollegiate sports** (some offering scholarships) include baseball (m), basketball, cross-country running, football (m), soccer, softball (w), swimming, tennis, volleyball (w).

Campus Safety

Student safety services include late-night transport/escort service, 24-hour emergency telephone alarm devices, 24-hour patrols by trained security personnel, and electronically operated dormitory entrances.

Applying

Valpo requires SAT I or ACT and a high school transcript, and in some cases an interview. It recommends an essay and 2 recommendations. Application deadline: 8/15; 3/1 priority date for financial aid. Deferred admission is possible.

Getting in Last Year
3,173 applied
80% were accepted
663 enrolled (26%)
40% from top tenth of their h.s. class
46% had SAT verbal scores over 600
44% had SAT math scores over 600
78% had ACT scores over 24
10% had SAT verbal scores over 700
13% had SAT math scores over 700
24% had ACT scores over 30
19 National Merit Scholars
27 valedictorians

Graduation and After
52% graduated in 4 years
18% graduated in 5 years
2% graduated in 6 years
23% pursued further study (6% law, 2% education, 2% medicine)
71% had job offers within 6 months
74 organizations recruited on campus

Financial Matters
$18,700 tuition and fees (2001–02)
$4870 room and board
86% average percent of need met
$15,250 average financial aid amount received per undergraduate

VANDERBILT UNIVERSITY

URBAN SETTING ■ PRIVATE ■ INDEPENDENT ■ COED
NASHVILLE, TENNESSEE

Web site: www.vanderbilt.edu
Contact: Mr. Bill Shain, Dean of Undergraduate Admissions, Nashville, TN
37240-1001
Telephone: 615-322-2561 or toll-free 800-288-0432 **Fax:** 615-343-7765
E-mail: admissions@vanderbilt.edu

Academics

Vanderbilt awards bachelor's, master's, doctoral, and first-professional **degrees**. Challenging opportunities include advanced placement credit, accelerated degree programs, student-designed majors, an honors program, double majors, independent study, and a senior project. Special programs include cooperative education, summer session for credit, off-campus study, study-abroad, and Army, Navy and Air Force ROTC.

The most frequently chosen **baccalaureate** fields are social sciences and history, engineering/engineering technologies, and biological/life sciences. A complete listing of majors at Vanderbilt appears in the Majors Index beginning on page 430.

The **faculty** at Vanderbilt has 690 full-time members, 97% with terminal degrees. The student-faculty ratio is 9:1.

Students of Vanderbilt

The student body totals 10,338, of whom 6,077 are undergraduates. 51.8% are women and 48.2% are men. Students come from 54 states and territories and 36 other countries. 20% are from Tennessee. 2.7% are international students. 5.9% are African American, 0.2% American Indian, 6.3% Asian American, and 3.8% Hispanic American. 94% returned for their sophomore year.

Facilities and Resources

Student rooms are linked to a campus network. 400 **computers** are available on campus that provide access to productivity and educational software. The 8 **libraries** have 1,668,985 books and 21,608 subscriptions.

Campus Life

There are 264 active organizations on campus, including a drama/theater group, newspaper, radio station, choral group, and marching band. 34% of eligible men and 48% of eligible women are members of national **fraternities** and national **sororities**.

Vanderbilt is a member of the NCAA (Division I). **Intercollegiate sports** (some offering scholarships) include baseball (m), basketball, cross-country running, football (m), golf, lacrosse (w), soccer, tennis, track and field (w).

Campus Safety

Student safety services include late-night transport/escort service, 24-hour emergency telephone alarm devices, 24-hour patrols by trained security personnel, student patrols, and electronically operated dormitory entrances.

Applying

Vanderbilt requires an essay, SAT I or ACT, a high school transcript, and 2 recommendations. It recommends SAT II Subject Tests and SAT II: Writing Test. Application deadline: 1/4; 2/1 priority date for financial aid. Early and deferred admission are possible.

Getting in Last Year
9,746 applied
46% were accepted
1,557 enrolled (34%)
74% from top tenth of their h.s. class
79% had SAT verbal scores over 600
87% had SAT math scores over 600
96% had ACT scores over 24
24% had SAT verbal scores over 700
36% had SAT math scores over 700
46% had ACT scores over 30
85 National Merit Scholars
30 class presidents
101 valedictorians

Graduation and After
32% pursued further study (20% arts and sciences, 7% law, 4% medicine)
63% had job offers within 6 months
250 organizations recruited on campus

Financial Matters
$25,847 tuition and fees (2001–02)
$8635 room and board
99% average percent of need met
$24,812 average financial aid amount received per undergraduate

VASSAR COLLEGE
SUBURBAN SETTING ■ PRIVATE ■ INDEPENDENT ■ COED
POUGHKEEPSIE, NEW YORK

Web site: www.vassar.edu
Contact: Dr. David M. Borus, Dean of Admission and Financial Aid, 124 Raymond Avenue, Poughkeepsie, NY 12604
Telephone: 845-437-7300 or toll-free 800-827-7270 **Fax:** 914-437-7063
E-mail: admissions@vassar.edu

Getting in Last Year
5,690 applied
34% were accepted
696 enrolled (36%)
61% from top tenth of their h.s. class
3.60 average high school GPA
93% had SAT verbal scores over 600
87% had SAT math scores over 600
44% had SAT verbal scores over 700
27% had SAT math scores over 700
37 class presidents
31 valedictorians

Graduation and After
81% graduated in 4 years
5% graduated in 5 years
1% graduated in 6 years
17% pursued further study (9% arts and sciences, 4% law, 2% medicine)
69% had job offers within 6 months
25 organizations recruited on campus

Financial Matters
$26,290 tuition and fees (2001–02)
$7160 room and board
100% average percent of need met
$20,835 average financial aid amount received per undergraduate (2000–01 estimated)

Academics
Vassar awards bachelor's and master's **degrees**. Challenging opportunities include advanced placement credit, student-designed majors, double majors, independent study, and a senior project. Special programs include internships, off-campus study, and study-abroad.

The most frequently chosen **baccalaureate** fields are social sciences and history, visual/performing arts, and English. A complete listing of majors at Vassar appears in the Majors Index beginning on page 430.

The **faculty** at Vassar has 246 full-time members, 95% with terminal degrees. The student-faculty ratio is 9:1.

Students of Vassar
The student body is made up of 2,439 undergraduates. 61.3% are women and 38.7% are men. Students come from 52 states and territories and 43 other countries. 33% are from New York. 4.3% are international students. 4.7% are African American, 0.4% American Indian, 8.6% Asian American, and 5.3% Hispanic American. 94% returned for their sophomore year.

Facilities and Resources
Student rooms are linked to a campus network. 300 **computers** are available on campus that provide access to Ethernet and the Internet. The **library** has 803,021 books and 5,887 subscriptions.

Campus Life
There are 100 active organizations on campus, including a drama/theater group, newspaper, radio station, and choral group. No national or local **fraternities** or **sororities**.

Vassar is a member of the NCAA (Division III). **Intercollegiate sports** include baseball (m), basketball, crew, cross-country running, fencing, field hockey (w), lacrosse, soccer, squash, swimming, tennis, volleyball.

Campus Safety
Student safety services include late-night transport/escort service, 24-hour emergency telephone alarm devices, 24-hour patrols by trained security personnel, student patrols, and electronically operated dormitory entrances.

Applying
Vassar requires an essay, SAT I and SAT II or ACT, a high school transcript, and 2 recommendations. It recommends an interview. Application deadline: 1/1; 1/10 for financial aid. Deferred admission is possible.

VILLANOVA UNIVERSITY

SUBURBAN SETTING ■ PRIVATE ■ INDEPENDENT RELIGIOUS ■ COED
VILLANOVA, PENNSYLVANIA

Web site: www.villanova.edu
Contact: Mr. Michael M. Gaynor, Director of University Admission, 800
  Lancaster Avenue, Villanova, PA 19085-1672
Telephone: 610-519-4000 **Fax:** 610-519-6450
E-mail: gotovu@villanova.edu

Academics

Villanova awards associate, bachelor's, master's, doctoral, and first-professional **degrees**. Challenging opportunities include advanced placement credit, accelerated degree programs, an honors program, double majors, independent study, and a senior project. Special programs include internships, summer session for credit, off-campus study, study-abroad, and Army, Navy and Air Force ROTC.

The most frequently chosen **baccalaureate** fields are business/marketing, social sciences and history, and engineering/engineering technologies. A complete listing of majors at Villanova appears in the Majors Index beginning on page 430.

The **faculty** at Villanova has 507 full-time members, 90% with terminal degrees. The student-faculty ratio is 13:1.

Students of Villanova

The student body totals 10,156, of whom 7,314 are undergraduates. 50.6% are women and 49.4% are men. Students come from 50 states and territories and 30 other countries. 32% are from Pennsylvania. 2.1% are international students. 2.8% are African American, 0.1% American Indian, 4.3% Asian American, and 4.6% Hispanic American. 94% returned for their sophomore year.

Facilities and Resources

Student rooms are linked to a campus network. 800 **computers** are available on campus that provide access to the Internet. The 3 **libraries** have 1,010,560 books and 5,338 subscriptions.

Campus Life

There are 100 active organizations on campus, including a drama/theater group, newspaper, radio station, television station, choral group, and marching band. 18% of eligible men and 34% of eligible women are members of national **fraternities** and national **sororities**.

Villanova is a member of the NCAA (Division I). **Intercollegiate sports** (some offering scholarships) include baseball (m), basketball, crew (w), cross-country running, field hockey (w), football (m), golf (m), lacrosse, soccer, softball (w), swimming, tennis, track and field, volleyball (w), water polo (w).

Campus Safety

Student safety services include late-night transport/escort service, 24-hour emergency telephone alarm devices, 24-hour patrols by trained security personnel, student patrols, and electronically operated dormitory entrances.

Applying

Villanova requires an essay, SAT I or ACT, a high school transcript, and activities resume. Application deadline: 1/7; 2/15 priority date for financial aid. Early and deferred admission are possible.

> **V**ision and education go hand in hand at Villanova. The University invests in students' futures by updating its facilities and resources. Three of its newest initiatives include the construction of the $20-million Center for Engineering Education and Research, the completion of $35 million in expansion and enhancement of the Mendel Science Center, and $20 million in renovation of the College of Commerce and Finance's Bartley Hall. Overall in the last 10 years, Villanova has dedicated more than $200 million to these initiatives and more, including 4 new apartment-style buildings, the new Student Health Center, and improvements to the computing infrastructure.

Getting in Last Year
10,291 applied
50% were accepted
1,743 enrolled (34%)
43% from top tenth of their h.s. class
3.64 average high school GPA
56% had SAT verbal scores over 600
73% had SAT math scores over 600
7% had SAT verbal scores over 700
14% had SAT math scores over 700
14 valedictorians

Graduation and After
79% graduated in 4 years
4% graduated in 5 years
2% graduated in 6 years
Graduates pursuing further study: 7% arts and sciences, 7% business, 4% law
78% had job offers within 6 months
375 organizations recruited on campus

Financial Matters
$23,727 tuition and fees (2001–02)
$8270 room and board
78% average percent of need met
$16,390 average financial aid amount received per undergraduate

VIRGINIA MILITARY INSTITUTE

SMALL-TOWN SETTING ■ PUBLIC ■ STATE-SUPPORTED ■ COED, PRIMARILY MEN
LEXINGTON, VIRGINIA

Web site: www.vmi.edu
Contact: Lt. Col. Tom Mortenson, Associate Director of Admissions, 309
   Letcher Avenue, Lexington, VA 24450
Telephone: 540-464-7211 or toll-free 800-767-4207 **Fax:** 540-464-7746
E-mail: admissions@vmi.edu

V MI offers a challenging curricular and cocurricular undergraduate experience, with the mission of producing educated and honorable men and women who will be leaders in all walks of life. Its 1,250 cadets pursue BA or BS degrees in 14 disciplines in the general fields of engineering, science, and liberal arts. VMI combines a full college curriculum within a framework of military discipline that emphasizes the qualities of honor, integrity, and responsibility. Undergirding all aspects of cadet life is the VMI Honor Code, to which all cadets subscribe.

Academics

VMI awards bachelor's **degrees**. Challenging opportunities include advanced placement credit, accelerated degree programs, an honors program, double majors, independent study, and a senior project. Special programs include internships, summer session for credit, study-abroad, and Army, Navy and Air Force ROTC. A complete listing of majors at VMI appears in the Majors Index beginning on page 430.

The **faculty** at VMI has 100 full-time members, 94% with terminal degrees. The student-faculty ratio is 11:1.

Students of VMI

The student body is made up of 1,311 undergraduates. Students come from 44 states and territories and 19 other countries. 53% are from Virginia. 3.1% are international students. 5.3% are African American, 0.5% American Indian, 3.8% Asian American, and 3.1% Hispanic American. 86% returned for their sophomore year.

Facilities and Resources

Student rooms are linked to a campus network. 200 **computers** are available on campus that provide access to the Internet. The 2 **libraries** have 507,133 books and 162,053 subscriptions.

Campus Life

There are 47 active organizations on campus, including a drama/theater group, newspaper, choral group, and marching band. No national or local **fraternities** or **sororities**.

VMI is a member of the NCAA (Division I). **Intercollegiate sports** (some offering scholarships) include baseball (m), basketball (m), cross-country running, football (m), golf (m), lacrosse (m), riflery, soccer (m), swimming, tennis (m), track and field, wrestling (m).

Campus Safety

Student safety services include 24-hour emergency telephone alarm devices, 24-hour patrols by trained security personnel, and student patrols.

Applying

VMI requires SAT I or ACT and a high school transcript. It recommends an essay, an interview, and 2 recommendations. Application deadline: 3/1; 3/1 priority date for financial aid.

Getting in Last Year
1,349 applied
63% were accepted
352 enrolled (42%)
15% from top tenth of their h.s. class
3.28 average high school GPA
29% had SAT verbal scores over 600
37% had SAT math scores over 600
42% had ACT scores over 24
5% had SAT verbal scores over 700
3% had SAT math scores over 700
7% had ACT scores over 30

Graduation and After
47% graduated in 4 years
14% graduated in 5 years
4% graduated in 6 years
Graduates pursuing further study: 9% arts and
   sciences, 7% engineering, 1% dentistry
98% had job offers within 6 months
40 organizations recruited on campus

Financial Matters
$5130 resident tuition and fees (2001–02)
$16,198 nonresident tuition and fees (2001–
   02)
$4838 room and board
93% average percent of need met
$12,838 average financial aid amount received
   per undergraduate

VIRGINIA POLYTECHNIC INSTITUTE AND STATE UNIVERSITY

SMALL-TOWN SETTING ■ PUBLIC ■ STATE-SUPPORTED ■ COED
BLACKSBURG, VIRGINIA

Web site: 00
Contact: Ms. Mildred Johnson, Associate Director for Freshmen Admissions,
201 Burruss Hall, Blacksburg, VA 24061
Telephone: 540-231-6267 **Fax:** 540-231-3242
E-mail: vtadmiss@vt.edu

Academics

Virginia Tech awards associate, bachelor's, master's, doctoral, and first-professional **degrees**. Challenging opportunities include advanced placement credit, accelerated degree programs, an honors program, double majors, independent study, and a senior project. Special programs include cooperative education, internships, summer session for credit, off-campus study, study-abroad, and Army and Air Force ROTC. A complete listing of majors at Virginia Tech appears in the Majors Index beginning on page 430.

The **faculty** at Virginia Tech has 1,242 full-time members. The student-faculty ratio is 23:1.

Students of Virginia Tech

The student body totals 26,490, of whom 21,869 are undergraduates. 40.1% are women and 59.9% are men. Students come from 52 states and territories and 104 other countries. 73% are from Virginia. 2.7% are international students. 5% are African American, 0.2% American Indian, 6.8% Asian American, and 2.2% Hispanic American. 90% returned for their sophomore year.

Facilities and Resources

Student rooms are linked to a campus network. The 5 **libraries** have 2,005,765 books and 18,281 subscriptions.

Campus Life

There are 437 active organizations on campus, including a drama/theater group, newspaper, radio station, television station, choral group, and marching band. 13% of eligible men and 15% of eligible women are members of national **fraternities**, national **sororities**, and local fraternities.

Virginia Tech is a member of the NCAA (Division I). **Intercollegiate sports** (some offering scholarships) include baseball (m), basketball, cross-country running, football (m), golf (m), lacrosse (w), soccer, softball (w), swimming, tennis, track and field, volleyball (w), wrestling (m).

Campus Safety

Student safety services include late-night transport/escort service, 24-hour emergency telephone alarm devices, 24-hour patrols by trained security personnel, student patrols, and electronically operated dormitory entrances.

Applying

Virginia Tech requires SAT I or ACT, a high school transcript, and a minimum high school GPA of 2.0. It recommends a minimum high school GPA of 3.3. Application deadline: 1/15; 3/1 priority date for financial aid. Early and deferred admission are possible.

Students wishing to learn in a high-technology environment choose Virginia Tech, the largest university in Virginia and the commonwealth's top research university. A leading magazine ranked Virginia Tech 5th in the nation for best value in schools specializing in science and technical programs. Tech was also named one of the most wired colleges in America for its innovative use of technology in the classroom (from English to engineering) and free student e-mail and Internet access. (Virginia Tech even prefers that students apply online!) Undergraduate research opportunities and cutting-edge facilities make Virginia Tech the high-tech choice.

Getting in Last Year
18,800 applied
66% were accepted
5,007 enrolled (40%)
39% from top tenth of their h.s. class
3.56 average high school GPA
39% had SAT verbal scores over 600
52% had SAT math scores over 600
5% had SAT verbal scores over 700
11% had SAT math scores over 700

Graduation and After
36% graduated in 4 years
31% graduated in 5 years
5% graduated in 6 years
13% pursued further study
79% had job offers within 6 months
475 organizations recruited on campus

Financial Matters
$3664 resident tuition and fees (2001–02)
$12,488 nonresident tuition and fees (2001–02)
$4032 room and board
68% average percent of need met
$7488 average financial aid amount received per undergraduate

WABASH COLLEGE

SMALL-TOWN SETTING ■ PRIVATE ■ INDEPENDENT ■ MEN ONLY
CRAWFORDSVILLE, INDIANA

Web site: www.wabash.edu
Contact: Mr. Steve Klein, Director of Admissions, PO Box 362, Crawfordsville, IN 47933-0352
Telephone: 765-361-6225 or toll-free 800-345-5385 **Fax:** 765-361-6437
E-mail: admissions@wabash.edu

As a college for men, Wabash helps students achieve their full potential—intellectually, athletically, emotionally, and artistically. Wabash prepares students for leadership in an ever-changing world. The College helps them learn to think clearly and openly and to explore a variety of interests. Independence and responsibility are emphasized and defined by the Gentlemen's Rule, which calls on students to conduct themselves as gentlemen at all times. With the guidance of professors who are accessible, a support staff that cares, and a nationwide network of alumni willing to offer assistance and encouragement, Wabash men frequently surpass even their own expectations.

Getting in Last Year
1,133 applied
55% were accepted
232 enrolled (38%)
36% from top tenth of their h.s. class
3.57 average high school GPA
46% had SAT verbal scores over 600
58% had SAT math scores over 600
73% had ACT scores over 24
10% had SAT verbal scores over 700
11% had SAT math scores over 700
17% had ACT scores over 30
2 National Merit Scholars
10 class presidents
9 valedictorians

Graduation and After
66% graduated in 4 years
3% graduated in 5 years
40% pursued further study (11% law, 10% arts and sciences, 9% theology)
60% had job offers within 6 months
40 organizations recruited on campus

Financial Matters
$19,243 tuition and fees (2001–02)
$6092 room and board
100% average percent of need met
$18,472 average financial aid amount received per undergraduate

Academics

Wabash awards bachelor's **degrees**. Challenging opportunities include advanced placement credit, accelerated degree programs, double majors, independent study, and a senior project. Special programs include cooperative education, internships, off-campus study, study-abroad, and Army ROTC.

The most frequently chosen **baccalaureate** fields are social sciences and history, English, and biological/life sciences. A complete listing of majors at Wabash appears in the Majors Index beginning on page 430.

The **faculty** at Wabash has 79 full-time members, 99% with terminal degrees. The student-faculty ratio is 11:1.

Students of Wabash

The student body is made up of 849 undergraduates. Students come from 35 states and territories and 14 other countries. 75% are from Indiana. 3.9% are international students. 6.6% are African American, 0.4% American Indian, 2.6% Asian American, and 5.2% Hispanic American. 86% returned for their sophomore year.

Facilities and Resources

Student rooms are linked to a campus network. 131 **computers** are available on campus that provide access to the Internet. The **library** has 416,798 books and 1,422 subscriptions.

Campus Life

There are 40 active organizations on campus, including a drama/theater group, newspaper, radio station, and choral group. 75% of eligible undergraduates are members of national **fraternities** and language houses.

Wabash is a member of the NCAA (Division III). **Intercollegiate sports** include baseball, basketball, cross-country running, football, golf, soccer, swimming, tennis, track and field, wrestling.

Campus Safety

Student safety services include late-night transport/escort service, 24-hour emergency telephone alarm devices, and 24-hour patrols by trained security personnel.

Applying

Wabash requires an essay, SAT I or ACT, a high school transcript, 1 recommendation, and a minimum high school GPA of 2.0. It recommends an interview and a minimum high school GPA of 3.0. Application deadline: 3/15; 3/1 for financial aid, with a 2/15 priority date. Early and deferred admission are possible.

WAKE FOREST UNIVERSITY

SUBURBAN SETTING ■ PRIVATE ■ INDEPENDENT RELIGIOUS ■ COED
WINSTON-SALEM, NORTH CAROLINA

Web site: www.wfu.edu
Contact: Martha Allman, Director of Admissions, PO Box 7305,
   Winston-Salem, NC 27109
Telephone: 336-758-5201 **Fax:** 336-758-6074
E-mail: admissions@wfu.edu

Academics

Wake Forest awards bachelor's, master's, doctoral, and first-professional **degrees**. Challenging opportunities include advanced placement credit, accelerated degree programs, student-designed majors, an honors program, double majors, independent study, and a senior project. Special programs include internships, summer session for credit, off-campus study, study-abroad, and Army ROTC.

The most frequently chosen **baccalaureate** fields are social sciences and history, business/marketing, and communications/communication technologies. A complete listing of majors at Wake Forest appears in the Majors Index beginning on page 430.

The **faculty** at Wake Forest has 427 full-time members, 89% with terminal degrees. The student-faculty ratio is 10:1.

Students of Wake Forest

The student body totals 6,216, of whom 3,987 are undergraduates. 51.1% are women and 48.9% are men. Students come from 50 states and territories and 23 other countries. 26% are from North Carolina. 0.8% are international students. 7% are African American, 0.2% American Indian, 2.6% Asian American, and 1.4% Hispanic American. 93% returned for their sophomore year.

Facilities and Resources

Student rooms are linked to a campus network. 150 **computers** are available on campus that provide access to personal computer and the Internet. The 4 **libraries** have 923,123 books and 16,448 subscriptions.

Campus Life

There are 125 active organizations on campus, including a drama/theater group, newspaper, radio station, television station, choral group, and marching band. 37% of eligible men and 50% of eligible women are members of national **fraternities** and national **sororities**.

Wake Forest is a member of the NCAA (Division I). **Intercollegiate sports** (some offering scholarships) include baseball (m), basketball, cross-country running, field hockey (w), football (m), golf, soccer, tennis, track and field, volleyball (w).

Campus Safety

Student safety services include late-night transport/escort service, 24-hour emergency telephone alarm devices, 24-hour patrols by trained security personnel, and electronically operated dormitory entrances.

Applying

Wake Forest requires an essay, SAT I, a high school transcript, and 1 recommendation. It recommends SAT II Subject Tests. Application deadline: 1/15; 2/1 priority date for financial aid. Early and deferred admission are possible.

Getting in Last Year

5,271 applied
46% were accepted
983 enrolled (41%)
62% from top tenth of their h.s. class
80% had SAT verbal scores over 600
85% had SAT math scores over 600
20% had SAT verbal scores over 700
28% had SAT math scores over 700
4 National Merit Scholars
29 class presidents
93 valedictorians

Graduation and After

77% graduated in 4 years
9% graduated in 5 years
1% graduated in 6 years
33% pursued further study (15% arts and
   sciences, 7% law, 5% medicine)
61% had job offers within 6 months
500 organizations recruited on campus

Financial Matters

$23,530 tuition and fees (2001–02)
$6760 room and board
91% average percent of need met
$18,976 average financial aid amount received
   per undergraduate

Wartburg College

Small-town setting ■ Private ■ Independent Religious ■ Coed
Waverly, Iowa

Web site: www.wartburg.edu
Contact: Doug Bowman, Dean of Admissions/Financial Aid, 100 Wartburg Boulevard, PO Box 1003, Waverly, IA 50677-0903
Telephone: 319-352-8264 or toll-free 800-772-2085 **Fax:** 319-352-8579
E-mail: admissions@wartburg.edu

> **W**artburg College encourages students to connect their classroom learning with opportunities to enhance their leadership skills, immerse themselves in another culture, engage in volunteer service, and "live their learning" in practical situations outside the classroom setting. The 1-month May Term offers a variety of courses led by Wartburg professors in the United States and abroad.

Getting in Last Year
1,562 applied
88% were accepted
470 enrolled (34%)
35% from top tenth of their h.s. class
3.50 average high school GPA
36% had SAT verbal scores over 600
51% had SAT math scores over 600
57% had ACT scores over 24
18% had SAT verbal scores over 700
15% had SAT math scores over 700
11% had ACT scores over 30
4 National Merit Scholars
43 valedictorians

Graduation and After
68% graduated in 4 years
5% graduated in 5 years
Graduates pursuing further study: 6% arts and sciences, 3% medicine, 1% education
74% had job offers within 6 months
80 organizations recruited on campus

Financial Matters
$16,565 tuition and fees (2001–02)
$4600 room and board
88% average percent of need met
$15,215 average financial aid amount received per undergraduate

Academics
Wartburg awards bachelor's **degrees**. Challenging opportunities include advanced placement credit, accelerated degree programs, student-designed majors, an honors program, double majors, independent study, and a senior project. Special programs include internships, summer session for credit, off-campus study, and study-abroad.

The most frequently chosen **baccalaureate** fields are business/marketing, education, and biological/life sciences. A complete listing of majors at Wartburg appears in the Majors Index beginning on page 430.

The **faculty** at Wartburg has 91 full-time members, 91% with terminal degrees. The student-faculty ratio is 14:1.

Students of Wartburg
The student body is made up of 1,649 undergraduates. 58.1% are women and 41.9% are men. Students come from 25 states and territories and 32 other countries. 79% are from Iowa. 4% are international students. 3.5% are African American, 0.1% American Indian, 1.1% Asian American, and 0.8% Hispanic American. 75% returned for their sophomore year.

Facilities and Resources
Student rooms are linked to a campus network. 200 **computers** are available on campus that provide access to the Internet. The **library** has 165,515 books and 718 subscriptions.

Campus Life
There are 94 active organizations on campus, including a drama/theater group, newspaper, radio station, television station, and choral group. No national or local **fraternities** or **sororities**.

Wartburg is a member of the NCAA (Division III). **Intercollegiate sports** include baseball (m), basketball, cross-country running, football (m), golf, soccer, softball (w), tennis, track and field, volleyball (w), wrestling (m).

Campus Safety
Student safety services include late-night transport/escort service, 24-hour emergency telephone alarm devices, 24-hour patrols by trained security personnel, and electronically operated dormitory entrances.

Applying
Wartburg requires SAT I or ACT, a high school transcript, and a minimum high school GPA of 2.0, and in some cases an interview. It recommends x recommendations and secondary school report. Application deadline: 3/1 priority date for financial aid. Deferred admission is possible.

WASHINGTON AND LEE UNIVERSITY
SMALL-TOWN SETTING ■ PRIVATE ■ INDEPENDENT ■ COED
LEXINGTON, VIRGINIA

Web site: www.wlu.edu
Contact: Mr. William M. Hartog, Dean of Admissions and Financial Aid,
  Lexington, VA 24450-0303
Telephone: 540-463-8710 **Fax:** 540-463-8062
E-mail: admissions@wlu.edu

Academics

W & L awards bachelor's and first-professional **degrees**. Challenging opportunities include advanced placement credit, accelerated degree programs, student-designed majors, an honors program, double majors, independent study, and a senior project. Special programs include internships, off-campus study, study-abroad, and Army ROTC. A complete listing of majors at W & L appears in the Majors Index beginning on page 430.

The **faculty** at W & L has 236 full-time members. The student-faculty ratio is 9:1.

Students of W & L

The student body totals 2,124, of whom 1,764 are undergraduates. 45.6% are women and 54.4% are men. Students come from 46 states and territories and 36 other countries. 13% are from Virginia. 4% are international students. 3.4% are African American, 0.1% American Indian, 1.5% Asian American, and 1% Hispanic American. 94% returned for their sophomore year.

Facilities and Resources

Student rooms are linked to a campus network. 224 **computers** are available on campus that provide access to e-mail and the Internet. The 5 **libraries** have 603,758 books and 2,856 subscriptions.

Campus Life

There are 120 active organizations on campus, including a drama/theater group, newspaper, radio station, television station, and choral group. 78% of eligible men and 74% of eligible women are members of national **fraternities**, national **sororities**, and local sororities.

W & L is a member of the NCAA (Division III). **Intercollegiate sports** include baseball (m), basketball, cross-country running, equestrian sports, field hockey (w), football (m), golf (m), lacrosse, soccer, swimming, tennis, track and field, volleyball (w), wrestling (m).

Campus Safety

Student safety services include late-night transport/escort service, 24-hour emergency telephone alarm devices, 24-hour patrols by trained security personnel, and electronically operated dormitory entrances.

Applying

W & L requires an essay, SAT I or ACT, 3 unrelated SAT II Subject Tests (including SAT II: Writing Test), a high school transcript, and 3 recommendations. It recommends an interview. Application deadline: 1/15; 2/1 priority date for financial aid. Deferred admission is possible.

Getting in Last Year
2,939 applied
35% were accepted
488 enrolled (48%)
77% from top tenth of their h.s. class
3.90 average high school GPA
89% had SAT verbal scores over 600
90% had SAT math scores over 600
100% had ACT scores over 24
36% had SAT verbal scores over 700
36% had SAT math scores over 700
49% had ACT scores over 30
33 National Merit Scholars
48 valedictorians

Graduation and After
86% graduated in 4 years
2% graduated in 5 years
25% pursued further study
67% had job offers within 6 months
80 organizations recruited on campus

Financial Matters
$19,345 tuition and fees (2001–02)
$5750 room and board
99% average percent of need met
$15,930 average financial aid amount received
  per undergraduate (2000–01)

WASHINGTON COLLEGE

SMALL-TOWN SETTING ■ PRIVATE ■ INDEPENDENT ■ COED
CHESTERTOWN, MARYLAND

Web site: www.washcoll.edu
Contact: Mr. Kevin Coveney, Vice President for Admissions, 300 Washington Avenue, Chestertown, MD 21620-1197
Telephone: 410-778-7700 or toll-free 800-422-1782
E-mail: admissions_office@washcoll.edu

Washington College (WC) has initiated a $40,000 scholarship program expressly for National Honor Society (NHS) members. Washington College NHS Scholarships are $10,000 annual awards renewable through the completion of 8 semesters (full-time enrollment and cumulative GPA of 3.0–4.0 required). To be eligible for WC/NHS Scholarship consideration, a student must apply for freshman admission no later than February 15 of the senior year, be admitted to Washington College, maintain NHS membership through graduation, and remit a $300 enrollment deposit no later than May 1 of the senior year. For more information, students can contact the Admission Office or visit the WC Web site at http://www.washcoll.edu.

Getting in Last Year
1,914 applied
73% were accepted
338 enrolled (24%)
42% from top tenth of their h.s. class
3.37 average high school GPA
40% had SAT verbal scores over 600
34% had SAT math scores over 600
54% had ACT scores over 24
7% had SAT verbal scores over 700
4% had SAT math scores over 700
8% had ACT scores over 30

Graduation and After
62% graduated in 4 years
4% graduated in 5 years
1% graduated in 6 years
39% pursued further study
90% had job offers within 6 months
40 organizations recruited on campus

Financial Matters
$22,300 tuition and fees (2001–02)
$5740 room and board
88% average percent of need met
$18,409 average financial aid amount received per undergraduate

Academics
WC awards bachelor's and master's **degrees**. Challenging opportunities include advanced placement credit, student-designed majors, double majors, independent study, and a senior project. Special programs include cooperative education, internships, off-campus study, and study-abroad.

The most frequently chosen **baccalaureate** fields are social sciences and history, biological/life sciences, and psychology. A complete listing of majors at WC appears in the Majors Index beginning on page 430.

The **faculty** at WC has 81 full-time members, 91% with terminal degrees. The student-faculty ratio is 12:1.

Students of WC
The student body totals 1,260, of whom 1,208 are undergraduates. 61.6% are women and 38.4% are men. Students come from 37 states and territories and 38 other countries. 50% are from Maryland. 5.2% are international students. 3.1% are African American, 0.3% American Indian, 1.6% Asian American, and 1.1% Hispanic American. 82% returned for their sophomore year.

Facilities and Resources
Student rooms are linked to a campus network. 100 **computers** are available on campus that provide access to e-mail and the Internet. The **library** has 231,576 books and 4,635 subscriptions.

Campus Life
There are 50 active organizations on campus, including a drama/theater group, newspaper, and choral group. 25% of eligible men and 25% of eligible women are members of national **fraternities** and national **sororities**.

WC is a member of the NCAA (Division III). **Intercollegiate sports** include baseball (m), basketball, crew, field hockey (w), lacrosse, soccer, softball (w), swimming, tennis, volleyball (w).

Campus Safety
Student safety services include late-night transport/escort service, 24-hour emergency telephone alarm devices, 24-hour patrols by trained security personnel, student patrols, and electronically operated dormitory entrances.

Applying
WC requires an essay, SAT I or ACT, a high school transcript, and 1 recommendation, and in some cases an interview. It recommends an interview. Application deadline: 2/15; 2/15 priority date for financial aid. Early and deferred admission are possible.

WASHINGTON UNIVERSITY IN ST. LOUIS

SUBURBAN SETTING ■ PRIVATE ■ INDEPENDENT ■ COED
ST. LOUIS, MISSOURI

Web site: www.wustl.edu
Contact: Ms. Nanette Tarbouni, Director of Admissions, Campus Box 1089, One Brookings Drive, St. Louis, MO 63130-4899
Telephone: 314-935-6000 or toll-free 800-638-0700 **Fax:** 314-935-4290
E-mail: admissions@wustl.edu

Learning across disciplines is a way of life at Washington University in St. Louis. Students enrolled in one of the undergraduate schools—Architecture, Art, Arts and Sciences, Business, and Engineering and Applied Science—are able to enroll in courses offered by any of the others. The University also offers the benefit of graduate programs in law, medicine (including occupational therapy and physical therapy), and social work. Students are challenged in the classroom and in labs and studios, where they work side-by-side with their professors on research and other special projects.

Academics

Washington awards bachelor's, master's, doctoral, and first-professional **degrees** and post-bachelor's certificates. Challenging opportunities include advanced placement credit, accelerated degree programs, student-designed majors, double majors, and independent study. Special programs include cooperative education, internships, summer session for credit, off-campus study, study-abroad, and Army and Air Force ROTC.

The most frequently chosen **baccalaureate** fields are engineering/engineering technologies, business/marketing, and social sciences and history. A complete listing of majors at Washington appears in the Majors Index beginning on page 430.

The **faculty** at Washington has 791 full-time members, 99% with terminal degrees. The student-faculty ratio is 7:1.

Students of Washington

The student body totals 12,187, of whom 6,772 are undergraduates. 51.4% are women and 48.6% are men. Students come from 52 states and territories and 104 other countries. 11% are from Missouri. 4.6% are international students. 7.6% are African American, 0.1% American Indian, 10% Asian American, and 3% Hispanic American. 96% returned for their sophomore year.

Facilities and Resources

Student rooms are linked to a campus network. 2,500 **computers** are available on campus that provide access to e-mail and the Internet. The 14 **libraries** have 1,462,427 books and 21,017 subscriptions.

Campus Life

There are 200 active organizations on campus, including a drama/theater group, newspaper, radio station, television station, and choral group. 25% of eligible men and 18% of eligible women are members of national **fraternities** and national **sororities**.

Washington is a member of the NCAA (Division III). **Intercollegiate sports** include baseball (m), basketball, cross-country running, football (m), soccer, softball (w), swimming, tennis, track and field, volleyball (w).

Campus Safety

Student safety services include late-night transport/escort service, 24-hour emergency telephone alarm devices, 24-hour patrols by trained security personnel, student patrols, and electronically operated dormitory entrances.

Applying

Washington requires an essay, SAT I or ACT, a high school transcript, and 2 recommendations. It recommends portfolio for art and architecture programs and a minimum high school GPA of 3.0. Application deadline: 1/15; 2/15 for financial aid. Early and deferred admission are possible.

Getting in Last Year
20,834 applied
23% were accepted
1,272 enrolled (26%)
89% from top tenth of their h.s. class
92% had SAT verbal scores over 600
97% had SAT math scores over 600
98% had ACT scores over 24
44% had SAT verbal scores over 700
59% had SAT math scores over 700
63% had ACT scores over 30
176 National Merit Scholars
21 class presidents
129 valedictorians

Graduation and After
75% graduated in 4 years
9% graduated in 5 years
2% graduated in 6 years
33% pursued further study (15% arts and sciences, 7% medicine, 5% law)
60% had job offers within 6 months
280 organizations recruited on campus

Financial Matters
$26,377 tuition and fees (2001–02)
$8216 room and board
100% average percent of need met
$22,173 average financial aid amount received per undergraduate (2000–01)

WEBB INSTITUTE

SUBURBAN SETTING ■ PRIVATE ■ INDEPENDENT ■ COED
GLEN COVE, NEW YORK

Web site: www.webb-institute.edu
Contact: Mr. William G. Murray, Executive Director of Student
    Administrative Services, Crescent Beach Road, Glen Cove, NY 11542-1398
Telephone: 516-671-2213 **Fax:** 516-674-9838
E-mail: admissions@webb-institute.edu

Getting in Last Year
69 applied
42% were accepted
20 enrolled (69%)
35% from top tenth of their h.s. class
3.60 average high school GPA
80% had SAT verbal scores over 600
100% had SAT math scores over 600
35% had SAT verbal scores over 700
55% had SAT math scores over 700

Graduation and After
79% graduated in 4 years
4% graduated in 6 years
18% pursued further study (18% engineering)
100% had job offers within 6 months
11 organizations recruited on campus

Financial Matters
38% average percent of need met
$2360 average financial aid amount received
    per undergraduate (2000–01 estimated)

Academics

Webb awards bachelor's **degrees**. Challenging opportunities include double majors, independent study, and a senior project. Special programs include cooperative education, internships, and off-campus study.

The most frequently chosen **baccalaureate** field is engineering/engineering technologies. A complete listing of majors at Webb appears in the Majors Index beginning on page 430.

The **faculty** at Webb has 8 full-time members, 50% with terminal degrees. The student-faculty ratio is 5:1.

Students of Webb

The student body is made up of 73 undergraduates. 21.9% are women and 78.1% are men. Students come from 23 states and territories and 2 other countries. 30% are from New York. 2.7% are Asian American. 90% returned for their sophomore year.

Facilities and Resources

Student rooms are linked to a campus network. 75 **computers** are available on campus that provide access to the Internet. The **library** has 40,545 books and 256 subscriptions.

Campus Life

Active organizations on campus include a choral group. 100% of eligible women are members of The Webb Women.

Intercollegiate sports include basketball, cross-country running, sailing, soccer, tennis, volleyball.

Campus Safety

Student safety services include 24-hour emergency telephone alarm devices, 24-hour patrols by trained security personnel, and electronically operated dormitory entrances.

Applying

Webb requires SAT I, SAT II: Writing Test, SAT II Subject Tests in math and either physics or chemistry, a high school transcript, an interview, 2 recommendations, proof of U.S. citizenship, and a minimum high school GPA of 3.5. Application deadline: 2/15; 7/1 priority date for financial aid.

WELLESLEY COLLEGE

SUBURBAN SETTING ■ PRIVATE ■ INDEPENDENT ■ WOMEN ONLY
WELLESLEY, MASSACHUSETTS

Web site: www.wellesley.edu
Contact: Ms. Janet Lavin Rapelye, Dean of Admission, 106 Central Street, Wellesley, MA 02481-8203
Telephone: 781-283-2270 **Fax:** 781-283-3678
E-mail: admission@wellesley.edu

Academics

Wellesley awards bachelor's **degrees** (double bachelor's degree with Massachusetts Institute of Technology). Challenging opportunities include advanced placement credit, student-designed majors, double majors, independent study, and a senior project. Special programs include internships, summer session for credit, off-campus study, study-abroad, and Army and Air Force ROTC.

The most frequently chosen **baccalaureate** fields are social sciences and history, psychology, and English. A complete listing of majors at Wellesley appears in the Majors Index beginning on page 430.

The **faculty** at Wellesley has 223 full-time members, 97% with terminal degrees. The student-faculty ratio is 9:1.

Students of Wellesley

The student body is made up of 2,273 undergraduates. Students come from 52 states and territories and 77 other countries. 19% are from Massachusetts. 6.9% are international students. 5.9% are African American, 0.4% American Indian, 24.9% Asian American, and 5.5% Hispanic American. 96% returned for their sophomore year.

Facilities and Resources

Student rooms are linked to a campus network. 200 **computers** are available on campus that provide access to electronic bulletin boards and the Internet. The 4 **libraries** have 689,627 books and 4,756 subscriptions.

Campus Life

There are 160 active organizations on campus, including a drama/theater group, newspaper, radio station, and choral group. No national or local **sororities**.

Wellesley is a member of the NCAA (Division III). **Intercollegiate sports** include basketball, crew, cross-country running, fencing, field hockey, golf, lacrosse, soccer, squash, swimming, tennis, volleyball.

Campus Safety

Student safety services include late-night transport/escort service, 24-hour emergency telephone alarm devices, 24-hour patrols by trained security personnel, and electronically operated dormitory entrances.

Applying

Wellesley requires an essay, SAT I and SAT II or ACT, a high school transcript, and 3 recommendations, and in some cases an interview. It recommends an interview. Application deadline: 1/15; 1/15 priority date for financial aid. Early and deferred admission are possible.

Wellesley College is a liberal arts institution for exceptional women. The College provides an individualized education, with an average class size of 20 students in more than 1,000 courses offered. Wellesley uses technology as a vital component of classroom teaching and offers cross-registration and a double-degree program with MIT. Located just 12 miles from Boston and its 250,000 college students, Wellesley is a multicultural community in which students learn as much from each other as from their classes. Women who attend Wellesley learn the skills necessary to successfully pursue any interest; Wellesley graduates are leaders in the laboratory, the classroom, the courtroom, the boardroom, and their communities—anywhere they choose.

Getting in Last Year
3,006 applied
43% were accepted
578 enrolled (44%)
66% from top tenth of their h.s. class
88% had SAT verbal scores over 600
85% had SAT math scores over 600
88% had ACT scores over 24
46% had SAT verbal scores over 700
33% had SAT math scores over 700
47% had ACT scores over 30

Graduation and After
84% graduated in 4 years
3% graduated in 5 years
1% graduated in 6 years
28% pursued further study

Financial Matters
$25,504 tuition and fees (2001–02)
$7890 room and board
100% average percent of need met
$20,891 average financial aid amount received per undergraduate

WELLS COLLEGE

RURAL SETTING ■ PRIVATE ■ INDEPENDENT ■ WOMEN ONLY
AURORA, NEW YORK

Web site: www.wells.edu
Contact: Ms. Susan Raith Sloan, Director of Admissions, MacMillan Hall, Aurora, NY 13026
Telephone: 315-364-3264 or toll-free 800-952-9355 **Fax:** 315-364-3227
E-mail: admissions@wells.edu

Wells College believes that the 21st century will be a time of unprecedented opportunity for women. Women who are prepared for leadership roles will have a distinct advantage. Wells College has an integrative liberal arts curriculum to prepare women for the leadership roles they will assume in all areas of life in this new century. Wells women are being prepared to become 21st-century leaders in a variety of fields: business, government, the arts, sciences, medicine, and education. The liberal arts curriculum, combined with a wide array of internships, outstanding study-abroad opportunities, leadership programs, and a wealth of cocurricular activities, helps Wells women realize their potential and career goals.

Academics

Wells awards bachelor's **degrees**. Challenging opportunities include advanced placement credit, accelerated degree programs, student-designed majors, double majors, independent study, and a senior project. Special programs include internships, off-campus study, study-abroad, and Air Force ROTC.

The most frequently chosen **baccalaureate** fields are social sciences and history, psychology, and visual/performing arts. A complete listing of majors at Wells appears in the Majors Index beginning on page 430.

The **faculty** at Wells has 49 full-time members, 100% with terminal degrees. The student-faculty ratio is 9:1.

Students of Wells

The student body is made up of 443 undergraduates. Students come from 30 states and territories and 8 other countries. 76% are from New York. 1.9% are international students. 4.7% are African American, 0.2% American Indian, 4.2% Asian American, and 4% Hispanic American. 69% returned for their sophomore year.

Facilities and Resources

Student rooms are linked to a campus network. 98 **computers** are available on campus that provide access to the Internet. The **library** has 248,390 books and 384 subscriptions.

Campus Life

There are 39 active organizations on campus, including a drama/theater group, newspaper, and choral group. No national or local **sororities**.

Wells is a member of the NCAA (Division III). **Intercollegiate sports** include field hockey, lacrosse, soccer, softball, swimming, tennis.

Campus Safety

Student safety services include late-night transport/escort service, 24-hour emergency telephone alarm devices, 24-hour patrols by trained security personnel, and electronically operated dormitory entrances.

Applying

Wells requires an essay, SAT I or ACT, a high school transcript, and 2 recommendations. It recommends an interview. Application deadline: 3/1; 2/15 priority date for financial aid. Early and deferred admission are possible.

Getting in Last Year
417 applied
88% were accepted
100 enrolled (27%)
26% from top tenth of their h.s. class
3.4 average high school GPA
36% had SAT verbal scores over 600
23% had SAT math scores over 600
60% had ACT scores over 24
6% had SAT verbal scores over 700
1% had SAT math scores over 700
7% had ACT scores over 30
1 valedictorian

Graduation and After
56% graduated in 4 years
1% graduated in 5 years
1% graduated in 6 years
8% pursued further study (4% arts and sciences, 2% medicine, 1% law)
39% had job offers within 6 months
5 organizations recruited on campus

Financial Matters
$13,050 tuition and fees (2001–02)
$6300 room and board
90% average percent of need met
$12,905 average financial aid amount received per undergraduate (2000–01)

WESLEYAN COLLEGE

SUBURBAN SETTING ■ PRIVATE ■ INDEPENDENT RELIGIOUS ■ WOMEN ONLY
MACON, GEORGIA

Web site: www.wesleyancollege.edu
Contact: Mr. Jonathan Stroud, Vice President for Enrollment and Marketing,
4760 Forsyth Road, Macon, GA 31210-4462
Telephone: 478-757-5206 or toll-free 800-447-6610 **Fax:** 478-757-4030
E-mail: admissions@wesleyancollege.edu

Academics

Wesleyan awards bachelor's and master's **degrees**. Challenging opportunities include advanced placement credit, accelerated degree programs, student-designed majors, an honors program, double majors, independent study, and a senior project. Special programs include internships, summer session for credit, off-campus study, and study-abroad.

The most frequently chosen **baccalaureate** fields are psychology, business/marketing, and communications/communication technologies. A complete listing of majors at Wesleyan appears in the Majors Index beginning on page 430.

The **faculty** at Wesleyan has 46 full-time members, 96% with terminal degrees. The student-faculty ratio is 11:1.

Students of Wesleyan

The student body totals 721, of whom 674 are undergraduates. Students come from 24 states and territories and 22 other countries. 81% are from Georgia. 11.7% are international students. 28.3% are African American, 0.3% American Indian, 3.3% Asian American, and 2.1% Hispanic American. 73% returned for their sophomore year.

Facilities and Resources

Student rooms are linked to a campus network. 35 **computers** are available on campus that provide access to the Internet. The **library** has 140,923 books and 650 subscriptions.

Campus Life

There are 40 active organizations on campus, including a drama/theater group, newspaper, and choral group. No national or local **sororities**.

Wesleyan is a member of the NCAA (Division III). **Intercollegiate sports** include basketball, equestrian sports, soccer, softball, tennis, volleyball.

Campus Safety

Student safety services include late-night transport/escort service, 24-hour emergency telephone alarm devices, 24-hour patrols by trained security personnel, and electronically operated dormitory entrances.

Applying

Wesleyan requires an essay, SAT I or ACT, a high school transcript, and 1 recommendation. It recommends an interview and 2 recommendations. Application deadline: 6/1. Early and deferred admission are possible.

Wesleyan College, a four-year liberal arts college founded in 1836, has the distinction of being the world's first degree-granting college for women. Located in Macon, Georgia, today it is recognized as one of the nation's most diverse and affordable selective colleges. Students value the College's tradition of service and its fun-filled class competitions, beautiful residence halls, and picturesque campus. Each student takes advantage of an internship or study-abroad experience. Wesleyan is committed to the goals of training women to understand and appreciate the liberal and fine arts and preparing them for careers through high-quality preprofessional programs.

Getting in Last Year
500 applied
74% were accepted
193 enrolled (52%)
36% from top tenth of their h.s. class
3.67 average high school GPA
39% had SAT verbal scores over 600
35% had SAT math scores over 600
55% had ACT scores over 24
10% had SAT verbal scores over 700
3% had SAT math scores over 700
9% had ACT scores over 30
3 National Merit Scholars
8 valedictorians

Graduation and After
26% pursued further study (6% arts and sciences, 5% business, 3% education)
68% had job offers within 6 months
75 organizations recruited on campus

Financial Matters
$9800 tuition and fees (2001–02)
$7250 room and board
85% average percent of need met
$10,749 average financial aid amount received per undergraduate

WESLEYAN UNIVERSITY

SMALL-TOWN SETTING ■ PRIVATE ■ INDEPENDENT ■ COED
MIDDLETOWN, CONNECTICUT

Web site: www.wesleyan.edu
Contact: Mrs. Nancy Hargrave Meislahn, Dean of Admission and Financial
Aid, Stewart M Reid House, 70 Wyllys Avenue, Middletown, CT
06459-0265
Telephone: 860-685-3000 **Fax:** 860-685-3001
E-mail: admissions@wesleyan.edu

For more than 160 years, Wesleyan University has championed the values of a liberal education in the arts and sciences. It seeks to train minds and open hearts and asks students to contribute to the good of society and to the world. About 30% of the undergraduates are students of color, while 10-12% are the first in their families to attend college. Wesleyan is committed to need-based financial aid and meeting the full demonstrated financial need of all students.

Getting in Last Year
7,014 applied
26% were accepted
722 enrolled (40%)
72% from top tenth of their h.s. class
85% had SAT verbal scores over 600
89% had SAT math scores over 600
100% had ACT scores over 24
48% had SAT verbal scores over 700
44% had SAT math scores over 700
75% had ACT scores over 30

Graduation and After
18% pursued further study
70% had job offers within 6 months
180 organizations recruited on campus

Financial Matters
$27,100 tuition and fees (2001–02)
$6950 room and board
100% average percent of need met
$23,549 average financial aid amount received
per undergraduate (2000–01)

Academics
Wesleyan awards bachelor's, master's, and doctoral **degrees** and post-master's certificates. Challenging opportunities include advanced placement credit, accelerated degree programs, student-designed majors, double majors, independent study, and a senior project. Special programs include internships, summer session for credit, off-campus study, study-abroad, and Air Force ROTC.

The most frequently chosen **baccalaureate** fields are social sciences and history, visual/performing arts, and area/ethnic studies. A complete listing of majors at Wesleyan appears in the Majors Index beginning on page 430.

The **faculty** at Wesleyan has 313 full-time members, 94% with terminal degrees. The student-faculty ratio is 9:1.

Students of Wesleyan
The student body totals 3,237, of whom 2,792 are undergraduates. 52.7% are women and 47.3% are men. Students come from 51 states and territories and 45 other countries. 10% are from Connecticut. 8.5% are international students. 7.8% are African American, 0.3% American Indian, 5.9% Asian American, and 5.8% Hispanic American. 95% returned for their sophomore year.

Facilities and Resources
Student rooms are linked to a campus network. 250 **computers** are available on campus that provide access to electronic portfolio and the Internet. The 4 **libraries** have 1,187,027 books and 2,719 subscriptions.

Campus Life
There are 200 active organizations on campus, including a drama/theater group, newspaper, radio station, and choral group. 4% of eligible men and 3% of eligible women are members of national **fraternities**, national **sororities**, local fraternities, and eating clubs.

Wesleyan is a member of the NCAA (Division III). **Intercollegiate sports** include baseball (m), basketball, crew, cross-country running, field hockey (w), football (m), golf, ice hockey, lacrosse, soccer, softball (w), squash, swimming, tennis, track and field, volleyball (w), wrestling (m).

Campus Safety
Student safety services include late-night transport/escort service, 24-hour emergency telephone alarm devices, 24-hour patrols by trained security personnel, student patrols, and electronically operated dormitory entrances.

Applying
Wesleyan requires an essay, SAT II: Writing Test, SAT I and SAT II or ACT, a high school transcript, and 3 recommendations. It recommends an interview. Application deadline: 1/1; 2/1 for financial aid. Early and deferred admission are possible.

WESTERN MARYLAND COLLEGE

SMALL-TOWN SETTING ■ PRIVATE ■ INDEPENDENT ■ COED
WESTMINSTER, MARYLAND

Web site: www.wmdc.edu
Contact: Ms. M. Martha O'Connell, Dean of Admissions, 2 College Hill,
   Westminster, MD 21157-4390
Telephone: 410-857-2230 or toll-free 800-638-5005 **Fax:** 410-857-2757
E-mail: admissio@wmdc.edu

Academics

WMC awards bachelor's and master's **degrees**. Challenging opportunities include advanced placement credit, student-designed majors, an honors program, double majors, independent study, and a senior project. Special programs include internships, summer session for credit, off-campus study, study-abroad, and Army and Air Force ROTC.

The most frequently chosen **baccalaureate** fields are social sciences and history, business/marketing, and communications/communication technologies. A complete listing of majors at WMC appears in the Majors Index beginning on page 430.

The **faculty** at WMC has 93 full-time members. The student-faculty ratio is 12:1.

Students of WMC

The student body totals 3,124, of whom 1,641 are undergraduates. 56.1% are women and 43.9% are men. Students come from 28 states and territories and 24 other countries. 71% are from Maryland. 4.3% are international students. 8% are African American, 0.1% American Indian, 1.6% Asian American, and 1.7% Hispanic American. 86% returned for their sophomore year.

Facilities and Resources

Student rooms are linked to a campus network. 162 **computers** are available on campus that provide access to the Internet. The **library** has 214,259 books and 1,090 subscriptions.

Campus Life

There are 136 active organizations on campus, including a drama/theater group, newspaper, radio station, television station, and choral group. 18% of eligible men and 14% of eligible women are members of national **fraternities**, national **sororities**, local fraternities, and local sororities.

WMC is a member of the NCAA (Division III). **Intercollegiate sports** include baseball (m), basketball, cross-country running, field hockey (w), football (m), golf (m), lacrosse, soccer, softball (w), swimming, tennis, track and field, volleyball (w), wrestling (m).

Campus Safety

Student safety services include late-night transport/escort service, 24-hour emergency telephone alarm devices, 24-hour patrols by trained security personnel, student patrols, and electronically operated dormitory entrances.

Applying

WMC requires an essay, SAT I or ACT, a high school transcript, and a minimum high school GPA of 2.5, and in some cases an interview. It recommends SAT II Subject Tests, an interview, and recommendations. Application deadline: 3/15; 3/1 priority date for financial aid. Early and deferred admission are possible.

> **H**ow students learn is influenced by where they learn, and the environment in which Western Maryland College (WMC) students and their professors work together has been winning over hearts for more than 130 years. Idyllic, historic, friendly, and strategically located (near Baltimore and Washington, D.C.), WMC remains committed to the liberal arts on a residential campus where undergraduate students are the focus. The Basic Liberal Arts Requirements (BLARS) are designed to provide a fundamental core of knowledge and to fuel students' thinking abilities. From there, students can choose from 60 programs of study.

Getting in Last Year
1,885 applied
77% were accepted
370 enrolled (26%)
61% from top tenth of their h.s. class
3.40 average high school GPA
29% had SAT verbal scores over 600
30% had SAT math scores over 600
6% had SAT verbal scores over 700
3% had SAT math scores over 700
1 National Merit Scholar
29 valedictorians

Graduation and After
51% graduated in 4 years
11% graduated in 5 years
40% pursued further study (11% arts and sciences, 9% business, 9% education)
76% had job offers within 6 months
118 organizations recruited on campus

Financial Matters
$20,900 tuition and fees (2001–02)
$5450 room and board
94% average percent of need met
$17,188 average financial aid amount received per undergraduate

---

WESTMINSTER COLLEGE

SUBURBAN SETTING ■ PRIVATE ■ INDEPENDENT ■ COED
SALT LAKE CITY, UTAH

Web site: www.wcslc.edu

Contact: Mr. Philip J. Alletto, Vice President of Student Development and Enrollment Management, 1840 South 1300 East, Salt Lake City, UT 84105-3697

Telephone: 801-832-2200 or toll-free 800-748-4753 **Fax:** 801-484-3252

E-mail: admispub@wsclc.edu

The only independent, private college in the state of Utah, Westminster serves the entire intermountain region and northwestern United States. The beautiful campus and setting reflect the College's combination of traditional private education and western pioneering spirit. Westminster is recognized nationally for excellent programs in business, education, arts and sciences, and nursing. It is continually ranked among the very top tier of colleges and universities in the western United States and has been named a "Top Value" in higher education. Student involvement, technology, and broad-based education, combined with close interaction with outstanding faculty members, are at the heart of a Westminster education.

Getting in Last Year
774 applied
90% were accepted
333 enrolled (48%)
36% from top tenth of their h.s. class
3.65 average high school GPA
51% had ACT scores over 24
7% had ACT scores over 30

Graduation and After
34% graduated in 4 years
12% graduated in 5 years
7% graduated in 6 years
48% pursued further study (14% business, 3% education, 2% arts and sciences)
113 organizations recruited on campus

Financial Matters
$14,780 tuition and fees (2001–02)
$4650 room and board
91% average percent of need met
$13,891 average financial aid amount received per undergraduate

Academics

Westminster College awards bachelor's and master's **degrees** and post-bachelor's certificates. Challenging opportunities include advanced placement credit, accelerated degree programs, student-designed majors, an honors program, double majors, independent study, and a senior project. Special programs include internships, summer session for credit, and Army, Navy and Air Force ROTC.

The most frequently chosen **baccalaureate** fields are business/marketing, health professions and related sciences, and education. A complete listing of majors at Westminster College appears in the Majors Index beginning on page 430.

The **faculty** at Westminster College has 112 full-time members, 84% with terminal degrees. The student-faculty ratio is 11:1.

Students of Westminster College

The student body totals 2,474, of whom 1,979 are undergraduates. 58.6% are women and 41.4% are men. Students come from 29 states and territories and 20 other countries. 92% are from Utah. 1% are international students. 0.3% are African American, 0.8% American Indian, 3% Asian American, and 5% Hispanic American. 77% returned for their sophomore year.

Facilities and Resources

Student rooms are linked to a campus network. 238 **computers** are available on campus that provide access to the Internet. The 2 **libraries** have 102,632 books and 1,807 subscriptions.

Campus Life

There are 41 active organizations on campus, including a drama/theater group, newspaper, and choral group. No national or local **fraternities** or **sororities**.

Westminster College is a member of the NAIA. **Intercollegiate sports** include basketball, golf, soccer (m), volleyball (w).

Campus Safety

Student safety services include late-night transport/escort service, 24-hour emergency telephone alarm devices, 24-hour patrols by trained security personnel, student patrols, and electronically operated dormitory entrances.

Applying

Westminster College requires SAT I or ACT, a high school transcript, and a minimum high school GPA of 2.5. It recommends an essay, an interview, 1 recommendation, and a minimum high school GPA of 3.0. Application deadline: rolling admissions. Early and deferred admission are possible.

WESTMONT COLLEGE

SUBURBAN SETTING ■ PRIVATE ■ INDEPENDENT RELIGIOUS ■ COED
SANTA BARBARA, CALIFORNIA

Web site: www.westmont.edu

Contact: Mrs. Joyce Luy, Director of Admissions, 955 La Paz Road, Santa Barbara, CA 93108

Telephone: 805-565-6200 ext. 6005 or toll-free 800-777-9011 **Fax:** 805-565-6234

E-mail: admissions@westmont.edu

Academics

Westmont awards bachelor's **degrees** and post-bachelor's certificates. Challenging opportunities include advanced placement credit, accelerated degree programs, student-designed majors, an honors program, double majors, independent study, and a senior project. Special programs include cooperative education, internships, summer session for credit, off-campus study, study-abroad, and Army and Air Force ROTC.

The most frequently chosen **baccalaureate** fields are social sciences and history, communications/communication technologies, and biological/life sciences. A complete listing of majors at Westmont appears in the Majors Index beginning on page 430.

The **faculty** at Westmont has 85 full-time members, 87% with terminal degrees. The student-faculty ratio is 13:1.

Students of Westmont

The student body is made up of 1,374 undergraduates. 62.5% are women and 37.5% are men. Students come from 41 states and territories. 66% are from California. 0.4% are international students. 0.6% are African American, 1.6% American Indian, 4.5% Asian American, and 6.7% Hispanic American. 85% returned for their sophomore year.

Facilities and Resources

Student rooms are linked to a campus network. 100 **computers** are available on campus that provide access to the Internet. The **library** has 156,348 books and 3,211 subscriptions.

Campus Life

There are 50 active organizations on campus, including a drama/theater group, newspaper, radio station, and choral group. No national or local **fraternities** or **sororities**.

Westmont is a member of the NAIA. **Intercollegiate sports** (some offering scholarships) include baseball (m), basketball, cross-country running, soccer, tennis, track and field, volleyball (w).

Campus Safety

Student safety services include late-night transport/escort service, 24-hour emergency telephone alarm devices, 24-hour patrols by trained security personnel, and electronically operated dormitory entrances.

Applying

Westmont requires an essay, SAT I or ACT, and a high school transcript, and in some cases an interview and recommendations. It recommends an interview, recommendations, and a minimum high school GPA of 3.0. Application deadline: 2/15; 3/1 priority date for financial aid.

Westmont. Intellectual. Spiritual. Personal. Stimulating. Rigorous. Challenging. Westmont is English lit, the fine arts, premed, economics and business, athletics, and nearly two dozen other courses of study. It's community service and service to God. It's small classes and personal relationships with professors. It's preparation for competitive grad schools and promising careers. It's living in one of the most beautiful places in the world—Santa Barbara. Westmont is learning how to live with other people and how to serve others. It's understanding that liberal arts is lifelong learning and development of skills that lead to leadership and contribution. Encounter Westmont, where character and wisdom meet.

Getting in Last Year
1,335 applied
75% were accepted
370 enrolled (37%)
44% from top tenth of their h.s. class
3.65 average high school GPA
53% had SAT verbal scores over 600
56% had SAT math scores over 600
76% had ACT scores over 24
13% had SAT verbal scores over 700
8% had SAT math scores over 700
7% had ACT scores over 30
12 National Merit Scholars
72 class presidents
39 valedictorians

Graduation and After
66 organizations recruited on campus

Financial Matters
$22,256 tuition and fees (2001–02)
$7492 room and board
75% average percent of need met
$16,235 average financial aid amount received per undergraduate

---

WHEATON COLLEGE

SUBURBAN SETTING ■ PRIVATE ■ INDEPENDENT RELIGIOUS ■ COED
WHEATON, ILLINOIS

Web site: www.wheaton.edu

Contact: Ms. Shawn Leftwich, Director of Admissions, 501 College Avenue,
Wheaton, IL 60187-5593

Telephone: 630-752-5011 or toll-free 800-222-2419 (out-of-state) **Fax:**
630-752-5285

E-mail: admissions@wheaton.edu

Getting in Last Year

1,870 applied
57% were accepted
574 enrolled (54%)
60% from top tenth of their h.s. class
3.69 average high school GPA
80% had SAT verbal scores over 600
80% had SAT math scores over 600
92% had ACT scores over 24
32% had SAT verbal scores over 700
30% had SAT math scores over 700
42% had ACT scores over 30
49 National Merit Scholars

Graduation and After

70% graduated in 4 years
13% graduated in 5 years
1% graduated in 6 years
21% pursued further study
70% had job offers within 6 months
197 organizations recruited on campus

Financial Matters

$16,390 tuition and fees (2001–02)
$5544 room and board
85% average percent of need met
$14,176 average financial aid amount received
  per undergraduate

Academics

Wheaton awards bachelor's, master's, and doctoral **degrees** and post-bachelor's
certificates. Challenging opportunities include advanced placement credit, student-
designed majors, double majors, independent study, and a senior project. Special
programs include internships, summer session for credit, off-campus study, study-abroad,
and Army and Air Force ROTC.

The most frequently chosen **baccalaureate** fields are English, philosophy, and trade
and industry. A complete listing of majors at Wheaton appears in the Majors Index
beginning on page 430.

The **faculty** at Wheaton has 181 full-time members, 92% with terminal degrees.
The student-faculty ratio is 11:1.

Students of Wheaton

The student body totals 2,844, of whom 2,386 are undergraduates. 51.2% are women
and 48.8% are men. Students come from 50 states and territories and 17 other countries.
21% are from Illinois. 1.3% are international students. 2.3% are African American, 0.3%
American Indian, 4.4% Asian American, and 2.9% Hispanic American. 92% returned for
their sophomore year.

Facilities and Resources

Student rooms are linked to a campus network. 150 **computers** are available on campus
that provide access to the Internet. The 2 **libraries** have 342,746 books and 3,264
subscriptions.

Campus Life

There are 97 active organizations on campus, including a drama/theater group,
newspaper, radio station, television station, and choral group. No national or local
fraternities or **sororities**.

Wheaton is a member of the NCAA (Division III). **Intercollegiate sports** include
baseball (m), basketball, cross-country running, football (m), golf, soccer, softball (w),
swimming, tennis, track and field, volleyball (w), wrestling (m).

Campus Safety

Student safety services include late-night transport/escort service, 24-hour patrols by
trained security personnel, and electronically operated dormitory entrances.

Applying

Wheaton requires an essay, SAT I or ACT, a high school transcript, and 2 recommendations. It recommends SAT II: Writing Test, SAT II Subject Test in French, German,
Latin, Spanish or Hebrew, and an interview. Application deadline: 1/15; 2/15 priority
date for financial aid. Deferred admission is possible.

WHITMAN COLLEGE

SMALL-TOWN SETTING ■ PRIVATE ■ INDEPENDENT ■ COED
WALLA WALLA, WASHINGTON

Web site: www.whitman.edu
Contact: Mr. John Bogley, Dean of Admission and Financial Aid, 345 Boyer
   Avenue, Walla Walla, WA 99362-2083
Telephone: 509-527-5176 or toll-free 877-462-9448 **Fax:** 509-527-4967
E-mail: admission@whitman.edu

Academics

Whitman awards bachelor's **degrees**. Challenging opportunities include advanced placement credit, student-designed majors, an honors program, double majors, independent
study, and a senior project. Special programs include internships, off-campus study, and
study-abroad.

The most frequently chosen **baccalaureate** fields are social sciences and history,
visual/performing arts, and biological/life sciences. A complete listing of majors at
Whitman appears in the Majors Index beginning on page 430.

The **faculty** at Whitman has 115 full-time members, 93% with terminal degrees.
The student-faculty ratio is 10:1.

Students of Whitman

The student body is made up of 1,439 undergraduates. 55.6% are women and 44.4% are
men. Students come from 45 states and territories and 22 other countries. 45% are from
Washington. 1.6% are international students. 1.5% are African American, 0.9%
American Indian, 6.9% Asian American, and 2.7% Hispanic American. 94% returned for
their sophomore year.

Facilities and Resources

Student rooms are linked to a campus network. 300 **computers** are available on campus
that provide access to course registration information and the Internet. The 2 **libraries**
have 325,245 books and 2,333 subscriptions.

Campus Life

There are 75 active organizations on campus, including a drama/theater group,
newspaper, radio station, and choral group. 36% of eligible men and 34% of eligible
women are members of national **fraternities** and national **sororities**.

Whitman is a member of the NCAA (Division III). **Intercollegiate sports** include
baseball (m), basketball, cross-country running, golf, skiing (cross-country), skiing
(downhill), soccer, swimming, tennis, track and field, volleyball (w).

Campus Safety

Student safety services include late-night transport/escort service, 24-hour emergency
telephone alarm devices, 24-hour patrols by trained security personnel, student patrols,
and electronically operated dormitory entrances.

Applying

Whitman requires an essay, SAT I or ACT, a high school transcript, and 1 recommendation. It recommends SAT II: Writing Test and an interview. Application deadline:
2/1; 11/15 priority date for financial aid. Early and deferred admission are possible.

Getting in Last Year
2,144 applied
54% were accepted
362 enrolled (31%)
62% from top tenth of their h.s. class
3.72 average high school GPA
81% had SAT verbal scores over 600
82% had SAT math scores over 600
95% had ACT scores over 24
30% had SAT verbal scores over 700
24% had SAT math scores over 700
45% had ACT scores over 30
16 National Merit Scholars
51 valedictorians

Graduation and After
60% graduated in 4 years
10% graduated in 5 years
1% graduated in 6 years
50 organizations recruited on campus

Financial Matters
$22,796 tuition and fees (2001–02)
$6290 room and board
96% average percent of need met
$16,700 average financial aid amount received
   per undergraduate

WHITTIER COLLEGE

Suburban setting ■ Private ■ Independent ■ Coed
Whittier, California

Web site: www.whittier.edu
Contact: Ms. Urmi Kar, Dean of Enrollment, 13406 E Philadelphia Street,
    PO Box 634, Whittier, CA 90608-0634
Telephone: 562-907-4238 **Fax:** 562-907-4870
E-mail: admission@whittier.edu

While the National Endowment for the Humanities has recognized Whittier College's curriculum as a model for liberal arts colleges and the College has produced 4 Rhodes scholars, students are encouraged to choose Whittier not just for its recognition but also for its substance. They should explore and appreciate the College's innovative curriculum, organized around the way people actually learn; a system of resident Faculty Masters, at whose homes students exchange insights on the world's events and cultures; team-taught and "paired" courses, natural arenas for heated discussion and mind-opening challenges; and professors who claim their success only when students declare their own.

Getting in Last Year
1,511 applied
80% were accepted
348 enrolled (29%)
25% from top tenth of their h.s. class
3.13 average high school GPA
28% had SAT verbal scores over 600
23% had SAT math scores over 600
32% had ACT scores over 24
6% had SAT verbal scores over 700
4% had SAT math scores over 700
5% had ACT scores over 30

Graduation and After
22% pursued further study (10% education,
  5% arts and sciences, 2% law)
61% had job offers within 6 months
25 organizations recruited on campus

Financial Matters
$21,336 tuition and fees (2001–02)
$7042 room and board

Academics

Whittier awards bachelor's, master's, and first-professional **degrees**. Challenging opportunities include advanced placement credit, accelerated degree programs, student-designed majors, double majors, independent study, and a senior project. Special programs include internships, summer session for credit, off-campus study, study-abroad, and Army and Air Force ROTC. A complete listing of majors at Whittier appears in the Majors Index beginning on page 430.

The **faculty** at Whittier has 96 full-time members, 96% with terminal degrees. The student-faculty ratio is 12:1.

Students of Whittier

The student body totals 2,170, of whom 1,263 are undergraduates. 57.8% are women and 42.2% are men. Students come from 33 states and territories and 20 other countries. 73% are from California. 4.3% are international students. 5.5% are African American, 1.1% American Indian, 7.8% Asian American, and 26.3% Hispanic American. 74% returned for their sophomore year.

Facilities and Resources

Student rooms are linked to a campus network. 150 **computers** are available on campus for student use. The 2 **libraries** have 225,337 books and 1,357 subscriptions.

Campus Life

There are 56 active organizations on campus, including a drama/theater group, newspaper, radio station, and choral group. 15% of eligible men and 15% of eligible women are members of local **fraternities** and local **sororities**.

Whittier is a member of the NCAA (Division III). **Intercollegiate sports** include baseball (m), basketball, cross-country running, football (m), golf (m), lacrosse, soccer, softball (w), swimming, tennis, track and field, volleyball (w), water polo.

Campus Safety

Student safety services include late-night transport/escort service, 24-hour emergency telephone alarm devices, 24-hour patrols by trained security personnel, and electronically operated dormitory entrances.

Applying

Whittier requires an essay, SAT I or ACT, a high school transcript, 2 recommendations, and a minimum high school GPA of 2.0, and in some cases a minimum high school GPA of 3.5. It recommends SAT II Subject Tests, an interview, and a minimum high school GPA of 2.5. Application deadline: rolling admissions; 3/2 for financial aid, with a 2/1 priority date. Deferred admission is possible.

WHITWORTH COLLEGE

SUBURBAN SETTING ■ PRIVATE ■ INDEPENDENT RELIGIOUS ■ COED
SPOKANE, WASHINGTON

Web site: www.whitworth.edu

Contact: Admissions Office, 300 West Hawthorne Road, Spokane, WA
99251-0001

Telephone: 800-533-4668 or toll-free 800-533-4668 (out-of-state) **Fax:**
509-777-3758

E-mail: admission@whitworth.edu

Academics

Whitworth awards bachelor's and master's **degrees**. Challenging opportunities include
advanced placement credit, student-designed majors, and a senior project. Special
programs include cooperative education, internships, summer session for credit, off-
campus study, study-abroad, and Army ROTC. A complete listing of majors at
Whitworth appears in the Majors Index beginning on page 430.

The **faculty** at Whitworth has 92 full-time members, 77% with terminal degrees.
The student-faculty ratio is 15:1.

Students of Whitworth

The student body totals 1,855, of whom 1,650 are undergraduates. Students come from
31 states and territories and 24 other countries. 55% are from Washington. 85%
returned for their sophomore year.

Facilities and Resources

Student rooms are linked to a campus network. 150 **computers** are available on campus
for student use. The **library** has 135,373 books and 725 subscriptions.

Campus Life

Active organizations on campus include a drama/theater group, newspaper, radio station,
and choral group. No national or local **fraternities** or **sororities**.

Whitworth is a member of the NCAA (Division III). **Intercollegiate sports** include
baseball (m), basketball, cross-country running, football (m), soccer, swimming, tennis,
track and field, volleyball (w).

Campus Safety

Student safety services include late-night transport/escort service, 24-hour emergency
telephone alarm devices, and 24-hour patrols by trained security personnel.

Applying

Whitworth requires an essay, SAT I or ACT, a high school transcript, and recommendations, and in some cases an interview. Application deadline: 3/1; 3/1 priority date for
financial aid. Early and deferred admission are possible.

Getting in Last Year
1,115 applied
90% were accepted
42% from top tenth of their h.s. class
3.60 average high school GPA
39% had SAT verbal scores over 600
40% had SAT math scores over 600
7% had SAT verbal scores over 700
5% had SAT math scores over 700
32 valedictorians

Graduation and After
42% graduated in 4 years
14% graduated in 5 years
4% graduated in 6 years
20% pursued further study
125 organizations recruited on campus

Financial Matters
$18,038 tuition and fees (2001–02)
$5900 room and board
86% average percent of need met
$15,543 average financial aid amount received
per undergraduate

WILLAMETTE UNIVERSITY

URBAN SETTING ■ PRIVATE ■ INDEPENDENT RELIGIOUS ■ COED
SALEM, OREGON

Web site: www.willamette.edu

Contact: Dr. Robin Brown, Vice President for Enrollment, 900 State Street,
Salem, OR 97301-3931

Telephone: 503-370-6303 or toll-free 877-542-2787 **Fax:** 503-375-5363

E-mail: undergrad-admission@willamette.edu

Getting in Last Year

1,634 applied
84% were accepted
476 enrolled (35%)
55% from top tenth of their h.s. class
3.71 average high school GPA
62% had SAT verbal scores over 600
63% had SAT math scores over 600
83% had ACT scores over 24
14% had SAT verbal scores over 700
14% had SAT math scores over 700
22% had ACT scores over 30
13 National Merit Scholars
34 class presidents
56 valedictorians

Graduation and After

70% graduated in 4 years
5% graduated in 5 years
165 organizations recruited on campus

Financial Matters

$23,272 tuition and fees (2001–02)
$6150 room and board
91% average percent of need met
$19,349 average financial aid amount received
per undergraduate (2000–01 estimated)

Academics

Willamette awards bachelor's, master's, and first-professional **degrees**. Challenging opportunities include advanced placement credit, accelerated degree programs, student-designed majors, an honors program, double majors, independent study, and a senior project. Special programs include cooperative education, internships, off-campus study, study-abroad, and Air Force ROTC.

The most frequently chosen **baccalaureate** fields are social sciences and history, foreign language/literature, and biological/life sciences. A complete listing of majors at Willamette appears in the Majors Index beginning on page 430.

The **faculty** at Willamette has 183 full-time members, 93% with terminal degrees. The student-faculty ratio is 10:1.

Students of Willamette

The student body totals 2,466, of whom 1,773 are undergraduates. 56% are women and 44% are men. Students come from 39 states and territories and 14 other countries. 42% are from Oregon. 1.1% are international students. 2.3% are African American, 1.9% American Indian, 7.3% Asian American, and 4.6% Hispanic American. 87% returned for their sophomore year.

Facilities and Resources

Student rooms are linked to a campus network. 200 **computers** are available on campus for student use. The 2 **libraries** have 279,574 books and 1,569 subscriptions.

Campus Life

There are 78 active organizations on campus, including a drama/theater group, newspaper, radio station, and choral group. 28% of eligible men and 22% of eligible women are members of national **fraternities** and national **sororities**.

Willamette is a member of the NCAA (Division III). **Intercollegiate sports** include baseball (m), basketball, crew, cross-country running, football (m), golf, soccer, softball (w), swimming, tennis, track and field, volleyball (w).

Campus Safety

Student safety services include late-night transport/escort service, 24-hour emergency telephone alarm devices, 24-hour patrols by trained security personnel, student patrols, and electronically operated dormitory entrances.

Applying

Willamette requires an essay, SAT I or ACT, a high school transcript, 1 recommendation, and a minimum high school GPA of 2.0, and in some cases an interview. It recommends an interview. Application deadline: 2/1; 2/1 priority date for financial aid. Early and deferred admission are possible.

WILLIAM JEWELL COLLEGE

SMALL-TOWN SETTING ■ PRIVATE ■ INDEPENDENT RELIGIOUS ■ COED
LIBERTY, MISSOURI

Web site: www.jewell.edu
Contact: Mr. Chad Jolly, Dean of Enrollment Development, 500 College Hill,
　Liberty, MO 64068
Telephone: 816-781-7700 or toll-free 800-753-7009 **Fax:** 816-415-5027
E-mail: admission@william.jewell.edu

Academics

William Jewell awards bachelor's **degrees** (also offers evening program with significant
enrollment not reflected in profile). Challenging opportunities include advanced placement credit, student-designed majors, an honors program, double majors, independent
study, and a senior project. Special programs include cooperative education, internships,
summer session for credit, and study-abroad.

　The most frequently chosen **baccalaureate** fields are business/marketing, education,
and psychology. A complete listing of majors at William Jewell appears in the Majors
Index beginning on page 430.

　The **faculty** at William Jewell has 84 full-time members, 85% with terminal degrees.
The student-faculty ratio is 11:1.

Students of William Jewell

The student body is made up of 1,089 undergraduates. 58.6% are women and 41.4% are
men. Students come from 32 states and territories and 12 other countries. 80% are from
Missouri. 2.4% are international students. 2.1% are African American, 0.5% American
Indian, 0.5% Asian American, and 1.5% Hispanic American. 75% returned for their
sophomore year.

Facilities and Resources

Student rooms are linked to a campus network. 160 **computers** are available on campus
that provide access to the Internet. The **library** has 248,749 books and 899 subscriptions.

Campus Life

There are 36 active organizations on campus, including a drama/theater group,
newspaper, radio station, and choral group. 41% of eligible men and 34% of eligible
women are members of national **fraternities** and national **sororities**.

　William Jewell is a member of the NAIA. **Intercollegiate sports** (some offering
scholarships) include baseball (m), basketball, cross-country running, football (m), golf,
soccer, softball (w), tennis, track and field, volleyball (w).

Campus Safety

Student safety services include late-night transport/escort service, 24-hour emergency
telephone alarm devices, 24-hour patrols by trained security personnel, and electronically operated dormitory entrances.

Applying

William Jewell requires SAT I or ACT, a high school transcript, and a minimum high
school GPA of 2.0. It recommends an essay, an interview, 2 recommendations, and a
minimum high school GPA of 2.5. Application deadline: rolling admissions; 3/1 priority
date for financial aid. Deferred admission is possible.

Getting in Last Year

635 applied
80% were accepted
243 enrolled (48%)
37% from top tenth of their h.s. class
3.66 average high school GPA
34% had SAT verbal scores over 600
48% had SAT math scores over 600
55% had ACT scores over 24
14% had SAT verbal scores over 700
7% had SAT math scores over 700
12% had ACT scores over 30
15 class presidents
10 valedictorians

Graduation and After

**19% pursued further study (10% arts and
　sciences, 4% medicine, 3% law)**
74% had job offers within 6 months
111 organizations recruited on campus

Financial Matters

$14,750 tuition and fees (2001–02)
$4390 room and board

WILLIAMS COLLEGE
SMALL-TOWN SETTING ■ PRIVATE ■ INDEPENDENT ■ COED
WILLIAMSTOWN, MASSACHUSETTS

Web site: www.williams.edu
Contact: Mr. Richard L. Nesbitt, Director of Admission, 988 Main Street, Williamstown, MA 01267
Telephone: 413-597-2211 **Fax:** 413-597-4052
E-mail: admission@williams.edu

Williams is a tightly knit residential community with a focus on the direct educational partnership between students and faculty members. The College emphasizes the continuities between academic and extracurricular life while maintaining a firm commitment to excellence in teaching, artistic endeavor, and scholarly research. Williams admits students without regard to financial need and provides financial assistance to meet 100% of demonstrated need. The College places a high priority on fostering a multicultural community—to promote an enriched exchange of ideas and to prepare its graduates for a world of increasing diversification.

Getting in Last Year
4,656 applied
24% were accepted
520 enrolled (46%)
92% had SAT verbal scores over 600
92% had SAT math scores over 600
59% had SAT verbal scores over 700
58% had SAT math scores over 700

Graduation and After
19% pursued further study
65% had job offers within 6 months
100 organizations recruited on campus

Financial Matters
$25,540 tuition and fees (2001–02)
$6930 room and board
100% average percent of need met
$23,215 average financial aid amount received per undergraduate

Academics
Williams awards bachelor's and master's **degrees**. Challenging opportunities include advanced placement credit, accelerated degree programs, student-designed majors, an honors program, double majors, independent study, and a senior project. Special programs include internships, off-campus study, and study-abroad.

The most frequently chosen **baccalaureate** fields are social sciences and history, psychology, and English. A complete listing of majors at Williams appears in the Majors Index beginning on page 430.

The **faculty** at Williams has 230 full-time members, 98% with terminal degrees. The student-faculty ratio is 9:1.

Students of Williams
The student body totals 2,048, of whom 1,997 are undergraduates. 48.2% are women and 51.8% are men. Students come from 51 states and territories and 32 other countries. 15% are from Massachusetts. 5.4% are international students. 6.8% are African American, 0.4% American Indian, 8.5% Asian American, and 6.8% Hispanic American. 97% returned for their sophomore year.

Facilities and Resources
Student rooms are linked to a campus network. 150 **computers** are available on campus for student use. The 10 **libraries** have 420,144 books and 2,853 subscriptions.

Campus Life
There are 110 active organizations on campus, including a drama/theater group, newspaper, radio station, choral group, and marching band. No national or local **fraternities** or **sororities**.

Williams is a member of the NCAA (Division III). **Intercollegiate sports** include baseball (m), basketball, crew, cross-country running, field hockey (w), football (m), golf (m), ice hockey, lacrosse, skiing (cross-country), skiing (downhill), soccer, softball (w), squash, swimming, tennis, track and field, volleyball (w), wrestling (m).

Campus Safety
Student safety services include late-night transport/escort service, 24-hour emergency telephone alarm devices, 24-hour patrols by trained security personnel, student patrols, and electronically operated dormitory entrances.

Applying
Williams requires an essay, SAT I and SAT II or ACT, a high school transcript, and 2 recommendations. Application deadline: 1/1; 2/1 for financial aid. Early and deferred admission are possible.

WITTENBERG UNIVERSITY

SUBURBAN SETTING ■ PRIVATE ■ INDEPENDENT RELIGIOUS ■ COED
SPRINGFIELD, OHIO

Web site: www.wittenberg.edu

Contact: Mr. Kenneth G. Benne, Dean of Admissions and Financial Aid, PO Box 720, Springfield, OH 45501-0720

Telephone: 937-327-6314 ext. 6366 or toll-free 800-677-7558 ext. 6314 **Fax:** 937-327-6379

E-mail: admission@wittenberg.edu

Academics

Wittenberg University awards bachelor's and master's **degrees**. Challenging opportunities include advanced placement credit, accelerated degree programs, student-designed majors, freshman honors college, an honors program, double majors, independent study, and a senior project. Special programs include cooperative education, internships, summer session for credit, off-campus study, study-abroad, and Army and Air Force ROTC. A complete listing of majors at Wittenberg University appears in the Majors Index beginning on page 430.

The **faculty** at Wittenberg University has 154 full-time members, 96% with terminal degrees. The student-faculty ratio is 14:1.

Students of Wittenberg University

The student body totals 2,269, of whom 2,216 are undergraduates. 55.4% are women and 44.6% are men. Students come from 41 states and territories and 27 other countries. 60% are from Ohio. 2.4% are international students. 6.3% are African American, 0.1% American Indian, 0.7% Asian American, and 0.7% Hispanic American. 85% returned for their sophomore year.

Facilities and Resources

Student rooms are linked to a campus network. 500 **computers** are available on campus that provide access to the Internet. The 3 **libraries** have 350,000 books and 1,300 subscriptions.

Campus Life

There are 100 active organizations on campus, including a drama/theater group, newspaper, radio station, and choral group. 15% of eligible men and 35% of eligible women are members of national **fraternities** and national **sororities**.

Wittenberg University is a member of the NCAA (Division III). **Intercollegiate sports** include baseball (m), basketball, cross-country running, field hockey (w), football (m), golf (m), lacrosse, soccer, softball (w), swimming, tennis, track and field, volleyball (w).

Campus Safety

Student safety services include crime prevention programs, late-night transport/escort service, 24-hour emergency telephone alarm devices, 24-hour patrols by trained security personnel, student patrols, and electronically operated dormitory entrances.

Applying

Wittenberg University requires an essay, SAT I or ACT, a high school transcript, and 1 recommendation, and in some cases an interview. It recommends SAT II Subject Tests and an interview. Application deadline: 3/15; 3/15 for financial aid, with a 2/15 priority date. Early and deferred admission are possible.

Getting in Last Year
2,415 applied
85% were accepted
580 enrolled (28%)
38% from top tenth of their h.s. class
3.50 average high school GPA
37% had SAT verbal scores over 600
39% had SAT math scores over 600
63% had ACT scores over 24
2% had SAT verbal scores over 700
5% had SAT math scores over 700
13% had ACT scores over 30
4 National Merit Scholars
35 class presidents
34 valedictorians

Graduation and After
63% graduated in 4 years
6% graduated in 5 years
1% graduated in 6 years
24% pursued further study (5% business, 5% medicine, 2% arts and sciences)
97% had job offers within 6 months
100 organizations recruited on campus

Financial Matters
$22,840 tuition and fees (2001–02)
$5776 room and board

Wofford College

URBAN SETTING ■ PRIVATE ■ INDEPENDENT RELIGIOUS ■ COED
SPARTANBURG, SOUTH CAROLINA

Web site: www.wofford.edu
Contact: Mr. Brand Stille, Director of Admissions, 429 North Church Street, Spartanburg, SC 29303-3663
Telephone: 864-597-4130 **Fax:** 864-597-4147
E-mail: admissions@wofford.edu

Getting in Last Year
1,209 applied
82% were accepted
303 enrolled (31%)
50% from top tenth of their h.s. class
3.83 average high school GPA
46% had SAT verbal scores over 600
52% had SAT math scores over 600
57% had ACT scores over 24
7% had SAT verbal scores over 700
9% had SAT math scores over 700
8% had ACT scores over 30
2 National Merit Scholars
7 class presidents
11 valedictorians

Graduation and After
73% graduated in 4 years
4% graduated in 5 years
2% graduated in 6 years
31% pursued further study (9% arts and sciences, 5% medicine, 4% business)
60% had job offers within 6 months

Financial Matters
$18,515 tuition and fees (2001–02)
$5480 room and board
84% average percent of need met
$13,717 average financial aid amount received per undergraduate

Academics

Wofford awards bachelor's **degrees**. Challenging opportunities include advanced placement credit, accelerated degree programs, student-designed majors, double majors, independent study, and a senior project. Special programs include internships, summer session for credit, off-campus study, study-abroad, and Army ROTC.

The most frequently chosen **baccalaureate** fields are business/marketing, social sciences and history, and biological/life sciences. A complete listing of majors at Wofford appears in the Majors Index beginning on page 430.

The **faculty** at Wofford has 75 full-time members, 91% with terminal degrees. The student-faculty ratio is 13:1.

Students of Wofford

The student body is made up of 1,107 undergraduates. 47.8% are women and 52.2% are men. Students come from 30 states and territories and 1 other country. 67% are from South Carolina. 0.1% are international students. 8.5% are African American, 0.2% American Indian, 1.7% Asian American, and 0.5% Hispanic American. 90% returned for their sophomore year.

Facilities and Resources

Student rooms are linked to a campus network. 225 **computers** are available on campus that provide access to the Internet. The **library** has 194,569 books and 642 subscriptions.

Campus Life

There are 68 active organizations on campus, including a drama/theater group, newspaper, and choral group. 56% of eligible men and 65% of eligible women are members of national **fraternities** and national **sororities**.

Wofford is a member of the NCAA (Division I). **Intercollegiate sports** (some offering scholarships) include baseball (m), basketball, cross-country running, football (m), golf, soccer, tennis, track and field, volleyball (w).

Campus Safety

Student safety services include late-night transport/escort service, 24-hour emergency telephone alarm devices, 24-hour patrols by trained security personnel, and electronically operated dormitory entrances.

Applying

Wofford requires an essay, SAT I or ACT, and a high school transcript. It recommends SAT II: Writing Test, an interview, and 2 recommendations. Application deadline: 2/1; 3/15 priority date for financial aid. Early and deferred admission are possible.

WORCESTER POLYTECHNIC INSTITUTE

SUBURBAN SETTING ■ PRIVATE ■ INDEPENDENT ■ COED
WORCESTER, MASSACHUSETTS

Web site: www.wpi.edu
Contact: Ms. Kristin Tichenor, Director of Admissions, 100 Institute Road,
    Worcester, MA 01609-2280
Telephone: 508-831-5286 **Fax:** 508-831-5875
E-mail: admissions@wpi.edu

Academics

WPI awards bachelor's, master's, and doctoral **degrees**. Challenging opportunities
include advanced placement credit, accelerated degree programs, student-designed
majors, double majors, independent study, and a senior project. Special programs include
cooperative education, summer session for credit, off-campus study, study-abroad, and
Army, Navy and Air Force ROTC.

The most frequently chosen **baccalaureate** fields are engineering/engineering
technologies, computer/information sciences, and biological/life sciences. A complete
listing of majors at WPI appears in the Majors Index beginning on page 430.

The **faculty** at WPI has 231 full-time members, 94% with terminal degrees. The
student-faculty ratio is 13:1.

Students of WPI

The student body totals 3,887, of whom 2,823 are undergraduates. 22.6% are women
and 77.4% are men. Students come from 51 states and territories and 40 other countries.
5.1% are international students. 1.4% are African American, 0.3% American Indian,
6.6% Asian American, and 2.5% Hispanic American. 92% returned for their sophomore
year.

Facilities and Resources

Student rooms are linked to a campus network. 1,000 **computers** are available on
campus that provide access to the Internet. The **library** has 170,000 books and 1,400
subscriptions.

Campus Life

There are 65 active organizations on campus, including a drama/theater group,
newspaper, radio station, and choral group. WPI has national **fraternities** and national
sororities.

WPI is a member of the NCAA (Division III). **Intercollegiate sports** include
baseball (m), basketball, cross-country running, field hockey (w), football (m), golf (m),
soccer, softball (w), swimming, tennis, track and field, volleyball (w), wrestling (m).

Campus Safety

Student safety services include late-night transport/escort service, 24-hour emergency
telephone alarm devices, 24-hour patrols by trained security personnel, and student
patrols.

Applying

WPI requires an essay, SAT I and SAT II or ACT, a high school transcript, and 1 recommendation. It recommends an interview. Application deadline: 2/1; 3/1 priority date for
financial aid. Early and deferred admission are possible.

Getting in Last Year
3,316 applied
74% were accepted
700 enrolled (28%)
45% from top tenth of their h.s. class
58% had SAT verbal scores over 600
83% had SAT math scores over 600
13% had SAT verbal scores over 700
29% had SAT math scores over 700
19 National Merit Scholars
50 valedictorians

Graduation and After
52% graduated in 4 years
18% graduated in 5 years
7% graduated in 6 years
150 organizations recruited on campus

Financial Matters
$24,890 tuition and fees (2001–02)
$7900 room and board
83% average percent of need met
$22,375 average financial aid amount received
    per undergraduate

XAVIER UNIVERSITY

SUBURBAN SETTING ■ PRIVATE ■ INDEPENDENT RELIGIOUS ■ COED
CINCINNATI, OHIO

Web site: www.xu.edu
Contact: Mr. Marc Camille, Dean of Admission, 3800 Victory Parkway,
    Cincinnati, OH 45207-5311
Telephone: 513-745-3301 or toll-free 800-344-4698 **Fax:** 513-745-4319
E-mail: xuadmit@xu.edu

Getting in Last Year
3,534 applied
83% were accepted
797 enrolled (27%)
31% from top tenth of their h.s. class
3.53 average high school GPA
46% had SAT verbal scores over 600
43% had SAT math scores over 600
68% had ACT scores over 24
8% had SAT verbal scores over 700
8% had SAT math scores over 700
14% had ACT scores over 30
6 National Merit Scholars
19 valedictorians

Graduation and After
56% graduated in 4 years
11% graduated in 5 years
1% graduated in 6 years
20% pursued further study (8% arts and sciences, 4% medicine, 4% law)
93% had job offers within 6 months
176 organizations recruited on campus

Financial Matters
$16,780 tuition and fees (2001–02)
$7230 room and board
79% average percent of need met
$11,552 average financial aid amount received per undergraduate (2000–01 estimated)

Academics

Xavier awards associate, bachelor's, master's, and doctoral **degrees** and post-bachelor's and post-master's certificates. Challenging opportunities include advanced placement credit, an honors program, double majors, independent study, and a senior project. Special programs include cooperative education, internships, summer session for credit, off-campus study, study-abroad, and Army and Air Force ROTC.

The most frequently chosen **baccalaureate** fields are business/marketing, liberal arts/general studies, and communications/communication technologies. A complete listing of majors at Xavier appears in the Majors Index beginning on page 430.

The **faculty** at Xavier has 263 full-time members, 80% with terminal degrees. The student-faculty ratio is 17:1.

Students of Xavier

The student body totals 6,660, of whom 4,006 are undergraduates. 58.2% are women and 41.8% are men. Students come from 45 states and territories and 43 other countries. 35% are from Ohio. 2.9% are international students. 9.5% are African American, 0.1% American Indian, 1.9% Asian American, and 1.3% Hispanic American. 88% returned for their sophomore year.

Facilities and Resources

Student rooms are linked to a campus network. 200 **computers** are available on campus that provide access to the Internet. The 2 **libraries** have 200,044 books and 1,586 subscriptions.

Campus Life

There are 90 active organizations on campus, including a drama/theater group, newspaper, radio station, and choral group. No national or local **fraternities** or **sororities**.

Xavier is a member of the NCAA (Division I). **Intercollegiate sports** (some offering scholarships) include baseball (m), basketball, cross-country running, golf, riflery, soccer, swimming, tennis, volleyball (w).

Campus Safety

Student safety services include campus-wide shuttle service, late-night transport/escort service, 24-hour emergency telephone alarm devices, and 24-hour patrols by trained security personnel.

Applying

Xavier requires an essay, SAT I or ACT, a high school transcript, and 1 recommendation. It recommends an interview. Application deadline: 2/1; 2/15 priority date for financial aid. Early and deferred admission are possible.

Yale University

URBAN SETTING ■ PRIVATE ■ INDEPENDENT ■ COED
NEW HAVEN, CONNECTICUT

Web site: www.yale.edu
Contact: Admissions Director, PO Box 208234, New Haven, CT 06520-8324
Telephone: 203-432-9300 Fax: 203-432-9392
E-mail: undergraduate.admissions@yale.edu

Getting in Last Year
14,809 applied
14% were accepted
1,296 enrolled (64%)
95% from top tenth of their h.s. class

Graduation and After
Graduates pursuing further study: 8%
    medicine, 6% arts and sciences, 6% law
62% had job offers within 6 months

Financial Matters
$26,100 tuition and fees (2001–02)
$7930 room and board
100% average percent of need met
$23,101 average financial aid amount received
    per undergraduate (2000–01 estimated)

Academics

Yale awards bachelor's, master's, doctoral, and first-professional **degrees** and post-master's certificates. Challenging opportunities include advanced placement credit, accelerated degree programs, student-designed majors, an honors program, double majors, independent study, and a senior project. Special programs include summer session for credit, study-abroad, and Army and Air Force ROTC.

The most frequently chosen **baccalaureate** fields are social sciences and history, biological/life sciences, and English. A complete listing of majors at Yale appears in the Majors Index beginning on page 430.

The **faculty** at Yale has 978 full-time members, 90% with terminal degrees. The student-faculty ratio is 7:1.

Students of Yale

The student body totals 11,136, of whom 5,286 are undergraduates. 49.3% are women and 50.7% are men. Students come from 55 states and territories and 74 other countries. 10% are from Connecticut. 7.4% are international students. 7.5% are African American, 0.7% American Indian, 13.7% Asian American, and 6% Hispanic American. 98% returned for their sophomore year.

Facilities and Resources

Student rooms are linked to a campus network. 350 **computers** are available on campus for student use. The 21 **libraries** have 10,800,000 books and 57,377 subscriptions.

Campus Life

There are 300 active organizations on campus, including a drama/theater group, newspaper, radio station, choral group, and marching band. Yale has national **fraternities** and national **sororities**.

Yale is a member of the NCAA (Division I). **Intercollegiate sports** include baseball (m), basketball, crew, cross-country running, fencing, field hockey (w), football (m), golf, gymnastics (w), ice hockey, lacrosse, soccer, softball (w), squash, swimming, tennis, track and field, volleyball (w).

Campus Safety

Student safety services include late-night transport/escort service, 24-hour emergency telephone alarm devices, 24-hour patrols by trained security personnel, and electronically operated dormitory entrances.

Applying

Yale requires an essay, SAT I and SAT II or ACT, a high school transcript, and 3 recommendations. It recommends an interview. Application deadline: 12/31; 2/1 priority date for financial aid. Early and deferred admission are possible.

YESHIVA UNIVERSITY

URBAN SETTING ■ PRIVATE ■ INDEPENDENT ■ COED
NEW YORK, NEW YORK

Web site: www.yu.edu
Contact: Mr. Michael Kranzler, Director of Undergraduate Admissions, 500
West 185th Street, New York, NY 10033-3201
Telephone: 212-960-5277 **Fax:** 212-960-0086
E-mail: yuadmit@ymail.yu.edu

Getting in Last Year
1,768 applied
78% were accepted
755 enrolled (55%)
3.4 average high school GPA

Graduation and After
Graduates pursuing further study: 17% law,
10% arts and sciences, 10% medicine
50 organizations recruited on campus

Financial Matters
$19,045 tuition and fees (2001–02)
$5950 room and board
69% average percent of need met
$11,666 average financial aid amount received
per undergraduate (1999–2000)

Academics

YU awards bachelor's, master's, doctoral, and first-professional **degrees** (Yeshiva College and Stern College for Women are coordinate undergraduate colleges of arts and sciences for men and women, respectively. Sy Syms School of Business offers programs at both campuses). Challenging opportunities include advanced placement credit, student-designed majors, an honors program, double majors, and a senior project. Special programs include internships, summer session for credit, off-campus study, and study-abroad. A complete listing of majors at YU appears in the Majors Index beginning on page 430.

The **faculty** at YU has 235 full-time members.

Students of YU

The student body totals 5,998, of whom 2,819 are undergraduates. 44.1% are women and 55.9% are men. Students come from 31 states and territories and 30 other countries. 85% returned for their sophomore year.

Facilities and Resources

142 **computers** are available on campus that provide access to the Internet. The 7 **libraries** have 995,312 books and 9,760 subscriptions.

Campus Life

Active organizations on campus include a drama/theater group, newspaper, radio station, and choral group. No national or local **fraternities** or **sororities**.

YU is a member of the NCAA (Division III). **Intercollegiate sports** include basketball, cross-country running (m), fencing (m), tennis, volleyball (m), wrestling (m).

Campus Safety

Student safety services include late-night transport/escort service, 24-hour emergency telephone alarm devices, and 24-hour patrols by trained security personnel.

Applying

YU requires an essay, SAT I or ACT, a high school transcript, an interview, and 2 recommendations. It recommends SAT II Subject Tests. Application deadline: 2/15. Early and deferred admission are possible.

APPENDIXES

Ten Largest Colleges

The University of Texas at Austin	50,616
The Ohio State University	48,477
University of Minnesota, Twin Cities Campus	46,597
University of Florida	46,515
Texas A&M University	44,618
University of Wisconsin–Madison	41,552
The Pennsylvania State University University Park Campus	40,828
University of Illinois at Urbana–Champaign	38,759
University of Michigan	38,248
University of California, Los Angeles	37,494

Ten Smallest Colleges

Webb Institute	73
The Curtis Institute of Music	168
College of the Atlantic	271
San Francisco Conservatory of Music	275
Mannes College of Music, New School University	278
Thomas Aquinas College	301
Corcoran College of Art and Design	372
Cleveland Institute of Music	382
Christendom College	407
Simon's Rock College of Bard	414

Colleges Accepting Fewer than Half of Their Applicants

Amherst College
Babson College
Bard College
Barnard College
Bates College
Berea College
Boston College
Boston University
Bowdoin College
Brandeis University
Brown University
Bucknell University
California Institute of Technology
California Polytechnic State University, San Luis Obispo
Carleton College
Carnegie Mellon University
Claremont McKenna College
Cleveland Institute of Music
Colby College
Colgate University
The College of St. Scholastica
College of the Holy Cross
The College of William and Mary
Columbia College (NY)
Columbia University, The Fu Foundation School of Engineering and Applied Science
Connecticut College
Cooper Union for the Advancement of Science and Art
Cornell University
The Curtis Institute of Music
Dartmouth College
Davidson College
Duke University
Emerson College

Emory University
Fairfield University
Fashion Institute of Technology
Florida International University
Georgetown University
The George Washington University
Grove City College
Hamilton College (NY)
Harvard University
Harvey Mudd College
Haverford College
Johns Hopkins University
The Juilliard School
Lafayette College
Lehigh University
Manhattan School of Music
Mannes College of Music, New School University
Maryland Institute, College of Art
Massachusetts College of Art
Massachusetts Institute of Technology
Middlebury College
Mount Holyoke College
Muhlenberg College
New York University
North Carolina School of the Arts
Northwestern University
Oberlin College
Occidental College
Parsons School of Design, New School University
Pepperdine University (Malibu, CA)
Pomona College
Princeton University
Rhode Island School of Design
Rice University
Sarah Lawrence College
Simon's Rock College of Bard
Skidmore College
Stanford University
State University of New York at Binghamton
Stevens Institute of Technology
Swarthmore College
Trinity College (CT)
Tufts University
Union College (NY)
United States Air Force Academy
United States Coast Guard Academy
United States Merchant Marine Academy
United States Military Academy
United States Naval Academy
University of California, Berkeley
University of California, Los Angeles
University of California, San Diego
University of Chicago
University of Miami
The University of North Carolina at Chapel Hill
University of Notre Dame
University of Pennsylvania
University of Richmond
University of Southern California
University of Virginia
Vanderbilt University

Vassar College
Villanova University
Wake Forest University
Washington and Lee University
Washington University in St. Louis
Webb Institute
Wellesley College
Wesleyan University
Williams College
Yale University

Single-Sex Colleges: Men Only
Morehouse College
Saint John's University (MN)
Wabash College

Single-Sex Colleges: Women Only
Agnes Scott College
Barnard College
Bryn Mawr College
College of Saint Benedict
Converse College
Mills College
Mount Holyoke College
Randolph-Macon Woman's College
Salem College
Scripps College
Smith College
Sweet Briar College
Wellesley College
Wells College
Wesleyan College

Predominantly African-American Colleges
Morehouse College

Colleges With Religious Affiliation

Baptist
Baylor University
Belmont University
Bethel College (MN)
Cedarville University
Georgetown College
Kalamazoo College
Mercer University
Oklahoma Baptist University
Samford University
Union University
Wake Forest University
William Jewell College

Brethren
Elizabethtown College
Juniata College

Christian (Unspecified)
Milligan College

Christian Church (Disciples of Christ)
Chapman University
Hiram College
Texas Christian University

Transylvania University

Church of the Nazarene
Point Loma Nazarene University

Churches of Christ
Harding University
Lipscomb University
Oklahoma Christian University
Pepperdine University (Malibu, CA)

Episcopal
University of the South

Friends
Earlham College
George Fox University

Interdenominational
Berry College
Biola University
Illinois College
Messiah College
Taylor University

Jewish
List College, Jewish Theological Seminary of America

Latter-day Saints (Mormon)
Brigham Young University

Lutheran
Augustana College (IL)
Augustana College (SD)
Concordia College (MN)
Gettysburg College
Gustavus Adolphus College
Luther College
Muhlenberg College
Pacific Lutheran University
St. Olaf College
Susquehanna University
Valparaiso University
Wartburg College
Wittenberg University

Methodist
Albion College
Albright College
Allegheny College
American University
Baldwin-Wallace College
Birmingham-Southern College
Centenary College of Louisiana
Cornell College
DePauw University
Drew University
Duke University
Emory University
Hamline University
Hendrix College
Huntingdon College
Lebanon Valley College
Lycoming College
McKendree College

Millsaps College
Mount Union College
North Central College
Ohio Northern University
Ohio Wesleyan University
Oklahoma City University
Randolph-Macon Woman's College
Seattle Pacific University
Simpson College
Southern Methodist University
Southwestern University
University of Evansville
Wesleyan College
Willamette University
Wofford College

Moravian
Salem College

Nondenominational
Asbury College
Azusa Pacific University
Gordon College (MA)
LeTourneau University
Northwestern College (MN)
Westmont College
Wheaton College (IL)

Presbyterian
Agnes Scott College
Alma College
Austin College
Buena Vista University
Centre College
Coe College
The College of Wooster
Covenant College
Davidson College
Eckerd College
Grove City College
Hanover College
Lafayette College
Lyon College
Macalester College
Maryville College
Presbyterian College
Rhodes College (TN)
Trinity University
University of Tulsa
Whitworth College

Reformed Churches
Calvin College
Central College
Hope College

Roman Catholic
Boston College
Canisius College
Carroll College (MT)
The Catholic University of America
Christendom College
Christian Brothers University

College of Saint Benedict
The College of St. Scholastica
College of the Holy Cross
Creighton University
Duquesne University
Fairfield University
Fordham University
Georgetown University
Gonzaga University
John Carroll University
Le Moyne College
Loyola College in Maryland
Loyola University Chicago
Loyola University New Orleans
Marquette University
Mount St. Mary's College
Providence College
Quincy University
Regis University
Rockhurst University
Saint Francis University
Saint John's University (MN)
Saint Joseph's University
Saint Louis University
Saint Mary's College of California
St. Norbert College
Santa Clara University
Seattle University
Siena College
Thomas Aquinas College
University of Dallas
University of Dayton
University of Notre Dame
University of St. Thomas (MN)
University of St. Thomas (TX)
University of San Diego
The University of Scranton
Villanova University
Xavier University

United Church of Christ
Heidelberg College
Ursinus College

Wesleyan
Indiana Wesleyan University
Oklahoma Wesleyan University

Public Colleges
Arkansas Tech University
California Polytechnic State University, San Luis Obispo
Clemson University
The College of New Jersey
The College of William and Mary
Colorado School of Mines
Colorado State University
Fashion Institute of Technology
Florida International University
Florida State University
Georgia Institute of Technology
Georgia State University
Iowa State University of Science and Technology

Mary Washington College
Massachusetts College of Art
Miami University
Michigan Technological University
New College of Florida
New Jersey Institute of Technology
New Mexico Institute of Mining and Technology
North Carolina School of the Arts
North Carolina State University
The Ohio State University
Oklahoma State University
The Pennsylvania State University University Park Campus
Queen's University at Kingston
Rutgers, The State University of New Jersey, New Brunswick
St. Mary's College of Maryland
Southwest Missouri State University
State University of New York at Binghamton
State University of New York College at Geneseo
State University of New York College of Environmental
    Science and Forestry
Texas A&M University
Texas Tech University
Truman State University
United States Air Force Academy
United States Coast Guard Academy
United States Merchant Marine Academy
United States Military Academy
United States Naval Academy
University at Buffalo, The State University of New York
The University of Alabama in Huntsville
The University of Arizona
University of Arkansas
University of California, Berkeley
University of California, Davis
University of California, Irvine
University of California, Los Angeles

University of California, Riverside
University of California, San Diego
University of California, Santa Barbara
University of California, Santa Cruz
University of Central Florida
University of Colorado at Boulder
University of Delaware
University of Florida
University of Georgia
University of Illinois at Chicago
University of Illinois at Urbana–Champaign
The University of Iowa
University of Maryland, Baltimore County
University of Maryland, College Park
University of Massachusetts Amherst
University of Michigan
University of Minnesota, Morris
University of Minnesota, Twin Cities Campus
University of Missouri–Columbia
University of Missouri–Kansas City
University of Missouri–Rolla
The University of North Carolina at Asheville
The University of North Carolina at Chapel Hill
University of Oklahoma
University of Pittsburgh
University of Rhode Island
University of South Carolina
The University of Texas at Austin
The University of Texas at Dallas
University of Virginia
University of Washington
University of Waterloo
University of Wisconsin–Madison
Virginia Military Institute
Virginia Polytechnic Institute and State University

INDEXES

Majors by College

Agnes Scott College
Anthropology; art; astrophysics; biochemistry; biology; chemistry; classics; creative writing; economics; English; French; German; history; interdisciplinary studies; international relations; literature; mathematics; music; philosophy; physics; political science; psychology; religious studies; sociology; Spanish; theater arts/drama; women's studies.

Albertson College of Idaho
Accounting; anthropology; art; biology; business administration; chemistry; computer science; creative writing; economics; English; exercise sciences; history; international business; international economics; mathematics; music; philosophy; physical education; physics; political science; (pre)medicine; psychology; religious studies; sociology; Spanish; sport/fitness administration; theater arts/drama.

Albion College
American studies; anthropology; art; biology; business administration; chemistry; computer science; economics; education; elementary education; English; environmental science; French; geology; German; history; human services; human services; international relations; mass communications; mathematics; modern languages; music; philosophy; physical education; physics; political science; (pre)law; (pre)medicine; (pre)veterinary studies; psychology; public policy analysis; religious studies; secondary education; sociology; Spanish; theater arts/drama; women's studies.

Albright College
Accounting; American studies; art; art education; biochemistry; biology; business administration; business marketing and marketing management; chemistry; clothing/apparel/textile studies; communications; computer science; criminology; early childhood education; economics; elementary education; English; environmental science; finance; forestry; French; history; information sciences/systems; interdisciplinary studies; international business; Latin American studies; mathematics; music; natural resources management; optics; organizational psychology; philosophy; physics; physiological psychology/psychobiology; political science; (pre)dentistry; (pre)law; (pre)medicine; (pre)veterinary studies; psychology; religious studies; secondary education; sociology; Spanish; special education; theater arts/drama; women's studies.

Alfred University
Accounting; applied art; art; art education; art history; athletic training/sports medicine; bilingual/bicultural education; biological and physical sciences; biology; biomedical technology; business administration; business economics; business education; business marketing and marketing management; ceramic arts; ceramic sciences/engineering; chemistry; clinical psychology; computer science; criminal justice studies; drawing; earth sciences; economics; education; electrical/electronics engineering; elementary education; English; environmental science; experimental psychology; finance; fine/studio arts; French; general studies; geology; German; gerontology; graphic design/commercial art/illustration; health services administration; history; information sciences/systems; interdisciplinary studies;

international business; literature; mass communications; materials science; mathematics; mathematics/computer science; mechanical engineering; medical laboratory technician; modern languages; philosophy; photography; physics; political science; (pre)dentistry; (pre)law; (pre)medicine; (pre)veterinary studies; printmaking; psychology; public administration; science education; sculpture; secondary education; sociology; Spanish; theater arts/drama.

Allegheny College
Art history; biology; chemistry; communications; computer science, other; computer/information sciences; economics; English; environmental science; fine arts and art studies, other; fine/studio arts; French; geology; German; history; international relations; mathematics; multi/interdisciplinary studies, other; music; neuroscience; philosophy; physics; political science; psychology; religious studies; Spanish; theater arts/drama; women's studies.

Alma College
Accounting; art; art education; athletic training/sports medicine; biochemistry; biological and physical sciences; biology; business administration; business marketing and marketing management; chemistry; computer science; dance; drawing; early childhood education; ecology; economics; education; elementary education; English; exercise sciences; French; German; gerontology; health science; history; humanities; information sciences/systems; international business; liberal arts and studies; literature; mass communications; mathematics; medical illustrating; modern languages; music; music (voice and choral/opera performance); music education; occupational therapy; philosophy; physics; political science; (pre)dentistry; (pre)law; (pre)medicine; (pre)theology; (pre)veterinary studies; psychology; public health; religious studies; secondary education; social sciences; sociology; Spanish; stringed instruments; theater arts/drama; wind and percussion instruments.

American University
African studies; American studies; anthropology; applied mathematics; art; art history; Asian studies; audio engineering; biochemistry; biology; broadcast journalism; business administration; business economics; business marketing and marketing management; business systems analysis and design; chemistry; computer science; criminal justice studies; development economics; economics; elementary education; enterprise management; environmental science; European studies; film/video production; finance; fine/studio arts; French; German; graphic design/commercial art/illustration; health science; history; human resources management; information sciences/systems; interdisciplinary studies; international business; international business marketing; international economics; international finance; international relations; Islamic studies; journalism; Judaic studies; Latin American studies; law and legal studies; liberal arts and studies; literature; management information systems/business data processing; mathematical statistics; mathematics; Middle Eastern studies; multimedia; music; peace and conflict studies; philosophy; physics; political science; (pre)dentistry; (pre)law; (pre)medicine; (pre)pharmacy studies;

(pre)veterinary studies; psychology; public relations; Russian; Russian/Slavic area studies; secondary education; sociology; Spanish; sport/fitness administration; theater arts/drama; women's studies.

Amherst College

African-American (black) studies; American studies; anthropology; art; Asian studies; astronomy; biology; chemistry; classics; computer science; dance; economics; English; European studies; fine/studio arts; French; geology; German; Greek (Ancient and Medieval); history; interdisciplinary studies; Latin (Ancient and Medieval); law and legal studies; mathematics; music; neuroscience; philosophy; physics; political science; psychology; religious studies; Russian; sociology; Spanish; theater arts/drama; women's studies.

Arkansas Tech University

Accounting; agricultural business; art; art education; biology; biology education; business administration; business education; chemistry; chemistry education; computer science; creative writing; early childhood education; economics; electrical/electronic engineering technology; electrical/electronics engineering; elementary education; engineering; engineering physics; English; English education; foreign languages education; foreign languages/literatures; French; general studies; geology; German; history; hospitality management; information technology; international relations; journalism; management science; mathematics; mathematics education; mechanical engineering; medical assistant; medical records administration; medical technology; middle school education; music; music education; natural resources protective services; natural sciences; nuclear engineering; nursing; office management; physical education; physical sciences; psychology; recreation/leisure facilities management; rehabilitation therapy; social studies education; sociology; Spanish; speech education; speech/rhetorical studies; sport/fitness administration; wildlife biology.

Art Center College of Design

Advertising; architectural environmental design; art; film studies; graphic design/commercial art/illustration; industrial design; photography; visual/performing arts.

Asbury College

Accounting; applied mathematics; art education; biblical studies; biochemistry; biology; business; chemistry; classics; computer/information sciences; elementary education; English; fine/studio arts; French; Greek (Ancient and Medieval); health/physical education; history; interdisciplinary studies; journalism; Latin (Ancient and Medieval); mathematics; middle school education; missionary studies; music; music education; philosophy; physical education; physical sciences; psychology; radio/television broadcasting technology; recreation/leisure facilities management; religious education; social sciences; social work; sociology; Spanish; speech/rhetorical studies.

Augustana College (IL)

Accounting; anthropology; art; art education; art history; Asian studies; biology; business administration; business marketing and marketing management; chemistry; classics; computer science; creative writing; earth sciences; economics; education; elementary education; engineering physics; English; environmental science; finance; fine/studio arts; French; geography; geology; German; history; jazz; Latin (Ancient and Medieval);

liberal arts and studies; literature; mass communications; mathematics; music; music (piano and organ performance); music (voice and choral/opera performance); music education; occupational therapy; philosophy; physical education; physics; political science; (pre)dentistry; (pre)law; (pre)medicine; (pre)veterinary studies; psychology; public administration; religious studies; sacred music; Scandinavian languages; secondary education; sociology; Spanish; speech therapy; speech-language pathology/audiology; speech/rhetorical studies; stringed instruments; theater arts/drama; wind and percussion instruments; women's studies.

Augustana College (SD)

Accounting; art; art education; athletic training/sports medicine; biology; business administration; business communications; chemistry; computer science; economics; education of the hearing impaired; elementary education; engineering physics; English; exercise sciences; foreign languages/literatures; French; German; health services administration; history; international relations; journalism; K-12 education; liberal arts and studies; management information systems/business data processing; mass communications; mathematics; medical technology; music; music education; nursing; philosophy; physical education; physics; political science; (pre)dentistry; (pre)law; (pre)medicine; (pre)veterinary studies; psychology; religious studies; secondary education; social studies education; social work; sociology; Spanish; special education; speech-language pathology/audiology; speech/theater education; sport/fitness administration; theater arts/drama.

Austin College

American studies; art; biology; business administration; chemistry; classical and ancient Near Eastern languages, other; classics; communications; computer science; economics; English; French; German; history; international economics; international relations; Latin (Ancient and Medieval); Latin American studies; mathematics; multi/interdisciplinary studies, other; music; philosophy; physical education; physics; political science; psychology; religious studies; sociology; Spanish.

Azusa Pacific University

Accounting; applied art; art; athletic training/sports medicine; biblical studies; biochemistry; biology; business administration; business marketing and marketing management; chemistry; communications; computer science; cultural studies; divinity/ministry; English; health science; history; international relations; liberal arts and studies; management information systems/business data processing; mathematics; music; natural sciences; nursing; philosophy; physical education; physics; political science; (pre)engineering; (pre)law; psychology; religious studies; social sciences; social work; sociology; Spanish; theology.

Babson College

Accounting; business administration; business communications; business marketing and marketing management; economics; entrepreneurship; finance; international business; investments and securities; management information systems/business data processing; operations research.

Baldwin-Wallace College

Accounting; art; art education; art history; arts management; athletic training/sports medicine; biology; broadcast journalism; business administration; business education; business marketing and marketing management; chemistry; computer science; criminal justice/law enforcement administration; dance; economics; education; elementary education; engineering science; English; environmental science; family/consumer studies; finance; fine/studio arts; French; geology; German; health education; history; home economics; home economics education; human services; information sciences/systems; interdisciplinary studies; international relations; mass communications; mathematics; medical technology; middle school education; music; music (piano and organ performance); music (voice and choral/opera performance); music business management and merchandising; music education; music history; music therapy; neuroscience; philosophy; physical education; physical therapy; physics; political science; (pre)dentistry; (pre)law; (pre)medicine; (pre)veterinary studies; psychology; religious studies; science education; secondary education; social work; sociology; Spanish; special education; speech-language pathology/audiology; sport/fitness administration; stringed instruments; theater arts/drama; wind and percussion instruments.

Bard College

Acting/directing; African studies; American government; American history; American studies; anthropology; archaeology; area studies; art; art history; Asian studies; biochemistry; biological and physical sciences; biology; chemistry; Chinese; city/community/regional planning; classics; comparative literature; creative writing; cultural studies; dance; drama/theater literature; drawing; Eastern European area studies; ecology; economics; English; environmental biology; environmental science; European history; European studies; film studies; film/video production; fine/studio arts; French; German; Greek (Ancient and Medieval); Greek (Modern); Hebrew; history; history of philosophy; history of science and technology; humanities; interdisciplinary studies; international economics; international relations; Italian; jazz; Judaic studies; Latin (Ancient and Medieval); Latin American studies; literature; mathematics; medieval/renaissance studies; modern languages; molecular biology; music; music (general performance); music (voice and choral/opera performance); music history; music theory and composition; natural sciences; painting; philosophy; photography; physical sciences; physics; play/screenwriting; political science; (pre)dentistry; (pre)law; (pre)medicine; (pre)veterinary studies; psychology; religious studies; Romance languages; Russian; Russian/Slavic area studies; sculpture; social sciences; sociology; Spanish; theater arts/drama; visual/performing arts; western civilization.

Barnard College

African studies; American studies; anthropology; applied mathematics; architecture; art history; Asian studies; astronomy; biochemistry; biology; biopsychology; chemistry; classics; comparative literature; computer science; dance; drama/theater literature; East Asian studies; Eastern European area studies; economics; English; environmental science; European studies; French; German; Greek (Ancient and Medieval); history; Italian; Latin (Ancient and Medieval); Latin American studies; mathematical statistics; mathematics; medieval/renaissance studies; Middle Eastern studies; music; philosophy; physics; physiological psychology/psychobiology; political science; (pre)medicine; psychology; religious studies; Russian; Russian/

Slavic area studies; Slavic languages; sociology; South Asian studies; Spanish; theater arts/drama; urban studies; women's studies.

Bates College

African studies; American studies; anthropology; art; biochemistry; biology; chemistry; Chinese; classics; East Asian studies; economics; English; environmental science; French; geology; German; history; interdisciplinary studies; Japanese; mathematics; medieval/renaissance studies; music; neuroscience; philosophy; physics; political science; psychology; religious studies; Russian; sociology; Spanish; speech/rhetorical studies; theater arts/drama; women's studies.

Baylor University

Accounting; acting/directing; aircraft pilot (professional); American studies; anthropology; applied mathematics; archaeology; architecture; art; art education; art history; Asian studies; biblical languages/literatures; biochemistry; biology; biology education; business; business administration; business economics; business education; business marketing and marketing management; business statistics; chemistry; chemistry education; classics; clothing/apparel/textile studies; communication disorders; communications; computer education; computer science; dietetics; drama and dance education; early childhood education; earth sciences; economics; education; education of the speech impaired; electrical/electronics engineering; elementary education; engineering; English; English composition; English education; enterprise management; environmental science; fashion design/illustration; finance; financial planning; fine/studio arts; foreign languages education; forensic technology; forestry; French; French language education; geography; geology; geophysics and seismology; German; German language education; Greek (Ancient and Medieval); health education; health/physical education; history; history education; home economics; human resources management; individual/family development; insurance and risk management; interdisciplinary studies; interior design; international business; international relations; journalism; Latin (Ancient and Medieval); Latin American studies; linguistics; management information systems/business data processing; mathematics; mathematics education; mechanical engineering; museum studies; music; music (general performance); music education; music history; music theory and composition; nursing; operations management; philosophy; physical education; physics; physics education; physiological psychology/psychobiology; political science; (pre)dentistry; (pre)law; (pre)medicine; psychology; public administration; reading education; real estate; religious studies; Russian; Russian/Slavic area studies; sacred music; science education; secondary education; social science education; social studies education; social work; sociology; Spanish; Spanish language education; special education; speech education; speech/rhetorical studies; sport/fitness administration; telecommunications; theater arts/drama; theater design; urban studies.

Belmont University

Accounting; advertising; applied mathematics; art; art education; behavioral sciences; biblical languages/literatures; biblical studies; bilingual/bicultural education; biochemistry; biological and physical sciences; biology; broadcast journalism; business administration; business economics; business education; business marketing and marketing management; chemistry; computer management; computer programming; computer science; counselor education/guidance; developmental/child psychology; divinity/ministry; early childhood education; economics; education; elementary education; engineering science; English; finance; fine/studio arts; Greek (Modern); health education; health services administration; history; hospitality management; hotel and restaurant management; information sciences/systems; international business; journalism; K-12 education; mass communications; mathematics; medical technology; music; music (piano and organ performance); music (voice and choral/opera performance); music business management and merchandising; music education; music history; nursing; pastoral counseling; pharmacology; philosophy; physical education; physics; political science; psychology; radio/television broadcasting; reading education; recreation and leisure studies; retail management; sacred music; secretarial science; social work; sociology; Spanish; special education; speech/rhetorical studies; theater arts/drama; western civilization.

Beloit College

Anthropology; art education; art history; Asian studies; biochemistry; biology; business administration; business economics; cell biology; chemistry; classics; comparative literature; computer science; creative writing; economics; education; elementary education; engineering; English; environmental biology; environmental science; European studies; fine/studio arts; French; geology; German; history; interdisciplinary studies; international relations; Latin American studies; literature; mass communications; mathematics; modern languages; molecular biology; museum studies; music; music education; philosophy; physics; political science; (pre)dentistry; (pre)law; (pre)medicine; psychology; religious studies; Romance languages; Russian; Russian/Slavic area studies; science education; secondary education; sociobiology; sociology; Spanish; theater arts/drama; women's studies.

Bennington College

Anthropology; architecture; art; biochemistry; biological and physical sciences; biology; ceramic arts; chemistry; Chinese; comparative literature; computer science; creative writing; dance; design/applied arts, other; developmental/child psychology; drawing; early childhood education; ecology; English; environmental biology; environmental science; European studies; film studies; fine/studio arts; French; German; history; history of philosophy; humanities; interdisciplinary studies; international relations; Italian studies; Japanese; jazz; liberal arts and studies; literature; mathematics; modern languages; music; music (voice and choral/opera performance); music history; natural sciences; philosophy; photography; physics; (pre)medicine; (pre)veterinary studies; printmaking; psychology; sculpture; social sciences; sociology; Spanish; stringed instruments; theater arts/drama; visual/performing arts.

Berea College

Agricultural business; agricultural sciences; art; art education; art history; biology; biology education; business administration; chemistry; child care/development; classics; developmental/child psychology; dietetics; early childhood education; economics; education; elementary education; English; English education; family/consumer studies; fine/studio arts; foreign languages education; French; French language education; German; German language education; history; home economics education;

hotel and restaurant management; industrial arts; industrial technology; mathematics; mathematics education; middle school education; music; music education; nursing; philosophy; physical education; physics; political science; (pre)dentistry; (pre)medicine; (pre)veterinary studies; psychology; religious studies; secondary education; sociology; Spanish; Spanish language education; theater arts/drama; women's studies.

Berry College

Accounting; animal sciences; anthropology; applied art; art; art education; art history; biochemistry; biology; biology education; broadcast journalism; business administration; business economics; business marketing and marketing management; chemistry; chemistry education; communications; computer science; computer/information sciences; early childhood education; economics; education; elementary education; English; English education; environmental science; finance; fine/studio arts; French; French language education; German; German language education; health education; history; history education; horticulture science; information sciences/systems; interdisciplinary studies; international relations; journalism; mass communications; mathematics; mathematics education; middle school education; music; music (piano and organ performance); music (voice and choral/opera performance); music business management and merchandising; music education; philosophy; physical education; physics; physics education; political science; (pre)dentistry; (pre)law; (pre)medicine; (pre)veterinary studies; psychology; public relations; religious studies; science education; secondary education; social sciences; sociology; Spanish; Spanish language education; speech/rhetorical studies; theater arts/drama.

Bethel College (MN)

Accounting; adult/continuing education; art; art education; art history; athletic training/sports medicine; biblical studies; biochemistry; biology; business administration; chemistry; child care/development; computer science; creative writing; cultural studies; early childhood education; economics; education; elementary education; English; environmental science; finance; fine/studio arts; health education; history; international relations; liberal arts and studies; literature; management information systems/business data processing; mass communications; mathematics; molecular biology; music; music education; nursing; philosophy; physical education; physics; political science; (pre)dentistry; (pre)law; (pre)medicine; (pre)veterinary studies; psychology; sacred music; science education; secondary education; social work; Spanish; speech/rhetorical studies; teaching English as a second language; theater arts/drama.

Biola University

Adult/continuing education; anthropology; art; biblical studies; bilingual/bicultural education; biochemistry; biology; business administration; clinical psychology; communication disorders; computer/information sciences; divinity/ministry; drawing; education; elementary education; English; exercise sciences; fine/studio arts; graphic design/commercial art/illustration; history; humanities; K-12 education; mathematics; missionary studies; music; nursing; pastoral counseling; philosophy; physical education; physical sciences; (pre)law; psychology; radio/television broadcasting; religious education; religious studies; secondary education; social sciences; sociology; Spanish; theology.

Birmingham-Southern College

Accounting; art; art education; art history; Asian studies; biology; business administration; chemistry; computer science; dance; drawing; early childhood education; economics; education; elementary education; English; fine/studio arts; French; German; history; human resources management; interdisciplinary studies; international business; mathematics; music; music (piano and organ performance); music (voice and choral/opera performance); music education; music history; painting; philosophy; physics; political science; (pre)dentistry; (pre)law; (pre)medicine; printmaking; psychology; religious studies; sculpture; secondary education; sociology; Spanish; theater arts/drama.

Boston College

Accounting; art history; biochemistry; biology; business administration; business marketing and marketing management; chemistry; classics; computer science; early childhood education; economics; elementary education; English; environmental science; finance; fine/studio arts; French; geology; geophysics and seismology; German; Hispanic-American studies; history; human resources management; individual/family development; interdisciplinary studies; Italian; management information systems/business data processing; mass communications; mathematics; music; nursing; operations research; philosophy; physics; political science; (pre)medicine; psychology; Russian; Russian/Slavic area studies; secondary education; Slavic languages; sociology; special education; theater arts/drama; theology.

Boston University

Accounting; acting/directing; aerospace engineering; American studies; anthropology; archaeology; area studies, other; art education; art history; astronomy; astrophysics; athletic training/sports medicine; bilingual/bicultural education; biochemistry; bioengineering; biological sciences/life sciences, other; biology; business administration; business marketing and marketing management; chemistry; chemistry education; classics; communication disorders; communications; computer engineering; computer science; dental laboratory technician; drama and dance education; drama/theater literature; drawing; early childhood education; earth sciences; East Asian studies; ecology; economics; education; education of the hearing impaired; electrical/electronics engineering; elementary education; engineering; engineering, other; English; English education; environmental science; ethnic/cultural studies, other; exercise sciences; film/video production; finance; foreign languages education; foreign languages/literatures; French; geography; geology; German; graphic design/commercial art/illustration; Greek (Ancient and Medieval); Greek (Modern); health science; history; hospitality management; hotel and restaurant management; industrial/manufacturing engineering; information sciences/systems; interdisciplinary studies; international business; international finance; international relations; Italian; journalism; journalism and mass communication, other; Latin (Ancient and Medieval); Latin American studies; linguistics; management information systems/business data processing; marine biology; marketing research; mass communications; mathematics; mathematics education; mathematics/computer science; mechanical engineering; medical technology; molecular biology; music (general performance); music (piano and organ performance); music

(voice and choral/opera performance); music education; music history; music theory and composition; neuroscience; nutritional sciences; occupational therapy; operations management; organizational behavior; painting; paralegal/legal assistant; philosophy; physical education; physical therapy; physics; physiology; political science; (pre)dentistry; psychology; public relations; radio/television broadcasting; recreation and leisure studies; rehabilitation therapy; religious studies; Russian; Russian/Slavic area studies; science education; sculpture; social sciences and history, other; social studies education; sociology; Spanish; special education; speech/theater education; systems engineering; teacher education, other; theater design; urban studies.

Bowdoin College

African studies; African-American (black) studies; anthropology; archaeology; art; art history; Asian studies; biochemistry; biology; chemistry; classics; computer science; economics; English; environmental science; fine/studio arts; French; geology; German; history; interdisciplinary studies; Latin American studies; mathematics; music; neuroscience; philosophy; physics; political science; (pre)medicine; psychology; religious studies; Romance languages; Russian; sociology; Spanish; women's studies.

Bradley University

Accounting; actuarial science; advertising; art; art history; biochemistry; biology; broadcast journalism; business administration; business economics; business marketing and marketing management; chemistry; civil engineering; civil engineering, other; communications; communications, other; computer/information sciences; construction engineering; criminal justice/law enforcement administration; early childhood education; ecology; economics; education of the emotionally handicapped; education of the mentally handicapped; education of the specific learning disabled; electrical/electronic engineering technology; electrical/electronics engineering; elementary education; engineering physics; English; environmental engineering; family resource management studies; finance; fine/studio arts; French; geology; German; health professions and related sciences, other; health science; history; industrial technology; industrial/manufacturing engineering; information sciences/systems; insurance and risk management; international business; international relations; journalism; liberal arts and studies; management information systems/business data processing; mathematics; mathematics, other; mechanical engineering; medical technology; molecular biology; music; music (general performance); music education; music theory and composition; nursing; philosophy; physical therapy; physics; political science; psychology; public relations; radio/television broadcasting; religious studies; social work; sociology; Spanish; speech/rhetorical studies; teacher education, specific programs, other; theater arts/drama.

Brandeis University

African studies; African-American (black) studies; American studies; anthropology; area, ethnic and cultural studies, other; art; biochemistry; biological sciences/life sciences, other; biology; biophysics; cell and molecular biology, other; chemistry; classical and ancient Near Eastern languages, other; comparative literature; computer science; economics; engineering physics; English; European studies; fine/studio arts; French; German; Greek (Ancient and Medieval); history; Islamic studies; Judaic studies; Latin (Ancient and Medieval); Latin American studies;

linguistics; mathematics; Middle Eastern studies; multi/interdisciplinary studies, other; music; neuroscience; philosophy; physics; political science; psychology; Russian; Russian/Slavic area studies; sociology; Spanish; theater arts/drama.

Brigham Young University

Accounting; agronomy/crop science; American studies; animal sciences; anthropology; art; art education; art history; Asian studies; astrophysics; biochemistry; biology; botany; business administration; business marketing and marketing management; chemical engineering; chemistry; chemistry education; Chinese; civil engineering; classics; communications; comparative literature; computer engineering; computer science; construction management; dance; design/visual communications; dietetics; drama and dance education; early childhood education; earth sciences; economics; electrical/electronic engineering technology; electrical/electronics engineering; elementary education; engineering; engineering technology; English; English education; European studies; family studies; family/community studies; food sciences; foreign languages education; French; French language education; geography; geology; German; German language education; graphic design/commercial art/illustration; health science; health/physical education; hearing sciences; history; history education; horticulture science; humanities; industrial arts education; industrial design; interior design; international relations; Italian; Japanese; Latin (Ancient and Medieval); Latin American studies; linguistics; mathematical statistics; mathematics; mathematics education; mechanical engineering; microbiology/bacteriology; Middle Eastern studies; molecular biology; music; music (general performance); music education; music theory and composition; nursing; nutritional sciences; philosophy; photography; physical education; physics; physics education; plant breeding; political science; Portuguese; psychology; range management; recreation/leisure facilities management; Russian; social studies education; social work; sociology; Spanish; Spanish language education; speech-language pathology; theater arts/drama; visual/performing arts; wildlife biology; wildlife management; zoology.

Brown University

African-American (black) studies; American studies; anthropology; applied mathematics; archaeology; architecture; art; art history; behavioral sciences; biochemistry; bioengineering; biology; biomedical science; biophysics; chemical engineering; chemistry; civil engineering; classics; cognitive psychology and psycholinguistics; comparative literature; computer engineering; computer science; creative writing; development economics; East Asian studies; economics; education; electrical/electronics engineering; engineering; engineering physics; English; environmental science; film studies; fine/studio arts; French; geochemistry; geology; geophysics and seismology; German; Hispanic-American studies; history; international relations; Italian; Italian studies; Judaic studies; Latin American studies; linguistics; literature; marine biology; materials engineering; mathematics; mathematics/computer science; mechanical engineering; medieval/renaissance studies; Middle Eastern studies; molecular biology; music; music, other; musicology; neuroscience; organizational behavior; philosophy; physics; political science; psychology; religious studies; Russian/Slavic area studies; sociology; South Asian studies; Spanish; theater arts/drama; urban studies; visual/performing arts; women's studies.

Bryn Mawr College

Anthropology; archaeology; art; art history; astronomy; biology; chemistry; classics; comparative literature; East Asian studies; economics; English; French; geology; German; Greek (Ancient and Medieval); history; Italian; Latin (Ancient and Medieval); mathematics; music; philosophy; physics; political science; psychology; religious studies; Romance languages; Russian; sociology; Spanish; urban studies.

Bucknell University

Accounting; anthropology; area studies; art; art history; biology; biopsychology; business administration; cell biology; chemical engineering; chemistry; civil engineering; classics; computer engineering; computer/information sciences; early childhood education; East Asian studies; economics; education; educational statistics/research methods; electrical/electronics engineering; elementary education; English; environmental science; fine/studio arts; French; geography; geology; German; history; humanities; interdisciplinary studies; international relations; Latin American studies; mathematics; mechanical engineering; music; music (general performance); music education; music history; music theory and composition; philosophy; physics; political science; psychology; religious studies; Russian; secondary education; sociology; Spanish; theater arts/drama; women's studies.

Buena Vista University

Accounting; art; arts management; athletic training/sports medicine; biological and physical sciences; biology; business administration; business economics; business education; business marketing and marketing management; chemistry; communications; computer science; criminal justice/law enforcement administration; economics; education; elementary education; English; finance; graphic design/commercial art/illustration; history; information sciences/systems; international business; liberal arts and studies; management information systems/business data processing; mass communications; mathematics; modern languages; music; music education; natural sciences; philosophy; physical education; physics; political science; (pre)dentistry; (pre)law; (pre)medicine; (pre)veterinary studies; psychology; public administration; public relations; radio/television broadcasting; religious studies; science education; secondary education; social sciences; social work; Spanish; special education; speech/rhetorical studies; theater arts/drama.

Butler University

Accounting; actuarial science; anthropology; arts management; athletic training/sports medicine; biology; business administration; business economics; business marketing and marketing management; chemistry; computer science; criminal justice studies; dance; economics; elementary education; English; finance; French; German; Greek (Modern); history; international business; international relations; journalism; Latin (Ancient and Medieval); liberal arts and studies; mathematics; medicinal/pharmaceutical chemistry; music; music (piano and organ performance); music (voice and choral/opera performance); music business management and merchandising; music education; music history; pharmacy; philosophy; physician assistant; physics; political science; psychology; public relations; religious studies; secondary education; sociology; Spanish; speech-language pathology/audiology; speech/rhetorical studies;

stringed instruments; telecommunications; theater arts/drama; wind and percussion instruments.

California Institute of Technology

Aerospace engineering; applied mathematics; astronomy; astrophysics; biochemistry; biology; business economics; cell biology; chemical engineering; chemistry; civil engineering; computer engineering; computer science; earth sciences; economics; electrical/electronics engineering; engineering; engineering physics; environmental engineering; geochemistry; geology; geophysics and seismology; history; literature; materials science; mathematics; mechanical engineering; molecular biology; neuroscience; nuclear physics; physical sciences; physics; social sciences.

California Polytechnic State University, San Luis Obispo

Aerospace engineering; agricultural business; agricultural engineering; agricultural sciences; agronomy/crop science; animal sciences; applied art; architectural engineering; architecture; art; biochemistry; biology; business administration; chemistry; city/community/regional planning; civil engineering; computer engineering; computer science; dairy science; developmental/child psychology; early childhood education; economics; electrical/electronics engineering; engineering science; English; environmental biology; environmental engineering; farm/ranch management; food sciences; forestry; graphic design/commercial art/illustration; graphic/printing equipment; history; horticulture science; human resources management; industrial technology; industrial/manufacturing engineering; journalism; landscape architecture; liberal arts and studies; management information systems/business data processing; materials engineering; mathematical statistics; mathematics; mechanical engineering; mechanical engineering technology; microbiology/bacteriology; music; nutrition science; ornamental horticulture; philosophy; physical education; physical sciences; physics; political science; (pre)medicine; psychology; recreation and leisure studies; social sciences; speech/rhetorical studies; trade and industrial education.

Calvin College

Accounting; American history; art; art education; art history; athletic training/sports medicine; biblical studies; bilingual/bicultural education; biochemistry; biological and physical sciences; biology; biotechnology research; business administration; business communications; chemical engineering; chemistry; civil engineering; classics; computer science; criminal justice/law enforcement administration; design/visual communications; economics; electrical/electronics engineering; elementary education; engineering; English; environmental science; European history; exercise sciences; film studies; fine/studio arts; French; geography; geology; German; Greek (Modern); history; interdisciplinary studies; international relations; Latin (Ancient and Medieval); mass communications; mathematics; mechanical engineering; music; music (general performance); music (piano and organ performance); music (voice and choral/opera performance); music conducting; music education; music history; music theory and composition; natural sciences; nursing; occupational therapy; philosophy; physical education; physical sciences; physics; political science; (pre)dentistry; (pre)law; (pre)medicine; (pre)veterinary studies; psychology; public administration; recreation and leisure studies; religious studies;

sacred music; science education; secondary education; social sciences; social work; sociology; Spanish; special education; speech-language pathology/audiology; speech/rhetorical studies; teaching English as a second language; theater arts/drama; theology.

Canisius College

Accounting; accounting, other; anthropology; art history; athletic training/sports medicine; biochemistry; biological sciences/life sciences, other; biology; biology education; business administration; business education; business marketing and marketing management; chemistry; chemistry education; computer science; criminal justice/law enforcement administration; design/visual communications; economics; education; elementary education; English; English education; entrepreneurship; environmental science; European studies; finance; French; French language education; German; German language education; history; humanities; international relations; liberal arts and studies; management information systems/business data processing; mass communications; mathematics; mathematics education; medical technology; middle school education; philosophy; physical education; physics; physics education; political science; psychology; public administration; religious studies; science education; secondary education; social sciences; social studies education; sociology; Spanish; Spanish language education; special education; urban studies.

Carleton College

African studies; American studies; anthropology; art history; Asian studies; biology; chemistry; classics; computer science; economics; English; fine/studio arts; French; geology; German; Greek (Ancient and Medieval); history; interdisciplinary studies; international relations; Latin (Ancient and Medieval); Latin American studies; mathematics; music; philosophy; physics; political science; psychology; religious studies; Romance languages; Russian; sociology; Spanish; women's studies.

Carnegie Mellon University

Applied mathematics; architecture; art; biochemistry; bioengineering; biology; biophysics; business administration; business economics; ceramic arts; chemical engineering; chemistry; civil engineering; cognitive psychology and psycholinguistics; computer engineering; computer science; computer/information sciences; creative writing; economics; electrical/electronics engineering; engineering; engineering design; English; environmental engineering; European studies; fine/studio arts; French; German; graphic design/commercial art/illustration; history; humanities; industrial design; information sciences/systems; interdisciplinary studies; Japanese; liberal arts and studies; literature; mass communications; materials engineering; materials science; mathematical statistics; mathematics; mechanical engineering; modern languages; music; music (general performance); music theory and composition; philosophy; physics; political science; polymer chemistry; psychology; Russian; sculpture; social sciences; Spanish; technical writing; theater arts/drama; western civilization.

Carroll College (MT)

Accounting; acting/directing; art; biology; biology education; business administration; business economics; chemistry; civil engineering; communications; computer science; education; elementary education; engineering; English; English education;

environmental science; finance; French; general studies; history; history education; international relations; Latin (Ancient and Medieval); mathematics; mathematics education; medical records administration; medical technology; nursing; philosophy; physical education; political science; (pre)dentistry; (pre)law; (pre)medicine; (pre)pharmacy studies; (pre)veterinary studies; psychology; public administration; public relations; religious education; religious studies; secondary education; social science education; social sciences; social work; sociology; Spanish; Spanish language education; sport/fitness administration; teaching English as a second language; technical writing; theater arts/drama; theater design; theology.

Case Western Reserve University

Accounting; aerospace engineering; American studies; anthropology; applied mathematics; art education; art history; Asian studies; astronomy; biochemistry; bioengineering; biological and physical sciences; biology; business administration; chemical engineering; chemistry; civil engineering; classics; communication disorders; comparative literature; computer engineering; computer science; dietetics; economics; electrical/electronics engineering; engineering; engineering physics; engineering science; English; environmental science; European studies; evolutionary biology; French; geology; German; gerontology; history; history of science and technology; international relations; materials engineering; materials science; mathematical statistics; mathematics; mechanical engineering; music; music education; nursing; nutrition science; philosophy; physics; plastics engineering; political science; psychology; religious studies; sociology; Spanish; systems engineering; theater arts/drama; women's studies.

The Catholic University of America

Accounting; anthropology; architecture; art; art education; art history; biochemistry; bioengineering; biology; biology education; business; business administration; chemical and atomic/molecular physics; chemistry; chemistry education; civil engineering; classics; communications; computer engineering; computer science; construction engineering; drama and dance education; early childhood education; ecology; economics; education; electrical/electronics engineering; elementary education; engineering; English; English education; finance; fine arts and art studies, other; French; French language education; general studies; German; German language education; history; history education; human resources management; interdisciplinary studies; international economics; international finance; Latin (Ancient and Medieval); mathematics; mathematics education; mechanical engineering; medical technology; music; music (general performance); music (piano and organ performance); music (voice and choral/opera performance); music education; music history; music theory and composition; nursing; painting; philosophy; physics; political science; psychology; religious education; religious studies; Romance languages; sculpture; secondary education; social work; sociology; Spanish; Spanish language education; theater arts/drama.

Cedarville University

Accounting; American studies; athletic training/sports medicine; biblical studies; biological and physical sciences; biology; biology education; broadcast journalism; business administration; business marketing and marketing management; chemistry; communication equipment technology; communications; computer

science; criminal justice/law enforcement administration; early childhood education; education; electrical/electronics engineering; elementary education; English; English education; environmental biology; finance; health education; health/physical education; history; information sciences/systems; international business; international relations; mathematics; mathematics education; mechanical engineering; medical technology; missionary studies; music; music (piano and organ performance); music (voice and choral/opera performance); music education; nursing; pastoral counseling; philosophy; physical education; political science; (pre)dentistry; (pre)law; (pre)medicine; (pre)veterinary studies; psychology; public administration; radio/television broadcasting; sacred music; science education; secondary education; secretarial science; social sciences; social studies education; social work; sociology; Spanish; Spanish language education; special education; speech education; speech/rhetorical studies; technical writing; theater arts/drama; theology.

Centenary College of Louisiana

Accounting; art; art education; arts management; biochemistry; biology; biophysics; business administration; business economics; chemistry; dance; drawing; early childhood education; economics; education; elementary education; English; environmental science; film studies; fine/studio arts; French; geology; German; health education; health science; history; interdisciplinary studies; K-12 education; Latin (Ancient and Medieval); liberal arts and studies; literature; mass communications; mathematics; middle school education; music; music (piano and organ performance); music (voice and choral/opera performance); music education; occupational therapy; philosophy; physical education; physical sciences; physical therapy; physics; political science; (pre)dentistry; (pre)law; (pre)medicine; (pre)veterinary studies; psychology; religious studies; sacred music; science education; secondary education; social sciences; sociology; Spanish; speech-language pathology/audiology; speech/rhetorical studies; stringed instruments; theater arts/drama; wind and percussion instruments.

Central College

Accounting; art; biology; business administration; chemistry; communications; computer science; economics; elementary education; English; environmental science; exercise sciences; French; general studies; German; history; information sciences/systems; interdisciplinary studies; international business; Latin American studies; linguistics; mathematics; mathematics/computer science; music; music education; philosophy; physics; political science; psychology; religious studies; secondary education; social sciences; sociology; Spanish; theater arts/drama; Western European studies.

Centre College

Anthropology; art; art history; biochemistry; biology; chemistry; classics; computer science; economics; elementary education; English; French; German; history; international relations; mathematics; molecular biology; music; philosophy; physics; physiological psychology/psychobiology; political science; (pre)dentistry; (pre)law; (pre)medicine; psychology; religious studies; secondary education; sociology; Spanish; theater arts/drama.

Chapman University

Accounting; advertising; American studies; applied mathematics; art; art history; athletic training/sports medicine; biochemistry;

biology; broadcast journalism; business administration; business economics; business marketing and marketing management; chemistry; comparative literature; computer science; creative writing; criminal justice/law enforcement administration; dance; economics; English; environmental science; European studies; exercise sciences; film studies; film/video production; finance; fine/studio arts; food sciences; French; graphic design/commercial art/illustration; health science; history; information sciences/systems; international business; journalism; Latin American studies; law and legal studies; liberal arts and studies; literature; mass communications; music; music (piano and organ performance); music (voice and choral/opera performance); music education; music therapy; peace and conflict studies; philosophy; physical education; political science; (pre)dentistry; (pre)law; (pre)medicine; (pre)veterinary studies; psychology; public relations; religious studies; social sciences; social work; sociology; Spanish; speech/rhetorical studies; stringed instruments; theater arts/drama; wind and percussion instruments; women's studies.

Christendom College

Classics; French; history; liberal arts and studies; literature; philosophy; political science; theology.

Christian Brothers University

Accounting; biology; biology education; business; business administration; business marketing and marketing management; chemical engineering; chemistry; chemistry education; civil engineering; computer engineering; computer science; economics; education; educational psychology; electrical/electronics engineering; elementary education; engineering physics; English; English education; environmental engineering; finance; history; history education; management information systems/business data processing; mathematics; mathematics education; mechanical engineering; natural sciences; physics; physics education; (pre)dentistry; (pre)law; (pre)medicine; (pre)pharmacy studies; (pre)theology; psychology; religious studies; technical writing.

Claremont McKenna College

Accounting; African-American (black) studies; American studies; art; Asian studies; biochemistry; biology; biophysics; chemistry; Chinese; classics; computer science; economics; engineering/industrial management; English; environmental science; European studies; film studies; French; German; Greek (Modern); history; international business; international economics; international relations; Italian; Japanese; Latin (Ancient and Medieval); Latin American studies; law and legal studies; literature; mathematics; Mexican-American studies; modern languages; music; philosophy; physics; physiological psychology/psychobiology; political science; (pre)dentistry; (pre)law; (pre)medicine; psychology; religious studies; Russian; Spanish; theater arts/drama; women's studies.

Clarkson University

Accounting; aerospace engineering; applied mathematics; biochemistry; biology; biophysics; biotechnology research; business administration; business economics; business marketing and marketing management; cell biology; chemical engineering; chemistry; civil engineering; communications; computer engineering; computer science; computer software engineering; computer/information sciences; economics; electrical/electronics

engineering; engineering; entrepreneurship; environmental engineering; environmental health; environmental science; finance; history; human resources management; humanities; industrial/manufacturing engineering; interdisciplinary studies; liberal arts and studies; management information systems/business data processing; materials engineering; materials science; mathematics; mechanical engineering; molecular biology; operations management; organizational psychology; physics; political science; (pre)law; (pre)medicine; (pre)veterinary studies; psychology; social sciences; sociology; structural engineering; technical writing; toxicology.

Clemson University

Accounting; agricultural business; agricultural economics; agricultural education; agricultural engineering; animal sciences; aquaculture operations and production management; architecture; architecture and related programs, other; art; biochemistry; biology; business administration; business management/administrative services, other; business marketing and marketing management; ceramic sciences/engineering; chemical engineering; chemistry; chemistry, other; civil engineering; computer engineering; computer/information sciences; early childhood education; economics; electrical/electronics engineering; elementary education; English; finance; food sciences; foreign languages/literatures; foreign languages/literatures, other; forest management; geology; health professions and related sciences, other; history; horticulture science; industrial arts education; industrial design; industrial/manufacturing engineering; information sciences/systems; landscape architecture; mathematics; mathematics education; mechanical engineering; medical technology; nursing; operations management; philosophy; physics; political science; polymer chemistry; (pre)medicine; (pre)pharmacy studies; (pre)veterinary studies; psychology; recreation/leisure facilities management; science education; science technologies, other; secondary education; sociology; special education; speech/rhetorical studies; visual and performing arts, other.

Cleveland Institute of Music

Audio engineering; music; music (piano and organ performance); music (voice and choral/opera performance); music education; stringed instruments; wind and percussion instruments.

Coe College

Accounting; African-American (black) studies; American studies; architecture; art; art education; Asian studies; athletic training/sports medicine; biochemistry; biological and physical sciences; biology; business administration; chemistry; classics; computer science; economics; education; elementary education; English; environmental science; fine/studio arts; French; German; history; interdisciplinary studies; liberal arts and studies; literature; mathematics; molecular biology; music; music education; nursing; philosophy; physical education; physical sciences; physics; political science; (pre)dentistry; (pre)law; (pre)medicine; (pre)veterinary studies; psychology; public relations; religious studies; science education; secondary education; sociology; Spanish; speech/rhetorical studies; theater arts/drama.

Colby College

African-American (black) studies; American studies; anthropology; art; art history; biochemistry; biology; cell biology;

chemistry; classics; computer science; earth sciences; East Asian studies; economics; English; environmental science; French; geology; German; history; international relations; Latin American studies; mathematics; molecular biology; music; philosophy; physics; political science; psychology; religious studies; Russian/Slavic area studies; sociology; Spanish; theater arts/drama; women's studies.

Colgate University
African studies; African-American (black) studies; anthropology; art; art history; Asian studies; astronomy; astrophysics; biochemistry; biology; chemistry; Chinese; classics; computer science; East Asian studies; economics; education; English; environmental biology; environmental science; French; geography; geology; German; Greek (Modern); history; humanities; international relations; Japanese; Latin (Ancient and Medieval); Latin American studies; mathematics; molecular biology; music; Native American studies; natural sciences; neuroscience; peace and conflict studies; philosophy; physical sciences; physics; political science; psychology; religious studies; Romance languages; Russian; Russian/Slavic area studies; social sciences; sociology; Spanish; theater arts/drama; women's studies.

The College of New Jersey
Accounting; art; art education; biology; biology education; business administration; business economics; chemistry; chemistry education; computer science; criminal justice/law enforcement administration; early childhood education; economics; education of the hearing impaired; elementary education; engineering science; English; English education; finance; fine/studio arts; graphic design/commercial art/illustration; history; history education; industrial arts education; international business; international relations; management information systems/business data processing; mathematical statistics; mathematics; mathematics education; music; music education; nursing; philosophy; physical education; physics; physics education; political science; (pre)law; (pre)medicine; psychology; secondary education; sociology; Spanish; Spanish language education; special education; speech/rhetorical studies; women's studies.

College of Saint Benedict
Accounting; art; art education; art history; biochemistry; biology; business administration; chemistry; classics; computer science; dietetics; economics; education; elementary education; English; fine/studio arts; forestry; French; German; history; humanities; liberal arts and studies; mathematics; mathematics/computer science; music; music education; natural sciences; nursing; nutrition science; occupational therapy; peace and conflict studies; philosophy; physical therapy; physics; political science; (pre)dentistry; (pre)law; (pre)medicine; (pre)pharmacy studies; (pre)theology; (pre)veterinary studies; psychology; religious education; secondary education; social sciences; social work; sociology; Spanish; speech/rhetorical studies; theater arts/drama; theology.

The College of St. Scholastica
Accounting; biochemistry; biology; business communications; business management/administrative services, other; chemistry; communications; computer/information sciences; economics; education; educational media design; English; exercise sciences; health science; health services administration; history; humanities; international business; international relations; K-12 educa-

tion; liberal arts and studies; management science; mathematics; medical laboratory technologies; music; natural sciences; nursing; occupational therapy; physical therapy; psychology; religious studies; social science education; social work.

College of the Atlantic
Architectural environmental design; art; biological and physical sciences; biology; botany; ceramic arts; computer graphics; drawing; ecology; economics; education; elementary education; English; environmental biology; environmental education; environmental science; evolutionary biology; human ecology; interdisciplinary studies; landscape architecture; law and legal studies; liberal arts and studies; literature; marine biology; maritime science; middle school education; museum studies; music; natural sciences; philosophy; (pre)veterinary studies; psychology; public policy analysis; science education; secondary education; wildlife biology; zoology.

College of the Holy Cross
Accounting; African studies; African-American (black) studies; art history; Asian studies; biochemistry; biology; biopsychology; chemistry; classics; economics; English; environmental science; fine/studio arts; French; German; gerontology; history; Italian; Latin American studies; literature; mathematics; Middle Eastern studies; music; peace and conflict studies; philosophy; physics; political science; (pre)dentistry; (pre)law; (pre)medicine; psychology; religious studies; Russian; sociology; Spanish; theater arts/drama; women's studies.

The College of William and Mary
African-American (black) studies; American studies; anthropology; art; art history; biology; biopsychology; business administration; chemistry; classics; computer science; cultural studies; East Asian studies; economics; English; environmental science; European studies; French; geology; German; Greek (Modern); history; interdisciplinary studies; international relations; Latin (Ancient and Medieval); Latin American studies; linguistics; mathematics; medieval/renaissance studies; modern languages; music; philosophy; physical education; physics; political science; psychology; public policy analysis; religious studies; Russian/Slavic area studies; sociology; Spanish; theater arts/drama; women's studies.

The College of Wooster
African studies; African-American (black) studies; archaeology; art; art history; Asian studies; biochemistry; biology; business economics; chemical and atomic/molecular physics; chemistry; classics; communications; comparative literature; computer science; economics; English; European studies; fine/studio arts; French; geology; German; Greek (Modern); history; interdisciplinary studies; international relations; Latin (Ancient and Medieval); Latin American studies; mass communications; mathematics; music; music (voice and choral/opera performance); music education; music history; music therapy; philosophy; physics; political science; (pre)dentistry; (pre)law; (pre)medicine; (pre)veterinary studies; psychology; religious studies; Russian; sociology; South Asian studies; Spanish; speech-language pathology/audiology; speech/rhetorical studies; theater arts/drama; urban studies; women's studies.

The Colorado College
Anthropology; art history; Asian studies; biochemistry; biology; chemistry; classics; comparative literature; creative writing;

dance; economics; economics, other; English; environmental science; ethnic/cultural studies, other; film studies; fine/studio arts; French; geology; German; history; history, other; liberal arts and studies, other; mathematics; mathematics/computer science; music; neuroscience; philosophy; physics; political science; psychology; quantitative economics; religious studies; Romance languages, other; Russian/Slavic area studies; social sciences and history, other; sociology; Spanish; theater arts/drama; women's studies.

Colorado School of Mines

Chemical engineering; chemistry; civil engineering; computer science; economics; electrical/electronics engineering; engineering; engineering physics; engineering science; environmental engineering; geological engineering; geophysical engineering; mathematics; mechanical engineering; metallurgical engineering; mining/mineral engineering; petroleum engineering.

Colorado State University

Accounting; agribusiness; agricultural economics; agricultural education; agricultural engineering; agricultural extension; agricultural sciences; agronomy/crop science; American studies; animal sciences; anthropology; applied mathematics; art; art education; art history; Asian studies; athletic training/sports medicine; biochemistry; biology; biology education; botany; business administration; business education; business marketing and marketing management; ceramic arts; chemical engineering; chemistry; chemistry education; civil engineering; clothing/apparel/textile studies; computer engineering; computer science; construction technology; creative writing; criminal justice studies; dance; dietetics; drawing; economics; electrical/electronics engineering; engineering physics; engineering science; English; English education; entomology; environmental engineering; environmental health; equestrian studies; exercise sciences; farm/ranch management; finance; fine/studio arts; fishing sciences and management; forestry sciences; French; French language education; geology; German; German language education; graphic design/commercial art/illustration; history; home economics; home economics education; horticulture science; hotel and restaurant management; humanities; individual/family development; industrial arts; industrial technology; information sciences/systems; interior design; journalism; landscape architecture; landscaping management; Latin American studies; liberal arts and studies; marketing/distribution education; mathematical statistics; mathematics; mathematics education; mechanical engineering; metal/jewelry arts; microbiology/bacteriology; music; music (general performance); music education; music therapy; natural resources management; nursery management; nutrition science; painting; philosophy; photography; physical education; physical sciences; physics; physics education; plant protection; political science; (pre)dentistry; (pre)law; (pre)medicine; (pre)veterinary studies; printmaking; psychology; public relations; radio/television broadcasting; range management; real estate; recreation/leisure facilities management; science education; sculpture; social sciences; social studies education; social work; sociology; soil conservation; soil sciences; Spanish; Spanish language education; speech/rhetorical studies; technical education; textile arts; theater arts/drama; trade and industrial education; turf management; water resources; wildlife management; zoology.

Columbia College (NY)

African-American (black) studies; American studies; anthropology; archaeology; architecture; architecture and related programs, other; art history; Asian-American studies; astronomy; astrophysics; biochemistry; biology; biophysics; biopsychology; chemical and atomic/molecular physics; chemistry; classics; comparative literature; computer science; dance; East Asian studies; economics; English; environmental biology; environmental science; film studies; French; geochemistry; geology; German; Greek (Ancient and Medieval); Greek (Modern); Hispanic-American studies; history; Italian; Italian studies; K-12 education; Latin American studies; linguistics; mathematical statistics; mathematics; medieval/renaissance studies; Middle Eastern studies; music; philosophy; physics; political science; psychology; religious studies; Russian; Russian/Slavic area studies; Slavic languages; sociology; Spanish; theater arts/drama; urban studies; visual/performing arts; women's studies.

Columbia University, The Fu Foundation School of Engineering and Applied Science

Applied mathematics; bioengineering; chemical engineering; civil engineering; computer engineering; computer science; electrical/electronics engineering; engineering mechanics; engineering/industrial management; environmental engineering; industrial/manufacturing engineering; materials science; mechanical engineering; operations research; physics.

Concordia College (MN)

Accounting; advertising; apparel marketing; architecture; art; art education; art history; biology; biology education; broadcast journalism; business; business administration; business education; chemistry; chemistry education; child care/development; classics; clothing and textiles; clothing/apparel/textile; communications; computer science; creative writing; criminal justice studies; dietetics; early childhood education; economics; education; elementary education; English; English education; environmental science; exercise sciences; family/consumer studies; fine/studio arts; French; French language education; German; German language education; health education; health services administration; health/physical education; history; history education; humanities; international business; international relations; journalism; Latin (Ancient and Medieval); mass communications; mathematics; mathematics education; medical laboratory technologies; medical technology; music; music (general performance); music (piano and organ performance); music (voice and choral/opera performance); music education; music theory and composition; nursing; nutrition science; occupational therapy; office management; ophthalmic/optometric services, other; philosophy; physical education; physical therapy; physics; physics education; political science; (pre)dentistry; (pre)engineering; (pre)law; (pre)medicine; (pre)theology; (pre)veterinary studies; psychology; public relations; radio/television broadcasting; religious studies; respiratory therapy; Russian/Slavic area studies; Scandinavian languages; science education; secondary education; social studies education; social work; sociology; Spanish; Spanish language education; speech/rhetorical studies; theater arts/drama.

Connecticut College

African studies; American studies; anthropology; architecture; art; art history; astrophysics; biochemistry; biology; botany; cell and molecular biology, other; chemistry; chemistry, other;

Chinese; classics; computer/information sciences; dance; East Asian studies; Eastern European area studies; ecology; economics; engineering physics; English; ethnic/cultural studies, other; film studies; French; German; history; human ecology; interdisciplinary studies; international relations; Italian; Japanese; Latin American studies; mathematics; medieval/renaissance studies; music; music education; music, other; neuroscience; philosophy; physics; physics education; political science; psychology; religious studies; Russian; sociology; Spanish; theater arts/drama; urban studies; women's studies; zoology.

Converse College

Accounting; applied art; art; art education; art history; art therapy; biochemistry; biology; business administration; business marketing and marketing management; chemistry; computer science; early childhood education; economics; education; elementary education; English; fine/studio arts; French; history; interior design; international business; mathematics; modern languages; music; music (piano and organ performance); music (voice and choral/opera performance); music education; music history; political science; (pre)dentistry; (pre)law; (pre)medicine; (pre)veterinary studies; psychology; religious studies; secondary education; sign language interpretation; sociology; Spanish; special education; stringed instruments; theater arts/drama.

Cooper Union for the Advancement of Science and Art

Architecture; art; chemical engineering; civil engineering; electrical/electronics engineering; engineering; graphic design/commercial art/illustration; mechanical engineering.

Corcoran College of Art and Design

Applied art; art; ceramic arts; drawing; fine/studio arts; graphic design/commercial art/illustration; photography; printmaking; sculpture.

Cornell College

Anthropology; architecture; art; art education; art history; biochemistry; biology; business economics; business education; chemistry; classics; computer science; cultural studies; economics; education; elementary education; English; environmental science; exercise sciences; French; geology; German; Greek (Modern); history; interdisciplinary studies; international business; international relations; Latin (Ancient and Medieval); Latin American studies; liberal arts and studies; mathematics; medieval/renaissance studies; modern languages; music; music education; philosophy; physical education; physics; political science; psychology; religious studies; Russian; Russian/Slavic area studies; secondary education; sociology; Spanish; speech/rhetorical studies; theater arts/drama; women's studies.

Cornell University

African studies; African-American (black) studies; agribusiness; agricultural business; agricultural economics; agricultural education; agricultural engineering; agricultural mechanization; agricultural sciences; agronomy/crop science; American studies; anatomy; animal sciences; anthropology; applied art; applied economics; archaeology; architectural engineering technology; architectural environmental design; architecture; art; art history; Asian studies; astronomy; atmospheric sciences; behavioral sciences; biochemistry; bioengineering; biology; biometrics; biostatistics; botany; business administration; cell biology; chemical engineering; chemistry; child care/development; Chinese; city/community/regional planning; civil engineering; classical and ancient Near Eastern languages, other; classics; clothing and textiles; communications; community services; comparative literature; computer science; consumer services; creative writing; crop production management; dairy science; dance; developmental/child psychology; dietetics; drawing; East Asian studies; Eastern European area studies; ecology; economics; education; electrical/electronics engineering; engineering; engineering physics; engineering science; English; entomology; environmental engineering; environmental science; European studies; family resource management studies; family/community studies; family/consumer studies; farm/ranch management; fine/studio arts; food sciences; French; genetics; geological engineering; geology; German; Greek (Modern); Hebrew; Hispanic-American studies; history; history of science and technology; home economics education; horticulture science; hotel and restaurant management; human ecology; human services; individual/family development; industrial/manufacturing engineering; information sciences/systems; interdisciplinary studies; interior architecture; international agriculture; international relations; Italian; Japanese; Judaic studies; labor/personnel relations; landscape architecture; Latin (Ancient and Medieval); Latin American studies; liberal arts and studies; linguistics; marine science; mass communications; materials engineering; materials science; mathematical statistics; mathematics; mechanical engineering; medieval/renaissance studies; microbiology/bacteriology; Middle Eastern studies; modern languages; molecular biology; music; Native American studies; natural resources management; neuroscience; nutrition science; nutritional sciences; operations research; ornamental horticulture; philosophy; photography; physics; physiology; plant breeding; plant pathology; plant sciences; political science; poultry science; (pre)law; (pre)medicine; (pre)veterinary studies; psychology; public policy analysis; religious studies; Romance languages; Russian; Russian/Slavic area studies; science/technology and society; sculpture; Slavic languages; sociobiology; sociology; soil sciences; Southeast Asian studies; Spanish; textile arts; theater arts/drama; urban studies; women's studies; zoology.

Covenant College

Biblical studies; biology; business administration; chemistry; computer science; economics; elementary education; English; health science; history; interdisciplinary studies; mathematics; music; natural sciences; nursing; philosophy; physics; (pre)engineering; (pre)law; (pre)medicine; psychology; sociology.

Creighton University

Accounting; American studies; art; art education; art history; atmospheric sciences; biology; business economics; business marketing and marketing management; chemistry; classics; computer science; economics; education; elementary education; emergency medical technology; English; environmental science; exercise sciences; finance; French; German; graphic design/commercial art/illustration; Greek (Modern); health services administration; history; international business; international relations; journalism; K-12 education; Latin (Ancient and Medieval); management information systems/business data processing; mass communications; mathematics; modern languages; music; nursing; philosophy; physics; political science; psychology; social work; sociology; Spanish; special education; speech/rhetorical studies; theater arts/drama; theology.

The Curtis Institute of Music

Music; music (piano and organ performance); music (voice and choral/opera performance); stringed instruments; wind and percussion instruments.

Dartmouth College

African studies; African-American (black) studies; anthropology; Arabic; archaeology; art history; Asian studies; astronomy; biochemistry; biology; chemistry; chemistry, other; Chinese; classics; cognitive psychology and psycholinguistics; comparative literature; computer science; creative writing; earth sciences; East and Southeast Asian languages, other; ecology; economics; engineering; engineering physics; English; environmental science; evolutionary biology; film studies; fine/studio arts; French; genetics; geography; German; Greek (Ancient and Medieval); Hebrew; Hispanic-American studies; history; Italian; Japanese; Latin (Ancient and Medieval); Latin American studies; linguistics; mathematics; Middle Eastern studies; molecular biology; multi/interdisciplinary studies, other; music; Native American studies; philosophy; physics; political science; psychology; religious studies; Romance languages; Russian; Russian/Slavic area studies; sociology; Spanish; theater arts/drama; women's studies.

Davidson College

Anthropology; art; biology; chemistry; classics; economics; English; French; German; history; mathematics; multi/interdisciplinary studies, other; music; philosophy; physics; political science; psychology; religious studies; sociology; Spanish; theater arts/drama.

Denison University

African-American (black) studies; anthropology; area studies; art; art history; biochemistry; biology; chemistry; classics; computer science; creative writing; dance; East Asian studies; economics; English; environmental science; film studies; fine/studio arts; French; geology; German; history; international relations; Latin American studies; mass communications; mathematics; music; organizational behavior; philosophy; physical education; physics; political science; psychology; religious studies; sociology; Spanish; speech/rhetorical studies; theater arts/drama; women's studies.

DePauw University

Anthropology; art history; athletic training/sports medicine; biology; chemistry; classics; computer science; earth sciences; East Asian studies; economics; elementary education; English; English composition; fine/studio arts; French; geography; geology; German; Greek (Modern); history; interdisciplinary studies; Latin (Ancient and Medieval); mass communications; mathematics; medical technology; music; music (general performance); music business management and merchandising; music education; music theory and composition; peace and conflict studies; philosophy; physics; political science; psychology; religious studies; Romance languages; Russian/Slavic area studies; sociology; Spanish; women's studies.

Dickinson College

American studies; anthropology; biochemistry; biology; chemistry; classics; computer science; dance; East Asian studies; economics; English; environmental science; fine/studio arts; French; geology; German; Greek (Ancient and Medieval); history; international business; international relations; Italian;

Judaic studies; Latin (Ancient and Medieval); mathematics; medieval/renaissance studies; molecular biology; music; philosophy; physics; political science; (pre)dentistry; (pre)law; (pre)medicine; psychology; public policy analysis; religious studies; Russian; Russian/Slavic area studies; sociology; Spanish; theater arts/drama; theater design; women's studies.

Drake University

Accounting; actuarial science; advertising; anthropology; art; art history; astronomy; biology; broadcast journalism; business; business administration; business education; business marketing and marketing management; chemistry; computer science; drawing; economics; elementary education; English; environmental science; finance; fine/studio arts; graphic design/commercial art/illustration; history; information sciences/systems; international business; international relations; journalism; mass communications; mathematics; military science; music; music (piano and organ performance); music (voice and choral/opera performance); music business management and merchandising; music education; pharmacy; pharmacy administration and pharmaceutics; philosophy; physics; political science; (pre)dentistry; (pre)law; (pre)medicine; (pre)veterinary studies; psychology; public relations; radio/television broadcasting; religious studies; sacred music; science education; sculpture; secondary education; sociology; speech/rhetorical studies; theater arts/drama.

Drew University

Anthropology; art; behavioral sciences; biochemistry; biology; chemistry; classics; computer science; economics; English; French; German; history; interdisciplinary studies; Italian; mathematics; mathematics/computer science; music; neuroscience; philosophy; physics; political science; psychology; religious studies; Russian; sociology; Spanish; theater arts/drama; women's studies.

Duke University

African-American (black) studies; anatomy; anthropology; art; art history; Asian studies; bioengineering; biology; chemistry; civil engineering; classics; computer science; economics; electrical/electronics engineering; English; environmental science; French; geology; German; Greek (Ancient and Medieval); history; international relations; Italian; Latin (Ancient and Medieval); linguistics; literature; materials science; mathematics; mechanical engineering; medieval/renaissance studies; music; philosophy; physics; political science; psychology; public policy analysis; religious studies; Russian; Russian/Slavic area studies; Slavic languages; sociology; Spanish; theater arts/drama; women's studies.

Duquesne University

Accounting; accounting, other; art history; athletic training/sports medicine; biochemistry; biology; biology education; business; business management/administrative services, other; business marketing and marketing management; chemistry; chemistry education; chemistry, other; classics; communications; computer science; early childhood education; education; educational media technology; elementary education; English; English education; English, other; environmental science; finance; fine/studio arts; foreign languages education; foreign languages/literatures; French language education; German language education; Greek (Ancient and Medieval); health services administration; health/medical preparatory programs, other; history; international business; international relations; investments and securities; journalism; journalism and mass communication, other; Latin (Ancient and Medieval); liberal arts and studies, other; logistics and materials management; management information systems/business data processing; management science; marketing management and research, other; mathematics; mathematics education; medical pharmacology and pharmaceutical sciences; microbiology/bacteriology; music (general performance); music education; music therapy; music, other; nursing; occupational therapy; philosophy; physical therapy; physician assistant; physics; physics education; political science; psychology; science education; secondary education; social sciences; social studies education; sociology; Spanish; Spanish language education; speech-language pathology; teacher education, specific programs, other; theater arts/drama; theology.

Earlham College

African-American (black) studies; art; Asian studies; biology; business administration; chemistry; classics; computer science; economics; education; English; environmental science; French; geology; German; history; interdisciplinary studies; international relations; Latin American studies; mathematics; music; peace and conflict studies; philosophy; physics; political science; (pre)law; (pre)medicine; psychology; religious studies; sociology; Spanish; theater arts/drama; women's studies.

Eckerd College

American studies; anthropology; art; biology; business administration; chemistry; communications; comparative literature; computer science; creative writing; economics; English; environmental science; French; German; history; human resources management; humanities; individual/family development; interdisciplinary studies; international business; international relations; literature; marine biology; mathematics; medical technology; modern languages; music; philosophy; physics; political science; (pre)dentistry; (pre)law; (pre)medicine; (pre)veterinary studies; psychology; religious studies; Russian; sociology; Spanish; theater arts/drama; women's studies.

Elizabethtown College

Accounting; anthropology; art; biochemistry; biology; biotechnology research; business administration; chemistry; communications; computer engineering; computer science; criminal justice studies; early childhood education; economics; education; elementary education; engineering; engineering physics; English; environmental science; French; German; history; industrial/manufacturing engineering; international business; mathematics; modern languages; music; music education; music therapy; occupational therapy; peace and conflict studies; philosophy; physics; political science; (pre)dentistry; (pre)law; (pre)medicine; (pre)veterinary studies; psychology; religious studies; science education; secondary education; social sciences; social work; sociology; Spanish.

Elmira College

Accounting; American studies; anthropology; art; art education; biochemistry; biology; biology education; business administration; business economics; business marketing and marketing management; chemistry; chemistry education; classics; criminal justice/law enforcement administration; economics; education;

elementary education; English; English education; environmental science; European studies; fine/studio arts; foreign languages education; foreign languages/literatures; French; French language education; Greek (Ancient and Medieval); history; history education; human services; human services; humanities; information sciences/systems; interdisciplinary studies; international business; international relations; Latin (Ancient and Medieval); liberal arts and studies; literature; mathematics; mathematics education; medical technology; mental health/rehabilitation; middle school education; modern languages; music; nursing; nursing science; philosophy; political science; (pre)dentistry; (pre)law; (pre)medicine; (pre)veterinary studies; psychology; religious studies; Romance languages; science education; secondary education; social science education; social sciences; social studies education; social work; sociology; Spanish; Spanish language education; speech education; speech-language pathology/audiology; theater arts/drama.

Embry-Riddle Aeronautical University (AZ)

Aerospace engineering; aircraft pilot (professional); aviation management; aviation/airway science; business administration; computer engineering; computer/information sciences; electrical/electronics engineering; engineering; engineering technology.

Emerson College

Acting/directing; advertising; broadcast journalism; business marketing and marketing management; communication disorders; communications; creative writing; dance; drama and dance education; education of the speech impaired; film studies; film/video production; interdisciplinary studies; journalism; mass communications; multimedia; play/screenwriting; public relations; publishing; radio/television broadcasting; radio/television broadcasting technology; speech therapy; speech-language pathology; speech-language pathology/audiology; speech/rhetorical studies; theater arts/drama; theater design; visual/performing arts.

Emory University

Accounting; African studies; African-American (black) studies; anthropology; art history; Asian studies; biology; biomedical science; business administration; business economics; business marketing and marketing management; chemistry; classics; comparative literature; computer science; creative writing; dance; Eastern European area studies; economics; education; elementary education; English; film studies; finance; French; German; Greek (Modern); history; human ecology; international relations; Italian; Judaic studies; Latin (Ancient and Medieval); Latin American studies; liberal arts and studies; literature; mathematics; medieval/renaissance studies; music; neuroscience; nursing; philosophy; physics; political science; psychology; religious studies; Russian; secondary education; sociology; Spanish; theater arts/drama; women's studies.

Eugene Lang College, New School University

Anthropology; creative writing; economics; education; English; history; humanities; interdisciplinary studies; international relations; liberal arts and studies; literature; music history; philosophy; political science; psychology; religious studies; social sciences; sociology; theater arts/drama; urban studies; women's studies.

Fairfield University

Accounting; American studies; art; biology; business administration; business marketing and marketing management; chemistry; clinical psychology; computer science; computer software engineering; economics; electrical/electronics engineering; engineering, other; English; finance; French; German; history; information sciences/systems; international relations; management information systems/business data processing; mass communications; mathematics; mechanical engineering; modern languages; music history; neuroscience; nursing; philosophy; physics; political science; psychology; religious studies; secondary education; sociology; Spanish.

Fashion Institute of Technology

Advertising; art; fashion design/illustration; fashion merchandising; graphic design/commercial art/illustration; industrial design.

Florida Institute of Technology

Aerospace engineering; aircraft pilot (professional); applied mathematics; astrophysics; atmospheric sciences; aviation management; aviation/airway science; biochemistry; biology; biology education; business administration; chemical engineering; chemistry; chemistry education; civil engineering; communications; computer education; computer engineering; computer science; ecology; electrical/electronics engineering; environmental science; humanities; information sciences/systems; interdisciplinary studies; marine biology; mathematics education; mechanical engineering; molecular biology; ocean engineering; oceanography; physics; physics education; psychology; science education.

Florida International University

Accounting; applied mathematics; architectural environmental design; art education; art history; biology; broadcast journalism; business administration; business marketing and marketing management; chemical engineering; chemistry; civil engineering; communications; computer engineering; computer science; computer/information sciences; construction technology; criminal justice studies; dance; dietetics; economics; education of the emotionally handicapped; education of the mentally handicapped; education of the specific learning disabled; electrical/electronics engineering; elementary education; English; English education; environmental science; exercise sciences; finance; fine/studio arts; foreign languages education; French; geography; geology; German; health education; health science; health services administration; history; home economics education; hospitality management; human resources management; humanities; information sciences/systems; insurance and risk management; interior design; international business; international relations; Italian; liberal arts and studies; mathematical statistics; mathematics; mathematics education; mechanical engineering; medical records administration; music; music education; nursing; occupational therapy; orthotics/prosthetics; philosophy; physical education; physics; political science; Portuguese; psychology; public administration; real estate; recreation/leisure facilities management; religious studies; science education; social science education; social work; sociology; Spanish; systems engineering; theater arts/drama; trade and industrial education; urban studies; women's studies.

Florida State University

Accounting; acting/directing; actuarial science; advertising; American studies; anthropology; applied economics; applied mathematics; art; art education; art history; Asian studies; atmospheric sciences; bilingual/bicultural education; biochemistry; bioengineering; biology; business; business administration; business communications; business marketing and marketing management; cell and molecular biology, other; chemical engineering; chemistry; child care/development; civil engineering; classics; clothing/apparel/textile studies; communications; community health liaison; computer engineering; computer science; computer software engineering; computer/information sciences; creative writing; criminology; dance; dietetics; early childhood education; Eastern European area studies; ecology; economics; education of the emotionally handicapped; education of the mentally handicapped; education of the specific learning disabled; education of the visually handicapped; electrical/electronics engineering; elementary education; English; English education; entrepreneurship; environmental engineering; environmental science; evolutionary biology; family/consumer studies; fashion design/illustration; fashion merchandising; film studies; film/video production; finance; fine/studio arts; foreign languages education; French; genetics; geography; geology; German; graphic design/commercial art/illustration; Greek (Modern); health education; history; home economics; home economics education; hospitality management; housing studies; human resources management; humanities; individual/family development; industrial/manufacturing engineering; insurance and risk management; interior design; international business; international relations; Italian; jazz; Latin (Ancient and Medieval); Latin American studies; liberal arts and studies; library science; linguistics; literature; management information systems/business data processing; marine biology; mass communications; materials engineering; mathematical statistics; mathematics; mathematics education; mechanical engineering; music; music (general performance); music (piano and organ performance); music (voice and choral/opera performance); music education; music history; music theory and composition; music therapy; nursing; nutrition science; nutrition studies; philosophy; physical education; physical sciences; physical sciences, other; physics; physiology; plant physiology; political science; (pre)dentistry; (pre)law; (pre)medicine; (pre)pharmacy studies; (pre)theology; (pre)veterinary studies; psychology; public relations; radio/television broadcasting; real estate; recreation/leisure facilities management; religious studies; Russian; Russian/Slavic area studies; science education; secondary education; social science education; social sciences; social work; sociology; Spanish; speech-language pathology/audiology; stringed instruments; theater arts/drama; theater design; vocational rehabilitation counseling; wind and percussion instruments; women's studies; zoology.

Fordham University

Accounting; African studies; African-American (black) studies; American studies; anthropology; art; art history; bilingual/bicultural education; biological and physical sciences; biology; broadcast journalism; business administration; business economics; business marketing and marketing management; chemistry; classics; comparative literature; computer management; computer science; computer/information sciences; creative writing; criminal justice/law enforcement administration; dance; Eastern European area studies; economics; education; elementary education; English; film studies; finance; fine/studio arts; French; German; graphic design/commercial art/illustration; Greek (Modern); Hispanic-American studies; history; information sciences/systems; interdisciplinary studies; international business; international relations; Italian; journalism; Latin (Ancient and Medieval); Latin American studies; liberal arts and studies; literature; management information systems/business data processing; mass communications; mathematics; medieval/renaissance studies; Middle Eastern studies; modern languages; music; music history; natural sciences; peace and conflict studies; philosophy; photography; physical sciences; physics; political science; (pre)dentistry; (pre)law; (pre)medicine; (pre)veterinary studies; psychology; public administration; radio/television broadcasting; religious studies; Romance languages; Russian; Russian/Slavic area studies; secondary education; social sciences; social work; sociology; Spanish; theater arts/drama; theology; urban studies; women's studies.

Franklin and Marshall College

African studies; American studies; anthropology; art; biochemistry; biology; business administration; chemistry; classics; economics; English; finance; French; geology; German; Greek (Ancient and Medieval); history; Latin (Ancient and Medieval); mathematics; music; neuroscience; philosophy; physics; political science; psychology; religious studies; sociology; Spanish; theater arts/drama.

Friends University

Accounting; applied art; art; art education; biblical studies; biology; business administration; business education; ceramic arts; chemistry; child care/development; communications; computer programming; computer science; computer/information sciences; dance; divinity/ministry; early childhood education; ecology; education; elementary education; English; graphic design/commercial art/illustration; health education; health services administration; history; human resources management; human services; industrial radiologic technology; interdisciplinary studies; international business; liberal arts and studies; literature; marriage and family counseling; mathematics; medical laboratory technician; music; music (piano and organ performance); music (voice and choral/opera performance); music business management and merchandising; music education; philosophy; physical education; political science; (pre)dentistry; (pre)engineering; (pre)medicine; (pre)veterinary studies; psychology; religious studies; sacred music; science education; secondary education; social sciences; sociology; Spanish; speech/rhetorical studies; stringed instruments; theology.

Furman University

Accounting; art; art history; Asian studies; biochemistry; biology; business administration; chemistry; communications; computer science; early childhood education; economics; education; elementary education; English; environmental science; exercise sciences; fine/studio arts; French; geology; German; Greek (Modern); history; Latin (Ancient and Medieval); mathematics; music; music (piano and organ performance); music (voice and choral/opera performance); music education; philosophy; physics; political science; (pre)dentistry; (pre)law; (pre)medicine; (pre)veterinary studies; psychology; religious studies; sacred music; secondary education; sociology; Spanish; special education; theater arts/drama; urban studies.

George Fox University

Art; athletic training/sports medicine; biblical studies; biology; biology education; business administration; business economics; chemistry; chemistry education; clinical psychology; cognitive psychology and psycholinguistics; communications; computer/information sciences; education (multiple levels); elementary education; engineering; English; English education; family resource management studies; fashion merchandising; health education; history; home economics; home economics education; human resources management; interdisciplinary studies; international relations; management information systems/business data processing; mathematics; mathematics education; missionary studies; music; music education; pastoral counseling; physical education; psychology; public relations; radio/television broadcasting; religious education; religious studies; social studies education; social work; sociology; Spanish; sport/fitness administration.

Georgetown College

Accounting; American studies; art; biology; business administration; business marketing and marketing management; chemistry; computer science; early childhood education; ecology; education; elementary education; English; environmental science; European studies; finance; French; German; history; information sciences/systems; international business; management information systems/business data processing; mass communications; mathematics; medical technology; music; music (piano and organ performance); music (voice and choral/opera performance); music education; philosophy; physical education; physics; political science; (pre)dentistry; (pre)law; (pre)medicine; psychology; recreation and leisure studies; religious studies; secondary education; sociology; Spanish; speech/rhetorical studies; theater arts/drama.

Georgetown University

Accounting; American studies; Arabic; art; biochemistry; biology; business administration; business marketing and marketing management; chemistry; Chinese; classics; comparative literature; computer science; economics; English; finance; French; German; history; interdisciplinary studies; international business; international economics; international relations; Italian; Japanese; liberal arts and studies; linguistics; mathematics; nursing; philosophy; physics; political science; Portuguese; psychology; religious studies; Russian; science/technology and society; social sciences and history, other; sociology; Spanish; women's studies.

The George Washington University

Accounting; American studies; anthropology; applied mathematics; archaeology; art; art history; Asian studies; biology; business administration; business economics; business marketing and marketing management; chemistry; Chinese; civil engineering; classics; computer engineering; computer science; computer/information sciences; criminal justice/law enforcement administration; dance; East Asian studies; economics; electrical/electronics engineering; emergency medical technology; engineering; English; environmental engineering; environmental science; European studies; exercise sciences; finance; fine/studio arts; French; geography; geology; German; history; human resources management; human services; humanities; industrial radiologic technology; interdisciplinary studies; international business; international relations; journalism; Judaic studies; Latin American studies; liberal arts and studies; mass communications; mathematical statistics; mathematics; mechanical engineering; medical laboratory technician; medical laboratory technologies; medical technology; Middle Eastern studies; music; nuclear medical technology; philosophy; physician assistant; physics; political science; (pre)dentistry; (pre)law; (pre)medicine; psychology; public policy analysis; radio/television broadcasting; radiological science; religious studies; Russian; Russian/Slavic area studies; sociology; Spanish; speech-language pathology/audiology; speech/rhetorical studies; systems engineering; theater arts/drama.

Georgia Institute of Technology

Aerospace engineering; applied mathematics, other; architecture; biology; business administration; business economics; chemical engineering; chemistry; chemistry, other; civil engineering; computer engineering; computer/information sciences; construction technology; earth sciences; electrical/electronics engineering; history of science and technology; industrial design; industrial/manufacturing engineering; international relations; management science; materials engineering; mathematics; mechanical engineering; modern languages; nuclear engineering; operations management; organizational psychology; physics; polymer chemistry; public policy analysis; science/technology and society; textile sciences/engineering.

Georgia State University

Accounting; actuarial science; African-American (black) studies; anthropology; art education; biology; business administration; business economics; business marketing and marketing management; chemistry; classics; computer/information sciences; criminal justice studies; dietetics; drawing; early childhood education; economics; English; film studies; finance; French; geography; geology; German; history; hotel and restaurant management; human resources management; insurance and risk management; interdisciplinary studies; journalism; liberal arts and studies; mathematics; medical records administration; medical technology; middle school education; music (general performance); nursing; operations research; philosophy; physical education; physical therapy; physics; political science; psychology; real estate; recreation/leisure facilities management; religious studies; respiratory therapy; social work; sociology; Spanish; speech/rhetorical studies; theater arts/drama; urban studies.

Gettysburg College

Accounting; African-American (black) studies; American studies; anthropology; area studies; art; art history; biochemistry; biological and physical sciences; biology; business administration; chemistry; classics; computer science; economics; education; elementary education; English; environmental science; fine/studio arts; French; German; Greek (Modern); health science; history; interdisciplinary studies; international business; international economics; international relations; Latin (Ancient and Medieval); Latin American studies; liberal arts and studies; literature; marine biology; mathematics; modern languages; music; music education; philosophy; physical education; physics; political science; (pre)dentistry; (pre)law; (pre)medicine; (pre)veterinary studies; psychology; religious studies; Romance languages; science education; secondary education; social sciences; sociology; South Asian studies; Spanish; theater arts/drama; western civilization; women's studies.

Gonzaga University

Accounting; art; Asian studies; biochemistry; biology; broadcast journalism; business administration; business economics; business marketing and marketing management; chemistry; civil engineering; computer engineering; computer science; criminal justice/law enforcement administration; economics; electrical/electronics engineering; elementary education; engineering; English; exercise sciences; finance; French; German; history; information sciences/systems; international business; international relations; Italian; journalism; liberal arts and studies; literature; mass communications; mathematics; mechanical engineering; music; music education; nursing; philosophy; physical education; physics; political science; psychology; public relations; religious studies; secondary education; sociology; Spanish; special education; speech/rhetorical studies; sport/fitness administration; theater arts/drama.

Gordon College (MA)

Accounting; art; biblical studies; biology; business administration; chemistry; communications; computer science; early childhood education; economics; education; elementary education; English; exercise sciences; foreign languages/literatures; French; German; history; international relations; mass communications; mathematics; modern languages; music; music (general performance); music education; philosophy; physics; political science; psychology; recreation and leisure studies; religious education; social work; sociology; Spanish; special education.

Goucher College

American studies; architectural history; art; biology; chemistry; computer science; dance; economics; education; elementary education; English; French; history; interdisciplinary studies; international relations; management science; mass communications; mathematics; music; philosophy; physics; political science; psychology; religious studies; Russian; sociology; Spanish; theater arts/drama; women's studies.

Grinnell College

African-American (black) studies; American studies; anthropology; art; biochemistry; biological and physical sciences; biology; chemistry; Chinese; classics; computer science; economics; English; environmental science; French; German; history; interdisciplinary studies; Latin American studies; linguistics; mathematics; music; philosophy; physics; political science; psychology; religious studies; Russian; science/technology and society; sociology; Spanish; theater arts/drama; Western European studies; women's studies.

Grove City College

Accounting; biochemistry; biology; business administration; business communications; business economics; business marketing and marketing management; chemistry; computer management; divinity/ministry; early childhood education; economics; electrical/electronics engineering; elementary education; English; finance; French; history; international business; literature; mass communications; mathematics; mechanical engineering; modern languages; molecular biology; music business management and merchandising; music education; philosophy; physics; political science; (pre)dentistry; (pre)law; (pre)medicine; (pre)veterinary studies; psychology; religious studies; science education; secondary education; sociology; Spanish.

Gustavus Adolphus College

Accounting; anthropology; art; art education; art history; athletic training/sports medicine; biochemistry; biology; biology education; business administration; business economics; chemistry; chemistry education; classics; computer science; criminal justice/law enforcement administration; dance; economics; education; elementary education; English; environmental science; French; geography; geology; German; health education; history; interdisciplinary studies; international business; Japanese; Latin American studies; mass communications; mathematics; mathematics education; music; music education; nursing; occupational therapy; philosophy; physical education; physical therapy; physics; physics education; political science; (pre)dentistry; (pre)law; (pre)medicine; (pre)veterinary studies; psychology; religious studies; Russian; Russian/Slavic area studies; sacred music; Scandinavian languages; secondary education; social sciences; social studies education; sociology; Spanish; speech/rhetorical studies; theater arts/drama; trade and industrial education.

Hamilton College (NY)

African studies; American studies; anthropology; art; art history; Asian studies; biochemistry; biology; chemistry; classics; comparative literature; computer science; creative writing; dance; East Asian studies; economics; English; fine/studio arts; French; geology; German; Greek (Modern); history; international relations; Latin (Ancient and Medieval); literature; mass communications; mathematics; modern languages; molecular biology; music; neuroscience; philosophy; physics; physiological psychology/psychobiology; political science; psychology; public policy analysis; religious studies; Russian/Slavic area studies; sociology; Spanish; theater arts/drama; women's studies.

Hamline University

Anthropology; art; art history; Asian studies; athletic training/sports medicine; biology; business administration; chemistry; criminal justice/law enforcement administration; East Asian studies; Eastern European area studies; economics; education; elementary education; English; environmental science; European studies; exercise sciences; fine/studio arts; French; German; health education; history; international business; international economics; international relations; Judaic studies; K-12 education; Latin American studies; law and legal studies; mass communications; mathematics; music; music education; occupational therapy; paralegal/legal assistant; philosophy; physical education; physical therapy; physics; political science; (pre)dentistry; (pre)law; (pre)medicine; (pre)veterinary studies; psychology; public administration; religious studies; Russian/Slavic area studies; science education; secondary education; social sciences; sociology; Spanish; speech/theater education; theater arts/drama; urban studies; women's studies.

Hampshire College

African studies; African-American (black) studies; agricultural sciences; American studies; anatomy; animal sciences; anthropology; applied mathematics; archaeology; architectural environmental design; architecture; art; art history; Asian studies; astronomy; astrophysics; behavioral sciences; biochemistry; biological and physical sciences; biology; biophysics; botany; business economics; Canadian studies; cell biology; chemistry; child care/development; city/community/regional planning; cognitive psychology and psycholinguistics; community services;

comparative literature; computer graphics; computer programming; computer science; computer/information sciences; creative writing; cultural studies; dance; developmental/child psychology; drawing; early childhood education; earth sciences; East Asian studies; Eastern European area studies; ecology; economics; education; elementary education; English; environmental biology; environmental health; environmental science; European studies; evolutionary biology; exercise sciences; family/consumer studies; film studies; film/video production; fine/studio arts; genetics; geochemistry; geography; geology; geophysics and seismology; graphic design/commercial art/illustration; health science; Hispanic-American studies; history; history of philosophy; history of science and technology; humanities; individual/family development; interdisciplinary studies; international business; international economics; international relations; Islamic studies; jazz; journalism; Judaic studies; labor/personnel relations; Latin American studies; law and legal studies; liberal arts and studies; linguistics; literature; marine biology; mass communications; mathematical statistics; mathematics; medieval/renaissance studies; Mexican-American studies; microbiology/bacteriology; Middle Eastern studies; molecular biology; music; music history; Native American studies; natural sciences; neuroscience; nutrition science; oceanography; peace and conflict studies; philosophy; photography; physical sciences; physics; physiological psychology/psychobiology; physiology; political science; (pre)medicine; (pre)veterinary studies; psychology; public health; public policy analysis; radio/television broadcasting; religious studies; Russian/Slavic area studies; sculpture; secondary education; social sciences; sociobiology; sociology; solar technology; South Asian studies; Southeast Asian studies; telecommunications; theater arts/drama; urban studies; women's studies.

Hanover College

Anthropology; art; art history; biology; business administration; chemistry; classics; computer science; economics; elementary education; English; French; geology; German; history; international relations; Latin American studies; mass communications; mathematics; medieval/renaissance studies; music; philosophy; physical education; physics; political science; psychology; sociology; Spanish; theater arts/drama; theology.

Harding University

Accounting; advertising; American studies; art; art education; art therapy; biblical languages/literatures; biblical studies; biochemistry; biological and physical sciences; biology; business administration; business marketing and marketing management; chemistry; child care/development; communication disorders; communications; computer engineering; computer science; computer/information sciences; criminal justice studies; data processing technology; dietetics; early childhood education; economics; education of the specific learning disabled; elementary education; English; exercise sciences; family/consumer studies; fashion merchandising; finance; French; general studies; graphic design/commercial art/illustration; health services administration; history; human resources management; humanities; interior design; international business; international relations; journalism; mass communications; mathematics; mathematics education; medical technology; missionary studies; music; music (piano and organ performance); music (voice and choral/opera performance); music education; nursing; painting; pastoral counseling; physical education; physics; political science; (pre)dentistry; (pre)law; (pre)medicine; (pre)veterinary studies; psychology; public administration; public relations; radio/television broadcasting; religious studies; sales operations; science education; social sciences; social work; Spanish; sport/fitness administration; stringed instruments; theater arts/drama.

Harvard University
African languages; African studies; African-American (black) studies; American studies; anthropology; applied mathematics; Arabic; archaeology; architectural engineering; architectural environmental design; art; art history; Asian studies; astronomy; astrophysics; atmospheric sciences; behavioral sciences; biblical languages/literatures; biblical studies; biochemistry; bioengineering; biological and physical sciences; biological technology; biology; biomedical science; biometrics; biophysics; cell biology; chemical engineering; chemistry; Chinese; city/community/regional planning; civil engineering; classics; cognitive psychology and psycholinguistics; comparative literature; computer engineering; computer engineering technology; computer graphics; computer programming; computer science; computer/information sciences; creative writing; cultural studies; earth sciences; East Asian studies; Eastern European area studies; ecology; economics; electrical/electronics engineering; engineering; engineering physics; engineering science; English; entomology; environmental biology; environmental engineering; environmental science; European studies; evolutionary biology; film studies; fine/studio arts; fluid and thermal sciences; folklore; French; genetics; geochemistry; geological engineering; geology; geophysical engineering; geophysics and seismology; German; Greek (Modern); Hebrew; Hispanic-American studies; history; history of philosophy; history of science and technology; humanities; individual/family development; information sciences/systems; interdisciplinary studies; international economics; international relations; Islamic studies; Italian; Japanese; Judaic studies; Latin (Ancient and Medieval); Latin American studies; liberal arts and studies; linguistics; literature; marine biology; materials engineering; materials science; mathematical statistics; mathematics; mechanical engineering; medieval/renaissance studies; metallurgical engineering; microbiology/bacteriology; Middle Eastern studies; modern languages; molecular biology; music; music history; natural resources conservation; neuroscience; nuclear physics; philosophy; physical sciences; physics; physiological psychology/psychobiology; political science; polymer chemistry; Portuguese; (pre)dentistry; (pre)law; (pre)medicine; (pre)veterinary studies; psychology; public policy analysis; religious studies; robotics; Romance languages; Russian; Russian/Slavic area studies; Scandinavian languages; Slavic languages; social sciences; sociobiology; sociology; South Asian studies; Southeast Asian studies; Spanish; systems engineering; theater arts/drama; urban studies; western civilization; women's studies.

Harvey Mudd College
Biology; chemistry; computer science; engineering; mathematics; physics.

Haverford College
African studies; anthropology; archaeology; art; art history; astronomy; biochemistry; biology; biophysics; chemistry; classics; comparative literature; computer science; East Asian studies; economics; education; English; French; geology; German;

Greek (Modern); history; Italian; Latin (Ancient and Medieval); Latin American studies; mathematics; music; neuroscience; peace and conflict studies; philosophy; physics; political science; (pre)law; (pre)medicine; (pre)veterinary studies; psychology; quantitative economics; religious studies; Romance languages; Russian; sociology; Spanish; urban studies; women's studies.

Heidelberg College
Accounting; anthropology; athletic training/sports medicine; biology; business administration; chemistry; computer science; economics; education; elementary education; English; environmental biology; German; health education; health services administration; history; information sciences/systems; international relations; mass communications; mathematics; music; music (piano and organ performance); music (voice and choral/opera performance); music business management and merchandising; music education; philosophy; physical education; physics; political science; (pre)dentistry; (pre)law; (pre)medicine; (pre)veterinary studies; psychology; public administration; public relations; religious studies; science education; secondary education; Spanish; special education; stringed instruments; theater arts/drama; water resources.

Hendrix College
Accounting; anthropology; art; biology; business economics; chemistry; computer science; economics; elementary education; English; French; German; history; interdisciplinary studies; international relations; mathematics; music; philosophy; physical education; physics; political science; psychology; religious studies; sociology; Spanish; theater arts/drama.

Hillsdale College
Accounting; American studies; art; biology; business administration; business marketing and marketing management; chemistry; classics; comparative literature; computer science; drafting and design technology; early childhood education; economics; education; elementary education; English; European studies; finance; French; German; history; interdisciplinary studies; international relations; K-12 education; mathematics; music; philosophy; physical education; physics; political science; (pre)dentistry; (pre)medicine; (pre)veterinary studies; psychology; religious studies; secondary education; sociology; Spanish; speech/rhetorical studies; theater arts/drama.

Hiram College
Art; art history; biology; business administration; chemistry; classics; computer science; economics; elementary education; English; environmental science; fine/studio arts; French; German; health science; history; international business; international economics; mass communications; mathematics; music; philosophy; physics; physiological psychology/psychobiology; political science; (pre)dentistry; (pre)law; (pre)medicine; (pre)veterinary studies; psychology; religious studies; secondary education; sociology; Spanish; theater arts/drama.

Hobart and William Smith Colleges
African studies; African-American (black) studies; American studies; anthropology; architecture; art; art history; Asian studies; biochemistry; biology; chemistry; Chinese; classics; comparative literature; computer science; dance; economics; English; environmental science; European studies; fine/studio arts; French; geology; Greek (Ancient and Medieval); history; interdisciplinary studies; international relations; Japanese; Latin

(Ancient and Medieval); Latin American studies; liberal arts and studies; mass communications; mathematics; medieval/renaissance studies; modern languages; music; philosophy; physics; political science; (pre)dentistry; (pre)law; (pre)medicine; (pre)veterinary studies; psychology; public policy analysis; religious studies; Russian; Russian/Slavic area studies; sociology; Spanish; theater arts/drama; urban studies; women's studies.

Hope College
Accounting; art history; athletic training/sports medicine; biochemistry; biology; business administration; chemistry; classics; communications; computer science; dance; economics; education of the emotionally handicapped; education of the specific learning disabled; elementary education; engineering; engineering physics; English; environmental science; exercise sciences; fine/studio arts; French; geology; geophysics and seismology; German; history; humanities; interdisciplinary studies; Latin (Ancient and Medieval); mathematics; music; music (general performance); music education; music history; music theory and composition; nursing; philosophy; physical education; physics; political science; psychology; religious studies; secondary education; social work; sociology; Spanish; theater arts/drama.

Huntingdon College
Accounting; American studies; applied art; art; art education; athletic training/sports medicine; biology; business administration; business economics; business marketing and marketing management; cell and molecular biology, other; chemistry; chemistry education; communications; computer graphics; computer science; creative writing; dance; drama and dance education; ecology; education; English; English education; environmental science; European studies; exercise sciences; history; history education; interdisciplinary studies; international business; international relations; liberal arts and studies; mathematics; mathematics education; multi/interdisciplinary studies, other; music; music (piano and organ performance); music (voice and choral/opera performance); music education; paralegal/legal assistant; physical education; physical therapy; political science; (pre)dentistry; (pre)law; (pre)medicine; (pre)veterinary studies; psychology; public administration; recreation and leisure studies; recreation/leisure facilities management; religious education; religious studies; secondary education; Spanish; speech/rhetorical studies; sport/fitness administration; theater arts/drama.

Illinois College
Accounting; art; biology; business administration; business economics; chemistry; computer science; cytotechnology; economics; education; elementary education; English; environmental science; finance; French; German; history; information sciences/systems; interdisciplinary studies; international relations; K-12 education; liberal arts and studies; management information systems/business data processing; mass communications; mathematics; medical technology; music; occupational therapy; philosophy; physical education; physics; political science; (pre)dentistry; (pre)law; (pre)medicine; (pre)veterinary studies; psychology; religious studies; secondary education; sociology; Spanish; speech/rhetorical studies; theater arts/drama.

Illinois Institute of Technology
Aerospace engineering; applied mathematics; architectural engineering; architecture; bioengineering; biology; biophysics; chemical engineering; chemistry; civil engineering; computer engineering; computer science; electrical/electronics engineering; engineering/industrial management; industrial technology; information sciences/systems; materials engineering; mechanical engineering; metallurgical engineering; physics; political science; psychology.

Illinois Wesleyan University
Accounting; applied art; art; art history; arts management; biology; business administration; chemistry; computer science; drawing; economics; education; elementary education; English; European studies; fine/studio arts; French; German; graphic design/commercial art/illustration; history; insurance and risk management; interdisciplinary studies; international business; international relations; Latin American studies; liberal arts and studies; mathematics; medical technology; music; music (piano and organ performance); music (voice and choral/opera performance); music business management and merchandising; music education; nursing; philosophy; physics; political science; (pre)dentistry; (pre)law; (pre)medicine; (pre)veterinary studies; psychology; religious studies; science education; secondary education; sociology; Spanish; stringed instruments; theater arts/drama; wind and percussion instruments.

Indiana Wesleyan University
Accounting; alcohol/drug abuse counseling; art; art education; athletic training/sports medicine; biblical languages/literatures; biblical studies; biology; business administration; business marketing and marketing management; ceramic arts; chemistry; communications; computer graphics; computer/information sciences; creative writing; criminal justice studies; cultural studies; economics; education; elementary education; English; English education; exercise sciences; finance; general studies; history; K-12 education; mathematics; mathematics education; medical technology; middle school education; music; music education; music theory and composition; nursing; painting; pastoral counseling; philosophy; photography; physical education; political science; (pre)dentistry; (pre)law; (pre)medicine; (pre)veterinary studies; printmaking; psychology; recreation/leisure facilities management; religious education; sacred music; science education; secondary education; social sciences; social studies education; social work; sociology; Spanish; special education; sport/fitness administration; theology.

Iowa State University of Science and Technology
Accounting; advertising; aerospace engineering; agricultural business; agricultural education; agricultural engineering; agricultural mechanization; agricultural sciences; agronomy/crop science; animal sciences; anthropology; architecture; art; atmospheric sciences; biochemistry; biology; biophysics; botany; business administration; business management/administrative services, other; business marketing and marketing management; ceramic sciences/engineering; chemical engineering; chemistry; city/community/regional planning; civil engineering; clothing/apparel/textile studies; community services; computer engineering; computer science; consumer services; dairy science; design/visual communications; developmental/child psychology; dietetics; early childhood education; earth sciences; ecology; economics; education; electrical/electronics engineering; elementary education; engineering; engineering science; engineering, other; English; enterprise management; entomol-

ogy; environmental science; family resource management studies; family/community studies; family/consumer studies; farm/ranch management; fashion design/illustration; finance; fish/game management; food products retailing; food services technology; forestry; French; genetics; geology; German; graphic design/commercial art/illustration; health education; health/physical education; history; home economics; home economics education; horticulture science; horticulture services; hotel and restaurant management; housing studies; industrial/manufacturing engineering; interdisciplinary studies; interior design; international agriculture; international business; international relations; journalism; landscape architecture; liberal arts and studies; linguistics; logistics and materials management; management information systems/business data processing; mass communications; mathematical statistics; mathematics; mechanical engineering; medical illustrating; metallurgical engineering; microbiology/bacteriology; music; music education; natural resources management; nutrition science; ornamental horticulture; philosophy; physics; plant protection; political science; (pre)dentistry; (pre)law; (pre)medicine; (pre)veterinary studies; psychology; public administration; religious studies; Russian; secondary education; sociology; Spanish; speech/rhetorical studies; technical writing; theater arts/drama; trade and industrial education; transportation technologies; visual/performing arts; wildlife biology; women's studies; zoology.

Ithaca College

Accounting; acting/directing; adapted physical education; anthropology; applied economics; applied mathematics; art; art history; arts management; athletic training/sports medicine; biochemistry; biology; biology education; broadcast journalism; business; business administration; business economics; business marketing and marketing management; chemistry; chemistry education; computer science; computer/information sciences; creative writing; dance; economics; education (multiple levels); education of the speech impaired; educational media design; English; English education; environmental science; exercise sciences; film studies; film/video production; finance; fine/studio arts; French; French language education; German; German language education; gerontology; health education; health facilities administration; health services administration; health/medical preparatory programs, other; health/physical education; history; human resources management; interdisciplinary studies; international business; jazz; journalism; K-12 education; labor/personnel relations; liberal arts and studies; marketing research; mass communications; mathematics; mathematics education; mathematics/computer science; middle school education; music; music (general performance); music (piano and organ performance); music (voice and choral/opera performance); music education; music theory and composition; nutrition science; nutrition studies; occupational therapy; organizational psychology; philosophy; photography; physical education; physical therapy; physics; physics education; political science; (pre)law; (pre)medicine; psychology; public health education/promotion; public relations; radio/television broadcasting; recreation and leisure studies; recreational therapy; rehabilitation therapy; science education; secondary education; social sciences; social studies education; socio-psychological sports studies; sociology; Spanish; Spanish language education; speech-language pathology/audiology; speech/rhetorical studies; sport/

fitness administration; telecommunications; theater arts/drama; theater design; visual/performing arts.

John Carroll University

Accounting; art history; Asian studies; biological and physical sciences; biology; business administration; business marketing and marketing management; chemistry; classics; computer science; early childhood education; East Asian studies; economics; education; elementary education; engineering physics; English; environmental science; finance; French; German; gerontology; Greek (Modern); history; humanities; interdisciplinary studies; international economics; international relations; K-12 education; Latin (Ancient and Medieval); literature; mass communications; mathematics; neuroscience; philosophy; physical education; physics; political science; (pre)dentistry; (pre)law; (pre)medicine; (pre)veterinary studies; psychology; public administration; religious education; religious studies; secondary education; sociology; Spanish; special education.

Johns Hopkins University

American studies; anthropology; applied mathematics; art history; behavioral sciences; bioengineering; biological and physical sciences; biology; biophysics; business; chemical engineering; chemistry; civil engineering; classics; cognitive psychology and psycholinguistics; computer engineering; computer/information sciences; creative writing; earth sciences; East Asian studies; economics; electrical/electronics engineering; electroencephalograph technology; engineering; engineering mechanics; English; environmental engineering; environmental science; film studies; French; geography; German; history; history of science and technology; industrial/manufacturing engineering; interdisciplinary studies; international relations; Italian; Latin American studies; liberal arts and studies; liberal arts and studies, other; literature; materials engineering; materials science; mathematics; mechanical engineering; Middle Eastern studies; music; music (general performance); music education; music theory and composition; natural sciences; neuroscience; nursing; philosophy; physics; physiological psychology/psychobiology; political science; psychology; public administration; public health; social sciences; sociology; Spanish.

The Juilliard School

Dance; music; music (piano and organ performance); music (voice and choral/opera performance); stringed instruments; theater arts/drama; wind and percussion instruments.

Juniata College

Accounting; anthropology; art history; biochemistry; biological and physical sciences; biology; biology education; botany; business administration; business marketing and marketing management; cell biology; chemistry; chemistry education; communications; communications, other; computer/information sciences; criminal justice studies; early childhood education; ecology; economics; education; elementary education; engineering; engineering physics; English; English education; environmental science; finance; fine/studio arts; foreign languages education; foreign languages/literatures; French; French language education; geology; German; German language education; health/medical preparatory programs, other; history; human resources management; humanities; interdisciplinary studies; international business; international relations; liberal arts and studies; management information systems/business data processing; marine biology; mathematics; mathematics education; microbiology/bacteriology; molecular biology; museum studies; natural sciences; peace and conflict studies; physical sciences; physics; physics education; political science; (pre)dentistry; (pre)law; (pre)medicine; (pre)pharmacy studies; (pre)theology; (pre)veterinary studies; professional studies; psychology; public administration; Russian; science education; secondary education; social sciences; social studies education; social work; sociology; Spanish; Spanish language education; special education; teacher education, specific programs, other; zoology.

Kalamazoo College
Anthropology; art; art history; biology; business economics; chemistry; classics; computer science; English; French; German; health science; history; interdisciplinary studies; mathematics; music; philosophy; physics; political science; psychology; religious studies; sociology; Spanish; theater arts/drama.

Kenyon College
African-American (black) studies; American studies; anthropology; art; art history; Asian studies; biochemistry; biology; chemistry; classics; computer science, other; creative writing; dance; economics; English; environmental science; fine/studio arts; French; German; Greek (Modern); history; humanities; interdisciplinary studies; international relations; Latin (Ancient and Medieval); law and legal studies; literature; mathematics; modern languages; molecular biology; music; natural sciences; neuroscience; philosophy; physics; political science; psychology; public policy analysis; religious studies; Romance languages; sociology; Spanish; theater arts/drama; women's studies.

Kettering University
Accounting; applied mathematics; business administration; business marketing and marketing management; chemistry; computer engineering; computer science; electrical/electronics engineering; engineering/industrial management; environmental science; finance; industrial/manufacturing engineering; information sciences/systems; mathematical statistics; mechanical engineering; operations management; physics; plastics engineering.

Knox College
African-American (black) studies; American studies; anthropology; art; art history; biochemistry; biology; chemistry; classics; computer/information sciences; creative writing; economics; education; English; environmental science; foreign languages/literatures; French; German; history; international relations; mathematics; music; philosophy; physics; political science; psychology; Russian; Russian/Slavic area studies; sociology; Spanish; theater arts/drama; Western European studies; women's studies.

Lafayette College
American studies; anthropology; art; art history; biochemistry; biology; business economics; chemical engineering; chemistry; civil engineering; computer science; economics; electrical/electronics engineering; engineering; English; environmental engineering; fine/studio arts; French; geology; German; history; international relations; mathematics; mechanical engineering; music; music history; philosophy; physics; political science; psychology; religious studies; Russian/Slavic area studies; sociology; Spanish.

Lake Forest College
African studies; American studies; anthropology; art history; Asian studies; biology; business economics; chemistry; communications; computer science; economics; education; elementary education; English; environmental science; European studies; finance; fine/studio arts; French; German; history; Latin American studies; mathematics; music; philosophy; physics; political science; (pre)dentistry; (pre)law; (pre)medicine; (pre)veterinary studies; psychology; secondary education; sociology; Spanish; women's studies.

Lawrence Technological University
Architecture; business administration; chemical engineering technology; chemistry; civil engineering; civil engineering technology; computer science; construction engineering; construction technology; electrical/electronic engineering technology; electrical/electronics engineering; engineering design; engineering technology; humanities; industrial technology; industrial/manufacturing engineering; information sciences/systems; interior architecture; mathematics; mechanical engineering; mechanical engineering technology; physics; technical writing.

Lawrence University
Anthropology; art history; biology; chemistry; classics; cognitive psychology and psycholinguistics; computer science; East Asian studies; ecology; economics; English; environmental science; fine/studio arts; French; geology; German; history; international economics; international relations; linguistics; mathematics; music; music (piano and organ performance); music (voice and choral/opera performance); music education; neuroscience; philosophy; physics; political science; (pre)dentistry; (pre)law; (pre)medicine; (pre)veterinary studies; psychology; religious studies; Russian; Russian/Slavic area studies; secondary education; Spanish; stringed instruments; theater arts/drama; wind and percussion instruments.

Lebanon Valley College
Accounting; actuarial science; biochemistry; biology; business administration; chemistry; communications technologies, other; computer science; economics; elementary education; English; French; German; health professions and related sciences, other; history; international business; liberal arts and studies; mathematics; medical technology; music; music business management and merchandising; music education; music, other; nuclear medical technology; philosophy; physics; physiological psychology/psychobiology; political science; (pre)dentistry; (pre)law; (pre)medicine; (pre)veterinary studies; psychology; religious studies; secondary education; social sciences; Spanish.

Lehigh University
Accounting; African studies; American studies; anthropology; architecture; art; Asian studies; biochemistry; biology; business administration; business economics; business marketing and marketing management; chemical engineering; chemistry; civil engineering; classics; cognitive psychology and psycholinguistics; computer engineering; computer science; economics; electrical/electronics engineering; engineering; engineering mechanics; engineering physics; English; environmental science; finance; French; German; history; industrial/manufacturing engineering; information sciences/systems; international business; international relations; journalism; materials engineering;

mathematical statistics; mathematics; mechanical engineering; molecular biology; music; natural sciences; neuroscience; philosophy; physics; political science; (pre)dentistry; (pre)medicine; psychology; religious studies; Russian/Slavic area studies; science/technology and society; sociology; Spanish; theater arts/drama; urban studies.

Le Moyne College
Accounting; applied mathematics; biochemistry; biological and physical sciences; biology; business administration; chemistry; communications; creative writing; criminology; economics; elementary education; English; English education; foreign languages education; French; history; information sciences/systems; international relations; labor/personnel relations; mathematics; mathematics education; philosophy; physician assistant; physics; political science; (pre)dentistry; (pre)law; (pre)medicine; (pre)pharmacy studies; (pre)veterinary studies; psychology; religious studies; science education; secondary education; social studies education; sociology; Spanish; theater arts/drama.

LeTourneau University
Accounting; aircraft mechanic/airframe; aircraft pilot (professional); aviation technology; biblical studies; bioengineering; biology; business administration; business marketing and marketing management; chemistry; computer engineering; computer engineering technology; computer science; drafting and design technology; electrical/electronic engineering technology; electrical/electronics engineering; elementary education; engineering; engineering technology; English; finance; history; information sciences/systems; interdisciplinary studies; international business; management information systems/business data processing; mathematics; mechanical engineering; mechanical engineering technology; missionary studies; natural sciences; physical education; (pre)dentistry; (pre)law; (pre)medicine; (pre)veterinary studies; psychology; religious studies; secondary education; sport/fitness administration; welding technology.

Lewis & Clark College
Anthropology; art; biochemistry; biology; chemistry; computer science; East Asian studies; economics; English; environmental science; French; German; Hispanic-American studies; history; international relations; mass communications; mathematics; modern languages; music; philosophy; physics; political science; (pre)dentistry; (pre)engineering; (pre)law; (pre)medicine; (pre)veterinary studies; psychology; religious studies; sociology; Spanish; theater arts/drama.

Lipscomb University
Accounting; American government; American studies; art; athletic training/sports medicine; biblical languages/literatures; biblical studies; biochemistry; biology; biology education; business administration; business economics; business marketing and marketing management; chemistry; computer science; dietetics; divinity/ministry; education; elementary education; engineering science; English; environmental science; exercise sciences; family/consumer studies; fashion merchandising; finance; fine/studio arts; food products retailing; French; French language education; German; graphic design/commercial art/illustration; health education; history; home economics; information sciences/systems; liberal arts and studies; mass communications;

mathematics; middle school education; music; music (piano and organ performance); music (voice and choral/opera performance); music education; nursing; philosophy; physical education; physics; political science; (pre)dentistry; (pre)law; (pre)medicine; (pre)veterinary studies; psychology; public administration; public relations; secondary education; social work; Spanish; speech/rhetorical studies; stringed instruments; theology; urban studies; wind and percussion instruments.

List College, Jewish Theological Seminary of America
Biblical studies; history; Judaic studies; literature; museum studies; music; philosophy; religious studies.

Loyola College in Maryland
Accounting; applied mathematics; art; biology; business; chemistry; classics; communications; computer/information sciences; creative writing; economics; education; electrical/electronics engineering; elementary education; engineering; English; finance; French; German; history; interdisciplinary studies; international business; mathematics; philosophy; physics; political science; psychology; religious studies; sociology; Spanish; special education; speech-language pathology.

Loyola University Chicago
Accounting; anthropology; art; art history; biochemistry; biology; business administration; business economics; business marketing and marketing management; ceramic arts; chemistry; classics; communications; communications, other; computer science; criminal justice studies; early childhood education; economics; elementary education; English; environmental science; finance; fine arts and art studies, other; French; German; Greek (Ancient and Medieval); history; human resources management; humanities; information sciences/systems; international relations; Italian; journalism; Latin (Ancient and Medieval); management information systems/business data processing; mathematical statistics; mathematics; mathematics/computer science; metal/jewelry arts; music; natural sciences; nursing; nutrition studies; operations management; philosophy; photography; physics; political science; (pre)dentistry; (pre)law; (pre)medicine; (pre)theology; (pre)veterinary studies; psychology; psychology, other; social psychology; social work; sociology; Spanish; special education; theater arts/drama; theology.

Loyola University New Orleans
Accounting; art; behavioral sciences; biology; business administration; business economics; business marketing and marketing management; chemistry; classics; communications; computer/information sciences; creative writing; criminal justice studies; economics; education; elementary education; English; finance; forensic technology; French; general studies; German; graphic design/commercial art/illustration; history; humanities; information sciences/systems; international business; jazz; mathematics; music; music (general performance); music (piano and organ performance); music business management and merchandising; music education; music theory and composition; music therapy; nursing; philosophy; physics; political science; psychology; religious education; religious studies; Russian; sacred music; social sciences; sociology; Spanish; theater arts/drama; visual/performing arts.

Luther College
Accounting; African studies; African-American (black) studies; anthropology; art; art education; arts management; biblical

languages/literatures; biology; biology education; business; business administration; business computer programming; business marketing and marketing management; chemistry; chemistry education; classics; computer management; computer programming; computer science; computer/information sciences; cytotechnology; dance; drama and dance education; early childhood education; economics; education; elementary education; English; English composition; English education; environmental biology; foreign languages education; French; French language education; German; German language education; Greek (Modern); health education; health/physical education; Hebrew; history; history education; interdisciplinary studies; international business; international relations; Latin (Ancient and Medieval); Latin American studies; management information systems/business data processing; mass communications; mathematical statistics; mathematics; mathematics education; medical technology; middle school education; modern languages; museum studies; music; music (general performance); music (piano and organ performance); music (voice and choral/opera performance); music business management and merchandising; music conducting; music education; music history; music theory and composition; nursing; philosophy; physical education; physics; physics education; physiological psychology/psychobiology; political science; (pre)dentistry; (pre)law; (pre)medicine; (pre)theology; (pre)veterinary studies; psychology; reading education; religious studies; Scandinavian area studies; Scandinavian languages; science education; secondary education; social science education; social work; sociology; Spanish; Spanish language education; special education; sport/fitness administration; stringed instruments; theater arts/drama; theology; wind and percussion instruments.

Lycoming College

Accounting; actuarial science; American studies; anthropology; archaeology; art; art education; art history; astronomy; biology; business administration; business marketing and marketing management; chemistry; computer science; creative writing; criminal justice/law enforcement administration; economics; education; elementary education; English; finance; fine/studio arts; French; German; graphic design/commercial art/illustration; history; interdisciplinary studies; international business; international relations; literature; mass communications; mathematics; medical technology; music; music education; philosophy; physics; political science; (pre)dentistry; (pre)law; (pre)medicine; (pre)veterinary studies; psychology; religious studies; secondary education; sociology; Spanish; theater arts/drama.

Lyon College

Accounting; art; biology; business administration; chemistry; computer science; economics; English; environmental science; history; mathematics; music; philosophy and religion, other; political science; psychology; Spanish; theater arts/drama.

Macalester College

Anthropology; art history; Asian studies; biology; chemistry; classics; communications; computer science; economics; English; environmental science; fine/studio arts; French; geography; geology; Greek (Modern); history; humanities; interdisciplinary studies; international relations; Latin (Ancient and Medieval); Latin American studies; linguistics; mathematics; music; neuroscience; philosophy; physics; political science; psychology;

religious studies; Russian; Russian/Slavic area studies; sociology; Spanish; theater arts/drama; urban studies; women's studies.

Maharishi University of Management

Acting/directing; agricultural sciences; agricultural sciences, other; art; biochemistry; biology; British literature; business; business administration; ceramic arts; chemistry; computer graphics; computer science; creative writing; design/visual communications; drawing; ecology; education; electrical/electronic engineering technology; electrical/electronics engineering; English; environmental biology; environmental science; exercise sciences; film/video production; graphic design/commercial art/illustration; health professions and related sciences, other; interdisciplinary studies; literature; management science; mathematics; multimedia; painting; (pre)law; (pre)medicine; psychology; sculpture; theater arts/drama; theater design; visual/performing arts; web page, digital/multimedia and information resources design.

Manhattan School of Music

Jazz; music; music (piano and organ performance); music (voice and choral/opera performance); stringed instruments; wind and percussion instruments.

Mannes College of Music, New School University

Music; music (piano and organ performance); music (voice and choral/opera performance); music conducting; music theory and composition; stringed instruments; wind and percussion instruments.

Marietta College

Accounting; art; athletic training/sports medicine; biochemistry; biology; business administration; business communications; business marketing and marketing management; chemistry; communications; computer science; economics; education; elementary education; English; environmental science; fine/studio arts; geology; graphic design/commercial art/illustration; history; human resources management; information sciences/systems; international business; journalism; liberal arts and studies; mathematics; music; petroleum engineering; philosophy; physics; political science; psychology; public relations; radio/television broadcasting; secondary education; Spanish; speech/rhetorical studies; theater arts/drama.

Marquette University

Accounting; advertising; African-American (black) studies; anthropology; athletic training/sports medicine; bilingual/bicultural education; biochemistry; bioengineering; biology; biomedical science; broadcast journalism; business administration; business economics; business marketing and marketing management; chemistry; civil engineering; classics; communications; computer engineering; computer science; creative writing; criminology; dental hygiene; economics; education; electrical/electronics engineering; elementary education; engineering; English; environmental engineering; exercise sciences; finance; French; German; history; history of philosophy; human resources management; industrial/manufacturing engineering; information sciences/systems; interdisciplinary studies; international business; international relations; journalism; management information systems/business data processing; mass communications; mathematical statistics; mathematics; mechanical engineering; medical laboratory technician; middle school education; molecular biology; nursing; nursing (midwifery); philosophy; physical therapy; physician assistant; physics; political science; (pre)dentistry; (pre)law; (pre)medicine; psychology; public relations; secondary education; social work; sociology; Spanish; speech-language pathology/audiology; speech/rhetorical studies; theater arts/drama; theology; women's studies.

Maryland Institute, College of Art

Art; art education; ceramic arts; drawing; fine/studio arts; graphic design/commercial art/illustration; interior design; multimedia; painting; photography; printmaking; sculpture; textile arts; visual/performing arts.

Maryville College

Area studies, other; art; art education; biochemistry; biology; biology education; business administration; chemical and atomic/molecular physics; chemistry; chemistry education; computer science; developmental/child psychology; economics; education; engineering; English; English education; environmental science; fine/studio arts; history; history education; international business; international relations; mathematics; mathematics education; mathematics/computer science; music; music (piano and organ performance); music (voice and choral/opera performance); music education; nursing; physical education; physics education; political science; psychology; recreation and leisure studies; religious studies; sign language interpretation; social science education; sociology; Spanish; Spanish language education; teaching English as a second language; technical writing; theater arts/drama; wind and percussion instruments.

Mary Washington College

American studies; architectural history; art; art history; biology; business administration; chemistry; classics; computer science; economics; elementary education; English; environmental science; fine/studio arts; French; geography; geology; German; history; interdisciplinary studies; international relations; Latin (Ancient and Medieval); liberal arts and studies; mathematics; modern languages; music; music education; philosophy; physics; political science; (pre)dentistry; (pre)law; (pre)medicine; (pre)veterinary studies; psychology; religious studies; secondary education; sociology; Spanish; theater arts/drama.

Massachusetts College of Art

Architecture; art education; art history; ceramic arts; fashion design/illustration; film/video production; fine/studio arts; graphic design/commercial art/illustration; industrial design; metal/jewelry arts; multimedia; painting; photography; printmaking; sculpture; textile arts.

Massachusetts Institute of Technology

Aerospace engineering; American studies; anthropology; applied mathematics; archaeology; architecture; bioengineering; biology; business administration; chemical engineering; chemistry; city/community/regional planning; civil engineering; cognitive psychology and psycholinguistics; computer engineering; computer science; earth sciences; East Asian studies; economics; electrical/electronics engineering; engineering; environmental engineering; environmental science; foreign languages/literatures; German; history; humanities; interdisciplinary studies; Latin American studies; liberal arts and studies; linguistics; literature; materials engineering; materials science; mathematics; mechanical engineering; music; naval architecture/marine

engineering; naval science; nuclear engineering; ocean engineering; philosophy; physics; political science; (pre)dentistry; (pre)law; (pre)medicine; (pre)veterinary studies; Russian; Russian/Slavic area studies; science/technology and society; Spanish; theater arts/drama; women's studies.

McKendree College

Accounting; art; art education; athletic training/sports medicine; biology; biology education; business administration; business education; business marketing and marketing management; chemistry; computer science; criminal justice/law enforcement administration; distribution operations; economics; elementary education; English; English education; finance; history; history education; information sciences/systems; international relations; K-12 education; marketing operations; mass communications; mathematics; mathematics education; medical technology; music; nursing; philosophy; physical education; political science; (pre)dentistry; (pre)law; (pre)medicine; (pre)veterinary studies; psychology; public relations; religious studies; secondary education; social science education; social sciences; social work; sociology; speech/rhetorical studies; speech/theater education.

Mercer University

Accounting; African-American (black) studies; art; art education; bioengineering; biology; business; business administration; business marketing and marketing management; chemistry; classics; communications; computer engineering; computer science; computer/information sciences; criminal justice/law enforcement administration; early childhood education; earth sciences; economics; education of the specific learning disabled; electrical/electronics engineering; elementary education; engineering/industrial management; English; English education; environmental engineering; environmental science; finance; foreign languages education; French; German; history; history education; human services; industrial/manufacturing engineering; information sciences/systems; international business; Latin (Ancient and Medieval); mathematics; mathematics education; mechanical engineering; middle school education; multi/interdisciplinary studies, other; music; music (general performance); music education; nursing; philosophy; physics; political science; psychology; religious studies; science education; social sciences; social studies education; sociology; Spanish; theater arts/drama.

Messiah College

Accounting; adapted physical education; art education; art history; athletic training/sports medicine; biblical studies; biochemistry; biology; biology education; business administration; business economics; business management/administrative services, other; business marketing and marketing management; chemistry; chemistry education; civil engineering; communications; computer science; dietetics; early childhood education; economics; elementary education; engineering; English; English education; environmental science; exercise sciences; family/community studies; fine/studio arts; French; French language education; German; German language education; history; human resources management; humanities; information sciences/systems; international business; journalism; mathematics; mathematics education; music; music education; nursing; philosophy; physical education; physics; political science; psychology; radio/television broadcasting; recreation and leisure studies; religious education; religious studies; social studies education; social work; sociology; Spanish; Spanish language education; theater arts/drama.

Miami University

Accounting; aerospace engineering; African-American (black) studies; American studies; anthropology; architectural environmental design; architecture; art; art education; art history; athletic training/sports medicine; biochemistry; biology; biology education; botany; business; business administration; business economics; business marketing and marketing management; chemistry; child care/development; city/community/regional planning; classics; computer systems analysis; computer/information sciences; creative writing; dietetics; early childhood education; earth sciences; economics; elementary education; engineering physics; engineering technology; engineering/industrial management; English; English education; exercise sciences; family/consumer studies; finance; fine/studio arts; French; geography; geology; German; Greek (Ancient and Medieval); health education; health/physical education; history; home economics; home economics education; human resources management; individual/family development; industrial/manufacturing engineering; interdisciplinary studies; interior design; international relations; journalism; Latin (Ancient and Medieval); linguistics; management information systems/business data processing; management science; mass communications; mathematical statistics; mathematics; mechanical engineering; medical technology; microbiology/bacteriology; middle school education; music; music (general performance); music education; nursing; operations management; operations research; organizational behavior; philosophy; physical education; physics; political science; (pre)dentistry; (pre)law; (pre)medicine; (pre)veterinary studies; psychology; public administration; purchasing/contracts management; religious studies; Russian; science education; secondary education; social studies education; social work; sociology; Spanish; special education; speech-language pathology; speech-language pathology/audiology; speech/rhetorical studies; sport/fitness administration; systems science and theory; technical writing; theater arts/drama; wood science/paper technology; zoology.

Michigan Technological University

Accounting; applied mathematics; biochemistry; biological technology; biology; business administration; business economics; business marketing and marketing management; chemical engineering; chemical engineering technology; chemistry; civil engineering; civil engineering technology; communications; computer engineering; computer programming; computer science; construction engineering; earth sciences; ecology; electrical/electronic engineering technology; electrical/electronics engineering; electromechanical technology; engineering; engineering mechanics; engineering physics; English; environmental engineering; finance; forest harvesting production technology; forestry; general studies; geological engineering; geology; geophysics and seismology; history; humanities; industrial/manufacturing engineering; information sciences/systems; management information systems/business data processing; materials engineering; mathematical statistics; mathematics; mechanical engineering; mechanical engineering technology; medical technology; metallurgical engineering; microbiology/bacteriology; mining/mineral engineering; operations management; physical sciences; physics; (pre)dentistry;

(pre)medicine; (pre)veterinary studies; science education; secondary education; social sciences; surveying; technical writing; ing.

Middlebury College

American studies; anthropology; art; art history; biochemistry; biological and physical sciences; biology; chemistry; Chinese; classics; computer science; dance; drawing; East Asian studies; Eastern European area studies; economics; education; English; environmental science; film studies; fine/studio arts; French; geography; geology; German; history; humanities; international economics; international relations; Italian; Japanese; liberal arts and studies; literature; mathematics; modern languages; molecular biology; music; natural sciences; philosophy; physical sciences; physics; political science; (pre)dentistry; (pre)law; (pre)medicine; (pre)veterinary studies; psychology; religious studies; Romance languages; Russian; Russian/Slavic area studies; secondary education; social sciences; sociology; Southeast Asian studies; Spanish; theater arts/drama; women's studies.

Milligan College

Accounting; advertising; art; biblical studies; biological and physical sciences; biology; broadcast journalism; business administration; business economics; chemistry; computer science; early childhood education; education; English; exercise sciences; health science; health services administration; history; humanities; journalism; mathematics; music; music (piano and organ performance); music (voice and choral/opera performance); music education; nursing; pastoral counseling; physical education; (pre)dentistry; (pre)medicine; (pre)veterinary studies; psychology; public relations; radio/television broadcasting; religious education; sacred music; science education; secondary education; sociology; theater arts/drama.

Millsaps College

Accounting; anthropology; art; biology; business administration; chemistry; classics; computer science; economics; education; English; European studies; French; geology; German; history; mathematics; music; philosophy; physics; political science; psychology; religious studies; sociology; Spanish; theater arts/drama.

Mills College

American studies; anthropology; art; art history; biochemistry; biology; business economics; chemistry; comparative literature; computer science; creative writing; cultural studies; dance; developmental/child psychology; early childhood education; economics; education; elementary education; English; environmental science; fine/studio arts; French; German; Hispanic-American studies; history; interdisciplinary studies; international relations; liberal arts and studies; mathematical statistics; mathematics; music; philosophy; (pre)medicine; psychology; public policy analysis; social sciences; sociology; theater arts/drama; women's studies.

Milwaukee School of Engineering

Architectural engineering; bioengineering; business; communications, other; computer engineering; computer software engineering; electrical/electronic engineering technology; electrical/electronics engineering; industrial/manufacturing engineering; international business; management information systems/business data processing; mechanical engineering; mechanical engineering technology; nursing.

Morehouse College

Accounting; adult/continuing education; African-American (black) studies; art; biology; business administration; business marketing and marketing management; chemistry; computer/information sciences; economics; elementary education; engineering; English; finance; French; German; history; interdisciplinary studies; international relations; mathematics; middle school education; music; philosophy; physical education; physics; political science; psychology; religious studies; secondary education; sociology; Spanish; theater arts/drama; urban studies.

Mount Holyoke College

African-American (black) studies; American studies; anthropology; art history; Asian studies; astronomy; biochemistry; biology; chemistry; classics; computer science; dance; economics; education; English; environmental science; European studies; film studies; fine/studio arts; French; geography; geology; German; Greek (Modern); history; interdisciplinary studies; international relations; Italian; Judaic studies; Latin (Ancient and Medieval); Latin American studies; mathematical statistics; mathematics; medieval/renaissance studies; music; philosophy; physics; political science; psychology; religious studies; Romance languages; Russian; Russian/Slavic area studies; social sciences; sociology; Spanish; theater arts/drama; women's studies.

Mount St. Mary's College

Accounting; American studies; art; art education; biochemistry; biology; business administration; business education; business marketing and marketing management; chemistry; developmental/child psychology; early childhood education; education; elementary education; English; French; gerontology; health services administration; history; international business; liberal arts and studies; mathematics; music; music (voice and choral/opera performance); music education; nursing; occupational therapy assistant; philosophy; physical therapy assistant; political science; (pre)dentistry; (pre)law; (pre)medicine; psychology; religious studies; secondary education; social sciences; sociology; Spanish; urban studies.

Mount Union College

Accounting; American studies; art; Asian studies; astronomy; athletic training/sports medicine; biology; business administration; chemistry; communications; computer science; design/visual communications; early childhood education; economics; English; English composition; environmental biology; exercise sciences; French; geology; German; history; information sciences/systems; interdisciplinary studies; international business; Japanese; mass communications; mathematics; middle school education; music; music (general performance); music education; philosophy; physical education; physics; political science; psychology; religious studies; sociology; Spanish; sport/fitness administration; theater arts/drama.

Muhlenberg College

Accounting; American studies; anthropology; art; art history; biochemistry; biology; business administration; chemistry; communications; computer science; dance; economics; elementary education; English; environmental science; fine/studio arts; French; German; history; human resources management; international economics; international relations; mathematics; music; natural sciences; philosophy; physical sciences; physics; political

science; (pre)dentistry; (pre)law; (pre)medicine; (pre)veterinary studies; psychology; religious studies; Russian/Slavic area studies; secondary education; social sciences; sociology; Spanish; theater arts/drama.

Nazareth College of Rochester

Accounting; American studies; art; art education; art history; art therapy; biochemistry; biology; biology education; business administration; business education; business marketing and marketing management; ceramic arts; chemistry; chemistry education; creative writing; drawing; economics; education; elementary education; English; English education; environmental science; fine/studio arts; foreign languages education; French; German; gerontology; graphic design/commercial art/illustration; history; history education; human resources management; information sciences/systems; information technology; interdisciplinary studies; international relations; Italian; literature; management information systems/business data processing; mathematics; mathematics education; modern languages; music; music education; music history; music therapy; nursing; philosophy; photography; physical therapy; political science; (pre)dentistry; (pre)law; (pre)medicine; (pre)veterinary studies; psychology; religious studies; science education; secondary education; social sciences; social studies education; social work; sociology; Spanish; special education; speech-language pathology/audiology; theater arts/drama; women's studies.

New College of Florida

Anthropology; art; biology; chemistry; classics; economics; environmental science; fine/studio arts; French; German; Greek (Ancient and Medieval); history; international relations; Latin (Ancient and Medieval); liberal arts and studies; literature; mathematics; medieval/renaissance studies; music; natural sciences; philosophy; physics; political science; psychology; public policy analysis; religious studies; Russian; social sciences; sociology; Spanish; urban studies.

New England Conservatory of Music

Jazz; music (piano and organ performance); music (voice and choral/opera performance); music history; music theory and composition; stringed instruments; wind and percussion instruments.

New Jersey Institute of Technology

Actuarial science; applied mathematics; architecture; bioengineering; biology; business administration; chemical engineering; chemistry; civil engineering; computer engineering; computer science; computer/information sciences; computer/information sciences, other; electrical/electronics engineering; engineering; engineering science; engineering technology; environmental engineering; environmental science; geophysical engineering; history; industrial/manufacturing engineering; information sciences/systems; mathematical statistics; mechanical engineering; nursing science; physics; science/technology and society; technical writing.

New Mexico Institute of Mining and Technology

Applied mathematics; astrophysics; atmospheric sciences; behavioral sciences; biological and physical sciences; biology; business administration; chemical engineering; chemistry; computer programming; computer science; electrical/electronics engineering; engineering; engineering mechanics; environmental biology; environmental engineering; environmental science; experimental psychology; geochemistry; geology; geophysics and seismology; information technology; interdisciplinary studies; liberal arts and studies; materials engineering; mathematics; mechanical engineering; medical technology; metallurgical engineering; mining/mineral engineering; petroleum engineering; physics; (pre)dentistry; (pre)medicine; (pre)veterinary studies; psychology; science education; technical writing.

New York School of Interior Design
Interior design.

New York University
Accounting; actuarial science; African-American (black) studies; anthropology; archaeology; art; art history; biochemistry; biology; biology education; business administration; business economics; business marketing and marketing management; chemical engineering; chemistry; chemistry education; city/community/regional planning; civil engineering; classics; communications; comparative literature; computer engineering; computer programming; computer science; computer/information sciences; dance; dental hygiene; diagnostic medical sonography; drama and dance education; drawing; early childhood education; East Asian studies; economics; education; education of the speech impaired; electrical/electronics engineering; elementary education; engineering; engineering physics; English; English education; European studies; film studies; film/video production; finance; fine/studio arts; foreign languages education; French; French language education; German; graphic design/commercial art/illustration; Greek (Modern); health services administration; Hebrew; history; hotel and restaurant management; human services; humanities; information sciences/systems; interdisciplinary studies; international business; international relations; Italian; jazz; journalism; Judaic studies; Latin (Ancient and Medieval); Latin American studies; liberal arts and studies; linguistics; management information systems/business data processing; marketing operations; mass communications; materials engineering; mathematical statistics; mathematics; mathematics education; mechanical engineering; medical radiologic technology; medical records technology; medieval/renaissance studies; Middle Eastern studies; middle school education; music; music (general performance); music (piano and organ performance); music (voice and choral/opera performance); music business management and merchandising; music education; music theory and composition; musical instrument technology; neuroscience; nursing; nutrition science; operations research; philosophy; photography; physical therapy assistant; physics; physics education; play/screenwriting; political science; Portuguese; (pre)dentistry; (pre)law; (pre)medicine; psychology; radio/television broadcasting; real estate; religious studies; respiratory therapy; Romance languages; Russian; science education; sculpture; secondary education; social sciences; social studies education; social work; sociology; Spanish; special education; sport/fitness administration; theater arts/drama; theater design; travel-tourism management; urban studies; women's studies.

North Carolina School of the Arts
Dance; film studies; film/video production; music; music (piano and organ performance); music (voice and choral/opera performance); theater arts/drama.

North Carolina State University
Accounting; aerospace engineering; agribusiness; agricultural and food products processing; agricultural business; agricultural education; agricultural engineering; agricultural sciences; agronomy/crop science; animal sciences; applied mathematics; architecture; arts management; atmospheric sciences; biochemistry; biology; biology education; botany; business administration; business marketing and marketing management; chemical engineering; chemistry; chemistry education; civil engineering; communications; computer engineering; computer science; construction engineering; creative writing; criminal justice/law enforcement administration; design/visual communications; economics; education; electrical/electronics engineering; engineering; English; English education; environmental engineering; environmental science; food sciences; forest management; French; French language education; geology; German; graphic design/commercial art/illustration; health occupations education; history; horticulture science; human resources management; industrial design; industrial/manufacturing engineering; landscape architecture; landscaping management; liberal arts and studies; marketing/distribution education; materials engineering; mathematical statistics; mathematics; mathematics education; mechanical engineering; microbiology/bacteriology; natural resources conservation; natural resources management; nuclear engineering; oceanography; philosophy; physics; plant protection; political science; poultry science; psychology; public policy analysis; recreation/leisure facilities management; religious studies; science education; secondary education; social studies education; social work; sociology; Spanish; Spanish language education; textile sciences/engineering; travel-tourism management; turf management; wood science/paper technology; zoology.

North Central College
Accounting; actuarial science; American history; anthropology; applied mathematics; art; art education; athletic training/sports medicine; biochemistry; biology; broadcast journalism; business administration; business education; business marketing and marketing management; chemistry; classics; computer science; early childhood education; economics; education; elementary education; English; exercise sciences; finance; French; German; health education; history; humanities; international business; international relations; Japanese; jazz; liberal arts and studies; literature; management information systems/business data processing; mass communications; mathematics; modern languages; music; music (piano and organ performance); music (voice and choral/opera performance); natural sciences; philosophy; physical education; physics; political science; (pre)dentistry; (pre)law; (pre)medicine; (pre)veterinary studies; psychology; public relations; religious studies; science education; secondary education; social sciences; sociology; Spanish; speech/rhetorical studies; theater arts/drama.

Northwestern College (MN)
Accounting; art education; athletic training/sports medicine; biblical studies; biology; business administration; business marketing and marketing management; communications; creative writing; criminal justice studies; early childhood education; elementary education; English; English education; finance; fine/studio arts; graphic design/commercial art/illustration; history; international business; journalism; liberal arts and studies;

management information systems/business data processing; mathematics; mathematics education; missionary studies; music; music (general performance); music (piano and organ performance); music (voice and choral/opera performance); music education; organizational behavior; pastoral counseling; physical education; (pre)theology; psychology; public relations; radio/television broadcasting; religious education; social sciences; social studies education; Spanish; sport/fitness administration; teaching English as a second language; technical writing; theater arts/drama; theology/ministry, other.

Northwestern University

African-American (black) studies; American studies; anthropology; applied mathematics; art; art history; Asian studies; astronomy; biochemistry; bioengineering; biological and physical sciences; biology; cell biology; chemical engineering; chemistry; civil engineering; classics; cognitive psychology and psycholinguistics; communication disorders; communications; community psychology; comparative literature; computer engineering; computer science; computer/information sciences; counseling psychology; dance; drama/theater literature; ecology; economics; education; education of the specific learning disabled; electrical/electronics engineering; engineering; engineering science; engineering, other; English; environmental engineering; environmental science; film studies; French; geography; geology; German; hearing sciences; history; humanities; industrial/manufacturing engineering; interdisciplinary studies; international relations; Italian; jazz; journalism; liberal arts and studies; linguistics; materials engineering; materials science; mathematical statistics; mathematics; mathematics education; mechanical engineering; molecular biology; music; music (general performance); music (piano and organ performance); music (voice and choral/opera performance); music education; music history; music theory and composition; music, other; neuroscience; organizational behavior; philosophy; physics; political science; (pre)medicine; psychology; public policy analysis; radio/television broadcasting; religious studies; secondary education; Slavic languages; social sciences and history, other; social/philosophical foundations of education; sociology; South Asian languages; Spanish; speech therapy; speech-language pathology; speech-language pathology/audiology; speech/rhetorical studies; theater arts/drama; urban studies; visual/performing arts; wind and percussion instruments; women's studies.

Oberlin College

African-American (black) studies; anthropology; archaeology; art; art history; biochemistry; biology; chemistry; classics; comparative literature; computer science; creative writing; dance; East Asian studies; ecology; economics; English; environmental science; fine/studio arts; French; geology; German; Greek (Modern); history; interdisciplinary studies; jazz; Judaic studies; Latin (Ancient and Medieval); Latin American studies; law and legal studies; mathematics; Middle Eastern studies; music; music (piano and organ performance); music (voice and choral/opera performance); music education; music history; neuroscience; philosophy; physics; physiological psychology/psychobiology; political science; psychology; religious studies; Romance languages; Russian; Russian/Slavic area studies; sociology; Spanish; stringed instruments; theater arts/drama; wind and percussion instruments; women's studies.

Occidental College

American studies; anthropology; art history; Asian studies; biochemistry; biology; business economics; chemistry; cognitive psychology and psycholinguistics; comparative literature; economics; environmental science; exercise sciences; fine/studio arts; French; geology; history; international relations; mathematics; music; philosophy; physics; physiological psychology/psychobiology; political science; psychology; public policy analysis; religious studies; sociology; Spanish; theater arts/drama; women's studies.

Oglethorpe University

Accounting; American studies; art; biology; business administration; business economics; chemistry; computer science; early childhood education; economics; education; elementary education; English; history; interdisciplinary studies; international relations; mass communications; mathematics; middle school education; philosophy; physics; political science; (pre)dentistry; (pre)law; (pre)medicine; (pre)veterinary studies; psychology; secondary education; social work; sociology; urban studies.

Ohio Northern University

Accounting; art; art education; athletic training/sports medicine; biochemistry; biology; broadcast journalism; business administration; ceramic arts; chemistry; civil engineering; computer engineering; computer science; creative writing; criminal justice/law enforcement administration; early childhood education; electrical/electronics engineering; elementary education; English; environmental science; French; graphic design/commercial art/illustration; health education; history; industrial arts; industrial technology; international business; international relations; mass communications; mathematical statistics; mathematics; mechanical engineering; medical technology; medicinal/pharmaceutical chemistry; middle school education; molecular biology; music; music business management and merchandising; music education; pharmacy; philosophy; physical education; physics; political science; psychology; public relations; religious studies; sociology; Spanish; speech/rhetorical studies; sport/fitness administration; theater arts/drama.

The Ohio State University

Accounting; actuarial science; aerospace engineering; African studies; African-American (black) studies; agricultural and food products processing; agricultural business; agricultural economics; agricultural education; agricultural engineering; agricultural plant pathology; agronomy/crop science; animal sciences; anthropology; Arabic; architecture; art; art education; art history; Asian-American studies; astronomy; athletic training/sports medicine; aviation management; aviation technology; biochemistry; biology; biotechnology research; botany; business administration; business economics; business home economics; business marketing and marketing management; ceramic arts; ceramic sciences/engineering; chemical engineering; chemistry; Chinese; city/community/regional planning; civil engineering; classics; clothing and textiles; clothing/apparel/textile studies; communications; communications, other; comparative literature; computer engineering; computer science; computer/information sciences; creative writing; criminal justice studies; criminology; cultural studies; dance; dental hygiene; design/visual communications; development economics; dietetics; drama and dance education; drawing; East Asian studies; economics; electrical/electronics engineering; engineering physics; English; entomology; environmental education; environmental science; exercise sciences; family resource management studies; finance; fine/studio arts; fishing sciences and management; folklore; food sciences; forestry; French; genetics; geography; geology; German; graphic design/commercial art/illustration; Greek (Modern); health professions and related sciences, other; Hebrew; history; history, other; horticulture science; hospitality management; human resources management; humanities; individual/family development; industrial arts education; industrial design; industrial/manufacturing engineering; information sciences/systems; insurance and risk management; interior design; international business; international relations; Islamic studies; Italian; Japanese; jazz; journalism; Judaic studies; landscape architecture; Latin American studies; linguistics; logistics and materials management; management information systems/business data processing; materials engineering; materials science; mathematics; mathematics, other; mechanical engineering; medical dietician; medical radiologic technology; medical records administration; medical technology; metallurgical engineering; microbiology/bacteriology; Middle Eastern studies; music; music (general performance); music (piano and organ performance); music (voice and choral/opera performance); music education; music history; music theory and composition; natural resources management; natural resources protective services; nursing; nursing science; nutrition studies; occupational therapy; operations management; painting; peace and conflict studies; pharmacy; philosophy; physical education; physical therapy; physics; plant sciences; political science; Portuguese; printmaking; psychology; radiological science; real estate; religious studies; respiratory therapy; Russian; Russian/Slavic area studies; sculpture; social sciences; social work; sociology; soil conservation; Spanish; special education; speech-language pathology/audiology; surveying; systems engineering; technical education; theater arts/drama; turf management; Western European studies; wildlife management; women's studies; zoology.

Ohio Wesleyan University

Accounting; African-American (black) studies; anthropology; art education; art history; art therapy; astronomy; biology; botany; broadcast journalism; business administration; business economics; chemistry; classics; computer science; creative writing; cultural studies; earth sciences; East Asian studies; economics; education; elementary education; engineering science; engineering, other; English; environmental science; fine/studio arts; French; general studies; genetics; geography; geology; German; health education; history; humanities; international business; international relations; journalism; K-12 education; literature; mathematical statistics; mathematics; medieval/renaissance studies; microbiology/bacteriology; multi/interdisciplinary studies, other; music; music education; neuroscience; philosophy; physical education; physics; political science; (pre)dentistry; (pre)law; (pre)medicine; (pre)theology; (pre)veterinary studies; psychology; public administration; religious studies; secondary education; sociology; Spanish; theater arts/drama; urban studies; women's studies; zoology.

Oklahoma Baptist University

Accounting; advertising; applied art; art; art education; athletic training/sports medicine; biblical languages/literatures; biblical studies; biological and physical sciences; biology; biology education; broadcast journalism; business administration; business

computer programming; business marketing and marketing management; chemistry; chemistry education; child care/development; child guidance; computer management; computer science; computer systems analysis; computer/information sciences; developmental/child psychology; divinity/ministry; drama and dance education; early childhood education; education; education of the emotionally handicapped; education of the mentally handicapped; education of the specific learning disabled; elementary education; English; English composition; English education; exercise sciences; finance; fine/studio arts; French; French language education; German; German language education; health/physical education; history; history education; human resources management; humanities; information sciences/systems; interdisciplinary studies; international business; international business marketing; journalism; management information systems/business data processing; marriage and family counseling; mass communications; mathematics; mathematics education; missionary studies; museum studies; music; music (piano and organ performance); music (voice and choral/opera performance); music education; music theory and composition; natural sciences; nursing; pastoral counseling; philosophy; physical education; physical sciences; physics; political science; (pre)dentistry; (pre)law; (pre)medicine; (pre)pharmacy studies; (pre)veterinary studies; psychology; public relations; radio/television broadcasting; recreation and leisure studies; religious education; religious studies; sacred music; science education; secondary education; social science education; social sciences; social studies education; social work; sociology; Spanish; Spanish language education; special education; speech education; speech/rhetorical studies; telecommunications; theater arts/drama; theology; wind and percussion instruments.

Oklahoma Christian University

Accounting; advertising; American government; art; art education; biblical studies; biochemistry; biological and physical sciences; biology; broadcast journalism; business; business administration; business marketing and marketing management; chemistry; child care/development; community services; computer engineering; computer science; creative writing; divinity/ministry; early childhood education; electrical/electronics engineering; elementary education; engineering; engineering physics; English; English education; family/community studies; graphic design/commercial art/illustration; history; information sciences/systems; interior design; journalism; liberal arts and studies; mass communications; mathematics; mathematics education; mechanical engineering; medical technology; missionary studies; music; music (voice and choral/opera performance); music education; pastoral counseling; physical education; (pre)law; psychology; public relations; radio/television broadcasting; religious education; religious studies; science education; secondary education; social studies education; Spanish; special education; speech/rhetorical studies; teaching English as a second language; theater arts/drama; wind and percussion instruments.

Oklahoma City University

Accounting; advertising; American studies; art; art education; art history; arts management; biochemistry; biological and physical sciences; biology; broadcast journalism; business; business administration; business economics; business marketing and marketing management; chemistry; computer science; corrections; criminal justice/law enforcement administration; dance; early childhood education; education; elementary education; English; film/video production; finance; fine/studio arts; French; German; graphic design/commercial art/illustration; history; humanities; international business; journalism; law enforcement/police science; liberal arts and studies; management information systems/business data processing; mass communications; mathematics; music; music (piano and organ performance); music (voice and choral/opera performance); music business management and merchandising; music education; music theory and composition; nursing; philosophy; physical education; physics; political science; (pre)dentistry; (pre)law; (pre)medicine; (pre)veterinary studies; psychology; public relations; radio/television broadcasting; religious education; religious studies; sacred music; science education; secondary education; sociology; Spanish; speech/rhetorical studies; speech/theater education; stringed instruments; theater arts/drama; theater design; wind and percussion instruments.

Oklahoma State University
Accounting; advertising; aerospace engineering; agricultural business; agricultural economics; agricultural education; agricultural sciences; aircraft pilot (professional); American studies; animal sciences; architectural engineering; architecture; art; aviation management; aviation technology; biochemistry; bioengineering; biology; botany; broadcast journalism; business; business economics; business marketing and marketing management; cell biology; chemical engineering; chemistry; child care/development; civil engineering; clothing and textiles; communication disorders; communications, other; computer engineering; computer management; computer science; computer/information sciences; construction management; construction technology; economics; education; electrical/electronic engineering technology; electrical/electronics engineering; elementary education; engineering; engineering technology; English; entomology; environmental science; family/community studies; family/consumer studies; fashion merchandising; finance; fine/studio arts; fire protection/safety technology; forestry; French; geography; geology; German; graphic design/commercial art/illustration; health science; health/physical education; history; home economics; horticulture science; hotel and restaurant management; human resources management; industrial arts; industrial technology; industrial/manufacturing engineering; information sciences/systems; interior design; international business; journalism; landscape architecture; landscaping management; management information systems/business data processing; management science; mathematical statistics; mathematics; mechanical engineering; mechanical engineering technology; medical technology; microbiology/bacteriology; music; music business management and merchandising; music education; nutrition science; philosophy; physical education; physics; plant sciences; political science; (pre)dentistry; (pre)law; (pre)medicine; (pre)veterinary studies; psychology; Russian; secondary education; sociology; Spanish; speech/rhetorical studies; technical writing; theater arts/drama; trade and industrial education; wildlife management; zoology.

Oklahoma Wesleyan University
Accounting; athletic training/sports medicine; behavioral sciences; biological and physical sciences; biology; business administration; business education; chemistry; divinity/ministry;

education; elementary education; English; exercise sciences; history; information sciences/systems; liberal arts and studies; linguistics; mass communications; mathematics; music; music (general performance); natural sciences; nursing; physical education; physical therapy; political science; (pre)dentistry; (pre)law; (pre)medicine; (pre)veterinary studies; religious studies; science education; secondary education; secretarial science; social sciences; teaching English as a second language; theology.

Pacific Lutheran University
Accounting; anthropology; art; art education; art history; biochemistry; biology; broadcast journalism; business administration; business marketing and marketing management; chemistry; Chinese; classics; computer engineering; computer science; early childhood education; earth sciences; economics; education; electrical/electronics engineering; elementary education; engineering physics; engineering science; English; environmental science; finance; fine/studio arts; French; geology; German; history; international business; international relations; journalism; literature; management information systems/business data processing; mass communications; mathematics; modern languages; music; music (piano and organ performance); music (voice and choral/opera performance); music education; nursing; philosophy; physical education; physics; political science; psychology; radio/television broadcasting; reading education; recreational therapy; religious studies; sacred music; Scandinavian languages; science education; secondary education; social work; sociology; Spanish; special education; theater arts/drama; women's studies.

Pacific University
Accounting; art; art education; athletic training/sports medicine; biology; broadcast journalism; business administration; business marketing and marketing management; chemistry; Chinese; computer science; creative writing; early childhood education; economics; education; elementary education; English; environmental science; exercise sciences; finance; French; German; health science; history; humanities; international relations; Japanese; journalism; liberal arts and studies; literature; mass communications; mathematics; modern languages; music; music education; philosophy; physics; political science; (pre)dentistry; (pre)medicine; psychology; radio/television broadcasting; secondary education; social work; sociology; Spanish; telecommunications; theater arts/drama.

Parsons School of Design, New School University
Architectural environmental design; architecture; art; art education; drawing; fashion design/illustration; fashion merchandising; graphic design/commercial art/illustration; industrial design; interior design; photography; sculpture.

The Pennsylvania State University University Park Campus
Accounting; acting/directing; actuarial science; adult/continuing education administration; advertising; aerospace engineering; African-American (black) studies; agribusiness; agricultural business; agricultural business, other; agricultural engineering; agricultural mechanization; agricultural sciences; agronomy/crop science; American studies; animal sciences; anthropology; applied economics; applied mathematics; architectural engineering; architecture; art; art education; art history; astronomy;

astrophysics; atmospheric sciences; biochemistry; bioengineering; biological and physical sciences; biological technology; biology; business; business administration; business economics; business marketing and marketing management; chemical engineering; chemistry; civil engineering; classics; communications; comparative literature; computer engineering; computer/information sciences; criminal justice studies; criminal justice/law enforcement administration; cultural studies; earth sciences; East Asian studies; economics; electrical/electronics engineering; elementary education; engineering science; English; environmental engineering; film studies; finance; fishing sciences and management; food sciences; forest products technology; forestry sciences; French; geography; geology; German; graphic design/commercial art/illustration; health services administration; history; horticulture science; hospitality management; hotel and restaurant management; individual/family development; industrial/manufacturing engineering; information sciences/systems; insurance and risk management; interdisciplinary studies; international business; international relations; Italian; Japanese; journalism; Judaic studies; labor/personnel relations; landscape architecture; landscaping management; Latin American studies; liberal arts and studies; logistics and materials management; management information systems/business data processing; mathematical statistics; mathematics; mechanical engineering; medieval/renaissance studies; metallurgical engineering; microbiology/bacteriology; mining/mineral engineering; molecular biology; music; music (general performance); music education; natural resources conservation; nuclear engineering; nursing; nutrition studies; petroleum engineering; philosophy; physics; political science; (pre)medicine; psychology; real estate; recreation/leisure facilities management; religious studies; Russian; secondary education; sociology; soil sciences; Spanish; special education; speech-language pathology/audiology; speech/rhetorical studies; telecommunications; theater design; turf management; visual/performing arts; wildlife biology; women's studies.

Pepperdine University (Malibu, CA)
Accounting; advertising; art; athletic training/sports medicine; biology; business administration; chemistry; communications; computer science; economics; education; elementary education; English; French; German; history; humanities; interdisciplinary studies; international business; international relations; journalism; liberal arts and studies; mathematics; music; music education; natural sciences; nutrition science; philosophy; physical education; political science; (pre)dentistry; (pre)law; (pre)medicine; psychology; public relations; religious education; religious studies; secondary education; sociology; Spanish; speech/rhetorical studies; telecommunications; theater arts/drama.

Pitzer College
African-American (black) studies; American history; American studies; anthropology; art; art history; Asian studies; Asian-American studies; biology; chemistry; classics; dance; economics; engineering; engineering/industrial management; English; environmental studies; European history; European studies; film studies; fine/studio arts; French; German; history; interdisciplinary studies; international relations; Latin American studies; linguistics; literature; mathematics; Mexican-American studies; neuroscience; philosophy; physics; political science; (pre)medicine; psychology; religious studies; Romance languages; Russian; science/technology and society; sociology; Spanish; theater arts/drama; women's studies.

Point Loma Nazarene University
Accounting; art; athletic training/sports medicine; biochemistry; biology; British literature; business administration; business communications; business home economics; chemistry; child care/development; communications; computer science; dietetics; economics; engineering physics; family studies; graphic design/commercial art/illustration; health/physical education; history; home economics; journalism; liberal arts and studies; management information systems/business data processing; mass communications; mathematics; music; music business management and merchandising; nursing; organizational psychology; philosophy; philosophy and religion, other; physics; political science; psychology; religious studies; Romance languages; sacred music; social sciences; social work; sociology; Spanish; speech/rhetorical studies; theater arts/drama.

Polytechnic University, Brooklyn Campus
Chemical engineering; chemistry; civil engineering; computer engineering; computer science; electrical/electronics engineering; information sciences/systems; liberal arts and studies; mathematics; mechanical engineering; physics; (pre)law; (pre)medicine; technical writing.

Pomona College
African-American (black) studies; American studies; anthropology; art; art history; Asian studies; astronomy; biochemistry; biology; cell biology; chemistry; Chinese; classics; computer science; dance; East Asian studies; ecology; economics; English; environmental science; film studies; fine/studio arts; French; geochemistry; geology; German; Hispanic-American studies; history; humanities; interdisciplinary studies; international relations; Japanese; liberal arts and studies; linguistics; mathematics; Mexican-American studies; microbiology/bacteriology; modern languages; molecular biology; music; neuroscience; philosophy; physics; political science; (pre)medicine; psychology; public policy analysis; religious studies; Romance languages; Russian; sociology; Spanish; theater arts/drama; women's studies.

Presbyterian College
Accounting; art; biology; business administration; chemistry; computer science; early childhood education; economics; education; elementary education; English; French; German; history; mathematics; modern languages; music; music education; philosophy; physics; political science; (pre)dentistry; (pre)law; (pre)medicine; (pre)veterinary studies; psychology; religious studies; social sciences; sociology; Spanish; special education; theater arts/drama.

Princeton University
Anthropology; architecture; art history; astrophysics; chemical engineering; chemistry; civil engineering; classics; comparative literature; computer engineering; East Asian studies; East European languages, other; ecology; economics; electrical/electronics engineering; engineering/industrial management; English; geology; German; history; mathematics; mechanical engineering; Middle Eastern studies; molecular biology; multi/interdisciplinary studies, other; music; philosophy; physics; political science; psychology; public administration; religious studies; Romance languages; sociology.

Providence College

Accounting; American studies; art history; biology; business administration; business economics; business marketing and marketing management; chemistry; community services; computer science; economics; English; environmental science; finance; fine/studio arts; fire science; French; health services administration; history; humanities; instrumentation technology; Italian; labor/personnel relations; liberal arts and studies; mathematics; music; paralegal/legal assistant; pastoral counseling; philosophy; political science; psychology; secondary education; social sciences; social work; sociology; Spanish; special education; systems science and theory; theology; visual/performing arts.

Queen's University at Kingston

Art education; art history; astrophysics; biochemistry; biology; business administration; Canadian studies; chemical and atomic/molecular physics; chemical engineering; chemistry; civil engineering; classics; cognitive psychology and psycholinguistics; computer engineering; computer engineering, other; computer hardware engineering; computer science; computer science, other; computer software engineering; computer/information sciences; economics; education; electrical/electronics engineering; elementary education; engineering; engineering physics; engineering science; English; environmental science; film studies; fine/studio arts; French; geography; geological engineering; geology; German; Greek (Modern); health education; health science; health/physical education; Hispanic-American studies; history; interdisciplinary studies; Italian; Judaic studies; Latin (Ancient and Medieval); Latin American studies; linguistics; mathematical statistics; mathematics; mechanical engineering; medieval/renaissance studies; mining/mineral engineering; music; music education; nursing; occupational therapy; philosophy; physical education; physical therapy; physics; physiology; political science; psychology; rehabilitation therapy; religious studies; robotics; science education; secondary education; sociology; Spanish; stringed instruments; theater arts/drama; women's studies.

Quincy University

Accounting; art; art education; arts management; athletic training/sports medicine; aviation management; aviation/airway science; biology; business administration; business marketing and marketing management; chemistry; communications; computer science; criminal justice/law enforcement administration; elementary education; engineering-related technology; English; environmental science; finance; fine/studio arts; history; human services; humanities; information sciences/systems; interdisciplinary studies; journalism; K-12 education; mathematics; medical technology; music; music business management and merchandising; music education; nursing; philosophy; physical education; political science; (pre)dentistry; (pre)medicine; (pre)veterinary studies; psychology; public relations; radio/television broadcasting; social work; sociology; special education; sport/fitness administration; theology.

Quinnipiac University

Accounting; actuarial science; advertising; applied mathematics; athletic training/sports medicine; biochemistry; biological and physical sciences; biology; broadcast journalism; business administration; business economics; business marketing and marketing management; chemistry; child care/development; communications, other; computer science; criminal justice studies; developmental/child psychology; economics; education; English; entrepreneurship; film studies; film/video production; finance; gerontology; health products/services marketing; health services administration; history; human resources management; human services; information sciences/systems; international business; international relations; journalism; laboratory animal medicine; law and legal studies; liberal arts and studies; literature; mass communications; mathematics; medical laboratory technologies; microbiology/bacteriology; nursing; occupational therapy; paralegal/legal assistant; physical therapy; physician assistant; physiological psychology/psychobiology; political science; (pre)dentistry; (pre)law; (pre)medicine; (pre)veterinary studies; psychology; public relations; radiological science; respiratory therapy; social sciences; sociology; Spanish; veterinary technology; web page, digital/multimedia and information resources design; zoology.

Randolph-Macon Woman's College

American studies; art; art history; biology; chemistry; classics; creative writing; dance; economics; English; environmental science; fine/studio arts; French; German; Greek (Ancient and Medieval); health professions and related sciences, other; history; international relations; Latin (Ancient and Medieval); liberal arts and studies; mass communications; mathematics; museum studies; music; music (voice and choral/opera performance); music history; philosophy; physics; political science; psychology; religious studies; Russian/Slavic area studies; sociology; Spanish; theater arts/drama.

Reed College

American studies; anthropology; art; biochemistry; biology; chemistry; Chinese; classics; dance; economics; English; fine/studio arts; French; German; history; international relations; linguistics; literature; mathematics; music; philosophy; physics; political science; psychology; religious studies; Russian; sociology; Spanish; theater arts/drama.

Regis University

Accounting; biochemistry; biology; business administration; chemistry; communications; computer science; criminal justice/law enforcement administration; economics; education; elementary education; English; environmental science; French; history; human ecology; humanities; liberal arts and studies; mathematics; medical records administration; neuroscience; nursing; philosophy; political science; (pre)dentistry; (pre)law; (pre)medicine; (pre)veterinary studies; psychology; religious studies; sociology; Spanish; visual/performing arts.

Rensselaer Polytechnic Institute

Aerospace engineering; air science; applied mathematics; architecture; biochemistry; bioengineering; biological and physical sciences; biology; biophysics; business administration; chemical engineering; chemistry; civil engineering; computer engineering; computer science; computer/information sciences; economics; electrical/electronics engineering; engineering; engineering physics; engineering science; engineering/industrial management; environmental engineering; environmental science; geology; German; industrial/manufacturing engineering; information sciences/systems; interdisciplinary studies; management information systems/business data processing; mass communications; materials engineering; mathematics; mechanical engineering; military science; natural sciences; naval science; nuclear engineering; philosophy; physical sciences; physics; (pre)dentistry; (pre)law; (pre)medicine; psychology; science education; science/technology and society; speech/rhetorical studies; systems engineering; technical writing; transportation engineering; water resources.

Rhode Island School of Design

Architecture; art; ceramic arts; clothing and textiles; drawing; fashion design/illustration; film studies; graphic design/commercial art/illustration; industrial design; interior design; metal/jewelry arts; photography; printmaking; sculpture; textile arts; theater arts/drama.

Rhodes College (TN)

Anthropology; art; art history; biochemistry; biology; business administration; chemistry; classics; computer science; economics; English; fine/studio arts; French; German; Greek (Modern); history; interdisciplinary studies; international business; international economics; international relations; Latin (Ancient and Medieval); mathematics; music; philosophy; physics; political science; psychology; religious studies; Russian/Slavic area studies; sociology; Spanish; theater arts/drama; urban studies.

Rice University

Anthropology; applied mathematics; architecture; art; art history; Asian studies; astronomy; astrophysics; biochemistry; bioengineering; biology; business administration; chemical engineering; chemistry; civil engineering; classics; computer engineering; computer/information sciences; ecology; economics; electrical/electronics engineering; English; environmental engineering; evolutionary biology; fine/studio arts; French; geology; geophysics and seismology; German; Greek (Ancient and Medieval); history; Latin (Ancient and Medieval); Latin American studies; linguistics; materials engineering; materials science; mathematical statistics; mathematics; mechanical engineering; multi/interdisciplinary studies, other; music; music (general performance); music history; music theory and composition; neuroscience; philosophy; physical and theoretical chemistry; physical education; physics; political science; psychology; public policy analysis; religious studies; Russian; Russian/Slavic area studies; sociology; Spanish; visual and performing arts, other; women's studies.

Ripon College

Anthropology; art; biochemistry; biology; business administration; chemistry; computer science; early childhood education; economics; education; elementary education; English; environmental science; French; German; history; interdisciplinary studies; Latin American studies; mathematics; music; music education; philosophy; physical education; physics; physiological psychology/psychobiology; political science; (pre)dentistry; (pre)law; (pre)medicine; (pre)veterinary studies; psychology; religious studies; Romance languages; secondary education; sociology; Spanish; speech/rhetorical studies; theater arts/drama.

Rochester Institute of Technology

Accounting; advertising; aerospace engineering; applied art; applied mathematics; art; automotive engineering technology; biochemistry; biological and physical sciences; biological sciences/life sciences, other; biology; biotechnology research; business administration; business marketing and marketing management; ceramic arts; chemistry; civil engineering technol-ogy; commercial photography; communications; computer engineering; computer engineering technology; computer graphics; computer programming; computer science; computer/information sciences; computer/information sciences, other; craft/folk art; criminal justice studies; criminal justice/law enforcement administration; design/visual communications; diagnostic medical sonography; dietetics; economics; electrical/electronic engineering technology; electrical/electronics engineering; electromechanical technology; engineering; engineering science; engineering technology; engineering, other; engineering-related technology; environmental science; film/video production; finance; fine/studio arts; food products retailing; food sales operations; furniture design; general studies; genetics; graphic design/commercial art/illustration; graphic/printing equipment; hospitality management; hospitality/recreation marketing; hotel and restaurant management; industrial design; industrial technology; industrial/manufacturing engineering; information sciences/systems; interdisciplinary studies; interior design; international business; international finance; management information systems/business data processing; marketing operations; marketing research; mathematical statistics; mathematics; mathematics/computer science; mechanical engineering; mechanical engineering technology; medical illustrating; medical technology; metal/jewelry arts; natural resources management; nuclear medical technology; occupational safety/health technology; optometric/ophthalmic laboratory technician; photographic technology; photography; physician assistant; physics; political science/government, other; polymer chemistry; (pre)dentistry; (pre)law; (pre)medicine; (pre)veterinary studies; psychology; public policy analysis; publishing; sculpture; sign language interpretation; social work; telecommunications; tourism/travel marketing; travel-tourism management.

Rockhurst University

Accounting; biology; business; business administration; business communications; business marketing and marketing management; chemistry; communications; community services; computer programming; computer science; computer systems analysis; creative writing; economics; education; elementary education; English; finance; French; history; human resources management; information sciences/systems; international relations; labor/personnel relations; management science; mathematics; medical laboratory technologies; nursing; philosophy; physics; political science; psychology; public relations; secondary education; social sciences; sociology; Spanish; speech-language pathology; theater arts/drama; theology.

Rollins College

Anthropology; art; art history; biology; chemistry; classics; computer science; economics; education; elementary education; English; environmental science; fine/studio arts; French; German; history; interdisciplinary studies; international business; international relations; Latin American studies; mathematics; music; music history; philosophy; physics; political science; (pre)dentistry; (pre)law; (pre)medicine; (pre)veterinary studies; psychology; religious studies; sociology; Spanish; theater arts/drama.

Rose-Hulman Institute of Technology

Biology; chemical engineering; chemistry; civil engineering; computer engineering; computer science; economics; electrical/electronics engineering; mathematics; mechanical engineering; optics; physics.

Rutgers, The State University of New Jersey, New Brunswick

Accounting; African studies; American studies; anthropology; art; art history; atmospheric sciences; biology; biomedical science; biometrics; biotechnology research; business administration; business marketing and marketing management; cell biology; ceramic arts; chemistry; Chinese; classics; communications; comparative literature; computer science; criminal justice/law enforcement administration; dance; drawing; East Asian studies; Eastern European area studies; ecology; economics; English; environmental science; evolutionary biology; exercise sciences; film studies; finance; food sciences; foreign languages/literatures; French; genetics; geography; geology; German; graphic design/commercial art/illustration; Greek (Ancient and Medieval); Hispanic-American studies; history; human ecology; interdisciplinary studies; Italian; jazz; journalism; Judaic studies; labor/personnel relations; Latin (Ancient and Medieval); Latin American studies; linguistics; management science; marine biology; mass communications; mathematical statistics; mathematics; medical technology; medieval/renaissance studies; microbiology/bacteriology; Middle Eastern studies; molecular biology; music; music education; nutritional sciences; painting; pharmacy; philosophy; photography; physics; physiology; political science; Portuguese; (pre)dentistry; (pre)law; (pre)medicine; printmaking; psychology; public health; religious studies; Russian; Russian/Slavic area studies; sculpture; sociology; Spanish; theater arts/drama; urban studies; women's studies.

Saint Francis University

Accounting; American studies; anthropology; biology; business administration; business marketing and marketing management; chemistry; computer programming; computer science; criminal justice/law enforcement administration; culinary arts; data processing technology; drafting; economics; education; elementary education; emergency medical technology; English; environmental science; finance; French; history; human resources management; international business; international relations; journalism; labor/personnel relations; literature; management information systems/business data processing; marine biology; mass communications; mathematics; medical technology; modern languages; nursing; occupational therapy; pastoral counseling; philosophy; physical therapy; physician assistant; political science; (pre)dentistry; (pre)law; (pre)medicine; (pre)veterinary studies; psychology; public administration; public relations; real estate; religious studies; science education; secondary education; social work; sociology; Spanish.

St. John's College (MD)

Interdisciplinary studies; liberal arts and studies; western civilization.

St. John's College (NM)

Classics; history of philosophy; liberal arts and studies; literature; western civilization.

Saint John's University (MN)

Accounting; art; art education; art history; biochemistry; biology; business administration; chemistry; classics; computer science; dietetics; economics; education; elementary education; English; fine/studio arts; forestry; French; German; history; humanities; mathematics; mathematics/computer science; music; music education; natural sciences; nursing; nutrition science; occupational therapy; peace and conflict studies; philosophy; physical therapy; physics; political science; (pre)dentistry; (pre)law; (pre)medicine; (pre)pharmacy studies; (pre)theology; (pre)veterinary studies; psychology; religious education; secondary education; social sciences; social work; sociology; Spanish; speech/rhetorical studies; theater arts/drama; theology.

Saint Joseph's University

Accounting; art; biology; business administration; business marketing and marketing management; chemistry; computer programming; computer science; criminal justice/law enforcement administration; economics; education; elementary education; English; environmental science; finance; food sales operations; French; German; health services administration; history; human services; humanities; interdisciplinary studies; international relations; labor/personnel relations; liberal arts and studies; management information systems/business data processing; mathematics; philosophy; physics; political science; psychology; public administration; purchasing/contracts management; secondary education; social sciences; sociology; Spanish; theology.

St. Lawrence University

African studies; anthropology; art; art history; Asian studies; biochemistry; biology; biophysics; Canadian studies; chemistry; computer science; creative writing; ecology; economics; English; environmental science; foreign languages/literatures; French; geology; geophysics and seismology; German; history; mathematics; modern languages; music; neuroscience; philosophy; physics; political science; psychology; religious studies; sociology; Spanish; theater arts/drama.

St. Louis College of Pharmacy

Pharmacy.

Saint Louis University

Accounting; aerospace engineering; aerospace engineering technology; aircraft pilot (professional); American studies; applied mathematics; art history; atmospheric sciences; aviation management; bioengineering; biology; business administration; business economics; business marketing and marketing management; chemistry; classics; communications; communications, other; computer software engineering; computer/information sciences; computer/information sciences, other; corrections; criminal justice studies; dietetics; economics; education (multiple levels); electrical/electronics engineering; engineering/industrial management; English; environmental science; exercise sciences; finance; fine/studio arts; French; geology; geophysics and seismology; German; Greek (Ancient and Medieval); health services administration; health/medical laboratory technologies, other; history; human resources management; humanities; international business; international relations; management information systems/business data processing; management science; mathematics; mechanical engineering; music; nuclear medical technology; nursing; occupational therapy; philosophy; physician assistant; physics; political science; psychology; public relations; Russian; social sciences; social work; sociology; Spanish; theater arts/drama; theology; urban studies.

Saint Mary's College of California

Accounting; anthropology; art; art education; art history; biology; business administration; chemistry; dance; economics; education; engineering; English; French; German; Greek (Modern); health education; history; interdisciplinary studies; international business; international relations; Latin (Ancient and Medieval); liberal arts and studies; literature; mass communications; mathematics; modern languages; music; nursing; philosophy; physical education; physics; political science; (pre)dentistry; (pre)law; (pre)medicine; (pre)veterinary studies; psychology; religious studies; secondary education; sociology; Spanish; theater arts/drama; theology; women's studies.

St. Mary's College of Maryland

Anthropology; art; biology; chemistry; computer science; economics; educational psychology; English; history; interdisciplinary studies; mathematics; modern languages; music; natural sciences; philosophy; physics; political science; psychology; public policy analysis; religious studies; sociology; theater arts/drama.

St. Norbert College

Accounting; art; biological and physical sciences; biology; business computer programming; chemistry; communications; economics; elementary education; English; French; geology; German; graphic design/commercial art/illustration; history; humanities; interdisciplinary studies; international business; international relations; K-12 education; management information systems/business data processing; mathematics; mathematics/computer science; medical technology; music; music education; philosophy; physics; political science; (pre)dentistry; (pre)engineering; (pre)law; (pre)medicine; (pre)veterinary studies; psychology; religious studies; sociology; Spanish.

St. Olaf College

American studies; art; art history; Asian studies; biology; chemistry; classics; cultural studies; dance; economics; English; ethnic/cultural studies, other; French; German; Greek (Ancient and Medieval); Hispanic-American studies; history; individual/family development; Latin (Ancient and Medieval); liberal arts and studies; mathematics; multi/interdisciplinary studies, other; music; music (general performance); music education; music, other; musicology; nursing; philosophy; physics; political science; psychology; religious studies; Russian; Russian/Slavic area studies; Scandinavian languages; social studies education; social work; sociology; Spanish; theater arts/drama; visual/performing arts; women's studies.

Salem College

Accounting; American studies; art history; arts management; biology; business administration; chemistry; economics; education; English; fine/studio arts; French; German; history; interdisciplinary studies; interior design; international business; international relations; mass communications; mathematics; medical technology; music; music (general performance); philosophy; physician assistant; psychology; religious studies; sociology; Spanish.

Samford University

Accounting; art; Asian studies; athletic training/sports medicine; biblical studies; biochemistry; biology; business administration; cartography; chemistry; classics; community services; computer science; counseling psychology; criminal justice/law enforcement administration; dietetics; early childhood education; elementary education; engineering physics; English; environmental science; exercise sciences; foreign languages/literatures; French; general studies; geography; German; graphic design/commercial art/illustration; Greek (Ancient and Medieval); health/physical education; history; human resources management; humanities; individual/family development; interior design; international business; international relations; journalism; Latin (Ancient and Medieval); Latin American studies; marine biology; mathematics; music (general performance); music (piano and organ performance); music (voice and choral/opera performance); music education; music theory and composition; nursing; philosophy; physical education; physics; political science; psychology; public administration; religious studies; sacred music; science education; science/technology and society; social science education; social sciences; sociology; Spanish; speech education; speech/rhetorical studies; theater arts/drama; visual/performing arts.

San Francisco Conservatory of Music

Music; music (general performance); music (piano and organ performance); music (voice and choral/opera performance); music theory and composition; stringed instruments; wind and percussion instruments.

Santa Clara University

Accounting; anthropology; art; art history; biological and physical sciences; biology; business administration; business economics; business marketing and marketing management; chemistry; civil engineering; classics; communications; computer engineering; computer science; economics; electrical/electronics engineering; engineering; engineering physics; English; finance; French; Greek (Ancient and Medieval); history; interdisciplinary studies; Italian; Latin (Ancient and Medieval); liberal arts and studies; management information systems/business data processing; mathematics; mechanical engineering; music; philosophy; physics; political science; psychology; religious studies; sociology; Spanish; theater arts/drama.

Sarah Lawrence College

African-American (black) studies; American studies; anthropology; art; art history; Asian studies; biological and physical sciences; biology; chemistry; classics; comparative literature; computer science; creative writing; dance; developmental/child psychology; drawing; early childhood education; Eastern European area studies; ecology; economics; education; English; environmental science; European studies; film studies; film/video production; fine/studio arts; French; genetics; geology; German; history; humanities; individual/family development; interdisciplinary studies; international relations; Italian; Latin (Ancient and Medieval); Latin American studies; liberal arts and studies; literature; marine biology; mathematics; modern languages; music; music (piano and organ performance); music (voice and choral/opera performance); music history; natural sciences; philosophy; photography; physics; political science; (pre)dentistry; (pre)law; (pre)medicine; psychology; public policy analysis; religious studies; Romance languages; Russian; sculpture; social sciences; sociology; Spanish; stringed instruments; theater arts/drama; urban studies; western civilization; wind and percussion instruments; women's studies.

Scripps College

African-American (black) studies; American studies; anthropology; art; art history; Asian studies; Asian-American studies; biochemistry; biology; chemistry; Chinese; classics; computer science; dance; East Asian studies; economics; English; environmental science; European studies; film/video and photographic arts, other; fine/studio arts; foreign languages/literatures; French; geology; German; Hispanic-American studies; history; international relations; Italian; Japanese; Judaic studies; Latin (Ancient and Medieval); Latin American studies; law and legal studies; linguistics; mathematics; Mexican-American studies; modern languages; molecular biology; music; neuroscience; philosophy; physics; physiological psychology/psychobiology; political science; psychology; religious studies; Russian; science/technology and society; sociology; Spanish; theater arts/drama; visual and performing arts, other; women's studies.

Seattle Pacific University

Accounting; art; art education; biochemistry; biology; biology education; business administration; business computer facilities operator; business economics; business systems analysis and design; chemistry; classics; clothing/apparel/textile studies; communications; computer science; economics; electrical/electronics engineering; engineering science; English; English education; European studies; exercise sciences; family/consumer studies; French; general studies; German; history; home economics education; Latin (Ancient and Medieval); Latin American studies; mathematics; mathematics education; mathematics, other; music; music education; nursing; nutrition science; organizational behavior; philosophy; physical education; physics; political science; (pre)dentistry; (pre)law; (pre)medicine; psychology; religious education; religious studies; Russian; science education; social science education; sociology; Spanish; special education; theater arts/drama; theology.

Seattle University

Accounting; applied mathematics; art; art history; biochemistry; biological and physical sciences; biology; business administration; business economics; business marketing and marketing management; chemistry; civil engineering; computer science; creative writing; criminal justice/law enforcement administration; diagnostic medical sonography; East Asian studies; economics; electrical/electronics engineering; English; environmental engineering; environmental science; finance; fine/studio arts; French; German; history; humanities; industrial/manufacturing engineering; insurance and risk management; international business; international economics; international relations; journalism; liberal arts and studies; management information systems/business data processing; mass communications; mathematics; mechanical engineering; medical technology; nursing; operations management; philosophy; photography; physics; political science; psychology; public administration; public relations; religious studies; social work; sociology; Spanish; theater arts/drama; Western European studies.

Siena College

Accounting; American studies; biology; business economics; business marketing and marketing management; chemistry; classics; computer science; economics; English; environmental science; finance; French; history; mathematics; philosophy; physics;

political science; (pre)dentistry; (pre)law; (pre)medicine; psychology; religious studies; secondary education; social work; sociology; Spanish.

Simon's Rock College of Bard

Acting/directing; African-American (black) studies; agricultural business; American studies; anthropology; applied mathematics; art history; Asian studies; biology; ceramic arts; chemistry; cognitive psychology and psycholinguistics; computer graphics; computer science; creative writing; cultural studies; dance; developmental/child psychology; drawing; ecology; environmental science; European studies; fine/studio arts; foreign languages/literatures; French; geography; geology; German; interdisciplinary studies; jazz; Latin American studies; liberal arts and studies; literature; mathematics; metal/jewelry arts; music; music theory and composition; natural sciences; painting; philosophy; photography; physics; play/screenwriting; political science; (pre)law; (pre)medicine; printmaking; psychology; religious studies; sculpture; Spanish; theater arts/drama; visual/performing arts; women's studies.

Simpson College

Accounting; advertising; art; art education; athletic training/sports medicine; biochemistry; biological and physical sciences; biology; business administration; business communications; chemistry; computer management; computer science; criminal justice/law enforcement administration; early childhood education; economics; education; elementary education; English; environmental biology; French; German; graphic design/commercial art/illustration; history; information sciences/systems; international business; international relations; mass communications; mathematics; medical technology; music; music (general performance); music education; philosophy; physical education; physical therapy; political science; (pre)dentistry; (pre)law; (pre)medicine; (pre)veterinary studies; psychology; religious studies; secondary education; social sciences; sociology; Spanish; speech/rhetorical studies; sport/fitness administration; theater arts/drama.

Skidmore College

American studies; anthropology; area, ethnic and cultural studies, other; art history; Asian studies; biochemistry; biological sciences/life sciences, other; biology; business; business management/administrative services, other; chemistry; classics; computer/information sciences; dance; economics; elementary education; English, other; exercise sciences; fine arts and art studies, other; French; geology; German; history; liberal arts and studies; literature; mathematics; music history; philosophy; physics; political science; psychology; psychology, other; religious studies; social sciences and history, other; social work; sociology; Spanish; theater arts/drama; women's studies.

Smith College

African-American (black) studies; American studies; anthropology; architecture; art; art history; astronomy; biochemistry; biology; chemistry; classics; comparative literature; computer science; dance; East Asian studies; economics; education; English; fine/studio arts; French; geology; German; Greek (Ancient and Medieval); history; interdisciplinary studies; Italian; Latin (Ancient and Medieval); Latin American studies; mathematics; medieval/renaissance studies; Middle Eastern studies; music; neuroscience; philosophy; physics; political science; Portuguese; psychology; religious studies; Russian; Russian/Slavic area studies; sociology; Spanish; theater arts/drama; women's studies.

Southern Methodist University
Accounting; advertising; African-American (black) studies; anthropology; applied economics; art history; biochemistry; biology; broadcast journalism; business administration; business marketing and marketing management; chemistry; computer engineering; computer science; creative writing; dance; economics; electrical/electronics engineering; English; environmental engineering; environmental science; European studies; film studies; finance; fine/studio arts; foreign languages/literatures; French; geology; geophysics and seismology; German; history; humanities; international relations; journalism; Latin American studies; management information systems/business data processing; management science; mathematical statistics; mathematics; mechanical engineering; medieval/renaissance studies; Mexican-American studies; music; music (general performance); music (piano and organ performance); music education; music theory and composition; music therapy; organizational behavior; philosophy; physics; political science; psychology; public policy analysis; public relations; quantitative economics; radio/television broadcasting; real estate; religious studies; Russian; Russian/Slavic area studies; social sciences; sociology; Spanish; theater arts/drama.

Southwestern University
Accounting; American studies; animal sciences; art; art education; art history; biology; business administration; chemistry; computer science; economics; English; experimental psychology; fine/studio arts; French; German; history; international relations; literature; mass communications; mathematics; modern languages; music; music (piano and organ performance); music education; music history; philosophy; physical education; physics; political science; psychology; religious studies; sacred music; social sciences; sociology; Spanish; theater arts/drama; women's studies.

Southwest Missouri State University
Accounting; agribusiness; agricultural education; agricultural sciences; agronomy/crop science; animal sciences; anthropology; art; art education; athletic training/sports medicine; biology; biology education; business; business administration; business education; business marketing and marketing management; cartography; cell biology; chemistry; chemistry education; city/community/regional planning; clothing/apparel/textile studies; communications; computer science; construction technology; criminal justice studies; dance; design/visual communications; dietetics; drafting; early childhood education; economics; electrical/electronic engineering technology; elementary education; engineering physics; English; English education; finance; foreign languages education; French; French language education; geography; geology; German; German language education; gerontology; history; history education; home economics education; horticulture science; hotel and restaurant management; housing studies; humanities; individual/family development; industrial arts education; insurance and risk management; journalism; Latin (Ancient and Medieval); management information systems/business data processing; mass communications; mathematics; mathematics education; mechanical engineering technology; medical radiologic technology; medical

technology; middle school education; molecular biology; music; music (general performance); music education; nursing; philosophy; physical education; physics; physics education; political science; psychology; public administration; recreation and leisure studies; religious studies; respiratory therapy; science education; social work; sociology; Spanish; Spanish language education; special education; speech education; speech-language pathology/audiology; technical writing; theater arts/drama; visual/performing arts; wildlife management.

Stanford University
African studies; American studies; anthropology; archaeology; art; Asian studies; biology; chemical engineering; chemistry; Chinese; civil engineering; classics; communications; comparative literature; computer science; earth sciences; East Asian studies; economics; electrical/electronics engineering; engineering; English; environmental engineering; environmental science; French; geology; geophysics and seismology; German; history; industrial/manufacturing engineering; interdisciplinary studies; international relations; Italian; Japanese; linguistics; materials engineering; materials science; mathematics; mathematics/computer science; mechanical engineering; Mexican-American studies; music; Native American studies; petroleum engineering; philosophy; physics; political science; psychology; public policy analysis; religious studies; science/technology and society; Slavic languages; sociology; Spanish; systems science and theory; theater arts/drama; urban studies; women's studies.

State University of New York at Binghamton
Accounting; African studies; African-American (black) studies; anthropology; Arabic; art; art history; biochemistry; biology; chemistry; classics; comparative literature; computer engineering; computer science; drawing; economics; electrical/electronics engineering; English; environmental science; film studies; fine/studio arts; French; geography; geology; German; Hebrew; history; industrial/manufacturing engineering; information sciences/systems; interdisciplinary studies; Italian; Judaic studies; Latin American studies; linguistics; literature; management science; mathematics; mathematics/computer science; mechanical engineering; medieval/renaissance studies; music; music (general performance); nursing; philosophy; physics; physiological psychology/psychobiology; political science; (pre)law; psychology; sociology; Spanish; theater arts/drama.

State University of New York College at Geneseo
Accounting; African-American (black) studies; American studies; anthropology; art; art history; biochemistry; biology; biophysics; business administration; chemistry; communications; comparative literature; computer science; early childhood education; economics; education; elementary education; English; fine/studio arts; French; geochemistry; geography; geology; geophysics and seismology; history; international relations; mathematics; music; natural sciences; philosophy; physics; political science; (pre)dentistry; (pre)law; (pre)medicine; (pre)veterinary studies; psychology; sociology; Spanish; special education; speech therapy; speech-language pathology/audiology; theater arts/drama; visual and performing arts; other.

State University of New York College of Environmental Science and Forestry
Architectural environmental design; biochemistry; biological and physical sciences; biology; biology education; biotechnology

research; botany; chemical engineering; chemistry; chemistry education; city/community/regional planning; construction engineering; ecology; entomology; environmental biology; environmental education; environmental engineering; environmental science; fish/game management; fishing sciences and management; forest engineering; forest management; forestry; land use management; landscape architecture; natural resources conservation; natural resources management; plant pathology; plant physiology; plant protection; plant sciences; polymer chemistry; (pre)dentistry; (pre)law; (pre)medicine; (pre)veterinary studies; recreation and leisure studies; science education; water resources; water resources engineering; wildlife biology; wildlife management; wood science/paper technology; zoology.

Stevens Institute of Technology

Biochemistry; bioengineering; chemical engineering; chemistry; civil engineering; computer engineering; computer science; electrical/electronics engineering; engineering/industrial management; English; environmental engineering; history; humanities; mathematical statistics; mechanical engineering; philosophy; physics; (pre)dentistry; (pre)law; (pre)medicine.

Susquehanna University

Accounting; art; art history; biochemistry; biology; business administration; business economics; business marketing and marketing management; chemistry; communications; computer science; creative writing; early childhood education; economics; elementary education; English; finance; French; geology; German; history; human resources management; information sciences/systems; international relations; journalism; mass communications; mathematics; music; music (piano and organ performance); music (voice and choral/opera performance); music education; philosophy; physics; political science; (pre)dentistry; (pre)law; (pre)medicine; (pre)veterinary studies; psychology; public relations; radio/television broadcasting; religious studies; sacred music; secondary education; sociology; Spanish; speech/rhetorical studies; stringed instruments; theater arts/drama; wind and percussion instruments.

Swarthmore College

Anthropology; area studies, other; art history; Asian studies; astronomy; astrophysics; biochemistry; biological sciences/life sciences, other; biology; chemical and atomic/molecular physics; chemistry; Chinese; classics; comparative literature; computer/information sciences; dance; economics; education, other; engineering; English; fine/studio arts; French; German; Greek (Ancient and Medieval); history; Latin (Ancient and Medieval); linguistics; mathematics; medieval/renaissance studies; music; philosophy; physics; physiological psychology/psychobiology; political science; psychology; religious studies; Russian; sociology; Spanish; theater arts/drama; visual and performing arts, other.

Sweet Briar College

Anthropology; art history; biochemistry; biology; business administration/management, other; chemistry; classics; computer science; creative writing; dance; economics; English; environmental science; European studies; fine/studio arts; French; general studies; German; Greek (Ancient and Medieval); history; interdisciplinary studies; international relations; Italian; Italian studies; Latin (Ancient and Medieval); mathematics;

mathematics, other; modern languages; music; philosophy; physics; political science; psychology; religious studies; sociology; Spanish; theater arts/drama.

Syracuse University

Accounting; advertising; aerospace engineering; African-American (black) studies; American studies; anthropology; applied art; architecture; art; art education; art history; behavioral sciences; biochemistry; bioengineering; biology; broadcast journalism; business administration; business marketing and marketing management; ceramic arts; chemical engineering; chemistry; child care/development; civil engineering; classics; clothing and textiles; communication disorders; computer engineering; computer graphics; computer science; computer/information sciences; consumer services; design/visual communications; dietetics; early childhood education; economics; education; electrical/electronics engineering; elementary education; engineering physics; English; English education; enterprise management; entrepreneurship; environmental engineering; environmental science; exercise sciences; family studies; family/community studies; fashion design/illustration; film studies; film/video production; finance; fine/studio arts; food products retailing; foreign languages/literatures; French; geography; geology; German; graphic design/commercial art/illustration; Greek (Modern); health education; health science; history; hospitality management; individual/family development; industrial design; information sciences/systems; interdisciplinary studies; interior design; interior environments; international relations; Italian; journalism; K-12 education; Latin (Ancient and Medieval); Latin American studies; linguistics; literature; mathematics; mathematics education; mechanical engineering; medieval/renaissance studies; metal/jewelry arts; middle school education; modern languages; music; music (general performance); music (piano and organ performance); music (voice and choral/opera performance); music business management and merchandising; music education; music theory and composition; natural sciences; nursing; nutrition science; nutrition studies; painting; philosophy; photography; physical education; physics; political science; (pre)dentistry; (pre)law; (pre)medicine; (pre)veterinary studies; printmaking; psychology; public policy analysis; public relations; radio/television broadcasting; religious studies; retail management; Russian; Russian/Slavic area studies; science education; sculpture; secondary education; social sciences; social studies education; social work; sociology; Spanish; special education; speech-language pathology/audiology; speech/rhetorical studies; stringed instruments; telecommunications; textile arts; theater arts/drama; theater design; wind and percussion instruments; women's studies.

Taylor University

Accounting; art; art education; athletic training/sports medicine; biblical languages/literatures; biblical studies; biology; business administration; business marketing and marketing management; chemistry; computer engineering; computer programming; computer science; creative writing; early childhood education; economics; education; elementary education; engineering physics; English; environmental biology; environmental science; finance; French; graphic design/commercial art/illustration; history; human resources management; information sciences/systems; international business; international economics; international relations; literature; management information systems/business data processing; mass communications;

mathematics; medical technology; middle school education; music; music (piano and organ performance); music (voice and choral/opera performance); music business management and merchandising; music education; natural sciences; philosophy; physical education; physics; political science; (pre)dentistry; (pre)law; (pre)medicine; (pre)veterinary studies; psychology; recreation and leisure studies; religious education; religious studies; sacred music; science education; secondary education; social sciences; social work; sociology; Spanish; sport/fitness administration; theater arts/drama; theology.

Texas A&M University
Accounting; aerospace engineering; agribusiness; agricultural animal breeding; agricultural animal husbandry and production management; agricultural business; agricultural economics; agricultural engineering; agricultural mechanization; agricultural sciences; agronomy/crop science; American studies; animal sciences; anthropology; applied mathematics; aquaculture operations and production management; architectural environmental design; atmospheric sciences; biochemistry; bioengineering; biological and physical sciences; biology; botany; business administration; business marketing and marketing management; cell biology; chemical engineering; chemistry; civil engineering; community health liaison; computer engineering; computer/information sciences; construction technology; curriculum and instruction; dairy science; earth sciences; economics; electrical/electronics engineering; engineering-related technology; English; entomology; environmental science; finance; food sciences; foreign languages/literatures; forestry; French; genetics; geography; geology; geophysics and seismology; German; health education; health/physical education; history; horticulture services; industrial/manufacturing engineering; interdisciplinary studies; journalism; landscape architecture; logistics and materials management; mathematics; mechanical engineering; microbiology/bacteriology; molecular biology; music; natural resources conservation; nuclear engineering; nutrition studies; ocean engineering; operations research; ornamental horticulture; petroleum engineering; philosophy; physics; plant sciences; political science; poultry science; psychology; range management; recreation/leisure facilities management; Russian; sales operations; sociology; Spanish; speech/rhetorical studies; theater arts/drama; zoology.

Texas Christian University
Accounting; advertising; aerospace engineering; art; art education; art history; Asian studies; astronomy; astrophysics; bilingual/bicultural education; biochemistry; biology; broadcast journalism; business administration; business marketing and marketing management; chemistry; classics; computer science; criminal justice studies; dance; dietetics; economics; education of the hearing impaired; elementary education; engineering; English; English education; enterprise management; entrepreneurship; environmental science; fashion design/illustration; fashion merchandising; finance; fine/studio arts; French; general studies; geology; graphic design/commercial art/illustration; health science; history; interior design; international business; international relations; journalism; Latin American studies; liberal arts and studies; marketing research; mass communications; mathematics; mathematics education; middle school education; military studies; music; music (general performance); music (piano and organ performance); music (voice and choral/opera performance); music education; music

history; music theory and composition; musicology; neuroscience; nursing; nutrition studies; philosophy; photography; physical education; physics; political science; printmaking; psychology; radio/television broadcasting; real estate; religious studies; science education; sculpture; secondary education; social studies education; social work; sociology; Spanish; special education; speech-language pathology/audiology; speech/rhetorical studies; teaching English as a second language; technical education; theater arts/drama; women's studies.

Texas Tech University
Accounting; acting/directing; advertising; agricultural animal husbandry and production management; agricultural business; agricultural economics; agricultural production; agricultural sciences; agronomy/crop science; animal sciences; anthropology; architectural engineering technology; architecture; art; art history; biochemistry; biological and physical sciences; biology; business administration; business administration/management, other; business marketing and marketing management; cell biology; chemical engineering; chemistry; child care/development; civil engineering; classics; clothing/apparel/textile studies; community health liaison; computer engineering; computer/information sciences; dance; dietetics; earth sciences; economics; electrical/electronic engineering technology; electrical/electronics engineering; engineering; engineering physics; engineering technology; engineering-related technology; English; environmental engineering; exercise sciences; family studies; fashion design/illustration; fashion merchandising; finance; fine/studio arts; fishing sciences and management; food sciences; French; general studies; geography; geology; geophysics and seismology; German; graphic design/commercial art/illustration; health/physical education; hearing sciences; history; home economics; horticulture science; horticulture services; hotel and restaurant management; individual/family development; industrial/manufacturing engineering; interdisciplinary studies; interior architecture; international business; journalism; landscape architecture; Latin American studies; liberal arts and studies; management information systems/business data processing; mathematics; mechanical engineering; mechanical engineering technology; microbiology/bacteriology; molecular biology; music; music (general performance); music theory and composition; natural resources conservation; nutrition studies; petroleum engineering; philosophy; physics; plant protection; political science; psychology; public relations; radio/television broadcasting; radio/television broadcasting technology; range management; recreation and leisure studies; Russian/Slavic area studies; social work; sociology; Spanish; speech/rhetorical studies; textile sciences/engineering; theater arts/drama; theater design; wildlife management; zoology.

Thomas Aquinas College
Interdisciplinary studies; liberal arts and studies; western civilization.

Transylvania University
Accounting; anthropology; art; art education; biology; business administration; chemistry; computer science; economics; elementary education; English; exercise sciences; fine/studio arts; French; history; K-12 education; mathematics; middle school education; music (general performance); music education; philosophy; physical education; physics; political science; psychology; religious studies; sociology; Spanish; theater arts/drama.

Trinity College (CT)

American studies; anthropology; art; art history; biochemistry; bioengineering; biology; chemistry; classics; comparative literature; computer science; creative writing; dance; economics; education; engineering; English; fine/studio arts; French; German; history; interdisciplinary studies; international relations; Italian; Judaic studies; mathematics; mechanical engineering; modern languages; music; neuroscience; philosophy; physics; political science; psychology; public policy analysis; religious studies; Russian; sociology; Spanish; theater arts/drama; women's studies.

Trinity University

Accounting; acting/directing; anthropology; art; art history; Asian studies; biochemistry; biology; business administration; business marketing and marketing management; chemistry; Chinese; classics; communications; computer/information sciences; economics; engineering science; English; European studies; finance; French; geology; German; history; humanities; international business; Latin American studies; management science; mathematics; music; music (general performance); music (voice and choral/opera performance); music theory and composition; philosophy; physics; political science; (pre)dentistry; (pre)law; (pre)medicine; (pre)veterinary studies; psychology; religious studies; Russian; sociology; Spanish; speech/rhetorical studies; theater arts/drama; theater design; urban studies.

Truman State University

Accounting; agricultural economics; agricultural sciences; agronomy/crop science; animal sciences; applied art; art; art history; biology; business administration; chemistry; classics; communication disorders; computer science; criminal justice/law enforcement administration; economics; English; equestrian studies; exercise sciences; finance; fine/studio arts; French; German; graphic design/commercial art/illustration; health science; history; journalism; law enforcement/police science; mass communications; mathematics; music; music (piano and organ performance); music (voice and choral/opera performance); nursing; philosophy; physics; political science; (pre)dentistry; (pre)law; (pre)medicine; (pre)veterinary studies; psychology; public health; religious studies; Russian; sociology; Spanish; speech/rhetorical studies; theater arts/drama.

Tufts University

African-American (black) studies; American studies; anthropology; archaeology; architectural engineering; art history; Asian studies; astronomy; behavioral sciences; biology; chemical engineering; chemistry; child care/development; Chinese; civil engineering; classics; computer engineering; computer science; developmental/child psychology; early childhood education; ecology; economics; electrical/electronics engineering; elementary education; engineering; engineering design; engineering physics; engineering science; English; environmental engineering; environmental science; experimental psychology; French; geology; geophysical engineering; German; Greek (Modern); history; industrial/manufacturing engineering; international relations; Judaic studies; Latin (Ancient and Medieval); mathematics; mechanical engineering; mental health/rehabilitation; music; philosophy; physics; political science; psychology; public health; Romance languages; Russian; Russian/Slavic area studies; secondary education; sociobiology; sociology; Southeast Asian studies; Spanish; special education; theater arts/drama; urban studies; women's studies.

Tulane University

Accounting; African studies; American studies; anthropology; architecture; art; art history; Asian studies; biochemistry; bioengineering; biology; business administration; business marketing and marketing management; cell biology; chemical engineering; chemistry; civil engineering; classics; cognitive psychology and psycholinguistics; computer engineering; computer science; computer/information sciences; earth sciences; ecology; economics; electrical/electronics engineering; engineering science; English; environmental biology; environmental engineering; environmental science; evolutionary biology; exercise sciences; finance; fine/studio arts; French; geology; German; Greek (Modern); Hispanic-American studies; history; information sciences/systems; international relations; Italian; Judaic studies; Latin (Ancient and Medieval); Latin American studies; liberal arts and studies; linguistics; mass communications; mathematics; mechanical engineering; medical illustrating; medieval/renaissance studies; molecular biology; music; paralegal/legal assistant; philosophy; physics; political science; Portuguese; psychology; religious studies; Russian; Russian/Slavic area studies; sociology; Spanish; sport/fitness administration; theater arts/drama; women's studies.

Union College (NY)

American studies; anthropology; biochemistry; biological and physical sciences; biology; chemistry; classics; computer/information sciences; economics; electrical/electronics engineering; English; fine/studio arts; foreign languages/literatures; geology; history; humanities; liberal arts and studies; mathematics; mechanical engineering; philosophy; physics; political science; psychology; social sciences; sociology.

Union University

Accounting; advertising; art; art education; athletic training/sports medicine; biblical languages/literatures; biblical studies; biological and physical sciences; biology; broadcast journalism; business administration; business economics; business education; business marketing and marketing management; chemistry; computer science; early childhood education; economics; education; elementary education; English; exercise sciences; family/community studies; finance; foreign languages/literatures; French; history; information sciences/systems; journalism; mass communications; mathematics; medical technology; music; music (general performance); music (piano and organ performance); music (voice and choral/opera performance); music business management and merchandising; music education; nursing; philosophy; philosophy and religion, other; physical education; physics; political science; (pre)dentistry; (pre)law; (pre)medicine; (pre)pharmacy studies; psychology; public relations; radio/television broadcasting; recreation/leisure facilities management; religious studies; sacred music; science education; secondary education; social work; sociology; Spanish; special education; speech/rhetorical studies; sport/fitness administration; teaching English as a second language; theater arts/drama; theological studies/religious vocations, other; theology.

United States Air Force Academy

Aerospace engineering; area studies; atmospheric sciences; behavioral sciences; biochemistry; biological and physical sciences; biology; business administration; chemistry; civil engineering; computer science; economics; electrical/electronics engineering; engineering; engineering mechanics; engineering science; English; environmental engineering; geography; history; humanities; interdisciplinary studies; law and legal studies; materials science; mathematics; mechanical engineering; military studies; operations research; physics; political science; social sciences.

United States Coast Guard Academy
Civil engineering; electrical/electronics engineering; management science; marine science; mechanical engineering; naval architecture/marine engineering; operations research; political science.

United States Merchant Marine Academy
Engineering/industrial management; maritime science; naval architecture/marine engineering.

United States Military Academy
Aerospace engineering; American studies; applied mathematics; Arabic; behavioral sciences; biological and physical sciences; biology; business administration; chemical engineering; chemistry; Chinese; civil engineering; computer engineering; computer science; East Asian studies; Eastern European area studies; economics; electrical/electronics engineering; engineering; engineering physics; engineering/industrial management; environmental engineering; environmental science; European studies; French; geography; German; history; humanities; information sciences/systems; interdisciplinary studies; Latin American studies; literature; mathematics; mechanical engineering; Middle Eastern studies; military science; modern languages; nuclear engineering; operations research; philosophy; physics; political science; Portuguese; (pre)law; (pre)medicine; psychology; public policy analysis; Russian; Spanish; systems engineering.

United States Naval Academy
Aerospace engineering; chemistry; computer science; economics; electrical/electronics engineering; engineering; English; history; mathematics; mechanical engineering; naval architecture/marine engineering; ocean engineering; oceanography; physics; political science; quantitative economics; systems engineering.

University at Buffalo, The State University of New York
Accounting; aerospace engineering; African-American (black) studies; American studies; anthropology; architectural environmental design; architecture; art; art history; biochemical technology; biochemistry; biology; biophysics; biotechnology research; business administration; chemical engineering; chemistry; civil engineering; classics; communication disorders; computer engineering technology; computer science; dance; economics; electrical/electronics engineering; engineering physics; English; environmental engineering; exercise sciences; film studies; fine/studio arts; French; geography; geology; German; history; industrial/manufacturing engineering; Italian; linguistics; mass communications; mathematics; mechanical engineering; medical technology; medicinal/pharmaceutical chemistry; music; music (general performance); Native American studies; nuclear medical technology; nursing; occupational therapy; pharmacy administration and pharmaceutics; philosophy; physics; political science; psychology; social sci-

ences; sociology; Spanish; speech-language pathology/audiology; theater arts/drama; women's studies.

The University of Alabama in Huntsville
Accounting; art; biology; business administration; business marketing and marketing management; chemical engineering; chemistry; civil engineering; computer engineering; computer/information sciences; electrical/electronics engineering; elementary education; English; finance; foreign languages/literatures; history; industrial/manufacturing engineering; management information systems/business data processing; mathematics; mechanical engineering; music; nursing; philosophy; physics; political science; psychology; sociology; speech/rhetorical studies.

The University of Arizona
Accounting; aerospace engineering; agricultural economics; agricultural education; agricultural engineering; agricultural sciences; animal sciences; anthropology; architecture; art education; art history; astronomy; atmospheric sciences; biochemistry; biology; biology education; business; business economics; business marketing and marketing management; cell biology; chemical engineering; chemistry; chemistry education; city/community/regional planning; civil engineering; classics; communication disorders; communications; computer engineering; computer/information sciences; consumer economics; creative writing; criminal justice/law enforcement administration; dance; drama and dance education; early childhood education; earth sciences; East Asian studies; ecology; economics; electrical/electronics engineering; elementary education; engineering; engineering physics; engineering, other; English; English education; enterprise management; environmental science; evolutionary biology; finance; fine/studio arts; foreign languages education; French; French language education; geography; geological engineering; geology; German; German language education; health education; health services administration; Hispanic-American studies; history; history education; home economics education; human resources management; humanities; individual/family development; industrial/manufacturing engineering; Italian; journalism; Judaic studies; landscape architecture; Latin American studies; liberal arts and studies; linguistics; management information systems/business data processing; materials science; mathematics; mathematics education; mechanical engineering; medical technology; microbiology/bacteriology; Middle Eastern studies; mining/mineral engineering; multi/interdisciplinary studies, other; music; music (general performance); music education; music, other; nuclear engineering; nursing; nutritional sciences; operations management; optics; philosophy; physical education; physics; physics education; physiology; plant sciences; political science; (pre)veterinary studies; psychology; public administration; radio/television broadcasting; religious studies; Russian; science education; secondary education; social science education; social studies education; sociology; soil sciences; Spanish; Spanish language education; special education; speech education; systems engineering; teacher education, specific programs, other; theater arts/drama; theater design; visual/performing arts; water resources engineering; wildlife management; women's studies.

University of Arkansas
Accounting; agribusiness; agricultural education; agricultural engineering; agronomy/crop science; American studies; animal

sciences; anthropology; architecture; art; biology; botany; business; business administration; business economics; business marketing and marketing management; chemical engineering; chemistry; civil engineering; classics; clothing/apparel/textile studies; communications; computer engineering; computer/information sciences; criminal justice studies; data processing technology; earth sciences; economics; electrical/electronics engineering; elementary education; English; finance; food sciences; French; geography; geology; German; health professions and related sciences, other; health/physical education; history; home economics; horticulture science; housing studies; individual/family development; industrial/manufacturing engineering; international business; international relations; journalism; landscape architecture; logistics and materials management; mathematics; mechanical engineering; microbiology/bacteriology; Middle Eastern studies; middle school education; multi/interdisciplinary studies, other; music (general performance); nursing; nutrition studies; ornamental horticulture; philosophy; physics; plant protection; political science; poultry science; (pre)medicine; psychology; public administration; recreation and leisure studies; social work; sociology; Spanish; special education; speech-language pathology/audiology; theater arts/drama; trade and industrial education; zoology.

University of California, Berkeley
African-American (black) studies; American studies; anthropology; applied mathematics; architecture; art; art history; Asian studies; Asian-American studies; astrophysics; bioengineering; business administration; chemical engineering; chemistry; Chinese; civil engineering; classics; comparative literature; computer/information sciences; cultural studies; earth sciences; economics; electrical/electronics engineering; engineering; engineering physics; English; environmental engineering; environmental science; film/video production; forestry sciences; French; genetics; geography; geology; geophysics and seismology; German; Greek (Ancient and Medieval); Hispanic-American studies; history; industrial/manufacturing engineering; interdisciplinary studies; Italian; Japanese; landscape architecture; Latin (Ancient and Medieval); Latin American studies; law and legal studies; linguistics; mass communications; materials engineering; mathematical statistics; mathematics; mechanical engineering; Middle Eastern studies; molecular biology; music; Native American studies; natural resources conservation; natural resources management; nuclear engineering; nutritional sciences; peace and conflict studies; petroleum engineering; philosophy; physical sciences; physics; political science; psychology; religious studies; Scandinavian languages; Slavic languages; social sciences; social work; sociology; Southeast Asian studies; Spanish; speech/rhetorical studies; theater arts/drama; women's studies.

University of California, Davis
Aerospace engineering; African studies; African-American (black) studies; agricultural business; agricultural economics; agricultural education; agricultural engineering; American studies; animal sciences; anthropology; art; art history; atmospheric sciences; biochemistry; bioengineering; biology; botany; cell biology; chemical engineering; chemistry; Chinese; civil engineering; clothing/apparel/textile studies; comparative literature; computer engineering; design/visual communications; East Asian studies; economics; electrical/electronics engineering;

engineering; English; entomology; environmental biology; food sciences; French; genetics; geology; German; history; horticulture science; individual/family development; international agriculture; international relations; Italian; Japanese; landscape architecture; linguistics; materials engineering; mathematical statistics; mathematics; mechanical engineering; Mexican-American studies; microbiology/bacteriology; music; Native American studies; natural resources conservation; nutrition science; philosophy; physical education; physics; physiology; political science; poultry science; psychology; range management; religious studies; Russian; sociology; Spanish; speech/rhetorical studies; theater arts/drama; women's studies; zoology.

University of California, Irvine
Anthropology; art; art history; biology; chemical engineering; chemistry; civil engineering; classics; cognitive psychology and psycholinguistics; comparative literature; computer engineering; computer science; computer/information sciences; criminology; cultural studies; dance; East Asian studies; ecology; economics; electrical/electronics engineering; engineering; English; environmental engineering; film studies; fine/studio arts; French; geography; German; history; human ecology; humanities; international relations; linguistics; literature; mathematics; mechanical engineering; music; philosophy; physics; political science; psychology; Russian; social sciences; sociology; Spanish; theater arts/drama; women's studies.

University of California, Los Angeles
Aerospace engineering; African languages; African-American (black) studies; American literature; American studies; anthropology; applied art; applied mathematics; Arabic; art; art history; Asian-American studies; astrophysics; atmospheric sciences; biochemistry; biology; business economics; cell biology; chemical engineering; chemistry; Chinese; civil engineering; classics; cognitive psychology and psycholinguistics; communications; comparative literature; computer engineering; computer science; design/visual communications; earth sciences; East Asian studies; ecology; economics; electrical/electronics engineering; English; European studies; exercise sciences; film studies; French; geochemistry; geography; geological engineering; geology; geophysical engineering; geophysics and seismology; German; Greek (Modern); Hebrew; history; international economics; international relations; Italian; Japanese; Judaic studies; Latin (Ancient and Medieval); Latin American studies; linguistics; marine biology; materials engineering; materials science; mathematics; mechanical engineering; Mexican-American studies; microbiology/bacteriology; Middle Eastern studies; molecular biology; music; musicology; neuroscience; nursing; philosophy; physics; physiological psychology/psychobiology; plant sciences; political science; Portuguese; psychology; radio/television broadcasting; religious studies; Russian; Russian/Slavic area studies; Scandinavian languages; Slavic languages; sociology; Southeast Asian studies; Spanish; theater arts/drama; women's studies.

University of California, Riverside
African-American (black) studies; anthropology; art history; Asian studies; Asian-American studies; biochemistry; biology; biomedical science; botany; business administration; business economics; chemical engineering; chemistry; Chinese; classics; comparative literature; computer science; creative writing; cultural studies; dance; economics; electrical/electronics

engineering; English; entomology; environmental engineering; environmental science; fine/studio arts; French; geology; geophysics and seismology; German; history; humanities; individual/family development; Latin American studies; liberal arts and studies; linguistics; mathematical statistics; mathematics; mechanical engineering; Mexican-American studies; music; Native American studies; neuroscience; philosophy; physical sciences; physics; physiological psychology/psychobiology; political science; (pre)law; psychology; public administration; religious studies; Russian; Russian/Slavic area studies; social sciences; sociology; Spanish; theater arts/drama; women's studies.

University of California, San Diego

Aerospace engineering; anthropology; applied mathematics; archaeology; art; art history; biochemistry; bioengineering; biology; biophysics; biotechnology research; cell biology; chemical and atomic/molecular physics; chemical engineering; chemistry; chemistry education; Chinese; classics; cognitive psychology and psycholinguistics; computer engineering; computer science; creative writing; cultural studies; dance; earth sciences; ecology; economics; electrical/electronics engineering; engineering; engineering physics; engineering science; English; environmental science; film studies; fine/studio arts; foreign languages/literatures; French; German; history; human ecology; interdisciplinary studies; Italian; Japanese; Judaic studies; Latin American studies; linguistics; literature; management science; mass communications; mathematics; mathematics education; mechanical engineering; medicinal/pharmaceutical chemistry; microbiology/bacteriology; molecular biology; multimedia; music; music history; natural resources management; philosophy; physics; physics education; physiology; political science; psychology; quantitative economics; religious studies; Russian; Russian/Slavic area studies; sociology; Spanish; structural engineering; systems engineering; theater arts/drama; urban studies; women's studies.

University of California, Santa Barbara

African-American (black) studies; anthropology; applied history; art history; Asian studies; Asian-American studies; biochemistry; biology; biopsychology; business economics; cell biology; chemical engineering; chemical engineering technology; chemistry; Chinese; classics; communications; comparative literature; computer science; dance; ecology; economics; electrical/electronic engineering technology; electrical/electronics engineering; English; environmental science; film studies; fine/studio arts; French; geography; geology; geophysics and seismology; German; history; interdisciplinary studies; Islamic studies; Italian; Japanese; Latin American studies; law and legal studies; linguistics; marine biology; mathematical statistics; mathematics; mechanical engineering; medieval/renaissance studies; Mexican-American studies; microbiology/bacteriology; Middle Eastern studies; molecular biology; music; pharmacology; philosophy; physics; physiology; political science; Portuguese; psychology; religious studies; Slavic languages; sociology; Spanish; theater arts/drama; women's studies; zoology.

University of California, Santa Cruz

American studies; anthropology; applied mathematics; art; art history; Asian studies; astrophysics; biochemistry; biology; botany; business economics; cell biology; chemistry; Chinese; classics; cognitive psychology and psycholinguistics; comparative literature; computer engineering; computer science; creative

writing; dance; developmental/child psychology; drawing; earth sciences; East Asian studies; ecology; economics; electrical/electronics engineering; English, other; environmental science; European history; family/community studies; film studies; film/video production; foreign languages/literatures; French; geology; geophysics and seismology; German; Greek (Ancient and Medieval); Hispanic-American studies; history; information sciences/systems; international economics; Italian; Italian studies; Japanese; Latin (Ancient and Medieval); Latin American studies; law and legal studies; linguistics; literature; marine biology; mathematics; mathematics education; molecular biology; music; peace and conflict studies; philosophy; photography; physics; physiological psychology/psychobiology; plant sciences; political science; printmaking; psychology; religious studies; Russian/Slavic area studies; sculpture; social psychology; sociology; South Asian studies; Southeast Asian studies; Spanish; theater arts/drama; theater design; women's studies.

University of Central Florida

Accounting; advertising; aerospace engineering; anthropology; art; art education; biology; business; business administration; business economics; business education; business marketing and marketing management; chemistry; civil engineering; communications; computer engineering; computer/information sciences; criminal justice studies; early childhood education; economics; electrical/electronic engineering technology; electrical/electronics engineering; elementary education; engineering technology; English; English education; environmental engineering; film/video production; finance; fine/studio arts; foreign languages education; foreign languages/literatures; forensic technology; French; health science; health services administration; history; hospitality management; humanities; industrial/manufacturing engineering; journalism; liberal arts and studies; management information systems/business data processing; mathematical statistics; mathematics; mathematics education; mechanical engineering; medical radiologic technology; medical records administration; microbiology/bacteriology; multimedia; music (general performance); music education; nursing; paralegal/legal assistant; philosophy; physical education; physics; political science; psychology; public administration; radio/television broadcasting; respiratory therapy; science education; social science education; social sciences; social work; sociology; Spanish; special education; speech-language pathology/audiology; speech/rhetorical studies; theater arts/drama; trade and industrial education.

University of Chicago

African studies; African-American (black) studies; American studies; anthropology; applied mathematics; Arabic; art; art history; Asian studies; behavioral sciences; biblical languages/literatures; biochemistry; biology; chemistry; Chinese; classics; computer science; creative writing; East Asian studies; Eastern European area studies; economics; English; environmental science; film studies; fine/studio arts; French; geography; geophysics and seismology; German; Greek (Ancient and Medieval); history; history of science and technology; humanities; interdisciplinary studies; Italian; Japanese; Judaic studies; Latin (Ancient and Medieval); Latin American studies; liberal arts and studies; linguistics; mathematical statistics; mathematics; medieval/renaissance studies; Middle Eastern studies; modern languages; music; music history; philosophy; physics; political science; psychology; public policy analysis; religious studies;

Romance languages; Russian; Russian/Slavic area studies; Slavic languages; social sciences; sociology; South Asian studies; Southeast Asian studies; Spanish.

University of Colorado at Boulder

Accounting; advertising; aerospace engineering; American studies; anthropology; applied mathematics; architectural engineering; architectural environmental design; art; Asian studies; astronomy; biochemistry; biology; broadcast journalism; business administration; business marketing and marketing management; cell biology; chemical engineering; chemistry; Chinese; civil engineering; classics; communication disorders; communications; computer engineering; computer science; computer/information sciences; cultural studies; dance; economics; electrical/electronics engineering; engineering physics; English; environmental engineering; environmental science; exercise sciences; film studies; finance; fine/studio arts; French; geography; geology; German; history; humanities; international relations; Italian; Japanese; journalism; linguistics; management information systems/business data processing; mass communications; mathematics; mechanical engineering; molecular biology; multi/interdisciplinary studies, other; music; music education; philosophy; physics; political science; psychology; religious studies; Russian/Slavic area studies; sociology; Spanish; theater arts/drama; visual and performing arts, other; women's studies.

University of Dallas

Art; art education; art history; biochemistry; biology; ceramic arts; chemistry; classics; computer science; economics; economics, other; education; elementary education; English; fine/studio arts; French; German; history; mathematics; painting; philosophy; physics; political science; (pre)dentistry; (pre)law; (pre)medicine; (pre)theology; printmaking; psychology; sculpture; secondary education; Spanish; theater arts/drama; theology.

University of Dayton

Accounting; American studies; applied art; art; art education; art history; biochemistry; biology; broadcast journalism; business administration; business economics; business marketing and marketing management; chemical engineering; chemistry; civil engineering; computer engineering; computer engineering technology; computer science; criminal justice/law enforcement administration; dietetics; early childhood education; economics; education; electrical/electronic engineering technology; electrical/electronics engineering; elementary education; English; environmental biology; environmental science; exercise sciences; finance; fine/studio arts; French; general studies; geology; German; graphic design/commercial art/illustration; health education; history; industrial technology; information sciences/systems; international business; international relations; journalism; management information systems/business data processing; mass communications; mathematics; mechanical engineering; mechanical engineering technology; music; music education; music therapy; nutrition science; philosophy; photography; physical education; physical sciences; physics; political science; (pre)dentistry; (pre)law; (pre)medicine; psychology; public relations; quantitative economics; radio/television broadcasting; religious education; religious studies; science education; secondary education; sociology; Spanish; special education; sport/fitness administration; theater arts/drama.

University of Delaware

Accounting; African-American (black) studies; agribusiness; agricultural business; agricultural economics; agricultural education; agricultural engineering; agricultural sciences; agronomy/crop science; animal sciences; anthropology; applied art; architectural history; art; art history; astronomy; astrophysics; athletic training/sports medicine; bilingual/bicultural education; biochemistry; biological technology; biology; biology education; biotechnology research; botany; business administration; business economics; business marketing and marketing management; chemical engineering; chemistry; chemistry education; child care/development; civil engineering; classics; communications; community services; comparative literature; computer engineering; computer science; computer/information sciences; consumer economics; criminal justice/law enforcement administration; developmental/child psychology; dietetics; early childhood education; East Asian studies; ecology; economics; education; electrical/electronics engineering; elementary education; engineering; English; English education; entomology; environmental engineering; environmental science; environmental technology; exercise sciences; family/community studies; family/consumer studies; fashion design/illustration; fashion merchandising; film studies; finance; food sales operations; food sciences; foreign languages education; foreign languages/literatures; French; geography; geology; geophysics and seismology; German; graphic design/commercial art/illustration; health education; health/physical education; history; history education; horticulture science; hotel and restaurant management; individual/family development; international relations; Italian; journalism; Latin (Ancient and Medieval); Latin American studies; liberal arts and studies; linguistics; mass communications; mathematics; mathematics education; mechanical engineering; medical technology; middle school education; music; music (piano and organ performance); music (voice and choral/opera performance); music education; music theory and composition; natural resources management; neuroscience; nursing; nursing science; nutrition science; nutrition studies; nutritional sciences; operations management; ornamental horticulture; paleontology; philosophy; physical education; physics; physics education; plant protection; political science; (pre)veterinary studies; psychology; public relations; recreation/leisure facilities management; Russian; science education; secondary education; sociology; soil conservation; soil sciences; Spanish; special education; teaching English as a second language; technical writing; theater design; wildlife management; women's studies.

University of Denver

Accounting; animal sciences; anthropology; art; art education; art history; Asian-American studies; biochemistry; biological and physical sciences; biology; biopsychology; business; business administration; business economics; business marketing and marketing management; chemistry; communications; computer engineering; computer/information sciences; construction management; creative writing; economics; electrical/electronics engineering; engineering; English; environmental science; finance; fine/studio arts; French; geography; German; graphic design/commercial art/illustration; history; hospitality management; hotel and restaurant management; international business; international relations; Italian; journalism; Latin American studies; mathematical statistics; mathematics; mechanical engineering; molecular biology; music; music (general performance);

musicology; operations research; philosophy; physics; political science; psychology; public administration; real estate; religious studies; Russian; social sciences; sociology; Spanish; theater arts/drama; women's studies.

University of Evansville

Accounting; anthropology; archaeology; art; art education; art history; arts management; athletic training/sports medicine; biblical studies; biochemistry; biology; business administration; business economics; business marketing and marketing management; ceramic arts; chemistry; civil engineering; classics; computer engineering; computer science; creative writing; criminal justice/law enforcement administration; drawing; economics; electrical/electronics engineering; elementary education; engineering/industrial management; English; environmental science; exercise sciences; finance; French; German; gerontology; graphic design/commercial art/illustration; health services administration; history; international business; international relations; law and legal studies; liberal arts and studies; literature; mass communications; mathematics; mechanical engineering; medical technology; music; music business management and merchandising; music education; music therapy; nursing; philosophy; physical education; physical therapy; physical therapy assistant; physics; physiological psychology/psychobiology; political science; (pre)dentistry; (pre)law; (pre)medicine; (pre)veterinary studies; psychology; religious studies; science education; sculpture; secondary education; sociology; Spanish; special education; theater arts/drama.

University of Florida

Accounting; advertising; aerospace engineering; agricultural economics; agricultural education; agricultural engineering; agronomy/crop science; American studies; animal sciences; anthropology; architecture; art education; art history; Asian studies; astronomy; botany; business administration; business marketing and marketing management; chemical engineering; chemistry; civil engineering; classics; computer engineering; computer/information sciences; construction technology; criminal justice studies; dairy science; dance; economics; electrical/electronics engineering; elementary education; engineering; English; entomology; environmental engineering; environmental science; exercise sciences; family/community studies; finance; fine/studio arts; food sciences; forestry; French; geography; geology; German; graphic design/commercial art/illustration; health education; health science; history; horticulture science; human resources management; industrial/manufacturing engineering; insurance and risk management; interdisciplinary studies; interior design; journalism; Judaic studies; landscape architecture; liberal arts and studies; linguistics; management science; materials engineering; mathematical statistics; mathematics; mechanical engineering; microbiology/bacteriology; music; music education; nuclear engineering; nursing; occupational therapy; pharmacy; philosophy; physical education; physical therapy; physics; plant pathology; plant sciences; political science; Portuguese; poultry science; psychology; public relations; radio/television broadcasting; real estate; recreation/leisure facilities management; rehabilitation therapy; religious studies; Russian; sociology; soil sciences; Spanish; special education; speech-language pathology/audiology; surveying; systems engineering; telecommunications; theater arts/drama; zoology.

University of Georgia

Accounting; advertising; African-American (black) studies; agricultural business; agricultural economics; agricultural education; agricultural engineering; agronomy/crop science; animal sciences; anthropology; art; art education; art history; astronomy; biochemistry; biological and physical sciences; biology; botany; broadcast journalism; business; business administration; business economics; business education; business marketing and marketing management; cell biology; chemistry; classics; clothing/apparel/textile studies; cognitive psychology and psycholinguistics; communication disorders; comparative literature; computer/information sciences; consumer economics; criminal justice studies; dairy science; dietetics; drama and dance education; early childhood education; ecology; economics; English; English education; entomology; environmental health; fashion merchandising; finance; fine/studio arts; fishing sciences and management; food sciences; foreign languages education; foreign languages/literatures; forestry; forestry sciences; French; genetics; geography; geology; German; Greek (Ancient and Medieval); health education; history; home economics education; horticulture services; housing studies; individual/family development; industrial arts education; insurance and risk management; international business; Italian; Japanese; journalism; landscape architecture; landscaping management; Latin (Ancient and Medieval); liberal arts and studies; linguistics; management information systems/business data processing; marketing/distribution education; mass communications; mathematical statistics; mathematics; mathematics education; microbiology/bacteriology; middle school education; music; music (general performance); music education; music theory and composition; music therapy; nutrition studies; pharmacy; philosophy; physical education; physics; plant protection; political science; poultry science; psychology; public relations; radio/television broadcasting technology; reading education; real estate; religious studies; Russian; science education; Slavic languages; social science education; social work; sociology; soil sciences; Spanish; special education; speech/rhetorical studies; sport/fitness administration; theater arts/drama; turf management; wildlife management; women's studies.

University of Illinois at Chicago

Accounting; African-American (black) studies; anthropology; architecture; art education; art history; biochemistry; bioengineering; biology; biology education; business administration; business marketing and marketing management; chemical engineering; chemistry; chemistry education; civil engineering; classics; computer engineering; computer/information sciences; criminal justice studies; economics; electrical/electronics engineering; elementary education; engineering physics; engineering/industrial management; English; English education; film/video production; finance; fine/studio arts; foreign languages education; French; French language education; geography; geology; German; German language education; graphic design/commercial art/illustration; health/physical education; history; history education; industrial design; industrial/manufacturing engineering; Italian; Latin American studies; management information systems/business data processing; mathematical statistics; mathematics; mathematics education; mathematics/computer science; mechanical engineering; medical dietician; medical records administration; medical technology; music; nursing; philosophy; photography; physical therapy; physics; physics education; political science; (pre)dentistry; (pre)law; psychology; Russian; science education; secondary education; Slavic languages; social science education; social work; sociology; Spanish; Spanish language education; speech/rhetorical studies; theater arts/drama.

University of Illinois at Urbana–Champaign

Accounting; actuarial science; advertising; aerospace engineering; agricultural and food products processing; agricultural economics; agricultural education; agricultural engineering; agricultural mechanization; agricultural sciences; agronomy/crop science; aircraft pilot (professional); animal sciences; anthropology; architecture and related programs, other; area studies, other; art education; art history; Asian studies; astronomy; biochemistry; bioengineering; biology; biophysics; botany; broadcast journalism; business; cell and molecular biology, other; cell biology; chemical engineering; chemistry; city/community/regional planning; civil engineering; classics; comparative literature; computer education; computer engineering; computer/information sciences; consumer economics; craft/folk art; dance; early childhood education; ecology; economics; electrical/electronics engineering; elementary education; engineering; engineering mechanics; engineering physics; English; English composition; English education; entomology; environmental science; finance; food sciences; foreign languages education; forestry; French; French language education; geography; geology; German; German language education; graphic design/commercial art/illustration; health/physical education; history; horticulture science; humanities; individual/family development; industrial design; industrial/manufacturing engineering; Italian; journalism; landscape architecture; Latin American studies; liberal arts and studies; linguistics; marketing operations; mass communications; materials science; mathematical statistics; mathematics; mathematics/computer science; mechanical engineering; microbiology/bacteriology; music; music (general performance); music (voice and choral/opera performance); music education; music history; music theory and composition; nuclear engineering; ornamental horticulture; painting; philosophy; photography; physics; physiology; political science; Portuguese; (pre)veterinary studies; psychology; public health, other; recreation and leisure studies; religious studies; Russian; Russian/Slavic area studies; sculpture; sociology; Spanish; Spanish language education; special education; speech-language pathology/audiology; speech/rhetorical studies; theater arts/drama.

The University of Iowa

Accounting; actuarial science; African studies; African-American (black) studies; air science; American history; American studies; anthropology; art; art education; art history; arts management; Asian studies; astronomy; athletic training/sports medicine; biochemistry; bioengineering; biology; broadcast journalism; business administration; business economics; business marketing and marketing management; ceramic arts; chemical engineering; chemistry; chemistry education; Chinese; civil engineering; classics; comparative literature; computer engineering; computer science; creative writing; dance; drama and dance education; drawing; earth sciences; Eastern European area studies; economics; education; electrical/electronics engineering; elementary education; engineering; engineering/industrial management; English; entrepreneurship; environmental engineering; environmental science; exercise sciences; film studies; film/video

production; finance; fine/studio arts; French; French language education; geography; geology; German; German language education; Greek (Modern); health education; history; history education; human resources management; industrial/manufacturing engineering; information sciences/systems; interdisciplinary studies; international business; international relations; Italian; Japanese; jazz; journalism; labor/personnel relations; Latin (Ancient and Medieval); Latin American studies; linguistics; literature; management information systems/business data processing; management science; mass communications; materials engineering; mathematical statistics; mathematics; mathematics education; mechanical engineering; medical technology; medieval/renaissance studies; metal/jewelry arts; microbiology/bacteriology; military science; museum studies; music; music (piano and organ performance); music (voice and choral/opera performance); music education; music history; music therapy; Native American studies; nuclear medical technology; nursing; painting; pharmacy; philosophy; photography; physics; political science; Portuguese; (pre)dentistry; (pre)law; (pre)medicine; (pre)pharmacy studies; (pre)veterinary studies; printmaking; psychology; public relations; radio/television broadcasting; recreation and leisure studies; recreational therapy; religious studies; Russian; science education; sculpture; secondary education; social sciences; social studies education; social work; sociology; Spanish; Spanish language education; speech education; speech therapy; speech-language pathology/audiology; speech/rhetorical studies; sport/fitness administration; stringed instruments; theater arts/drama; wind and percussion instruments; women's studies.

University of Maryland, Baltimore County

African-American (black) studies; American studies; anthropology; applied mathematics; art; art history; biochemistry; biology; chemical engineering; chemistry; classics; computer engineering; computer science; dance; economics; emergency medical technology; engineering science; English; environmental science; film studies; French; geography; German; health science; health services administration; history; information sciences/systems; interdisciplinary studies; linguistics; mathematical statistics; mathematics; mechanical engineering; modern languages; music; philosophy; photography; physics; political science; (pre)dentistry; (pre)law; (pre)medicine; (pre)veterinary studies; psychology; Russian; social work; sociology; Spanish; theater arts/drama; visual/performing arts.

University of Maryland, College Park

Accounting; aerospace engineering; African-American (black) studies; agricultural economics; agricultural sciences; agronomy/crop science; American studies; animal sciences; anthropology; architecture; art education; art history; astronomy; biochemistry; biology; broadcast journalism; business; business administration/management, other; business marketing and marketing management; cartography; chemical engineering; chemistry; Chinese; civil engineering; classics; communications; computer engineering; computer science; computer/information sciences; criminology; dance; dietetics; drama and dance education; early childhood education; ecology; economics; education; electrical/electronics engineering; elementary education; engineering; engineering, other; English; English education; environmental science; family/community studies; finance; fine/studio arts; food sciences; foreign languages education; French; geography; geology; German; health education; history; horticulture science;

human resources management; Italian; Japanese; journalism; Judaic studies; landscape architecture; linguistics; mass communications; materials engineering; mathematics; mathematics education; mechanical engineering; microbiology/bacteriology; music; music (general performance); music education; natural resources conservation; nuclear engineering; nutrition science; operations management; philosophy; physical education; physical sciences; physics; plant sciences; political science; (pre)veterinary studies; psychology; Russian; Russian/Slavic area studies; science education; secondary education; social studies education; sociology; Spanish; special education; speech-language pathology; theater arts/drama; turf management; women's studies.

University of Massachusetts Amherst

Accounting; African-American (black) studies; animal sciences; anthropology; applied economics; architectural environmental design; art history; astronomy; biochemistry; biological and physical sciences; biology; business administration; business marketing and marketing management; chemical engineering; chemistry; Chinese; civil engineering; classics; communication disorders; communications; comparative literature; computer engineering; computer science; crop production management; dance; earth sciences; economics; education; electrical/electronics engineering; English; environmental science; equestrian studies; exercise sciences; finance; fine/studio arts; food sciences; forestry; French; general studies; geography; geology; German; history; horticulture services; horticulture services, other; hospitality management; humanities; industrial/manufacturing engineering; interdisciplinary studies; interior design; Italian; Japanese; journalism; Judaic studies; landscape architecture; landscaping management; law and legal studies; linguistics; mathematics; mechanical engineering; medical technology; microbiology/bacteriology; Middle Eastern studies; music; music (general performance); natural resources management; nursing; nutrition studies; ornamental horticulture; philosophy; physics; plant sciences; political science; Portuguese; (pre)dentistry; (pre)medicine; (pre)veterinary studies; psychology; Russian/Slavic area studies; social sciences and history, other; sociology; Spanish; sport/fitness administration; theater arts/drama; turf management; wildlife management; women's studies; wood science/paper technology.

University of Miami

Accounting; advertising; aerospace engineering; African-American (black) studies; American studies; anthropology; Arabic; architectural engineering; architecture; art; art history; athletic training/sports medicine; atmospheric sciences; biochemistry; bioengineering; biology; broadcast journalism; business administration; business economics; business marketing and marketing management; ceramic arts; chemistry; chemistry, other; civil engineering; classics; communications; communications, other; computer engineering; computer science; computer systems analysis; creative writing; criminology; dance; ecology; education; education administration/supervision, other; electrical/electronics engineering; elementary education; engineering science; English; enterprise management; environmental engineering; environmental health; environmental science; exercise sciences; film studies; film/video production; finance; fine/studio arts; French; general studies; geography; geological sciences, other; geology; German; graphic design/commercial art/illustration; health professions and related sciences, other; health/medical preparatory programs, other; history; human resources management; industrial/manufacturing engineering; information sciences/systems; international business; international relations; Italian; jazz; journalism; Judaic studies; Latin American studies; law and legal studies, other; liberal arts and studies; marine biology; mass communications; mathematics; mechanical engineering; medical microbiology; music; music (general performance); music (piano and organ performance); music (voice and choral/opera performance); music business management and merchandising; music education; music theory and composition; music therapy; musicology; natural resources management; nursing; oceanography; painting; philosophy; photography; physical education; physics; physics, other; physiological psychology/psychobiology; political science; Portuguese; (pre)dentistry; (pre)law; (pre)medicine; (pre)pharmacy studies; (pre)veterinary studies; printmaking; psychology; public policy analysis; public relations; radio/television broadcasting; real estate; religious studies; Russian; sculpture; secondary education; social sciences and history, other; sociology; Spanish; special education; stringed instruments; theater arts/drama; toxicology; visual/performing arts; wildlife management; wind and percussion instruments; women's studies.

University of Michigan

Accounting; aerospace engineering; African studies; African-American (black) studies; American studies; anthropology; applied art; applied mathematics; Arabic; archaeology; architecture; art education; art history; Asian studies; astronomy; athletic training/sports medicine; atmospheric sciences; biblical studies; biochemistry; biology; biomedical science; biometrics; biophysics; botany; business administration; cell biology; ceramic arts; chemical engineering; chemistry; Chinese; civil engineering; classics; comparative literature; computer engineering; computer science; creative writing; dance; dental hygiene; design/visual communications; drawing; ecology; economics; education; electrical/electronics engineering; elementary education; engineering; engineering physics; engineering science; English; environmental engineering; environmental science; European studies; exercise sciences; film studies; French; general studies; geography; geology; German; graphic design/commercial art/illustration; Greek (Modern); Hebrew; Hispanic-American studies; history; humanities; industrial design; industrial/manufacturing engineering; interdisciplinary studies; interior design; international relations; Islamic studies; Italian; Japanese; jazz; journalism; Judaic studies; landscape architecture; Latin (Ancient and Medieval); Latin American studies; liberal arts and studies; linguistics; literature; mass communications; materials engineering; materials science; mathematical statistics; mathematics; mechanical engineering; medical technology; medieval/renaissance studies; metal/jewelry arts; metallurgical engineering; Mexican-American studies; microbiology/bacteriology; Middle Eastern studies; molecular biology; multimedia; music; music (piano and organ performance); music (voice and choral/opera performance); music education; music history; music theory and composition; natural resources management; naval architecture/marine engineering; nuclear engineering; nursing; nutrition science; oceanography; painting; pharmacy; philosophy; photography; physical education; physics; play/screenwriting; political science; printmaking; psychology; radiological science; recreation and leisure studies; religious studies; Romance languages; Russian; Russian/Slavic area studies; Scandinavian area studies; sculpture; secondary education; social sciences; sociology; South Asian studies; Southeast Asian studies; Spanish; speech/rhetorical studies; sport/fitness administration; stringed instruments; textile arts; theater arts/drama; theater design; visual/performing arts; wildlife biology; wind and percussion instruments; women's studies; zoology.

University of Minnesota, Morris

Art history; biology; business administration; chemistry; computer science; economics; education; elementary education; English; European studies; fine/studio arts; French; geology; German; history; human services; K-12 education; Latin American studies; liberal arts and studies; management science; mass communications; mathematical statistics; mathematics; music; philosophy; physical therapy; physics; political science; (pre)dentistry; (pre)law; (pre)medicine; (pre)pharmacy studies; (pre)veterinary studies; psychology; secondary education; social sciences; sociology; Spanish; speech/rhetorical studies; speech/theater education; theater arts/drama; women's studies.

University of Minnesota, Twin Cities Campus

Accounting; actuarial science; aerospace engineering; African studies; African-American (black) studies; agricultural business; agricultural education; agricultural engineering; agricultural sciences; agronomy/crop science; American studies; animal sciences; anthropology; architecture; art; art education; art history; astronomy; astrophysics; biochemistry; biology; botany; business education; business marketing and marketing management; cell biology; chemical engineering; chemistry; Chinese; civil engineering; clothing and textiles; comparative literature; computer science; construction management; dance; dental hygiene; developmental/child psychology; early childhood education; East Asian studies; ecology; economics; education; electrical/electronics engineering; elementary education; emergency medical technology; English; English education; environmental science; European studies; family/community studies; film studies; finance; fish/game management; foreign languages education; forest management; forestry; French; genetics; geography; geological engineering; geology; geophysics and seismology; German; graphic design/commercial art/illustration; Greek (Modern); Hebrew; history; home economics education; industrial/manufacturing engineering; insurance and risk management; interior design; international business; international relations; Italian; Japanese; journalism; Judaic studies; landscape architecture; Latin (Ancient and Medieval); Latin American studies; linguistics; management information systems/business data processing; mass communications; materials engineering; materials science; mathematics; mathematics education; mechanical engineering; medical technology; Mexican-American studies; microbiology/bacteriology; Middle Eastern studies; mortuary science; music; music education; music therapy; Native American studies; natural resources management; neuroscience; nursing; nutrition science; occupational therapy; philosophy; physical education; physical therapy; physics; physiology; plant sciences; political science; Portuguese; (pre)dentistry; (pre)law; (pre)medicine; (pre)veterinary studies; psychology; public health; recreation/leisure facilities management; religious studies; Russian; Russian/Slavic area studies; Scandinavian languages; science education; social science education; socio-psychological sports studies; sociology; soil sciences; South Asian studies; Spanish; speech-language pathology/audiology; theater arts/drama; urban studies; women's studies; wood science/paper technology.

University of Missouri–Columbia

Accounting; advertising; agricultural business; agricultural economics; agricultural education; agricultural mechanization; agricultural sciences; animal sciences; anthropology; archaeology; art; art education; atmospheric sciences; biochemistry; bioengineering; biology; broadcast journalism; business administration; business economics; business marketing and marketing management; chemical engineering; chemistry; civil engineering; classics; clothing/apparel/textile studies; communications; computer engineering; computer science; developmental/child psychology; dietetics; early childhood education; economics; education; electrical/electronics engineering; elementary education; English; family/consumer studies; finance; fish/game management; food sciences; forestry; French; geography; geology; German; history; hotel and restaurant management; housing studies; individual/family development; industrial/manufacturing engineering; interdisciplinary studies; international business; journalism; liberal arts and studies; linguistics; mass communications; mathematical statistics; mathematics; mechanical engineering; microbiology/bacteriology; middle school education; music; music education; nuclear medical technology; nursing; nutrition science; occupational therapy; philosophy; physical therapy; physics; plant sciences; political science; psychology; publishing; radio/television broadcasting; radiological science; real estate; recreation and leisure studies; religious studies; respiratory therapy; Russian; Russian/Slavic area studies; science education; social work; sociology; South Asian studies; Spanish; theater arts/drama.

University of Missouri–Kansas City

Accounting; American studies; art; art history; biology; business administration; chemistry; civil engineering; computer science; criminal justice/law enforcement administration; dance; dental hygiene; early childhood education; earth sciences; economics; education; electrical/electronics engineering; elementary education; English; fine/studio arts; French; geography; geology; German; health/physical education; history; information sciences/systems; interdisciplinary studies; Judaic studies; liberal arts and studies; mass communications; mathematical statistics; mathematics; mechanical engineering; medical laboratory technician; music; music (piano and organ performance); music (voice and choral/opera performance); music education; music therapy; nursing; pharmacy; philosophy; physical education; physics; political science; psychology; secondary education; sociology; Spanish; stringed instruments; theater arts/drama; urban studies; wind and percussion instruments.

University of Missouri–Rolla

Aerospace engineering; applied mathematics; architectural engineering; biology; business; business administration; ceramic sciences/engineering; chemical engineering; chemistry; civil engineering; computer engineering; computer science; computer/information sciences, other; economics; electrical/electronics engineering; engineering/industrial management; English; geological engineering; geology; geophysics and seismology; history; information sciences/systems; mechanical engineering; metallurgical engineering; mining/mineral engineering; nuclear engineering; petroleum engineering; philosophy; physics; (pre)dentistry; (pre)law; (pre)medicine; psychology; secondary education.

The University of North Carolina at Asheville

Accounting; art; atmospheric sciences; biology; business administration; chemistry; classics; computer science; economics; English; environmental science; fine/studio arts; French; German; history; journalism and mass communication, other; liberal arts and studies; mathematics; music; music, other; operations management; philosophy; physics; political science; psychology; sociology; Spanish; theater arts/drama.

The University of North Carolina at Chapel Hill

African-American (black) studies; American studies; anthropology; applied mathematics; area, ethnic and cultural studies, other; art history; Asian studies; biology; business administration; chemistry; classics; communications; comparative literature; dental hygiene; early childhood education; East European languages, other; economics; elementary education; English; environmental health; environmental science; fine/studio arts; geography; geology; German; health services administration; health/medical biostatistics; health/physical education; history; human resources management; Latin American studies; liberal arts and studies; linguistics; mass communications; mathematics; medical radiologic technology; medical technology; middle school education; music; music (general performance); nursing; nutrition studies; peace and conflict studies; philosophy; physics; political science; psychology; public policy analysis; recreation/leisure facilities management; religious studies; Romance languages; Russian; Russian/Slavic area studies; sociology; theater arts/drama; women's studies.

University of Notre Dame

Accounting; aerospace engineering; American studies; anthropology; Arabic; architecture; art history; biochemistry; biology; business; business administration/management, other; business marketing and marketing management; chemical engineering; chemistry; chemistry, other; Chinese; civil engineering; classics; computer engineering; computer/information sciences; computer/information sciences, other; design/visual communications; economics; electrical/electronics engineering; English; environmental engineering; environmental science; finance; fine/studio arts; French; geology; German; Greek (Ancient and Medieval); history; Italian; Japanese; Latin (Ancient and Medieval); liberal arts and studies; management information systems/business data processing; mathematics; mechanical engineering; medieval/renaissance studies; music; philosophy; philosophy and religion, other; physics; physics, other; political science; (pre)medicine; psychology; religious studies; Russian; science education; sociology; Spanish; theater arts/drama; theology.

University of Oklahoma

Accounting; advertising; aerospace engineering; African-American (black) studies; aircraft pilot (professional); anthropology; architectural environmental design; architecture; area studies; art; art history; astronomy; astrophysics; atmospheric sciences; biochemistry; botany; broadcast journalism; business administration; business economics; business marketing and marketing management; ceramic arts; chemical engineering; chemistry; civil engineering; classics; communications; computer engineering; computer science; construction technology; criminology; dance; early childhood education; economics; electrical/electronics engineering; elementary education; energy manage-ment technology; engineering; engineering physics; English; English education; environmental engineering; environmental science; film/video production; finance; fine/studio arts; foreign languages education; French; geography; geological engineering; geology; geophysics and seismology; German; health/physical education; history; industrial/manufacturing engineering; interior architecture; international business; journalism; liberal arts and studies, other; library science; linguistics; management information systems/business data processing; mathematics; mathematics education; mechanical engineering; medical laboratory technologies; microbiology/bacteriology; music; music (piano and organ performance); music (voice and choral/opera performance); music education; music theory and composition; Native American studies; petroleum engineering; philosophy; philosophy and religion, other; physics; political science; (pre)dentistry; (pre)medicine; (pre)veterinary studies; printmaking; professional studies; psychology; public administration; public relations; radio/television broadcasting; real estate; religious studies; Russian; science education; sculpture; social studies education; social work; sociology; Spanish; special education; stringed instruments; theater arts/drama; visual and performing arts, other; wind and percussion instruments; women's studies; zoology.

University of Pennsylvania

Accounting; actuarial science; African studies; African-American (black) studies; American studies; anthropology; architectural environmental design; architecture; art; art history; biochemistry; bioengineering; biology; biophysics; business administration; business marketing and marketing management; business quantitative methods/management science, other; chemical engineering; chemistry; civil engineering; classics; communications; comparative literature; computer engineering; computer/information sciences; East Asian studies; economics; electrical/electronics engineering; elementary education; English; entrepreneurship; finance; folklore; French; geology; German; health facilities administration; health professions and related sciences, other; history; history of science and technology; human resources management; humanities; insurance and risk management; interdisciplinary studies; international relations; Italian; Judaic studies; Latin American studies; law and legal studies; liberal arts and studies; liberal arts and studies, other; linguistics; management information systems/business data processing; management science; materials engineering; mathematical statistics; mathematics; mechanical engineering; multi/interdisciplinary studies, other; music; nursing; nursing, other; operations management; organizational behavior; philosophy; physics; physiological psychology/psychobiology; political science; (pre)dentistry; psychology; public policy analysis; real estate; religious studies; Romance languages; Russian; sociology; South Asian studies; Spanish; systems engineering; theater arts/drama; transportation engineering; urban studies; women's studies.

University of Pittsburgh

Accounting; African-American (black) studies; anthropology; applied mathematics; art history; bioengineering; biological and physical sciences; biology; British literature; business; business marketing and marketing management; chemical engineering; chemistry; child care/development; Chinese; civil engineering; classics; communications; computer engineering; computer science; corrections; creative writing; dental hygiene; dietetics;

ecology; economics; electrical/electronics engineering; engineering physics; English; ethnic/cultural studies, other; film studies; finance; fine/studio arts; French; geological sciences, other; geology; German; health professions and related sciences, other; history; history of science and technology; humanities; industrial/manufacturing engineering; interdisciplinary studies; Italian; Japanese; law and legal studies; liberal arts and studies; linguistics; materials engineering; mathematical statistics; mathematics; mathematics, other; mechanical engineering; medical records administration; medical technology; metallurgical engineering; microbiology/bacteriology; molecular biology; music; neuroscience; nursing; occupational therapy; pharmacy; philosophy; physical education; physical sciences; physics; political science; psychology; public administration; rehabilitation/therapeutic services, other; religious studies; Russian; Slavic languages; social sciences; social work; sociology; Spanish; speech-language pathology/audiology; speech/rhetorical studies; theater arts/drama; urban studies.

University of Puget Sound
Art; Asian studies; biology; business; business computer programming; chemistry; classics; communications; computer science; creative writing; economics; English; exercise sciences; French; geology; German; history; interdisciplinary studies; international business; international economics; international relations; mathematics; music; music (general performance); music business management and merchandising; music education; natural sciences; occupational therapy; philosophy; physics; political science; (pre)dentistry; (pre)law; (pre)medicine; (pre)veterinary studies; psychology; religious studies; sociology; Spanish; theater arts/drama.

University of Redlands
Accounting; anthropology; art history; Asian studies; biology; business; business administration; chemistry; computer science; creative writing; economics; education; elementary education; English; environmental science; fine/studio arts; French; German; history; interdisciplinary studies; international relations; liberal arts and studies; literature; management information systems/business data processing; mathematics; music; music (general performance); music (piano and organ performance); music (voice and choral/opera performance); music education; music history; music theory and composition; philosophy; physics; political science; psychology; religious studies; secondary education; sociology; Spanish; speech therapy; speech-language pathology/audiology.

University of Rhode Island
Accounting; animal sciences; anthropology; apparel marketing; applied economics; art; art history; bioengineering; biology; business administration; business marketing and marketing management; chemical engineering; chemistry; civil engineering; classics; clothing/apparel/textile studies; communication disorders; communications; comparative literature; computer engineering; computer/information sciences; consumer economics; dental hygiene; dietetics; economics; electrical/electronics engineering; elementary education; English; environmental science; finance; fishing sciences and management; French; geology; German; health services administration; history; human services; individual/family development; industrial/manufacturing engineering; interdisciplinary studies; international business; Italian; journalism; landscape

architecture; Latin American studies; liberal arts and studies; management information systems/business data processing; marine biology; mathematics; mechanical engineering; medical technology; microbiology/bacteriology; music; music (general performance); music education; music theory and composition; natural resources conservation; natural resources management; nursing; nutrition studies; ocean engineering; pharmacy; philosophy; physical education; physics; political science; psychology; public policy analysis; quantitative economics; secondary education; sociology; Spanish; turf management; wildlife management; women's studies; zoology.

University of Richmond
Accounting; American studies; art; art education; art history; biology; business administration; business economics; business marketing and marketing management; chemistry; classics; computer science; criminal justice/law enforcement administration; Eastern European area studies; economics; education; elementary education; English; environmental science; European studies; finance; fine/studio arts; French; German; Greek (Modern); health education; history; human resources management; interdisciplinary studies; international business; international economics; international relations; journalism; Latin (Ancient and Medieval); Latin American studies; legal administrative assistant; management information systems/business data processing; mathematics; middle school education; molecular biology; music; music history; philosophy; physical education; physics; political science; psychology; religious studies; secondary education; sociology; Spanish; speech/rhetorical studies; theater arts/drama; urban studies; women's studies.

University of Rochester
Anthropology; applied mathematics; art history; astronomy; biochemistry; bioengineering; biological and physical sciences; biology; cell biology; chemical engineering; chemistry; classics; cognitive psychology and psycholinguistics; comparative literature; computer engineering technology; computer science; earth sciences; economics; electrical/electronics engineering; engineering; engineering science; English; environmental science; evolutionary biology; film studies; fine/studio arts; French; genetics; geology; German; health science; history; interdisciplinary studies; Japanese; jazz; linguistics; mathematical statistics; mathematics; mechanical engineering; microbiology/bacteriology; music; music education; music history; music theory and composition; natural sciences; neuroscience; optics; philosophy; physics; political science; psychology; religious studies; Russian; Russian/Slavic area studies; sign language interpretation; Spanish; women's studies.

University of St. Thomas (MN)
Accounting; actuarial science; advertising; alcohol/drug abuse counseling; art history; behavioral sciences; biochemistry; biology; broadcast journalism; business administration; business administration/management, other; business communications; business marketing and marketing management; chemistry; classics; communications; comparative literature; computer/information sciences; creative writing; criminology; drama and dance education; East Asian studies; economics; electrical/electronics engineering; elementary education; English; enterprise management; environmental science; finance; French; geography; geology; German; Greek (Ancient and Medieval); health education; health science; health/physical education; his-

tory; human resources management; interdisciplinary studies; international business; international relations; journalism; journalism and mass communication, other; K-12 education; Latin (Ancient and Medieval); mass communications; mathematics; mathematics education; mechanical engineering; music; music business management and merchandising; music education; music, other; operations management; peace and conflict studies; philosophy; physical education; physics; political science; psychology; public health education/promotion; public relations; publishing; real estate; religious studies; Russian; Russian/Slavic area studies; science education; secondary education; social sciences; social studies education; social work; sociology; Spanish; speech/theater education; teacher education, specific programs, other; theater arts/drama; theology; women's studies.

University of St. Thomas (TX)
Accounting; biology; business administration; business marketing and marketing management; chemistry; communications; economics; education; elementary education; English; environmental science; finance; fine/studio arts; French; general studies; history; international relations; liberal arts and studies; management information systems/business data processing; mathematics; music; music education; pastoral counseling; philosophy; political science; (pre)dentistry; (pre)law; (pre)medicine; psychology; secondary education; Spanish; theater arts/drama; theology.

University of San Diego
Accounting; anthropology; art; biology; business administration; business economics; chemistry; computer science; economics; education; electrical/electronics engineering; English; French; Hispanic-American studies; history; humanities; industrial/manufacturing engineering; international relations; liberal arts and studies; marine science; mass communications; mathematics; music; oceanography; philosophy; physics; political science; (pre)medicine; psychology; religious studies; sociology; Spanish; urban studies.

The University of Scranton
Accounting; biology; biophysics; business administration; business administration/management, other; business marketing and marketing management; chemistry; chemistry, other; communications; computer engineering; computer science; criminal justice studies; early childhood education; economics; electrical/electronics engineering; elementary education; English; enterprise management; entomology; environmental science; exercise sciences; finance; foreign languages/literatures; French; German; gerontology; Greek (Ancient and Medieval); health services administration; history; human resources management; human services; information sciences/systems; information technology; international business; international relations; Italian; Japanese; Latin (Ancient and Medieval); management science; mathematics; mathematics, other; medical technology; neuroscience; nursing; occupational therapy; operations management; philosophy; physical therapy; physics; political science; Portuguese; psychology; religious studies; Russian; secondary education; Slavic languages; sociology; Spanish; special education; theater arts/drama.

University of South Carolina
Accounting; advertising; African-American (black) studies; anthropology; art education; art history; biology; broadcast journalism; business administration; business economics; business marketing and marketing management; chemical engineering; chemistry; civil engineering; classics; computer engineering; computer/information sciences; criminal justice/law enforcement administration; economics; electrical/electronics engineering; English; European studies; exercise sciences; experimental psychology; finance; fine/studio arts; French; general retailing/wholesaling; geography; geology; geophysics and seismology; German; history; hospitality management; insurance and risk management; international relations; Italian; journalism; Latin American studies; liberal arts and studies; management science; marine biology; mathematical statistics; mathematics; mechanical engineering; music; music education; nursing; office management; philosophy; physical education; physics; political science; public relations; real estate; religious studies; sociology; Spanish; sport/fitness administration; theater arts/drama; women's studies.

University of Southern California
Accounting; acting/directing; aerospace engineering; African-American (black) studies; American literature; American studies; anthropology; architectural engineering; architecture; art; art history; Asian-American studies; astronomy; audio engineering; biochemistry; bioengineering; biology; biophysics; British literature; broadcast journalism; business administration; chemical engineering; chemistry; Chinese; city/community/regional planning; civil engineering; classics; comparative literature; computer engineering; computer science; creative writing; cultural studies; dental hygiene; East Asian studies; economics; education; electrical/electronics engineering; engineering mechanics; engineering/industrial management; English; environmental engineering; environmental science; exercise sciences; film studies; film/video production; fine/studio arts; French; geography; geology; German; gerontology; Greek (Ancient and Medieval); health science; Hispanic-American studies; history; history of philosophy; industrial/manufacturing engineering; interdisciplinary studies; international relations; Italian; Japanese; jazz; journalism; Judaic studies; K-12 education; landscape architecture; Latin (Ancient and Medieval); linguistics; marine biology; mass communications; mathematics; mechanical engineering; Mexican-American studies; molecular biology; music; music (general performance); music (piano and organ performance); music (voice and choral/opera performance); music business management and merchandising; music theory and composition; natural resources management; neuroscience; nursing; petroleum engineering; philosophy; physical sciences; physics; physiological psychology/psychobiology; play/screenwriting; political science; psychology; public administration; public relations; radio/television broadcasting; radio/television broadcasting technology; religious studies; Russian; sociology; Spanish; stringed instruments; structural engineering; systems engineering; theater arts/drama; theater design; urban studies; water resources; water resources engineering; wind and percussion instruments; women's studies.

The University of Texas at Austin
Accounting; advertising; aerospace engineering; American studies; anthropology; Arabic; archaeology; architectural engineering; architecture; art; art history; Asian studies; astronomy; biochemistry; bioengineering; biology; botany; business; business administration; business administration/management, other; business marketing and marketing management; chemical engineering; chemistry; civil engineering; classics; clothing/ap-

parel/textile studies; communication disorders; communications; community health liaison; computer/information sciences; dance; design/visual communications; ecology; economics; electrical/electronics engineering; English; ethnic/cultural studies, other; finance; fine/studio arts; foreign languages/literatures; French; geography; geological sciences, other; geology; geophysics and seismology; German; Greek (Ancient and Medieval); health/physical education; Hebrew; history; home economics; humanities; individual/family development; interior design; Islamic studies; Italian; journalism; Latin (Ancient and Medieval); Latin American studies; liberal arts and studies; linguistics; management information systems/business data processing; mathematics; mechanical engineering; medical technology; microbiology/bacteriology; Middle Eastern studies; molecular biology; music; music (general performance); music history; music theory and composition; nursing; nutrition studies; petroleum engineering; pharmacy; philosophy; physical sciences, other; physics; political science; Portuguese; psychology; public relations; radio/television broadcasting; religious studies; Russian; Russian/Slavic area studies; Scandinavian languages; Slavic languages; social work; sociology; Spanish; theater arts/drama; visual/performing arts; zoology.

The University of Texas at Dallas
Accounting; American studies; applied mathematics; art; biology; business; business marketing and marketing management; chemistry; cognitive psychology and psycholinguistics; computer engineering; computer science; computer/information sciences; criminology; economics; electrical/electronics engineering; ethnic/cultural studies, other; geography; geology; history; humanities; industrial/manufacturing engineering; interdisciplinary studies; international business; literature; management information systems/business data processing; mathematical statistics; mathematics; neuroscience; organizational behavior; physics; political science; psychology; public administration; sociology; speech-language pathology/audiology; visual/performing arts.

University of the Pacific
Art; art history; biochemistry; bioengineering; biology; business administration; chemistry; chemistry, other; civil engineering; classics; communications; computer engineering; computer science; economics; education; electrical/electronics engineering; engineering physics; engineering/industrial management; English; environmental science; exercise sciences; fine/studio arts; French; geology; German; graphic design/commercial art/illustration; history; information sciences/systems; interdisciplinary studies; international relations; Japanese; mathematics; mechanical engineering; music; music (piano and organ performance); music (voice and choral/opera performance); music business management and merchandising; music education; music history; music theory and composition; music therapy; pharmacy; philosophy; physical sciences; physics; political science; psychology; religious studies; social sciences; sociology; Spanish; special education; speech-language pathology/audiology; theater arts/drama.

University of the Sciences in Philadelphia
Biochemistry; biology; chemistry; computer science; computer/information sciences; environmental science; health science; medical pharmacology and pharmaceutical sciences; medical technology; microbiology/bacteriology; occupational therapy;

pharmacology; pharmacy; pharmacy administration and pharmaceutics; pharmacy, other; physical therapy; physician assistant; (pre)dentistry; (pre)medicine; (pre)veterinary studies; psychology; science education; toxicology.

University of the South
American studies; anthropology; applied art; art; art history; Asian studies; biology; chemistry; classics; comparative literature; computer science; drawing; economics; English; environmental science; European studies; fine/studio arts; forestry; French; geology; German; Greek (Modern); history; international relations; Latin (Ancient and Medieval); literature; mathematics; medieval/renaissance studies; music; music history; natural resources management; philosophy; physics; political science; psychology; religious studies; Russian; Russian/Slavic area studies; social sciences; Spanish; theater arts/drama.

University of Tulsa
Accounting; anthropology; applied mathematics; art; art history; arts management; athletic training/sports medicine; biochemistry; biology; broadcast journalism; business administration; business marketing and marketing management; chemical engineering; chemistry; communications; computer science; economics; education; electrical/electronics engineering; elementary education; engineering; engineering physics; English; environmental science; exercise sciences; finance; French; geology; geophysics and seismology; German; history; information sciences/systems; international business; law and legal studies; management information systems/business data processing; mathematics; mechanical engineering; music; music (piano and organ performance); music (voice and choral/opera performance); music education; nursing; petroleum engineering; philosophy; physics; political science; psychology; religious studies; sociology; Spanish; special education; speech-language pathology/audiology; sport/fitness administration.

University of Virginia
Aerospace engineering; African-American (black) studies; anthropology; applied mathematics; architecture; art; astronomy; biology; business; chemical engineering; chemistry; city/community/regional planning; civil engineering; classics; comparative literature; computer engineering; computer/information sciences; cultural studies; economics; electrical/electronics engineering; engineering; English; environmental science; French; German; history; international relations; Italian; liberal arts and studies; mathematics; mechanical engineering; music; nursing; philosophy; physical education; physics; political science; psychology; religious studies; Slavic languages; sociology; Spanish; speech-language pathology/audiology; systems engineering; theater arts/drama.

University of Washington
Accounting; aerospace engineering; African-American (black) studies; air science; anthropology; applied mathematics; architectural urban design; architecture; art; art history; Asian studies; astronomy; atmospheric sciences; bilingual/bicultural education; biochemistry; biology; biology education; biostatistics; botany; business; business administration; Canadian studies; cell biology; ceramic arts; ceramic sciences/engineering; chemical engineering; chemistry; Chinese; city/community/regional planning; civil engineering; classics; communications; comparative literature; computer engineering; computer science;

computer/information sciences; construction management; creative writing; criminal justice/law enforcement administration; cultural studies; dance; data processing technology; dental hygiene; East Asian studies; economics; education; education (multiple levels); electrical/electronics engineering; elementary education; engineering; English; environmental health; environmental science; European studies; fishing sciences and management; forest engineering; forest management; forestry; forestry sciences; French; general studies; geography; geology; geophysics and seismology; German; graphic design/commercial art/illustration; Greek (Ancient and Medieval); history; history of science and technology; humanities; industrial design; industrial/manufacturing engineering; information sciences/systems; interdisciplinary studies; interior architecture; international business; international relations; Italian; Japanese; Judaic studies; landscape architecture; Latin (Ancient and Medieval); Latin American studies; liberal arts and studies; linguistics; management information systems/business data processing; management science; materials engineering; mathematical statistics; mathematics; mechanical engineering; medical technology; metal/jewelry arts; metallurgical engineering; Mexican-American studies; microbiology/bacteriology; Middle Eastern studies; military science; molecular biology; music; music (general performance); music (piano and organ performance); music (voice and choral/opera performance); music education; music history; music theory and composition; musical instrument technology; musicology; Native American studies; natural resources management; naval science; nursing; nursing (maternal/child health); nursing (public health); occupational therapy; oceanography; orthotics/prosthetics; painting; pharmacy; philosophy; photography; physical therapy; physician assistant; physics; political science; printmaking; psychology; public administration; public health; religious studies; Romance languages; Russian; Russian/Slavic area studies; Scandinavian area studies; Scandinavian languages; science education; sculpture; secondary education; Slavic languages; social sciences; social work; sociology; South Asian studies; Southeast Asian studies; Spanish; speech-language pathology/audiology; speech/rhetorical studies; stringed instruments; teaching English as a second language; technical writing; textile arts; theater arts/drama; wildlife management; women's studies; wood science/paper technology; zoology.

University of Waterloo

Accounting; actuarial science; anthropology; applied mathematics; architecture; art history; arts management; biochemistry; biological and physical sciences; biology; biology education; biotechnology research; business administration; business administration/management, other; Canadian studies; chemical and atomic/molecular physics; chemical engineering; chemistry; chemistry education; city/community/regional planning; civil engineering; classics; computer engineering; computer science; computer software engineering; earth sciences; economics; electrical/electronics engineering; engineering; English; environmental engineering; environmental science; exercise sciences; film studies; fine/studio arts; French; French language education; geochemistry; geography; geological engineering; geology; German; health science; history; human resources management; interdisciplinary studies; international relations; liberal arts and studies; mathematical statistics; mathematics; mathematics education; mathematics/computer science;

mechanical engineering; medieval/renaissance studies; music; operations research; ophthalmic/optometric services; philosophy; physics; physics education; political science; psychology; recreation and leisure studies; religious studies; Russian; Russian/Slavic area studies; social work; sociology; Spanish; speech/rhetorical studies; systems engineering; theater arts/drama; women's studies.

University of Wisconsin–Madison

Accounting; actuarial science; advertising; African languages; African studies; African-American (black) studies; agricultural business; agricultural economics; agricultural education; agricultural engineering; agricultural sciences; agronomy/crop science; American studies; animal sciences; anthropology; applied art; applied mathematics; art; art education; art history; Asian studies; astronomy; biochemistry; bioengineering; biology; botany; broadcast journalism; business administration; cartography; cell biology; chemical engineering; chemistry; child care/development; Chinese; civil engineering; classics; clothing and textiles; comparative literature; computer engineering; computer science; construction management; consumer services; dairy science; developmental/child psychology; dietetics; early childhood education; earth sciences; economics; electrical/electronics engineering; elementary education; engineering; engineering mechanics; engineering physics; English; entomology; environmental engineering; experimental psychology; family/consumer studies; farm/ranch management; fashion merchandising; finance; food sciences; forestry; French; genetics; geography; geology; geophysics and seismology; German; Greek (Modern); Hebrew; Hispanic-American studies; history; history of science and technology; home economics; home economics education; horticulture science; industrial/manufacturing engineering; insurance and risk management; interior design; international relations; Italian; Japanese; journalism; labor/personnel relations; landscape architecture; Latin (Ancient and Medieval); Latin American studies; linguistics; mass communications; mathematical statistics; mathematics; mechanical engineering; medical technology; metallurgical engineering; microbiology/bacteriology; mining/mineral engineering; molecular biology; music; music education; natural resources management; nuclear engineering; nursing; nutrition science; occupational therapy; pharmacology; pharmacy; philosophy; physical education; physician assistant; physics; political science; Portuguese; poultry science; psychology; public relations; radio/television broadcasting; real estate; recreation and leisure studies; Russian; Scandinavian languages; science education; secondary education; Slavic languages; social sciences; social work; sociology; Southeast Asian studies; Spanish; special education; speech therapy; surveying; theater arts/drama; toxicology; urban studies; water resources; wildlife management; women's studies; zoology.

Ursinus College

Accounting; anthropology; applied mathematics; art; athletic training/sports medicine; biochemistry; biology; business administration; chemistry; classics; computer science; creative writing; East Asian studies; ecology; economics; education; English; environmental science; French; German; Greek (Modern); health education; health science; history; international relations; Japanese; Latin (Ancient and Medieval); liberal arts and studies; mass communications; mathematics; modern languages; music; philosophy; physical education; physical therapy; physics; political science; (pre)dentistry; (pre)law; (pre)medicine; (pre)veterinary studies; psychology; religious studies; Romance languages; secondary education; sociology; South Asian studies; Spanish.

Valparaiso University

Accounting; American studies; art; art education; art history; astronomy; athletic training/sports medicine; atmospheric sciences; biological and physical sciences; biology; business administration; business marketing and marketing management; chemistry; civil engineering; classics; communications; computer science; criminology; East Asian studies; economics; education; electrical/electronics engineering; elementary education; engineering; English; environmental science; European studies; exercise sciences; finance; fine/studio arts; French; geography; geology; German; health/physical education; history; interdisciplinary studies; international business; international economics; international relations; liberal arts and studies; mathematics; mechanical engineering; music; music (general performance); music business management and merchandising; music education; music theory and composition; nursing; philosophy; physical education; physics; political science; (pre)theology; psychology; sacred music; secondary education; social sciences; social work; sociology; Spanish; sport/fitness administration; theater arts/drama; theology.

Vanderbilt University

African studies; African-American (black) studies; American studies; anthropology; art; astronomy; bioengineering; biology; chemical engineering; chemistry; civil engineering; classics; cognitive psychology and psycholinguistics; computer engineering; computer science; early childhood education; East Asian studies; ecology; economics; education; electrical/electronics engineering; elementary education; engineering; engineering science; English; European studies; French; geology; German; history; human resources management; individual/family development; interdisciplinary studies; Latin American studies; mass communications; mathematics; mechanical engineering; molecular biology; music; music (piano and organ performance); music (voice and choral/opera performance); philosophy; physics; political science; Portuguese; psychology; religious studies; Russian; secondary education; sociology; Spanish; special education; stringed instruments; theater arts/drama; urban studies; wind and percussion instruments.

Vassar College

African studies; American studies; anthropology; art history; Asian studies; astronomy; biochemistry; biology; chemistry; classics; cognitive psychology and psycholinguistics; computer science; economics; elementary education; English; environmental science; film studies; fine/studio arts; French; geography; geology; German; Hispanic-American studies; history; interdisciplinary studies; international relations; Italian; Judaic studies; Latin (Ancient and Medieval); Latin American studies; mathematics; medieval/renaissance studies; music; philosophy; physics; physiological psychology/psychobiology; political science; psychology; religious studies; Russian; science/technology and society; sociology; theater arts/drama; urban studies; women's studies.

Villanova University

Accounting; art history; astronomy; astrophysics; biology; business administration; business economics; business marketing and marketing management; chemical engineering; chemistry; civil engineering; classics; computer engineering; computer science; criminal justice/law enforcement administration; economics; education; electrical/electronics engineering; elementary education; English; finance; French; geography; German; history; human services; information sciences/systems; international business; liberal arts and studies; management information systems/business data processing; mass communications; mathematics; mechanical engineering; natural sciences; nursing; philosophy; physics; political science; (pre)dentistry; (pre)law; (pre)medicine; (pre)veterinary studies; psychology; religious studies; secondary education; sociology; Spanish.

Virginia Military Institute

Biology; chemistry; civil engineering; computer science; economics; electrical/electronics engineering; English; history; international relations; mathematics; mechanical engineering; modern languages; physics; psychology.

Virginia Polytechnic Institute and State University

Accounting; aerospace engineering; agricultural economics; agricultural education; agricultural mechanization; agronomy/crop science; animal sciences; architecture; art; biochemistry; biology; business; business administration; business education; business marketing and marketing management; chemical engineering; chemistry; civil engineering; clothing and textiles; communications; computer engineering; computer science; construction technology; consumer and homemaking education; dairy science; dietetics; early childhood education; economics; electrical/electronics engineering; engineering; engineering science; English; environmental science; finance; food sciences; forestry; French; geography; geology; German; health education; history; horticulture science; human resources management; human services; industrial arts education; industrial design; industrial/manufacturing engineering; information sciences/systems; interdisciplinary studies; international relations; landscape architecture; management information systems/business data processing; marketing/distribution education; materials engineering; mathematical statistics; mathematics; mechanical engineering; mining/mineral engineering; music; nutrition science; ocean engineering; philosophy; physics; political science; poultry science; psychology; sociology; Spanish; theater arts/drama; trade and industrial education; travel-tourism management; urban studies.

Wabash College

Art; biology; chemistry; classics; economics; English; French; German; Greek (Modern); history; Latin (Ancient and Medieval); mathematics; music; philosophy; physics; political science; (pre)law; (pre)medicine; (pre)veterinary studies; psychology; religious studies; Spanish; speech/rhetorical studies; theater arts/drama.

Wake Forest University

Accounting; anthropology; applied mathematics; art; art history; biology; business; chemistry; classics; communications; computer/information sciences; economics; education; elementary education; English; exercise sciences; finance; French; German; Greek (Ancient and Medieval); history; Latin (Ancient and Medieval); management science; mathematics;

music; philosophy; physician assistant; physics; political science; psychology; religious studies; Russian; sociology; Spanish; theater arts/drama.

Wartburg College

Accounting; art; art education; arts management; biochemistry; biology; broadcast journalism; business administration; business marketing and marketing management; chemistry; computer science; early childhood education; economics; elementary education; engineering; English; English composition; finance; French; German; graphic design/commercial art/illustration; history; history education; information sciences/systems; international business; international relations; journalism; mass communications; mathematics; mathematics education; medical technology; music; music (general performance); music education; music theory and composition; music therapy; occupational therapy; philosophy; physical education; physics; political science; psychology; public relations; religious studies; sacred music; secondary education; social science education; social work; sociology; Spanish; speech/theater education; sport/fitness administration.

Washington and Lee University

Accounting; anthropology; archaeology; art history; biology; business administration; chemical engineering; chemistry; classics; computer science; East Asian studies; economics; engineering physics; English; fine/studio arts; foreign languages/literatures; forestry; French; geology; German; history; interdisciplinary studies; journalism; mathematics; medieval/renaissance studies; music; neuroscience; philosophy; physics; political science; psychology; public policy analysis; religious studies; Russian/Slavic area studies; sociology; Spanish; theater arts/drama.

Washington College

American studies; anthropology; art; biology; business administration; chemistry; economics; English; environmental science; French; German; history; humanities; international relations; Latin American studies; liberal arts and studies; mathematics; music; philosophy; physics; physiological psychology/psychobiology; political science; (pre)dentistry; (pre)law; (pre)medicine; (pre)veterinary studies; psychology; sociology; Spanish; theater arts/drama.

Washington University in St. Louis

Accounting; advertising; African studies; African-American (black) studies; American literature; American studies; anthropology; applied art; applied mathematics; Arabic; archaeology; architectural engineering technology; architecture; architecture and related programs, other; area, ethnic and cultural studies, other; art; art education; art history; Asian studies; biochemistry; bioengineering; biological and physical sciences; biological sciences/life sciences, other; biology; biology education; biophysics; biopsychology; British literature; business; business administration; business economics; business marketing and marketing management; ceramic arts; chemical engineering; chemistry; chemistry education; Chinese; civil engineering; civil engineering technology; classics; cognitive psychology and psycholinguistics; communications; comparative literature; computer engineering; computer science; computer/information sciences; computer/information sciences, other; creative writing; cultural studies; dance; design/visual communications; drama and dance education; drama/theater literature; drawing; earth sciences; East and Southeast Asian languages, other; East Asian studies; economics; education; electrical/electronics engineering; elementary education; engineering; engineering physics; engineering science; English; English, other; environmental science; ethnic/cultural studies, other; European studies; fashion design/illustration; film studies; finance; fine/studio arts; French; French language education; German; German language education; graphic design/commercial art/illustration; Greek (Ancient and Medieval); health professions and related sciences, other; Hebrew; history; history education; human resources management; information sciences/systems; interdisciplinary studies; international business; international economics; international finance; international relations; Islamic studies; Italian; Japanese; Judaic studies; K-12 education; Latin (Ancient and Medieval); Latin American studies; liberal arts and studies; literature; marketing management and research, other; marketing operations/marketing and distribution, other; mathematical statistics; mathematics; mathematics education; mathematics/computer science; mechanical engineering; medieval/renaissance studies; Middle Eastern studies; middle school education; modern languages; multi/interdisciplinary studies, other; music; music (voice and choral/opera performance); music history; music theory and composition; natural resources conservation; natural sciences; neuroscience; operations management; painting; philosophy; philosophy and religion, other; photography; physical sciences; physics; physics education; political science; (pre)dentistry; (pre)medicine; (pre)pharmacy studies; (pre)veterinary studies; printmaking; psychology; religious studies; Romance languages; Russian; Russian/Slavic area studies; science education; science/technology and society; sculpture; secondary education; social science education; social sciences; social studies education; social/philosophical foundations of education; Spanish; Spanish language education; systems engineering; systems science and theory; theater arts/drama; urban studies; women's studies.

Webb Institute

Naval architecture/marine engineering.

Wellesley College

African studies; African-American (black) studies; American studies; anthropology; archaeology; architecture; art history; astronomy; astrophysics; biochemistry; biology; chemistry; Chinese; classics; cognitive psychology and psycholinguistics; comparative literature; computer science; East Asian studies; economics; English; environmental science; ethnic/cultural studies, other; film studies; fine/studio arts; French; geology; German; Greek (Ancient and Medieval); history; international relations; Islamic studies; Italian; Italian studies; Japanese; Judaic studies; Latin (Ancient and Medieval); Latin American studies; linguistics; mathematics; medieval/renaissance studies; music; neuroscience; peace and conflict studies; philosophy; physics; political science; psychology; religious studies; Russian; Russian/Slavic area studies; sociology; Spanish; theater arts/drama; women's studies.

Wells College

African-American (black) studies; American studies; anthropology; art; art history; biochemistry; biology; business administration; chemistry; computer science; creative writing; dance; economics; education; elementary education; engineering;

English; environmental science; fine/studio arts; French; German; history; international relations; mathematics; molecular biology; music; philosophy; physics; political science; (pre)dentistry; (pre)law; (pre)medicine; (pre)veterinary studies; psychology; public policy analysis; religious studies; secondary education; sociology; Spanish; theater arts/drama; women's studies.

Wesleyan College

Accounting; advertising; American studies; art history; biology; business administration; chemistry; communications; computer/information sciences; early childhood education; economics; education; English; fine/studio arts; history; humanities; interdisciplinary studies; international business; international relations; mathematics; middle school education; music; philosophy; physical sciences; physics; political science; psychology; religious studies; social sciences; sociology; Spanish.

Wesleyan University

African-American (black) studies; American studies; anthropology; art history; astronomy; biochemistry; biology; chemistry; classics; computer science; dance; earth sciences; East Asian studies; Eastern European area studies; economics; English; environmental science; film studies; fine/studio arts; French; German; history; humanities; interdisciplinary studies; Italian; Latin American studies; mathematics; medieval/renaissance studies; molecular biology; music; neuroscience; philosophy; physics; political science; psychology; religious studies; Romance languages; Russian; Russian/Slavic area studies; science/technology and society; social sciences; sociology; Spanish; theater arts/drama; women's studies.

Western Maryland College

Art; art history; biochemistry; biology; business administration; chemistry; communications; economics; English; exercise sciences; French; German; history; mathematics; music; philosophy; physics; political science; psychology; religious studies; social work; sociology; Spanish; theater arts/drama.

Westminster Choir College of Rider University

Liberal arts and studies; music; music (piano and organ performance); music (voice and choral/opera performance); music conducting; music education; music theory and composition; sacred music.

Westminster College (UT)

Accounting; aircraft pilot (professional); art; aviation management; biology; biology education; business; business administration; business economics; business information/data processing, other; business marketing and marketing management; chemistry; communications; computer science; early childhood education; elementary education; English; finance; history; human resources management; international business; mathematics; nursing; philosophy; physics; political science; psychology; social science education; social sciences; sociology; special education.

Westmont College

Anthropology; art; art education; biology; business; business economics; chemistry; communications; computer science; dance; economics; education; elementary education; engineering physics; English; English education; exercise sciences; French; history; liberal arts and studies; mathematics; mathematics

education; modern languages; music; neuroscience; philosophy; physical education; physics; political science; (pre)dentistry; (pre)law; (pre)medicine; (pre)pharmacy studies; (pre)theology; (pre)veterinary studies; psychology; religious studies; secondary education; social science education; social sciences; sociology; Spanish; theater arts/drama.

Wheaton College (IL)

Anthropology; archaeology; art; biblical studies; biology; business economics; chemistry; computer science; economics; elementary education; engineering, other; English; environmental science; exercise sciences; French; geology; German; history; international relations; mathematics; multi/interdisciplinary studies, other; music; music (general performance); music business management and merchandising; music education; music history; music theory and composition; music, other; nursing, other; philosophy; physical sciences; physics; political science; psychology; religious education; religious studies; social studies education; sociology; Spanish; speech/rhetorical studies; theology/ministry, other.

Whitman College

Anthropology; art; art history; Asian studies; astronomy; biochemistry; biology; biophysics; chemistry; classics; economics; English; environmental science; French; geology; German; history; mathematics; molecular biology; music; philosophy; physics; political science; psychology; sociology; Spanish; theater arts/drama.

Whittier College

Art; biochemistry; biology; business administration; chemistry; developmental/child psychology; early childhood education; economics; English; French; history; international relations; liberal arts and studies; mathematics; music; philosophy; physical education; physics; political science; psychology; religious studies; social work; sociology; Spanish; theater arts/drama.

Whitworth College

Accounting; American studies; art; art education; art history; arts management; athletic training/sports medicine; biology; business administration; chemistry; computer science; economics; elementary education; English; fine/studio arts; French; history; international business; international relations; journalism; mass communications; mathematics; music; music (piano and organ performance); music (voice and choral/opera performance); music education; nursing; peace and conflict studies; philosophy; physical education; physics; political science; (pre)dentistry; (pre)law; (pre)medicine; (pre)veterinary studies; psychology; religious studies; secondary education; sociology; Spanish; special education; speech/rhetorical studies; theater arts/drama.

Willamette University

American studies; art; art history; Asian studies; biology; chemistry; classics; comparative literature; computer science; economics; English; environmental science; exercise sciences; fine/studio arts; French; German; Hispanic-American studies; history; humanities; international relations; mathematics; music; music education; music therapy; philosophy; physical education; physics; political science; (pre)dentistry; (pre)law; (pre)medicine; (pre)veterinary studies; psychology; religious studies; sociology; Spanish; speech/rhetorical studies; theater arts/drama.

William Jewell College

Accounting; art; biochemistry; biology; business administration; cell biology; chemistry; computer science; drama and dance education; economics; education; elementary education; English; French; history; information sciences/systems; interdisciplinary studies; international business; international relations; mathematics; medical technology; molecular biology; music; music (general performance); music education; music theory and composition; nursing; philosophy; physics; political science; (pre)dentistry; (pre)law; (pre)medicine; (pre)veterinary studies; psychology; religious studies; sacred music; secondary education; Spanish; speech education; speech/rhetorical studies; theater arts/drama.

Williams College

American studies; anthropology; art history; Asian studies; astronomy; astrophysics; biology; chemistry; Chinese; classics; computer science; economics; English; fine/studio arts; French; geology; German; history; Japanese; literature; mathematics; music; philosophy; physics; political science; psychology; religious studies; Russian; sociology; Spanish; theater arts/drama.

Wittenberg University

American studies; art; art education; art history; Asian studies; behavioral sciences; biochemistry; biological and physical sciences; biology; botany; business administration; business economics; business marketing and marketing management; cartography; cell biology; ceramic arts; chemistry; communications; comparative literature; computer graphics; computer science; creative writing; developmental/child psychology; drawing; earth sciences; East Asian studies; economics; education; elementary education; English; environmental biology; environmental science; finance; fine/studio arts; French; geography; geology; German; graphic design/commercial art/illustration; history; humanities; interdisciplinary studies; international business; international relations; liberal arts and studies; literature; marine biology; mathematics; microbiology/bacteriology; middle school education; modern languages; music; music (piano and organ performance); music (voice and choral/opera performance); music education; natural sciences; philosophy; physical sciences; physics; physiological psychology/psychobiology; political science; (pre)dentistry; (pre)law; (pre)medicine; (pre)veterinary studies; psychology; religious studies; Russian/Slavic area studies; science education; sculpture; secondary education; social sciences; sociology; Spanish; special education; technical writing; theater arts/drama; theology; urban studies.

Wofford College

Accounting; art history; biology; business economics; chemistry; computer science; economics; English; finance; French; German; history; humanities; international business; international relations; mathematics; philosophy; physics; political science; (pre)dentistry; (pre)law; (pre)medicine; (pre)veterinary studies; psychology; religious studies; sociology; Spanish.

Worcester Polytechnic Institute

Actuarial science; aerospace engineering; applied mathematics; biochemistry; bioengineering; biological technology; biology; biomedical science; business administration; cell biology; chemical engineering; chemistry; civil engineering; computer engineering; computer science; computer/information sciences; economics; electrical/electronics engineering; engineering design; engineering mechanics; engineering physics; engineering/industrial management; environmental engineering; environmental science; fluid and thermal sciences; genetics; history; history of science and technology; humanities; industrial/manufacturing engineering; information sciences/systems; interdisciplinary studies; management information systems/business data processing; materials engineering; materials science; mathematics; mechanical engineering; medicinal/pharmaceutical chemistry; metallurgy; microbiology/bacteriology; molecular biology; music; nuclear engineering; philosophy; physics; science/technology and society; social sciences; technical writing.

Xavier University

Accounting; advertising; art; athletic training/sports medicine; biological and physical sciences; biology; biology education; business; business administration; business economics; business marketing and marketing management; chemical engineering; chemistry; chemistry education; classics; computer science; corrections; criminal justice studies; early childhood education; economics; education; elementary education; English; entrepreneurship; environmental science; finance; fine/studio arts; French; German; history; human resources management; industrial radiologic technology; international relations; liberal arts and studies; management information systems/business data processing; mathematics; medical technology; middle school education; music; music education; nursing science; occupational therapy; philosophy; physics; physics education; political science; psychology; public relations; radio/television broadcasting; science education; social sciences; social work; sociology; Spanish; special education; sport/fitness administration; teacher education, other; theology.

Yale University

African studies; African-American (black) studies; American studies; anthropology; applied mathematics; archaeology; architecture; art; art history; astronomy; astrophysics; bioengineering; biology; cell and molecular biology, other; chemical engineering; chemistry; Chinese; classics; cognitive psychology and psycholinguistics; computer/information sciences; cultural studies; East Asian studies; ecology; economics; electrical/electronics engineering; engineering physics; engineering science; English; environmental engineering; environmental science; ethnic/cultural studies, other; evolutionary biology; film studies; foreign languages/literatures, other; French; geological sciences, other; German; Greek (Ancient and Medieval); history; humanities; Italian; Japanese; Judaic studies; Latin (Ancient and Medieval); Latin American studies; linguistics; literature; mathematics; mathematics/computer science; mechanical engineering; molecular biology; multi/interdisciplinary studies, other; music; philosophy; physics; political science; Portuguese; psychology; religious studies; Russian; Russian/Slavic area studies; sociology; South Asian languages; Spanish; systems science and theory; theater arts/drama; women's studies.

Yeshiva University

Accounting; biology; business administration; business marketing and marketing management; chemistry; classics; computer science; early childhood education; economics; education; elementary education; English; finance; French; Hebrew; history; interdisciplinary studies; Judaic studies; management information systems/business data processing; mass communications; mathematics; music; philosophy; physics; political science; (pre)dentistry; (pre)law; (pre)medicine; psychology; sociology; speech-language pathology; speech-language pathology/audiology; speech/rhetorical studies; theater arts/drama.

GEOGRAPHIC INDEX OF COLLEGES